Market Discipline
across Countries
and Industries

Market Discipline across Countries and Industries

edited by

Claudio Borio
Bank for International Settlements

William C. Hunter
*University of Connecticut and
formerly Federal Reserve Bank of Chicago*

George G. Kaufman
*Loyola University Chicago and
Federal Reserve Bank of Chicago*

Kostas Tsatsaronis
Bank for International Settlements

The MIT Press
Cambridge, Massachusetts
London, England

MIT Press books may be purchased at special quantity discounts for business or sales promotional use. For information, please email special_sales@mitpress.mit.edu or write to Special Sales Department, The MIT Press, 5 Cambridge Center, Cambridge, MA 02142.

This book was set in Times by the Federal Reserve Bank of Chicago and was printed and bound in the United States of America.

Library of Congress Cataloging-in-Publication Data

Market discipline across countries and industries / edited by Claudio Borio ... [et al.].
   p. cm
   Papers presented at a conference cosponsored by the Federal Reserve Bank of Chicago and the Bank for International Settlements, held on Oct. 30 to Nov. 1, 2003, at the Federal Reserve Bank of Chicago.
   Includes index.
   ISBN 0-262-02575-2 (alk. paper)
   1. Capital market—Congresses. 2. Internal finance—Congresses. 3. Banks and banking, International—Congresses. 4. Risk management—Congresses. I. Borio, C. E. V.

HG4523.M267 2004
332—dc22

2004050028

Contents

Acknowledgments ix

Preface xi

Part I: Keynote Addresses

1   Market Discipline and Public Policy: The Role of the IMF
    Anne O. Krueger 3

2   Three Observations on Market Discipline
    Malcolm Knight 11

3   Effective Market Discipline: The Roles of Auditors, Companies,
    and Analysts
    Susan Schmidt Bies 17

4   A Review of the New Basel Capital Accord
    Jaime Caruana 25

Part II: Theory of Market Discipline

5   Market Discipline: Players, Processes, and Purposes
    Robert R. Bliss 37

6   Market Discipline in Banking: Where Do We Stand?
    Jean-Charles Rochet 55

7   Market Discipline for Financial Institutions and Sovereigns
    Hal S. Scott 69

8   Comments on the Theory of Market Discipline
    Kostas Tsatsaronis 79

Part III: Evidence of Market Discipline in Banking

9 Market Discipline of U.S. Financial Firms: Recent Evidence
and Research Issues
Mark J. Flannery and Stanislava Nikolova 87

10 Bank Market Discipline and Indicators of Banking System Risk:
The European Evidence
Reint Gropp 101

11 Weakening Market and Regulatory Discipline in the Japanese
Financial System
Mitsuhiro Fukao 119

12 Market Discipline in Emerging Economies:
Beyond Bank Fundamentals
Eduardo Levy-Yeyati, Maria Soledad Martinez Peria,
and Sergio L. Schmukler 135

13 Inside the "Black Box" of Market Discipline
David T. Llewellyn 147

Part IV: Evidence of Market Discipline in Other Industries

14 Market Discipline in Insurance and Reinsurance
Scott E. Harrington 159

15 Conflicts of Interest and Market Discipline
Ingo Walter 175

16 Market Discipline and Corporate Control
Clifford W. Smith, Jr. 187

Part V: Evidence of Market Discipline for Countries

17 Capital Controls: Mud in the Wheels of Market Discipline
Kristin J. Forbes 197

18 Equity Integration in Times of Crisis
Robert P. Flood and Andrew K. Rose 211

19 Assessing the Evidence on Market Discipline for Countries
Andrew G. Haldane 225

Part VI: Current State of Corporate Governance

20   U.S. Corporate Governance: What Went Wrong and Can It Be Fixed?
     Franklin R. Edwards 237

21   Corporate Governance in Europe: Competition versus Harmonization
     Marco Becht and Colin Mayer 255

22   Evolving Corporate Governance in Japan
     Hugh Patrick 269

23   Quis Custodiet Ipsos Custodes? Controlling Conflicts of Interest in
     the Financial Industry?
     Eugene N. White 287

Part VII: Interaction of Market Discipline and Public Policy

24   The Role and Limitations of Financial Accounting and Auditing
     for Market Discipline
     George J. Benston 303

25   Fair Values and Financial Statement Volatility
     Mary E. Barth 323

26   Enron and Effective Corporate Governance
     Charles M. Elson 335

27   Interaction of Market Discipline and Public Policy: Discussion
     Shyam Sunder 341

Part VIII: Interaction of Market Discipline and Public Policy

28   Can the Unsophisticated Market Provide Discipline?
     Gerard Caprio and Patrick Honohan 349

29   How Can the Invisible Hand Strengthen Prudential Supervision? and
     How Can Prudential Supervision Strengthen the Invisible Hand?
     Richard J. Herring 363

30   Healing with Destabilizing 'Market Discipline'
     Daniel Cohen and Richard Portes 381

31   Comments on Market Discipline and Public Policy
     Charles Freedman 397

Part IX: Policy Panel

32 Reestablishing Market Discipline as Part of Bank Regulation
Charles W. Calomiris 407

33 Comment on Policy
Christine M. Cumming.. 417

34 Market Discipline—Interaction with Public Policy
Patricia Jackson 423

Conference Program 427

Index 435

Acknowledgments

Both the conference and this volume represent a joint effort of the Federal Reserve Bank of Chicago and the Bank for International Settlements, and many persons at each institution aided in their preparation and successful execution. The four editors served as the principal organizers of the conference program. They would like to thank all the persons who contributed their efforts. At the risk of omitting some, in particular, they thank Ella Dukes, Shirley Harris, Loretta Novak, and Aretha Sims, who supervised the arrangements, and Julia Baker, Mary Jo Cannistra, Jennifer Cornman, Howard Deehan, John Dixon, Lana Henderson, Helen O'D. Koshy, Hala Leddy, Michael McConnaughay, Rita Molloy, Yvonne Peeples, Elizabeth Taylor, Barbara Van Brussell, and Kristine Wolstenholme, who helped in the preparation of the conference and the proceedings volume. Special mention must be accorded Kathryn Moran (Federal Reserve Bank of Chicago), who had primary responsibility for preparing the program information and shepherding the book from manuscript review to final copy, as well as to Loretta Ardaugh (Federal Reserve Bank of Chicago), who supervised the administrative procedures.

Preface

The Federal Reserve Bank of Chicago and the Bank for International Settlements in Basel, Switzerland, cosponsored a conference on "Market Discipline: The Evidence across Countries and Industries," on October 30 to November 1, 2003, at the Federal Reserve Bank of Chicago. This was the fifth annual international conference sponsored by the Chicago Fed in partnership with a major official international institution focusing on important current issues in global economics and finance. Previous conferences were cosponsored with the World Bank and the International Monetary Fund. The conference attracted speakers and other participants from more than 25 countries. The papers published in this volume were presented at the conference by government officials, regulators, and academics representing a broad range of countries and industries, from small emerging economies to large industrial economies.

The role and ability of market discipline in affecting corporate behavior and performance has received increased attention in recent years. Evidence on the effectiveness of market discipline is of particular importance in banking and finance as longstanding government discipline in the form of prudential regulation appears to be becoming less effective as financial institutions and financial markets become larger and more complex. Most recently, market discipline has been introduced as the third pillar in the three-pillar prudential framework for banking proposed by the Basel Committee on Banking Supervision to supplement capital standards and supervisory review. A major purpose of this conference was to develop evidence on how market discipline operates in industries that are not government regulated and in sovereign countries, how successful or unsuccessful it has been, and how it may transfer to a regulated industry.

As a result, the conference sessions addressed the following areas:

- The theory of market discipline,
- Evidence of market discipline in banking,
- Evidence of market discipline in other industries,
- Evidence of market discipline for countries,
- Current state of corporate governance, and
- Interaction of market discipline and public policy.

The conference speakers were selected to represent a wide range of views. We were pleased to have Susan Schmidt Bies, Member, Board of Governors of the Federal Reserve System; Jaime Caruana, Governor, Bank of Spain and Chairman, Basel Committee on Banking Supervision; Malcolm D. Knight, General Manager, Bank for International Settlements; and Anne Krueger, First Deputy Managing Director, International Monetary Fund as keynote speakers. The conference brought together a diverse group of academics and policymakers and provided a forum for an important free interchange of ideas that hopefully will serve to enhance macroeconomic and microeconomic policies in the future. It is in the pursuit of these objectives that the papers delivered at the conference are published in this volume to reach a larger audience.

PART I

KEYNOTE ADDRESSES

Chapter 1

Market Discipline and Public Policy: The Role of the IMF

Anne O. Krueger*
International Monetary Fund

1. Introduction and Theme

As such a distinguished gathering as this testifies, market discipline is an increasingly important topic for policymakers—in both the public and private sectors—around the world. The Federal Reserve Bank of Chicago and the Bank for International Settlements are to be congratulated for having the foresight to organize such an excellent conference.

I think it is fair to say that the past couple of decades have witnessed a major shift in the attitude of many policymakers around the world. They have become increasingly aware of the importance of markets, and market-friendly policies. They have also come to realize—many of them for the first time—the benefits that the discipline of the markets can bring—provided, of course, that they seek to use the markets for public policy purposes instead of trying to fight them.

This morning I want to look a little more closely at what those benefits are, and to examine how national authorities can best exploit those benefits in their response to markets. I want to argue that sensible market-oriented policies will help provide governments with a buttress against domestic and global instability. And I want to outline some of the ways in which the International Monetary Fund (IMF) is seeking to help in this process.

2. Looking Back

It is hard to believe now, but there was a time, not all that long ago, when many governments treated the markets—and above all, the financial markets, with suspicion. I am not referring here just to those countries that were part of the communist empire. Even what might have been thought of as relatively enlightened governments in the industrial world feared, or mistrusted market forces. Britain's prime minister,

Harold Wilson, muttered darkly about the "gnomes of Zurich" in the wake of the devaluation crisis that nearly toppled his government in 1967. It was, of course, much easier to blame the power of the financial markets rather than his government's misguided economic policies.

In truth, governments relied for too long on policies that were essentially hostile to markets. It took time, and a great deal of effort on the part of many economists, for policymakers to learn quite how inefficient many of these measures were. In too many countries, governments could not resist the temptation constantly to extend their sphere of economic control—to micromismanage, if you like—even though neither their experience nor, indeed, their track record, gave any reason to expect them to be successful in generating economic wealth in the way that markets can do so well.

In one respect, public policymakers did display entrepreneurial flair: in devising ways for interfering with the markets. Credit rationing, for example, ensured that capital was allocated inefficiently—going all too often to favored economic actors, rather than those who could use it most effectively. Price controls meant that public sector utilities were—and in some countries still are—starved of much-needed investment funds. State-owned enterprises engaged in a wide variety of activities that, given proper price signals, would have been left to the private sector and been carried out in much more economic ways. In many cases, there was an absence of meaningful commercial codes for property rights: and in some countries, there still is.

But we are now seeing a revolution in the way governments, in both industrial and emerging economies, view the markets. The shift in attitudes has not been smooth. But shift there has been. And the progress in many emerging market economies has been particularly striking. Of course, policy reform in these countries is, inevitably, a more uneven process. They often start from a more extreme position, with very tight restrictions on markets. They have had to fight vested interests even more fiercely than industrial economies to make headway in freeing markets and adopting market-friendly policies.

But it is also striking to see some of the results that I believe can, at least in part, be ascribed to the greater willingness to recognize the potential gains to be had from enabling markets to operate more effectively. Twenty years ago, for instance, most developing and emerging market countries had double or even triple digit inflation. We sometimes forget how remarkable it is that nowadays, inflation in these countries is rarely into double-digit territory, and countries—such as Zimbabwe—with triple digit inflation are now extreme and rare cases.

And if we take the case of Chile, a country that has embraced markets earlier, more wholeheartedly, and more successfully than most emerging market economies, the results are unambiguous. This is a country that went from triple digit inflation to economic stability and prosperity in barely a single generation. Bad regulation—and by that I mean regulation intended expressly to prevent markets from operating effectively—was dismantled. A proper fiscal and monetary framework was put in place. Trade barriers were lowered. Accompanying that has been a series of reforms aimed at helping the markets function more effectively—such as those in the financial sector, for example, including the privatization of pensions.

The Chileans realized that it is not enough simply to embrace the market at the rhetorical level. Governments must construct a policy framework that enables markets to thrive. Yes, that means freeing markets from the sort of regulation that was intended to curb them. But it also means putting policies in place aimed at fostering macroeconomic stability—including budgetary discipline in the public sector. It means a readiness to let price signals work. It means, especially, establishing property rights and an effective judicial framework. It means efforts to combat bribery and corruption.

It also requires effective, well-designed measures that encourage competition and limit the scope for market-distorting behavior in the private sector. Markets can only flourish if policies are in place that provide appropriate incentives. Opening economies to international trade and world prices is one crucially important means of achieving this. In the Chilean case, high tariff and non-tariff barriers have been replaced with a uniform tariff of 6 percent.

Many other countries have successfully opened up their economies. Among emerging markets, trade barriers are a small fraction of their levels of 20 to 30 years ago, and even low-income countries have reduced them significantly.

3. The Role of the IMF

But markets do not function well in an environment of high inflation or high real interest rates. A major part of the Fund's role has been to work with our members to reduce fiscal deficits and improve the functioning of the financial system.

Improving fiscal controls is difficult, but essential. Better tax administration, more efficient tax structures (with fewer exemptions and broader bases at low rates) effective budgeting and expenditure controls are all essential. And this is a major part of the Fund's work. It is noteworthy that, even in Sub-Saharan Africa, those countries that have successfully implemented Fund programs, improving fiscal balance and public administration, have experienced a significant acceleration of their growth rates relative to other Sub-Saharan countries and their own past growth performance. And, as that has happened, the importance of a stable macroeconomic framework and good governance has been increasingly recognized as vital for good economic performance and growth.

Helping member governments develop and improve markets, to enable them to function effectively, is an increasingly important part of the Fund's work. In recent years, the Fund has been particularly concerned to help its members—all 184 of them—to develop sound economic policies aimed at promoting growth—policies that can help governments exploit the opportunities that markets can bring.

Most of the Fund's work in this area is not high profile. Significantly, though, it is work that is supported by many of those critical of other aspects of the Fund's activities. It is important. And we believe it is delivering results—though sometimes not as rapidly as we would like.

Helping governments to put the right arrangements in place is a coordinated effort, across countries and industries. The Fund works closely with the Bank for International Settlements (BIS)—and I know Malcolm Knight will be speaking at lunchtime—and the Financial Stability Forum. We cooperate closely with various international bodies, including the Basel Committee on Banking Supervision, International Organization of Securities Commissions (IOSCO) on securities regulation, International Association of Insurance Advisors (IAIS) on insurance supervision, International Accounting

Standards Board (IASB) on accounting, and International Fiscal Association (IFA) on auditing. These groups play a major role in setting standards in their areas of expertise. Thomas Jones gave an eloquent account of the work of the IASB last night. I think he brought home how great are the challenges that these international bodies face—at the intellectual and political levels.

The IMF tries to draw all these strands of work together. The most obvious way we can do this is in the surveillance work we do with every member state. As you know, every member has what we call Article 4 consultations with the Fund, whether or not a Fund program is currently in place. These consultations continue to be an important way of monitoring policy and providing timely advice. Such advice is, from time to time, unwelcome—fortunately, the Fund has never sought to win a popularity contest!

Our Article 4 surveillance work has, if anything, become even more important in recent years. That is partly because we have added to our armory. Most of you will probably be familiar with the Financial Sector Assessment Program (FSAP) introduced in 1999, a joint effort by the Fund and the World Bank, at least insofar as it involves low-income countries. Resilient, well-regulated financial systems are essential for macroeconomic and financial stability in a world of increased capital flows. The FSAP was designed to support member countries' own efforts to strengthen their financial systems. It aims to facilitate early detection of financial sector vulnerabilities, identification of key developmental needs, and to prioritize policy responses and provide technical assistance when needed to strengthen supervisory and reporting frameworks. The work under the program is supported by experts from a range of national agencies and standard-setting bodies.

The FSAP also forms the basis of Financial System Stability Assessments (FSSAs), in which IMF staff address issues of relevance to IMF surveillance, including risks to macroeconomic stability stemming from the financial sector and the capacity of the sector to absorb macroeconomic shocks. Nearly sixty such assessments have now been prepared.

Alongside this work, we have worked closely with our members—again in conjunction with the World Bank—to help them put in place relevant standards and codes, which give rise to Reports on the Observance of Standards and Codes (ROSC). The reports summarize the extent to which countries have made progress towards observing certain internationally recognized standards and codes. There are 12 areas in which we support development and adherence to codes. These comprise data dissemination, fiscal transparency, monetary and financial policy transparency, banking supervision, securities regulation, insurance supervision, payments systems, anti-money laundering and countering the financing of terrorism, corporate governance, accounting, auditing, and insolvency and creditor rights. The financial sector ROSCs are an integral part of the Financial Sector Assessment program. The ROSCs are prepared and published at the request of the member country. They are used to help sharpen policy discussions of both the Fund and the Bank with national authorities, and in the private sector (including by rating agencies) for risk assessment.

We have also stepped up our efforts to provide technical assistance. Again, this is hardly the sort of work that makes the front pages. But I believe it is a vital part of our work. In the past the importance of having the right institutional and judicial frameworks in place was often overlooked. Nowadays, we recognize that such arrangements are critical ingredients in developing market-friendly and sustainable policies. We can provide assistance—and encouragement—to countries who need to revise their judicial frameworks, reform institutions, develop bankruptcy laws, strengthen property rights, construct equitable and efficient tax regimes, and reduce corruption. Many countries need help in establishing, for instance, proper systems for monitoring and reporting public expenditure, the collection of reliable statistics, and payments systems. The Fund provides expertise and training in these areas.

4. Transparency

One of the most important changes in the way we work as an institution, and the way we are encouraging our member countries to work, is our attitude to transparency. One of the charges that Fund critics most frequently articulated was that we were a secretive institution, busily deciding the fate of national economies behind closed doors. This criticism hit home—not least because it was true! The Fund had no tradition of public engagement. The institution hated being in the public eye. And, to be fair, most member governments quite liked it that way. It meant they could fudge matters when they received unpalatable advice.

The critics still complain of the IMF's secretive ways—conspiracy theorists, after all, love to attack faceless and nameless bureaucrats. But now, I'm pleased to say, those critics are wrong. The Fund might give the impression sometimes of being slow to change. But on the issue of transparency, the institution has undergone a dramatic—and swift—revolution. It's a revolution that many of the critics are finally beginning to notice.

We are now one of the most transparent organizations in the world. Our website is packed with information that until recently the Fund would never have dreamed of publishing. Information junkies could overdose on the amount of detailed material we now regularly release.

There were two motives behind this drive for transparency. One was an attempt to deflect criticism—only partially successful, as I have said, because, as we have now learned, critics are not always influenced by facts.

The second and more important motive was an attempt to lead by example. Transparency—of policy objectives, of decision-making, and the decision-making process—is more than just a fad. It is clearly one of the most effective ways to engage markets and gain their confidence. Markets loathe uncertainty. The markets can price in bad news, and even unwelcome policies: What they do not know, though, they cannot price.

So transparency works in two ways. First, it provides markets with clear evidence of policy intentions and actions. Second, it reinforces the drive to make those policies sound, since governments are under greater pressure to deliver sustainable policies.

This is a battle I can confidently say we are winning. We have persuaded most member governments that transparency is a desirable objective. Indeed, with the support of our members, we have recently introduced a modification to our procedures as they relate to publication of Article 4 consultations. The standard presumption is now in favor of publication of such reports. The fewer the number of countries that prefer to withhold information, the more suspicious will be the markets of those countries that do so.

We should not underestimate quite how far we have come in this regard. We see an increasing number of emerging market economies in particular working to engage more openly with the financial markets. Governments are beginning to recognize the benefits of explaining to market practitioners what they are doing, and what they hope to achieve. In some cases, formal consultative procedures have been established. All this helps to build confidence in both directions. Markets trust open governments more than secretive ones; and open governments find it easier to understand how markets work and to explain their policies. The better and more detailed the explanation, the fewer surprises that governments are then likely to spring on unsuspecting markets.

And transparency brings results. Carrots are always better than sticks in the battle to convert reluctant skeptics. A recent IMF working paper showed that improving transparency does lower borrowing costs, as measured by sovereign spreads. The research also found that markets respond not just to the *publication* of reports such as Article 4 consultations, or Reports on the Observance of Standards and Codes, but to the *content* of those reports. This, of course, is entirely consistent with the argument that transparency reinforces the pressure for the development of sound economic policies.

I cannot resist noting that both inside and outside the Fund, some of the most vehement critics of transparency are now some of its most enthusiastic advocates. Nothing succeeds like success!

5. Crisis Prevention

All the work I have described comes under the very broad heading of crisis prevention. It reflects the Fund's core aim—unchanged since we were established nearly sixty years ago—of helping to provide a stable international financial system that in turn can help promote growth and international trade. Stand-by agreements, for example, are intended to provide a cushion for governments affected by market turbulence, but whose fundamental policies appear sound.

Take the recent case of Brazil. In mid-2002, the country was gearing up for its presidential election in November. Brazil had a large debt burden, but it appeared to be sustainable. Its macroeconomic policies were sound. But investors apparently doubted that these policies would be sustained by the successor government. The IMF support announced at that time of investor uncertainty during the pre-election period came about only after all the presidential candidates have indicated that they would abide by the accompanying program. This committed the incoming government to maintenance of the fiscal and monetary framework and thus reassured the financial markets. The new government's commitment to sound and sustainable policies has been maintained and markets have to date remained calm. A year ago, the spread on Brazilian bonds was about 2,400 basis points—it is now about 650.

It can certainly be argued that the market pressures during the summer of 2002 helped persuade Brazilian politicians and the public alike of the importance of adhering to the macroeconomic framework—and Brazilians are beginning to feel the benefits.

6. Crisis Resolution

Of course, even if the Fund were always right in its Article 4 assessments, governments would not necessarily follow the advice on offer. There are many reasons why a government might want to delay acting on external advice or might choose to ignore it altogether. And unless a government seeks financial assistance from the Fund, the staff ultimately has little leverage in persuading reluctant governments to introduce reform. But failure to heed warnings by the Fund will certainly lead to crisis in some cases. Crises will also erupt because of unexpected economic shocks.

The Fund's role in crises resolution remains important; and it is, of course, still the most high-profile aspect of our work. Even at this stage, the IMF is still seeking to help governments adjust their policies in ways that make them more market-friendly, although it is also seeking to give governments some protection from the impact of market turbulence. As with Brazil, the markets themselves provide a signal to governments and the public of the importance of developing and adhering to a sound macroeconomic framework.

The IMF programs for countries seeking financial assistance are agreed jointly between them and the Fund. Nowadays such programs will always include a shift towards greater transparency, economic sustainability, and institutional reform. Markets base their assessment of a country's economic prospects on a wide range of factors: the right objectives must be in place, of course, but so must be convincing ways of delivering those policy aims. Implementation is often a problem.

Measures to restore economic stability and a commitment to longer-term economic reform are critical elements in the process of crisis resolution. Equally important in the immediate aftermath of a crisis, though, is a speedy and orderly resolution to the debt problem that in many cases precipitated trouble in the first place. Here we have, I think, made some progress recently. The wide-ranging public debate we initiated on the sovereign debt restructuring mechanism did much to focus people's minds on what constitutes the most effective response. Already, one tangible result of this debate has been the adoption of collective action clauses (CAC) by ten countries that have issued bonds under New York law this year. Both governments and market practitioners had previously been reluctant to extend the use of CACs beyond the jurisdictions—such as English law—where they have long been standard.

Resistance to CACs reflected fears that the markets would demand a penalty for bond issues where they were included. It soon became apparent, though, that such bond issues attract no such penalty. There have been some sovereign bond issues that did not include CACs this year, but most such bonds issued in New York now include them as standard. Indeed, interest has now shifted towards refinement of these clauses.

Work is now under way—and much of it is in the private sector—to build on this success by examining the opportunities for aggregation across different types and maturities of debt. The most recent bond issues by Uruguay represent a first step in that direction. The challenge, though, is to find a formula that best balances the benefits to be had against the risks that this could be vulnerable to abuse. Most concern centers on two issues: the scope for inter-creditor discrimination and the possibility of manipulation by the sovereign debtor.

7. Conclusion

In terms of recognizing what benefits markets can bring, I think we have come a long way in recent years. In most cases, I think we have won the philosophical battle. Governments around the world are now, by and large, ready to acknowledge the role that markets do and should play in the domestic and international economies. Globalization has brought home to those whose instinct is perhaps to remain suspicious that governments and markets have, at the least, to establish an effective and productive way of working together.

Of course, governments will always be tempted—to take the easy path, to resist or ignore unwelcome market pressure, to postpone difficult and unpopular reforms. Markets can have an important role in helping governments stick to the right path— and in so doing help those governments deliver the stability and prosperity that their citizens want.

The IMF also has a role in keeping governments on the straight and narrow. By encouraging governments to see what benefits the markets can bring, and to help them exploit those benefits to the full, the Fund is working with the markets, not against them. It truly is a collaborative process.

*Anne O. Krueger is first deputy managing director at the International Monetary Fund.

Chapter 2

Three Observations on Market Discipline

Malcolm Knight[*]
Bank for International Settlements

We certainly all agree that market discipline is an indispensable element of a well-functioning economy. When market discipline is strong, it serves to guide funds to their most productive uses with due regard to risk. That is because market forces can raise the cost or restrict the volume of funding for those activities that have unattractive risk/return trade-offs. By threatening the demise of enterprises with poor risk/return profiles, market discipline can deter the wasteful use of scarce resources and excessive risk-taking.

Market discipline is clearly a necessary condition for financial stability, even if it is not a sufficient condition. In the repressed financial systems that existed in many countries well into the 1980s, where there were many types of interest rate and capital controls, financial system instability could remain hidden for years. But these repressed financial environments created ponderous inefficiencies, stifled incentives to price and manage risks, and resulted in "covert" insolvencies that only became exposed, sometimes with severe financial consequences, once these systems were opened to the healthy rigors of competition. There is by now a solid consensus that strengthening market discipline within a clear prudential framework can help to achieve a better balance between financial system stability and economic efficiency.

In my remarks today, I want to take a forward-looking perspective and stress three observations about market discipline on which there is no such consensus. In my view, these three issues merit greater attention from the academic and policymaking communities. The first observation identifies a limitation of market discipline; the next two observations draw out some policy implications of this limitation. In particular, they highlight two existing gaps that will need to be addressed in the strategies aimed at boosting market discipline if these strategies are to be effective. Filling these gaps will require improving the information available to exercise discipline, and sharpening market participants' incentives to enforce discipline.

My first observation: Market discipline is less effective in restraining a generalized overextension of risk-taking than it is in restraining excessive risk-taking by individual firms. And it is generalized overextension that lies behind the forms of financial instability that have the greatest macroeconomic costs.

My second observation: As regards policies designed to improve market information, we need to understand better what types of information are best suited to identifying the buildup of aggregate risk, as opposed to firm-specific risk, in the financial system. Call this, if you will, the "information gap." The disclosure of such information is an essential complement to improving the markets' ability to identify the risk profiles of individual institutions.

My third observation: As regards policies that target incentives to control risks, a key challenge is to find ways of narrowing the gap between individually rational behavior and courses of action that are collectively desirable. This "incentives gap" in part reflects the inevitable endogeneity of aggregate risk with respect to collective behavior.

Let me expand on each of these observations.

1. My First Observation: Market Discipline's Limitations Are in the Large, Not So Much in the Small

Experience indicates that markets are at their best when identifying a risky institution in an otherwise healthy financial system—the black sheep in the flock, as it were. As long as sufficient information about the financial condition of the firm exists, and as long as there is little prospect of external assistance that might insulate claimants from losses, market prices and funding conditions will tend to reflect the firm's relative riskiness. In fact that is why it is not uncommon for supervisors to rely partly on market intelligence and market reactions to spot early signs of distress in individual institutions.

At the same time, experience also indicates that markets find it harder to identify and limit excessive exposure to risk in financial systems as a whole. Evidence for this view comes from the many banking crises that have punctuated economic history and that have become more frequent since the financial liberalization that has taken place in many countries over the past quarter century. The root cause of these crises typically was not the increased fragility of a few institutions whose subsequent failure spread to others through contagion. Rather, it was the buildup of widely shared exposures across the financial system to macroeconomic risks, which were in turn closely associated with business fluctuations.

I think there are two reasons why markets are less good at identifying and mitigating systemic risk than the risks run by individual institutions.

The first has to do with *perceptions of risk.* It is no doubt easier to measure the cross-sectional dimension of risk than its time dimension, especially that of system-wide risk. The benchmark to assess cross-sectional risk, namely average behavior at a point in time, is more easily identifiable. In particular, it is less dependent on our limited knowledge of the causes of business fluctuations and on competing and controversial paradigms about the interaction between the financial and the real economy. Above all, there is less of a temptation to justify outliers. In the cross-sectional dimension, all that is required is for one institution to be "wrong," that is, an outlier. In the system-wide time dimension, somehow most institutions must be "wrong" at the same time. The burden of proof is higher; discounting past experience is easier. Paradoxically, the reluctance to question average behavior makes average behavior more questionable.

The second reason has to do with *incentives to take on risk*. Actions that may appear reasonable for individual economic agents may collectively result in undesirable outcomes. This is true both for the managers of firms and for those who provide the external financial capital to firms. For instance, during booms fear of loss of tangible short-term profit opportunities can numb risk aversion and encourage overextension. It can do so by boosting credit expansion, asset prices, and real expenditures beyond sustainable levels in a self-reinforcing process. And during downswings or in response to signs of financial strains, rational individual retrenchment can result in a "rush for the exits" that creates generalized financial distress. This fundamental endogeneity of risk is very difficult to price into individual financial instruments.

I think that this line of reasoning helps to explain why risk perceptions, and the willingness to take on risk, move in such a highly procyclical way, thereby tending to amplify business fluctuations. It helps to clarify why markets may fail to prevent the buildup of aggregate risks sufficiently promptly. And it underscores the need to address the "macroprudential" dimension of financial stability in order to strengthen market discipline. By this I mean the dimension that highlights the role of shared system-wide exposures, the intimate relationship between the macroeconomy and the financial system, and the endogeneity of aggregate risk with respect to collective decisions.

2. My Second Observation: Better Information—Both in the Large and in the Small

By now, there is a well-established consensus on the need to improve the disclosure of the risk profile of individual financial institutions. The steps taken to strengthen pillar 3 in the new Basel Capital Accord are just the latest example of this. And yet, vital as they are, these steps are not sufficient to address generalized, as opposed to institution-specific, overextension. To this end, we need to close the corresponding "information gap." In particular, we need to sharpen market participants' ability to identify the risk profile of the financial system as a whole, and we need to explore how best to disclose that information to the financial markets so as to strengthen their disciplinary role. Such disclosure, if sufficiently timely, can make market participants more cautious.

Admittedly, this task is far from straightforward. Indeed, it is complicated by the same factors that make it so difficult for markets to identify generalized overextension in the financial system. At the same time, one can make some informed guesses about its contours. First, in order to identify such vulnerabilities with sufficient lead-time, the assessment should pay particular attention to conditions during economic booms, the phase in which risk builds up. Second, it would have to consider both the likelihood and the severity of potential stress. Consequently, one might expect indicators of asset price misalignments and of excessive leverage to figure prominently. Third, it would have to be based on some form of aggregate information, with the degree and form of aggregation depending on the type of vulnerability considered.

Some encouraging progress has been made in recent years. Research by my colleagues at the Bank for International Settlements and elsewhere suggests that it may be possible to develop simple indicators of generalized overextension that are capable of foreseeing fairly well, and with a reasonable lead time, the types of banking crises that have struck a number of countries since the 1980s. Much effort has also been devoted to developing system-wide macro-stress tests. In particular, the International Monetary Fund's Financial Sector Assessment Programs (FSAPs) have confirmed the heuristic value of these exercises. And broadly based evaluations of financial vulnerabilities now feature regularly in the activities of international policy forums such as the Committee on the Global Financial System (CGFS) and the Financial Stability Forum (FSF).

Even so, this work is only in its infancy, and there are many challenges ahead. Much more research is needed to develop the necessary analytical frameworks and to elaborate and assess indicators of vulnerability. For instance, little has been done beyond the analysis of traditional banking crises: Financial market distress, as illustrated in the autumn 1998 turbulence, remains largely unaddressed. The fact that episodes of serious financial instability are, by their very nature, rare, makes it hard to reach conclusions with the necessary confidence. And the onward rush of structural change in the financial system further adds to the need for caution. On the positive side, the continuous advances in risk management and disclosure at the level of individual institutions promise to improve the raw material on which system-wide risk assessments could be made.

3. My Third Observation: The Need for Better Incentives—Not Just Safety Nets

It is not much of an exaggeration to say that for a long time the prescriptions to improve the incentives to exercise market discipline were a short-hand for "reducing the scope of financial safety nets." No doubt ill-designed safety nets can numb the incentives to behave prudently. After all, insulating creditors and investors from losses weakens the ultimate disciplinary sanction of a market economy. And since insulation is more likely in the event of generalized distress, as opposed to institution-specific distress, this may also be a factor behind the comparative difficulty that markets face in limiting generalized overextension. Policymakers have rightly devoted much attention to this problem in recent years. Prominent examples include the implementation of "structured early intervention" mechanisms in a number of countries, and the search for a more balanced burden sharing with the private sector in managing sovereign debt restructuring problems.

And yet, if the main source of distortions in private incentives is the gap between individually rational and collectively desirable courses of action, the problem is more endemic and, consequently, the right answers are harder to identify.

The problem is more endemic because the conditions that give rise to this "incentives gap" are quite common. As noted, the gap arises whenever two conditions hold: An individual action comes to be seen as more reasonable as the number of economic agents doing the same thing increases, and systemic risk is an increasing function of that number. In particular, the gap is not the result of the moral hazard induced by safety nets, but is much more "primitive." In fact, safety nets are sometimes seen as a second-best response to this gap. The obvious example is liquidity-driven bank runs.

The right answers are harder to identify because there need be nothing "irrational" about the corresponding forms of behavior. For instance, the widespread existence of short time horizons is not an irrational feature of economic life. Rather, it often reflects well-grounded contractual arrangements that try to address the uneven distribution of information between the parties in an economic relationship. For example, the need to monitor closely the performance of asset managers or corporate managers may encourage an "excessive" reliance on short-term performance indicators, such as quarterly portfolio returns or share returns.

This is a largely unexplored area, and I have hardly any specific suggestions to make. Generally, however, in order to narrow the "incentives gap," we need to give more thought to what forms of unintrusive public intervention can help agents internalize some of the unintended consequences of their collective behavior. We also need to recognize that there are inevitable limits to the worthy search for "incentive compatible" prudential standards, because the perspectives of private agents and public authorities necessarily diverge. Finally, the effort should focus more on prevention rather than cure. Hence the desirability of encouraging the buildup of cushions in good times, as risk builds up, so as to be able to run them down, up to a point, in bad times, as risks materialize.

To conclude, there is considerable scope to strengthen market discipline, particularly in the time dimension, as the economic cycle unfolds. We all agree on the goal. However, there are still many open questions about the best means to achieve it. I have tried to suggest that the questions are deeper and broader than sometimes thought. I hope that my remarks can encourage us to move a bit further towards identifying the right questions to ask in order to identify the source and dynamics of systemic risk, as a first step towards providing the answers for reinforcing market discipline.

*Malcolm Knight is the general manager at the Bank for International Settlements.

Chapter 3

Effective Market Discipline: The Roles of Auditors, Companies, and Analysts

Susan Schmidt Bies*
Board of Governors of the Federal Reserve System

I want to thank the Federal Reserve Bank of Chicago and the Bank for International Settlements for the opportunity to speak to you tonight. This conference addresses the important and timely topic of market discipline. Last evening Tom Jones spoke about the challenges in achieving high-quality, convergent, international accounting standards. My remarks, too, will touch on the importance of sound accounting and auditing, but I will also focus on the growing importance of transparent disclosures to the effective functioning of financial markets. Further, I will discuss how information users, particularly those who provide analysis to investors, can improve the quality and accessibility of their analysis. I will use some recent research on pension fund accounting to illustrate this issue. And, at the risk of setting a bleak tone for the remainder of the evening, I will also discuss the difficulties associated with achieving meaningful disclosure.

Accounting standards and appropriate disclosure are complex issues, and achieving proper and useful disclosure is not an easy task. Disclosure is not just a greater volume of information but information provided in context. Companies need to make disclosures in a way that promotes and encourages transparency. In the long run, useful disclosures will benefit well-managed companies by allowing these firms to gain access to funds in the marketplace at rates that reflect their sound management.

Of course, investors cannot be left completely off the hook—a point too often ignored. Analysts and stakeholders have an obligation to carefully analyze disclosed information and demand better disclosure if what is provided is not adequate or useful. Only then can they promote and achieve market discipline, in the classic sense of buying and selling securities, or taking a more activist approach in proxy voting and in initiating reforms.

1. Audit Quality

Most firms favor accounting standards and disclosure that help to faithfully portray the economics of a transaction, although a few companies in recent years have not been completely transparent about their practices. In these latter situations, financial reports have neither reflected nor been consistent with the way the business has actually been run or the risks to which the business has actually been exposed. Many, if not most, of these recent cases reflect fraud and breakdowns in auditing rather than inadequate accounting standards. Markets must be able to rely on the quality of work of outside auditors. In 2002, we were reminded that markets do in fact harshly discipline companies that have misled markets about their performance. But we also saw a general run-up in debt spreads in 2002, as more corporate accounting and fraud abuses became known and the market became concerned about the general quality of audits. Thus, weaknesses in a few companies and major audit firms significantly raised the cost of capital broadly across markets.

That is why the work of the new Public Company Accounting Oversight Board is so important—to reestablish the trust that investors can rely on the quality of audits. International accounting standards are moving toward an approach based on principles rather than the approach based on prescriptive rules that is familiar in the United States. The more complex and dynamic the business world becomes, the more important it is that accounting be based on strong principles that provide the framework for proper accounting of new types of transactions. However, I strongly believe that accounting standards based on principles cannot achieve the high-quality, reliable information that markets demand unless the quality of audits improves and there is insistence on high professional standards and integrity for corporate financial officers and auditors. I hope the efforts of the newly formed Public Company Accounting Oversight Board to enforce a higher professional standard at accounting firms will help restore consistency in financial reporting in U.S. financial markets. The International Accounting Federation's recent proposal to create a Public Interest Oversight Board should be supported by regulators in all counties to ensure that this renewed emphasis on high-quality professionalism for accountants and auditors becomes the standard.

Further, this summer, bank regulators in the United States adopted guidance that would permit the regulators to debar an accountant from auditing a financial institution. The bank regulators have had this statutory power since the 1991 passage of the Federal Deposit Insurance Corporation Improvement Act but, until 2001, had never seen weaknesses in audit quality that were widespread enough to require guidance. In the past two years, however, we have seen such significant breaches in audit quality at financial institutions that formal guidance was adopted to communicate clearly that we will not tolerate the poor quality of audits and attestations that we were seeing at several banking organizations.

2. Meaningful Disclosures and Financial Innovations

What constitutes meaningful disclosure can be discussed in the context of the rapid and dramatic pace of financial innovations and risk-management practices in the past few decades. During this period, firms acquired effective new tools to manage financial risk, one of which was securitization. Securitization helps a firm manage the risk of a concentrated exposure by transferring some of that exposure outside the firm. By pooling a diverse set of assets and issuing marketable securities, firms obtain liquidity and reduce funding costs. Of course, moving assets off the balance sheet and into special purpose entities, with the attendant creation of servicing rights and high-risk residual interests retained by firms, generates its own risks and reduces transparency unless the firm takes additional disclosure steps.

Firms also use derivatives to manage their risk exposures. Firms face risks from price fluctuations in currency, commodity, energy, and interest rate markets. More recently, firms have used a relatively new type of derivative, credit derivatives, which allow firms to purchase protection against the risk of loss from the default of a given entity. By purchasing such protection, financial and nonfinancial firms alike can limit or reduce their exposures to given borrowers or counterparties. Credit derivatives also allow financial firms to achieve a more-diversified credit portfolio by acquiring credit exposure to borrowers with which they do not have a lending relationship. For example, European insurance companies reportedly have used credit derivatives to acquire exposure to European corporations that, because they rely primarily on bank lending, have little publicly traded debt outstanding.

The improvements in technology, the quick pace of financial innovation, and the evolving risk-management techniques almost ensure that businesses will increasingly use almost limitless configurations of products and services and sophisticated financial structures. A byproduct of these developments will be that outsiders will have ever more difficulty understanding the risk positions of many large, complex organizations. These developments represent significant challenges to standard setters and to firms. For market discipline to function, accounting boards must innovate to accurately capture these developments.

Company managers must also do their part, by ensuring that public disclosures clearly identify all significant risk exposures—whether on or off the balance sheet—and their effects on the firm's financial condition and performance, cash flow, and earnings potential. With regard to securitizations, derivatives, and other innovative risk-transfer instruments, accounting measurement of a company's balance sheet at a point in time may be insufficient to convey the full effect of a company's financial risk profile. Therefore, disclosures about how risks are being managed and the underlying basis for values and other estimates must be included in financial reports.

Unlike typical accounting reports, information generated by risk management tends to be oriented less to a particular time and more to a description of the risks. To take an example from the world of banking, where the discipline of risk management is relatively well developed, a fair value report might say that the value of a loan portfolio is $300 million and has dropped $10 million from the previous report. However, the bank's internal risk report would show much more extensive information, such as the interest rate and credit quality of the assets and the range of values the portfolio would take under alternative future scenarios. Thus unlike a user of the fair value report, the user of a risk-management report could determine whether changes in value were due to declining credit quality, rising interest rates, or sales or payoffs of loans. Corporate risk officers have developed other types of reports that provide information on the extent to which the total return in a particular line of business compensates for the line's comprehensive risk. A reader of such a report can determine whether the growing lines of business have risk exposures that tend to offset those in other business lines—thereby resulting in lower volatility for the earnings of the corporation as a whole.

Complex organizations should continue to improve their risk-management and reporting functions. When they are comfortable with the reliability and consistency of the information in these reports, they should begin disclosing this information to the market, perhaps in summary form, paying due attention to the need for keeping proprietary business data confidential. The test for useful disclosure should be the question, Are we—the firm and its accountants—providing investors with what is needed to evaluate accurately the risk position of the firm? Disclosure that meets this test would not only provide more qualitative and quantitative information about the firm's current risk exposure to the market but also help the market assess the quality of the risk oversight and risk appetite of the organization. And, by reducing uncertainty, it would lower the cost of, and increase access to, market funding.

I particularly want to emphasize that disclosure need not be in a standard framework nor exactly the same for all organizations. Rather, we should all be insisting that each entity disclose the information that its investors need to evaluate the entity's risk profile in the most convenient and useful way. And we should keep in mind that disclosure without context may not be meaningful. Transparency means that the information presented allows an accurate understanding of the transaction that has transpired and challenges firms to present information that fosters market discipline. That is why pillar 3 in the Basel II accord is so important.

3. The Importance of Reading Disclosures: Defined-Benefit Pension Plans

The complexities and difficulties of establishing sound accounting standards and meaningful disclosure are illustrated by the treatment of expenses associated with defined-benefit pension plans. Though the details of pension accounting will surely cause many eyes to glaze over and make you all wish you were out "trick or treating" tonight, I do want to use this accounting standard as an example. In recent years we have seen how the actuarial principles on which these standards are based can produce, quite frankly, some very misleading measures of corporate earnings and balance sheets. Moreover, "full disclosure" of the underlying details, by itself, does not appear to be a panacea.

The most widely criticized aspect of the U.S. accounting standard for defined-benefit pensions is the treatment of investment returns. In effect, firms use expectations of the long-term return on assets in defined-benefit plans to calculate current-period pension cost (income) while disguising the volatility actually occurring in the portfolio. At the same time, they use a spot rate to discount the future liabilities. This accounting is reconciled with the economic reality by gradual amortization of the discrepancies between the assumed and the actual returns experienced on pension assets. As many of you are aware, this smoothing feature created very large distortions between economic reality and the pension-financing cost accruals embedded in the income statement. Of course, this begs the question of whether the market was actually hoodwinked by the accounting for pension expenses and liabilities, a question that became quite relevant after the stock market tumbled—along with interest rates—in the early 2000s.

A study recently undertaken by staff at the Federal Reserve Board tackled that very question.[1] The study adopts the premise that most of what investors need to know about the true pension-financing costs, not the smoothed costs, is most accurately reflected in two numbers disclosed in the pension footnote. These two numbers are the fair market value of pension assets and the present value of outstanding pension liabilities. The net financing cost in the income statement, a potentially misleading measure, can be thought of as a translation of these balance-sheet figures into an expected flow.

The study then asks two questions: First, how close is the correspondence between the fair market value of net pension assets—that is, the value of assets net of liabilities reported in the footnotes—and its wayward twin, the net financing cost accrual embedded in the income statement? Second, when these two measures provide conflicting information, which measure does the market employ to value the firm?

The study finds that, in normal times—that is, when asset prices have not been subject to unusually large swings—these two measures of pension plan value usually give fairly consistent signals of the pension plan's condition. In such times, the valuation implications of using one measure over the other would be fairly modest for most firms. However, by late 2001, after stock prices and interest rates had tumbled for eighteen months, these two measures of pension finances gave very different, in many cases highly contradictory, signals of the pension plan finances and their valuation implications.

What is more, the study finds that, when these measures do diverge, stock prices are much more prone to reflect the misleading net financing cost rather than the more direct measure of the pension assets and liabilities disclosed in the footnotes. For many firms, the implied valuation discrepancies were quite large in 2001, when the average discrepancy was 5 percent to 10 percent. In other words, the average firm with a defined-benefit plan in 2001 may have been 5 percent to 10 percent overvalued relative to an otherwise similar firm without a defined-benefit plan.

What lessons should we take away? Well, to begin with, the findings suggest that wholesale disclosure, by itself, does not automatically create transparency. Arguably, there are two additional requirements. First, the disclosures must be provided in a way that facilitates their incorporation into a financial analysis of the firm. And second, transparency requires that investors, at least those having the wherewithal, assume the responsibility of doing their homework.

For instance, key information from the pension balance sheet can be readily incorporated into a valuation model only if investors or analysts can easily identify its evil twin, the financing cost accrual, and exclude it from their preferred measure of earnings. But the information needed to make this adjustment has not been presented in a way that encourages or even facilitates such an approach. And though certainly some analysts and investors had their eye on the ball, too many apparently could not be bothered.

The Financial Accounting Standards Board (FASB) and the International Accounting Standards Board (IASB) are actively pursuing reforms to pension accounting and disclosure. The new annual disclosures proposed in the draft should give a clearer picture of plan assets and the risks they harbor. In particular, companies will be required to disclose in their annual financial reports the actual and targeted percentages of plan assets that fall into various investment categories—in particular, stocks, debt securities, and real estate. Sponsors will also be required to report the long-run rates of return that they are assuming for each category.

Another piece of information that is not currently in the proposal, but probably ought to be, is the amount invested in the firm's own stock. Whereas investing pension assets in general equities increases the sponsor's risk, investing in a firm's own stock boosts this effect since it is equivalent to increasing the firm's balance-sheet leverage. When the company gets into financial difficulties, the ability to contribute to the pension plan will be the weakest just when the declining value of those plan assets requires larger contributions.

Disclosure regarding cash flow information—that is, actual contributions—is also to be enhanced. In particular, the proposal is that sponsors will be required to detail contributions intended for the fiscal year that was just begun, showing contributions required by funding regulations, additional discretionary contributions, and any noncash contributions.

The FASB is proposing that some of the annual pension disclosures be reported on a quarterly basis. Currently, none of this information is updated except when the annual report is released. The proposal has firms reporting quarterly net pension cost broken out into its various components as well as disclosing substantial unanticipated contributions to their plans. If implemented, these proposed disclosures will shed a fair amount of additional light on this murky area of pension accounting.

4. Investor Information

Finally, I turn to the role of users of financial information. The objective of accounting and disclosure is to make relevant, transparent information available to the market. But as we have just seen for pensions, the leading analysts did not focus on information available about the funding status of defined-benefit pension plans when they were added to earnings per share each quarter. Thus, the analysts did not communicate that these "pennies" were just timing differences and should not be included in long-term earnings forecasts.

As organizations become more complex and financial innovations become more arcane to the average investor, the question arises as to how the typical investor can receive good analysis of the companies they are considering for investment. The serious nature of the conflicts of interest between sell-side analysts and investment bankers has lead to major restructuring of the research function at investment banks. We have seen a reduction in these staffs as firms begin to try to find a way to cover the expense of the research function by other means.

As a result, investors are currently finding it hard to get any information about some companies because alternative sources of analysis that are accessible to the average investor have not yet replaced the sell-side information. Consider the companies among the Standard & Poor's (S&P) 500; presumably these large firms should have the most analyst coverage since they are more likely to be in investors' portfolios. However, if you go to sources of analyst reports, there are firms among the S&P 500 that have less than two earnings estimates by analysts posted! Further, as a result of Sarbanes–Oxley, Securities and Exchange Commission actions, and recent shareholder suits, some firms have decided not to give earnings guidance. Thus, for many investors, receiving good independent analysis about companies that they want to consider for investment has become a problem. I hope that more attention will shift to improving information that goes to investors. Without improved information, we will not see the full effect that better accounting, disclosure, audit quality, and corporate governance could have on strengthening financial markets.

5. Conclusion

In conclusion, timely, accurate, and credible financial information for market participants is critical to the successful functioning of market discipline. Because not all concepts can be easily measured and fit into a rigid accounting framework, investors need to rely also on enhanced disclosures to provide a faithful portrayal of economic transactions. However, disclosure by itself is not necessarily equivalent to transparency. Rather, firms need to provide information in ways that allow and encourage investors to process it, and as I emphasized earlier, the form of disclosure need not be the same across firms. And if analysts and shareholders do not use the information at hand, even the best disclosure is useless. For all these reasons, disclosures may need to be reevaluated as circumstances dictate. Success is in the interest of everyone, not least of all the companies themselves, because disclosure reduces uncertainty and their financing costs.

*Susan Schmidt Bies is a member of the Board of Governors of the Federal Reserve System.

Notes

1. Julia Coronado and Steve Sharpe, 2003, "Did pension accounting contribute to a stock market bubble?," *Brookings Papers on Economic Activity*, July.

Chapter 4

A Review of the New Basel Capital Accord

Jaime Caruana*
Basel Committee on Banking Supervision and Bank of Spain

1. Overview

I would like to thank President Moskow, Malcolm Knight, and the staffs of the Federal Reserve Bank of Chicago and of the Bank for International Settlements for organizing and hosting this timely conference. It is a pleasure for me to join your discussion in Chicago today. I can think of few venues better situated to talk about markets and to explore the links between transparency, corporate governance, and the role markets can play to encourage prudent risk-taking.

Bank regulators in recent years have begun to view markets as an ally to our system of supervision. We have consequently sought to incorporate market discipline directly into the supervisory framework. Markets value well-capitalized and well-managed institutions as much as supervisors do, and can create rewards for banks that manage their risks appropriately. Yet banks can be very complex institutions and no market discipline is possible without widespread public access to timely, accurate, and comprehensive information on a bank's exposures, its risk management processes, and its outlook for the future.

I'd like to discuss this morning why the Basel Committee believes that applying transparency and market discipline approaches in the New Capital Accord will help us achieve our objectives to reinforce the safety and soundness of the banking system.

My first point will be that, despite its name, the New Capital Accord is about much more than just capital. It is also about maintaining a level playing field and about strengthening incentives to foster sound risk management through three pillars: risk-sensitive minimum capital requirements, coordinated supervisory review, and—importantly, given the theme of this conference—enhanced market discipline through greater transparency. The New Accord is therefore much more comprehensive than its 1988 forerunner.

Second, I'll comment on the rationale behind the compound approach followed by the Basel Committee that blends rules, discretion, and market-based incentives.

It could be viewed as a portfolio of different policy approaches that allow supervisors to achieve or at least draw close to a kind of efficient frontier.

Third, I'll share with you key issues that the committee faced in drafting the market discipline component of the New Accord and, specifically, I will mention some of the concerns that arose in our public consultations. Mainly:

- Proprietary versus public information,

- Principles versus rules, and

- Consistency of accounting standards and the New Basel Accord.

Finally, I will review the present status of the accord, the significant progress made in our last meeting in Madrid and I will outline the next steps in its rapid finalization, as well as our plans for keeping it fit for the future.

2. Basel II: A New, Comprehensive Approach to Achieve Greater Financial Stability

To begin, I would like to reemphasize the importance of market discipline to banking supervision, especially in a rapidly changing environment. Supervisors seek improvements in the public's access to information on a bank's condition precisely to bolster the ability of rating agencies, of business counterparties, and even of investors or depositors to evaluate the profile of a bank's risks and the quality of its controls. Yet as safety and soundness regulators, we wish to fortify the stability and resilience of the financial system. In our view this goal requires not just greater transparency, but also significant advances in the state of the art of risk management and adequate capital when unexpected losses materialize.

For the first time, the Capital Accord will include not only explicit economic incentives expressed in the minimum capital requirements but also implicit incentives built into the processes for supervisory review and market disclosure.

I think it is helpful to recall why so many central banks, regulatory agencies, and commercial banks have devoted their best resources to ensuring the success of the New Accord. The existing accord, as you know, was already considered a milestone in banking regulation. It offered the first internationally accepted "yardstick" for capital adequacy and a simple measure of risk. It had received praise for reversing a downward trend in bank capital levels and for serving as a benchmark measure of a bank's financial health around the world.

But the 1988 Accord was a blunt instrument that quickly fell behind the times. Advances in technology, in banking products, and in risk management changed the way that leading banks measure and manage their risks. By the mid-1990s, bankers and supervisors agreed that the original accord no longer offered the largest and most sophisticated organizations a meaningful measure of risk.

Under the leadership of William McDonough, former president of the Federal Reserve Bank of New York and my predecessor as chairman of the Basel Committee, the committee seized the opportunity to achieve more than a simple update of the capital requirements. Bill brought tireless energy to the project and convinced industry leaders, bank supervisors, and central bankers that we should pursue a far greater objective that would incorporate market discipline and also encourage advances in risk management across the industry.

While he has moved on to new challenges as head of the Public Company Accounting Oversight Board in Washington, the U.S. delegation to the Basel Committee remains in excellent hands. The hard work of leaders such as Roger Ferguson, the Vice Chairman of the Federal Reserve, and Jerry Hawke, the U.S. Comptroller of the Currency, and of other U.S. supervisors in the negotiations, has strengthened the quality of the capital rules. They have helped ensure that the New Accord will be flexible, forward-looking, and fit for the service of twenty-first century banking.

3. Basel II: A Blend of Reinforcing Policy Approaches

The long-term objective of fostering greater financial stability led to our decision to supplement the revised minimum capital requirements, which constitute the first pillar of the New Accord, with two equally important pillars.

Although this may be an oversimplification, one could argue that each of the three pillars can be viewed as representing a different policy approach for a regulatory/supervisory framework. The first pillar emphasizes the adoption of uniform rules. The second pillar relies more on the use of discretion in setting requirements for individual banks. And the third pillar can be expressive of a market-based approach.

Each of these choices individually considered has its merits, but also certain downsides. The point I want to make is that the risk/reward features of each of the three options—rules, discretion, and market discipline—have their own particularities and are not totally correlated. From a portfolio theory point of view it could be argued that the optimum result is achieved through using a combination of all three approaches, and that this combination is far better than any of the individual options alone.

Rules constitute a very direct approach and one that offers the greatest clarity to institutions on what supervisors expect from banks, thereby leading to a higher level of transparency from both the perspective of the banks and the supervisors, and promoting comparability between institutions.

However, adopting a rules-based option alone, even if they are market friendly, entails certain disadvantages. It tends to be inflexible and therefore might preclude innovation. It could also fail to take account of bank or business line specificities.

This is why the committee decided to complement the minimum capital requirements with the second pillar, known as supervisory review. This allows a discretionary approach according to the situation of specific banks or types of business—very much like the principles-based policy approach. The benefits of such an approach are flexibility and adaptability to specific needs, both now and over time as situations and responses change.

But this approach alone would also have its shortcomings. Market participants could find it difficult to compare banks. The lack of a common standard across institutions might actually reduce transparency, since markets might not know or understand why supervisors established particular requirements for certain banks but not for others. This approach alone could also raise competitive equality problems, making it more difficult to ensure a level playing field, one of the key objectives of the Basel Accord.

The third option would be a market-driven solution. As I have already said, the committee has recognized the importance of market discipline in the third pillar of the New Accord. It draws on the power of markets to create strong incentives for banks, incentives to help ensure that banks manage their risks properly and do not hold unrealistically low amounts of capital for their risk.

There is a lot of merit in this approach, yet all of us know that markets sometimes behave inefficiently. They can overreact to certain minor events yet still overlook significant indicators of risk in the short run. Likewise, markets are not always able to capture some externalities on their own, such as the interests of the broader public. They sometimes focus on the immediate needs of direct participants rather than those of depositors or customers or they can be too short-sighted in their time horizon. I think the thoughtful comments made by Malcolm Knight yesterday about gaps and limitations of market discipline clarify these kinds of issues most constructively.

So it is clear that no single one of these three options provides all of the benefits that supervisors seek. We want rules to provide clarity and strong incentives. We want the ability to use discretion to manage diversity, to tailor requirements to the specific businesses of each bank. Finally, we want markets to provide economic incentives for institutions to improve bank management and disclose information that is relevant to end-users' needs.

What I am saying is that the "efficient frontier" can best be achieved through a combination of the three pillars, given the reinforcing/diversifying effects of each. Each pillar provides something that the other cannot and is essential to achieving our overall objective of financial stability.

I realize that this presentation of the three pillars as items of a portfolio of policy options is an oversimplification, but I think it helps us visualize why we think that the most "efficient frontier" involves a mixture of minimum rules, tempered by supervisory discretion, and supplemented by market-based incentives.

4. Current Industry Practices and Issues That Arose in Consultations

Let me now move to current industry practices and how transparency is incorporated into the Basel framework.

In deciding to revise the 1988 Accord, the Basel Committee thought carefully about what improvements to banks' public reporting would mirror the New Accord's incentive-based approach to foster improvements in risk management. In recent years, the committee has noted some improvements in the quality of bank reporting worldwide. Annual surveys conducted by the committee suggest that the extent of banks' public disclosures has increased markedly in some areas.

Still, important deficiencies remain. For example, in 2001—the most recent date for which comparative global information is available—the most prevalent disclosures covered accounting and presentation policies, on a bank's capital structure and its measures of capital adequacy, and, for those that had them, on the kind of market risk models the bank used. Few banks disclosed much about their credit risk models, the types of credit risk mitigation techniques that they employed, or even the external or internal ratings assigned to their credit exposures.

The relative paucity of data available publicly on a typical bank's credit risk profile appears inconsistent with the fact that, for most banks, credit risk remains the single most important source of potential loss. At present, market participants seem to know only little about the extent of most banks' exposure to credit risk. One could conclude that it seems unrealistic today to assume that they have enough knowledge of a bank's position to exercise properly a benign influence on its handling of credit risk. Disclosure practices do not seem to have kept pace with the very rapid evolution in the ways that banks take on, measure, and ultimately manage their risk positions.

4.1 Incorporating Market Discipline into the New Basel Accord

To improve the ability of markets to contribute to greater stability in the banking sector, the New Accord will contain a series of disclosure requirements. The committee views pillar 3 as a further refinement of accounting standards requirements as they should apply to banks in the light of the specific risks they face. Some of the requirements may furthermore be tied to a bank's eligibility for adopting an advanced approach to credit or operational risk or for recognizing the benefits of particular instruments and transactions in mitigating risks.

We based our decisions on the information that should be disclosed on the following principles: that market participants require an understanding of how the capital requirements apply to the consolidated banking organization; that they should know what risks banks face, to what degree, and how they assess those risks; and that they should have details on what capital they hold.

More generally, by emphasizing principles in the disclosure rules—that banks should have a formal disclosure policy approved by the board, that internal measurement tools must be credible, that they must adequately capture risk, and that they must be used by banks in the daily management of their operations and not just for regulatory capital purposes—transparency may actually result in more consistency in the application of advanced approaches than detailed quantitative criteria.

4.2 Issues That Arose in Consultation

The process for transcribing these principles into rules for the New Accord has involved extensive discussion among supervisors, representatives of the accounting profession, and financial institutions. This past summer alone, for example, the committee received over 200 public comments on the proposals set out in our third consultative paper, or "CP3" as we call it. The third pillar attracted a degree of controversy among many banks mainly in earlier drafts of the rules, but thanks to the very positive discussions that the committee had with the industry and with accounting standards-setting bodies, all the pillars of CP3 now enjoy broad support. This brings me to the next part of my address, in which I'll cover the key concerns that arose during consultations.

4.3 Proprietary versus Public Information

Certainly, an early concern about the market discipline component of the New Accord was that the required disclosures appeared to go far beyond what banks traditionally reported publicly. In some institutions' opinion, the committee was seeking to require the disclosure of information previously considered confidential. While the committee is mindful of the concern that some information should remain private, we believe that concepts of public versus proprietary information require some reflection. In order to determine whether information should be disclosed, consideration should also be given to end-users' needs. For example, in order for shareholders, creditors, and counterparties to appreciate the risks of their own exposures to a bank, they must understand that bank's appetite for risk and its approach to, and methodologies for, managing risk. What should drive this debate is what a bank itself would want to know before making an investment or credit decision, rather than the concerns that some have about what had formerly been considered secret.

The committee believes it has struck an appropriate balance between meaningful disclosure and protection of proprietary and confidential information.

4.4 Principles versus Rules

A second concern that arose in consultations was the committee's decision to adopt specific rules for disclosure, rather than articulate broad principles for transparency. But on this point, many institutions seem caught up in a contradiction. On the one hand, banks suggest that we avoid overly detailed guidance on public reporting that might create burdensome and inflexible rules. On the other, nearly all banks have urged the committee to provide clarity to ensure the consistent application of the New Accord across jurisdictions. Understandably, some banks are concerned that, in the absence of specific rules, competitors in other countries might be subject to less scrutiny than they are.

We recognize that a principles-based approach offers benefits, especially in terms of simplicity and flexibility. But our main intention is to offer markets a clearer picture of a bank's risk profile, regardless of what jurisdiction that bank may call home. To promote both greater insight into a bank's true risks and a more level playing field for all banks, we advocate disclosure rules based on principles rather than looser principles that might be subject to local interpretation. Likewise, the committee rejected proposals for supplemental disclosures that would be optional under the New Accord.

This has admittedly resulted in disclosure requirements that are more detailed and perhaps less elegant than a simple expression of principles might be. But perhaps supervisors can take some comfort from the physicist who recommended that "if you are out to describe the truth, leave elegance to the tailor."

4.5 Consistency of Accounting Standards and the New Basel Accord

One cannot discuss transparency and market discipline without considering the mechanics through which financial data are recorded and reported. And this brings me to a final key observation raised in comment letters, namely the industry's position that if we are to leverage market discipline through better reporting, the committee should clarify the differences between accounting standards and supervisory objectives.

Numerous institutions have called on the committee to continue to align the regulatory framework more closely with the converging standards in accounting worldwide. Many industry representatives have noted quite correctly that a greater degree of accordance is warranted especially now that the New Basel Accord includes explicit disclosure requirements intended to promote greater insight into a bank's risk profile. Likewise, the Basel Committee's treatment of provisions and the valuation of financial instruments must keep pace with changes in the relevant accounting standards.

We have made a considerable effort to see that the narrower focus of pillar 3 does not conflict with the broader accounting requirements, and we have liaised closely with our colleagues in the International Accounting Standards Board in pursuit of this objective. In fact, the committee views pillar 3 as a further refinement of the accounting standards requirements as they should apply to banks in the light of the specific risks that they face. The committee is convinced that such specificity is both appropriate and necessary for prudential reasons.

Market discipline, and hence financial stability, is strengthened when accounting and disclosure requirements reflect sound risk-management principles and represent the control practices that banks adopt. Consequently, we recognize our responsibility to participate actively in the development of national and international accounting standards. When designing standards for the disclosure of components of capital, for loan reporting, and for other topics of mutual concern, we have sought out the views of accounting standards-setting bodies. This dialogue will continue.

Where regulatory and accounting principles may not yet be fully consistent, we have sought to align our requirements as best as possible with international accounting standards and to resolve other matters reasonably and based on our understanding of the potential direction that accounting standards might take in the future. Because we recognize that there is still much to be done in this area we will continue to monitor pillar 3 in the light of accounting and market developments. I should add that we are seeking new opportunities for discussion with accounting standards-setting bodies and private sector accounting professionals.

5. The Status of the New Accord

The committee is currently reviewing carefully these responses and other issues that the industry raised. In relation to pillar 3, we are evaluating closely what should be reported publicly, versus what can remain confidential. We are refining the rules so that they will help secure a more level playing field without being overly burdensome. We are aligning our reporting requirements with those emerging from accounting standards.

In terms of the way forward, as you may know, in mid-October the committee reached an important agreement on a work plan for taking these and other issues into account, and significant progress was made on major issues. What is most important to the committee is the quality and consistency of the New Accord. At the same time, we recognized the need to provide banks with as much certainty as possible while they plan and prepare for the adoption of the new rules. In our last meeting in Madrid, the members of the committee agreed on the importance of finalizing the New Accord expeditiously and in a manner that is technically and prudentially sound.

We noted in a statement to the press that we expect to address the remaining issues and complete the text of the New Accord in the coming months and no later than mid-year 2004. This period of time will also allow us to take careful note of valuable information coming from domestic consultations under way in some jurisdictions, including the process for the Advance Notice of Proposed Rulemaking in the United States.

The committee also discussed the importance of ensuring that the calibration of the New Accord achieves its objectives. Accordingly, prior to implementation, a further review of the calibration will be conducted on the basis of additional information, such as further impact assessments in some jurisdictions and the monitoring of banks' parallel calculations.

In terms of specific issues, a number of areas were identified where major improvements were possible: the expected versus unexpected losses calibration issue, securitization, credit cards commitments, and risk-mitigation techniques. At present, we have offered for public review a proposal to resolve a fundamental concern raised by the industry on the treatment of expected versus unexpected losses. I would encourage those interested to read the statement outlining our proposed revision on our website and to share any thoughts you may have by the end of this year. We have also simplified the proposals for securitization exposures, as we decided to replace the "supervisory formula" approach to unrated tranches with a simpler rule.

Also, as we draw closer to finalization, the committee has intensified its efforts to facilitate a consistent implementation of the New Accord. A set of principles has been outlined for the cross-border application of the New Accord to promote closer practical cooperation and information exchange among supervisors. These implementation issues are very important to promote consistency and to reduce the burden on internationally active banks.

There are, however, other areas that we can already identify as part of our future work plan to advance risk management, to promote greater transparency, and to strengthen the stability of the financial sector. Given that I have mentioned in this presentation the benefits of utilizing the diversification effects of different approaches in the search for an efficient frontier, I'd like to conclude with just one of the potential items on our agenda for future work once the New Accord is implemented.

This item would be to consider the benefits of full credit risk models in the calculation of minimum capital requirements. In theory, a bank's capital requirements would then reflect to the greatest degree the economic benefits of diversification in its balance sheet. In fact, the committee did at one point evaluate whether advanced banks should be permitted to estimate the degree to which their assets might behave similarly or default together in the New Basel Accord.

As you know, we decided that we are not quite there yet. We know that some banks are making commendable progress in thinking about ways to estimate the value of diversification. Nonetheless, we remain concerned about the degree of confidence one might have in those estimates, given the relative lack of data available. Likewise, we have not yet seen evidence that there is a critical mass of banks that would today consistently meet the "use" test spelled out in the New Accord. In the coming years, and we can start very soon, we look forward to continuing this dialogue with banks, banking associations, and researchers to find ways to move Basel in the direction of full credit risk models.

Although banks and supervisors have much to do in the years ahead, we are confident that the development of an incentives-based capital framework, accompanied by more consistent and focused supervisory review and a concurrent enhancement of market discipline, will improve the management of risk across the industry, promote broader financial stability and resilience, and ensure that the banking system is better able to promote sustainable growth in the economy.

*Jaime Caruana is the chairman of the Basel Committee on Banking Supervision and governor of the Bank of Spain.

PART II

THEORY OF MARKET DISCIPLINE

Chapter 5

Market Discipline: Players, Processes, and Purposes

Robert R. Bliss*

Federal Reserve Bank of Chicago

1. Introduction

The study of market discipline has a long tradition in financial economics.[1] However, since the debates surrounding the introduction of deposit insurance in 1933, it was not until the late 1990s that there was a resurgence of interest in the regulatory community in the potential benefits of increased market discipline of financial institutions in general and banks in particular became widely accepted.[2] Now regulators have joined academics and regulatory economists in calling for enhanced market discipline of financial institutions. Today, regulators extol market discipline as a desirable or even necessary supplement to regulatory discipline in their speeches. Market discipline forms the third of three pillars of the Basel II proposal, and the Gramm–Leach–Bliley legislation required the study of subordinated debt proposals as a means of enhancing market discipline. Despite this growing awareness of the issue and the already voluminous literature on various aspects of market discipline, relatively little attention has been given to what market discipline is and how it works.[3] This may be because the discussion of market discipline has been driven in large part by proposed remedies, which have defined the problem in terms of the proffered solutions.[4]

This paper steps back and asks what market discipline is, what problems it addresses, how it works, how it interacts with regulatory discipline, and how it relates to other issues in finance. I will argue that market discipline consists of those mechanisms that have evolved to solve information and incentive problems inherent in modern large corporations so that capital markets can function.[5] Market discipline is both a very old issue and a very complex one.

2. What Is the Problem?

In 1776 Adam Smith thought that joint-stock companies, the precursors to our modern corporations, were doomed. He observed that "… [joint-stock companies] have … very seldom succeeded without an exclusive privilege [legal monopoly]; and frequently have not succeeded with one."[6] Smith based his analysis both on the empirical evidence of frequent failures of joint stock companies[7] and on a theoretical argument that we now call the principal–agent problem.

> The directors of such [joint-stock] companies … being the managers rather of other people's money than their own, it cannot well be expected, that they should watch over it with the same anxious vigilance with which partners in a private copartnery frequently watch over their own. … Negligence and profusion, therefore, must always prevail, more or less, in the management of the affairs of such a company.[8]

And yet today joint-stock companies are the dominant form of business organization in industrialized countries. While Adam Smith was correct in his identification of the central problem with the corporate form, his conclusion has become dated. Markets have evolved to solve, imperfectly, to be sure, but sufficiently for their purposes, the problem of how providers of capital can induce managers to watch over their investments with sufficient anxious vigilance; in other words, markets have learned to discipline managers.

3. The Components of Market Discipline

To begin our discussion of market discipline and the mechanisms by which it operates, it is important to recognize that market discipline involves two key functions: monitoring and influence (Bliss and Flannery, 2002). Monitoring requires the market participants to have the incentives and ability to monitor the actions of the firm and its managers. The incentives to monitor depend on the cost/benefit trade-offs of doing so. Costs depend on transparency and easily accessible information. Benefits depend on the size of the exposure, thus many diffuse stockholders may monitor less than a few large block holders. The ability component involves both access to necessary information about the firm (transparency) and the ability to properly interpret that information (competence). The results of market monitoring may show up in equity prices, yield spreads, or willingness to invest or transact; or they may take more opaque forms such as collateral requirements and net position adjustments.[9]

Monitoring is a necessary but not sufficient condition for market discipline. For market discipline to be effective there must be feedback from the monitors which induces firm managers adjust their behavior. Bliss and Flannery (2002) call this "influence." Influence can come directly from market participants, called direct discipline, or it can come from other agents, such as regulators, using the information provided by market monitoring to inform actions that influence managers' decisions, called indirect discipline.

Furthermore, discipline can take one of two forms. Ex post discipline comes in response to managerial actions. Actions the markets disapprove of may be "punished" in various ways, the most drastic being a withdrawal of funding that may lead to illiquidity and possible insolvency. More subtly, and no doubt more pervasive, properly aligned incentives, including the threat of adverse consequences, may induce managers to undertake actions which are in the first place consistent with the markets' interests. This is called ex ante discipline.

4. Why the Call for More Market Discipline?

Financial institutions have become increasingly complex and opaque. This is particularly true of the largest financial organizations with large derivatives positions and off-balance-sheet activities. Securitizations and associated residuals present challenges to both accountants and supervisors attempting to value the firm's assets and liabilities. This is coupled with the increasing concentration in the financial markets, particularly for derivatives. Thus, while the largest firms are becoming difficult to examine and supervise prudentially, the potential adverse impact of their failure is also increasing.

The regulatory calls for *increased* market discipline point to a perception that what market discipline there is may be insufficient. This is itself due in part to real or perceived regulatory distortions. Deposit insurance creates a class of bank counterparties with diminished incentives to monitor.[10] However, insured depositors may be ineffective monitors, frequently lacking the competence to make informed valuation and risk assessments. More importantly, deposit insurance means that banks are able to raise funds from investors who may not have strong incentives to monitor, thus undermining other potential sources of discipline (risk-sensitive uninsured creditors). While insured depositors enjoy *de jure* protection, there is also a concern among many regulators and academics that market participants may perceive *de facto* protection of the counterparties of very large banks. This is either too big to fail or "too big to be allowed to implode quickly."[11]

Regulators have become increasingly uncomfortable with shouldering the primary burden for supervising large financial institutions. They realize that the complexity and valuation of modern financial engineering products may be beyond the ken of most examiners. This problem is exacerbated by a scarcity of regulatory resources. The regulatory logic for increased market discipline presumes that market participants may be collectively more able to monitor banks activities than understaffed regulators or at least to provide a more continuous oversight. Furthermore, some market participants, for instance derivatives counterparties, may be individually better able to undertake the complex assessments required.

Regulators seek to leverage the perceived abilities of markets in two ways. The first is to use the signals provided by market monitoring as an input when deciding how to allocate regulatory resources (producing indirect market discipline). The second is to have at-risk market participants directly influence managers to take the desired actions, thus supplementing regulatory discipline with direct market discipline. Other commentators have suggested that market monitoring is needed to influence the regulators rather than the regulated. Evidence of regulatory forbearance during the savings and loan crisis and attendant concerns regarding regulatory incentives have not been entirely ameliorated by prompt corrective action (PCA) rules legislated under the

Federal Deposit Insurance Corporation Improvement Act (FDICIA) of 1991. Proposals to reduce forbearance range from using sub-debt yield spreads to trigger mandatory regulatory actions to simply providing a public signal of bank quality that will raise the political costs of regulatory forbearance.[12]

5. Agency Costs and Market Discipline

Discussions of market discipline frequently assume, without qualification, that market discipline would obtain if only regulatory distortions such as too big to fail were eliminated and transparency increased. However, the highly idealized view of the relevant economic agents implicit in these discussions masks critical issues that impact the functioning of market discipline mechanisms (both monitoring and influence). The idealized worldview underlying subordinated debt proposals ignores what are called principal–agent problems, or simply agency problems.

A formal theory of agency was first developed by Jensen and Meckling (1976) and applied to the modern corporation by Fama (1980) and Fama and Jensen (1983). Agency costs are created by the separation of ownership, or more generally the provision of capital, and control (management) in an environment characterized by information asymmetries, costly monitoring, and incomplete contracting. These unavoidable costs arise because investors cannot reliably ensure that managers will act in the investors' interest and not the managers'—that is, equity (and bond) holders cannot perfectly control managers. There is an extensive empirical literature analyzing the determinants, extent, and magnitude of agency costs in the economy.[13] The success of corporate capitalism clearly demonstrates that the benefits of separation of investment and management far outweigh the agency costs that this separation gives rise to. However, it would be incorrect to conclude that agency costs are negligible. Rather, the mechanisms of market discipline are in general sufficiently well developed to lower these costs to the point where the benefits of the corporate form can be realized.

Agency costs can be mitigated by various mechanisms: delegated monitors (boards of directors, regulatory supervision), reducing information costs (required disclosures of relevant information), and reducing managers' incentives to abuse their position (fiduciary, fraud, and insider trading laws; threat of a takeover; and performance incentives such as managerial stock options). However, agency costs cannot be entirely eliminated, thus market discipline of managers is inevitably imperfect. We must seek to understand what market discipline can do and how, rather than to view it as a panacea, and we do this by first examining how market discipline works in the general, that is for most unregulated corporations, where market forces are the source of discipline. We can then intelligently approach the question of how market discipline functions in a heavily regulated environment and how that environment might be modified to increase the power of market disciplinary mechanisms.

Equity holders and bondholders can surely influence managers in extremis. For example, when money market participants refused to roll over Penn Central's commercial paper in 1971, management was forced to take action. They filed for Chapter 11 bankruptcy protection from the firm's creditors. Equity holders can also vote out management, and poor firm performance increases the likelihood of managerial turnover.

Sufficiently disgruntled equity holders may create an environment that facilitates a hostile takeover.

Direct and reasonably certain discipline of managers is possible only in certain circumstances. The market for corporate control (takeovers) and direct control by large external equity holders who have effective-control blocks are forms of market discipline.[14] Major equity holders can themselves effect changes in board composition or form, at relatively low cost, coalitions to do so, inducing the board to change management. Major investors or other firms can mount hostile takeovers, which if successful will result in a change in management. These situations, while they represent the ultimate sanction against management (other than prosecution for malfeasance), are rare events and affect only the top managers of a few very large firms. Informal or ad hoc restriction of derivatives dealing to highly rated counterparties is another form of market discipline, by preventing managers from engaging in certain forms of excessive risk-taking if they wish to participate in those markets. Empirical evidence confirms the existence, though not the invariable effectiveness, of all these disciplinary forces.

Labor market discipline is another form of market discipline. For many senior managers, the hope of more lucrative jobs at other firms induces them to work to establish their reputations as value-enhancing agents acting in the equity holders' interests.[15,16] Examining the post-resolution placement of bank managers following a number of Texas bank failures in the 1980s, Cannella, Fraser, and Lee (1995) find results consistent with the managerial labor market discriminating between managers who were likely to have been responsible for their bank's problems and those who were not. Managers likely to have been responsible for bank failures tended not to be subsequently employed in the industry, while those arguably not responsible were frequently employed by other banks. Farrell and Whidbee (2000) find a similar result for outside directors. In this case, outside directors who were aligned with forcibly removed chief executive officers (CEOs), owned little equity, and made poor choices in replacing the CEO, on average, subsequently lost their positions. Directors who were not aligned with the fallen leader (and/ or had large equity stakes) not only kept their current directorships, but also were appointed to additional directorships at other firms.

However, policy proposals for using market discipline to enhance banking supervision usually envisage something more commonplace, constructive, and benign than precipitating bankruptcy or replacing management through takeovers. Yet we have virtually no empirical evidence, outside the managerial labor market literature, concerning equity holder and bondholder market influence in less extreme situations.[17]

Only a few papers look at banking and corporate control (agency cost) issues. Most of the economics of regulation literature (which considers, among other things, the incentives of regulators) is concerned with market power regulation (for example, utilities) or safety regulation (for example, airlines), rather than financial safety regulation. To draw implications from our review of the corporate literature for the problem of bank regulation, we can only make tentative extrapolations of the existing theory and consider the few existing empirical studies.

The theoretical effects of bank regulation, supervision, and deposit insurance on agency costs are potentially ambiguous. Examiners are in an excellent position to act as delegated monitors. They have unparalleled access to information, and they can compel remedial action. Only the board of directors is in as strong a position to monitor and discipline management. Early empirical investigations of this hypothesis found little evidence that the supervisors' theoretical comparative advantage translated into measurable benefits. However, DeYoung, Flannery, Lang, and Sorescu (2001), using an improved research methodology and a unique data set, find strong evidence that exams do reveal information that is not known to the market. Thus, examiners functioning as effective delegated monitors may serve to reduce agency costs.

On the other hand, much of the information examiners develop is confidential, and other aspects of bank regulation may have a negative effect. Deposit insurance obviously eliminates most, if not all, incentives for insured creditors to monitor. Explicit too-big-to-fail policies in the 1980s undermined the incentives of uninsured creditors as well. This effect may have continued even after the passage of FDICIA in 1991, while the credibility of regulators in foreswearing forbearance remained untested. Even if one can argue that regulators will now let individual banks fail, imposing costs on uninsured creditors, one can also argue that diversified holders of uninsured claims might still rely on regulators' unwillingness to allow a large number of banks to fail. These factors would tend to increase free-riding and, therefore, undermine market discipline.[18]

One of the few studies that directly examines the agency cost consequences of bank regulations is Prowse (1997). Prowse examines the frequency of friendly mergers, hostile takeovers, management turnover initiated by the board of directors, and intervention by regulators in U.S. bank holding companies (BHCs) from 1987 to 1992, and compares this with data on the frequency of the first three of these corporate control events in nonfinancial firms. Prowse concludes that

> … while market-based mechanisms of corporate control in BHCs appear to operate in the same [broad] fashion as manufacturing firms they may be weakened because hostile takeovers are precluded by regulation and bank boards of directors are not as aggressive in removing poorly performing managers. These weaknesses leave intervention by regulators as the primary force in disciplining management. (Prowse, 1997, p. 525)

This evidence suggests that, whatever the informational benefits of examination, one effect of regulation on banks is to reduce the effectiveness of other corporate governance mechanisms. However, we cannot say anything on the basis of this sparse evidence as to whether regulatory discipline has been effective in *replacing* the market's usual disciplinary mechanisms.

6. The Players: Incentives, Goals, and Conflicts

I have suggested that market discipline is, in large part, the solution to the principal–agent problem that is inherent in the separation of management of the modern corporation from the providers of capital (equity and debt) on which the corporation depends.[19] This problem definition leads to identification of three players who needed to be considered and whose roles and incentives need to be understood: managers, equity holders, and bondholders (or more generally uninsured suppliers of credit, including uninsured depositors).

Firms (banks) are not players per se. While they may have legal identities under the law, firms are incapable of making decisions or having incentives.[20] While it is common to talk of firms doing such and such, it is important for this discussion to recognize that the actions that firms take are decided by their managers (excepting when compelled to act by courts or regulators).

To this set of players I add two others. When discussing contemporary market discipline of banks one cannot ignore regulators. The functioning of market discipline in unregulated corporations, the basis for most of our understanding of the subject, cannot be translated to regulated banks without understanding how regulators distort the incentives and mechanisms involved. Lastly, securities (derivatives) market participants provide a powerful influence on the actions of large financial institutions involved in those markets, and so constitute a potential source of financial market discipline.

Excluded from the list of players to be considered are insured depositors who may have little or no incentive to exert market discipline; borrowers, who may have incentives to monitor their creditors to ensure against loss of the lending relation;[21] and insurers, who tend to discipline through ex post litigation rather than ex ante monitoring, though this ex post litigation may still provide ex ante discipline. These exclusions are arbitrary and others may wish to introduce these players into an expanded analysis.

Bondholders (uninsured creditors and depositors) are the easiest agents to analyze. The bondholders' contract with the firm is predicated on transparent and predictable information about the risks they are taking, rather than the level of risk per se. Bondholders lend for a fixed term at a fixed rate or at a rate tied to short-term market interest rates. Critically, their maximum return is fixed—they have no "upside potential." Bondholders bear the credit risk associated with the risk-taking of the firms they lend to. However, this does not mean that bondholders avoid risk-taking. Creditors happily lend to risky firms; approximately 15 percent of new bond issues are rated below investment grade (Bliss, 2001), and bond issuers tend to be even higher quality than bank borrowers. What creditors need is for the risks they are taking to be transparent so that they can correctly price the risk (through the coupon rate). Since the coupon is usually fixed with respect to changes in credit risk, subsequent changes in perceived credit risk (newly revealed information or actual changes in risk) can impact the value of the bondholder's claim. Because bondholders' principal is returned when their claim matures, unless the firm become insolvent, they can reassess the risk profile of the creditor and either adjust the coupon on new lending or decline to lend in the future if they are too much in doubt as to the condition of the borrower.

Equity holders have a more complex attitude towards firm risk. Equity holders have both upside potential, if the firm prospers, and downside potential, if the firm fails. A simple model of equity holders' incentives based on Black–Scholes (1972) analyzes equity as a call option on the value of a levered firm. In this single-period analysis, bondholders are captives (they do not price risk), and equity holders will seek to maximize the value of their option by inducing managers to increase firm risk. This analysis, however, ignores some salient features of the equity holder's decision problem. Equity holders have a perpetual claim on the net cash flows of the firm, and present value of future dividends is lost when the firm fails. Furthermore, bondholders price risk, so increased risk (should) result in increased interest expense and reduced net profits (for a given expected return on assets). Equity holders may thus be expected to consider both expected profits and risk simultaneously, factoring in the bondholders' responses, rather than just focusing on asset risk as in the simple Black–Scholes model. Merton (1978) suggests that as the firm approaches insolvency the equity holders become increasingly risk averse as the likelihood of loss of their future dividend stream increases. However, equity holders of a firm that is economically insolvent or likely to become so, but not yet formally in bankruptcy, have little to lose and may prefer the firm's manager take on excessive risk in the hopes of a reversal of fortunes before the otherwise inevitable detection of the insolvency.

Managers are at the heart of the principal–agent problem, and face conflicting interests. On the one hand managers are agents for the owners, the equity holders, and are supposed to act in their interest.[22] On the other hand, managers may act in their own interests rather than that of their principals. This is because they are in a position to profit personally from their actions—through perquisite consumption, self-dealing, outright expropriation, or simply shirking—and it is impossible for equity holders to perfectly monitor the managers actions and to contract so as to entirely prevent such malfeasance.

Derivatives market participants are in unique position. Their profits derive from the profitability of the positions they take and the spreads they earn from dealing. Derivatives market participants are exposed to the credit risk of their counterparties, though except in the case of credit derivatives, that is not their raison d'être.[23] The institutional structure of the derivatives market leads markets participants to manage counterparty credit risk so as to control and minimize this component, rather than consciously accept and price credit risk as bondholders do.[24] This is made possible by legally protected collateral and netting arrangements that apply to derivatives "master agreements" and a few other financial contracts, such as payments systems and clearing houses, but do not apply to most financial contracts.[25] Derivatives market participants can and do simply decline to deal with counterparties who are considered to be not creditworthy and unable to post sufficient collateral. Furthermore, derivatives contracts contain close-out rights that enable counterparties to terminate existing contracts if the firm becomes insolvent and fails to meet certain conditions (for example, maintain a given minimum rating on its debt). Bergman et al. (2003) argue that while this alters the derivatives market participants' incentives to monitor, it does not eliminate them. Furthermore, derivatives markets participants, particularly large dealer firms, are considered to be among the most sophisticated monitors both in terms of the skills they possess and the resources they can devote to monitoring.

Regulators have the most complex incentives of any of the players. As agents for the public good, bank regulators have a general goal of ensuring the soundness of the financial system, the avoidance of panics, and limiting systemic risk. Thus, unlike other players, regulators may be expected to take into account the external consequences of bank (and not nonbank financial institution) failures. Systemic risk considerations appear in banking legislation (to permit exceptions to normal bank closure rules), and the Federal Reserve has intervened on an ad hoc basis when it thought that market stability was threatened (the 1987 stock market crash, Long-Term Capital Management, the millennium date change). However, regulatory monitoring for the most part focuses on the safety and soundness of individual banks.

Monitoring consists of standardized information collection and verification (call reports for banks and Y-9 reports for bank holding companies), this information being made publicly available relatively quickly. This data collection is supplemented by on-site examinations, the reports of which are not made public. Examiners influence bank (and bank holding) company managers through a variety of mechanisms—required reclassification of loans, memoranda of understanding, capital directives, etc.—some of which are public, and some of which are not. Criticism of regulatory forbearance in the late 1980s and early 1990s led Congress to pass PCA legislation[26] which limited, in theory, supervisors' discretion in dealing with problem banks.[27] Nonetheless, since PCA triggers are defined in terms of bank book capital and considerable uncertainty remains as to how and when to revalue problem assets (and liabilities), considerable discretion remains. The exercise of this discretion in the execution of their duties brings regulators (examiners, supervisors) incentives into play.

Like managers, regulators have incentives inherent in the function they are performing on behalf of others and as well as personal incentives. The "others" for whom the regulators are working are complex. There is the public, who relies on regulators to keep the financial system safe. There are the taxpayers who rely on the regulators to ensure that the deposit insurance system is self-financing and does not result in further costs to the taxpayer as happened during the savings and loan crisis.[28] There is the deposit insurance system itself, the soundness of which requires proper management of bank failures so as to minimize losses to the insurance fund.[29]

Regulators also face their own personal incentives. At the most basic level is that of self-preservation. In the U.S., regulatory authorities compete for business. Since there are multiple regulators, the type of charter determines which regulator supervises a given bank. But the choice of charter lies with the bank. The number of banks being supervised determines the number of examiners and supervisors employed. This calculus is exacerbated at those regulator agencies that are funded through examination fees. This market for regulators creates the potential that regulators may at the margin act in their own interest rather than risk driving away clients.[30] Regulators are also subject to political pressures in the exercise of their duties. In the past, this descended to political interference in specific bank closure decisions (most notably during the savings and loan crisis). PCA is designed to discourage this by requiring the forbearance be formalized at the highest (regulatory) levels and in a public manner. Nonetheless, more subtle political influence may remain.[31] Larger policy decisions which impact the functioning of the regulatory system, such as bank fees and deposit insurance limit, are still determined through the political process. Lastly, there is the possibility of "regulatory capture" arising from the close working relation between the regulators and the regulated, and the remoteness of those in whose interest the regulation is being carried out. This potential is of course inherent in many regulatory agencies. Movement of staff from the regulatory agency to the regulated industry may contribute to regulatory capture.

7. Relations among Players

Ceteris paribus, equity holders and bondholders of solvent firms share an aversion to lower expected and realized rates of return.[32] Neither benefits from malfeasance or mismanagement by managers. This may seem trivial, but it is often overlooked that bondholders and equity holders have common as well as potentially divergent, interests. Most failures are due to poor management or poor investments rather than to ex ante rational risk-taking followed by a bad outcome. Thus, equity holders' and bondholders' interests are aligned with respect to firm profitability. With respect to risk, over a wide range bondholders simply prefer that risk be predictable, while equity holders' attitude towards risk may vary with the solvency of the firm.

Proponents of mandatory sub-debt note that sub-debt holders, like regulators (the insurance fund), do not benefit from the upside potential that may attend increased risk-taking (while equity holders and manager do). Mandatory sub-debt proponents conclude that sub-debt and regulatory incentives are therefore aligned and the market discipline by sub-debt holders will be directed towards the same goals that regulators have. This may be true for solvent institutions; both players wish the firm to remain solvent. But in other important ways the goals and incentives differ. As noted earlier, bondholders price risk until it becomes too great then they withhold investment. For various reasons regulators price risk only crudely and only "withhold" (deposit insurance) in extreme cases when the bank is closed. Most banks currently pay nothing for the deposit insurance guarantees they enjoy, and the banks that are classified as weak and pay fees do not pay fees that are economically related to the risks they impose on the fund. Thus, bondholders and regulators differ in their attitude towards risk-taking; the former being compensated, the latter not.

When a bank approaches insolvency the interests of bondholders and regulators diverge further. When a bank approaches insolvency the subordinated debt holders become the *de facto* residual claimants and may begin to act (in so far as they can) like equity holders. This is particularly true if the firm is so insolvent that their claim has little current value. Sub-debt holders may then favor "going for broke" rather than immediate liquidation, while more senior claimants (including the FDIC) may be better off liquidating while the assets still cover a good portion of their claim.

In insolvency, the regulators (FDIC) and subordinated debt holders can become adversaries. There have been several instances where subordinated debt holders or the bankruptcy trustees have sued regulators over the manner in which failed banks were resolved.[33] The FDIC as both receiver (or conservator) and major creditor has a natural conflict of interest. Least cost resolution mandates least cost to the deposit insurance fund, not to the subordinated creditors.[34] Furthermore, subordinated creditors have little standing to be heard when a failed bank is being resolved. This may help to explain why most subordinated debt is issued at the holding company rather than the bank level. Creditors enjoy much more clearly defined protections under the bankruptcy code used to resolve holding companies, than under banking law used to resolve banks.

While all players, except perhaps managers prefer greater transparency when a bank is solvent, when a bank becomes troubled the managers and regulators generally prefer opacity. Bank ratings which signal deteriorating bank quality are non-public and may not be even voluntarily disclosed. While some regulatory actions taken against troubled banks are made public, it is often the case that regulatory concerns are not made public. This usually happens while supervisors are working with managers to attempt to resolve the problem.

The justification for not always making regulatory concerns public is that such information might cause the public to panic and withdraw funds, making a workout infeasible. This concern for regulatory control of the situation when a bank is in trouble, highlights an important point: Regulators want ex ante discipline to minimize the incidence of troubled banks, but they do not want ex post discipline that reduces their options when dealing with a troubled bank.[35]

8. Conclusion

Market discipline is a complex phenomenon. It has its roots in the fundamental problem of the corporate structure—the separation of ownership of capital (both equity and debt) and control, which lies with managers. Markets, together with governments and courts, have evolved a number of mechanisms by which markets are able to discipline managers, imperfectly to be sure, but sufficiently for the corporate form of business organization to be remarkably successful.

Regulatory discipline of banks was introduced because it was perceived that market discipline was not sufficiently able to deal with these particularly important institutions. Regulatory discipline contains elements specifically designed to replace market discipline—bank supervision, restrictions on certain activities, regulatory approval of mergers, regulatory insolvency procedures. This undermines market discipline by encouraging free-riding and by weakening some of the mechanisms that function in unregulated markets (for instance, hostile takeovers). Market discipline of banks is further weakened by deposit insurance, weakening incentives of a large class of creditors to monitor, and by perceptions of *de facto* too-big-to-fail treatment of large institutions. The current calls for an increased role of market discipline in bank regulation do not seek to roll back these distortions. Rather they seek to strengthen market discipline within the existing framework of regulatory discipline.

This paper takes a step back from specific proposals to take an overview of market discipline. When one considers the incentives and goals of the major participants in the process, it becomes apparent that bringing increased market discipline to bear in bank regulation is not as simple as some proposals may presume. Small amounts of subordinated debt may prove weak inducements to managers to alter their behavior, and sub-debt signals may not be enough to overcome incentive problems faced by regulators. Increased transparency will certainly aid in market monitoring, but will do little in itself to increase market influence.

In the end, the call for increased market discipline must grapple with a fundamental contradiction. Regulators want market discipline, but on their own terms. They want increased ex ante market discipline, but they also want to retain those elements of regulatory discipline that weaken ex post (and to a lesser extent ex ante) market discipline, particularly their control of the process for resolving weak and troubled banks.[36] Whether the two forms of market discipline can be neatly separated remains to be seen. Getting market discipline "just right" is likely to be a challenge.

*Robert R. Bliss is a senior financial economist and economic advisor at the Federal Reserve Bank of Chicago. The author thanks Doug Evanoff, George Kaufman, and participants in the Bank for International Settlements and the Federal Reserve Bank of Chicago's 2003 *Conference on Market Discipline: The Evidence across Countries and Industries* for comments and discussion. The analysis and conclusions expressed herein represent the author's personal opinion, which do not necessarily coincide with those of the Federal Reserve System or the Federal Reserve Bank of Chicago. Portions of this paper appear in Bliss, 2001, "Market discipline and subordinated debt: A review of some salient issues," Federal Reserve Bank of Chicago, *Economic Perspectives*, First Quarter, pp. 24–45.

Notes

1. The term market discipline is also used in contexts other than the financial market discipline this paper is concerned with. Among these is product market discipline which penalizes inefficient firms and poor products—the so called "invisible hand." Adam Smith argued that this form of discipline is natural to a market economy undistorted by monopolies, tariffs, and other frictions.

2. Proponents of mandatory subordinated debt deserve much of the credit for the resurgence of interest in the role of market discipline in banking.

3. Exceptions include Bliss (2001), Bliss and Flannery (2002), Llewellyn and Mayes (2003), and Hamalainen, Hall, and Howcroft (2003).

4. For instance, many advocates of mandatory subordinated debt associate the term "market discipline" with a positive relation between firm risk and that firm's subordinated debt yield spreads. While such a risk/yield relation is a necessary condition for a subordinated-debt proposal to be effective, to so narrowly identify market discipline unnecessarily limits the discussion, precluding a full consideration of the issues and alternative solutions. The proponents of enhanced transparency have assumed that greater transparency will increase market discipline, without defining the term or examining how this might (or might not) work.

5. These issues may apply to a lesser degree in closely held corporations. However, the large financial institutions we are most concerned with do not fall into the category. For ease of exposition in this paper "corporations" will refer to large corporations with many non-manager stockholders.

6. Smith, 1796 [1776], Vol. III, Book 5, p. 124.

7. When Adam Smith was writing, the frauds and "irrational exuberance" of the bubbles associated with the South Sea Company (Britain) and Mississippi Company (France) were within living memory. Joint-stock companies were considered to be against the public interest and were prohibited (in Britain) except by act of Parliament.

8. Ibid.

9. Counterparties such as derivatives dealers can adjust their exposures to weak firms by management of their net positions (the difference between their in-the-money and out-of-the-money positions vis-à-vis a given counterparty). Such adjustments would not be readily apparent to third parties who have access only to limited aggregate information. See Bergman et al. (2003) for further discussion.

10. As Kaufman and Seelig (2002) point out, in many countries insured depositors are not paid immediately when their bank fails and so still have an incentive to monitor. In some countries the deposit insurance is implicit rather than explicit and the resulting uncertainty may produce incentives to monitor. Other countries such as the UK have partial deposit insurance so that all depositors are at some risk. In the U.S., where insured depositors have immediate access to their funds, depositors with accounts under the insured limit have no incentives to monitor.

11. Greenspan (2000) raised the concern that the precipitous collapse of large complex financial institutions might present unacceptable social costs and suggested that while failure should not be prevented, the process might require regulatory intervention. The workout and unwinding of Long-Term Capital Management is an example. Bliss (2003) discusses potential problems that might arise to impede the orderly resolution of such firms.

12. See Kwast et al. (1999) for a detailed discussion of various subordinated debt proposals and Bliss (2001) for an analysis of these and related issues.

13. Shleifer and Vishny (1997) and Short (1994) provide useful introductions to this literature.

14. Managers, on the other hand, can sometimes protect (immunize) themselves against involuntary replacement through golden parachutes and antitakeover amendments. Fama (1980) notes that adversarial resolution of manager/investor conflicts is very expensive. While golden parachutes apparently reward outgoing managers for failure, they may constitute the least costly means of removing managers who are willing to use the firm's (investors') own resources to contest their removal.

15. This labor market discipline is an important source of managerial discipline; indeed Fama (1980) argues that "[t]he viability of the large corporation with diffuse security ownership is better explained in terms of a model where the primary disciplining device comes through managerial labor markets, both within and outside the firm, ..."

16. An alternative possibility is that risk-averse entrenched managers may seek to protect their current positions by taking too few risks (satisficing). This has led to a literature on managerial compensation designed to align managers incentives with those of the equity holders—executive stock options being a topical example.

17. Bliss and Flannery (2002) and Calomiris and Powell (2000) are two exceptions. Bliss and Flannery find little clear evidence of ex post equity or bond market influence on U.S. bank holding companies, while Calomiris and Powell purport to find evidence consistent with bondholder influence in Argentina under very different circumstances.

18. Park (2000) develops a formal model in which senior-debt holders monitor firms for moral hazard problems and junior-debt holders free-ride. This is consistent with observed debt priority, ownership, and maturity structure in nonbanks. The reasons that junior-debt holders do not monitor (benefits accrue first to senior claimants) carry over to subordinated bank debt. It is less clear that Park's arguments for why senior-debt holders do monitor (gain full benefit of their monitoring efforts) would carry over to bank supervisors, who are agents rather than principals with their own funds at risk. On the other hand, Park argues that senior-debt holders will tend to have lower monitoring costs, an observation that carries over to supervisors who are *paid* to monitor.

19. The bulk of the corporate finance literature on principal–agent problems centers on conflicts between managers and equity holders. Another literature in banking focuses on conflicts between equity holders/managers and bondholders, assuming away the manager versus

equity holder conflicts. The salient issue is the separation of control and risk bearing, and since interests of equity holders and bondholders differ, this paper will consider all three parties separately.

20. The anthropomorphizing of firms may be a convenient device when analyzing equity holder/bondholder conflicts, though it presumes that managers are perfectly aligned with equity holders.

21. There is little evidence that borrowers run from weak lenders, perhaps because weak firms tend to offer inducements—lower credit standards, underpriced credit—to attract business.

22. This is the Anglo-American perspective. In some other countries managers are required to act in the interests of a broader set of "stakeholders," including employees, the local community, environmental interests, and so forth.

23. Bondholders take on credit risk in return for an agreed promised return and a priority of their claim vis-à-vis equity holders and other subordinated claimants (sub-debt, preferred stock) to the firm's cash flows when solvent and assets under insolvency

24. This distinction is one of degrees. Bondholders sometimes manage credit risk through the use of bond covenants, though these have become less common, and through collateralized lending (for example, mortgage bonds, repurchase agreements). Poor credit risks may be excluded from certain credit markets entirely.

25. Enforceable netting results in the combination of multiple contracts into a single legal obligation for the net value. This usually requires that the individual transactions take place under a governing master agreement. Credit exposures under such contracts are thus limited to net of the position values across all the included transactions. Where netting is not permitted multiple contracts between a solvent and an insolvent counterparty are treated separately in insolvency. See Bergman et al. (2003) for a detailed discussion of netting rules and their economic implications.

26. 12 USC 1831o(e)(2)(E).

27. Examination refers to the on-site information gathering and supervision to the decision-making. These functions usually are collocated in supervisory agencies, with field examiners collecting the information, but supervisory management making the final decisions.

28. In the U.S., the deposit insurance fund is funded by fees assessed on troubled banks and when the fund falls below prescribed limits by fees assessed on all depository institutions. Losses incurred by the FDIC in resolving banks are charged to the fund. Thus, at least in principle, the FDIC is the agent of all the depository institutions in its management of the fund. It remains to be seen whether in fact massive losses to the fund would be made good by the member banks as required by law, with possible severe repercussions for bank lending, or whether the taxpayer would be called on to recapitalize the fund. The recent possibility that the fund might slip slightly below its minimum level requiring top-up fees from all depository institutions, has already exposed the political sensitivity of the issue.

29. 12 USC 1823(c)(4).

30. There is little direct evidence of this effect (see Rosen, 2003), and banks already in trouble may have difficulty changing charters. However, the lack of uniformity of examination fees across regulators is controversial, as are changes in client base that might impact staffing—witness the institutional resistance to merging the Office of the Comptroller of the Currency and the Office of Thrift Supervision (OTS).

31. The reluctance of the OTS to take early vigorous action against Superior Savings in 2000 has been attributed by some commentators to the political clout of the Pritzker family which co-owned the institution.

32. For insolvent firms, further losses cannot change the position of equity holders who are already wiped out. The same logic applies successively to other claimants in reverse order of priority as the losses wipe out successive creditor classes.

33. MCorp, BNEC, and NextBank are examples.

34. Under depositor preference, the FDIC shares on a pro rata basis with uninsured depositors any losses resulting from insufficient recoveries from liquidation of assets. Thus, there is no conflict of interest between the FDIC and uninsured *depositors*. The conflict is limited to other non-depositor creditors.

35. Bliss (2003) has noted that close-out rights under derivatives master agreements may frustrate this desire to control bank resolution in the case of large complex financial organizations. Currently close-out of bank master agreements solely due to appointment of the FDIC as conservator is prohibited and efforts are underway to expand this prohibition to other causes except actual default (see Bergman et al., 2003). However, closeout (winding down positions and demands for increased collateral) cannot be prevent prior to the FDIC taking over the bank, should problems become public before the regulators close the bank.

36. Evanoff (1993) referred to this as "the razor's edge."

References

Avery, Robert B., Terrence M. Belton, and Michael A. Goldberg, 1986, "Market discipline in regulating bank risk: New evidence from the capital markets," Board of Governors of the Federal Reserve System, Research Paper in Banking and Financial Economics, No. 86.

Bergman, William, Robert R. Bliss, Christian Johnson, and George Kaufman, 2003, "Netting, financial contracts, and banks: The economic implications," in *Market Discipline in Banking: Theory and Evidence*, Vol. 15, *Research in Financial Services*, G. Kaufman (ed.), Amsterdam: Elsevier Press.

Black, Fisher, and Myron Scholes, 1972, "The valuation of option contracts and a test of market efficiency," *Journal of Finance*, Vol. 27, No. 2, May, pp. 399–417.

Bliss, Robert R., 2003, "Resolving large complex financial organizations," in *Market Discipline in Banking: Theory and Evidence*, Vol. 15, *Research in Financial Services*, G. Kaufman (ed.), Elsevier Press, Amsterdam.

_____, 2001, "Market discipline and subordinated debt: A review of some salient issues," *Economic Perspectives*, Federal Reserve Bank of Chicago, First Quarter, pp. 24–45.

Bliss, Robert R., and Mark Flannery, 2002, "Market discipline in the governance of U.S. bank holding companies: Monitoring vs. influence," *European Finance Review*, Vol. 6, No. 3, pp. 361–395.

Calomiris, Charles W., and Andrew Powell, 2000, "Can emerging market bank regulation establish credible discipline: The case of Argentina 1992–1999," in *Prudential Supervision: What Works and What Doesn't?* Frederic S. Mishkin (ed.), Chicago: NBER Press and University of Chicago Press.

Cannella, Albert A., Donald R. Fraser, and D. Scott Lee, 1995, "Firm failure and managerial labor markets: Evidence from Texas banking" *Journal of Financial Economics*, Vol. 38, No. 2, June, pp. 185–210.

DeYoung, Robert, Mark J. Flannery, William W. Lang, and Sorin M. Sorescu, 2001, "The informational content of bank exam ratings and subordinated debt prices," *Journal of Money, Credit and Banking*, November, pp. 900–925.

Evanoff, Douglas D., 1993, "Preferred sources of market discipline," *Yale Journal on Regulation*, Vol. 10, No. 2, Summer, pp. 347–367.

Fama, Eugene F., 1980, "Agency problems and the theory of the firm," *Journal of Political Economy*, Vol. 88, No. 2, April, pp. 288–307.

Fama, Eugene F., and Michael C. Jensen, 1983, "Separation of ownership and control," *Journal of Law and Economics*, Vol. 26, No. 2, June, pp. 301–325.

Farrell, Kathleen A., and David A. Whidbee, 2000, "The consequences of forced CEO succession for outside directors," *Journal of Business*, Vol. 73, No. 4, October, pp. 597–527.

Greenspan, Alan, 2000, "Question and answer session following the keynote address," *Proceedings of the 36th Annual Conference on Bank Structure and Competition: The Changing Financial Industry Structure and Regulation: Bridging States, Countries, and Industries*, Chicago: Federal Reserve Bank of Chicago.

Hamalainen, Paul, Maximilian Hall, and Barry Howcroft, 2003, "Market discipline: A theoretical framework for regulatory policy development," in *Market Discipline in Banking: Theory and Evidence*, Vol. 15, *Research in Financial Services*, G. Kaufman (ed.), Amsterdam: Elsevier Press.

Jensen, Michael C., and William H. Meckling, 1976, "Theory of the firm: Managerial behavior, agency costs, and ownership structure," *Journal of Financial Economics*, Vol. 3, No. 4, October, pp. 305–360.

Kaufman, George G., and Steven A. Seelig, 2002, "Post-resolution treatment of depositors at failed banks: Implications for the severity of banking crises, systemic risk, and too big to fail," *Economic Perspectives*, Federal Reserve Bank of Chicago, Second Quarter, pp. 27–40.

Kwast, Myron L., Daniel M. Covitz, Diana Hancock, James V. Houpt, David P. Adkins, Norah Barger, Barbara Bouchard, John F. Connolly, Thomas F. Brady, William B. English, Douglas D. Evanoff, and Larry D. Wall, 1999, "Using subordinated debt as an instrument of market discipline," report of a Study Group on Subordinated Notes and Debentures, Board of Governors of the Federal Reserve System, staff study, No. 172, December.

Llewellyn, David T., and David G. Mayes, 2003, "The role of market discipline in handling problem banks," Bank of Finland, working paper.

Martinez Peria, Maria Soledad, and Sergio L. Schmukler, 2001, "Do depositors punish banks for bad behavior? Market discipline, deposit insurance, and banking crises," *Journal of Finance*, Vol. 56, No. 3, June, pp. 1029–1051.

Merton, Robert C., 1978, "On the cost of deposit insurance when there are surveillance costs," *Journal of Business*, Vol. 51, July, pp. 439–452.

_____, 1977, "An analytic derivation of the cost of deposit insurance and loan guarantees: An application of modern option pricing theory," *Journal of Banking and Finance*, Vol. 1, June, pp. 3–11.

Myers, Stewart C., and Nicholas S. Majluf, 1984, "Corporate financing and investment decisions when firms have information that investors do not have," *Journal of Financial Economics*, Vol. 13, No. 2, pp. 184–221.

Park, Cheol, 2000, "Monitoring and structure of debt contracts," *Journal of Finance*, Vol. 55, No. 5, October, pp. 2157–2195.

Prowse, Stephen, 1997, "Corporate control in commercial banks," *Journal of Financial Research*, Vol. 20, No. 4, Winter, pp. 509–527.

Rosen, Richard, 2003, "Is three a crowd? Competition among regulators in banking," *Journal of Money, Credit, and Banking*, Vol. 35, No. 6, pp. 967–998.

Shleifer, Andrei, and Robert W. Vishny, 1997, "A survey of agency costs," *Journal of Finance*, Vol. 52, No. 2, June, pp. 737–783.

Short, Helen, 1994, "Ownership, control, financial structure, and the performance of firms," *Journal of Economic Surveys*, Vol. 8, No. 3, pp. 203–249.

Smith, Adam, 1796, *The Wealth of Nations*, London: A. Strahan, originally published in 1776.

Chapter 6

Market Discipline in Banking: Where Do We Stand?

Jean-Charles Rochet*
*Toulouse University, Institut d'Economie Industrielle,
and Toulouse Business School*

1. Introduction

The profound mutations experienced by the banking industry in the last three decades have prompted governments and international institutions to envisage thorough reforms of supervisory-regulatory systems. Market discipline is generally thought to be a fundamental element of these reforms.[1] Indeed, the rapidly increasing sophistication and internationalization of banking operations makes it impossible for bank supervisors to continue controlling thoroughly the activities of all banks. Therefore it is natural to envisage a partial substitution of bank supervisors by private investors for the monitoring of banks. However the precise methods by which market discipline can be implemented are not obvious.

The Basel Committee on Banking Supervision (BCBS), in its successive consultative papers (1999, 2001, 2003) on the reform of the Basel Accord, gives a lot of attention to the design of the new capital ratio (see the comments in Décamps et al., 2004, and Rochet, 2003), but is much less specific about market discipline. The committee only puts forward the need for an "increased transparency," without discussing any[2] concrete proposal for implementing market discipline, such as the mandatory sub-debt proposals put forward by several U.S. economists.[3]

In any case, the interactions between banking regulation and market discipline are less than clear. The objective of this note is to clarify the logical structure of the arguments supporting market discipline for banks and to review empirical evidence on the mechanisms through which this market discipline may function.

This paper is structured as follows: We start by recalling the objectives and methods of bank regulation. Then we examine why and how market discipline can help improve efficiency of the regulatory/supervisory system. We then discuss in more detail the limits to transparency, the roles of direct and indirect market discipline, and conclude by indicating some directions that need to be explored further both by academic researchers and regulators.

2. Why Regulate Banks and How?

Before clarifying why and how market discipline can help bank regulators, it is important to recall why banks are regulated in the first place. Although the topic is still debated in the academic literature (see Bhattacharya and Thakor, 1993; Freixas and Rochet, 1995; and Santos, 2000, for extended surveys), a large consensus seems to have emerged. It is now widely accepted that bank regulation and supervision have essentially two purposes:

- Protect small depositors, by limiting the frequency and cost of individual bank failures. This is often referred to as *microprudential* regulation.[4]

- Protect the banking system as a whole, by limiting the frequency and cost of systemic banking crises. This is often referred to as *macroprudential* regulation.

  Notice that, from the point of view of economic analysis, these two types of regulations have very different justifications:

- Microprudential regulation is justified by the (presumed)[5] inability of small depositors to control the use of their money by bankers. This is why most countries have organized deposit insurance funds (DIFs hereafter) that guarantee small deposits against the risk of failure of their bank. The role of bank supervisors is then to represent the interests of depositors (or rather of the DIF) vis-à-vis banks managers and shareholders.[6,7]

- Macroprudential regulation is justified by the (partial) failure of the market to deal with aggregate risks, and by the public good component of financial stability. Like for other public goods, the total willingness to pay of individual banks (or more generally of investors) for financial stability is less that the social value of this financial stability. This is because each individual (bank or investor) free-rides on the willingness of others to pay for financial stability.

  These differences imply in particular that, while microprudential regulation (and supervision) can in principle be dealt with at a purely private level (it amounts to a collective representation problem for depositors), macroprudential regulation has intrinsically a public good component. This being said, governments have traditionally controlled both dimensions of regulation, which is the source of serious time consistency problems[8] (this is because democratic governments cannot commit to long-run decisions that will be made by their successors) leading to political pressure on supervisors, regulatory forbearance, and mismanagement of banking crises.

  In our discussion of why and how market discipline can help regulate banks, these two elements will play a crucial role.

- Market discipline can help regulators limiting political pressure and forbearance in microprudential regulation.

- However, it would be dangerous to rely extensively on market discipline for macroprudential regulation, since this regulation is precisely justified by the failure of the market to deal with macro shocks and financial instability.

Once the principles for the two types of bank regulation are established, it is important to question how these principles can be put into application and how banking regulation should be organized. I claim that there is a crucial need to reexamine this question in depth. Indeed, the traditional vision of bank regulation, in many countries, was extremely paternalistic. Roughly speaking, it was accepted that bank supervisors were there to tell banks what they had to do. Banks were protected from too much competition in exchange for "helping" governments on different occasions: bailing out insolvent institutions, lending at subsidized rates to certain sectors of the industry, financing public deficits, not to mention (in certain countries) more extreme forms of support like financing political campaigns or providing good jobs to the friends and families of politicians.

This traditional view of banking regulation was abandoned in the 1990s under the pressures of international competition, increased sophistication of financial markets and instruments, and also with the revelation in many countries of the intrinsic weakness of governments for preventing and resolving banking crises in a prompt and efficient way. The two crucial mottoes in this period were guaranteeing a "level playing field" for international competition (which essentially meant preventing governments from subsidizing domestic banks through implicit bailout commitments) and forcing supervisors to adopt prompt corrective action (PCA) measures when a bank starts showing signs of financial distress. The two main instruments developed for these purposes where the first Basel Accord (BCBS, 1988) and the Federal Deposit Insurance Corporation Improvement Act (FDICIA)[9] in the U.S. in 1991. Even though these two reforms were basically successful (as illustrated by the spectacular increase in banks capital ratios in most developed countries between 1990 and today),[10] the Basel Accord was heavily criticized for having provoked a "credit crunch"[11] and regulatory arbitrage,[12] while PCA was never implemented, or even seriously considered outside the U.S. Besides, both reforms only concern microprudential regulation. As argued by Borio (2003) there is an urgent need for a conceptualization and international harmonization of macroprudential regulation systems.

Surprisingly, the on-going reform of the Basel Accord (BCBS 1999, 2001, 2003) has taken different directions: even though the Basel Committee pays lip service to "supervisory action" and "market discipline" (called pillars 2 and 3 of the New Accord), it has spent most of its time and energy revising the capital requirement of Basel 1 (which was viewed as too crude).[13] The proposals for this new capital requirement have been modified several times and are still apparently the object of an intense bargaining with the banking profession. The BCBS apparently wants to go very deep into the details of risk-management methods by banks and give the choice to banks between applying "standard" formulas (defined by the BCBS in consultation with the profession) and using their own methods, which would have then to be validated by the Basel Committee. I view this strange situation as the consequence of a failed attempt to return to the old, paternalistic, approach to banking regulation. The

BCBS initially wanted to impose its own "standard" version of the management of banking risks. Large banks reacted by imposing their own risk-management methods, and the BCBS were forced to allow for these "advanced" methods and grant many exceptions to their standard formulas, taking into account particular situations for specific countries or specific industries.

As we argue in Décamps et al. (2004) and Rochet (2003), the BCBS should spend less time and energy refining an already extremely complex capital regulation that will ultimately be bypassed in some way or another by the largest and most sophisticated banks. By contrast, there is an urgent need (once again) to guarantee a level playing field in international banking. The development of large and complex banking organizations with multinational activities implies that supervisory authorities of different countries need urgently to harmonize their institutional practices. As we now explain, market discipline can be useful in this respect.

3. Why Market Discipline and How?

Conceptually, market discipline can be used by banking authorities in two different ways:

- *Direct* market discipline, which aims at inducing market investors to *influence*[14] the behavior of bank managers, and works as a *substitute* to prudential supervision.

- *Indirect* market discipline, which aims at inducing market investors to *monitor* the behavior of bank managers, and works as a *complement* to prudential supervision. The idea is that indirect market discipline provides new, objective, information that can be used by supervisors for improving their control on problem banks, but also to implement PCA measures that limit forbearance.

The instruments for implementing market discipline are essentially of three types:

- *Imposing more transparency,* that is, forcing bank managers to disclose publicly various types of information that can be used by market participants for a better assessment of banks' management.

- *Changing the capital structure of banks*, for example forcing bank managers to issue periodically subordinated debt.

- *Using market information* to improve the efficiency of supervision.

We now successively examine these three types of instruments.

4. The Limits to Transparency

In a recent empirical study of disclosure in banking, Baumann and Nier (2003) find that more disclosure tends to be beneficial to banks: It decreases stock volatility, increases market values, and increases the usefulness of accounting data. However, as argued by D'Avolio et al. (2001) "market mechanisms ... are unlikely themselves to solve the problems raised by misleading information. ... For the future of financial markets in the United States, disclosure [of accurate information] is likely to be critical for continued progress." In other words, financial markets will not themselves generate enough information for investors to allocate their funds appropriately and efficiently, and on some occasions will even tend to propagate misleading information. This means that disclosure of accurate information has to be imposed by regulators. A good example of such regulations are the disclosure requirements imposed in the U.S. by the Securities and Exchange Commission (and in other countries by the agencies regulating security exchanges) for publicly traded companies. However, the banking sector is peculiar in two respects: Banks' assets are traditionally viewed as "opaque,"[15] and banks are subject to regulation and supervision, which implies that bank supervisors are already in possession of detailed information on the banks' balance sheets. Thus it may seem strange to require public disclosure of information already possessed by regulatory authorities: Why can't these authorities disclose the information themselves,[16] or even publish their regulatory ratings (BOPEC, CAMELS[17] and the like)? There are basically two reasons for this:

- First, as argued by Rochet and Vives (2002), too much disclosure may trigger bank runs and/or systemic banking crises. This happens in any situation where coordination failures may occur between many dispersed investors.

- Second, as we explain below, the crucial benefit of market discipline is to limit the possibilities of regulatory forbearance by generating "objective" information that can be used to force supervisors to intervene before it is too late when a bank is in trouble. This would not be possible if the information was disclosed by the supervisors themselves.

In any case, there are intrinsic limits to transparency in banking: we have to recall that the main economic role of banks is precisely to allocate funds to projects of small and median enterprises, that are "opaque" to outside investors. If these projects were transparent, commercial banks would not be needed in the first place.

5. Changing the Liability Structure of Banks

The economic idea behind *direct market discipline* is that, by changing the liability structure of banks (for example forcing banks to issue uninsured debt of a certain maturity), one can change the incentives of bank managers and shareholders. In particular some proponents of the mandatory sub-debt proposal claim that informed investors may "influence" bank managers. This idea has been discussed extensively in the academic literature on corporate finance: short-term debt can in theory be used to mitigate the debt overhang problem (Myers, 1984) and the free cash flow problem (Jensen, 1986). In the banking literature, Calomiris and Kahn (1991) and Carletti (1999) have shown how demandable debt could be used in theory to discipline bank managers. The sub-debt proposal has been only analyzed formally in very few articles: Levonian (2001) uses a Black–Scholes–Merton type of model (where the bank's return on assets and closure date are exogenous) to show that mandatory sub-debt is typically not a good way to prevent bankers from taking too much risk.[18] Décamps et al. (2004) and Rochet (2003) modify this model by endogenizing the bank's return on assets and closure date. They find that under certain conditions (sufficiently long maturity of the debt, sufficient liquidity of the sub-debt market, limited scope for asset substitution by the bank managers) mandating a periodic issuance of subordinated debt could allow regulators to reduce equity requirements (tier 1). However it would always increase total capital requirements (tier 1 + tier 2).

In any case, empirical evidence for direct market discipline is weak: Bliss and Flannery (2001) find very little support for equity or bond holders influencing U.S. bank holding companies.[19] It is true that studies of crisis periods, either in the recent crises in emerging countries (see Martinez Peria and Schmukler, 2001, or Calomiris and Powell, 2000), during the Great Depression (see Calomiris and Mason, 1997) or the U.S. savings and loan crisis (see Park and Peristiani, 1998), have found that in extreme circumstances, depositors and other investors were able to distinguish between "good" banks and "bad" banks and "vote with their feet." There is no doubt indeed that depositors and private investors have the possibility to provoke bank closures, and thus ultimately discipline bankers. But it is hard to see this as "influencing" bank managers, and is not necessarily the best way to manage banking failures or systemic crises. This leads me to an important dichotomy within the tasks of regulatory/supervisory systems: One is to limit the *frequency* of bank failures, the other is to *manage* them in the most efficient way once they become unavoidable. I am not aware of any piece of empirical evidence showing that depositors and private investors can directly influence bank managers before their bank becomes distressed (that is, help supervisors in their first task). As for the second task (that is, managing closures in the most efficient way) it seems reasonable to argue that supervisors should in fact aim at an orderly resolution of failures, that is, exactly *preventing* depositors and private investors to interfere with the closure mechanism.

6. Using Market Information

The most convincing mechanism through which market discipline can help bank supervision is indirect: By *monitoring* banks, private investors can generate new, "objective" information on the financial situation of these banks. This information can then be used to complement the information already possessed by supervisors. There is a large academic literature on this question.[20] Most empirical studies of market discipline, indeed, focus on market monitoring, that is, indirect market discipline. The main questions examined by this literature are: what is the informational content of prices and returns of the securities issued by banks? More precisely, is this information new with respect to what supervisors already know? Also, are bond yields and spreads good predictors of bank risk?

Flannery (1998) reviews most of the empirical literature on these questions. More recent contributions are Jagtiani et al. (2000) and DeYoung et al. (2001). The main stylized facts are:

• Bond yields and spreads contain information not contained in regulatory ratings and vice versa. More precisely, bank closures can be predicted more accurately by using both market data and regulatory information than by using each of them separately.[21,22]

- Sub-debt yields typically contain bank risk premia. However in the U.S. this is only true since explicit too-big-to fail policies were abandoned (that is after 1985–86). This shows that market discipline can work only if regulatory forbearance is not anticipated by private investors.

- However as shown by Covitz et al. (2003) bond and sub-debt yields can also reflect other things than bank risk. In particular, liquidity premia are likely to play an important role.

In any case, even if there seems to be a consensus that complementing the information set of banking supervisors by market information is useful, it seems difficult to justify, on the basis of existing evidence, mandating banks to issue subordinated debt for the sole purpose of generating additional information. The argument that subordinated debt has the same profile as (uninsured) deposits and can thus be used to replace foregone market discipline (due to deposit insurance) is not convincing.

Indeed, as pointed out by Levonian (2001), the profile of sub-debt changes according to the region of scrutiny: it indeed behaves like deposits (or debt) in the region where the bank starts have problems, but like equity when the bank comes closer to the failure region. This is related to a basic weakness of most empirical studies of indirect market discipline, that have used cross-sectional data sets containing a vast majority of well-capitalized banks. Remember that the problem at stake is the dynamic behavior of undercapitalized banks. Thus what we should be interested in is instead the informational content of sub-debt yields for predicting banks' problems. That is, empirical studies should essentially focus on panel data involving only problem banks.

Finally, most of the academic literature (both theoretical and empirical) has focused on the asset substitution effect, exemplified by some spectacular cases, like those of "zombie" savings and loans in the U.S. crisis of the 1980s. However, as convincingly argued by Bliss (2001), "poor investments are as problematic as excessively risky projects. … Evidence suggests that poor investments are likely to be the major explanation for banks getting into trouble." Thus there is a need for a more thorough investigation of the performance of weakly capitalized banks. Is asset substitution the only problem, or is poor investment choice also at stake?

In fact, the crucial aspect about using market regulation to improve banking supervision is probably the possibility of limiting regulatory forbearance by triggering PCA, based on "objective" information. As soon as stakeholders of any sort (private investors, depositors, managers, shareholders, or employees of a bank in trouble) can check that supervisors have done their job, that is have reacted soon enough to "objective" information (provided by the market) on the bank's financial situation, the scope for regulatory forbearance will be extremely limited. Of course, the challenge is to design (ex ante) sufficiently clear rules (that is, set up a clear agenda for the regulatory agency) specifying how regulatory action has to be triggered by well specified market events.

7. Conclusion

A few conclusions emerge from our short review.

*   First it seems that supervision and market discipline are more complements than substitutes: One cannot work efficiently without the other. Without credible closure policies implemented by supervisors, market discipline is ineffective. Conversely, without the objective data generated by prices and yields of banks bonds and equity, closure policy is likely to be plagued by "ambiguity" and forbearance.

*   Second, *indirect* market discipline (private investors *monitoring* bank managers) seems to be more empirically relevant than *direct* market discipline (private investors *influencing* bank managers). Given that large bank holding companies (for which more intense supervision is crucial) already issue sub-debt and are publicly held (and therefore are already subject to market discipline), it seems difficult to recommend interfering in their financial policy by mandating regular issuance of a certain type of subordinated debt.[23]

*   Third, more attention should be directed to the precise ways in which supervisory action can be gradually triggered by market signals. Instead of spending so much time and energy on refining pillar 1 of the New Basel Accord, the Basel Committee should concentrate on this difficult issue, crucial to creating a level playing field for international banking.

There is also clearly a lot more to be done, both by academics and regulators, if one really wants to understand the interactions between banking supervision and market discipline. In particular, very little attention has been drawn[24] so far to macroprudential regulation: how to prevent and manage systemic banking crises. It seems clear that market discipline is probably not a good instrument for improving macroprudential regulation. Indeed, market signals often become erratic during crises, and the very justification of macroprudential regulation is that markets do not deal efficiently with aggregate shocks of sufficient magnitude. Macroprudential control lies therefore almost exclusively on the shoulders of bank supervisors, in coordination with the central bank and the Treasury. A difficult question is then how to organize the two dimensions (macro and micro) of prudential regulation in such a way that systemic crises are efficiently managed by governments and central banks, while individual bank closure decisions remain protected from political interference.

*Jean-Charles Rochet is a professor of mathematics and economics at Toulouse University and the Toulouse Business School, and research director at the Institut d'Economie Industrielle.

Notes

1. This illustrated by the fact that "market discipline" or "disclosure" is considered by the Basel Committee on Bank Supervision as the third pillar of the New Basel Accord.

2. This absence of discussion is criticized by the U.S. Shadow Financial Regulatory Committee (2000).

3. Recent references on the sub-debt proposal are Calomiris (1998), Evanoff and Wall (2000, 2001, 2002, and 2003), Hancock and Kwast (2001), and Sironi (2001).

4. See for example Borio (2003) or Crockett (2001) for a justification of this terminology.

5. The supporters of the "Free Banking School" challenge this view.

6. Contrary to what is often asserted, the need for a microprudential regulation is not a consequence of any "mispricing" of deposit insurance (or other form of government subsidies) but simply of the existence of deposit insurance.

7. This is the "representation theory" of Dewatripont and Tirole (1994).

8. A similar time consistency problem used to exist for monetary policy, until independence was granted to the central banks of many countries.

9. The consequences of FDICIA are assessed in Jones and King (1995) and Mishkin (1996).

10. See for example Furfine (2001) or Flannery and Rangan (2003).

11. On this, see for example Berger and Udell (1994), Bernanke and Lown (1991), Jackson et al. (1999), Peek and Rosengren (1995), and Thakor (1996).

12. See Jones (2000).

13. In particular, the weights used in the computation of the capital ratio were too coarse, leading to distortions in asset allocations: see Furlong and Keeley (1990), Jackson et al. (1999), Jones (2000), Kim and Santomero (1988), and Rochet (1992).

14. This distinction between influencing and monitoring is due to Bliss and Flannery (2001).

15. Morgan (2002) provides indirect empirical evidence on this opacity by comparing the frequency of disagreements among bond rating agencies about the values of firms across sectors of activity. He shows that these disagreements are much more frequent, all else being equal, for banks and insurance companies than for other sectors of the economy.

16. One could also argue that the information of supervisors is "proprietary" information that could be used inappropriately by the bank's competitors if publicly disclosed. This is not an argument against regulatory disclosure since regulators can select which pieces of information they disclose.

17. BOPEC stands for the BHC's bank subsidiaries, other nonbank subsidiaries, parent company, earnings, and capital adequacy. CAMELS stands for capital adequacy, asset quality, management, earnings, liquidity, and sensitivity.

18. The reason is that sub-debt behaves like equity in the region close to liquidation (which is precisely the region where influencing managers becomes crucial) so sub-debt holders have the some incentives as shareholders to take too much risk.

19. A recent article by Covitz et al. (2003) partially challenges this view. However, Covitz et al. (2003) focus exclusively on funding decisions. More specifically they find that in the U.S., riskier banks are less likely to issue sub-debt. This does not necessarily imply that mandating sub-debt issuance would prevent banks from taking too such risk.

20. See for example DeYoung et al. (2001) Evanoff and Wall (2001, 2002, and 2003), Flannery (1998), Flannery and Sorescu (1996), Gropp et al. (2002), Hancock and Kwast (2001), Jagtiani et al. (2000), and Pettway and Sinkey (1980).

21. A similar point was made earlier by Pettway and Sinkey (1980). They showed that both accounting information and equity returns were useful to predict bank failures.

22. Berger et al. (2000) obtain similar conclusions by testing causality relations between changes in supervisory ratings and in stock prices.

23. The only convincing argument for mandating regular issuance of a standardized form of sub-debt is that it may improve liquidity of such a market, and therefore increase informational content of prices and yields.

24. Borio (2003) is one exception.

References

Basel Committee on Banking Supervision, 2003, "The New Basel Capital Accord," third consultative document, Basel, Switzerland.

_____, 2001, "Overview of the New Basel Capital Accord," second consultative document, Basel, Switzerland.

_____, 1999, "A new capital adequacy framework," consultative paper, Basel, Switzerland.

_____, 1988, "International convergence of capital measurement and capital standards," paper, Basel, Switzerland.

Baumann, Ursel, and Erland Nier, 2003, "Disclosure in banking: What matters most?," paper presented at the New York Federal Reserve Bank-Chazen Institute conference, New York, October.

Berger, Allen, S. M. Davies, and Mark J. Flannery, 2000, "Comparing market and regulatory assessments of bank performance: Who knows what when?," *Journal of Money, Credit, and Banking*, Vol. 24, No. 7, pp. 641–667.

Berger, Allen, and Geoffrey F. Udell, 1994, "Did risk-based capital allocate bank credit and cause a credit crunch in the U.S.?," *Journal of Money Credit, and Banking*, Vol. 26, pp. 585–628.

Bernanke, Ben, and Cara Lown, 1991, "The Credit Crunch," *Brookings Papers on Economic Activity*, Vol. 2, pp. 205–247.

Bhattacharya, Sudipto, and Anjan V. Thakor, 1993, "Contemporary banking theory," *Journal of Financial Intermediation*, Vol. 3, pp. 2–50.

Bliss, Robert R., 2001, "Market discipline and subordinated debt: A review of some salient issues," Economic Perspectives, Federal Reserve Bank of Chicago, First Quarter, pp. 24-45.

Bliss, Robert, and Mark Flannery, 2001, "Market discipline in the governance of U.S. bank holding companies: Monitoring versus influencing," *European Finance Review*, Vol. 6, pp. 363–395.

Borio, Claudio, 2003, "Towards a macro-prudential framework for financial supervision and regulation?," Bank for International Settlements, Basel, working paper, No. 128.

Calomiris, Charles W., 1998, "Blueprints for a new global financial architecture," paper, available at www.house.gov/jec/imf/blueprnt.htm.

Calomiris, Charles W., and Charles Kahn, 1991, "The role of demandable debt in Structuring optimal debt contracts," *American Economic Review*, Vol. 81, pp. 497–513.

Calomiris, Charles W., and James Mason, 1997, "Contagion and bank failures during the Great Depression," *American Economic Review*, Vol. 87, pp. 863–883.

Calomiris, Charles W., and Peter Powell, 2000, "Can emerging markets bank regulators establish credible discipline? The case of Argentina," Banco Central de la Republica Argentina, mimeo.

Carletti, Elena, 1999, "Bank moral hazard and market discipline," London School of Economics, Financial Markets Group, mimeo.

Covitz, Daniel M., Diana Hancock, and Myron L. Kwast, 2003, "Market discipline in banking reconsidered: The role of deposit insurance reform and funding manager decisions," paper presented at the New York Federal Reserve Bank-Chazen Institute Conference, New York, October.

Crockett, Andy, 2001, "Market discipline and financial stability," speech delivered at the Banks and Systemic Risk conference, Bank of England, London.

D'Avolio, G., E. Gildor, and Andrei Shleifer, 2001, "Technology, information production, and market efficiency," proceedings of the Jackson Hole conference, Federal Reserve Bank of Kansas City.

Décamps, Jean-Paul, Benoît Roger, and Jean-Charles Rochet, 2004, "The 3 pillars of Basel 2: Optimizing the mix," *Journal of Financial Intermediation*, forthcoming.

Dewatripont, Matthias, and Jean Tirole, 1994, *The Prudential Regulation of Banks*, Cambridge, MA: MIT Press.

DeYoung, Robert, Mark Flannery, Walter W. Lang, and Sorin M. Sorescu, 2001, "The informational content of bank exam ratings and subordinated debt prices," *Journal of Money, Credit, and Banking*, Vol. 33, No. 4, pp. 900–925.

Evanoff, Douglas D., and Larry R. Wall, 2003, "Subordinated debt and prompt corrective regulatory action," Federal Reserve Bank of Chicago, working paper, No. WP 2003-03.

_____, 2002, "Measures of the riskiness of banking organizations: Subordinated debt yields, risk-based capital," Federal Reserve Bank s of Chicago and Atlanta, working paper.

_____, 2001, "SND yield spreads as bank risk measures," *Journal of Financial Services Research*, Vol. 20, pp. 121–146.

_____, 2000, "Subordinated debt and bank capital reform," Federal Reserve Bank of Chicago, working paper, No. WP-2000-07.

Flannery, Mark, 1998, "Using market information in prudential bank supervision: A review of the U.S. empirical evidence," *Journal of Money, Credit, and Banking*, Vol. 30, No. 3, pp. 273–305.

Flannery, Mark, and Kasturi Rangan, 2003, "Market forces in the banking industry: Evidence from the capital buildup in the 1990s," paper presented at the American Finance Association meeting, Washington, DC.

Flannery, Mark, and Sorin Sorescu, 1996, "Evidence of bank market discipline in subordinated debenture yields," *Journal of Finance*, Vol. 51, No. 4, pp. 1347–1377.

Freixas, Xavier, and Jean-Charles Rochet, 1995, *Microeconomics of Banking*, Cambridge, MA: MIT Press.

Furfine, Craig, 2001, "Bank portfolio allocation: The impact of capital requirements, regulatory monitoring, and economic conditions," *Journal of Financial Services Research*, Vol. 20, No. 1, pp. 33–56.

Furlong, F., and N. Keeley, 1990, "A reexamination of mean-variance analysis of bank capital regulation," *Journal of Banking and Finance*, Vol. 14, No. 1, pp. 69–84.

Gorton, Gary, and Anthony Santomero, 1990, "Market discipline and bank subordinated debt," *Journal of Money, Credit, and Banking*, Vol. 22, pp. 119–128.

Gropp, Reint, Jukka Vesala, and G. Vulpes, 2002, "Equity and bond market signals as leading indicators of bank fragility," European Central Bank, Frankfurt, Germany, working paper, No. 150.

Hancock, Diana, and Myron Kwast, 2001, "Using subordinated debt to monitor bank holding companies: Is it feasible?," *Journal of Financial Services Research*, Vol. 20, pp. 147–188.

Hancock, Diana, A. J. Laing, and James A. Wilcox, 1995, "Bank capital shocks: Dynamic effects on securities, loans, and capital," *Journal of Banking and Finance*, Vol. 19, pp. 661–677.

Jackson, Patricia, Craig Furfine, H. Groeneveld, Diana Hancock, D. Jones, William Perraudin, L. Redecki, and N. Yoneyama, 1999, "Capital requirements and bank behavior: The impact of the Basel Accord," Basel Committee on Bank Supervision, working paper, No. 1.

Jagtiani, Julapa, George Kaufman, and Catherine Lemieux, 2000, "Do markets discipline banks and bank holding companies?," Federal Reserve Bank of Chicago, working paper.

Jensen, Michael, 1986, "Agency cost of free cash-flow, corporate finance and takeovers," *American Economic Review*, Vol. 76, pp. 323–339.

Jones, David, 2000, "Emerging problems with the Basel Accord: Regulatory capital arbitrage and related issues," *Journal of Banking and Finance*, Vol. 24, pp. 35–58.

Jones, D., and K. King, 1995, "The implementation of prompt corrective action: An assessment," *Journal of Banking and Finance*, Vol. 19, pp. 491–510.

Kim, D., and Anthony Santomero, 1988, "Risk in banking and capital regulation," *Journal of Finance*, Vol. 43, pp. 1219–1233.

Levonian, Mark, 2001, "Subordinated debt and the quality of market discipline in banking," Federal Reserve Bank of San Francisco, mimeo.

Martinez Peria, S., and Sergio Schmukler, 2001, "Do depositors punish banks for 'bad' behavior? Market discipline, deposit insurance, and banking crises," *Journal of Finance*, Vol. 56, No. 3, pp. 1029–1051.

Mishkin, Frederic, 1996, "Evaluating FDICIA," Federal Reserve Bank of New York, mimeo.

Morgan, Don, 2002, "Rating banks: Risk and uncertainty in an opaque industry," *American Economic Review*, Vol. 92, No. 4, pp. 874–888.

Myers, Stuart, 1984, "The capital structure puzzle," *Journal of Finance*, Vol. 39, pp. 575–592.

Park, S., and Stavros Peristiani, 1998, "Market discipline by thrift depositors," *Journal of Money Credit and Banking*, Vol. 26, pp. 439–459.

Peek, Joe, and Erik Rosengren, 1995, "Bank capital regulation and the credit crunch," *Journal of Banking and Finance*, Vol. 19, pp. 679–692.

Pettway, Richard, and Joseph Sinkey, 1980, "Establishing on site bank examination priorities: An early-warning system using accounting and market information," *Journal of Finance*, Vol. 35, No. 1, pp. 137–150.

Rochet, Jean-Charles, 2003, "Rebalancing the 3 pillars of Basel 2," paper presented at the New York Federal Reserve Bank-Chazen Institute Conference, New York, October.

_____, 1992, "Capital requirements and the behavior of commercial banks," *European Economic Review*, Vol. 43, pp. 981–990.

Rochet, Jean-Charles, and Xavier Vives, 2002, "Coordination failures and the lender of last resort: Was Bagehot right after all?," London School of Economics, Financial Markets Group, discussion paper.

Santos, João, 2000, "Bank capital regulation in contemporary banking theory: A review on the literature," Bank for International Settlements, Basel, Switzerland, working paper, No. 30.

Sironi, Andrea, 2001, "An analysis of European banks' SND issues and its implications for the design of a mandatory subordinated debt policy," *Journal of Financial Services Research*, Vol. 19, pp. 233–266.

Thakor, Anjan, 1996, "Capital requirements, monetary policy, and aggregate bank lending," *Journal of Finance*, Vol. 51, No. 1, pp. 279–324.

U.S. Shadow Financial Regulatory Committee, 2000, "Reforming bank capital standards," Washington, DC.

Chapter 7

Market Discipline for Financial Institutions and Sovereigns

Hal S. Scott*
Harvard Law School

This paper explores how market discipline works for financial institutions, a highly regulated industry, and sovereigns. It is organized into two parts: 1) an assessment of what market discipline (MD) is and how it applies to banks and sovereigns and 2) mechanisms to induce greater MD discipline for banks and sovereigns.

1. How Market Discipline Works

1.1 Definition

Market discipline can be defined in different ways. One could equate market discipline with the classical conditions for perfect markets, including perfect information and competition, lack of agency problems, and no externalities. But such "perfect" conditions are rarely found in most markets in the real world, even unregulated ones. Similarly, agency costs exist for all firms, regulated and unregulated alike. It is hard to attribute the failures in corporate governance reflected in the recent accounting and other corporate scandals to the fact that firms were *regulated*. This is not to say lack of corporate governance, as measured by independent boards and audit committees, is not a problem for financial institutions, but rather to say it is no more a problem for financial institutions than other firms.

1.2 Safety Net Distortion

Market discipline for financial institutions (mainly banks) and sovereigns is undermined by the provision of safety nets, publicly supplied credit or guarantees, which relieve debtors from risk, thereby creating both debtor and creditor moral hazard. Debtors may borrow more or incur more risk, and creditors may supply more funds, and at better prices, than would be the case without such safety nets.

The safety nets take somewhat different forms for banks and sovereigns. In the former case, they consist of deposit insurance and bailouts (lending by central banks or governments to insolvent banks). In the latter case, they consist of loans to non-creditworthy or defaulting sovereigns by multilateral institutions, principally the International Monetary Fund (IMF), or particular countries (official bilateral credits). The rationales for the two safety nets also differ. In the case of banks, concerns of systemic risk are the principal justification for the safety nets. The idea is that the failure of one bank could trigger those of others, ultimately disrupting an entire economy.

In the case of sovereigns, the international safety net may be used to stem a country banking crisis. In many cases, financial crises are caused by the inability of banks to service their foreign debt. Korea and Turkey are recent prominent examples (Scott and Wellons, 2003). But there may also be a concern about country contagion, a financial meltdown in one country extending to others. In addition, there is a large political component of sovereign safety nets; countries and the multilaterals they control lend to countries whose support they seek to maintain.

There is, of course, an intense debate about whether these systemic risk concerns are real (Scott, 2004), either in the case of banks or sovereigns, and thus whether these public safety nets are justified. This debate is largely beyond the scope of this paper. The point here is that the existence of such safety nets can undermine market discipline.

1.3 Market Discipline Requisites

This paper formulates three general requirements for finding an acceptable level of market discipline: 1) a market in the financial instruments of the issuer; 2) enforceable credit contracts; and 3) a market for corporate control.

1.3.1 Capital Instruments

Market discipline requires a mechanism through which the market can penalize excessive risk-taking. Ordinarily, such discipline comes from losses or ultimately the failure of the firm. It is not obvious why one would demand that the issuer have instruments traded in the market. After all, many firms may be in perfectly competitive markets that penalize excessive risks taken, and not issue such instruments. But banks and sovereigns are different. Given our concern with the possible systemic consequences of bank failure and losses to public safety nets designed to minimize systemic risk, we must have confidence that the market provides sufficient solvency signals to permit instrument holders to demand management changes, or that creditors or regulators be able to intervene before a banks' capital becomes negative.

Sovereigns are also different. As with banks, there is concern with systemic consequences—here both economic and political—and the need to avoid calls on public safety nets (new official or multilateral credits). In addition, sovereigns, unlike banks, are not private actors, and are thus generally less responsive to private incentives to avoid losses. This can be a problem for state-owned banks but it is always a problem for sovereigns. It may be essential in the case of sovereigns that capital instrument holders be at risk if sovereigns are to be subject to any MD. Also, unlike the case with banks, there is no fallback to regulation if MD fails. It is thus even more crucial that there be market discipline for sovereigns than it is for banks.

Market discipline from capital markets could, in principle, be provided from equity or debt investments. But debt instruments more directly provide signals of default risk through interest rates. While default risk in theory might be extracted from equity prices (Gropp et. al., 2002), this may be difficult to do in practice.

Market discipline with respect to debt instruments requires that key terms, including supply, price, and maturity, in both the primary and secondary markets, be determined by risk. For this to occur, the instrument must be traded and priced, thus excluding, for example, a long-term credit facility arranged between a securities firm borrower and a bank creditor. Credit arrangements must also be capable of modulation in response to risk. Thus, senior and junior positions, and collateral and guarantee provisions, must be possible. These mechanisms assume credit suppliers have sufficient knowledge about risk to price it or design mechanisms to control or minimize it.

This does not require perfect information since the market typically makes price or collateral adjustments to compensate for lack of information; it only requires that the market have a fairly good idea as to what it is missing, so that discounts or level of required collateral will not be excessive. It is wrong, in my view, to say that market discipline cannot exist for banks because of the opaqueness of their loan portfolios. Assets of other largely unregulated firms, like biotech or entertainment firms, may be much more difficult to value. It may be enough for the market to know commonly disclosed aggregate data about loan portfolios such as number and type of borrowers.

There are obvious deficiencies in information available to creditors of banks and sovereigns. In the case of banks, there is the difficulty of accounting for loans. There is also the problem that banks may be discouraged by regulators from making disclosures, either because the regulators fear the market reaction could trigger a run on the bank or a run on the regulators themselves (insolvent banks reflect poorly on the regulators).

The problem in banking is that there is generally no capital instrument, immune from bailouts, through which judgments about the performance of the issuer can be reflected. The true risks of instruments will be distorted by the prospect of bailouts. Thus, the bank will not pay the same kind of price for inadequate performance or disclosure as will issuers without capital instruments protected by safety nets. The same is even more the case for sovereigns.

1.3.2 Legal Mechanisms to Foreclose on or Restructure Debt

Another key element of MD is that default on debt will result in losses to the issuer. This requires that there be legal mechanisms to foreclose on debt, and if necessary, to force debtors into bankruptcy or reorganization where value available for creditors may be maximized. In short, the potential discipline from capital market instruments requires that these instruments be enforceable.

Banks have some difficulty in issuing enforceable debt contracts. On the one hand, they can issue a range of debt, secured and unsecured, bank creditors can generally enforce debt contracts, and insolvent banks can go bankrupt and be restructured. However, the decision to invoke the bankruptcy process is left to regulators, for example, the Federal Deposit Insurance Corporation in the United States, rather than to private creditors, the usual case in other industries. Further, the actual bankruptcy process for banks is often within the control of the regulators themselves.

The problem is more severe for sovereigns. Political and constitutional dictates may preclude active use of secured credit or guarantee arrangements; debt contracts are less modulated. Secured credit may be difficult to enforce—the days of gunboat diplomacy to seize a country's assets are long gone. The escrow arrangements for the zero coupon U.S. Treasuries securing payments on Brady Bonds appear to be a highly unusual exception.

There is generally no process for dealing with default, as the extended crisis in Argentina clearly illustrates. Countries are not liquidated, and there is no regular process, as with companies, for dealing with insolvency (or inability to pay). As with banking, the process of dealing with sovereign default is largely managed by the public, for example, the IMF, rather than the private sector.

1.3.3 Market for Corporate Control

Another essential element for MD is a market in corporate control. Poor performance by managers, reflected in the prices of capital instruments (higher debt yields, lower share prices), or potential defaults, should be capable of resulting in takeovers, friendly or unfriendly. A market for corporate control, at least for unfriendly takeovers, is itself dependent upon the existence of capital market instruments that can be used to gain control of a firm.

Takeovers of banks present significant obstacles as compared with takeovers of firms in most other industries. This was well illustrated in the U.S. by the extremely rare hostile takeover of Irving Trust Company by the Bank of New York in 1988. Regulators have to approve the acquirer, a process which can take substantial time with attendant risk for both the acquirer and the target. Second, regulators may insist that the acquirer restore the acquired bank to health by injecting additional capital, adding expense. Third, extremely restrictive antitrust rules may be applied, for example, review of the effect on competition in multiple local banking markets. These rules may reflect the unwillingness of regulators to put other banks at a competitive risk from the merged institution.

Of course, where sovereigns are involved, takeovers are a non-event, except in war, and even then are generally unrelated to poor economic performance. One might argue that countries with strong democratic arrangements do permit change in control and that poor economic performance may trigger such changes. However, it is unlikely that the changes will depend on the degree to which sovereign debt—particularly that owed to foreign creditors—is honored. Indeed, as Argentina most recently illustrates, political advantage may result from default.

2. Mechanisms to Improve Market Discipline

2.1 Banks

The most important improvement that could be made to increase market discipline for banks would be to decrease or eliminate safety nets. This requires, however, that one accept the added systemic risk that may result, or independently attempt to decrease that risk. In banking, changes in payment arrangements—migration to real-time gross settlement systems like Fedwire, conversion of end-of-day net settlement systems to continuous settlement as in CHIPS (clearing house interbank payments system), or the reduction of Herstatt risk (foreign exchange settlement risk) through the use of the CLS Bank, have reduced systemic risk. Limits also exist on interbank placements, and deposit insurance acts to prevent bank runs. Further, one can provide that safety nets like central bank lending to insolvent institutions will only occur after a determination that systemic risk is a real concern, the approach taken in 1991 in the Federal Depositors Insurance Corporation Improvement Act (FDICIA). And one can try to make risky banks pay more for deposit insurance than less risky banks, thus internalizing the cost of public support.

The removal of safety nets would, of course, permit more accurate risk-based pricing of capital instruments. A more modest step is to insure that banks issue some instruments that are immune from bailouts. The proposal of the Shadow Financial Regulatory Committee to require banks to issue bailout-proof subordinated debt is intended to accomplish this result (Shadow Financial Regulatory Committee, 2001).

Other measures have been adopted to decrease risk, such as activities restrictions and capital requirements, but these approaches, as most command and control regulation, can have perverse effects. Activity restrictions may actually prevent risk-reducing diversification and capital requirements may not achieve their objective, e.g. most analysts believe that present Basel rules require too much capital for good risks and too little for bad risks (a result that may also occur under the approach of Basel II) (Crouhy et. al., 2004).

Other improvements could be made. A more private creditor-friendly bankruptcy process could be designed, regulators could abandon efforts to block banks from making damaging disclosures (and could even disclose more of their own information about banks) (Hoenig, 2003) and rules more favorable to acquisitions could be adopted.

2.2 Sovereigns

2.2.1 Safety Nets

As with banks, a principal problem is with safety nets. Limitations on multilateral lending to sovereigns have been proposed, such as in the Bank of England–Bank of Canada proposals (Haldane and Krueger, 2001), but so far no restrictions have been adopted or even seriously considered. Further, there has been almost no discussion of limiting bilateral official credit. The lack of movement on this front largely reflects the present reality that the international system has no acceptable alternative way to deal with financial crises.

Reform in the sovereign debt area has focused on improving the process of dealing with insolvency. This could in theory improve market discipline by providing better legal mechanisms which, in turn, might mean less need for public support. If sovereigns and their creditors had effective means for decreasing and restructuring debt, less public support might be needed. However, these processes may take a long time to use when a crisis does arise, and there may well be the same pressure, in the short term, for public support.

Two approaches to dealing with insolvency have been actively considered, providing for collective action clauses (CACs) (Taylor, 2002) in bond covenants and the creation of a legal process for debt restructuring, the so-called sovereign debt restructuring mechanism (SDRM) (Krueger, 2001 and 2002).

2.2.2 CACs

There are several different types of bond covenants that could be subject to CACs. The primary attention has been on CACs that permit a majority of creditors to change the payment terms in outstanding bonds. Traditionally, sovereign debt issued under UK law has included such CACs, permitting 75 percent of creditors (by value) to take action, whereas debt issued under U.S. law (over 60 percent of present debt) has required creditor unanimity (unanimity action clauses or UACs). U.S. law actually only requires this result for corporate bonds, not sovereign ones—so parties have freely chosen UACs over CACs.

The Group of 7 (G-7) countries, led by the United States (with Undersecretary of the Treasury John Taylor as the champion) have urged emerging market countries to use British-style CACs. This effort has borne some fruit. For example, Mexico, Brazil, and Uruguay switched in 2003 from using UACs to CACs in substantial new 2003 bond issues. However, it unclear to what extent speculative grade issuers (who are most likely to use such clauses) will or will have to pay a premium for use of CACs (Eichengreen et. al., 2003, believe they have). If the cost is significant, the use of CACs may be limited. In addition, some of the recent CAC issues have effectively required a higher than 75 percent majority requirement. For example, in the Uruguay $5.1 billion issue in May 2003, all debt holders "controlled" by the sovereign, such as state banks, are to be excluded in obtaining the required 75 percent. It is unclear, just how much easier this stringent collective action rule makes restructuring than a complete unanimity requirement.

There are other problems about the effectiveness of CACs. First, it is questionable whether they will really ever be used. As Argentina has most recently demonstrated, creditors and debtors would rather obtain public support. While this may be bad for sovereigns in the long run, since it increases debt costs, in the short run it permits them to avoid painful adjustments. Creditors also benefit by avoiding losses. Second, there is a severe "aggregation" problem. Some bonds may have CACs, and others may not, and those issues with CACs may have different majority requirements. It is unclear what rules would apply across different bonds. Uruguay's recent issue attempts to deal with this problem by using a super CAC, providing that all future bonds issued in the same series would require the same 75 percent CAC, and that collective action across all bondholders in the series could be taken by a 85 percent majority of creditors, and 66.6 percent of the holders of each separate bond issue. But this aggregation solution could be easily undone if Uruguay were to decide in the future to issue a new "series" of bonds without CACs or with different CACs, or not subject to aggregation.

In short, it may be extremely difficult, if not impossible, to use private contracts—bond covenants—to achieve real coordinated majority action requirements across different debt instruments, where different creditors extend credit to the same debtor over time. Indeed, this explains why we have bankruptcy laws for corporate debt, and why some think we need a SDRM for sovereign debt. The marginal price increases, if any, associated with the recent conversions to CACs by some countries may indicate that these clauses will have a marginal effect on the sovereign debt risk process.

2.2.3 SDRM

The SDRM proposal put forward by the IMF in 2002 failed to get support from the G-7, particularly the United States. It is officially on hold, but could always be reactivated if CACs were found wanting. The key elements of the SDRM are: 1) at a debtor's request, a majority of creditors could impose a standstill on payments and a stay of creditor litigation for a fixed duration, for example, 90 days; 2) facilitation of new financing by providing that, upon consent of a super-majority of existing creditors, old claims would be subordinate to new money (so-called debtor in possession or DIP financing); 3) during the SDRM process, priority creditors (multilaterals like the IMF and World Bank, and possibly countries) would still be paid—outside of restructuring, but some parallel restructuring of their debt would occur; 4) a restructuring plan could be approved by a super-majority of creditors, informed by the IMF's view of the sustainability of the resulting debt burden; and 5) an independent tribunal (maybe a judicial organ) would adjudicate issues like lack of equitable treatment or valuation of claims.

It is highly unlikely that such a procedure will be adopted in the near future due to opposition from the United States and most creditor groups (who see this as making restructuring too easy). Even if SDRM were to be adopted, it would not by itself necessarily increase market discipline. Like CACs, it is unclear it would ever be used. It can only be triggered by debtors who may prefer not to use it, and instead obtain additional multilateral or official bilateral funding.

2.2.4 Another Suggestion: Reform of Sovereign Immunity Laws

Some more limited measures may be possible. The IMF has made major efforts to improve the disclosure of country finances. Better information may lead to more realistic debt terms. The IMF has also used its conditionality requirements and financial sector assessment program, FSAP, to promote macroeconomic measures and structural reforms that might reduce crises in the future. However, it is unclear whether such measures actually do reduce risk.

One additional possibility would be to expose sovereigns to more threat from creditor foreclosure actions. This can be analyzed with reference to the United States. Under U.S. law, creditors of defaulting sovereigns can get judgments in U.S. courts against defaulting sovereigns, but cannot easily attach assets in satisfaction of such judgments. Absent a waiver of sovereign immunity, the only attachable assets are those used in connection with the issue of such debt—and it is hard to imagine what those assets might be. This has not, in fact, proved to be a problem since sovereigns commonly waive sovereign immunity. While this opens up U.S. assets to seizure (except those specifically excluded by statute, such as central bank assets), U.S. courts will not enforce the attachment of assets outside the U.S.

What assets would a sovereign have in the U.S.—or other countries—that are now available for seizure? As the *Elliott Associates* case demonstrates, payment of interest on existing debt is an important asset available for seizure outside the sovereign issuer's country. Payments in foreign currency to foreign creditors require a transfer of funds through the payment system of the country of the currency to foreign accounts of the creditors. In addition, payments from other countries to defaulting sovereigns, for example, in connection with imports from the defaulting sovereign, may also be exposed to seizures. Any doubt that such assets are available for seizure could be removed by clarifying statutory enactments.

Countries own substantial commercial ventures, state-owned enterprises (SOEs). While the SOEs are separate corporate entities, sovereigns do own them, and the stock in such enterprises could be available for attachment. If such stock is held in the defaulting sovereign's own country, foreign courts, like those in the U.S., cannot attach them. This outcome could be changed by a law giving the U.S. courts the power to order the delivery of such stock to creditors. If such an order were not complied with, U.S. courts could allow the creditors to levy on the assets of the SOE. This would result in a possible conflict of claims between the creditors of the sovereign and those of the SOE, but this conflict could be resolved by giving the sovereign's creditors a claim subordinated to all of the SOEs creditors—a pure equity interest.

Interestingly, Jeremy Bulow (2002) has proposed a reform of sovereign immunity laws going in the exact opposite direction. He has recommended increasing sovereign immunity protection on the theory that creditors who are more at risk from sovereign default will be more careful in lending to those sovereigns in the first place. It seems odd, however, to address potential sovereign default problems by decreasing creditor remedies. Bulow is obviously focused on the creditor moral hazard problem—the fact that creditors are not sufficiently at risk because of public bailouts. But, as long as such bailouts exist, creditors will be relatively indifferent to their remedies—like CACs they will not have to use them. Indeed, as long a such bailouts exist, creditors will be relatively indifferent to an *increase* or *decrease* in their rights.

Absent bailouts, however, or given that bailouts are not always assured or complete, one would want the market to discipline debtors as well as creditors. Creditors should be disciplined by uncompensated losses and debtors should be disciplined by creditors exercising their rights. The latter could be promoted, in my judgment, by decreasing sovereign immunity protection. At the margin of the safety net, this should lead to fewer defaults and cheaper credit.

*Hal S. Scott is the Nomura Professor of International Financial Systems at Harvard Law School.

References

Bulow, Jeremy, 2002, "First world governments and third world debt," *Brookings Papers on Economic Activity*, Vol. 1, pp. 229–253.

Crouhy, Michael, Dan Galai, and Robin Mark, 2004, "The use of internal models: Comparison of the new Basel credit proposals with available internal models for credit risk," in *Capital Adequacy Beyond Basel: Banking, Securities and Insurance*, Hal Scott (ed.), New York: Oxford University Press, forthcoming.

Eichengreen, Barry, Kenneth Kletzer, and Ashoka Mody, 2003, "Crisis resolution: Next steps," Santa Cruz Center for International Economics, working paper, November.

Gropp, Reint, Jukka Vesala, and Giuseppe Vulpes, 2002, "Equity and bond market signals as leading indicators of bank fragility," European Central Bank, working paper, No. 150, June.

Haldane, Andy, and Mark Krueger, 2001, "The revolution of international financial crises: Private finance and public funds," Bank of Canada, working paper, November.

Hoenig, Thomas, 2003, "Should more supervisory information be publicly disclosed?," *Economic Review*, Federal Reserve Bank of Kansas City, Vol. 88-3, pp. 5–14.

Kreuger Anne, 2002, "New approaches to sovereign debt restructuring: An update on our thinking," remarks at the Conference on Sovereign Debt Workouts, Institute for International Economics, April 1.

_____, 2001, "International financial architecture for 2002: A new approach to sovereign debt restructuring," remarks at the National Economists' Club Annual Members Dinner, November 26.

Scott, Hal, 2004, *International Finance: Policy and Regulation*, London: Sweet & Maxwell, Ch. 3, forthcoming.

Scott, Hal, and Philip Wellons, 2003, *International Finance: Transactions, Policy and Regulation*, New York: Foundation Press, 10th edition, pp. 1309–1312, 1325–1329.

Shadow Financial Regulatory Committee, 2001, "The Basel Committee's revised capital accord proposal," Statement No. 169, February 26.

Taylor, John, 2002, "Sovereign debt restructuring: A U.S. perspective," remarks at the Conference on Sovereign Debt Workouts: Hopes and Hazards, Institute for International Economics, April 2.

Chapter 8

Comments on the Theory of Market Discipline

Kostas Tsatsaronis*

Bank for International Settlements

Market discipline can be viewed generally as the influence that "outsiders" (that is, stakeholders with no executive decision making power) exert on "insiders" (that is, the decision-makers in an economic unit) that encourages value enhancing behavior by the latter. Irrespective of whether this influence takes the form of ex ante guidance or ex post sanction, it is important to recognize that the objectives are decidedly "macro" in the sense of being inclusive of the views of all stakeholders. In this respect, the encouragement of market discipline is hardly controversial. The trickier issues have to do with the extent of its effectiveness and its applicability in particular economic settings.

The three papers in this opening session deal with a number of broad issues relating to the effectiveness of market discipline in the context of financial firms (especially banks) and in the case of sovereigns. Clearly, the disciplinary force of market forces influences the governance of other economic units such as non-financial firms (as it will be discussed in later sessions). Arguably, the two cases dealt with in this session are of particular interest both from the academic and policy perspectives because of the particularities of the nexus of information and incentives that characterize them. The production of financial intermediation services is typically characterized by greater opacity and fragility of the producer's balance sheet. While there are other informationally intensive economic sectors, financial intermediation is alone in that it relies critically on leverage as an input to production of its services. The case of sovereign financing also presents a unique framework where the definition and enforceability of property rights of counterparties are more limited compared to the case of private sector contracts.

The three papers provide similar descriptions of what can market discipline accomplish in these different contexts and then move on to discuss how these objectives are to be accomplished. In this regard they focus on two sets of issues. The first relates to what are the necessary conditions for market forces to operate properly and maximize their disciplinary influence on insider decision-makers. The second set of issues relates to the interaction between the architecture and specific application of policy (both in the national and international levels) on one hand, and the effectiveness of market discipline on the other. I will structure my main comments around those two main issues. As the authors did I will also restrict my focus if the case of financial institutions and countries, although many of my comments are applicable to other cases as well.

1. What Are the Requirements for Effective Market Discipline?

As the authors correctly point out, market discipline requires that outside stakeholders possess adequate information about the behavior of insider decision-makers but also, importantly, that their incentives to act upon this information are not distorted. These twin requirements are quite distinct from whether they have the means to influence this behavior. Discussions on how to promote market discipline often focus on this latter condition, while in my opinion the former two are more basic requirements for effective discipline.

The role of information availability in promoting effective discipline in is quite clear and not particularly controversial. Stakeholders need to be able to make independent assessments of the current condition of the economic unit and to evaluate the behavior of the insiders in promoting their interests. Disclosure and the accounting framework play a key role in this respect. Accounts should present a clear and accurate description of the financial condition of the firm and provide outsiders with the necessary elements to make their own assessments. The quality of the information provided through the regular reporting channels is at least as important as the quantity and extent of disclosures. Timeliness and representativeness of disclosures are fundamental. However, in an economic environment where traditional sectoral and national boundaries become increasingly devoid of their economic significance, comparability of reporting standards across industries and countries becomes a critical issue. Furthermore, as the operations of firms and the associated financing structures become more complex it becomes important that accounting standards encompass the representation not only of the current value of assets and liabilities, but also the balance of risks going forward. While this challenges the more narrow interpretations of accounts as objective reports firmly grounded on current facts and free of conjectures about the future, it is fully consistent with the view that the accounting framework should give a full picture of the current condition of the firm which includes its near term outlook. Thinking in this direction has already begun as witnessed by the paper by Mary Barth in another session of this conference.

The working principle of market discipline is that outsiders have important stakes in the economic unit that they have an incentive to protect. An important characteristic of these stakes is their diversity. The interests of equity holders differ significantly from those of debt holders and also from those that are counterparties to the firm in the securities markets. In addition the incentives of stakeholders differ by the type of claimant. Professional asset managers subjected to the rigors of a quarterly portfolio performance reporting cycle will arguably behave differently compared to institutional investors that have their own funds at stake. Retail investors, with stakes that are relatively small but that represent a larger component of their personal financial wealth, may yet have a different attitude towards financial risk and reward. This diversity of perspectives is a source of strength for the market economy: the proverbial invisible hand will balance these perspectives in proportion to their corresponding size and to the relative strength of the holders' opinions.

At the same time, however, one should recognize the complexity of the interactions among these different perspectives can give rise to self-reinforcing asset price dynamics that can at times run contrary to value creation. A key factor that can lead to such dynamics is the influence of short horizon decision making which leads market participants to subordinate the longer-term value objective to that of achieving nearer-term gains. Asset managers under the pressure of frequent performance appraisal cycles, institutional investors constrained by statutory and regulatory requirements, or securities markets counterparties seeking liquidity in a fast-moving market environment are prone to succumb to the concreteness of current market trends on occasion even ignoring their own beliefs regarding fundamental value. The resulting herd-like behavior of participants creates its own dynamics and can exacerbate asset price movements in either direction. A reduced diversity in participant perspectives can be detrimental to the ability of the market to accurately assess risk. Episodes of persistent market over-reaction abound in economic history books as well as in current day newspaper headlines. Whether the object of speculation was tulips or the power of computer chips, the fundamentals of speculative manias remain the same. Conversely, panic in the face of sudden losses can at times trigger abrupt withdrawals and generalized retraction from risk-taking that is equally self-reinforcing. Contagion, asset price overshooting, and market seizure can have long-lasting economic implications for those dependent on external financing. The experiences of three iconic value investors with the recent technology bubble serve as a reminder of the limits to the ability of contrarian investors to resist market trends. Warren Buffet had to face several annual meetings of shareholders concerned with the apparent failure of the company holdings to reflect the "new realities" of the late 1990s, before he could make a triumphant "I told you so" speech in 2000. Julian Robertson and George Soros, however, did not have the financial stamina to withstand the pressures on the market value of their funds stemming from their decision to doubt the optimism of others in the "new economy" valuations.

The pronounced and persistent overshooting of asset prices highlights an important shortcoming of current risk assessment technology. Markets are better in judging relative risk at a given point in time, than making consistent risk assessments across time. This shortcoming is evidenced in the cyclical patterns or credit ratings, bond spreads, and other premiums that characterize different asset classes. While these measures give a consistent depiction of the balance between risk and reward associated with different securities at a given point in time, over time they tend to co-move systematically with each other and often with the overall state of the business cycle. The root of such systematic patterns can be found partly in a changing economic environment, which conditions market participants' future outlook, but also in those participants' shifting attitudes towards risk. These shifts typically reflect changes in the effective attitude towards risk suggested by the response to asset market conditions (for example as traders being obliged, independently of their own views, to shift towards more defensive postures when pressed against their risk budget ceilings in the wake of an adverse market move), or quite simply under- or over-estimation of the actual risks involved due to generalized euphoria or pessimism about future prospects. The self-reinforcing nature of these mechanisms has often led commentators to label this as the endogenous element of financial risk: aggregate risk that is built up from the collective impact of individual actions. It must be noted, that the responses of individual players are fully justified from their particular perspective. There is nothing irrational at the "micro" level. The suboptimality of the "macro" outcome is the result of these perspectives failing to take account of the complementarities between individual actions.

In this respect a key question to be addressed is to what extent are markets sufficiently disciplined themselves to be relied upon to discipline firms and countries. The arguments presented above suggest that market forces alone cannot be fully relied upon to deliver a consistent influence on decision makers. Endogenous responses to changing conditions and shifting attitudes towards risk over time imply that the market is likely to be more or less permissive towards various types of risk at any particular point in time.

2. Market Discipline and Public Policy: Complements of Substitutes?

Markets do not operate in the void. The specifics of the policy framework affect critically the ability of outside stakeholders to influence decision makers. Hence, all three papers consider a number of issues related to the interactions between market discipline and policy, and more specifically how it affects the availability of information and the incentives of outsiders. Views diverge as to whether policy and market discipline are substitutes to each other (in the sense that policy intervention necessarily decreases the effectiveness of market discipline) or whether there are important complementarities between the two (in other words, there is scope for mutually reinforcing influence). With a liberal dose of added interpretation of my own, I would classify Hal Scott and to a lesser extent Jean-Charles Rochet as siding with the substitutability view, while Robert Bliss suggests that the two can play complementary roles. My personal views are more sympathetic to the latter.

I mentioned above the important role of information in enabling outsiders to form their own assessment of the current condition and future prospects of an economic unit in order to be able to exert influence on decision makers. While demand by outsiders does lead to the voluntary disclosure of information by those that are seeking external finance, a prime example being the development of credit ratings, the quantity and quality of this information cannot be taken for granted. In fact, there seems to be an undersupply of information both in terms of what is reported but also, importantly, how it is reported. Mandatory requirements provide a useful coordination device that can improve the quantity of available information in the aggregate, establish common formats that facilitate comparisons across reporters, and minimize distortions to the competitive playing field.

In the case of regulated industries, such as finance, supervisors gather information about the firm that is not necessarily available to outside investors. A question arises as to whether such information should be disclosed. This is a complicated and under-researched question. One's answer to it would be conditioned by whether they view the supervisor as a facilitator of market discipline or as an independent source of discipline. I personally see scope for the official sector collecting commercially sensitive information and disclosing it only in a sufficiently aggregated form as to inform decisions of market participants without undermining individual competitive positions.

The architecture of the policy framework and the way this framework is implemented play a key role in shaping the incentives of outsiders in providing effective governance. Safety nets, whether they apply to financial firms or to the case of sovereign borrowing, are a clear case in point. By limiting downside risk they reduce the returns to monitoring and influence behavior. At the same time, however, a well-designed framework that reduces the negative externalities that are associated with financial crises can allow outsiders to hold insiders accountable for their own decisions and not penalize them for the impact of factors that are beyond their control.

In discussing the impact of policy actions on incentives the three papers refer to the recent proposals for the introduction of mandatory issuance of subordinated debt by banks. These proposals are an example of policy contributing to the strengthening of market discipline, by creating a class of stakeholders in banking organizations that have stronger incentives than other debt holders to keeping the bank safe, but at the same time the upside potential of their investment is capped at the contracted return. There are several merits to this idea including the fact that in many cases it is likely to increase private sector scrutiny of banks and coupled with mandated minimum frequency of issuance it can provide a lever for effective governance by outsiders. However, there are a number of points that I would like to mention in conjunction with these proposals. The fact that there is not sufficient issuance of subordinated debt at present, attests to the fact that markets left on their own do not always produce the mechanisms to exert sufficient discipline on decision makers. In fact, it is not clear from existing evidence that subordinated debt holders are more effective in disciplining bank management than other outside stakeholders. Even if these proposals were to be adopted, it is unclear who would be the holders of these securities, clearly there does not seem to be a large unsatisfied demand at the moment. Will supply create its own demand? And if this debt is held by unsophisticated investors, does the limited gain in private sector monitoring justify another official restriction on the capital structure of banking institutions? Finally, I am not oblivious to the fact that information from subordinated debt prices should be formally incorporated into supervisory strategy of dealing with problem institutions. Prices reflect investors' assessment of the likelihood of future events including the probability of supervisory intervention. As such there is the risk that supervisory monitoring of market prices is akin to looking itself in the mirror. In fact, if market participants have full faith in the ability of the supervisory authority to promptly intervene prices of subordinated debt should not move at all!

I do not mean to imply that there are no important trade-offs between policy intervention and the disciplinary capacity of market forces. Overly prescriptive regulation can discourage creativity of entrepreneurs and destroy value creating potential in the economy. An unclear policy framework is a source of uncertainty that can numb the private sector creativity. Ambiguity is not typically constructive. Similarly, excessive use of policy discretion and forbearance in dealing with the inevitable (and on occasion necessary) crisis can also breed moral hazard.

I would like stress, however, that neither policy nor market forces are sufficient by themselves to bring about the optimal balance between stability and efficiency. They are both necessary. Markets and regulators have different perspectives. The regulatory perspective is in many ways similar to that of an insurance underwriter: The focus is on downside risk. Moreover, regulators are typically obliged to consider the overall picture abstracting from the particularities and idiosyncrasies of individual institutions. Such a macro perspective emphasizes the commonalities in risks and interactions among individual components of the financial system. There are important differences in the horizon of analysis: The official sector can typically afford to take a longer-term view, not being subject to the same incentive constraints as market participants. Finally, supervisors gain access to different types of information than outside stakeholders and can thus form a different opinion about the prospects of the firm, and, to steal a term from Robert Bliss, they have "unparalleled power" to discipline insiders. As I mentioned earlier, policy can also play a coordinating role in establishing standards of disclosure that are adopted by everybody, thus minimizing the inefficiencies of competing methodologies.

Many recent policy initiatives have emphasized these complementarities. Regulatory and supervisory frameworks have become increasingly more transparent by establishing ex ante rules and procedures and, importantly, following them ex post. The private sector is increasingly involved in the rulemaking process and one basic principle adopted by policymakers is that the regulatory framework should work as much as possible with the grain of the market rather than against it. Hence, I differ from Jean-Charles Rochet's interpretation of the Basel II in that I view the philosophy of the new accord as an example where regulation has moved closer to what is current best practice in the market rather than trying to impose a rigid rule to all. Similarly in the case of sovereigns, the official sector has engaged the private sector in the process of designing new disclosure guidelines, in the effort to build a new framework for sovereign default, and in the introduction of CACs and the cost-sharing in the resolution of crises.

In conclusion, there are ample opportunities for policymakers and market participants to work together in disciplining insiders in firms and governments. This two-way interaction also implies that market forces can also be a healthy source of discipline for policymakers as two of the papers suggested. I would add that the regulatory and policy framework can also be useful in keeping markets in check.

*Kostas Tsatsaronis is head of financial institutions and infrastructure in the Research and Policy Analysis Division of the Monetary and Economic Department at the Bank for International Settlements. These comments represent opinions of the author and should not be interpreted as necessarily reflecting the views of the Bank for International Settlements.

PART III

EVIDENCE OF MARKET DISCIPLINE
IN BANKING

Chapter 9

Market Discipline of U.S. Financial Firms: Recent Evidence and Research Issues

Mark J. Flannery*
University of Florida

and

Stanislava Nikolova
University of Florida

The potential for market discipline of financial firms has attracted increasing attention from academics and supervisors. Not only have financial economists written numerous papers on the topic, but the Basel Committee on Bank Supervision identifies market discipline as one of the three "pillars" on which effective regulatory oversight should be based. After initial resistance, some supervisors have come to recognize the potential benefits of market participation in bank supervision:

> The real pre-safety-net discipline was from the market, and we need to adopt policies that promote private counterparty supervision as the first line of defense for a safe and sound banking system. (Greenspan, 2001)

Market discipline also appears to suit a financial sector in which financial institutions are increasingly complex:

> I believe that market discipline is a particularly attractive tool for encouraging safety and soundness in a rapidly evolving environment. Market discipline is inherently flexible and adaptive with respect to innovations, since market participants have incentives to change the ways that they evaluate risks as innovations are adopted. (Meyer, 1999)

In short, involving counterparties in bank supervision may reduce the costs and improve the quality of prudential oversight.

Researchers have investigated whether market information is accurate and timely, and whether it can enhance the supervisory process. In this paper, we review the recent empirical evidence on these issues. In the process, we try to summarize what is known, and to identify the most important things we still need to learn. Our charge is to concentrate on the U.S. evidence, which requires us to omit several interesting foreign studies.

1. Defining Market Discipline

Supervision has among its primary goals the identification and correction of problems that might lead to a financial firm's failure. At its most basic level, therefore, supervisors seek information about their firms' failure probabilities, which they have historically assessed via mandatory financial reporting and periodic on-site examinations. "Market discipline" describes a situation in which private sector agents—equity holders and debt holders—produce information that helps supervisors recognize problem situations and implement appropriate corrective measures. Bliss and Flannery (2001) describe two distinct components of market discipline—market monitoring and market influence. Effective *monitoring* occurs when investors can accurately assess changes in a firm's condition, and promptly impound those changes into the firm's stock and bond prices. Market *influence* describes the ability of market participants to affect a firm's financial decisions. Both facets of market discipline can theoretically complement government supervision.

Berger (1991) points out that market discipline requires private investors to face costs that increase as firms undertake risks, and to take action as a result of these costs. These investor reactions fall into three broad classes. First, investors can monitor bank condition and require higher coupon rates from riskier banks. When a supervisor observes higher rates (if they are paid), she knows that at least some investors have noticed a change in the bank's probability of failure. So monitoring creates information that supervisors can use. But what if the bank refuses to pay higher rates? This is the second class of investor reactions: at least some investors will withdraw uninsured funds from the bank (Billet et al., 1998). In response, the bank must raise new funds elsewhere and/or curtail its activities. This interaction generates no price signal for supervisors, but the shift from uninsured to insured sources of funds conveys information about the market's assessment. Moreover, the withdrawal of uninsured money probably forces the institution to shrink, which is what supervisors might also prescribe for an institution whose risk has risen. So in this case investors' actions influence the bank's position. The third class of actions forces the bank to restore its initial default probability. Supervisors would observe neither a rate change nor a withdrawal of uninsured liabilities if the threat of either action leads the bank to restore its capital ratio—either by reducing asset size or raising (retaining) new equity. This constitutes market influence, and if managers value their debt ratings we can expect investors or the rating agencies to force at least some corrections that are consistent with what supervisors would like to have done.

Before we discuss each class of market action at greater length, we should emphasize that market discipline requires private investors to bear the costs of their bank becoming more likely to fail. Obviously, a supervisory system that provides implicit guarantees against creditor losses cannot expect to secure much benefit from market discipline.

We have relatively little empirical evidence about the ability of market participants to influence financial firms' decisions, which is likely the result of market influence being hard to identify (Rajan, 2001). The basic problem is that market prices impound expected future actions. The impact of any shock on a firm's value therefore depends on the shock itself and the managers' anticipated reaction to the shock. A small decline in share value following a negative shock could mean either that the shock was small and managers were not expected to respond at all, or that the shock was large but investors anticipated that appropriate managerial action could offset part of its effect on the firm. (See also section 5 below.)

Moreover, the decisions of a financial firm reflect both the influence of market participants and the existing regulatory framework, making it difficult to isolate the effect of either one. In an effort to draw inferences about the effectiveness of market discipline *per se*, researchers must compare the behavior of similar firms operating under different supervisory arrangements. For example, Nier and Bauman (2002) use a sample of banks from 32 countries and document a positive association between capital and risk after controlling for government guarantees. Gunther et al. (2000) studied Texas banks in 1910, when they had access to two alternative insurance plans. One plan charged a flat-rate premium while the other required additional security if the financial state of the bank deteriorated. The authors find that banks choosing the latter, were better capitalized and less risky. These capitalization and risk differences persisted or increased over time

Compared with identifying effective market influence, studying market monitoring is relatively easy. Moreover, monitoring is a logical prerequisite for influence. It is therefore not surprising that most of the market discipline research has addressed three main questions about monitoring:

- Does the market accurately reflect information about financial firms' condition?

- Does the market incorporate information in a timely manner?

- Does that information differ from the information available to supervisors?

To many financial economists, it seems odd to pose these questions so explicitly, since the efficiency of market prices has strong support for asset prices in general. Its high profile in studying financial firms may reflect an unusually high cost of the misperception of a financial firm's true condition—for example, because bank failures are unusually costly. Alternatively, banking firms may be more difficult to understand from the outside—a question evaluated by Morgan (2002), Morgan and Stiroh (2001), and Flannery et al. (2004), albeit with different conclusions. Strategically, it was also important to establish the accuracy of market monitoring in order to counteract a common supervisory impression that their inside information was generally (and necessarily!) more accurate than market prices.

Market participants' ability to evaluate a bank's financial condition is typically detected as an association between market prices of the bank's claims and indicators of its asset value and risk exposures. The most common such indicators are the risk composition of the bank's asset portfolio, its capitalization status, its regulatory or credit agency rating, or its failure. Evidence of the market's monitoring ability can also be found in various event studies, which document how bank claim prices respond to *new* information about the bank's condition. Finally, even if the market is found to have accurate and timely information, the question still remains of whether its information can be valuable to regulators. Researchers address this question by investigating the marginal contribution of market indicators to supervisory models, or by using market indicators to forecast regulatory ratings.

2. Evidence of Market Discipline in Debt Prices

Market discipline in the debt markets can be manifested as a change in the cost of uninsured funds. As the perceived risk of a banking firm increases, holders of the firm's uninsured liabilities will require a higher promised return to compensate for higher expected losses.

The early search for evidence of market discipline in debt prices investigated the contemporaneous relationship between bank risk indicators and subordinated debt yields or large deposit rates. A number of recent studies follow this same approach. They document that issuance and secondary-market risk premiums on traded subordinated notes and debentures are correlated with accounting measures of risk, asset portfolio composition, credit agency or regulatory ratings, and probability of undercapitalization or of failure (Jagtiani and Lemieux, 2001; Morgan and Stiroh, 2001; Sironi, 2002; Evanoff and Wall, 2002; Jagtiani et al., 2002; and Krishnan et al., 2003). The analysis of the rates on large uninsured CDs (certificates of deposit) yields mixed results. Hall et al. (2002) focus on banks that have a satisfactory regulatory rating and document a positive relation between CD yields and measures of bank risk. On the other hand, Jagtiani and Lemieux (2001) find no evidence of market discipline in the uninsured CD market for a small sample of bank holding companies (BHCs) with failing subsidiaries. An innovative approach to the issue is offered by Furfine (2001), who examines the existence of market discipline in a debt market overlooked by previous studies—the overnight federal funds market. The evidence there is expected to be the strongest since counterparties are likely to be more sophisticated than the average investor, and loans are likely to impose significant expected losses given their size and lack of collateral. Consistent with this expectation, the author documents that interest rates paid on federal funds transactions reflect differences in credit risk across borrowers.

Another approach to investigating the existence of market monitoring is by testing whether the prices of uninsured debt claims respond to relevant news in a rational manner. If the debt holders of a financial firm are concerned with their expected losses, then they will adjust the valuation of their claims as new information about the firm's default probability is revealed. Two recent event studies provide evidence of market discipline by documenting that the prices of uninsured financial-firm liabilities respond to news in a reasonable manner. Harvey et al. (2003) examine whether the Federal Reserve's announcement that trust-preferred stock can be included in tier 1 capital affected the value of bank debt. The authors find that following the announcement, credit spreads of banks that subsequently issued trust-preferred stock decrease. This is consistent with the hypothesis that debt markets value the default probability decrease from the addition of trust-preferred stock to capital. Allen et al. (2001) examine changes in debt valuation for BHCs that decide to convert to financial holding companies (FHC) under the Gramm–Leach–Bliley Act. They find that conversions result in lower yield spreads consistent with the lower risk likely to be attained through greater diversification.

Another recent change in the market discipline literature has been a shift from contemporaneous affirmation to forecasting. While earlier studies focused on contemporaneous associations between uninsured liability prices and indicators of firm risk, new ones explore whether information in current prices corresponds to *future* outcomes. This question is intuitively appealing since prices reflect expectations of future cash flows. Analysis of the forecasting ability of subordinated debenture credit spreads demonstrates that these can explain one-quarter-ahead regulatory ratings better than capital ratios could (Evanoff and Wall, 2001), they can improve the forecasting accuracy of supervisory rating models four quarters prior to inspection (Krainer and Lopez, 2003), and they are more closely correlated with bank risk measures in the 12 months prior to bank failure (Jagtiani and Lemieux, 2001). Thus, prices of subordinated debentures reflect not only the current condition of financial firms, but its future condition as well.

3. Evidence of Market Discipline in Debt Quantities

Market discipline in the debt markets can be detected not only as a change in the cost of uninsured funds, but also as a change in their availability. If holders of uninsured liabilities believe that a financial firm is becoming increasingly risky, they might react by withdrawing or withholding their investment. In addition, financial firms undertaking more risk are faced with higher borrowing costs of uninsured funds and can choose to use insured funds instead. These supply-side and demand-side changes of uninsured debt quantity in response to changes in perceived risk would be evidence of market monitoring and influence respectively. Consistent with the existence of market discipline, recent studies document that as the financial condition of banks (Billet et al., 1998; Jagtiani and Lemieux, 2001; and Hall et al., 2002) or thrifts (Goldberg and Hudgins, 1996; Park and Peristiani, 1998; and Goldberg and Hudgins, 2000) worsens, these institutions increase their reliance on insured deposits. McDill and Maechler (2003) also ask whether uninsured depositors discipline banks by withdrawing their funds but they explicitly account for the simultaneous determination of deposit quantities and rates. When a bank's fundamentals deteriorate, they find a shift in both its demand for uninsured funds and the market's supply of such funds. That is, the volume of uninsured deposits at a deteriorating bank falls, even though the bank responds by offering higher rates.

It is a widespread regulatory concern that the effects of market discipline on the quantity of deposits can have undesirable consequences. One often-cited reason for this concern is that depositors will withdraw funds suddenly in a "run" to reduce looming losses, rather than doing so gradually as changes in a bank's risk profile occur. While some believe that "runs" can cause even a healthy bank to fail, Calomiris and Mason (1997) find no evidence to support such a belief. They analyze the 1932 Chicago banking panic and find that failing banks could be distinguished from non-failing banks at least six months before the panic. They conclude that failures reflected the relative weakness of failing banks in the face of a common asset value shock.

Another cited reason for regulatory concern is that depositors may use information about one bank to infer incorrectly the condition of others. One bank's failure may thus trigger contagious runs and widespread panics. Existing studies have documented that bank-specific news events, such as announcements about the quality of a bank's portfolio (Docking et al., 1997) and about formal supervisory actions at the bank (Jordan et al., 2000), do affect the valuation of other banks. As in Calomiris and Mason (1997), these studies find evidence of rational, information-based spillover, as opposed to an indiscriminate contagion.

4. Evidence of Market Discipline in Equity Prices

Although most of the research has evaluated market discipline by examining debt prices or quantities, a few studies have looked at equity prices. This limited research indicates that share prices reflect a bank's current condition, and can perhaps help predict future changes. Recent event studies document that equity prices promptly impound new information about a bank's condition: Moody's downgrades (Billet et al., 1998), loan-loss reserve increases (Docking et al., 1997), and announcements of formal supervisory actions (Jordan et al., 2000) result in negative abnormal equity returns. In addition, as we discuss below, equity market indicators can help predict changes in a firm's financial condition one to two years before these changes materialize (Elmer and Fissel, 2001; Berger et al., 2000; Curry et al., 2001; and Krainer and Lopez, 2002).

5. Influencing Bank Capitalization?

Market discipline need not manifest itself as a change in the cost or availability of uninsured funds. Since any firm's default probability is a function of both asset risk and leverage, a financial firm can keep its default probability constant if it balances changes in risk with changes in capital. The causality in the relationship between risk and capital can flow in either direction. Banks might decide to increase risk and then build up capital to reduce the probability of default. Alternatively, they can first accumulate capital and then choose to substitute into riskier activities, perhaps because they need to take on more risk in order to pay for their higher overall financing cost. An incipient increase in risk or reduction in capitalization can generate debt price or quantity pressure to adjust bank capital to its perceived risk exposure. Such behavior is consistent with market influence even though it can leave the quantities and prices of uninsured liabilities unaffected.

Early evidence of the interdependence between bank risk and capital can be found in Cargill (1989) and Swindle (1995). Cargill (1989) documents that CAMEL (capital adequacy, asset quality, management, earnings, and liquidity) ratings are not significant in explaining interest rates on large uninsured CDs. Using essentially the same data, Swindle (1995) finds that regulatory capital ratio changes are a function of CAMEL ratings. The results in the two studies suggest that increases in risk can be compensated for by increases in equity, thus leaving the risk to debt holders unchanged. More recently, Shrieves and Dahl (1992) and Calomiris and Wilson (1998) find that increases in bank risk are positively related to increases in bank capital. Finally, Flannery and Rangan (2003) document that the substantial capital buildup by large BHCs during the 1990s is likely due to the increased risk exposure and risk aversion of bank counterparties as implicit and explicit government guarantees have decreased.

6. Using Market Discipline to Enhance Bank Supervision

We find it encouraging to learn that market information is frequently mentioned in formal supervisory reports (Feldman and Schmidt, 2003). However, it is "not clearly integrated into or supportive of a supervisory assessment (p. 1)." If market assessments are to influence supervisors, we must design procedures through which market information is incorporated meaningfully into the supervisory process. This incorporation can take three general forms. First, market information may help supervisors assess a firm's current condition. Second, it can act as an early warning signal of the firm's future condition. Third, it can permit (or require) supervisors to address problems promptly.

Assessing a firm's current condition should be viewed as a "forecasting" problem: given available information, what is the firm's true default probability? Statistical theory indicates that combining two estimates will produce a more accurate assessment than either one alone, provided the estimators' prediction errors are not perfectly correlated. So long as market information accurately reflects bank condition, on average, combining market and supervisory information should yield a more accurate assessment of the firm's true condition.

We have already cited studies that document the relationship between market signals and bank risk. Does this market information add value to supervisory information? A number of studies show that equity-market and debt-market indicators can marginally increase the explanatory power of BOPEC (BHC's bank subsidiaries, other nonbank subsidiaries, parent company, earnings, and capital adequacy) or CAMEL forecasting models. Berger et al. (2000) find that supervisory assessments are less accurate than equity-market indicators in reflecting the bank's condition except when the supervisory assessment is based on recent inspections. Gunther et al. (2001) show that equity data in the form of expected default frequency can add value when included in BOPEC forecasting models. Curry et al. (2001) find that adding simple equity-market indicators (price, return, and dividend information) adds explanatory power to CAMEL rating forecasting models based on accounting information. Evanoff and Wall (2001) show that yield spreads are slightly better than capital ratios in predicting bank condition. Krainer and Lopez (2003) find that equity- and debt-market indicators predict subsequent BOPEC ratings and that including these in a BOPEC off-site monitoring model helps identify additional risky firms.

Only a small subset of the above papers (Krainer and Lopez, 2002, 2003; and Gropp et al., 2001) assess the model's forecasting ability not in terms of R^2 statistics alone (which treat all errors as equally important), but by examining the model's propensity for specific kinds of errors. In the context of bank supervision, we conjecture that a type 1 error—failing to identify a true problem—is more costly than a type 2 error—falsely classifying a sound bank as troubled. Krainer and Lopez (2002, 2003) are encouraged when their market-augmented decision rule slightly reduces the number of false negatives, even though the market information adds little to the model's R^2 statistic.

At the present time, it appears that market information adds rather little to the explanatory power of models that rely exclusively on accounting information. Given that supervisors actually know more than is contained in these accounts, this is a low threshold for judging the performance of market information. Further research in this area is clearly important. Without a substantial increase in predictive abilities, however, market information is unlikely to help supervisors identify problems at an early stage.

Even if market information cannot systematically improve supervisory assessments of current or future conditions, contemporaneous affirmation of supervisory information can still provide substantial value. Supervisory judgments can be buttressed by market data, provided that market data is properly interpreted. By re-affirming supervisors' judgments, market information may enable supervisors to act sooner when they perceive a problem. Conversely, market information may cause appropriate forbearance if it suggests that the supervisory view is too bearish.

A second use for market information also requires only that market signals provide an unbiased contemporaneous assessment of bank condition: Supervisors can be required to take specific actions when a market signal becomes adverse enough. Sufficiently accurate market signals might usefully serve as a tripwire to forestall supervisory forbearance, as investigated by Evanoff and Wall (2000). If market signals are noisy, a strict rule of this sort will generate type 1 and type 2 errors. Nevertheless, the cost of these errors might be lower than the cost of errors made under the alternative supervisory procedures.

7. Stock or Bond Market Indicators?

Most of the existing literature on market discipline of financial firms has focused on information in debt prices or credit spreads, largely because the debt holders' payoffs most closely resemble those of regulators. However, this advantage of debt market prices is balanced out by a number of disadvantages. To start with, debt prices are notoriously difficult for a researcher to collect. While some corporate bonds trade on NYSE (New York Stock Exchange) and Amex (American Stock Exchange), they account for no more than 2 percent of market volume (Nunn et al., 1986). The accuracy of bond data is also problematic. Data on OTC (over the counter) trades or quotes are not collected into a single database. Indeed, Hancock and Kwast (2001) compare bond yield data from four sources and find that the correlations between different sources are only about 70 percent to 80 percent. Moreover, many bond prices are based on matrix valuation rather than on actual trades, and Warga and Welch (1993) document that there are large disparities between matrix prices and dealer quotes. Even for bond transaction prices, Saunders et al. (2002) show that the corporate bond market is characterized by a small number of bidders, slow trade execution, and large spreads between the best and second-best price bids.

Another factor that may limit the usefulness of debt prices as a tool of market discipline is that debt issuance has been endogenous. According to Covitz et al. (2001), managers tend to issue new debentures or other uninsured claims disproportionately when market investors are relatively bullish about the firm. The result is a weaker connection between new issue rates and the bank's true condition. This possibility has lead some researchers to suggest that debenture issuance should be mandated at regular intervals (Calomiris, 1998; Ferguson, 1999; Kwast et al., 1999; Meyer, 1999; Benink and Schmidt, 2000; Evanoff and Wall, 2000; and U.S. Shadow Regulatory Committee, 2000). Although there is evidence that the implementation of these proposals can be valuable, the existing literature has not assessed the cost (if any) of forcing banks to issue debt regardless of market demand for it. Even if there were no self-selection problem and bond data were readily available and accurate, extracting risk information from debt spreads is complicated. The typical approach is to use debt prices and calculate yield spreads as the difference between a corporate yield and the yield on a Treasury security of the same maturity. After adjusting for redemption and convertibility options, sinking fund provisions, and other relevant features, spreads are assumed to measure credit risk. However, corporate yields differ from Treasury yields for a number of reasons other than credit risk (see Elton et al., 2001; Huang and Huang, 2002; Delianedis and Geske, 2001; and Longstaff, 2004). They include premiums for tax, liquidity, and expected recovery differences between corporate and Treasury bonds, as well as compensation for common bond-market factors. This new understanding of the composition of bond spreads raises new questions about their interpretation.

Saunders (2001) points out that contingent-claim models of firm valuation imply that in prefect markets both equity and debt prices will reflect the same information about firm market value and portfolio risk. Why not extract market information from share prices? In contrast to debt markets, equity markets are liquid and deep. Accurate equity prices can be obtained frequently, and more financial firms have traded equity than traded debt. Despite these data advantages, researchers have been reluctant to embrace the idea that share prices can convey valuable information to supervisors. Junior bonds have payoffs similar to those of the federal safety net, making their price changes easier to interpret in most cases. By contrast, the value of any safety net subsidies is impounded in the bank's share price. As a result, equity price increases do not unambiguously correspond to a lower expected claim on the federal safety net. Indeed, under some circumstances, an insured institution's equity value can rise simply because its portfolio risk has risen—which leaves the bank's failure probability higher than before.[1] This calls for using equity-market indicators other than prices or returns to extract information about firm risk. Such indicators are proposed by Moody's KMV (Crosbie and Bohn, 2002) and Gropp et al. (2001), who combine equity prices, firm leverage, and historical equity volatility to construct equity-based default risk measures.

To the extent that debt (or equity) prices contain noise, or fail to conform to the Black–Scholes assumptions used to "back out" risk parameters, using both securities (where they are available) might provide more accurate information. Gropp et al. (2001) and Krainer and Lopez (2003) document the advantage of this approach by showing that a model using both equity-market and debt-market indicators to forecast bank risk, outperforms a model using either set of indicators alone. Nikolova (2003) proposes a structural way to combine information from equity and debt prices. She observes that if a firm's equity is modeled as a call on its assets and the same firm's risky debt is modeled as risk-free debt short a put, then the equity-call and debt-put models can be combined in a system of equations and simultaneously solved for the market value and volatility of assets. The resulting asset volatility is entirely forward-looking. Nikolova finds that risk measures produced by this approach are more closely related to indicators of bank condition. They also have higher explanatory power in forecasting material changes in bank condition up to three quarters before these changes materialize.

8. Financial Conglomerates: How Big a Cloud?

Our discussion thus far reflects an implicit assumption in the literature that the legal entity issuing a market security is the same as the entity whose safety concerns supervisors. Yet the U.S. has long maintained a distinction between "banking" and "nonbanking" financial activities, and much has been written about our need to limit the activities covered by the social safety net. With the passage of the Gramm–Leach–Bliley Financial Modernization Act of 1999, this issue becomes more compelling. For a financial conglomerate combining traditional (U.S.) banking, investment banking, and insurance, which parts should the safety net protect? Market discipline will help assess the condition of protected activities only if the relevant subsidiaries issue stand-alone securities. Even then, supervisors must understand the extent to which real or imagined guarantees from the parent to the subsidiaries' claim holders affect the stand-alone security prices. Intra-conglomerate guarantees may strip the relevant information out of the rate spread for example, on subsidiary debentures. The *de facto* separation of subsidiaries within a bank holding company has often been discussed in the U.S. without reaching consensus. At this point in time, however, we must reconsider this issue if market discipline is to supplement government supervision of the financial system.

9. Summary and Conclusions

Recent research into market disciplinary forces in banking has refined the idea of market discipline and how it may complement traditional supervisory methods. The initial focus on bond or deposit credit spreads has expanded to include studies of funding composition: the balance between insured and uninsured sources of funds. Researchers have also begun to recognize that equity prices may contain relevant information about a firm's condition, even if shareholders' interests are not always aligned with those of the safety net. We have also made progress judging the marginal value of market information in the supervisory process, moving toward more sophisticated indicators of information, such as the number of type 1 and type 2 errors associated with market-augmented classification rules. Assessing a bank's condition from the outside is essentially a forecasting problem and treating it this way helps to focus the relevant questions and issues. Along with these conceptual (and empirical) advances, the increased conglomerization of financial service corporations in the U.S. raises questions about the relation between market discipline and the extent of the federal safety net.

We conclude by listing the open research and policy questions that seem most important for pushing forward the use of market discipline as a complement to more traditional methods of safety and soundness supervision.

- We need to determine the best method of extracting information from security prices and the best procedure for meaningfully incorporating this information into supervisory processes.

- We need further information about the marginal contribution of market information to the "type 1–type 2" accuracy of various forecasting models.

- Financial economists and supervisors should try to articulate an appropriate loss function for forecasting and classification models. How expensive are undiagnosed problems versus false alarms?

- The emergence of financial conglomerates complicates supervisory uses of market discipline, and requires a reconsideration of how extensive should the federal safety net be.

*Mark J. Flannery is an Eminent Scholar Chair in finance at the University of Florida. Stanislava Nikolova is a doctoral student in finance at the University of Florida.

Notes

1. This perverse price reaction occurs only when the bank is very highly levered. Subordinate debt shares the same feature in some situations.

References

Allen, L., J. Jagtiani, and J. Moser, 2001, "Further evidence on the information content of bank examination ratings: A study of BHC-to-FHC conversion applications," *Journal of Financial Services Research*, Vol. 20, pp. 213–232.

Benink, H., and R. Schmidt, 2000, "Agenda for banking in Europe," in *Bank Fragility and Regulation: Evidence from Different Countries and Different Times*, G. Kaufman (ed.), Greenwich, CT: JAI Press.

Berger, A., 1991, "Market discipline in banking," *Proceedings of a Conference on Bank Structure and Competition*, Federal Reserve Bank of Chicago, pp. 419–437.

Berger, A., S. Davies, and M. Flannery, 2000, "Comparing market and regulatory assessments of bank performance: Who knows what when?," *Journal of Money, Credit, and Banking*, Vol. 32, pp. 641–667.

Billet, M., J. Garfinkel, and E. O'Neal, 1998, "The cost of market versus regulatory discipline in banking," *Journal of Financial Economics*, Vol. 48, pp. 333–358.

Bliss, R., and M. Flannery, 2001, "Market discipline in governance of U.S. bank holding companies: Monitoring vs. influencing," in *Prudential Supervision: What Works and What Doesn't*, F. Mishkin, (ed.), Chicago: National Bureau of Economic Research and University of Chicago Press.

Calomiris, C., 1998, *Blueprints for a New Global Financial Architecture*, Washington, DC: American Enterprise Institute.

Calomiris, C., and J. Mason, 1997, "Contagion and bank failures during the Great Depression: The June 1932 Chicago banking panic," *American Economic Review*, Vol. 87, pp. 863–883.

Calomiris, C., and B. Wilson, 1998, "Bank capital and portfolio management: The 1930s 'capital crunch' and scramble to shed risk," National Bureau of Economic Research, working paper, No. 6649.

Cargill, T., 1989, "CAMEL ratings and the CD market," *Journal of Financial Services Research*, Vol. 3, pp. 347–358.

Covitz, D., D. Hancock, and M. Kwast, 2001, "Market discipline and the decision to issue subordinated debt: Is required issuance really necessary?," Federal Reserve System, working paper.

Crosbie, P., and J. Bohn, 2002, "Modeling default risk," Moody's KMV, white paper, available at www.moodyskmv.com/.

Curry, T., P. Elmer, and G. Fissel, 2001, "Regulator use of market data to improve the identification of bank financial distress," Federal Deposit Insurance Corporation, working paper, No. 2001-01.

Delianedis, G., and R. Geske, 2001, "The components of corporate credit spreads: Default, recovery, tax, jumps, liquidity, and market factors," University of California, Los Angeles, Anderson School, working paper, No. 22-01.

Docking, D., M. Hirschey, and E. Jones, 1997, "Information and contagion effects of bank loan-loss reserve announcements," *Journal of Financial Economics*, Vol. 43, pp. 219–239.

Elmer, P., and G. Fissel, 2001, "Forecasting bank failure from momentum patterns in stock returns," Federal Deposit Insurance Corporation, working paper.

Elton, E., M. Gruber, D. Agrawal, and C. Mann, 2001, "Explaining the rate spread on corporate bonds," *Journal of Finance*, Vol. 56, pp. 247–277.

Evanoff, Douglas D., and Larry D. Wall, 2002, "Measures of the riskiness of banking organizations: Subordinated debt yields, risk-based capital, and examination ratings," *Journal of Banking and Finance*, Vol. 26, pp. 989–1009.

_____, 2001, "Sub-debt yield spreads as bank risk measures," *Journal of Financial Services Research*, Vol. 20, No. 2/3, pp. 121–146.

_____, 2000, "Subordinated debt and bank capital reform," Federal Reserve Bank of Chicago, working paper.

Feldman, R., and J. Schmidt, 2003, "Supervisory use of market data in the Federal Reserve System," Federal Reserve Bank of Minneapolis, working paper.

Ferguson, R., 1999, "Evolution of financial institutions and markets: Private and policy implications," speech at New York University, New York.

Flannery, M., and K. Rangan, 2003, "What caused the bank capital build-up of the 1990s?," University of Florida, working paper.

Flannery, M., S. Kwan, and M. Nimalendran, 2004, "Market evidence on the opaqueness of banking firms' assets," *Journal of Financial Economics*, forthcoming.

Furfine, C., 2001, "Banks as monitors of other banks: Evidence from the overnight federal funds market," *Journal of Business*, Vol. 74, pp. 33–57.

Goldberg, L,. and S. Hudgins, 2000, "Depositor discipline and changing strategies for regulating thrift institutions," *Journal of Financial Economics*, Vol. 63, pp. 263–274.

_____, 1996, "Response of uninsured depositors to impending S&L failures: Evidence of depositor discipline," *Quarterly Review of Economics and Finance*, Vol. 36, pp. 311–325.

Greenspan, A., 2001, "The financial safety net," remarks to the 37th Annual Conference on Bank Structure and Competition, Federal Reserve Bank of Chicago, Chicago, IL May 10, available at www.federalreserve.gov/boarddocs/speeches/2001/20010510/default.htm/.

Gropp, R., J. Vesala, and G. Vulpes, 2001, "Equity and bond market signals as leading indicators of bank fragility," European Central Bank, working paper.

Gunther, J., L. Hooks, and K. Robinson, 2000, "Adverse selection and competing deposit insurance systems in pre-depression Texas," *Journal of Financial Services Research*, Vol. 17, pp. 237–258.

Gunther, J., M. Levonian, and R. Moore, 2001, "Can the stock market tell bank supervisors anything they don't already know?," *Economic and Financial Review*, Second Quarter, pp. 2–9.

Hall, J., T. King, A. Meyer, and M. Vaughan, 2002, "Did FDICIA enhance market discipline? A look at evidence from the jumbo-CD market," Federal Reserve Bank of St. Louis, working paper, No. 2002-2.

Hancock, D., and M. Kwast, 2001, "Using subordinated debt to monitor bank holding companies: Is it feasible?," *Journal of Financial Services Research*, Vol. 20, pp. 147–188.

Harvey, K., M. Collins, and J. Wansley, 2003, "The impact of trust-preferred issuance on bank default risk and cash flow: Evidence from the debt and equity securities markets," *The Financial Review*, Vol. 38, pp. 235–256.

Huang, J., and M. Huang, 2002, "How much of the corporate–Treasury yield spread is due to credit risk?," Pennsylvania State University, working paper.

Jagtiani, J., and C. Lemieux, 2001, "Market discipline prior to failure," *Journal of Economics and Business*, Vol. 53, pp. 313–324.

Jagtiani, J., G. Kaufman, and C. Lemieux, 2002, "The effect of credit risk on bank and bank holding companies bond yield: Evidence from the post-FDICIA period," *Journal of Financial Research*, Vol. 25, pp. 559–576.

Jordan, J., J. Peek, and E. Rosengren, 2000, "The market reaction to the disclosure of supervisory actions: implications for bank transparency," *Journal of Financial Intermediation*, Vol. 9, pp. 298–319.

Krainer, J., and J. Lopez, 2003, "Using security market information for supervisory monitoring," Federal Reserve Bank of San Francisco, working paper.

_____, 2002, "Incorporating equity market information into supervisory monitoring models," Federal Reserve Bank of San Francisco, working paper.

Krishnan, C., P. Ritchken, and J. Thomson, 2003, "Monitoring and controlling bank risk: Does risky debt serve any purpose?," Case Western Reserve University, working paper.

Kwast, Myron L., and Members of the Federal Reserve System Study Group on Subordinated Notes and Debentures, 1999, "Using subordinated debt as an instrument of market discipline," report of a Study Group on Subordinated Notes and Debentures, M. Kwast (chair), Board of Governors of the Federal Reserve System, staff study, No. 172, December.

Longstaff, F., 2004, "The flight-to-quality premium in U.S. Treasury bond prices," *Journal of Business*, Vol. 7, No. 3, forthcoming.

McDill, K., and A. Maechler, 2003, "Dynamic depositor discipline in U.S. banks," Federal Deposit Insurance Corporation and International Monetary Fund, working paper.

Meyer, Laurence H., 1999, "Market discipline as a complement to bank supervision and regulation," speech before the Conference on Reforming Bank Capital Standards, New York.

Morgan, Donald P., 2002, "Rating banks: Risk and uncertainty in an opaque industry," *American Economic Review*, Vol. 92, No. 4, pp. 874–888.

Morgan, Donald P., and Kevin J. Stiroh, 2001, "Market discipline of banks: The asset test," *Journal of Financial Services Research*, Vol. 20, No. 2/3, pp. 195–208.

Nier, E., and U. Baumann, 2002, "Market discipline, disclosure, and moral hazard in banking," Bank of England, working paper.

Nikolova, S., 2003, "Bank risk reflected in security prices: Combining equity and debt market information to assess bank condition," University of Florida, working paper.

Nunn, K., J. Hill, and T. Schneeweis, 1986, "Corporate bond price data sources and return/risk measurement," *Journal of Financial and Quantitative Analysis*, Vol. 21, pp. 197–208.

Park, S., and S. Peristiani, 1998, "Market discipline by thrift depositors," *Journal of Money, Credit, and Banking*, Vol. 30, pp. 347–364.

Rajan, Raghuram G., 2001, "Comment on 'Market discipline in the governance of U.S. bank holding companies: Monitoring versus influencing'," in *Prudential Supervision: What Works and What Doesn't*, Frederic Mishkin (ed.), Chicago: University of Chicago Press, pp. 143–145.

Saunders, Anthony, 2001, "Comment on Evanoff and Wall/Hancock and Kwast," *Journal of Financial Services Research*, Vol. 20, No. 2/3, pp. 189–194.

Saunders, Anthony, A. Srinivasan, and I. Walter, 2002, "Price formation in the OTC corporate bond markets: A field study of the inter-dealer market," *Journal of Economics and Business*, Vol. 54, pp. 95–110.

Shrieves, R., and D. Dahl, 1992, "The relationship between risk and capital in commercial banks," *Journal of Banking and Finance*, Vol. 16, pp. 439–457.

Sironi, A., 2002, "Strengthening banks' market discipline and leveling the playing field: Are the two compatible?," *Journal of Banking and Finance*, Vol. 26, pp. 1065–1091.

Swindle, S., 1995, "Using CAMEL ratings to evaluate regulator effectiveness at commercial banks," *Journal of Financial Services Research*, Vol. 9, pp. 123–141.

U.S. Shadow Regulatory Committee, 2000, *Reforming Bank Capital Regulation*, Washington, DC: AEI Press.

Warga, A., and I. Welch, 1993, "Bondholder losses in leveraged buyouts," *Review of Financial Studies*, Vol. 6, pp. 959–982.

Chapter 10

Bank Market Discipline and Indicators of Banking System Risk: The European Evidence

Reint Gropp*
European Central Bank

1. Introduction

There is considerable interest among bank supervisors and central banks in the availability and quality of market signals on banks' current and prospective financial condition and risks. This interest is based on two ideas. One, the increased cost of raising new debt or equity in the primary capital markets could exert direct market discipline on banks. Namely, the anticipation of higher re-financing cost may constrain banks' risk-taking and the manifestation of higher refinancing cost (and in the limit the inability of banks to access capital markets) may impose constraints on banks' ability to grow without first reducing their exposure to risks. Second, the prices of banks' outstanding securities (both bonds and stocks) could provide a signal about banks' financial conditions to supervisors, private investors and central banks. The monitoring and potential corrective actions, especially by market participants and supervisors, are referred to as indirect market discipline. In particular, supervisors may use secondary market signals as screening devices or inputs into early warning models geared at identifying banks, which should be more closely examined.[1]

For market signals to be accurate, market participants must have adequate information about banks' behavior. Especially for large complex banking organizations, balance sheets and profit and loss totals may provide an incomplete and insufficiently detailed picture. Data on the composition of banks' credit exposures, capital and its composition, banks' off-balance-sheet activities and the associated risks and information about the banks' exposures to liquidity, operational and market risk may be necessary. This is recognized in pillar 3 of the New Basel Accord, which envisions such information to be made available to the market.[2]

This paper first discusses some conceptual issues relating to market discipline, including a description of mandatory subordinated debt proposals, which may provide a reference point for the likely effectiveness of market discipline. After that, I summarize the findings of a recent report on banks' issuance of marketable securities by the Basel Committee.[3] Next, I summarize the evidence whether the prices of these instruments reflect banks' risk in the European Union (EU) and examine the predictive properties of market indicators for future individual bank instability. In the final section of the paper, I ask the question whether useful information about the banking system as a whole can be extracted by aggregating market indicators of individual banks into country level indicators.

2. What Is Market Discipline?

Equity holders, as the owners of the bank can exercise market discipline in a very immediate and direct way, as they have the right to replace management. The reason why in spite of this equity holders have not been considered strong candidates for providing market discipline in banking is also clear: Equity holders, once their equity stake has sufficiently deteriorated have an interest in the bank taking on *more* risk rather than less. Depositors are also not strong candidates for disciplining banks. One, if they are covered by deposit insurance, they have no incentive to monitor banks. Second, even if they are uninsured, it is frequently argued that they may be to unsophisticated and fragmented to exercise discipline effectively.

Instead the literature has placed great hopes on subordinated debt as a mechanism for disciplining banks. In particular mandatory subordinated debt requirements have long been viewed in the academic literature as a relatively elegant, market-based way to regulate banks. Subordinated debt holders, given their subordinated status relative to other creditors of the banks such as senior debt holders and depositors, should have particularly strong incentives to monitor the risk-taking of the bank. Given that they do not benefit in an unlimited way on upside gains, subordinated debt holders can be expected to have a natural concern to limit risk-taking. Of course, this is only true as long as the bank has some equity left; without equity, subordinated debt holders face the same incentives to gamble as equity holders.

It has, however, also been realized that the actual power over management of subordinated debt holders may be limited. Hence, more recent subordinated debt proposals have relied on specific features to strengthen the effectiveness of the discipline arising from subordinated debt holders. These features include put options, where subordinated debt have the right to demand early repayment of their claims, and the convertibility of subordinated debt into equity (Cooper and Fraser, 1998; Evanoff, 1993). Most recently, Calomiris (1999) proposes caps on the spread over government bonds on primary issues, in order to impose funding constraints on banks that are perceived to be highly risky.

Currently there is no subordinated debt requirement in place. As we will see, virtually none of the subordinated debt outstanding in the EU exhibits the features that authors have argued may strengthen the hand of subordinated debt holders. Hence, the "tests" for the effectiveness of market discipline are weak and cannot reject the hypothesis that market discipline would be effective in the presence of a mandatory debt requirement, which asked banks to issue debt frequently, regularly, and, say, at interest rates below a pre-specified spread. The absence of these as well as other features from current subordinated debt also suggests that imposing mandatory subordinated debt requirements would impose a cost on banks. The benefits accrue to society as a whole (in form of a more stable banking system) and weighing these benefits against the costs should guide policymakers in their decision as to whether the introduction of mandatory schemes may be desirable.

Somewhat less ambitious than direct market discipline is the idea of indirect market discipline. Indirect market discipline, that is, supervisors using market information to identify weak banks, "only" requires relatively liquid and deep secondary markets and that investors truly have their money at stake. Further, they rely on some comparability of market prices across banks, which suggests that banks should issue sufficiently standardized securities.

3. Subordinated Debt and Equity Markets in Europe

The Basel Committee on Bank Supervision has recently published a comprehensive summary of subordinated debt and equity markets in member countries.[4] The main conclusions of the report can be summarized as follows. Subordinated debt issues are widespread in Europe. During 1990–2001, there were approximately 4,000 issuances of subordinated debt in the EU countries covered in the report (U.S.: 820). In value terms, subordinated debt issues amounted to more than $260 billion (U.S.: $93 billion). The issuing banks represent more than 50 percent of the total assets in the banking system in all EU countries covered. However, of the 4,000 issuances, almost 3,500 took place in Germany and of those, 2,000 were issued by small publicly owned savings banks. While this suggests that very small institutions can also issue subordinated debt, the debt was almost always privately placed and very small in face value.[5]

Indirect market discipline requires the *public* issuance of subordinated debt. The report finds that there were 1400 public placements of subordinated debt (U.S.: 820) valued at $168 billion (U.S.: $93 billion). Public placements have been quite frequent by banks in Germany, the UK, and the Netherlands. The report also concludes that the euro may have facilitated deeper and more liquid subordinated debt markets for the smaller euro area countries, decreasing the cost of issuance and broadening the investor base. Further, the report finds that banks tend to issue subordinated debt less than twice a year and average initial term to maturity tends to be in excess of 10 years. This compares unfavorably to most proposals for subordinated debt requirements, which would view a frequency of issuance of at least four times a year and an average initial term to maturity of around 2 years as optimal. Subordinated debt markets have grown steadily during the 1990s, with respect to the number of institutions issuing, the frequency of issuance, as well as the average size of issues.

The report's data for equity markets is considerably more sketchy.[6] Total number of issues for the three EU countries, for which data are available (Belgium, Germany, and the UK), has been 126 issues (U.S.: 16) with a value of $58 billion (U.S.: $7 billion). There seems to be considerable potential for equity markets to provide indirect market discipline. Equity markets are deep and liquid, and have become even deeper and more liquid during the past decade. The interpretability of equity signals is easy, once they have been appropriately adjusted to eliminate their call option character, for example, KMV Corporations's distance to default. Hence, equity-market signals generally avoid the problems in using debt market signals highlighted in Hancock and Kwast (2001). Hancock and Kwast show that spreads calculated from different subordinated issues of the same bank may give conflicting signals about the fragility of the bank. In addition, subordinated debt markets are inherently illiquid, because most issues are traded in over-the-counter markets with proprietary pricing.

Overall, the conclusions that emerge from the report suggest that market discipline may—for the present time at least—be limited to the largest institutions. In total, as a lower bound the report identifies around 10 such institutions in Europe and reports an upper bound of around 100 banks. At the same time, given their complexity, the extent of off-balance-sheet operations and their international orientation, this may be precisely where traditional tools of supervisors may most usefully be complemented by market discipline.

4. Evidence on Market Discipline for Individual Banks

4.1 Market Prices and Contemporaneous Risk

In the literature on market discipline, the question of whether market prices reflect contemporaneous risk taking of banks has been most extensively discussed. There are two closely related issues. One, do *primary* market spreads reflect banks risk? And second, do *secondary* market spreads reflect banks risk? Without going into detail here, both questions have been answered in the affirmative in a rich body of literature using U.S. data.[7]

Sironi (2003) examines the first question for a sample of EU banks. He argues that the spread of subordinated debt over the corresponding maturity risk-free bonds (government bonds) is a function of five main factors. One, the spread reflects the economic and financial condition of the issuing bank. Second, it reflects the time to maturity of the issue, as this affects its default risk premium. Third, the spread reflects the depth and liquidity of the market for the bond. Fourth, the spread reflects any explicit or implicit government guarantees perceived by investors. Fifth, the spread reflects the degree to which government bonds are indeed "risk free."[8] Hence, Sironi estimates the following (subscript i denotes issue):

$$Spread_i = f(Risk_i, Matu_i, Amount_i, Country_i, Curr_i, Year_i) + \varepsilon_i.$$

In the specification, the coefficient on *Risk* is of central interest. Sironi uses four different proxies for banks' risk: 1) the issue rating; 2) the issuer rating; 3) financial strength rating, which is intended to evaluate the strength of the bank irrespective of the safety net; and 4) a number of balance-sheet indicators that are believed to be related to risk. Allowing for non-linear effects, Sironi finds a monotonically increasing effect of lower issue and issuer ratings on spreads. He also finds that public banks enjoy a funding advantage of about 40 basis points relative to private banks with the same financial strength rating. At the same time, Sironi finds that there is only a weak relationship between accounting measures of risk, such as leverage or problem loans, and spreads. This is somewhat difficult to interpret from a market discipline perspective. Does this mean that spreads do not accurately reflect banks' risk (bad news for market discipline)? Or does it mean that spreads contain information not already in accounting variables (good news for market discipline)?

Sironi also finds that the correlation of spreads and ratings may have strengthened over time in the EU. In particular, he finds that there was no relationship between ratings and spreads before 1996. He argues that the reason may be the loss of monetary policy authority, combined with the desire in many countries to satisfy the strict budget rules of the Maastricht Treaty (no more than 3 percent of gross domestic product, GDP, deficit and less than 60 percent of GDP total government debt). To check on this interpretation he runs separate regressions for European Monetary Union (EMU) and non-EMU countries before and after 1996, and finds that non-EMU countries' bank spreads were correlated before and after 1996 with ratings, while EMU countries were not. Sironi claims that this confirms the idea that the "improvement in market discipline" was related to EMU.[9] Further, Sironi finds that given all other factors, including risk profile, maturity, liquidity etc., UK banks pay a higher premium over the risk-free rate on their subordinated debt. This is a very interesting finding, which is confirmed in Gropp et al. (2002) in the context of the ability of spreads to predict bank fragility.[10]

An important technical consideration emerges in the context of regressions of the form run by Sironi (2003). As Sironi is considering primary market spreads, his results may suffer from selection bias. Banks may access subordinated debt markets only if the conditions are favorable. This is the converse of the core idea of market discipline: Only banks satisfying markets have access to new funds and therefore, under some additional conditions, without new funds the size of "misbehaving" banks is forced to shrink. We only observe primary market spreads for banks that actually decide to access the market for funds and we do not observe those that do not. This would suggest modeling the spread as

$$S = f(Risk, X),$$

where the vector X contains other factors aside from risk explaining the spread. We do not observe S, however. Let S^* represent the observed spread for banks that actually access the market. We can define an indicator variable

$$I = 1 \; if \; S^* = S$$

$$I = 0 \; otherwise,$$

where I distinguishes banks that accessed the market from those that did not. One would then model the decision of banks to access the market as the following discrete choice probit model

$$Prob(I = 1) = \psi(Z),$$

where Z represents a vector of variables that affect the decision of banks to issue subordinated debt and $\psi()$ the cumulative normal distribution. The vector Z would include variables measuring the 1) the need for external funds; 2) the relative attractiveness to issue subordinated debt rather than other forms of external funding; and 3) the likelihood of wanting to access the market but not being able to due to prohibitively high interest rates. It is clear that there will be a significant amount of overlap between the variables included in X and those included in Z. For the model to yield improved estimates of the relationship between proxies of $Risk$ and the spread, however, one would need at least one instrument, which is related to points 1 to 3 above and unrelated to the level of the observed spread.

This discussion suggests that primary market spreads may generally not be very suitable for examining the degree to which market prices reflect the riskiness of the bank, without properly controlling for the selection problem. At the same time, arguing that the selection problem is not important is equivalent to suggesting that market discipline may not be operational in the sense of Calomiris (1999): Even risky banks have access to subordinated debt markets and are not financing constrained. Examining secondary market prices may be a solution. However, aside from also suffering from selection (albeit to a lesser degree), they raise a number of new problems, mainly relating to liquidity premia and taxes. Recent papers have argued that secondary market spreads over the risk-free rate may be dominated by tax considerations and liquidity premia and that default risk accounts for only between 5 percent and 20 percent of the total spread.[11] These problems suggest that an event study approach using secondary market spreads may be a way forward. Gropp and Richards (2001), instead of modeling spreads as a function of variables that are conjectured to be some measure of risk, consider 186 issuer ratings changes of leading international ratings agencies (Moody's, Standard and Poor's, and Fitch/IBCA) during 1989 to 2000 for a sample of EU banks. They then test for abnormal returns in subordinated debt and equity prices in a short (one day) window surrounding the announcement. This has the advantage of avoiding the selection problem described above and the approach also does not need to rely on assumptions about the relative importance of default risk relative to other factors in the level of spreads.

Gropp and Richards find statistically significant and economically substantial effects of a ratings change on stock prices. They also find that the reason for the ratings change matters. Ratings downgrades, which were motivated by an increase in risk (that is, the standard deviation around an earnings expectation) increased stock prices, while downgrades due to a deterioration of earnings potential resulted in a decline in stock prices. This is in line with earlier evidence on corporate stock prices (Goh and Ederington, 1993) and consistent with the notion that the pay-off to stock holders is the same as a call option on the underlying assets.

For subordinated debt, Gropp and Richards fail to detect any significant relationship between ratings changes and returns. When examining why, it may be useful to recall that there are two alternative views of the information about default risk in ratings. One view is that the rating agencies have access to publicly available information only and that the agencies generally lag the market in processing that information. According to this view, rating changes should not affect market prices, if capital markets are efficient in semi-strong form. Proponents of this view argue that the frequency with which rating agencies review companies is too low even to generate timely summaries of relevant public information. An alternative view is that rating agencies are specialists at obtaining and processing information, and thereby generate information on default risk that was not previously in the public domain. Consequently based on this view, rating changes should affect securities prices. Ultimately any test as the one in Gropp and Richards is a joint test of two hypotheses: Do rating agencies bring valuable information to the market and do spreads accurately reflect this information. The result that equity prices do react to ratings changes, while bond prices do not, disentangles the two effects. Ratings appear to contain new information, but bond prices do not reflect risks accurately.

While Gropp and Richards find little evidence of liquidity as the cause of the non-significance and small reaction of bond prices to rating changes, they cannot reject two explanations for the non-reaction of bond prices to ratings changes.[12] One, there may be extensive implicit safety nets and subordinated debt holders may expect to be bailed out in case of problems in any event. Second, there is some evidence that the reaction of subordinated bond prices to new information as long as the bank is far from default should be quite small and may be difficult to detect econometrically.[13]

While the literature has largely focused on examining banks' securities' prices, a more direct way to test for market discipline is to examine quantities. In fact, the mandatory subordinated debt proposals (for example, Calomiris, 1999) explicitly relied on the idea that risky banks are forced to reduce their assets, because they would be unable to access capital markets. In Europe, Birchler and Mächler (2001) examine whether there is market discipline from uninsured depositors in a sample of Swiss banks during 1987–98. They find that depositors are responsive to bank balance-sheet characteristics suggesting higher risk and that state guarantees matter, in the sense that depositors do not withdraw their deposits from weak banks that enjoy a state guarantee. Birchler and Mächler's results also are economically highly relevant. They find that variations in banks specific fundamentals can explain 75 percent of the variation in uninsured savings deposits.

Birchler and Mächler use a specific feature of the Swiss deposit insurance system to identify these effects. Each depositor is insured up to 30,000 Swiss francs (CHF). However, there is also a cap per bank: Total insurance per bank is limited to CHF1 billion. Hence, a bank with many small depositors, the effective insurance per depositor may fall short of CHF30,000. Birchler and Mächler find that banks above the cap experience a drop in insured deposits and an increase in uninsured deposits. Both findings are consistent with market discipline. This evidence contradicts notions that depositors may be too fragmented to effectively monitor banks (free-rider problem) or not sophisticated enough. Further it dispels the idea that market discipline can only arise from publicly traded instruments at very large banks. This is of great importance in the European context, as there are many small, non-public banks. Their results also highlight the importance of credible limits to deposit insurance.

The literature has devoted relatively less attention to the question of whether banks indeed change their behavior in response to adverse signals from the market. A change of behavior may come about because supervisors observing adverse market signals may impose behavioral changes as part of their regular supervisory review. Or bank managers themselves may find it necessary to change risk exposures, risk management or other business practices, because it has become highly expensive to raise fresh capital.

Gropp and Vesala (2002) explore this question for EU banks. They place the issue in the context of deposit insurance. Generally deposit insurance is viewed as detrimental to market discipline as insured depositors no longer have the incentive to monitor banks. Gropp and Vesala (2002) stress that while this is true, explicit deposit insurance may in fact foster market discipline by other creditors of the bank, such as subordinated debt holders, equity holders, and uninsured depositors. Deposit insurance may act as a pre-commitment device for policymakers to limit the safety net to small depositors, credibly exposing all other creditors to risk and therefore increasing their incentives to provide market discipline.

The authors use time-series and cross-sectional variation in the existence of explicit deposit insurance in the EU to identify market "influencing." In response to the EU Deposit Insurance Directive of 1994, those countries without it (Finland, Sweden, Portugal, Greece) were required to introduce deposit insurance. If in response to the introduction of explicit deposit insurance, banks with lots subordinated debt, banks with low charter values and banks that are not considered too-big-to-fail reduced their risk-taking, this would be evidence of an increase in the effectiveness of market discipline. The paper presents evidence supporting the idea. Interestingly, they also find an increase in insured deposit finance after the introduction of explicit deposit insurance, suggesting a tendency by banks to try to offset the more stringent market discipline of the uninsured creditors, evidence which is consistent with Birchler and Mächler's (2001) findings regarding Swiss banks.[14]

4.2 Do Market Indicators Predict Bank Fragility?

Gropp et al. (2002, 2003) examine the question of whether market indicators are able to predict bank fragility for a sample of EU banks during 1991 to 2001. If they did, there would be a strong case for bank supervisors to incorporate market information into their early warning models or at least monitor market prices to identify weak banks deserving more attention. First, Gropp et al. (2003) show that the "distance to default" (KMV Corporation, 1999) does not suffer from the "equity bias" and is strictly declining in asset volatility. The distance to default combines stock price information with stock volatility and leverage and measures the number of standard deviations away from default, where default is defined as the point at which assets are just equal to liabilities. This property makes the distance to default a useful indicator from a supervisory perspective. In addition to the distance to default, the authors examine subordinated debt spreads. The research is hampered by some data constraints, which arise in the European context. One, formal bankruptcies have been extremely rare events in Europe and consistent CAMEL (capital adequacy, asset quality, management, earnings, and liquidity) or BOPEC (the bank holding company bank subsidiaries, other nonbank subsidiaries, parent company, earnings, and capital adequacy) ratings do not exist in EU countries. Hence, Gropp et al. (2002) use a downgrade in the Fitch/IBCA individual rating to C or below as their dependent variable. Fitch/IBCA's individual rating is designed to measure the true condition of banks as such without taking into account the possibility of public support. Grade C or below was selected as the cut-off point, because banks downgraded to C or below either experienced a government intervention or a parent bank intervention within a year.

First, the authors test whether the two market indicators have *unconditional* power in predicting downgrades. They find that spreads are able to accurately classify 62 percent of the downgrades six months ahead of time and the distance to default by 74 percent twelve months before the downgrade. It turns out that spreads have predictive power only up to six months, whereas the distance to default has some predictive ability as much as two years ahead of the downgrade. They argue that the lack of a measurable signal from spreads further away from the default point is a function of the pay-off structure of subordinated debt. Subordinated debt holders are senior to equity holders in case of default and therefore exhibit only a relatively muted reaction to adverse shocks far away from default. This in turn results in a low signal to noise ratio. Further, the authors find that spreads only have predictive power for banks, which are not publicly owned or covered by a generous implicit safety net.

Second, the authors examine whether market indicators add information to accounting information in predicting downgrades. While they find this to be the case, at least in case of the distance to default, the test is quite weak as they only had access to annual publicly available accounting data, rather than the more detailed and higher frequency reports banks generally file with supervisors. Overall there may be a stronger case to use equity indicators, such as the distance to default, for indirect market discipline rather than subordinated debt spreads. Finally they identify thresholds for the distance to default and the spread, which maximize the discriminatory power in terms of detecting downgrades. The results suggest that a distance of default of below 3 and a spread of above 100 basis points may be useful as trigger points, especially if observed over several months.

5. Market Indicators and Banking System Risk

One potential use of market information has received much less attention. This is the question of whether we can aggregate market prices of *individual* financial institutions into indicators of banking *system* risk. Can we construct a sensible macroprudential indicator from microprudential market information? Borio (2003) has argued forcefully for the need of taking such a macroprudential perspective. Table 10.1 replicates Borio's summary of the differences between macro- and microprudential perspectives with respect to financial stability. The macroprudential approach is concerned with the financial system and ultimately with limiting output losses due to financial crises. This implies that the avoidance of distress in individual institutions, while still sufficient, is not a necessary condition for success (Borio, 2003). This implies that the failure of an individual institution is only insofar of concern as this failure has systemic implications. In addition, correlations in risk exposures across institutions are central from the macroprudential perspective.

What does this imply for the design of distress indicators? Clearly, they should reflect risks in the system as a whole and they should be all encompassing, in the sense that they should reflect different sources of risk. Borio and Lowe (2002) propose to use indicators, which may signal the buildup of imbalances in an economy.

Proximate objective	Limit financial system-wide distress	Limit of individual institutions
Ultimate objective	Avoid output (GDP) costs	Consumer (investor/ depositor) protection
Model of risk	(In part) Endogenous	Exogenous
Correlations and common exposures across institutions	Important	Irrelevant
Calibration of prudential controls	In terms of systemwide distress; top down	In terms of risks of individual institutions; bottom up

Source: Borio, 2003, Table 1.

Table 10.1: The Macro- and Microprudential Perspectives Compared

Their choice of variables is based on the observation that recently (during the 1980s and 1990s) many crises have followed a very similar pattern: relatively high growth associated with increases in asset prices and lending, as well as very high investment. Risk premia decline. Overall, favorable economic developments mask overinvestment in some sectors, creating imbalances and distortions. At some point, often triggered by some relatively benign event, the process goes into reverse and the ensuing contraction results in widespread instability. These patterns suggest that the ratio of private sector credit to GDP, equity prices, and real effective exchange rates should be leading candidates as indicators of financial instability. Further, Borio and Lowe (2002) suggest that the use of cumulative deviations from trend provide clearer signals of imbalances, which may be building up, rather than flows or stocks.

Borio and Lowe test the properties of these indicators in a sample of 34 countries during 1960 to 1999. The sample spans 40 crises in 27 countries. Using combinations of the three variables, the authors are able to predict that a crisis will take place with up to 75 percent accuracy, although the timing of the crises appears to be more elusive.

Building on this evidence, we propose that indicators based on market prices of individual banks may also be useful in the spirit of Borio and Lowe (2002). Given their all-encompassing nature, using market indicators does not require one to subscribe to one particular theory about the root of financial crises. While the stylized patterns in Borio and Lowe (2002) and Borio (2003) reasonably describe many crises of the 1980s and 1990s, there is clearly no guarantee that future crises will follow a similar pattern. Indeed, Padoa-Schioppa (2003) has argued the exact opposite: Lending boom-bust patterns will cease to be a major reason for banking crises. He argues that this is due to vastly improved risk-management techniques available to and used by major banks, as well as the increasing integration of financial systems across borders. Future crises will frequently be rooted in liquidity problems in money markets, other financial markets, and payment systems. Contagion may also play an important role blurring the difference between macro shocks and idiosyncratic shocks. This line of reasoning also highlights a further advantage of market indicators of banking system risk: their high frequency. Crises, which arise due to liquidity shortages in money markets or payment systems, may be much quicker moving than crises of the past.

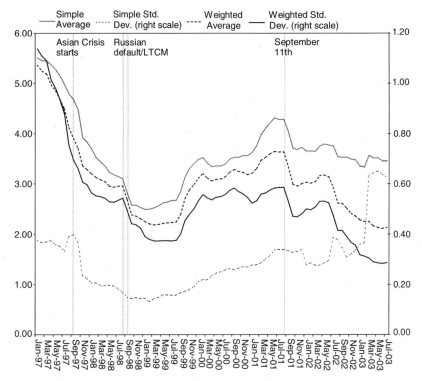

Figure 10.1: Distance to Default for EU Banks

It would go beyond the scope of this paper to fully explore this issue. We will merely sketch how one might want to construct banking system stability indicators from individual banks' distances to default. We start from the results in Gropp et al. (2002), which imply that the distance to default is able to predict individual bank fragility with considerable lead time. Hence, one might be able, through aggregating the indicators for individual banks, to obtain a useful indicator for the entire banking system or at least for the group of banks, for which equity prices can be obtained. While the individual distances to defaults reflect a combination of idiosyncratic and systemic risk, the aggregation, at least as long as it is across a sufficient number of banks should remove the idiosyncratic component of risk.[15] The available sample, which is determined by the availability of equity prices in the EU, consists of 67 banks. While relative to the population of banks these numbers seem small, their market share is above 50 percent of total banking system assets in almost all EU countries.

In figure 10.1 we present simple averages and asset-weighted averages of the distances to default of EU banks, as well as the associated standard deviations. We have also indicated recent events, which were widely recognized as systemic or otherwise important.[16] In figure 10.1, we see that the asset-weighted and the simple average distance to default move together for most of the sample period. However, the asset-weighted distance to default is consistently below the simple average, suggesting that

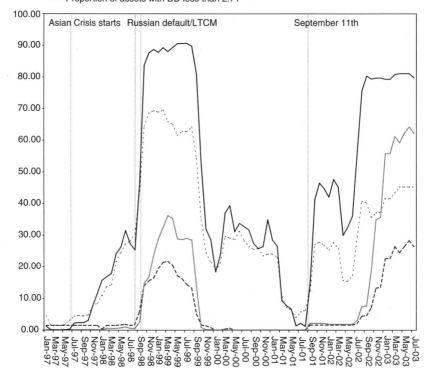

Figure 10.2: Threshold Indicator: Distance to Default

larger banks were weaker. Conceptually, weighting by assets makes some sense, as in the spirit of Borio (2003), we should be interested in assets "at risk," rather than number of banks "at risk." The indicators react strongly at the time of the Russia default/LTCM crisis and the terror attacks of September 11. As expected, the events of September 11 are completely unanticipated. Russia's default on the other hand, seems to be preceded by declining distances to default already several months before.

Even more closely corresponding to Borio's (2003) notion of "setting acceptable tail losses for the portfolio as whole," we can plot the proportion of banking assets (or banks) that are below a certain threshold distance to default.[17] In figure 10.2, we use two thresholds: a distance to default of 1.96, corresponding to a probability of failure within a year of 5 percent and a distance to default of 2.71, corresponding to a probability of failure within a year of 0.7 percent.[18] The latter threshold has its correspondence in the difference between investment grade and speculative grade credit quality and was also found to work well in detecting weak individual banks in Gropp et al. (2002).[19]

Figure 10.2 shows that using threshold indicators may significantly improve the precision of the signal on the fragility of the banking system. Let us focus on the proportion of assets below a threshold. The proportion of banking assets below investment grade quality (threshold less than 2.71) was steadily increasing in the year before Russia's default (from 0 percent of assets to around 50 percent of banking assets in October of 1998). After Russia's default, the increase quickened, reaching a peak of around 90 percent of assets from November 1998 to September 1999. The decline during the following several months is equally steep as the ascent. As one would expect, the events of September 11 were completely unanticipated by the indicator, but subsequently resulted in an increase to 50 percent of assets below investment grade quality. Very interesting is the substantial increase in the indicator beginning in the late spring of 2002. This increase may have been the result of rumors surrounding a number of larger EU banks (especially large German banks) of dramatic increases in interbank market spreads and losses involving credit derivatives. The high level of assets below investment grade has persisted through 2003. Similar patterns also emerge from the more stringent threshold of a distance to default of below 1.96. In fact, this threshold may give a much more accurate signal of a crisis, rather than just weakness, which is evidenced by its "non-reaction" to the terror attacks of September 11.[20]

6. Conclusions

This paper reviewed the empirical evidence on bank market discipline in the EU. The evidence is mixed. While the size of subordinated debt and equity markets in the EU suggest substantial potential for market discipline, the evidence that this potential has in fact been effective is weak. The reasons for this assessment are manifold. One, market participants need to have adequate information about banks. At least in the EU, one may need to await the implementation of pillar 3 of the New Basel Accord. Nevertheless, financial innovation will tend to be a step ahead of regulators and banks' opaqueness may have only increased by trends towards off-balance-sheet operations and by the use of financial instruments whose precise risk characteristics may be difficult to understand. Second, the institutional structure must be conducive to market discipline. Some creditors of the bank must credibly be left out of the safety net, and, indeed, expect to lose their money in case the bank fails. In case of the creditors of very large, systemically important banks such a commitment by the authorities may lack credibility. Possibly a pre-agreed set of rules for how to deal with failing banks may help. In our view, an explicit deposit insurance system should be part of such a set of rules, as it permits a reimbursement of small depositors without coming under pressure to reimburse other creditors of the bank. Third, in the absence of rate caps and in the absence of forced frequent renewals of subordinated debt (Calomiris, 1999), the pressure exercised by subordinated debt holders remains weak. Fourth, while direct market discipline may be hampered by many of the considerations mentioned above, there may be substantial value in supervisors incorporating market prices into early warning models. In particular, equity based measures such as the distance to default or implied default probabilities seem to have substantial unexplored potential. In our view, such indicators have three fundamental advantages over accounting data: They represent the views of a large number of market participants condensed in one convenient price, they are inherently forward looking and they are available at a high frequency. Fifth, market discipline in small banks may not only be desirable, but also feasible. This is an important point in light of the arguments advanced by Borio (2003) and others (for example, Crockett, 2000) that the concern of supervisors to preserve the health of each individual bank may be misguided. If supervisors could leave the "regulation" of small banks to markets, this may free resources for the more important macroprudential task of preserving the stability of the banking system as a whole.

It seems that we need more research looking inside the "black box" of market discipline. What are the mechanisms by which the market exercises discipline? What is their effectiveness? To answer these question, we believe it may be necessary to move beyond funding cost; rather, market discipline should be examined in the context of the broader question of bank's corporate finance decisions. This means extending the analysis beyond subordinated debt and equity and examining the full menu of funding options available to banks. Ultimately, market discipline of banks should be closely related to the balance of power between the different stakeholders in the bank (supervisors, management, subordinated debt holders, senior debt holders, uninsured depositors, and insured depositors) and how this balance can result in an outcome in which banks take the socially optimal amount of risk.

In the latter part of this paper, we sketch how one might go about constructing banking system fragility indicators from market information. We show that a threshold indicator based on the distance of default, that is, an indicator, which specifies the percentage of banking system assets, which the market expects to fail with a certain probability, may yield useful signals from a macroprudential perspective. We suggest that such indicators may usefully complement other information, especially information about imbalances building up in an economy, to more precisely predict and ultimately avoid financial crises.

*Reint Gropp is a senior economist in the Directorate General Research of the European Central Bank. The author would like to thank Claudio Borio, Kostas Tsatsaronis, Jukka Vesala, and participants of the Bank for International Settlements/Federal Reserve Bank of Chicago conference "Market Discipline: The Evidence across Countries and Industries" for helpful discussions. All views expressed in this paper are those of the author and not those of the ECB or its Executive Board.

Notes

1. The distinction between direct and indirect market discipline was first proposed in Board of Governors of the Federal Reserve System (1999).

2. Basel Committee (2003a).

3. Basel Committee (2003b).

4. Basel Committee (2003b). The report covers Belgium, France, Germany, The Netherlands, Spain, Sweden, and the United Kingdom in the EU. See also Sironi (2001) for data on European subordinated debt markets and Board of Governors of the Federal Reserve System (1999) for data on U.S. subordinated debt markets.

5. Apparently some of this debt is marketed to retail investors, who are willing to purchase it precisely because the issuing bank is publicly owned or at least publicly guaranteed.

6. The U.S. equity data used in the study only include the 50 largest bank holding companies.

7. See, for example, Flannery (1998) for a summary of the early evidence and more recently Morgan and Stiroh (2001).

8. During some periods, some EU countries government bonds may been quite far from riskless (for example, Italy).

9. Alternatively, however, the performance of rating agencies in continental Europe may have improved. This possibility is consistent with his findings as his non-EMU sample is dominated by the UK (plus a few banks from Switzerland, Denmark, and Sweden).

10. Gropp and Olters (2002) develop a model in which difference in spreads for fundamentally equivalent banks are explained by differences in the financial system (banks based in non-UK Europe and market based in the UK), which in turn has effects on the institutional structure governing the resolution of bank failures. In contrast to authorities in continental Europe, authorities in the UK may have been able to build a reputation of toughness with respect to claimants on the bank other than insured depositors. Hence, the probability of a full reimbursement of subordinated debt holders in case the bank fails may be significantly lower in the UK compared to continental Europe even in case of very large and systemically important banks.

11. See Elton et al. (2001) and Huang and Huang (2003). The evidence is for corporate bonds.

12. Inter alia, they find no reaction to rating changes of bonds, which are included in a major global bond index, and there is no improvement in the results from correcting for non-trading bias.

13. See Gropp et al. (2003).

14. Bliss and Flannery (2002) is the only study attempting to test for market discipline (as opposed to market monitoring) in a sample of U.S. banks. They conclude "day to day market discipline remains, for the moment, more a matter of faith than of empirical evidence."

15. While this is true, if there is contagion, the aggregated indicator will reflect cases in which individual banks are hit by an idiosyncratic shock, which then is transmitted (through, for example, money market or payment system exposures, or ownership links) to other banks. In fact one use of market indicators may be to use them to detect such links (see Gropp and Moerman, 2004).

16. The onset of the Asian crisis in Thailand in July 1997, Russia's sovereign debt default in late August 1998, the Long-Term Capital Management (LTCM) crisis about a month later, and the terrorist attacks of September 11, 2001.

17. One should interpret the following as x percent of large publicly traded banks' assets are below a certain threshold.

18. The associated expected default frequencies are based on normality. Gropp and Moerman (2004) show that this assumption may be violated in reality. Nevertheless, the figures may serve as an illustration.

19. See also European Central Bank (2003).

20. We did a similar analysis for spreads but found that spreads may be much less suited as systemic indicators of bank fragility. The signals were substantially more volatile and they tend to be lagging the events that we have identified.

References

Basel Committee on Bank Supervision, 2003a, *Third Consultative Paper on the New Basel Capital Accord*, Basel, Switzerland, April.

Basel Committee on Bank Supervision, 2003b, "Markets for bank subordinated debt and equity in Basel Committee member countries," working paper, No. 12, August.

Birchler, U., and A. Mächler, 2001, "Do depositors discipline Swiss banks?," Studienzentrum Gerzensee, working paper, No 01.06, November.

Bliss, R., and M. Flannery, 2002, "Market discipline in the governance of U.S. bank holding companies: Monitoring vs. influencing," *European Finance Review*, Vol. 6, pp. 363–395.

Board of the Governors of the Federal Reserve System, 1999, "Using subordinated debt as an instrument of market discipline," staff study, No. 172, December.

Bordo, M., B. Eichengreen, D. Klingbiel, and M. Martinez-Peria, 2001, "Financial crises: Lessons from the past 120 Years," *Economic Policy*, April.

Borio, C., 2003, "Towards a macroprudential framework for financial supervision and regulation?," Bank for International Settlements, working papers, No 128, February.

Borio, C., and P. Lowe, 2002, "Assessing the risk of banking crises," *BIS Quarterly Review*, Basel, December, pp. 43–54.

Calomiris, C., 1999, "Building an incentive-compatible safety net," *Journal of Banking and Finance,* Vol. 23, pp. 1499–1519.

Cooper, K., and D. Fraser, 1998, "The rising cost of bank failures: A proposed solution," *Journal of Retail Banking,* Vol. 10, pp. 5–12.

Crockett, A., 2000, "Marrying the micro- and macroprudential dimensions of financial stability," speech held at the 11th International Conference of Banking Supervisors, Basel, September 20–21.

Elton E., M. Gruber, D. Agrawal, and C. Mann, 2001, "Explaining the rate spread on corporate bonds," *Journal of Finance,* Vol. 56, No. 1, pp. 247–277.

European Central Bank, 2003, *EU Banking Sector Stability,* Frankfurt, November.

Evanoff, D., 1993, "Preferred sources of market discipline," *Yale Journal on Regulation*, Vol. 10, pp. 347–367.

Flannery, M., 1998, "Using market information in prudential banking supervision: A review of U.S. evidence," *Journal of Money, Credit and Banking*, Vol. 30, pp. 273–305.

Goh, Jeremy, and Louis Ederington, 1993, "Is a bond rating downgrade bad news, good news, or no news for stockholders?," *Journal of Finance*, December.

Gropp, R., and G. Moerman, 2004, "Measurement of contagion in banks' equity prices," *Journal of International Money and Finance*, forthcoming.

Gropp, R., and J. Olters, 2002, "The political economy of bank bail-outs" European Central Bank, working paper, March.

Gropp, R., and A. Richards, 2001, "Rating agency actions and the pricing of debt and equity of European banks: What can we infer about private sector monitoring of bank soundness?," *Economic Notes*, Vol. 30, No. 3, pp. 373–398.

Gropp, R., and J. Vesala, 2003, "Deposit insurance, moral hazard, and market monitoring," European Central Bank, working paper, December.

Gropp, R., J. Vesala, and G. Vulpes, 2003, "Market indicators, bank fragility and indirect market discipline," *Policy Review*, Federal Reserve Bank of New York.

_____, 2002, "Equity and bond market signals as leading indicators of bank fragility," European Central Bank, working paper, No 150, July.

Hancock, D., and M. Kwast, 2001, "Using subordinated debt to monitor bank holding companies: Is it feasible?," *Journal of Financial Services Research,* Vol. 20, pp. 147–187.

Huang, J., and M. Huang, 2003, "How much of the corporate–Treasury yield spread is due to credit risk?," Stanford University, working paper, May.

KMV Corporation, 1999, *Modeling Risk*, KMV Corporation, San Francisco.

Krainer, J., and J. Lopez, 2003, "Forecasting bank supervisory ratings using securities market information," *Journal of Money, Credit, and Banking.*

Morgan, D., and K. Stiroh, 2001, "Market discipline of banks: The asset test," *Journal of Financial Services Research*, Vol. 20, pp. 195–208.

Padoa-Schioppa, T., 2003, "Central banks and financial stability: Exploring a land in between," in *The Transformation of the Financial System*, Gaspar, Hartmann, and Sleijpen (eds.), Second European Central Bank Central Banking Conference, Frankfurt.

Sironi, A., 2003, "Testing for market discipline in the European banking industry: Evidence from subordinated debt issues," *Journal of Money, Credit, and Banking*, Vol. 35, No. 3, pp. 443–472.

_____, 2001, "An analysis of European banks' SND issues and its implications for the design of a mandatory subordinated debt policy," *Journal of Financial Services Research,* Vol. 20, No. 2-3, pp. 233-266.

Sironi, A., J. Stiglitz, and A. Weiss, 1981, "Credit rationing in markets with imperfect information," *American Economic Review,* Vol. 71, pp. 393–410.

Chapter 11

Weakening Market and Regulatory Discipline in the Japanese Financial System

Mitsuhiro Fukao*
Keio University

1. Japanese Financial Crisis and Bank Supervision

Japanese banks incurred heavy losses in the early 1990s due to the crush of the bubble economy of the 1980s. However, most banks could survive this shock thanks to the thick cushion of accumulated profit and latent profit in their stock portfolios. However, in the second half of 1990s, some banks started to run out of this cushion due to the rapidly accumulating loan losses under the accelerating deflation. Banks could not obtain sufficient profit margins on their commercial lending activities because borrowers faced fairly high real borrowing costs due to deflation. Moreover, the Bank of Japan's zero-interest rate policy wiped out the banks' rents from their zero-interest demand deposit. As a result, the capital injections to banks by the government in 1998 and 1999 could not revitalize the banking sector and the public money that had been injected into the system had been depleted as a quasi-subsidy to the banking sector.

In the second half of 1990s, the primary supervisor of banks changed its name from Ministry of Finance, Financial Supervisory Agency to Financial Services Agency. Generally speaking, these supervisors allowed banks to understate the amount of bad loans. They also allowed undercapitalized banks to operate under a very lenient application of capital requirement rules. The only exception was the period between 1998 and 1999 when the Financial Rehabilitation Commission supervised the regulators. In my opinion, this forbearance policy was induced by the following factors. Firstly, regulators had to pay attention to some borrowers from banks, such as small- and medium-sized companies who supported many politicians. Secondly, the regulator did not want to sentence death to weak banks that followed all the instructions of the regulator, including the request to save still weaker banks than themselves.

Market forces did play an important role of disciplining unsound banks until late 1990s. However, as the financial institutions weakened under a prolonged weak economy, the government gradually expanded the protection of bank creditors. As a result, the market forces were disarmed by the government.

As the Japanese financial system gradually deteriorated in the late 1990s, the government expanded the financial safety net to avoid systemic crisis and to protect various type of creditors. At first, only the depositors were protected by the deposit insurance system. When the interbank market lost liquidity in late 1997, following the first default of borrowing by Sanyo Securities in the call market, the protection of creditors was extended to interbank instruments. When Long-Term Credit Bank (LTCB) of Japan and Nippon Credit Bank were nationalized in 1998, the government protected the interest of life insurance companies that held subordinated loans of these banks. Finally, when Resona Bank faced a crisis in 2003, even the shareholders of the bank were protected.

2. Market Discipline and Financial Crisis in 1997–98

As the financial conditions of banks deteriorate, the market put pressure on weaker financial institutions. In November 1997, the failure of Sanyo Securities, Hokkaido Takushoku Bank, and Yamaichi Securities sharply increased financial instability. These events generated a severe credit crunch in the Japanese financial market, inducing an extremely serious recession. Then what has caused this enormous problem for Japan? In my opinion, there are two factors behind this financial crisis.

One is the crash of the stock and real estate market bubble in the 1990s. The second is the loss of confidence in the accounting and auditing system in Japan. We note that the actual amount of bad loans discovered at failed financial institutions has been far larger than the amount published prior to the failure. The Hokkaido Takushoku Bank was forced into bankruptcy even though it posted profits and paid dividends for the year to March 1997. Financial statements for that year reported ¥0.3 trillion in capital; inspections after the failure found a negative equity of ¥1.2 trillion as of March 31, 1998. This indicates a window-dressing of almost ¥1.5 trillion.

Likewise, Yamaichi Securities was hiding ¥260 billion of losses on securities investments—worth more than one-half of its equity capital—which neither the Ministry of Finance inspections nor the Bank of Japan examinations were reportedly able to uncover.

Depositors and investors of bank debentures issued by long-term credit banks imposed some market discipline. Deposits flew out of banks with low credit ratings because depositors feared that they would not be able to withdraw their deposits quickly if their banks were closed. LTCB and Nippon Credit Bank faced a rapid early redemption of their debentures in 1997 because their debentures were not covered explicitly by the deposit insurance system. Stock prices of weaker banks fell sharply and triggered mild bank runs in some cases.

These financial institution failures have exacerbated suspicions both at home and abroad regarding the financial statements and supervision of Japanese financial institutions. It was this mistrust of financial statements that widened the "Japan premium" charged in overseas markets, blocked the domestic call market (which is used for short-term interbank loans), and multiplied the number of cash-pressed financial institutions turning to the Bank of Japan for loans. Japanese financial markets clearly experienced a kind of credit crunch because of a rash of failures, declining asset prices, and growing mistrust of financial statements and regulators.[1]

This credit crunch in turn cut into corporate investment and hiring, increased bankruptcy rates, and reduced consumption and housing investments because workers feared for losing their jobs. That resulted in a further contraction of credit in what became a vicious cycle. In other words, unreliable financial statements had proved to be a serious impediment to the functioning of a market economy.

However, the absence of the market for corporate control and the extensive cross-shareholding generally prevented strong shareholder pressure on banks. The largest shareholders of major Japanese banks were generally large life-insurance companies or other banks. Under most circumstances, cross-shareholders would not vote against the will of the management. As a result, banks did not carry out major restructuring until they obtained capital injection from the government in 1999. One senior director of a major bank told me that when his bank reported a big loss for the first time in many years, he was stunned to find that hardly any major shareholders complained at the annual meeting.

3. The Expanding Safety Net

The Deposit Insurance Law established the DIC (Deposit Insurance Corporation) in 1971.[2] The initial role was to protect depositors of failed financial institutions up to ¥1 million per person by direct payout of insured deposits. The limit of coverage was increased twice to ¥10 million by 1986 and the DIC obtained a new power to assist mergers of failed institution and a sound one to protect depositors.

The DIC find had never been used until 1992 when it assisted Iyo Bank in the rescue of Toho-Sogo Bank. It was relatively easy to find a willing buyer when bank branches carried a regulatory rent. Until early 1990s, deposit interest rates were controlled below the market rates. Moreover, the establishment of new branches was also controlled by the Ministry of Finance. As a result, when there is a weak bank, it was relatively easy to find a rescuer that want to obtain a new subsidiary or new branches with negative equity. However, in the early 1990s, the ceilings on deposit interest rates were removed and the regulation on branching was considerably loosened. This change made the job of bank regulators much more difficult.

After a few failures of small financial institutions in 1994 and 1995, the DIC Law was amended in 1996 to allow the DIC to fully protect depositors beyond the normal ¥10 million as a temporary emergency measure until March 2001. At the end of 1997, the DIC obtained the power to purchase bad loans from failing financial institutions when they collectively create a new bank. The borrowing limit of DIC from the Bank of Japan and private financial institutions was also raised from ¥1 trillion to ¥10 trillion.

In spite of the full protection of all the deposits beyond the limit of normal coverage, public concern over the soundness of financial system became extremely intense after the successive failures of Sanyo Securities, Hokkaido Takushoku Bank, and Yamaichi Securities in late 1997. Depositors were not sure that the DIC had enough money to honor the commitment of the government to protect all the deposits.

In October 1998, just before the LTCB went bankrupt, the Financial Revitalization Act and Bank Recapitalization Act were enacted in a disorderly atmosphere.

4. The Financial Revitalization Act and Bank Recapitalization Act of 1998

The purposes of these two laws could be summarized as follows: The Financial Revitalization Act is a special law regarding the resolution of insolvent deposit financial institution; Bank Recapitalization Act, on the other hand, concerns the capital injection to those financial institutions which are solvent, but losing the confidence of investors and depositors so that they are facing difficulties to raise capital in the market on their own.[3]

When the regulatory authority judges that a financial institution has a negative equity, or likely to stop repaying the deposits in the near future, the Financial Revitalization Act is to be applied. By putting the institution under national receivership, the law tries to protect their customers including both depositors and borrowers. After the effective nationalization, however, this act attempts to privatize the institution promptly, by making the management efficient, injecting capital, and disposing of its bad loans. Public funds are going to be used to protect the depositors and to replenish its damaged capital base. On the other hand, when a financial institution is solvent but undercapitalized, the Bank Recapitalization Act is to be applied. Public funds are going to be injected to its capital base. By doing this, it will be possible to stabilize the performance of financial institutions and restore the credibility towards them.

The Financial Revitalization Act was applied to the Long-Term Credit Bank of Japan in October 1998 and to the Nippon Credit Bank in December of the same year, and both banks were put under national control. The outstanding shares were wiped out and they were nationalized without compensation to the existing shareholders.

At the time of the legislation of the two acts, the Deposit Insurance Law was also amended. As a result, a principle of the resolution of failed financial institution was established and a new mechanism for rehabilitating solvent but undercapitalized ones. The DIC obtained the following temporary roles in this process: to act as an administrator of failing institutions, to establish bridge banks to keep failed institutions running, to own stocks of temporarily nationalized institutions and choose directors for them, to purchase bad loans from financial institutions, and to purchase shares of undercapitalized institutions so as to bolster their capital position.

5. Further Amendments to the Deposit Insurance Law

In May 2000, Deposit Insurance Law was amended to provide a permanent resolution scheme for failing banks because the Financial Revitalization Act and Bank Recapitalization Act were scheduled to expire at the end of March 2001. In this amendment, procedures of systemic exception from the minimum cost principle became a permanent feature of the system in one of its article. Table 11.1 summarizes Article 102 of the Deposit Insurance Law of May 2000 that stipulates the measures against a financial crisis.

Under this article, the Prime Minister may take the following measures for the concerned financial institution when such measures are necessary to avoid very

Article 102 of Deposit Insurance Company Law

Type 1 measure

If the financial institution is
solvent and has not failed:

DIC underwrites shares of the financial
institution. Government can impose a
reduction of stated capital.

Type 2 measure

If the financial institution is
insolvent or has failed:

DIC provides aid beyond the minimum
cost of resolution to protect creditors of the
financial institution. The institution will be
controlled by the financial receiver.

Type 3 measure

If the financial institution has failed
and is insolvent and if type 2 measure
is insufficient to achieve stability:

Nationalization of the financial institution
without compensation to existing shareholders.

Note: Failed institution means that it had stopped the payment of deposits or it is highly likely to stop it.
Source: Prepared by the author.

Table 11.1: Measures against Financial Crisis

serious disruptions to the stability of the financial system of the country or the region
where the institution operates. The decision has to be taken after a deliberation of a
Council for Financial Crisis that consists of the Prime Minister, the Chief Cabinet
Secretary, the Minister for Financial Stability, the Commissioner of the Financial
Services Agency, the Minister of Finance, and the Governor of the Bank of Japan.

The type 1 measure corresponds to Bank Recapitalization Act and the type 2 and
type 3 measures correspond to Financial Revitalization Act. The Prime Minister can
protect all creditors of a bank if he thinks that such a measure is necessary to avoid
serious disruptions in the financial market.

The termination of full protection of deposits was postponed for one year from
the end of March 2001. In March 2002, while the full protection of time deposits was
removed, the government postponed the removal of the full protection of payment
deposits once again. The fund had ¥10 trillion added to the ¥17 trillion for the protection of depositors. While the government pledges to remove the full protection payment deposits in March 2004, they introduced a permanent protection of all
zero-interest deposits with payment services at the end of 2002.

6. Problems in Article 102 of the Deposit Insurance Law

Type 2 and type 3 measures of Article 102 should be applied to financial institutions in the same way as the normal bankruptcy procedures are applied, although
public funds are used to protect their creditors. When the going concern value of a
financial institution exceeds the liquidation value, reorganization would be desirable. But when the going concern value is less than the liquidation value, an orderly
and gradual liquidation would be desirable. In both cases, shareholders' capital will
be cancelled and the board members will have to resign.

We can point out the following problems arising from type 2 and type 3 measures of the Article 102.

Firstly, when a financial institution is put under national control, the nationalized bank has to honor existing employment contracts, since the judicial status of the bank is maintained. As a result, unlike the case of bankruptcy of an ordinary corporation where most employees are dismissed, the employees of a failed financial institution are well protected, although their compensation can be cut up to 25 percent. Moreover, all the liabilities to workers will be protected in the same manner as other liabilities. Therefore, even a very generous retirement allowance will be protected with the public fund.

Secondly, in the resolution of an insolvent financial institution under Financial Revitalization Act, all of its subordinated debt will be protected. The subordination clauses of this debt are triggered only when the issuing financial institutions apply to the court for protection under the bankruptcy code or reorganization order. Since this resolution procedure is not counted as a formal bankruptcy procedure, all the subordinated debt of Japanese financial institutions are treated as ordinary debt and protected by the public funds. In this regard, the primary problem lies in the past financial supervisory policy that allowed banks to count such "subordinated debt" as their Bank for International Settlements (BIS) capital.

In the resolution procedures for Long-Term Credit Bank of Japan and Hokkaido Takushoku Bank, for example, their subordinated debt did not work as capital. Therefore, it is necessary to reexamine the contracts of subordinated debt. Those debts to which subordination clause are not applicable within the framework of type 2 and type 3 measures should be excluded from the BIS capital with a short transition period.

One major problem in applying the type 1 measure, capital injection to a solvent bank, or type 2 and 3 measures, bankruptcy procedure, would be the choice of measure for a particular financial institution.

The government can underwrite a capital increase of a particular bank under type 1 measure, only when the bank has positive equity capital. In addition, the stocks or preferred shares bought by the government must be marketable. Thus, in order for the government to recapitalize a particular bank, the business condition of the bank needs to become stable through the capital increase, and also there is an expectation of a reasonable return on the injected public fund.

In case of type 2 and type 3 measures, on the other hand, a financial institution can be placed under the national control (outright nationalization in the type 3 measure) or under the national receivership with an assignment of financial receivers (type 2 measure). To put a bank under effective national control so as to protect their depositors and borrowers, one of the following conditions needs to be satisfied; that is, the bank has negative equity capital, the bank has stopped repaying their deposits, or there is a strong possibility of suspending the repayment.

Whether the financial institution has negative equity or whether there is a possibility of suspending repayment of deposits would decide the measure to be applied. In practice, however, to which category the bank is going to be classified depends upon the judgment of the authority. Between a well-capitalized bank and an insolvent bank, there are numerous financial institutions that are more or less marginally capitalized.

Whether a particular bank can survive or not depends not only upon the management but also on the macroeconomic conditions domestic or overseas.

7. The Rescue of Resona Bank

The first application of Article 102 of DIC Law is the case of the Resona Bank rescue in 2003. Resona Bank is the biggest bank under Resona Holdings, a bank holding company, with assets of more than ¥30 trillion. Resona Group was formed by an integration of Daiwa Bank in Osaka and Asahi Bank in Tokyo with the fifth largest group of banks, just after so-called four mega bank groups.

The Resona Group banks supplemented their capital with massive deferred tax assets (DTA). Banks usually generate DTA with the following two factors:

1. Japanese tax rule allows loss carry-forward for five years but no loss carry-backward. Combined tax rates of national and local corporate tax is about 40 percent. As a result, when banks accumulate losses in taxable income, they can show DTA up to 40 percent of estimated taxable income in the coming five years. This DTA will be unwound when the bank earns taxable income.

2. Rules on the write-off of bad loans are stricter in tax rules than in accounting rules. As a result, sometimes a bank can recognize loan losses in their financial statements but cannot recognize losses in their tax statements. The over-paid tax on loan losses can be carried as DTA. The DTA will be unwound when the bank can recognize loan losses under tax rules.

In short, the DTA are the net present value of future tax shelter due to accumulated loan losses. The DTA have real value only when a bank can generate taxable income in the near future. The DTA have no liquidation value because the tax authority will not reimburse the DTA in the case of a bankruptcy of the bank. Therefore, the quality of DTA as an asset is low unless the bank is very profitable.

As table 11.2 shows, Resona Bank had more than ¥400 billion of DTA which was larger than its shareholders' equity, ¥366 billion. Moreover, Resona Bank reported losses in the past three years that ended in March 2003. In order to realize ¥400 billion of DTA in the coming five years, the bank has to earn ¥200 billion of taxable income every year and after tax return on equity (ROE) has to be as high as 32 percent:

Taxable income (¥200 billion) × tax rate (40%) × 5 years = ¥400 billion

After tax income (¥120 billion)/Equity (¥366 billion) = 32.7%.

This is clearly an unrealistic scenario. In fact, Asahi & Co. that had been auditing Asahi Bank, refused to allow Resona Bank to show any DTA on their financial statement for March 2003. However, Shin Nihon & Co. that had been auditing Daiwa Bank allowed Resona Bank to keep ¥400 billion of DTA. The Resona management took the more lenient opinion of Shin Nihon & Co. and terminated the auditing contract with Asahi & Co. The FSA apparently agreed with Shin Nihon & Co. and the Resona management and treated Resona Bank a solvent financial institution.

Even with the lenient audit, Resona bank could not satisfy BIS capital rules and the bank asked FSA to give about ¥2 trillion of capital injection under type 1 measure of Article 102 of the DIC Law. The FSA invoked prompt corrective action on May 17

Assets		Liabilities	
Cash and due from banks	1,703	Deposits	22,354
Trading assets	511	NCDs	414
Securities	5,114	Money market liabilities	5,315
Loans	21,444	Other liabilities	2,041
Premises and equipments	646		
Deferred tax assets	**401**	Total liabilities	30,124
Loan loss reserves	−666		
Other assets	1,337	**Shareholders' equity**	**366**
Total Assets	30,490	Total Liabilities and equity	30,490

Note: Loan guarantees amounting 4,432 billion yen were removed from both the assets and liabilities of Japanese balance sheet. Under the Japanese accounting standards, the total amount of guarantees has to be shown on the balance sheet.
Source: Resona Bank disclosure materials.

Table 11.2: Consolidated Balance Sheet of Resona Bank, March 2003, in Billion Yen

and it also convened a Council for Financial Crisis on the same day. The Prime Minister decided to provide Resona Bank ¥1.96 trillion of capital through DIC. The DIC exchanged the stock of Resona Bank with that of Resona Holdings, a listed company. The DIC obtained ¥296 billion of common stocks and ¥1,664 billion of preferred stocks. In this exchange, the government effectively bought common stock of Resona Holdings at 52 yen per share that was the prevailing stock price of Resona Holdings just before the announcement of public assistance.

This injection of public money to the Resona Group started a strong rally in the Tokyo Stock Exchange. The share prices of major banks recovered sharply. In my opinion, this rally was the reaction to a big surprise to the market regarding the Resona rescue. While the existing shares of Long-Term Credit Bank and Nippon Credit Bank were wiped out, the shareholders of Resona Bank were protected by public money. This was certainly a perverse but effective way to support bank stock prices.

After this injection of public money, the newly appointed Resona management undertook reexamination of their books. On October 10, the management revised the projected current profit of Resona Group for the mid-term ending September 2003 from ¥22 billion of profit to ¥1,760 billion of loss. The downward revision was huge, ¥1,788 billion in just four months, amounting 93 percent of the injected capital. The downward revision of Resona Bank alone includes ¥435 billion of additional loan loss reserves and ¥330 billion of resolution costs of related companies.

Certainly, the safety net always generates some form of moral hazard among creditors of banks. Especially when there is an element of systemic risk in the banking sector, it would be necessary to use a very strong medicine even though it has severe side effects. However, the fact that FSA has to protect even the subordinated creditors and shareholders indicates that FSA has completely failed in keeping the financial system reasonably sound. As a result, Japanese stock market is losing the capability of giving price signal to investors; after the rescue of Resona Bank, the stock prices of fragile banks and companies rose more than sound companies. According to many observes of Tokyo Stock Exchange, the recovery of stock prices since May 2003 is due to the increasing confidence in the eventual bailout of bank shareholders by the Japanese government. Many analysts call this recovery a "moral-hazard rally."

The protection of equity holders is spreading to industrial companies and to life-insurance companies. In recent years, banks sometimes wrote off a part of the debt of insolvent borrowers without wiping out shareholders' equity. For example, IRCJ (Industrial Revitalization Corporation Japan), a government-sponsored company for corporate rehabilitation, decided to waive a part of the debt of Mitsui Mining while allowing the existing shareholders to keep somewhat less than a half of the equity. The government also sponsored a new law that would allow mutual life-insurance companies to write off a part of the policyholders' claims, a senior liability, without requiring the companies to write off surplus notes (similar to redeemable preferred stocks) and subordinated debts. This new law became effective in August 2003. Since major banks provide a large amount of surplus notes and subordinated debts to life-insurance companies, this law would protect banks, the junior claimant, then policy-holders, the senior claimant.

8. Absence of Regulatory Discipline by the FSA

As the financial system gradually deteriorated, the government expanded the protection from depositors to owners of subordinated debt and bank shares. As a result, the market forces were removed one after another. Under such conditions, the disciplinary forces of bank supervisors would become much more important. Unfortunately, however, this force is not working in Japan.

Capital requirements on banks are very important regulatory instrument to move the incentive of bank management in the right direction and to protect the funds of the deposit insurance system. However, the FSA has failed to use capital requirements and prompt corrective action properly.

Figure 11.1 shows the degree of insolvency of all the failed deposit taking financial institutions from the introduction of prompt corrective action in April 1998 to September 2002. Altogether, 132 institutions have failed out of 976 DIC protected financial institutions that existed at the end of March 1998. The degree of insolvency is defined as follows:

Degree of insolvency = DIC grants to protect all depositors/Total disclosed debt just before the failure.

The average degree of insolvency was 25.1 percent. The DIC protected financial institutions includes commercial banks, shinkin banks, credit unions, and labor banks (rokin). The average degree of insolvency of failed institutions is about the same among different groups and the size of the institutions. Even big banks showed relatively large degrees of insolvency; Hokkaido Takushoku Bank, 18.8 percent; Long-Term Credit Bank, 11.6 percent; and Nippon Credit Bank, 29.3 percent.

In spite of the declining net asset of banks, all the banks have been complying with BIS capital requirements. Under the Japanese accounting rules on banks and lenient application by the regulators, BIS capital ratios have been manipulated in many ways:

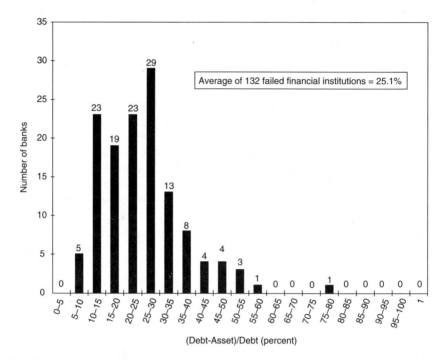

Average of 132 failed financial institutions = 25.1%

(Debt-Asset)/Debt (percent)

Note: Estimated from the DIC assistance to failed deposit taking institutions and the disclosed financial statements.
See Fukao and Japan Center for Economic Resarch (2003).

Figure 11.1: Degree of Insolvency of Failed Deposit Taking Financial Institutions, April 1998 to September 2002

1. Banks underreserved against bad loans as explained above. This tends to increase bank capital by the same amount.

2. Banks kept large amounts of deferred tax assets in spite of the fact that most of them have been losing money for the past 10 years. Table 11.3 shows the share of DTA in the core capital of major Japanese financial groups. The DTA of Resona Bank and Mitsui Trust Holdings is larger than their core capital. The DTA of other banking groups is also very large compared with its core capital; more than half for UFJ and Sumitomo Mitsui Financial Group. If we apply the U.S. capital requirement rule that sets the limit of DTA up to 10 percent of core capital, most major Japanese banks cannot comply with BIS capital requirements.

3. The friendly life insurance companies hold stocks and subordinated loans of banks. At the end of March 2003, major 10 life-insurance companies held ¥1.1 trillion of bank shares and ¥4.4 trillion of subordinated loans. Banks, in turn, held ¥1.0 trillion of surplus notes and ¥0.9 trillion of subordinated loans of life-insurance companies. In addition, life-insurance companies held a portion of preferred capital notes of banks that are issued through their special purpose entities in tax haven countries. This practice is a so-called double gearing and

	Core capital (A) billion Yen	Net DTA (B) billion Yen	Ratio (B/A) percent
Mitsubishi Tokyo Financial Group	3,338	1,303	39.0
UFJ Holdings	2,665	1,522	57.1
Resona Holdings	635	522	82.2
Resona Bank	366	401	109.6
Saitama Resona Bank	155	44	28.4
Sumitomo Mitsui Financial Group	3,168	1,842	58.1
Mizuho Financial Group	4,322	2,105	48.7
Mistui Trust Holdings	341	346	101.5

Notes: Net DTA means deferred tax assets minus deferred tax liabilities.
Source: Disclosure materials of individual banks.

Table 11.3: The Ratio of Deferred Tax Asset in the Core Capital of Major Japanese Banks, March 2003

the cross-held quasi capital should not be treated as genuine capital of banks or life insurance companies.

In order to normalize Japanese financial system, we have to carry out following measures: restore profitability in the banking sector, recapitalize banks, rollback excessive safety net provisions, and restore regulatory discipline on the banking sector.

9. Measures to Restore Market Discipline: Restoring Profitability in the Banking Sector

First and foremost, we have to restore profitability in the banking sector.[4] Banks are losing money by high level of loan losses and very thin profit margin. The banking sector is running out of capital, and it is surviving with government guarantee of their liabilities and occasional injection of public capital. In order to stabilize the banking sector, it is necessary to increase the lending margin of banks by about one percentage point. Borrowers are already facing relatively high real interest rates even under the zero-interest policy by the Bank of Japan. This is due to gradual acceleration of deflation. Therefore, an increase in the average lending rate is likely to depress the Japanese economy and will aggravate the deflation. In order to avoid this adverse effect, it is necessary to raise nominal interest rates without raising the real cost of debt for weakened borrowers. Only way to do this is to stop deflation and have a mild inflation. By raising trend inflation rate from minus 2 percent to plus 2 percent, for example, banks can raise average lending rate from current 2 percent to 4 percent. At the same time, the real cost of debt for borrowers will fall from 4 percent to 2 percent.

Banks certainly have to control their costs and develop profitable lines of business. Most banks are downsizing their operations under strong pressure from FSA to show profit. But they are neglecting positive measures such as investing in human capital and new information technologies because of low profit.

One important reason of low profit is the competition with government sponsored financial institutions. In Japanese financial markets, the presence of government financial institutions (GFIs) is extremely large. In the loan market, the GFI share reaches 30 percent to 40 percent in rural prefectures, although it is only 26 percent overall. They are especially dominant in housing loans. Their lending rates are similar to those for short-term loans from private banks, but the average term is much longer. The GFIs obtain subsidies of about ¥1 trillion per year as direct subsidy and indirect subsidy of zero-cost capital. These are estimated to provide a 60 basis point cost advantage relative to private financial institutions.[5]

In deposit and life-insurance markets, Japan Post has been a dominant player. It holds deposits of ¥240 trillion which is about the size of four largest private banking groups combined. The total assets of postal life insurance are about three times of Nippon Life, the largest private life insurance company. Japan Post does not pay corporate tax, deposit insurance fees, or policyholder protection fund fees. The total cost advantage is about ¥600 billion per year.[6] Its deposits and insurance policy are fully guaranteed by the government. There are more than 24,000 post offices, giving the system a branch network larger than all the city and regional banks combined. The largest private banking group, Mizuho, has only about 600 offices. Japan Post does not charge account-maintenance fees, so it is difficult for private banks to charge such fees without alienating a large number of customers.

In order to restore profitability in the Japanese banking sector, the government has to remove the competitive advantages of GFIs such as free government guarantees of their debts and tax advantages.

10. Measures to Restore Market Discipline: Capitalizing Japanese Banks

It is necessary to note that a simple injection of government capital to weakened banks will not stabilize the banking sector. Banks making losses will eventually deplete the injected money. For example, Resona Bank received ¥808 billion of core capital and ¥100 billion of subordinated loans from the government in 1999 when it was two separate banks—Daiwa Bank and Asahi Bank. In the spring of 2003, Resona Bank had depleted it capital and it received ¥1,960 billion of additional capital from the government.

In order to revitalize the banking sector, the government has to do two things: allow banks to obtain enough lending margin that is consistent with the expected credit costs, and recapitalize only profitable and solvent banks. Key points are as follows:

1. The government provides public funds to recapitalize a bank only when the bank successfully raises additional capital on their own efforts in the market. By doing so, the bank would have to make themselves more attractive to investors.

2. If the net worth of the bank before the public capital injection is depleted by the loss arisen after the capital increase, pre-existing ordinary shares should be canceled with no compensation, and the preferred shares held by the government are to be converted into ordinary shares.

3. The public funds can only be used to recapitalize the bank itself, rather than its subsidiaries or holding company.

In reality, the government has been providing disguised subsides as government capital to insolvent banks. As a result, the banking sector cannot recover profitability because healthier banks face unfair competition with unhealthy banks that are receiving disguised subsidies.

11. Measures to Restore Market Discipline: Rolling Back Excessive Safety Net

We have to remove the government guarantee of almost all of the banking sector liabilities. The government introduced a permanent protection of all the zero-interest payment deposits. Since the interest rates on time deposits are very close to zero, depositors do not mind keeping most of their deposits in payment accounts. This measure has weakened the pressure for restructuring among banks. As soon as we stabilize financial system, we have to introduce risk-adjusted deposit insurance premium and terminate the unlimited protection of payment deposits. The government should not bail out shareholders and subordinated creditors of insolvent banks. The protection of the shareholders of Resona Bank seriously undermined the function of Japanese stock market.

12. Restoring Regulatory Discipline to the Banking Sector

The FSA has to redefine BIS core capital of banks by eliminating deferred tax assets and double gearing among banks and life-insurance companies. Under current FSA policy, banks can keep an almost unlimited amount of DTA on their balance sheet. This put a tremendous pressure on accountants that have to set a limit on DTA for their clients. In the final days of Resona Bank, Satoshi Hirata, a CPA of Asahi & Co, apparently killed himself. He had been auditing Asahi Bank, which became Resona Group by a merger, for a long period of time. When Asahi & Co management took a strict stance against Resona Bank's DTA, he was caught between Resona Bank and Asahi & Co. Current accounting rules on DTA are clearly too ambiguous to be used for BIS capital rules. The FSA should limit the use of DTA in the core capital of banks.

The FSA should also restrict double gearing among banks, life insurance companies, and bank customers. In the effort to increase their capital, many banks resorted measures dangerously close to double gearing. Some banks also used their subsidiaries to raise additional capital. We list only well-known cases:

1. In February 2003, Sumitomo Mitsui Financial Group (SMFG) raised capital by issuing ¥150.3 billion ($ 1.27 billion) of preferred shares to the Goldman Sachs Group (GSG). At the same time, SMFG provided $ 1.375 billion of cash collateral to GSG so as to guarantee the following credit loss protection contract to a GSG subsidiary that will conduct credit-extension activities. SMFG will share 95 percent of losses of the subsidiary up to $ 1 billion for 20 years. SMFG will also share 70 percent of losses of the subsidiary up to $ 1.125 billion for 5 years.[7]

2. UFJ Bank established a wholly owned subsidiary, UFJ Strategic Partner Co. and Merrill Lynch bought ¥120 billion preferred equity. This subsidiary will accept

assignment of the problem loans of UFJ bank and it will manage them. The preferred equity from Merrill Lynch is counted as tier 1 capital of UFJ bank after consolidation. Since the preferred equity is the senior part of the total capital of the subsidiary, ¥325 billion, the risk for Merrill Lynch is limited.[8]

3. Mizuho Financial Group raised ¥1,200 billion in preferred equity. The equity was mostly subscribed by its Japanese customers and friendly life-insurance companies. There were 75 large subscribers that bought more than ¥3 billion. Mizuho Bank and Mizuho Corporate Bank are among top three shareholders of 32 of the 75 large subscribers. Top three subscribers are Daiichi Life, ¥45 billion; Yasuda Life, ¥33 billion; and Sompo Japan Insurance, ¥31.5 billion. Mizuho Corporate Bank is among the top two shareholders of the three companies.

The FSA should pay careful attention to the capital structures of big financial groups rather than superficial BIS ratios. Without the restoration of sound banking sector, we cannot expect market forces to discipline banks in a constructive way.

*Mitsuhiro Fukao is a professor of economics in the Faculty of Business and Commerce of Keio University. The author would like to thank David Llewellyn for his helpful comments at the conference.

Notes

1. Fukao (1998a) documents the process of financial crisis in 1997.

2. See Deposit Insurance Corporation of Japan (2002, 2003).

3. See Fukao (2000) for the details of these acts.

4. See Fukao (2003) for a detailed analysis of the profitability of Japanese banking sector.

5. See Fukao (1998b) for an estimation of government subsidies to GFIs.

6. See Japan Center for Economic Research (2001) on the cost advantage of the Postal Saving system.

7. See the Goldman Sachs Group (2003).

8. See UFJ Holdings (2003).

References

Deposit Insurance Corporation of Japan, 2003, *Annual Report 2003*, Japanese edition.

_____, 2002, *The New Deposit Insurance System*, Tokyo.

Fukao, Mitsuhiro, 2003, "Financial sector profitability and double-gearing," National Bureau of Economic Research, working paper, No. 9368.

_____, 1998a, "Japanese financial instability and weaknesses in the corporate governance structure," *Seoul Journal of Economics*, Vol. 11, No. 4, Winter, pp. 381–422.

_____, 1998b, "Overview of fiscal investment and loan program and its problems," in *Economic Analysis of Fiscal Investment and Loan Program, (Zaisei Toyushi no Keizai Bunseki)*, in Japanese, Tokyo: Nihon Keizai Shinbun Sha, pp. 1-23.

_____, 2000, "Recapitalizing Japan's banks: The functions and problems of Financial Revitalization Act and Bank Recapitalization Act," *Keio Business Review*, No. 38, pp. 1–16.

Fukao, Mitsuhiro, and Japan Center for Economic Research, 2003, *Examining the Banking Crisis (Kensho Ginko Kiki)*, in Japanese, Tokyo: Japan Economic Journal.

Goldman Sachs Group, Inc., 2003, Form 8-K, January 15.

Japan Center for Economic Research, 2001, *Deflation and Financial System Reform (Defure to Kinyu Shisutemu Kaikaku)*, in Japanese, financial research report, No. 5.

UFJ Holdings, Inc., 2003, "Execution of corporate separation and investors' agreement with Merrill Lynch," February 14.

Chapter 12

Market Discipline in Emerging Economies: Beyond Bank Fundamentals

Eduardo Levy-Yeyati*
Universidad Torcuato Di Tella

Maria Soledad Martinez Peria
World Bank

and

Sergio L. Schmukler
World Bank

1. Introduction

The recent wave of financial crises has renewed the interest in market discipline in banking systems. This interest is not merely academic, but it is also apparent in recent policy initiatives such as the latest capital proposal by the Basel Committee on Banking Supervision.[1] The New Basel Capital Accord put forward by this body has three main components or "pillars." Pillar 3 lays out a number of disclosure requirements that banks are recommended to comply with in order to enhance market discipline. As stated in Bank for International Settlements (2001), "market discipline has the potential to reinforce minimum capital standards (pillar 1) and the supervisory review process (pillar 2), and so promote safety and soundness in banks and financial systems."

Market discipline in banking is commonly understood as a situation in which private sector agents face costs that are positively related to the risks undertaken by banks and react on the basis of these costs (Berger, 1991).[2] This reaction may materialize via prices (such as when depositors demand higher interest) or via quantities (for example, when depositors withdraw funds). Traditionally, the empirical literature has studied market discipline by testing market sensitivity to bank fundamentals, which, if present, has been interpreted as conducive to more prudent risk-taking practices and a healthier banking sector as a whole (hence, the emphasis on information disclosure as a prudential tool).

Both institutional and systemic factors may, however, have important effects on market discipline, at least as it has been traditionally defined. Institutional factors may affect market discipline indirectly, by influencing the degree to which agents react to changes in bank fundamentals. The existence of well-functioning markets, the degree of government ownership of banks, the presence of guarantees, and the level of disclosure and transparency may affect the incentives of and the information available to market participants to respond to the idiosyncratic risk of banks.

Systemic risks (driven by macroeconomic factors) may affect market discipline both directly and indirectly. On the one hand, given bank fundamentals, worsening economic conditions can threaten the value of market participants' assets (such as the value of bank deposits) directly provoking adverse market responses. On the other hand, macroeconomic factors may induce a market reaction indirectly, by bringing about a deterioration of bank fundamentals, in particular for institutions heavily exposed to those risks.[3] Given the influence of macroeconomic factors, the failure to find empirical evidence of market reaction to bank fundamentals does not imply the absence of market discipline. Rather, it reflects the fact that the informational content of *observed* fundamentals diminishes as market participants (such as depositors) react to *expected* changes in future fundamentals driven by large systemic shocks. Thus, for any given level of bank risk, bank fundamentals are likely to become less informative as the systemic component increases and market participants respond accordingly.

As noted, the empirical literature on market discipline has mostly focused on market reaction to bank fundamentals.[4] However, this work has largely ignored how institutional and macroeconomic factors may affect their findings.[5] Moreover, the view of market sensitivity as a disciplining device is indeed questionable when market reaction is driven by macroeconomic conditions largely beyond the control of bank managers.[6] The impact of institutional and macroeconomic factors on market sensitivity and its implications for market discipline are the subjects of this paper.

2. Institutional Factors and Market Discipline

In principle, various economic agents can exercise market discipline; bondholders, stockholders, credit rating agencies, and depositors are the usual candidates. Their ability to monitor and discipline financial firms depends crucially on the existence of deep, well-functioning markets where price and quantity movements convey useful information about the solvency of firms. When it comes to bond and stock markets, this point is not as trivial at it may sound. In the U.S., arguably the country with the most developed capital markets, only 15 percent of all banks issue equity, and a similar proportion of financial institutions have publicly traded debt outstanding (Flannery, 1998). In emerging economies, in part as a result of smaller firm size and relatively higher transaction costs, debt and equity issuance is likely to be even more rare (figure 12.1, panel A). Moreover, secondary markets tend to be very thin (figure 12.1, panel B). Therefore, price and quantity movements may become noisy signals of the underlying fundamentals, undermining their potential as a market discipline tool. This

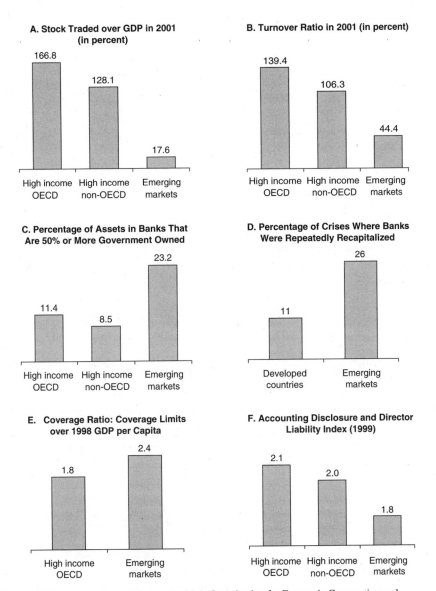

A. Stock Traded over GDP in 2001 (in percent)

166.8 — High income OECD
128.1 — High income non-OECD
17.6 — Emerging markets

B. Turnover Ratio in 2001 (in percent)

139.4 — High income OECD
106.3 — High income non-OECD
44.4 — Emerging markets

C. Percentage of Assets in Banks That Are 50% or More Government Owned

11.4 — High income OECD
8.5 — High income non-OECD
23.2 — Emerging markets

D. Percentage of Crises Where Banks Were Repeatedly Recapitalized

11 — Developed countries
26 — Emerging markets

E. Coverage Ratio: Coverage Limits over 1998 GDP per Capita

1.8 — High income OECD
2.4 — Emerging markets

F. Accounting Disclosure and Director Liability Index (1999)

2.1 — High income OECD
2.0 — High income non-OECD
1.8 — Emerging markets

Notes: GDP is gross domestic product. OECD is Organization for Economic Cooperation and Development. The figures show institutional features of developed and emerging economies. The composition of the country groups varies across figures due to limitations in the availability of data. Sources: World Bank Development indicators; Barth, Caprio, and Levine (2001); and Demirgüç-Kunt and Sobaci (2001).

Figure 12.1: Institutional Factors and Market Discipline

is clearly reflected in the fact that all existing studies of market discipline in emerging economies focus exclusively on the behavior of depositors.[7]

Government ownership of banks, more pervasive in emerging economies (figure 12.1, panel C), is another institutional factor that may influence market discipline for a number of reasons.[8] First, government-owned banks are not publicly held, which already rules out stockholders as candidates for bank monitoring. Second, public banks are often perceived (usually correctly) as protected by implicit government guarantees, due not only to their size and systemic impact, but also to their role as vehicles for political lending. Finally, government ownership may contaminate market discipline in the private sector, both through the anticipation of a *pari passu* treatment of private institutions (which extends the guarantee and relaxes discipline across the board) and through contagion once a crisis is underway, as measures to protect public banks may have deleterious effects on the system as a whole.

Market discipline is also undermined by policies that credibly protect market agents from suffering losses. For example, "too big to fail" policies, which tend to be more prevalent in developing countries (figure 1, panel D), reduce the incentives of bank stakeholders to monitor risk.[9] Deposit insurance schemes (DIS) are also likely to dampen market sensitivity.[10] Furthermore, they tend to be more generous in emerging economies (figure 1, panel E).[11] However, because they are frequently underfunded, their credibility is likely to be questioned, particularly at times of systemic crisis when fiscal solvency is also at stake. While, relative to developed countries, the net effect of a generous but undependable DIS is ex ante ambiguous, there is some indication that the credibility component tends to dominate.[12]

Last, but certainly not least, for market discipline to work, market participants must have access to the right information in a timely fashion. Emerging economies, while progressing rapidly, still tend to fare poorly on these fronts (figure 1, panel F).[13]

In sum, market discipline, as typically measured in the academic literature, may be difficult to observe in a context in which some of the institutional constraints mentioned above are at play. Even if the institutional environment is conducive to an effective market monitoring, the relative importance of systemic risks in emerging economies may mask the link between market behavior and bank-specific fundamentals to the point of making it empirically unobservable. To this issue we turn next.

3. Systemic Risks and Market Discipline

Institutional differences notwithstanding, perhaps the main distinctive factor influencing market discipline in emerging economies is the relative importance of systemic vis-à-vis idiosyncratic risks. The underlying sources of systemic risk are by now well known. On the one hand, relatively large real shocks combined with a strong dependence on highly procyclical international capital flows (coupled with narrow domestic markets) yield large output volatility and a perilous propensity to fall into deep recessions. The latter can drastically deteriorate the repayment capacity of bank debtors and, in turn, bank solvency. On the other hand, the karma of weak domestic currencies often leads to the dollarization of domestic savings or, if this option is not allowed, to the shortening of deposits ready to fly away from banks to the foreign currency. The associated exchange rate and rollover risks tend to feed back on systemic financial fragility.

It is immediate to see how these systemic sources may overshadow the informational content of observed bank fundamentals. To the extent that banks are subject to large systemic risks that might threaten the value of their assets, depositors and investors will respond to fluctuations in those risks no matter how healthy bank fundamentals look or how well hedged banks appear ex ante. Classic examples of systemic factors that can have a direct effect on market reactions include exchange rate risk and confiscation risk. Pure currency risk (as, for example, in the case of a "peso problem") could lead to deposit flight in those countries where onshore dollarization is restricted.[14] A run may also be induced by the threat of confiscation by an insolvent government unable to rescue a few troubled "too-big-to-fail" institutions.[15] Finally, systemic risks might overshadow the role of *observed* bank fundamentals due to their impact on *expected* changes in future fundamentals (for example, through rapidly deteriorating nonperforming ratios or, in the event of a currency run, through a liquidity crunch that can quickly become a solvency problem due to the collapse of the market value of bank assets).

In sum, the lack of evidence of market discipline, as traditionally defined, does not imply that market participants are not sensitive to risk or that bank withdrawals are random, as the existing (largely U.S.-based) literature would conclude. Rather it suggests that markets respond to a broader set of risks, which in the context of emerging economies are primarily driven by macroeconomic conditions.

The recent currency-cum-bank run in Argentina is a clear example of how markets, and in particular depositors, respond to systemic risks.[16] In 1998, right before the beginning of the protracted recession that led to the crisis, Argentina was ranked among the most solid banking sectors within emerging countries based on standard fundamentals.[17] Even by the end of 2000, Argentina could have been characterized as having a well-capitalized, highly liquid, strongly provisioned banking sector. Fundamentals, however, played a limited role in the run up to a crisis driven largely by systemic factors such exchange rate and default risk. It is not surprising, then, that banks were affected across the board, irrespective of their ownership structure and their financial condition.

This is clearly illustrated in figure 12.2. Panels A and B of figure 12.2 show the shift in the distribution of interest rates and changes in deposits across banks between the period December 2000 to June 2001 and the period July 2001 to December 2001. The figure shows that in the second half of 2001 interest rate hikes and deposit withdrawals affected all banks in the financial system. From panels C and D in figure 12.2, it is clear that the interest rate and deposit movements that occurred in the second half of 2001 coincided with increases in currency risk, expressed in the non-deliverable forward (NDF) premium, and default or country risk, as measured by the Emerging Market Bond Index (EMBI) spread. Moreover, figure 12.3 illustrates that deposit withdrawals and interest rate increases were more pronounced in banks with higher exposure to systemic risk (in this case measured by the exposure to exchange rate risk). Thus, these two figures suggest that depositors were indeed sensitive to how systemic risk would affect the value of their deposits, findings that are also confirmed by a more rigorous econometric analysis in Levy-Yeyati, Martinez Peria, and Schmukler (2003).[18]

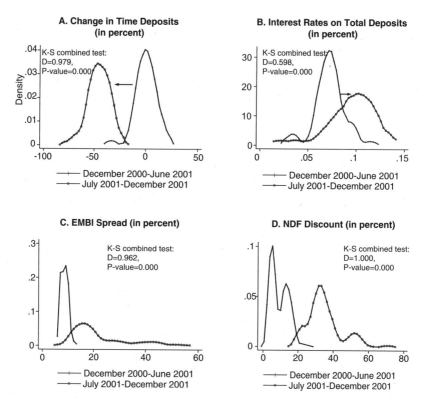

Figure 12.2: Deposits, Interest Rates, and Systemic Risk: Kernel Distributions

Overall, these findings are not surprising. A long recession as a result of a defla-
tionary real exchange rate adjustment pushed (private and public) dollarized debtors to
the verge of bankruptcy, fueling expectations of a currency realignment and fostering
further dollarization of bank deposits. In turn, anticipation of the devastating balance-
sheet effect of a nominal devaluation made it clear to depositors that the exit of the
currency board would entail either massive bank insolvency or, given the perceived
insolvency of the government, a debtor bailout in the form of a forceful conversion of
dollar contracts at below market rates. These factors led to a run from the system.

Interestingly, for the sake of our argument, which of these two scenarios was in the
mind of fleeing depositors at any point in time is immaterial. Under the first scenario,
observed fundamentals conveyed no relevant information about bank risk, as they would
worsen sharply overnight. Under the second, the recovery value of deposits was fully
dependent on the conversion rate picked by the government, irrespective of the health
of individual banks. As a result, market discipline was then imposed on the market as a
whole, following closely the evolution of the systemic indicators that were perceived as
the best predictors of the impending currency collapse.

A. Percent Change in Time Deposits

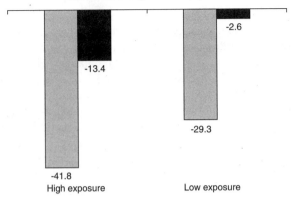

B. Change in Interest Rates on Time Deposits (percentage points)

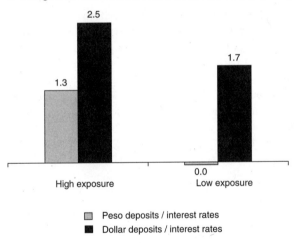

☐ Peso deposits / interest rates
■ Dollar deposits / interest rates

Notes: The figures show the percent change in time deposits and the change in interest rates (in percentage points) by currency during December 2000 - November 2001, differentiating banks with high and low exposure to exchange rate risk.
Source: Central Bank of Argentina.

Figure 12.3: Change in Deposits and Interest Rates by Bank Exposure to Exchange Rate Risk, December 2000–November 2001

4. Conclusions

The quest for market discipline embedded in Basel's pillar 3 and in recent proposals to get banks to issue subordinated debt moves in the right direction, by addressing the supervisor's limitations (both in terms of human capital and as a result of agency problems) to enforce compliance with prudential regulations. However, in the context of emerging markets, the discussion and analysis of market discipline should take into account two important factors that have been largely ignored so far. First, institutional constraints affecting incentives and information accuracy may narrow the scope for market discipline in emerging economies. Second, systemic risks may overshadow the role of bank fundamentals in driving market responses. Bank fundamentals, useful indicators of bank health in tranquil times, may fail to capture macroeconomic risk exposures that tend to materialize in the run-up to a crisis, and may be slow to incorporate the impact of macroeconomic risk once the latter becomes apparent. This is particularly so in crisis-prone emerging economies, where risk is of a systemic nature to a larger degree, as the recent Argentine episode illustrates.

In this light, we argue that the narrow definition of market discipline implicit in the empirical as well as the prudential literature needs to be revisited considerably for emerging economies. The incidence of systemic risk, while accounting for the weaker explanatory power of bank fundamentals in crisis periods, indicates that the information set to which market participants respond is wider than usually considered, and that market sensitivity to risk is quite robust when both idiosyncratic and systemic factors are taken into account. From a prudential perspective, our argument calls for a distinction between market responses to idiosyncratic factors, on one hand, and to systemic factors, on the other. Market responses to idiosyncratic risk can truly discipline bank managers, forcing them to run sound banks with healthy fundamentals. However, market responses to systemic risk may at times be independent of the soundness of bank fundamentals. In this environment, the only action that managers can take to limit adverse market responses is to minimize (to the extent possible) their banks' exposure to systemic factors.

*Eduardo Levy-Yeyati is a professor at the Universidad Torcuato Di Tella. Maria Soledad Martinez Peria and Sergio Schmukler are both senior economists in the Development Research Group of The World Bank. Juan Miguel Crivelli, Federico Droller, and Marina Halac provided excellent research assistance. We are grateful to Francisco Gismondi, Claudio Irigoyen, Ricardo Martinez, and Luciana Rios-Benso for their help with the data on Argentina. For useful comments and suggestions we thank David Llewellyn, Roberto Rigobon, and participants at the conference "Market Discipline: The Evidence across Countries and Industries," cosponsored by the Federal Reserve Bank of Chicago and the Bank for International Settlements. The views expressed in this paper are entirely those of the authors and do not necessarily represent the views of the World Bank.

Notes

1. Other recent initiatives to enhance market discipline include proposals to make it mandatory for banks to issue subordinated debt. See Calomiris (1997, 1999) and Evanoff and Wall (2000).

2. In the case of rating agencies, because they do not have a direct economic stake in the financial firms, the costs they suffer if they fail to rate banks according to their risk is primarily reputational.

3. Take, for example, the impact of currency risk. If convertibility to a foreign currency is not an option, it may lead depositors to flee from the domestic banks irrespective of their individual health. Also, banks that are particularly sensitive to exchange rate risk might see their fundamentals deteriorate after a pronounced currency depreciation, and might suffer greater losses in deposits vis-à-vis less exposed banks.

4. For a review of the U.S. literature on market discipline by stockholders, bondholders, and depositors see Flannery (1998). Sironi (2003) offers evidence of discipline by subordinated debt holders in the European banking industry. Studies of depositor market discipline in developing countries are more limited, with this literature emerging only in the late 1990s. Some of these papers are Barajas and Steiner (2000) for Colombia, Bundevich and Franken (2003) for Chile, Ghosh and Das (2003) for India, and Schumacher (2000) for Argentina.

5. Some exceptions are Martinez Peria and Schmukler (2001) and Demirgüç-Kunt and Huizinga (2003), who study the impact of deposit insurance.

6. See Cordella and Levy-Yeyati (1998) for an analytical discussion of the link between information disclosure, market discipline, and the nature of the underlying risk.

7. High costs of issuance and the presence of illiquid markets might also help explain why initiatives that promote regulations requiring banks in developing countries to issue subordinated debt as a vehicle for market discipline are likely to fail. In late 1996, in what is the only emerging market experiment to date, Argentina adopted a regulation according to which banks had to issue a subordinated liability for some two percent of their deposits each year. However, the plan was derailed by the increase in the domestic cost of capital that followed the Russian crisis, right after the regulation became effective in 1998. Repeatedly, the central bank was forced to relax the enforcement of the regulation by pushing forward the date for compliance, broadening the range of liabilities that banks could issue to meet the requirement, and reducing the penalties for non-compliance. Nonetheless, Calomiris and Powell (2001) find a positive correlation between those banks that issued subordinated debt and those that exhibited stronger fundamentals.

8. Using data collected by Barth, Caprio, and Levine (2001), figure 1, panel C shows that the percentage of banking system assets in banks that are 50 percent or more government owned averages 23 percent among emerging economies, while the corresponding statistic is 11 percent for high income Organization for Economic Cooperation and Development (OECD) countries and 8.5 percent for high income non-OECD countries.

9. As the figure shows, out of the 40 crisis events reported in Honohan and Klingebiel (2003), recapitalizations with the use of fiscal funds occurred in 26 percent of the crises in emerging markets and in 11 percent in developed countries. Crony capitalism and regulatory capture can have comparable consequences, as depositors anticipate that even medium-sized institutions may be ultimately favored by regulatory forbearance of rescue packages if they fall in distress.

10. Demirgüç-Kunt and Huizinga (2003), using a bank-level database comprising 30 (developed and developing) countries, find that explicit deposit insurance dampens the interest sensitivity to bank fundamentals.

11. Using information gathered by Demirgüç-Kunt and Sobaci (2001), Figure 1, panel e shows that coverage ratios (coverage limits over 1998 GDP per capita) average 2.4 among emerging markets and 1.8 among high-income OECD countries.

12. Martinez Peria and Schmukler (2001) find evidence of a comparable market response among insured and uninsured depositors in Argentina, Chile, and Mexico, which they attribute to the lack of confidence in the existing insurance schemes or implicit guarantees due to lack of funding or long delays in repayments.

13. Barth, Caprio, and Levine (2001) construct an index of *accounting disclosure and director liability* based on 1) whether the income statement includes accrued or unpaid interest or principal on non-performing loans, 2) whether banks are required to produce consolidated financial statements, including nonbank financial affiliates or subsidiaries, and 3) whether bank directors are legally liable if the information disclosed is erroneous or misleading. The index ranges between 0 and 3 depending on whether countries comply with none, some, or all of the above.

14. It is interesting to note that preventing these types of currency-induced runs was one of the reasons behind the lifting of restrictions on foreign currency deposits in many emerging economies.

15. The placing of deposit rate caps and the ulterior suspension of deposit convertibility in Argentina in November-December 2001 may be explained, at least in part, using this argument.

16. For a detailed description and analysis of how the recent Argentine crisis unfolded, as well as the condition of the financial sector prior to the crisis, see De la Torre, Levy-Yeyati, and Schmukler (2003)

17. The World Bank (1998) ranked Argentina second among 12 emerging economies based on CAMELOT scores (the World Bank's version of the CAMEL rating).

18. Using bank level panel estimations and vector autoregression analysis with data for the system as a whole, the authors show that most of the evolution of deposit and interest rates during the crisis period is explained by macroeconomic indicators (such as currency and country risk), as well as indicators of bank exposure to those risks (such as the share of government debt and the ratio of dollar assets over bank capital). In particular, they find that peso and dollar deposits reacted negatively to increases both in individual banks' exposure to government default risk and in the country risk premium, while interest rates rose in response to these variables. The exchange rate risk premium, on the other hand, had a negative (positive) impact on peso deposits (interest rates) and a positive (negative) effect on dollar deposits (interest rates).

References

Bank for International Settlements, 2001, "Working paper on pillar 3—market discipline," Basel Committee on Banking Supervision, working paper, September.

Barajas, Adolfo, and Roberto Steiner, 2000, "Depositor behavior and market discipline in Colombia," *International Monetary Fund Seminar Series*, Vol. 51, September, pp. 1–39.

Barth, James R., Gerard Caprio, Jr., and Ross Levine, 2001, "The regulation and supervision of banks around the world: A new database," in *Brookings-Wharton Papers on Financial Services*, Robert E. Litan and Richard Herring (eds.), Washington, DC: Brookings Institution Press.

Berger, Allen N., 1991, "Market discipline in banking," in *Proceedings of a Conference on Bank Structure and Competition*, Federal Reserve Bank of Chicago.

Budnevich, Carlos L., and Helmut M. Franken, 2003, "Disciplina de mercado en la conducta de los depositantes y rol de las agencias clasificadoras de riesgo: el caso de Chile," *Economía Chilena*, Vol. 6, August, pp. 45–70.

Calomiris, Charles W., 1999, "Building an incentive-compatible safety net," *Journal of Banking and Finance*, Vol. 23, October, pp. 1499–1519.

_____, 1997, *The Postmodern Bank Safety Net: Lessons from Developed And Developing Economies*, Washington, DC: American Enterprise Institute Press.

Calomiris, Charles W., and Andrew Powell, 2001, "Can emerging market bank regulators establish credible discipline? The case of Argentina, 1992–1999," in *Prudential Supervision*, Frederic S. Mishkin (ed.), Chicago: University of Chicago Press.

Cordella, Tito, and Eduardo Levy-Yeyati, 1998, "Public disclosure and bank failures," *IMF Staff Papers*, Vol. 45, March, pp. 110–131.

De la Torre, Augusto, Eduardo Levy-Yeyati, and Sergio Schmukler, 2003, "Living and dying with hard pegs: The rise and fall of Argentina's currency board," *Economia*, Vol. 3, Spring, pp. 43–107.

Demirgüç-Kunt, Aslı, and Harry Huizinga, 2003, "Market discipline and deposit insurance," *Journal of Monetary Economics*.

Demirgüç-Kunt, Aslı, and Tolga Sobaci, 2001, "Deposit insurance around the world," *World Bank Economic Review*, Vol. 15, September, pp. 481–490.

Evanoff, Douglas D., and Larry D. Wall, 2000, "Subordinated debt as bank capital: A proposal for regulatory reform," *Economic Perspectives*, Vol. 25, May, pp. 40–53.

Flannery, Mark J., 1998, "Using market information in prudential bank supervision: A review of the U.S. empirical evidence," *Journal of Money, Credit, and Banking*, Vol. 30, August, pp. 273–305.

Ghosh, Saibal, and Abhiman Das, 2003, "Market discipline in the Indian banking sector: An empirical exploration," NSE Research Initiative, working paper.

Honohan, Patrick, and Daniela Klingebiel, 2003, "The fiscal cost implications of an accommodating approach to banking crises," *Journal of Banking and Finance*, Vol. 27, August, pp. 1539–1560.

Levy-Yeyati, Eduardo, Maria Soledad Martinez Peria, and Sergio Schmukler, 2003, "Market discipline and systemic risk in emerging economies," World Bank, mimeo.

Martinez Peria, Maria Soledad, and Sergio Schmukler, 2001, "Do depositors punish banks for 'bad' behavior? Market discipline, deposit insurance, and banking crises," *Journal of Finance*, Vol. 56, June, pp. 1029–1051.

Schumacher, Liliana, 2000, "Bank runs and currency run in a system without a safety net: Argentina and the 'tequila' shock," *Journal of Monetary Economics*, Vol. 46, August, pp. 257–277.

Sironi, Andrea, 2003, "Testing for market discipline in the European banking industry: Evidence from subordinated debt issues," *Journal of Money, Credit, and Banking*, Vol. 35, June, pp. 443–472.

World Bank, 1998, "Argentina: Financial sector review," report, No. 17864-AR, September.

Chapter 13

Inside the "Black Box" of Market Discipline

David T. Llewellyn*
Loughborough University

1. Introduction

As an initial point of perspective on these four excellent papers by Mutsuhiro Fukao, Mark J. Flannery and Stanislava Nikolova, Reint Gropp, and Eduard Levy-Yeyati, Maria Soledad Martinez Peria, and Sergio L Schmukler, there will probably be general agreement on three propositions: 1) market discipline has the *potential* to contribute to the two objectives of a regulatory/supervisory regime: namely to reduce the probability of bank failures for systemic reasons and to minimize the costs of those bank failures that do occur; 2) because of various structural and policy-made impediments, the potential role that market discipline has is greater than what it currently is in practice; and 3) it is not feasible to rely on market discipline alone and market discipline is not a realistic sole alternative to regulation and supervision by official agencies. Therefore, a central issue in regulatory and supervisory strategy is how market discipline in its various forms can be harnessed and enhanced within a broader regime which includes regulation, official supervision, intervention arrangements in the event of bank failure, incentive structures, and reform of corporate governance arrangements. Market discipline alone is insufficient and is not to be viewed in isolation from other components of a regulatory regime (Llewellyn, 2002, and the paper by Rochet in this volume). Market discipline therefore needs to be part of a holistic approach to achieve the twin objectives. In this context Flannery and Nikolova remind us that involving bank counterparties in supervision may reduce the overall cost of supervision and raise the quality of prudential oversight.

While the potential role is important, the operation of market discipline is nevertheless something of a "black box" in that it is not always clear precisely how it is envisaged to operate to discipline the risk-taking and management of banks. The merit of the four papers is that they contribute substantially to opening the box. The general theory is well established: In principle, well-informed creditors (widened below to encompass all stakeholders) have the resources, expertise, market knowledge and incentives to monitor the behavior of banks. While their private incentives may not always be perfectly aligned with society's twin objectives (because of, for instance, externalities) they are at least consistent with them. As is clear from each of the papers, the keys are information and incentive structures.

We have four excellent papers that, in their different ways with different perspectives, certainly increase our understanding of the role of market discipline in banking markets both in terms of theory and practice. All the papers (and most especially those of Flannery and Nikolova and Gropp) include substantial elements of valuable survey material. Flannery and Nikolova focus mainly on the U.S. experience while Gropp focuses on Europe. Fukao offers a fascinating case study of Japan (where virtually everything that could undermine market discipline actually did so) and the Levy-Yeyati, Martinez-Peria, and Schmukler (LYMPS) paper concentrates on the experience of emerging market economies and notably Argentina. It is impossible to do justice to the full richness of these wide-ranging and comprehensive papers and the insights they offer. We try here, therefore, to aggregate the papers by drawing on all of them for some general conclusions and observations about the role of market discipline. We attempt to outline some general themes within a paradigm suggested in Llewellyn and Mayes (2003) and also the various impediments to the effectiveness of this role as outlined in the four papers.

2. Four Key Issues

Four key issues lie at the center of the debate over the role of market discipline in banking:

1. What the precise channels of influence are: *direct* (such as price and quantity adjustments and incentive structures), and *policy influences* such as when market signals may enhance the role of official supervisory arrangements and interventions.

2. What the required conditions are for effective market discipline.

3. The nature and form of the impediments to the role of market discipline which may be *structural* in nature (such as the absence of markets) or *policy induced* (such as perceptions that banks will be rescued).

4. The role that regulatory and other official agencies may play to enhance the power and effectiveness of market discipline.

Each of the four papers addresses these issues in different ways with a constructive mix of theory and empirical evidence. These central issues may also form an agenda for future research.

Flannery and Nikolova make the useful point that market information can be used by supervisors in two ways: by offering information about the condition of a bank, and an incentive towards intervention in a prompt corrective action (PCA) regime. Market discipline can also help the supervisor through bonding and minimizing the pressures for forbearance. However, they also note that to be useful in helping supervisors predict future bank distress, market information needs to have strong predicative power which to date they do not have.

3. Inside the Black Box

While many published papers focus on different aspects of the role of market discipline, a more holistic paradigm might be helpful in considering the four papers. The central questions are how precisely is market discipline envisaged to work, and what are the precise channels of influence? We draw here on a paradigm suggested in Llewellyn and Mayes (2003) to identify the components inside the black box of market discipline. In particular, the paradigm outlines the requirements for effectiveness of market discipline.

The starting point is the concept of the stakeholder monitor (SHM) which encompasses all those agents who have an interest in the risk characteristics, safety, and performance of a bank. These include supervisory agencies, rating agencies, depositors, suppliers of marketable debt, subordinated debt holders, shareholders, other banks in the market, and fund managers. SHMs incur costs in monitoring banks but are also potentially exposed to costs in the event of a bank failure. The key is, therefore, the incentive structure of different SHMs to incur the costs, and the incentive structure faced by bank managers to avoid the costs of market sanctions which may be price and/or quantity adjustments. SHM incentives will be weak the higher is the cost of monitoring and the lower is the cost to them in the event of a bank failure. In this regard, there is potential for public policy to enhance the role of market discipline to the extent that it can lower the cost of private monitoring (by, for instance, information disclosure requirements) and raising the private cost of failure (for example, a commitment to no bailouts).

The general sequencing of the process moves from information $\rightarrow$ SHM monitoring $\rightarrow$ SHM action $\rightarrow$ changes in prices and/or quantities $\rightarrow$ sanctions on the bank $\rightarrow$ corrective action by the bank. The requirements for effective market discipline are summarized as follows:

1. Relevant, timely, accurate, and consistent information disclosure. This also requires, for instance, an appropriate accounting infrastructure, which has sometimes been absent in the case of Japan (Fukao paper).

2. A sufficient number of stakeholder monitors capable of analyzing information. Clearly, this is often not the case with state banks as shown in the LYMPS paper.

3. Incentives for SHMs to incur the costs of monitoring. This is the key in that effectiveness requires that SHMs be exposed to loss in the event of a bank failure. Evidently, not all SHMs will be exposed to loss at all times and this depends in part on the intervention arrangements within the overall regulatory regime. Flannery and Nikolova make the general point that a supervisory regime which provides guarantees cannot expect a great deal from market discipline. The greater the probability of forbearance, rescue, or insurance, the weaker will be the incentives. In practice, there are many impediments in this area (which are both structural and policy-induced) and each of the papers cite examples of them. In effect, anything that protects a SHM against the consequences of excessive risk-taking by banks, the weaker will be the incentive to monitor.

4. SHMs need to adjust their behavior on the basis of information about the bank. Clearly, if monitoring does not lead to appropriate bank behavior (that is, behavior to avoid

losses) there is little point in incurring he costs of monitoring. The Flannery and Nikolova paper focuses on two examples of adjustment: a rise in the cost of insured deposits through a higher risk premium, and the withdrawal of uninsured funds from the bank. Equally, supervisors (who are also part of the SHM group) can also adjust their behavior towards supervised institutions on the basis of market signals. This is the first stage in equilibrating behavior in a market discipline regime.

5.   There need to be markets through which market discipline can operate. There need to be relevant markets through which price and quantity adjustments can be made. This is emphasized in particular in the Gropp paper. The way that market discipline operates may be different between different markets such as the deposit market and the market for subordinated debt.

6.   Market adjustments need to produce efficient prices. The existence of markets is a necessary but not a sufficient condition for effective market discipline. Markets need to be efficient in the sense of prices reflecting risk characteristics of individual banks and banks in general. It is well established that bad regulation (such as the imposition of inappropriate capital requirements) creates distortions in the banking industry (such as mispricing of risks, misallocation of capital within the bank, and effective subsidies to some asset classes) which can impair efficiency and consumer welfare. Equally, inefficient pricing in markets also creates distortions. This raises the general issue of how well markets process information. In this context, Gropp poses two questions: Do primary and secondary market spreads reflect risk, and do they lead to market discipline via official supervisors? As always, there may be noise in the data and most especially in illiquid markets. For instance, movements in subordinate debt (SD) prices may not always reflect risk because of the endogeneity problem when banks faced with higher risk premia may switch to alternative sources of funds. In which case the observed higher premium may also reflect a higher liquidity premium as a result of the smaller volume of SD issue. This is one argument in favor of making subordinated debt issues mandatory: It increases the efficiency of pricing signals. However, Flannery and Nikolova suggest that movement from uninsured to insured deposits itself conveys information to supervisors about market views. Gropp is skeptical about the role of subordinated debt in a market disciplining regime because of deposit insurance, the sometimes weak liquidity of the market, noise in the data, and the endogeneity problem in interpreting premia. On the other hand, he also notes that the presence of (limited) deposit insurance might, under some circumstances, enhance the role of market discipline because it places a greater cost of default onto others. This means that it is not necessary for all SHMs to act to discipline banks.

7.   SHM reactions to market signals need to be rational. SHMs need to adjust rationally to market signals and not, for instance, be subject to the same errors, misperceptions, myopia, or false analysis as the banks themselves. If, for instance, SHMs are subject to the same herding behavior as their banks, market signals will become distorted.

8.   There need to be equilibrating quantity and price adjustments. As noted in the papers, in general, market discipline works through the cost of capital, the cost of

deposits, the cost of other debt, and the supply of deposits and debt. While many papers make a distinction between price and quantity adjustments, this distinction is both difficult to measure and may be inappropriate because price and quantity adjustments may occur simultaneously. Thus, if depositors become concerned about the risk profile of a bank the supply curve of deposits will shift, and the new equilibrium will involve different prices and quantities.

9. Managers need to have incentives to respond to market price and quantity signals. If, for any reason, managers do not respond to signals (or the threat of signals) and do not change behavior, market discipline will not be effective. The effectiveness of market discipline requires that managers respond to market signals, whether that be in the form of a rise in the price of debt or a decline in the availability of funds. In the final analysis, the objective of market discipline is to change bank behavior. Gropp makes the point that there is little research into how managers respond to market signals. Flannery and Nikolova suggest that there is little evidence regarding the impact of market signals on management behavior. The more general point is that remarkably little is known about the incentive structures faced by bank managers. It is, however, known that such incentives can be dysfunctional as, for instance, when reward structures are based on the volume of business and when mangers adopt herd behavior or excessively short-termist behavior. In particular, what are the incentives of managers to lower the risk profile of a bank in the face of adverse market signals? There is a host of principal–agent issues here. Reactions may, under some circumstances, be perverse as, for instance, when in the face of adverse price movements, banks switch to market-insensitive funding. Also, if a bank is hardly at all dependent on subordinated debt it may choose to ignore adverse market signals.

Each of the papers give examples of where some of these conditions have been present and where market discipline works reasonably effectively. Equally, and most especially in the case of Japan (Fukao), they also point to many instances where the effectiveness and efficiency of market discipline are weakened because these required conditions are not met. In some cases (and Japan is a prime example) it is public policy that undermines the requirements for effective market discipline.

4. The Impediments to Market Discipline

Several impediments to the effectiveness of market discipline are identified in each of the four papers which confirms the starting proposition that the potential for market discipline to operate effectively to lower the probability of bank failure and minimize the cost of those bank failures that do occur is greater than actual experience. However, the papers also indicate that experience varies substantially between countries along a spectrum with the U.S. probably being at one end and Japan at the other. LYMPS discern that market discipline is generally more effective in industrial than in developing countries, and Gropp suggests that within Europe it is probably more effective in the UK than in other countries. Impediments can be divided into two broad categories: *structural* (or "institutional" in the terminology of LYMPS) and *policy induced.*

The papers identify several examples within each category. LYMPS show how institutional impediments are often more powerful in many emerging market economies than in industrial countries. They identify in particular: lack of information and weak disclosure requirements, the greater number of state-owned banks, a greater inclination towards forbearance, a more extensive deposit-insurance schemes, fewer, more volatile, and less efficient markets, and greater macroeconomic risks. They argue, for instance, that the existence of a significant publicly owned banking sector weakens market discipline: there are no external owners, the market believes that a state-owned bank will automatically be rescued, and it might be believed in the market that this would also extend to other banks. This combination of factors males it more difficult for market discipline to operate, and also lowers the incentives for SHMs to conduct costly monitoring

The papers identify impediments in each of the routes within the paradigm outlined above. Clearly, in many countries there are information problems with respect to availability, timing and accuracy. As noted by Fukao, in some countries (for example, Japan) the basic accountancy infrastructure is weak. In some countries, and sometimes because of the role of state-owned banks, there are few stakeholder monitors to undertake effective monitoring. Incentives for SHMs to incur the cost of monitoring are also weakened when the losses likely to be incurred with a failed bank are low: the too-big-to-fail (TBTF) issue, full-cover deposit insurance, the perception of forbearance, and bailouts. It might also be the case that, because private investors know that banks are also supervised by an official agency, there is little value in themselves incurring monitoring costs. This may be because the official agency is perceived as having superior information, superior expertise, and economies of scale. The free-rider problem may also inhibit private monitoring. Private monitors might also believe that they are only duplicating, in a socially wasteful manner, the same activity as official agency supervisors. In some countries the relevant markets might not exist and may be very illiquid and inefficient. Herding behavior and collective "over-shooting" may also impede the emergence of efficient price signals. Equally, some of the impediments applicable to market participants may also be relevant in reducing the incentive of managers to respond: expectations of bailouts, TBTF, dysfunctional incentives, etc. In many instances, weak corporate governance arrangements within banks may also create adverse incentives in bank managers.

Official intervention arrangements (safety net) in the event of bank failure are mentioned in all of the papers. Gropp in particular emphasizes that intervention arrangements have an important impact on the effectiveness of market discipline. Such arrangements have powerful implications in that they have incentive effects for future behavior, influence the costs of failed banks, create moral hazard, and affect the market credibility of the intervention agency (central bank, government, etc.). In this regard there is a strong case for a rules-based approach to intervention rather than discretion. With a clearly defined, and credible, set of rules as to when and how intervention is to be made, the credibility of the agency is enhanced, the probability of forbearance is lowered, there is a smaller likelihood that the agency will itself "gamble for resurrection," political influence is likely to be weaker, and there should be less bargaining for economic rents. In effect, a rules system (such as in a PCA program) is likely to enhance the effectiveness of market discipline because market participants have more clarity about the private costs of a bank failure. SHMs therefore have a greater incentive to incur the costs of private monitoring.

The LYMPS paper shows how institutional and systemic (macroeconomic) factors impact the efficiency of market discipline in emerging market economies. The authors argue that macroeconomic factors influence prices and deposit–withdrawals from banks which are not motivated by perceptions of bank risk. The authors argue that depositors are prone to respond to macroeconomic risks irrespective of the state of banks. They cite evidence from Venezuela in particular. This has the effect of distorting market signals. In particular, they detect that the informational value of market data may be reduced if there are systemic problems or macroeconomic instability. In the case of Argentina, they find evidence that macroeconomic factors have been important influences on interest rate and deposit data. They show convincingly that, while market discipline may appear to be weak, it is more effective if allowance is made for the distorting effects of macroeconomic factors. This is an important finding when considering the potential effectiveness of market discipline in developing countries. As in any area, the absence of measurement does not mean that something is not operating.

The most powerful case of impediments to market discipline is found in the fascinating paper by Fukao on the experience of Japan. The paper elegantly plots the total collapse of market discipline because many of the potential impediments were created by public agencies and the government. Here is a powerful case study of how public policy intervention can totally erode the power of market discipline. Fukao points to many examples of impediments that have been created largely by policymakers and supervisory agencies: bad accounting allowing an understatement of bad loans, regulatory leniency over capital requirements, massive forbearance and late intervention, supervisory officials not remaining in their posts for very long which creates incentives to delay action, the protection (after 1997) of even interbank deposits, excessive and growing safety net facilities, protection offered to all subordinated debt holders which are protected by public funds, weak corporate governance arrangements, most especially with respect to cross-shareholdings and their effect on weakening shareholder pressure. Most astonishingly, protection was extended even to shareholders of banks who, in the final analysis, are ultimately responsible for the good governance of banks. The government extended the safety net to protect virtually all stakeholders, leading to the erosion of all market discipline on banks. Perhaps the best example of the perversity of responses in this environment cited by Fukao is found in the stock market reaction after the rescue of Resona Bank: Stock market prices rose more for fragile banks than for stronger banks! This "moral hazard rally" was due to enhanced expectations of subsequent bailouts.

The crisis in the Japanese banking industry, and the reasons for totally ineffective market discipline, represents a combination of bad public policy, weak corporate governance, excessive safety net arrangements, and perverse incentive structures. The role of market discipline collapses if all stakeholders are protected. The Japanese experience represents an extreme case of forbearance as the supervisory authority does not close deposit-taking institutions until they are deeply insolvent. Japan clearly needs a PCA program.

In his paper Gropp suggests that market discipline is more powerful in the U.S. than in Europe (largely because the required conditions are more prevalent in the U.S.) and that within Europe market discipline is more powerful in the UK than elsewhere. He argues in both cases that this is largely a reflection of a more credible no-bailout policy. He argues that in the case of the UK the probability of a full reimbursement of subordinated debt holders in the event of a bank failure may be significantly lower than in other European countries even in the case of very large and systemically significant banks. However, as he argues, "this has yet to be tested." This may indeed be the case, though other factors are almost certainly at work. In the UK case, compared with other European countries, the absence of any state or cooperative banks is probably relevant. Also, the general cultural difference that the UK stock market is more shareholder-value driven than is the case in many other European countries is probably also a factor. The general role of the capital market is greater in the UK than elsewhere in Europe.

5. What Have We Learned?

The four papers are rich in analysis, empirical investigation, and insights. We learn a lot about the role of market discipline through the papers bringing together many of the disparate threads in the debate. We have tried here to synthesize much of the analysis by establishing a general paradigm for the effectiveness of market discipline in banking markets. Several important conclusions emerge from the four papers.

- Market discipline has a potentially powerful role both directly and through signals passed to supervisory agencies.

- Through shifting the supply curve of funds, such discipline operates through both price and quantities and sometimes both simultaneously. Gropp suggests that quantity adjustments may be the more powerful of the two.

- When conditions are right, market discipline does work in practice.

- However, there are many structural and policy-induced impediments to the effective operation of market discipline, the extent and power of which vary between countries. Overall, and through such mechanisms as the safety net, forbearance, bailouts etc., public policy has a massive potential to impede the operation, and effectiveness, of market discipline in banking.

- Amongst the many factors that determine the power of market discipline, information and incentive structures hold the key.

- The power and effectiveness of market discipline might also be greater than indicated by the tests for empirical evidence because of the distorting effect of macroeconomic instability (LYMPS), and the endogeneity issue (Gropp).

- One major country (Japan) has experienced a total collapse of market discipline largely because of inappropriate public policy interventions.

- Equity prices are a problematic indicator not the least because of the potential for equity holders to choose a "gamble for resurrection" strategy with the effect that they may opt for a higher risk profile when the condition of the bank is deteriorating. Here is a case where the incentives of a SHM may not be perfectly aligned with the social objectives of systemic stability.

- The manner of intervention arrangements in the event of bank distress has a major impact on incentive structures for future behavior both by banks and their various stakeholders.

- Market data is often of more value in market discipline than accountancy data because of its high frequency, it represents the aggregate view of the markets, and it tends to be forward-looking in nature.

There is an interesting methodological problem that none of the papers mentioned when discussing the empirical evidence regarding the role of market discipline. Empirical tests to some extent understate the role that market discipline plays because bank behavior is to a degree influenced by the known *threat* of market discipline. If market discipline worked powerfully always and everywhere, its beneficial impact would not be measurable because banks would adjust behavior to guard against adverse movements in market prices and quantities.

6. Positive Policy Action

Our central proposition is that market discipline has a potentially important, though limited, role to play in any regulatory regime. It is not a substitute for regulation and official supervision but, as argued in Rochet (2004), is complementary to these other mechanisms. The skill in regulatory strategy lies in integrating market discipline within a holistic approach which includes regulation, official supervision, a focus on incentive structures, appropriate intervention arrangements in the case of bank distress, and improvements in banks' corporate governance arrangements. There is much that public policy intervention can do to enhance the role and effectiveness of market discipline. Central to the effectiveness of market discipline is the requirement that stakeholders should stand to lose through a bank failure. This suggests a requirement to limit deposit insurance and other safety-net mechanisms. This needs to be coupled with a credible commitment to a no-bailout policy. Both would become more credible within the context of a prompt corrective action regime where intervention arrangements were not only more predictable but graduated beginning at an early state in the emergence of bank distress. In some countries, market discipline would also be aided by the removal of market and competitive distortions so that all banks compete on equal terms. At a more basic level, policy makers need to give higher priority to refining information disclosure requirements on banks, and also addressing corporate governance weaknesses.

In effect, there is a potentially powerful role for policy makers to remove some of the many impediments that limit the role and power of market discipline.

*David T. Llewellyn is a professor of money and banking at Loughborough University.

References

Llewellyn, D. T., 2002, "Alternative approaches to regulation and corporate governance in financial firms," in *Financial Risks, Stability, and Globalisation*, O.E.G. Johnson (ed.), Washington, DC: International Monetary Fund.

Llewellyn, D. T., and D. Mayes, 2003, "The role of market discipline in handling problem banks," Bank of Finland, discussion paper, No. 21-2003, September.

Rochet, Jean-Charles, 2004, "Market discipline in banking: Where do we stand?,"*Market Discipline: The Evidence across Countries and Industries*, Boston: MIT Press.

PART IV

EVIDENCE OF MARKET DISCIPLINE
IN OTHER INDUSTRIES

Chapter 14

Market Discipline in Insurance and Reinsurance

Scott E. Harrington*

University of South Carolina

The magnitude of market discipline and the extent to which it can substitute for or augment regulation of financial intermediaries are of considerable interest and importance in the United States and abroad. The Basel II proposal, with its market discipline pillar, and the question of whether banks should be required to issue subordinated debt to promote market discipline have been widely debated. With respect to insurance markets, important policy issues include: 1) the on-going formulation of risk-based capital requirements for European Union (EU) insurers, 2) whether state-based risk-based capital requirements for U.S. insurers should be made more stringent, and 3) whether U.S. insurers should have the option of federal chartering and regulation. Whether financial conglomerates should be subject to consolidated regulation and whether solvency regulation should be harmonized across countries also are being debated.

This paper provides an overview of market discipline in insurance/reinsurance. I focus on market discipline in its broad (direct) sense: the extent to which product and capital markets discipline risk-taking by insurers. Much discussion of bank regulation focuses on the related issue of how market information may augment efficient solvency regulation in the context of deposit insurance and attendant moral hazard. I pay particular attention to product market discipline, that is, the extent to which demand by policyholders is sensitive to insolvency risk and thereby motivates insurers to manage their risk, with attendant implications for the design and implementation of regulatory capital requirements and other aspects of solvency regulation.

I begin with a brief description of the principal risks facing insurers. I next broadly consider the major factors that affect insurance market discipline: 1) the risk sensitivity of insurance demand, and 2) the potential loss of specific assets and other financial distress costs that also discipline insurer risk-taking, including potential bankruptcy costs associated with debt financing by insurance holding companies. I then discuss insurer financial strength ratings and summarize empirical evidence on market discipline and moral hazard. I conclude with brief discussion of policy implications and suggestions for additional research.

1. Insurers' Risk

1.1 Property/Casualty Insurance

The main risks that affect property–casualty (P/C) insurers (and reinsurers) are underwriting risk, credit risk, asset (market) risk, and interest rate risk.[1] Asset risk for U.S. P/C insurers has traditionally been modest, reflecting heavy investments in government and highly rated corporate bonds. Many EU insurers and reinsurers have had relatively greater holdings of common stocks, with adverse consequences during the past few years. Many P/C insurers have larger asset than liability durations, but interest rate risk is relatively modest, in part because payments to policyholders are not highly correlated with interest rate increases. Credit (counterparty) risk is largely related to reinsurance transactions, which are widely employed to manage underwriting risk.

Underwriting risk encompasses pricing and reserve (unpaid claim liability) risks associated with the possibility of large errors in predicting ultimate claim costs. Pricing risk involves possible divergence between ultimate costs and conditional forecasts of costs at the time policies are priced. Reserve risk involves possible divergence between ultimate costs and conditional forecasts of costs after claims have occurred (or are projected to have occurred) but before they are paid. Natural or man-made catastrophes can create large, sudden increases in costs. More benign changes in weather and unexpected changes in property repair costs also create risk. For long-tail coverages, such as general business liability, ultimate claims may not be known for many years after policies are priced and sold (for example, as in the cases of asbestos and environmental claims). Underwriting risk is amplified by intense price competition in many P/C insurance markets, which may arguably encourage prices to become too low during "soft market" episodes of the insurance cycle due to moral hazard, winner's curse effects, or other influences (see Harrington and Danzon, 1994). Subsequent negative shocks to capital have occasionally led to very hard markets characterized by scarce capital, large rate increases, and less favorable coverage terms, often with material effects on real activity.[2]

Property/casualty insurers hold relatively large amounts of capital compared with life insurers and commercial banks, which in turn produces relatively large tax and agency costs.[3] Depending on the jurisdiction, double taxation of returns from investing capital to support the sale of policies significantly increases the cost of capital and the prices needed to offer coverage, especially for low probability events with large potential severities (see Harrington and Niehaus, 2003). P/C insurers reduce risk and economize on costly capital by diversifying across policies of a given type and region, across types of coverage, and geographically. They also transfer significant amounts of risk through reinsurance, which achieves additional risk spreading, including across national borders, thus reducing the amount of capital held by ceding insurers and the aggregate amount of capital held by insurers and reinsurers to back coverage.

1.2 Life Insurance

Life/health/annuity (life) insurers' primary risks traditionally have arisen from the asset side of the balance sheet, as was illustrated by asset quality problems in U.S. real estate and high-yield bond markets during the late 1980s and early 1990s and by large drops in the value of U.S. and especially EU life insurers' equity portfolios during 1999 to 2001. Significant reductions in asset values and increases in interest rates can cause policyholders to withdraw funds and/or reduce life insurers' sales and conceivably force some assets to be sold at temporarily depressed prices. Reductions in interest rates can cause the value of promised payments and guaranteed interest credits to increase in relation to asset values and investment income. Although life insurers also face some mortality/morbidity risk, volatility on these dimensions has been relatively modest and generally is managed effectively by transferring the risk to specialized reinsurers. As noted above, U.S. life insurer capital levels in relation to assets are much smaller than those for P/C insurers and more comparable to those for banks.

2. Risk Sensitivity of Demand

The main factors affecting the sensitivity of insurance demand to insolvency risk are: 1) the scope of government mandated guarantees of insurers' obligations to policyholders, 2) the ability of risk-sensitive policyholders or their representatives to assess insurers' insolvency risk, and 3) the scope of the judgment proof problem, which causes some buyers to seek low prices regardless of insolvency risk.

2.1 Government Guarantees

Certain obligations of insolvent insurers are subject to government guarantees in the United States and other major countries, thus protecting some policyholders from the full consequences of insurer default. In the United States, all states have guaranty systems for both P/C and life insurers. The guarantees apply to direct insurance only; they exclude reinsurance. With the exception of New York, state guaranty systems are financed with ex post assessments on solvent insurers. Assessments are proportional to insurers' premiums; they are not risk based.

Guarantees of insolvent insurers' obligations reduce incentives of some buyers to trade with financially strong insurers. Reduced risk-sensitivity of demand by direct insurance buyers could in turn affect the risk sensitivity of insurers' demand for reinsurance. Limits on the amounts and types of direct insurance losses covered by guarantees, however, should provide many insurance buyers with substantial incentives to deal with financially sound insurers. (It generally would be prohibitively expensive or simply impractical for buyers to buy relatively small policies from multiple insurers in order to multiply the amount of guaranty fund protection.) P/C insurance guaranty fund limits typically are $300,000 or less per claim and much smaller than many commercial policyholders' policy limits. Limits on the amount of premium payments that are protected by guaranty funds (for example, $10,000 for fixed price contracts and no coverage of premium refunds on retrospectively rated policies purchased by many medium to large businesses) also reduce the scope of protection for many commercial buyers. Moreover, over half the states modified their guaranty fund statutes during the last two decades to exclude most protection for "large" commercial policyholders. Limits on life insurer guaranty coverage are likewise less than the policy limits or funds invested for many personal and commercial policyholders, and most life insurance guaranty funds provide only partial guarantees of investment returns. In addition to coverage limits, policyholders of insolvent insurers could experience delays in claims payment or premium refunds, and insurers cannot advertise guaranty fund protection. Moreover, many policyholders could regard the state guaranty system as less credible than federal deposit insurance, and there appears to be little or no implicit federal guaranty of insurers' obligations.

Significant limitations on insurance guarantees are efficient because they encourage market discipline. The conventional systemic risk rationale for deposit insurance is theoretically and empirically less applicable to insurance. While subject to debate, most observers agree that systemic risk is relatively low in insurance markets compared with banking, especially for P/C insurance. Low probability events with large losses can simultaneously damage many P/C insurers, and their impact is spread broadly through product line and geographic diversification and especially through reinsurance, which creates material contractual interdependence among insurers. As noted, large shocks can disrupt P/C insurance markets with adverse effects on real activity. Reductions in asset values may affect many life insurers at once, and some policyholders may seek to withdraw funds following negative shocks, perhaps causing some insurers to unload assets at temporarily depressed prices. But shocks to P/C and life insurers do not threaten the payment system, and there is little or no evidence of "pure" contagion associated with major events in either sector, as opposed to rational, information-based flights to quality (which is discussed later in this paper).

2.2 Costly Search and Transparency/Opacity

A variety of private sector institutions help match policyholders with financially strong insurers, including the widespread use of insurance intermediaries (agents and brokers), an extensive system of private ratings of insurers' claims paying abilities, secured lenders' monitoring of the quality of insurance protection on collateral, and knowledgeable corporate staff who oversee risk-management and insurance programs for many medium to large businesses. Even so, some personal insurance and small business insurance policyholders might find it difficult to identify high quality insurers or knowledgeable advisors, thus reducing the effective risk sensitivity of demand and providing a traditional rationale for regulatory monitoring and restrictions on insurer risk-taking. This problem might have some effect on reinsurance markets if it increases the demand by primary insurers for low-quality reinsurance.

In addition, many insurance companies have opaque characteristics, increasing the likelihood that some policyholders will be attracted to low prices or high promised investment returns without recognizing that they could indicate relatively high insolvency risk. Valuation of P/C insurers' unpaid claim liabilities for long-tailed liability and workers' compensation insurance is problematic, as is valuation of some life insurers' privately-placed fixed income investments and many commercial real estate investments. Many insurance organizations have complex ownership structures. Most insurers have elaborate reinsurance arrangements, sometimes involving dozens of reinsurers. While the primary function of those arrangements is to diversify risk, they reduce transparency and can sometimes be used to hide financial problems.

2.3 Compulsory Insurance and Judgment Proof Buyers

Almost all states require automobile owners to purchase specified minimum amounts of auto liability insurance. All states require employers governed by state workers' compensation systems to either buy workers' compensation insurance or meet financial strength requirements to qualify as a self-insurer. The purchase of environmental liability and professional liability insurance is likewise compulsory for many entities. Liability and workers' compensation insurance buyers with few assets to protect will often seek low-priced coverage with little concern for insolvency risk. Thus, the combination of compulsory insurance requirements and judgment-proof or near judgment-proof buyers reduces the risk sensitivity of demand.

3. Specific Assets and Financial Distress Costs

Like other firms, insurers' incentives to manage risk depend in part on the expected costs of financial distress and the extent to which expected financial distress costs are borne by owners ex ante. Financial distress can reduce the value of an insurer's firm-specific assets and impose losses (ex post) on a variety of stakeholders, including managers, employees, and agents/brokers. The risk of such losses ex post helps motivate insurer risk management ex ante.

3.1 Potential Loss of Franchise Value

Insurance production and distribution often involve the creation of firm-specific assets (franchise value) that could diminish or evaporate if the insurer experiences financial distress. As emphasized in both the banking and insurance literatures, franchise value can provide incentives for adequate capitalization and other forms of risk management even when the risk sensitivity of demand is dulled by guarantees or information problems.[4] Risk sensitivity of demand amplifies those incentives because financial difficulty will then reduce both new and renewal business.

Insurers' firm-specific assets arise in four main ways. First, attracting and providing coverage to new customers typically requires relatively high upfront costs, which insurers expect to recover from higher margins on renewal business. Thus, renewal premiums often include quasi-rents as a return for the initial investment in creating the customer relationship. Second, insurers may obtain valuable private information over time about their continuing policyholders' risks of loss. Third, some insurers make substantial investments in developing a brand name or reputation for quality service. Fourth, some insurers' investments in underwriting expertise and distribution systems generate valuable growth opportunities. In each case, much of the value of these investments could be lost in the event of financial distress or insolvency. Loss of quasi-rents and/or growth opportunities is especially likely in insurance given that unexpected reductions in assets values or increases in claim costs can affect many insurers at once, thus reducing the ability of other insurers to acquire the operations of distressed companies.

Insurers' franchise values are difficult to measure. Ratios of the market value of equity to the book value of equity provide a rough metric for publicly traded entities. Using data reported by *Yahoo! Finance* as of October 10, 2003, for publicly traded U.S. P/C insurers, the median, mean, and weighted (by book equity) mean values of market-to-book equity ratios were 1.17, 1.25, and 1.57, respectively. Because P/C insurers hold relatively large amounts of equity capital compared with life insurers and banks, the data suggest sizable franchise values for many insurers in relation to balance-sheet assets. But the market-to-book metric is crude. The reporting of P/C insurance claim liabilities on an undiscounted basis, for example, tends to reduce book equity and increase the market-to-book ratio apart from any franchise value. Possible understatement (overstatement) of claim liabilities tends to inflate (depress) book equity. Investments in bonds classified under generally accepted accounting principles (GAAP) as "hold to maturity" are valued at book rather than market, and so on. Using the same source, the market-to-book ratios for life insurers averaged less than one (median of 0.92, mean of 0.98, and weighted-mean of 1.16). While low market-to-book ratios could suggest relatively small franchise values for life insurers on average, the ratios have been significantly depressed by unexpectedly low interest rates in a long-term contractual environment. Low interest rates have reduced insurers' investment yields and substantially increased the market value of many life insurers' liabilities, which reflect, *inter alia*, relatively high guaranteed interest rates on some obligations.

3.2 Effects of Financial Distress on Insurance Intermediaries

The bulk of U.S. insurance is distributed through exclusive agents or independent agents and brokers. Exclusive agents primarily or exclusively represent a single insurance company or group of affiliated insurers. They generally make substantial investments in developing a book of business that would be lost if the insurer(s) issuing the policies became insolvent. This implies that exclusive agency insurers (direct writers) will have to provide credible assurance of continued financial viability to attract and develop exclusive agents. Independent agents and brokers arrange or distribute insurance for numerous insurers. Other things equal, they make smaller investments in developing relationships with any one insurer than exclusive agents. However, independent agents and brokers make substantial investments in relationships with their policyholder clients. The insolvency of an insurer could damage those relationships if it imposes costs on policyholders. Insolvencies also impose direct costs on the agent/broker, such as the cost of transferring business to other insurers and can produce costly litigation for alleged failure of the agent or broker to protect policyholders' interests.

3.3 Bankruptcy Costs and Control Changes

Many insurers issue conventional debt, almost always at the holding company level. Again using data reported by *Yahoo! Finance* as of October 2003, the median, mean, and weighted (by book equity) mean ratios of long-term debt to equity were 21, 29, and 41 percent, respectively, for P/C insurers and 17, 23, and 33 percent for life insurers. I also tabulated total (short- plus long-term) debt-to-equity ratios and ratios of total debt to total liabilities (including liabilities to policyholders) in 1997 for 172 insurance holding companies using data from *Best's Holding Company Guide, GAAP, United States, 1998 Edition.* (A. M. Best subsequently dropped this publication from its product line). On average total debt represented about 6 percent of liabilities for P/C entities and 5 percent of liabilities for life entities. The average ratio of total debt-to-equity was 18 percent for P/C insurers and 28 percent for life insurers. The average ratio of debt-to-equity is materially larger (about 40 percent) for the largest insurers in both sectors.

Debt finance presumably allows insurers to lower their cost of capital, including tax and agency costs. According to conventional theory, the possible direct bank-ruptcy costs associated with debt finance will be borne by issuers ex ante and help motivate them to reduce the probability of bankruptcy. More important, although the bulk of debt issued by U.S. insurers is senior debt at the holding company level, it generally is effectively subordinated to the claims of subsidiary insurers' policyhold-ers—unless the holding company is willing and able to let the underlying insurance subsidiary fail in the event of financial difficulty (see Cummins and Lamm-Tennant, 1994, for further discussion). Even though many or most of the issues are effectively subordinated to policyholder claims, the bulk of insurer debt is investment grade (Standard & Poor's rating of Baa or above; see Harrington, 2003).

Insurers' debt finance creates an additional category of stakeholder monitors that should be risk sensitive and should press for efficient risk management. It also in-creases the likelihood of a control change if insurance operations deteriorate, which in turn could encourage managers to reduce risk. It creates a set of hard claims that could dissuade excessive risk-taking ex ante and limit risk-taking ex post, especially compared with opaque, long-tailed claim liabilities that can be further extended by end-game claim settlement strategies. Four years prior to its insolvency in 2001, Re-liance Group Holdings (Reliance) had one of the highest debt-to-equity ratios (94 percent) among the sample of P/C entities described above. Reliance's debt obliga-tions eventually led to a crisis at maturity that precipitated, seriatim, substantial de-clines in its stock price, debt ratings, and policyholder ratings; a sharp reduction in its ability to sell coverage and generate more liabilities; and the ultimate regulatory clo-sure of its insurance subsidiaries.

Credit ratings on insurance entity debt issues also provide another source of in-formation that can be used by interested parties in assessing insurer financial strength. Hence, although the details may differ significantly from the design features of man-datory subordinated debt proposals for banks (for example, U.S. Shadow Financial Regulatory Committee, 2000), insurer debt finance should provide some of the ben-efits of market discipline that motivate such proposals.

4. Rating Agencies and Financial Strength Ratings

The A. M. Best Company, Standard & Poor's (S&P), and Moody's are the three most well-known agencies that rate insurers' claims paying ability (financial strength ratings or policyholder ratings). A. M. Best has the broadest coverage of U.S. insurers. Research shows that Best's ratings help predict insolvencies compared with U.S. regulatory screening systems and risk-based capital ratios, and that they are sensibly related to insurers' reported financial characteristics (for example, Pottier and Sommer, 1999, 2002). Best's bases its ratings of most insurers on analysis of public information and private discussions with management. Standard & Poor's bases its ratings of many companies on the analysis of public information only.[5] Conventional wisdom is that a Best's rating of A– (or the comparable rating at Standard & Poor's or Moody's) is a prerequisite for an insurer to be a meaningful player in the markets for most commercial P/C coverages.

As of June 2003, the vast majority of both personal and commercial P/C insurance was written by rated insurers with A. M. Best ratings of A– and above (see Harrington, 2003). Insurers with a Best's rating of A and above wrote a large majority of premiums. Insurers with low ratings and unrated insurers on average were quite small in relation to higher rated insurers. Standard & Poor's rating distributions generally were similar, with insurers with ratings of A– or above writing the bulk of coverage. The main difference was a smaller proportion of premiums written by insurers with the highest S&P rating (Aaa) than for the highest A. M. Best rating (A++). In the fall of 2003, executives of several large international reinsurers announced that they regarded the requirements for an S&P Aaa rating as too stringent and would no longer seek to achieve or maintain an Aaa rating.

Whether insurer policyholder/financial strength ratings are insufficiently accurate, biased upward due to relationships between agencies and insurers, and/or too slow to react to bad news has often been debated but is difficult to resolve empirically. Executives of major insurers and other insurer stakeholders often speak and act as if they have a keen interest in the ratings assigned to their companies. Independent agents and brokers make extensive use of ratings. Rating agency methodologies (for example, risk-based capital models) and competition among rating agencies have evolved considerably during the past 15 years. The overall evidence seems broadly consistent with substantial demand for information about (or certification of) insurer financial strength and with risk-sensitive demand for large portions of insurance markets.

5. Other Evidence of Market Discipline and Moral Hazard

A number of studies exploit cross-state variation in insurance guaranty fund characteristics or adoption dates to test whether guarantees have increased risk-taking. Lee, Mayers, and Smith (1997), for example, provide evidence that asset risk increased for stock property/casualty insurers following the introduction of guaranty funds (also see Lee and Smith, 1999, and Downs and Sommer, 1999). Brewer, Mondschean, and Strahan (1997) provide evidence that life insurer asset risk is greater in states where guaranty fund assessments against surviving insurers are offset against state premium taxes and thus borne by taxpayers, which may reduce financially strong insurers' incentives to press for efficient regulatory monitoring.

A variety of studies document unusually large premium growth prior to the insolvencies of some P/C insurers (Grace, Harrington, and Klein, 1998; Bohn and Hall,

1999; also see Harrington and Danzon, 1994), which could in some cases be plausibly related to under pricing and excessive risk-taking. (The EU evidence appears similar in this respect; see McDonnell, 2002.) More anecdotal evidence suggests that excessive risk-taking could have contributed to a number of "major" insurer insolvencies and perhaps many minor ones. Several highly publicized P/C insurer insolvencies during the late 1980s (Mission Insurance Group, Transit Casualty, Ideal Mutual) were associated with rapid premium growth and reinsurance arrangements in which underwriting and pricing authority was delegated to intermediaries ("managing general agents") who bore little or no risk of loss if claims exceeded premiums. Analogous problems arose in many Lloyds' of London syndicates.

The Reliance insolvency, which is expected to produce over $1 billion in guaranty fund assessments, and of several other P/C insurers during 2000 to 2002 were related in part to a similar arrangement. The entities participated in a reinsurance arrangement (the Unicover pool), where the managing general agency (Unicover) rapidly generated an enormous volume of reinsurance for workers' compensation medical claims, apparently at deeply discounted prices. The complex arrangement spread the liabilities among numerous reinsurers, with substantial liabilities flowing in to several large life-health insurers with little or no prior experience in workers' compensation. The insolvency of PHICO Insurance Company, a relatively large medical malpractice insurer, also was preceded by rapid growth and expansion at allegedly deeply discounted prices.

However, the extent to which these insolvencies were caused by excessive ex ante risk-taking due to inadequate market (and regulatory) discipline, unexpected loss shocks on risky business, ex post risk-taking following such shocks, and/or simple fraud or incompetence is less than transparent and difficult to disentangle. As information surfaced about operating losses, stock price declines (for publicly traded entities) and rating downgrades followed, which substantially curtailed the insurers' ability to continue writing business. Reliance executives fought desperately to avoid losing an A– rating. Their failure was terminal.

The highly publicized insolvencies in 1990 and 1991 of First Executive Corporation, First Capital Corporation, and Mutual Benefit Life also suggest some degree of excessive ex ante risk-taking but again the evidence again is not sharp. Without regulatory intervention both First Executive and First Capital might have remained viable despite the temporary collapse of the junk bond market (for example, DeAngelo, DeAngelo, and Gilson, 1995, 1996). Mutual Benefit's insolvency/reorganization following reductions in the value of its commercial real estate holdings produced only modest guaranty fund assessments. It is clear in each case that demand was risk sensitive: as more bad news surfaced, more policyholders withdrew their funds (DeAngelo, DeAngelo, and Gilson, 1995, 1996; also see Harrington, 1992).[6] The evidence also suggests market discipline from insurance company equity holders, that equity holders anticipated a flight to quality following these events, and that there was little or no "pure" contagion. Fenn and Cole (1994) and Brewer and Jackson (2002), for example, find that life insurer stock price declines during the high-yield bond and commercial real estate market slumps of 1989–91 were concentrated among firms with problem assets.[7]

Empirical work on market discipline in banking has analyzed the relation between bank risk and yields and flows of deposits, CDs, and subordinated debt (for an overview, see, for example, Flannery, 1998). Substantial evidence indicates that credit spreads on uninsured deposits and subordinated debt are generally positively related to bank risk and that uninsured deposit growth is negatively related to bank risk. Crabbe and Post (1994) find that outstanding commercial paper issued by bank holding companies declined following rating downgrades by Moody's. There thus far have been fewer insurance studies along these lines, in part due to data and measurement issues. P/C insurers, for example, do not report volume of coverage or premium rates per unit of coverage. (The information would not be very comparable across firms if they did.) It is very difficult to make inferences about (ex ante) price differences across insurers because conditional expectations of claim costs when policies are sold are not observable. Like other research on insurance prices, Sommer (1996) and Phillips, Cummins, and Allen (1998) employ measures of property/casualty insurers' premiums in relation to realized claim costs as proxies for the price of coverage. Consistent with risk sensitive demand and market discipline, they find that the price proxies are negatively to insolvency risk.

Zanjani (2002) provides evidence that life insurance policy termination rates are greater for insurers with lower A. M. Best ratings, but he finds that terminations are not reliably related to rating changes. Epermanis and Harrington (2003) provide evidence of changes in P/C insurer premium growth surrounding changes in Best's ratings. We conduct control group comparisons of premium growth for firms with rating changes versus those without for a sample of 9,446 firm-year observations during 1992–99 and regression tests for 7,961 firm-year observations during 1993–99. Consistent with risk-sensitive demand and attendant market discipline, we generally find economically and statistically significant premium declines in the year of and the year following rating downgrades. Figure 1 highlights the results of our simplest comparisons, which define abnormal premium growth as premium growth for a downgraded or upgraded insurer in a given year less mean premium growth for insurers in the same broad rating category pre-downgrade or upgrade. Year 0 (−1, +1) is the year of (year before, year after) the rating change. Similar results were obtained with control group comparisons that also conditioned on firm size and with least squares and random effects regressions that conditioned on a variety of other characteristics that could affect insurers' premium growth. In general and as illustrated in figure 1, premium declines were greater for firms with relatively low pre-downgrade ratings (Best's rating of either A− or B++ and below). Our results also indicate that rating upgrades for relatively low-rated insurers were accompanied by increased premium growth.

Consistent with less complete guaranty fund protection and greater risk sensitivity of demand for commercial insurance compared with personal automobile and homeowners' insurance, we also find that abnormal premium growth for downgraded insurers with pre-downgrade ratings of A− or below was negatively related to the proportion of an insurer's premiums in commercial insurance. For downgraded insurers with A− ratings and at least 50 percent of their premiums in commercial insurance prior to being downgraded, premiums declined by an average of 15 percent to 20 percent during the downgrade year alone. We also find a negative relation between

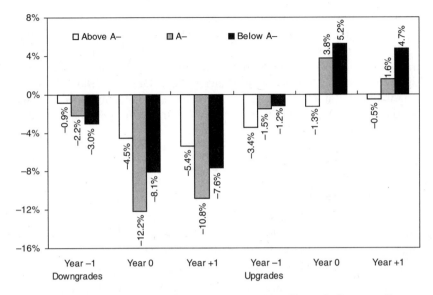

**Figure 14.1: Mean Abnormal P/C Insurer Premium Growth Surrounding
A.M. Best Rating Changes by Pre-Change Rating Category,
1992–1999**

downgraded firms' premium growth and firm size for firms with A– or lower ratings
prior to being downgraded. Our overall findings suggest material market discipline
for rated insurers, especially those that write relatively large amounts of commercial
insurance.

6. Policy Implications and Further Research

The overall evidence suggests that market discipline is reasonably strong in most
insurance markets, despite guaranty fund protection, the opacity of some insurers'
balance sheets, and other factors that dull policyholders' incentives to insure with
financially strong insurers. This conclusion has a number of policy implications. Those
for regulatory capital requirements are perhaps the most important. Given significant
market discipline, the benefits of stringent risk-based capital requirements, which
will have limited accuracy under the best of circumstances, will be small. The costs
from distorting decisions of sound insurers will be comparably large. As a result, risk-
based capital requirements should be designed not to bind the decisions of most insurers, and simple requirements are likely to be as effective as more complex rules
(see Harrington, 2002, for detailed discussion).

Current capital requirements for U.S. and EU insurers are fairly loose. The bulk
of insurers hold substantially more capital than the amounts required to avoid some
form of regulatory intervention. The U.S. risk-based capital requirements are complex; EU capital requirements are (for the time being) relatively simple. A variety of

evidence indicates that the U.S. requirements are not very accurate despite their complexity (for example, Cummins, Harrington, and Klein, 1995; Grace, Harrington, and Klein, 1998; Pottier and Sommer, 2002). In July 2003, the National Association of Insurance Commissioners (NAIC) proposed doubling required risk-based capital for P/C insurers. Widespread industry resistance has thus far dissuaded the NAIC from pushing that proposal. More stringent and elaborate capital requirements for insurance and reinsurance in the European Union are in the works. Given insurance market discipline, these initiatives strike me as misguided.

Additional implications of reasonably strong market discipline in most insurance markets include:

1. The primary focus of regulation for most markets should be prompt corrective action and efficient closure and liquidation of insolvent insurers.

2. Regulatory solvency monitoring should attempt to focus relatively more attention on 1) market segments where market discipline is weakest due to more complete guarantees, costly search, and the judgment proof problem; and on 2) associated indicators of excessive risk-taking.

3. Significant limits on guaranty protection, such as those in the U.S. state system, are advantageous because they promote market discipline and are consistent with relatively low systemic risk levels in insurance. Broader and more complete guarantees should be avoided; narrower coverage in some cases could be advantageous.

4. Any adoption of optional federal chartering of insurers in the U.S., or regulatory changes designed to harmonize solvency regulation across sectors or borders should recognize cross-sector and cross-border differences in and avoid undermining market discipline.

Additional research would be beneficial in a number of areas. It would be helpful to know more about 1) the relations between insurer debt finance, insurer insolvency risk, debt ratings, and policyholder/financial strength ratings; 2) the magnitude of insurer franchise value and its relation to risk-taking and ratings; 3) policyholder characteristics that are correlated with risk sensitivity of demand at the insurance entity level, and 4) the extent to which debt/policyholder ratings and measures of franchise value (based on market prices and/or other indicators) and the risk-sensitivity of demand might be incorporated formally into regulatory monitoring and prompt corrective action systems.

*Scott E. Harrington is the W. Frank Hipp Professor of Insurance and professor of finance at Moore School of Business of the University of South Carolina. This is an edited version of the paper prepared for the Conference on Market Discipline: Evidence across Countries and Industries cosponsored by the Federal Reserve Bank of Chicago and the Bank for International Settlements. The original version (Harrington, 2003) provides additional references, charts, and tables.

Notes

1. These subsections draw heavily from Harrington (2002), which includes detailed discussion of insurer/reinsurer capital regulation and policy initiatives in the United States and the European Union.

2. Effects on real activity were widely reported during the mid-1980s U.S. liability insurance crisis and more recently in the U.S. medical care sector. Odell and Weidenmier (2002) document real and monetary linkage following the San Francisco earthquake and associated insurance payments during 1906–07.

3. Capital to asset ratios for U.S. non-life insurers in the late 1990s averaged about 40 percent, compared with 10 percent to 11 percent for life insurers and commercial banks. Harrington and Niehaus (2003) contain detailed analysis of the tax costs of insurer capital in the U.S.

4. See Harrington (2003) for references.

5. Pottier and Sommer (1999) provide an empirical analysis of factors correlated with differences in ratings among Best's, Standard & Poor's, and Moody's.

6. DeAngelo, DeAngelo, and Gilson suggest that the withdrawals may have been aggravated by disproportionately negative media coverage and /or premature announcements by regulators.

7. Cummins and Lewis (2003) find that stock prices of property/casualty insurers with the highest A. M. Best ratings rebounded significantly following the World Trade Center attack, whereas those for lower rated insurers did not.

References

Bohn, James, and Brian Hall, 1999, "The moral hazard of insuring the insurers," in *The Financing of Catastrophe Risk*, K. Froot (ed.), Chicago: University of Chicago Press.

Brewer, Elijah, and William Jackson, 2002, "Intra-industry contagion and the competitive effects of financial distress announcements: Evidence from commercial banks and insurance companies," Federal Reserve Bank of Chicago, working paper, No. 2002-23.

Brewer, Elijah, Thomas Mondschean, and Philip Strahan, 1997, "The role of monitoring in reducing the moral hazard problem associated with government guarantees: Evidence from the life insurance industry," *Journal of Risk and Insurance*, Vol. 64, pp. 302–322.

Crabbe, Leland, and Mitchell Post, 1994, "The effect of a rating downgrade on outstanding commercial paper," *Journal of Finance*, Vol. 49, pp. 39–56.

Cummins, J. David, Scott Harrington, and Robert Klein, 1995, "Insolvency experience, risk-based capital, and prompt corrective action in property-liability insurance," *Journal of Banking and Finance*, Vol. 19, pp. 511–527.

Cummins, J. David, and Joan Lamm-Tennant, 1994, "Capital structure and the cost of equity capital in the property-liability insurance industry," *Insurance Mathematics and Economics*, Vol. 15, pp. 187–201.

Cummins, J. David, and Christopher Lewis, 2003, "Catastrophic events, parameter uncertainty, and the breakdown of implicit long-term contracting: The case of terrorism insurance," *Journal of Risk and Uncertainty*, Vol. 26, pp. 153–178.

DeAngelo, Harry, Linda DeAngelo, and Stuart Gilson, 1996, "Perceptions and the politics of finance: Junk bonds the regulatory seizure of First Capital Life," *Journal of Financial Economics,* Vol. 41, pp. 475–512.

_____, 1995, "The collapse of First Executive Corporation: Junk bonds, adverse publicity, and the 'run on the bank' phenomenon," *Journal of Financial Economics,* Vol. 36, pp. 287–336.

Downs, David, and David Sommer, 1999, "Monitoring, ownership, and risk-taking: The impact of guaranty funds," *Journal of Risk and Insurance,* Vol. 66, pp. 477–497.

Epermanis, Karen, and Scott Harrington, 2003, "Market discipline in insurance: Evidence from premium growth surrounding changes in policyholder ratings," University of South Carolina, working paper, September.

Fenn, George, and Rebel Cole, 1994, "Announcements of asset-quality problems and contagion effects in the life insurance industry," *Journal of Financial Economics,* Vol. 35, pp. 181–198.

Flannery, Mark, 1998, "Using market information in prudential bank supervision: A review of the U.S. empirical evidence," *Journal of Money, Credit and Banking,* Vol. 30, pp. 273–305.

Grace, Martin, Scott Harrington, and Robert Klein, 1998, "Risk-based capital and solvency screening in property-liability insurance," *Journal of Risk and Insurance,* Vol. 65, pp. 213–243.

Harrington, Scott, 2003, "Market discipline in insurance and reinsurance," paper presented at Federal Reserve of Chicago and Bank for International Settlements cosponsored Conference on Market Discipline: The Evidence across Countries and Industries, Chicago, October 31.

_____, 2002, "Capital adequacy in insurance and reinsurance," in *Capital Adequacy Beyond Basel: Banking, Securities, and Insurance,* Hal Scott (ed.), London: Oxford University Press.

_____, 1992, "The solvency of the insurance industry," in *Proceedings of the 28th Annual Conference on Bank Structure and Competition,* Chicago: Federal Reserve Bank of Chicago.

_____, 1991, "Should the Feds regulate insurance company solvency?," *Regulation: Cato Review of Business and Government,* Spring, pp. 53–60.

Harrington, Scott, and Patricia Danzon, 1994, "Price cutting in liability insurance markets," *Journal of Business,* Vol. 67, pp. 511–538.

Harrington, Scott, and Greg Niehaus, 2003, "Capital, corporate income taxes, and catastrophe insurance," *Journal of Financial Intermediation,* October, pp. 365–389.

Lee, Soon-Jae, David Mayers, and Clifford W. Smith, Jr., 1997, "Guaranty funds and risk-taking: Evidence from the insurance industry," *Journal of Financial Economics,* Vol. 44, pp. 3–24.

Lee, Soon-Jae, and Michael Smith, 1999, "Property-casualty insurance guaranty funds and insurer vulnerability to misfortune," *Journal of Banking and Finance,* Vol. 23, pp. 1437–1456.

McDonnell, William, 2002, "Managing risk: Practical lessons from recent 'failures' of EU insurers," Financial Services Authority, discussion paper series, No. 20.

Odell, Kerry, and Marc Weidenmier, 2002, "Real shock, monetary aftershock: The San Francisco Earthquake and the Panic of 1907," National Bureau of Economic Research, working paper, No. 9176.

Phillips, Richard, J. David Cummins, and Franklin Allen, 1998, "Financial pricing in the multiple-line insurance company," *Journal of Risk and Insurance,* Vol. 65, pp. 597–636.

Pottier, Steven, and David Sommer, 2002, "The effectiveness of public and private sector summary risk measures in predicting insurer insolvencies," *Journal of Financial Services Research,* Vol. 21, pp. 101–116.

_____, 1999, "Property-liability insurer financial strength ratings: Differences across rating agencies," *Journal of Risk and Insurance,* Vol. 66, pp. 621–642.

Sommer, David, 1996, "The impact of firm risk on property-liability insurance prices," *Journal of Risk and Insurance,* Vol. 63, pp. 501–514.

U.S. Shadow Financial Regulatory Committee, 2000, *Reforming Bank Capital Regulation—A Proposal By the U.S. Shadow Financial Regulatory Committee,* Washington, DC: American Enterprise Institute.

Zanjani, George, 2002, "Market discipline and government guarantees in life insurance," Federal Reserve Bank of New York, working paper.

Chapter 15

Conflicts of Interest and Market Discipline

Ingo Walter*
New York University

Potential conflicts of interest are a fact of life in financial intermediation. Under perfect competition and in the absence of asymmetric information, exploitation of conflicts of interest cannot rationally take place. Consequently, the necessary and sufficient conditions for agency costs associated with conflict of interest exploitation center on market and information imperfections. Arguably, the bigger and broader the financial intermediaries, the greater the agency problems associated with conflict-of-interest exploitation. It follows that efforts to address the issue through improved transparency and market discipline are central to creating viable solutions to a problem that repeatedly seems to shake public confidence in financial markets.

In recent years, the role of banks, securities firms, insurance companies, and asset managers in alleged conflict-of-interest-exploitation—involving a broad array of abusive retail market practices, in acting simultaneously as principals and intermediaries, in facilitating various corporate abuses, and in misusing private information—suggests that the underlying market imperfections are present even in highly developed financial systems. Certainly the prominence of conflict-of-interest problems so soon after the passage of the U.S. Gramm–Leach–Bliley Act of 1999, which removed some of the key structural barriers to conflict exploitation built into the U.S. regulatory system for some 66 years, seems to have surprised many observers.

Moreover, recent evidence suggests that the collective decision process in the management of major financial firms impairs pinpointing responsible individuals, and that criminal indictment of entire firms runs the risk of adverse systemic effects. Monetary penalties and negotiated settlements neither admitting nor denying guilt seem to have emerged as the principal external mechanisms to address conflict of interest exploitation. Market discipline operating through the share price may, under appropriate corporate governance, represent an important additional line of defense.

Part 1 of this paper proposes a taxonomy of conflicts between the interests of the financial firm's owners and managers and those of its clients, including situations where the firm is confronted by conflicts of interest between individual clients or types of clients. Some of these conflicts have been discussed extensively in the literature, while others seem to have surfaced more recently. Mapped onto this taxonomy is the distinction between conflicts of interest that arise in wholesale and retail domains, characterized by very different degrees of information asymmetry and fiduciary obligations, and conflicts that arise on the interface between the two domains. Part 2 of the paper relates this conflict-of-interest taxonomy to the strategic profile of financial services firms, linking potential conflicts of interest exploitation to the size and breadth of financial firms and illustrating how those conflicts can be compounded in large multi-line financial institutions. Part 3 reviews regulatory and market discipline-based constraints on conflict- of-interest exploitation, including issues of granularity and immediacy, and considers linkages between the two types of constraints. Part 4 presents the conclusions and some implications for public policy. A more comprehensive discussion if these issues is contained in Walter (2003).

1. A Conflict of Interest Taxonomy

There are essentially two types of conflicts of interest confronting firms in the financial services industry under market imperfections.

Type 1 conflicts between a firm's own economic interests and the interests of its clients, usually reflected in the extraction of rents or mispriced transfer of risk. In addition to direct firm-client conflicts, indirect conflicts of interest could involve collusion between the firm and a fiduciary acting as agent for the ultimate clients.

Type 2 conflicts of interest between a firm's clients, or between types of clients, which place the firm in a position of favoring one at the expense of another.

They may arise either in interprofessional activities carried out in *wholesale* financial markets or in activities involving *retail* clients. The distinction between these two market "domains" is important because of the key role of information and transactions costs, which differ dramatically between the two broad types of market participants. Their vulnerability to conflict-exploitation differs accordingly, and measures designed to remedy the problem in one domain may be inappropriate in the other. In addition there are what we shall term "transition" conflicts of interest, which run between the two domains—and whose impact can be particularly troublesome. In the following sections, we enumerate the principal conflicts of interest encountered in financial services firms arranged by *type* and by *domain* (see table 15.1).

2. Conflicts of Interest in Wholesale Financial Markets

In wholesale financial markets involving professional transaction counterparties, corporations, and sophisticated institutional investors, the asymmetric information and competitive conditions necessary for conflicts of interest to be exploited are arguably of relatively limited importance. *Caveat emptor* and limited fiduciary obligations rule in a game that all parties fully understand. Nevertheless, several types of conflicts of interest seem to arise.

Principal transactions. A financial intermediary may be involved as a principal with a stake in a transaction in which it is also serving as adviser, lender, or underwriter,

Wholesale Domain	Domain-Transition	Retail Domain
Type 1 **Firm-client conflicts** Principal transactions Typing Misuse of fiduciary role Board memberships Spinning Investor loans Self-dealing Front-running **Type 2** **Inter-client conflicts** Misuse of private information Client interest incompatibility	**Type 1** **Firm-client conflicts** Suitability Stuffing Conflicted research Spinning Laddering Bankruptcy-risk shifting Late trading and market timing	**Type 1** **Firm-client conflicts** Biased client advice Involuntary cross-selling Churning Laddering Inappropriate margin lending Failure to execute Misleading disclosure and reporting Misuse of personal information

Table 15.1: A Conflict of Interest Taxonomy

creating an incentive to put its own interest ahead of those of its clients or trading counterparties. Or the firm may engage in misrepresentation beyond the ability of even highly capable clients to uncover.

Tying. A financial intermediary may use its lending power to influence a client to use its securities or advisory services as well—or the reverse, denying credit to clients that refuse to use other (more profitable) services. Costs are imposed on the client in the form of higher-priced or lower-quality services in an exercise of market power. This differs from cross-subsidization, in which a bank (possibly pressured by clients) engages in lending on concessionary terms in order to be considered for securities or advisory services. There may be good economic reasons for such cross-selling initiatives, whose costs are borne by the bank's own shareholders. The line between tying and cross-selling is often blurred, and its effectiveness is debatable. In 2003, the Federal Reserve helped to clarify the concept of tying, imposing a fine of $3 million on WestLB for violating anti-tying regulations.

Misuse of fiduciary role. Mutual fund managers who are also competing for pension fund mandates from corporations may be hesitant to vote fiduciary shares against the management of those companies, to the possible detriment of their own shareholders. Or the asset management unit of a financial institution may be pressured by a corporate banking client into voting shares in that company for management's position in a contested corporate action such as a proxy battle. The potential gain (or avoidance of loss) in banking business comes at the potential cost of inferior investment performance for the firm's fiduciary clients, and violates its duty of loyalty.

Board interlocks. The presence of bankers on boards of directors of nonfinancial companies may cause various bank functions such as underwriting or equity research to differ from arms-length practice. This displacement may impose costs on the bank's shareholders or on clients. Although constrained by legal liability issues, director interlocks can compound other potential sources of conflict, such as simultaneous lending, advisory and fiduciary relationships.

Spinning. Securities firms involved in initial public offerings may allocate shares to officers or directors of client firms on the understanding of obtaining future business, creating a transfer of wealth to those individuals at the expense of other investors.

Investor loans. In order to ensure that an underwriting goes well, a bank may make below-market loans to third-party investors on condition that the proceeds are used to purchase securities underwritten by its securities unit.

Self-dealing. A multifunctional financial firm may act as trading counterparty for its own fiduciary clients, as when the firm's asset management unit sells or buys securities for a fiduciary client while its affiliated broker-dealer is on the other side of the trade.

Front-running. Financial firms may exploit institutional, corporate, or other whole-sale clients by executing proprietary trades in advance of client trades that may move the market.

All of the foregoing represent exploitation of Type 1 conflicts, which set the firm's own interest against those of its clients in wholesale, interprofessional transactions. Type 2 conflicts dealing with differences in the interests of multiple wholesale clients seems to center predominantly on two issues:

Misuse of private information. As a lender, a bank may obtain certain private information about a client. Such proprietary information may be used in ways that harm the interests of the client. For instance, it may be used by the bank's investment banking unit in pricing and distributing securities for another client, or in advising another client in a contested acquisition.

Client interest incompatibility. A financial firm may have a relationship with two or more clients who are themselves in conflict. For example, a firm may be asked to represent the bondholders of a distressed company and subsequently be offered a mandate to represent a prospective acquirer of that corporation. Or two rival corporate clients may seek to use their leverage to impede each other's competitive strategies. Or firms may underprice initial public offerings (IPO) to the detriment of a corporate client in order to create gains for institutional investor clients from whom they hope to obtain future trading business.

3. Conflicts of Interest in Retail Financial Services

Asymmetric information is intuitively a much more important driver of conflict-of-interest exploitation in retail financial services than in interprofessional wholesale financial markets. Retail issues all appear to involve Type 1 conflicts, setting the interests of the financial firm against those of its clients.

Biased client advice. When financial firms have the power to sell affiliates' products, managers may fail to dispense "dispassionate" advice to clients based on a financial stake in promoting high-margin "house" products. Sales incentives may also encourage promotion of high-margin third-party products, to the ultimate disadvantage of the customer. The incentive structures that underlie such practices are rarely transparent to the retail client. Even when the firm purports to follow a so-called "open architecture" approach to best-in-class product selection, such arrangements normally will be confined to suppliers of financial services with whom it has distribution agreements.

Involuntary cross-selling. Retail clients may be pressured to acquire additional financial services on unfavorable terms in order to access a particular product, such as the purchase of credit insurance tied to consumer or mortgage loans. Or financial firms with discretionary authority over client accounts may substitute more profitable services such as low-interest deposit accounts for less profitable services such as higher-interest money market accounts, without explicit instructions from the client.

Churning. A financial firm that is managing assets for retail or private clients may exploit its agency relationship by engaging in excessive trading, which creates higher costs and may lead to portfolio suboptimization. Commission-based compensation is the usual cause of churning, which can also arise in institutional portfolios—average U.S. equity mutual fund turnover rose from 17 percent annually in the 1950s to almost 110 percent in the early 2000s.

Inappropriate margin lending. Clients may be encouraged to leverage their investment positions through margin loans from the firm, exposing them to potentially unsuitable levels of market risk and high credit costs. Broker incentives tied to stock margining usually underlie exploitation of this conflict of interest.

Failure to execute. Financial firms may fail to follow client instructions on market transactions if doing so benefits the firm. Or payments may be delayed to increase the float.

Misleading disclosure and reporting. Financial firms may be reluctant to report unfavorable investment performance to clients if doing so threatens to induce outflows of assets under management. Whereas a certain degree of puffery in asset management performance reviews is normal and expected, there is undoubtedly a "break-point" where it becomes exploitive if not fraudulent.

Violation of privacy. The complete and efficient use of internal information is central to the operation of financial services firms, including such functions as cross-selling and risk assessment. This may impinge on client privacy concerns or regulatory constraints on misuse of personal information, and raises conflict-of-interest issues that tend to be increasingly serious as the activity lines of a particular firm become broader.

4. Wholesale–Retail "Transition" Conflicts

Conflicts of interest between the *wholesale* and *retail* domains—characterized by very different information asymmetries—can be either Type 1 or Type 2, and sometimes both.

Suitability. A classic domain-transition conflict of interest exists between a firm's "promotional role" in raising capital for clients in the financial markets and its obligation to provide suitable investments for retail clients. Since the bulk of a firm's earnings usually come from capital-raising side, and given the information asymmetries that exist, exploiting such conflicts can have adverse consequences for retail investors.

Stuffing. A financial firm that is acting as an underwriter and is unable to place the securities in a public offering may seek to ameliorate its exposure to loss by allocating unwanted securities to accounts over which it has discretionary authority (Schotland, 1980). This conflict of interest is unlikely to be exploited in the case of closely monitored institutional portfolios in the wholesale domain. But in the absence of effective legal and regulatory safeguards, it could be a problem in the case of discretionary trust accounts in the retail domain.

Conflicted research. Analysts working for multifunctional financial firms wear several hats and are subject to multiple conflicts of interest. In such firms, the researcher may be required to: 1) provide unbiased information and interpretation to investors, both directly and through retail brokers and institutional sales forces; 2) assist in raising capital for clients in the securities origination and distribution process; 3) help in soliciting and supporting financial and strategic advisory activities centered in corporate finance departments; and 4) support various management and proprietary functions of the firm. These diverse roles are fundamentally incompatible, and raise intractable agency problems at the level of the individual analyst, the research function, the business unit, and the financial firm as a whole. The extent of this incompatibility has been reflected, for example, in the post-IPO performance of recommended stocks (Michaely and Womack, 1999), contradictory internal communications released in connection with regulatory investigations, evidence on researcher compensation, and the underlying economics of the equity research function in securities firms. Other evidence seems to suggest that efforts to exploit this conflict of interest are generally unsuccessful in terms of investment banking market share and profitability (Ljungqvist et al., 2003).

It is argued that equity research conflicts are among the most intractable. Researchers cannot serve the interests of buyers and sellers at the same time. No matter how strong the firewalls, as long as research is not profitable purely on the basis of the buy-side (for example, by subscription or pay-per-view), the conflict can only be constrained but never eliminated as long as sell-side functions are carried out by the same organization. And even if research is purchased from independent organizations, those organizations could face the same inherent conflicts if they expect to develop further business commissioned by their financial intermediary clients.

Market-timing and late-trading. Important clients tend to receive better service than others, in the financial services sector as in most others. When such discrimination materially damages one client segment to benefit another, however, a conflict of interest threshold may be breached and the financial firm's actions may be considered unethical or possibly illegal, with potentially serious consequences for the value of its franchise. Such cases came to light in 2003, involving both criminal fraud charges and civil settlements regarding "late trading" and "market timing" by hedge funds in the shares of mutual funds, shifting returns from ordinary investors to the hedge funds in exchange for other business solicited by the mutual fund managers involved.

Laddering. Banks involved in initial public offerings may allocate shares to institutional investors who agree to purchase additional shares in the secondary market, thereby promoting artificial prices intended to attract additional (usually retail) buyers who are unaware of these private commitments. A related conflict involves providing bank loans to support the price of a security in the aftermarket (Saunders, 1995).

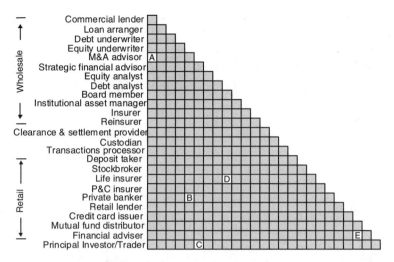

Figure 15.1: Indicative Financial Services Conflict Matrix

Shifting bankruptcy risk. A bank with credit exposure to a client whose bankruptcy risk has increased, to the private knowledge of the banker, may have an incentive to assist the corporation in issuing bonds or equities to the general public, with the proceeds used to pay-down the bank debt. Such behavior can also serve to redistribute wealth between different classes of bondholders and equity investors, and represents one of the "classic" conflicts of interest targeted by the 1933 separation of commercial and investment banking in the United States.

5. Conflicts of Interest and Strategic Profiles of Financial Firms

We posit that the broader the activity-range of financial firms in the presence of imperfect information 1) the greater the likelihood that the firm will encounter potential conflicts of interest; 2) the higher will be the potential agency costs facing clients; and 3) the more difficult and costly will be the internal and external safeguards necessary to prevent conflict exploitation. If true, competitive consequences associated with conflict-exploitation can offset the realization of economies of scope in financial services firms. Scope economies are intended to generate benefits on the demand side through cross-selling (revenue synergies) and on the supply side through more efficient use of the firm's business infrastructure (cost synergies). As a result of conflict exploitation the firm may initially enjoy revenue and profitability gains at the expense of clients. Subsequent adverse legal, regulatory, and reputational consequences—along with the managerial and operational cost of complexity—can be considered diseconomies of scope.

The potential for conflict-of-interest exploitation in financial firms can be depicted in a matrix such as figure 15.1. The matrix lists on each axis the main types of retail and wholesale financial services, as well as infrastructure services such as clearance, settlement, and custody. Cells in the matrix represent potential conflicts of interest. Some of these conflicts are basically intractable, and remediation may require changes in organizational structure. Others can be managed by appropriate changes in incentives, functional separation of business lines, or internal compliance initiatives. Still others may not be sufficiently serious to worry about. And in some cases it is difficult to imagine conflicts of interest arising at all.

For example, in figure 15.1 cell D is unlikely to encompass activities that pose serious conflicts of interest. Others cells, such as C, have traditionally been ring-fenced using internal compliance systems. Still others such as B and E can be handled by assuring adequate transparency. But there are some, such as A, which have created major difficulties in particular circumstances (such as advising on a hostile takeover when the target is a banking client), and for which easy answers seem elusive.

The foregoing discussion suggests that conflicts of interest are essentially two-dimensional—either between the interests of the firm and those of its client (Type 1), or between clients in conflict with one another (Type 2). They can also be multidimensional, however, spanning a number of different stakeholders and conflicts at the same time. This suggest that the broader the range of services that a financial firm provides to an individual client in the market, the greater the possibility that conflicts of interest will be compounded in any given case, and (arguably) the more likely they are to damage the market value of the financial firm's business franchise once they come to light.

6. Constraining Exploitation of Conflicts of Interest

From a public policy perspective, efforts to address exploitation of conflicts of interest in the financial services sector should logically focus on improving market efficiency and transparency. Compelling arguments have been made that regulation can materially improve the efficiency of financial systems. The greater the information asymmetries and transaction cost inefficiencies that exist (inefficiencies that are at the core of the conflict-of-interest issue), the greater is the potential gain from regulation that addresses these inefficiencies (Kane, 1987). In the United States, periodic efforts in this direction go back almost a century, often in response to perceived market abuses. A recent example is the Securities and Exchange Commission's Regulation FD (fair disclosure) of 1999, governing the flow of corporate information to the financial markets, with a clear potential for ameliorating certain conflicts of interest.

Nonetheless, the history of U.S. and other relatively well-developed financial markets chronicles a litany of conflict-of-interest exploitation involving all of the major bracket U.S. securities firms, four of the top six UK merchant banks (prior to their acquisition by larger financial firms), all of the major Japanese securities houses, as well as various commercial banks, asset managers, insurance companies, and financial conglomerates. So what is left of market imperfections and information asymmetries, even under intense competition and regulatory oversight, appears to allow plenty of scope for persistent conflict exploitation on the part of financial intermediaries. It suggests a continuing role for external control through firm-specific regulation and market discipline and internal control through improved corporate governance, incentive structures, and compliance initiatives.

If external regulatory constraints on conflict-of-interest exploitation are frequently politicized and difficult to devise, calibrate and bring to bear on specific problems without collateral damage, what is the alternative? As a general matter, it can be argued that regulatory constraints and litigation are relatively blunt instruments in dealing with exploitation of conflicts of interest in financial firms, conflicts that are often extremely granular and sometimes involve conduct that is "inappropriate" or "unethical" rather than "illegal." So the impact of conflict exploitation on the market value of a financial firm may provide a more consistent, incentive-compatible, and durable basis for firm-specific, internal defenses against exploitation of conflicts of interest. Here we shall argue that constraints on conflicts of interest that are rooted in market discipline can be substantially more cost-effective and surgical than constraints based on external regulation. Given the persistence of market inefficiencies and information asymmetries they can, acting in combination, have powerful deterrent effects on conflict of interest exploitation.

Revenues. Exploitation of conflicts of interest, whether or not they violate legal and regulatory constraints, can have a powerful effect on reputations, leading to revenue erosion as clients defect to competitors. In the case of Bankers Trust's 1995 exploitation of conflicts of interest in derivatives trading with Procter & Gamble Inc. and Gibson Greetings Inc., revenue losses from client defections dwarfed the $300 million in customer restitution the firm was forced to pay. It left the firm mortally wounded, subsequently to be acquired by Deutsche Bank AG in 1999. In the case of conflict-of-interest exploitation at Arthur Andersen in 2002, reputation losses and client defections virtually assured the liquidation of the firm well before its indictment and conviction on criminal charges. Less dramatically, Putnam Investments lost $14 billion in assets (out of $263 billion) in the week following disclosure of alleged late trading and market timing in its mutual funds.

Costs. Increased regulatory pressure and market impacts of conflict exploitation can jointly force the creation of a robust compliance infrastructure and other managerial safeguards that may reduce operating efficiency. This includes organizational changes and separation of functions that may impair realization of revenue economies of scope. Compliance itself is an expensive business in terms of direct outlays as well as separation of business units by "Chinese walls" or into distinct legal entities, which can erode operating efficiency. Also on the cost side is the impact of regulatory penalties in civil and criminal litigation and class action settlements.

Risks. The likelihood of exploitation of conflicts of interest and its consequences clearly is incorporated in the valuation of financial firms in the marketplace. A high degree of sensitivity to conflict exploitation and its revenue and cost impacts should be associated with greater earnings volatility and a lower share price, all else equal.

One can argue that regulation-based and market-based *external* controls, through the corporate governance process, create the basis for *internal* controls which can be either *prohibitive* (as reflected in Chinese walls and compliance systems, for example) or *affirmative*, involving the behavioral "tone" and incentives set by senior management together with reliance on the loyalty and professional conduct of employees. The more complex the financial services organization—perhaps most dramatically in the case of global financial services conglomerates, where comprehensive regulatory insight is implausible—the greater the challenge of sensible conflict-of-interest regulation, suggesting greater reliance on the role of market discipline. The logic runs as follows.

First, market discipline can leverage the effectiveness of regulatory actions. When they are announced—and especially when they are amplified through aggressive investigative reporting by independent media—regulatory actions can have a serious adverse effect on a financial firm's share price as well as its debt rating. In turn, this affects its cost of capital, its ability to make strategic acquisitions, its vulnerability to takeover, and management compensation. Such effects simply reflect the market's response to the prospective impact of regulatory actions on revenues, costs (including derivative civil litigation), and exposure to risk. Assuming appropriate corporate governance, boards and managements should be sensitive both to regulatory constraints and prospective market reactions with regard to exploitation of conflicts of interest. That is, they should be aware that violations of regulatory constraints designed to limit conflict-of-interest exploitation may be greatly amplified by market reactions—in the extreme including absorption by other firms, breakup, or bankruptcy. This awareness ought to be reflected in compensation arrangements as well as in the firm's organizational structure.

Second, even in the absence of explicit legal or regulatory constraints, actions that are widely considered to be "unfair" or "unethical" or that otherwise violate accepted behavioral norms will tend to trigger market discipline. In a competitive context, this will affect firm valuation through the revenue and risk dimensions in particular. Avoiding conflict-of-interest exploitation is likely to reinforce the value of the firm as a going concern and, with properly structured incentives, management's own compensation. In a firm well known for tying managers' remuneration closely to the share price, Citigroup chief executive officer Sanford Weill in 2002 noted in a message to employees, "There are industry practices that we should all be concerned about, and although we have found nothing illegal, looking back, we can see that certain of our activities do not reflect the way we believe business should be done. That should never be the case, and I'm sorry for that."

Third, since they tend to be more granular and provide constant reinforcement in metrics that managers can understand (market share, profitability, and the stock price) market discipline constraints can reach the more opaque areas of conflict-of-interest exploitation, and deal with those issues as they occur in real time, which external regulation normally cannot do.

Fourth, since external regulation bearing on conflicts of interest tends to be linked to information asymmetries and transaction costs, it should logically differentiate between the wholesale and retail domains, discussed earlier. Often this is not feasible, resulting in overregulation in some areas and underregulation in others. Market discipline-based constraints can help alleviate this problem by permitting lower overall levels of regulation and bridging fault-lines between wholesale and retain financial market domains. Few things are as reputation-sensitive as hawking the "risk-free" rump-ends of structured asset-backed securities deals—so-called toxic waste—to retirees in trailer homes trying to make ends meet. Moreover, just as market discipline can reinforce the effectiveness of regulation, it can also serve as a precursor of sensible regulatory change.

Finally, market structure and competition between strategic groups of financial firms can help reinforce the effectiveness of market discipline. For example, private information accessible to a bank as lender to a corporate acquisition target would almost certainly preclude its affiliated investment banking unit from acting as an adviser to a potential acquirer. An entrepreneur may not want his or her private banking affairs handled by a bank that also controls his or her business financing. A broker may be encouraged by a firm's compensation arrangements to sell in-house mutual funds or externally managed funds with high fees under "revenue sharing" arrangements, as opposed to funds that would better suit the client's needs. Market discipline that helps avoid exploitation of such conflicts may be weakened if most of the competition is coming from a monoculture of similarly structured firms which face precisely the same issues. But if the playing field is also populated by a mixed bag of aggressive insurance companies, commercial banks, thrifts, broker–dealers, fund managers, and other "monoline" specialists, market discipline may be much more effective—assuming competitors can break through the fog of asymmetric information.

7. Conclusions

Based on a taxonomy of potential conflicts of interest in financial services firms, how these conflicts relate to their strategic positioning, and the conditions that underlie their exploitation, we conclude that market discipline—though the reputation-effects on the franchise value of financial intermediaries—can be a powerful complement to and potential substitute for external regulation.

Market discipline is an often-overlooked sanction. It greatly reinforces regulatory mechanisms, particularly when there are too-big-to-fail considerations and constraints on criminal prosecution. In turn, it relies on a favorable legal framework, including controversial elements such as the Martin Act and class action litigation. Alongside measures to improve transparency and market efficiency, an important public policy objective is to make market discipline more effective, notably through better corporate governance and internal reward systems more closely aligned to the interests of shareholders. Still, "accidents" will continue to happen, sometimes repeatedly and sometimes repeatedly within the same firm. There is no panacea. Nirvana is too expensive.

*Ingo Walter is the Charles Simon Professor of Applied Financial Economics at the Stern School of Business, New York University.

References

Kane, Edward J., 1987, "Competitive financial reregulation: An international perspective," in *Threats to International Financial Stability*, R. Portes and A. Swoboda (eds.), Cambridge, UK: Cambridge University Press.

Ljungqvist, Alexander, Felicia Marston and William J. Wilhelm, 2003, "Competing for securities underwriting mandates: Banking relationships and analyst recommendations," New York University, Stern School of Business, Finance Department, working paper, May.

Michaely, Roni, and Kent Womack, 1999, "Conflict of interest and the credibility of underwriter analyst recommendations," *Review of Financial Studies*, Vol. 12, pp. 653-686.

Saunders, Anthony, 1985, "Conflicts of interest: An economic view," in *Deregulating Wall Street*, Ingo Walter (ed.), New York: John Wiley.

Schotland, R. A., 1980, *Abuse on Wall Street: Conflicts of Interest in the Securities Markets*, Westport, CT: Quantum Books.

Smith, Roy C., and Ingo Walter, 1997, *Street Smarts: Linking Professional Conduct and Shareholder Value in the Securities Industry*, Boston: Harvard Business School Press.

Walter, Ingo, 2003, "Conflicts of interest and market discipline among financial services firms," New York University, Stern School of Business, Department of Finance, working paper.

Chapter 16

Market Discipline and Corporate Control

Clifford W. Smith, Jr.*
University of Rochester

1. Introduction

The modern corporation can be viewed as a network of contracts: some are explicit, others implicit. The array of parties to these contracts—for instance, stockholders, managers, bondholders, and customers—have interests that sometimes are common but frequently are inconsistent. To control the resulting conflicts of interest, there is an extensive set of mechanisms. Among the most important are the organization's internal structures and policies; competition in product, labor, and capital markets (including mechanisms in the external market for corporate control); as well as external constraints imposed by laws and regulations.

Some of these control mechanisms are privately adopted within the firm and essentially are under the complete control of the firm's owners, the board of directors, and its managers. Other mechanisms that provide effective incentives and constraints operate largely externally—the firm's owners and managers can affect these mechanisms only indirectly. I array the major mechanisms in figure 16.1 with internal mechanisms at the top of this spectrum and external mechanisms at the bottom.

Among the more important internal mechanisms are the firm's choice of ownership, organizational, and financial structures. At the external end of this spectrum are legal/regulatory constraints. Other mechanisms lie somewhere between these extremes. For example, firms regularly engage external organizations to provide products and services that have the effect of providing certification or bonding of the firm's products, contracts, or information. For instance, employing a public accounting firm to audit the books and certify the firm's financial statements also subjects the firm's managers to periodic scrutiny and makes certain forms of malfeasance more likely to be detected. I now briefly review these major mechanisms and outline the roles they play in controlling these basic conflicts.

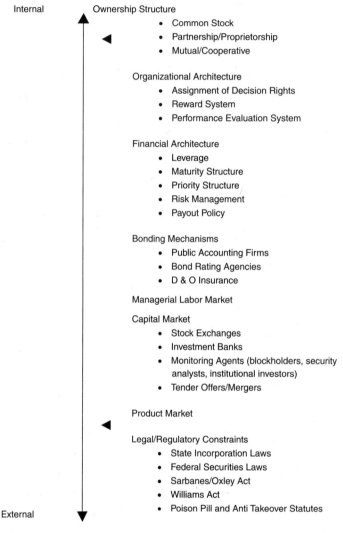

Figure 16.1: Spectrum of Corporate Control Mechanisms

2. Ownership Structure

One particularly important feature of the organization is the distribution of the residual profits. Organizations vary remarkably along this dimension. In a sole proprietorship, the owner/manager is the residual claimant. In a partnership, the claims are shared by the partners. In a large public corporation, these claims often are held by thousands of shareholders who take little direct interest in managing the company. In a mutual, ownership and customer claims are merged. In a cooperative, supplier and ownership claims are merged. In most of these large organizations, management authority is delegated to professional managers, who often have small (or no) ownership positions in the organization. At establishment, individuals have incentives to forecast potential conflicts within the organization and select the form of organization that maximizes expected total value.

Problems arise within organizations because of the separation of ownership and control. These problems are costly to resolve. Given these costs, there must be offsetting benefits that promote the prominence of organizations with substantial separation of ownership and control like large corporations. One of the most significant benefits is that capital is raised from many investors who share in the risk of the organization. Individual shareholders place only a small fraction of their wealth in a given company. Diversification lowers the cost at which risk-averse investors are willing to supply capital to corporations (see Fama and Jensen, 1983). This benefit, however, comes at the cost of having to control the incentive conflicts between managers and owners. Thus, in smaller operations, where raising large amounts of capital is less of an issue, one is more likely to find sole proprietorships, small partnerships, and closely held corporations where there is less separation of ownership and control.

3. Organizational Architecture

The practical implementation of any concept of corporate governance rests on the organizational underpinning of the firm. Fundamentally, I use the term organizational architecture to refer to three key elements of organizational design: the assignment of decision rights, the performance evaluation system, and the set of rewards offered to managers and employees (see Brickley, Smith, and Zimmerman, 2004).

A basic challenge in designing firms is to maximize the likelihood that decision-makers have both the relevant information to make good decisions as well as the incentives to use the information productively. The challenge of determining customer demands while reducing costs is complicated by the fact that important information for economic decision-making generally is dispersed among an array of different individuals within the firm. Furthermore, this information often is expensive to transfer. Communicating information is likely to be cumbersome—both texture and timelines are lost. Requiring that this information be transmitted to headquarters for approval before it can be acted upon would result in many lost opportunities. A second complication is that decision makers might not have appropriate incentives to make effective decisions even if they possess the relevant information—there are incentive problems.

A critical responsibility of the board of directors and senior management is to decide how to assign decision rights among employees of the firm. For instance, does the chief executive officer (CEO) make most major decisions or are decisions delegated to lower-level managers? Once a firm grows beyond a certain size, the CEO is unlikely to possess the relevant information for all major decisions. Consequently, the CEO faces three basic alternatives in designing organizational architecture: 1) make most major decisions, despite lacking relevant information, 2) attempt to acquire the relevant information to make better decisions, 3) decentralize decision rights to individuals with better information (see Jensen and Meckling, 1995, and Christie, Joye, and Watts, 2003). In the first case, incentive problems are limited and the development of a detailed control system is less critical. However without relevant information the CEO is likely to make suboptimal decisions. The second option can enhance decision-making. Yet obtaining and processing information can be both costly and time consuming. The third choice assigns decision-making authority to employees with the relevant information. Of course, CEOs can choose a mix of these basic alternatives; executives are likely to retain some decisions while delegating others. The optimal choice depends primarily on the business environment and strategy of the firm as well as the specific expertise of the CEO. For example, one potential drawback of decentralization is the costs of transferring information among the various decentralized decision-makers in coordinating efforts across the organization.

Through the delegation of decision rights, employees are granted authority over the use of company resources. Employees, however, are not owners. Thus, employees have fewer incentives to worry about the efficient use of company resources than do owners. To help control these incentive problems, managers develop control systems. That is, management structures the other two basic pieces of the organization's architecture, the reward and performance-evaluation systems that help to align the interests of the decision-makers with those of the owners. In the firm, an optimal control system depends on how decision rights are partitioned in the firm, and vice versa.

The structure of rewards within the firm is designed with at least two important objectives 1) to attract and retain qualified employees, and 2) to motivate employees to be more productive. All aspects of employment that reward employees for engaging in productive activities—including compensation promotions, titles, office location, perquisites, and layoffs—are components of the reward system.

Identifying employees that perform well or poorly requires a performance-evaluation system. Thus the firm's reward system uses as an input the firm's performance-evaluation system—the two systems are linked. The internal accounting system is at the center of most firms' performance evaluation systems; it is complemented by employee performance-review procedures.

Although the CEO and senior executives play a major role in framing the basic architecture for the firm, organizational decisions are made by managers throughout the organization. For example, when the CEO delegates a set of decisions rights to divisional managers, these managers must decide what decisions to make themselves and what decisions to delegate to their subordinates. These subordinates then are faced with similar organizational questions. The overall architecture of a firm is determined through this process, ultimately involving the board of directors as well as managers throughout the organization (see Brickley, Smith, and Zimmerman, 2004).

4. Financial Architecture

The structure of a firm's financial policies establishes important incentives. For high-growth firms, the underinvestment problem associated with heavy debt financing (see Myers, 1977) and the flotation costs of high dividends (see Easterbrook, 1984) make both policies potentially quite costly. But, for mature firms with limited growth opportunities, high leverage and dividends can have substantial benefits from controlling the free cash flow problem—the temptation of managers to over-invest in mature businesses or make diversifying acquisitions. (see Jensen, 1986). Moreover, companies with extensive investment opportunities can be expected to issue debt with shorter maturities, not only to protect lenders against the greater uncertainty associated with growth firms, but also to preserve their own financing flexibility and future ability to invest (see Barclay and Smith, 1995). Growth companies also are likely to choose private over public sources of debt because renegotiating a troubled loan with a banker (or a small group of private lenders) will generally be much easier than getting hundreds of widely dispersed bondholders to restructure the terms of a public bond issue. Effective firms insure that their financial architectures and organizational architectures are coordinated.

5. Bonding Mechanisms

Firms use reported accounting numbers in a variety of ways. For instance, they are employed in covenants in debt agreements (see Smith and Warner, 1979), in incentive compensation contracts (see Smith and Watts, 1982), and in union contracts. Long before the Securities and Exchange Commission, firms retained the services of public accounting firms to certify their accounting statements. By making the accounting numbers more credible, the numbers are more useful. And by reducing the risk of manipulation, the contract terms to which various parties to the firm—lenders, employees, investors—are willing agree are more favorable (see Watts, 1977, and DeAngelo, 1981).

Similarly, firms that raise capital in public capital markets regularly hire investment bankers to underwrite the security issues. A number of authors have argued that investment bankers are effective in monitoring aspects of the firm (see Rozeff, 1982, Easterbrook, 1984, and Smith, 1986). Such monitoring is quite valuable because of the material difference in access to information between managers and current shareholders as well as potential investors. Thus, in addition to a marketing function, the investment banker also performs a certification function analogous to that of public accounting firms, bond rating agencies (see Wakeman, 1981), or insurance companies (see Mayers and Smith, 1981). In each case, although the monitoring activity is expensive, it increases firm value because periodic exposure of the firm's decision makers to effective monitoring makes the terms under which external parties are willing to transact with the firm more favorable.

6. Product, Labor, and Capital Markets

The interplay of supply and demand in product, labor, and capital markets imposes important constraints on managerial decisions. Successful firms must offer products to customers at prices that cover costs. Thus, competition in the marketplace provides strong pressures for efficient decisions—including organizational decisions. Competition among firms in product markets dictates that only those firms with low costs survive. If firms adopt inefficient, high-cost policies—competition experts pressure on these firms to either adapt or close.

Given a firm's business strategy, its organizational decisions—including its governance decisions—can have an important impact on profitability and value. Appropriate organizational decisions can lower costs by promoting efficient production. Firms that experience governance problems raise questions among customers about production quality, delivery reliability, and service responsiveness. Thus, product prices can fall as a direct result of these problems. In addition, such firms regularly lose many valued employees and must increase compensation in order to keep others. What makes this problem particularly difficult is that the most productive employees frequently have the greatest external opportunities and thus would be among the first to leave. And in an organization where employees with longstanding working relationships are an important component of productivity, having several key individuals leave affects profitability not just in the short run, but over a longer period, as well.

Efficient capital markets rapidly and accurately process public information and reflect that information in security prices. Over time, this allocates more capital to firms with better crafted governance policies for they have fewer problems. Moreover by establishing well-bonded policies (for example, listing on the New York Stock Exchange with its more restrictive governance requirements), investors forecast fewer future problems and thus are willing to pay higher prices now.

Firms that access public capital markets regularly hire investment bankers to underwrite the issue. Although retaining a bulge-bracket investment banker is more expensive than having a rights offering, the certification provided by the investment banker—in effect renting the reputational capital of the investment bank for the transaction—provides a better-bonded transaction. Moreover, having shares traded in public capital markets subjects the firm's managers to monitoring by stock analysts, institutional investors, and other blockholders. Finally, if the difference between actual and potential market value becomes too great, a public firm can be the target of a hostile takeover in which a tender offer is made directly to the firm's owners.

7. Legal/Regulatory Constraints

Governance policies and mechanisms are constrained by various laws and regulations. For example, state incorporation laws, the federal securities laws, and the Sarbanes–Oxley Act stipulate certain shareholder rights, limit board composition and require disclosure of various policy choices. Most of these constraints impose a floor on various policy choices, for example, limiting the participation of non-independent directors on certain board committees. However, some legislation impeded the operation of the market for corporate control. For instance, the Williams Act prohibits certain quite effective terms in tender offers.

8. Conclusions

This analysis of corporate control mechanisms yields several implications: First, it is important to understand that each contracting party generally has incentives to resolve these conflicts in the least costly manner. By so doing, there are additional gains from trade to share among the parties. For instance, managers have incentives to increase a firm's profits because firms with inefficient managers can be taken over by other firms and the management team replaced. Also, inefficient firms eventually go out of business in a competitive market. Thus, incentives exist to negotiate contracts and adopt policies and procedures that provide monitoring and bonding activities to the point where their marginal cost equals the marginal gain from reducing the foregone value. This means that within the contracting process, incentives exist to produce an efficient utilization of resources.

Second, when the press reports a corporate control failure, in business meetings throughout the economy, managers and directors address three basic questions: 1) Is this problem occurring within my organization? 2) Can we do anything to reduce the likelihood of a similar future failure here? 3) Can we credibly convince external parties that such a failure is unlikely? Thus, the most rapid, effective, and flexible response to a corporate control failure comes from within the internal systems of the organization.

Third, corporate control mechanisms are an integrated system. Although critically important components of the system are established within the firms—ownership structure, organizational architecture (including board structure), and financial architecture—these choices are construed by external laws and regulations. The firm makes its labor, capital, and product choices mindful of the impact of its decisions on external markets. By voluntarily contracting with external parties and institutions—for instance, by retaining one of the four national public accounting firms or a major investment banker or listing on the New York Stock Exchange—it better bonds its governance activities and thus receives better terms as it contracts in these markets. Despite the widely reported governance failures of companies like Enron, Tyco, World Com, and Adelphia, tens of thousands of public firms have uniformly avoided such problems. Thus, I believe that these governance failures are so widely reported for the same reason that commercial aircraft crashes are—they are rare events.

Fourth, corporate governance failures (like most airplane crashes) are rarely associated with a single source of failure. Because there are so many layers in the process, failure generally requires a cascade of problems.

Fifth, regulation in this area imposes both compliance costs and opportunity costs. The compliance costs are more direct and have been discussed more extensively. But I believe they are the smaller and less important component. By regulating corporate control mechanisms, firms are limited in their ability to craft customized policies for their special circumstances. Since regulation rarely allows firms to contract around the legal requirements, such regulation imposes a one-size-fits-all solution on a diverse set of firms. Thus, even if 95 percent of firms would benefit from a ban on corporate loans to executives, for instance, that other 5 percent would bear costs. Moreover, such regulation reduces firm's ability to experiment with alternate governance mechanisms, thereby reducing the role of organizational innovation. This problem is insidious, specifically because this cost is extremely small at the time the regulation is adopted but can cumulate to an extraordinary size over time.

*Clifford W. Smith, Jr., is the Louise and Henry Epstein Professor of Business Administration in the William E. Simon Graduate School of Business Administration at the University of Rochester.

References

Barclay, M. J., and C. W. Smith, Jr., 1995, "The maturity structure of corporate debt," *Journal of Finance*, Vol. 50, No. 2, pp. 609–631.

Brickley, J. A., C. W. Smith, Jr., and J. L. Zimmerman, 2004, *Managerial Economics and Organizational Architecture*, third edition, Burr Ridge, IL: McGraw-Hill/Irwin.

Christie, A. A., M. P. Joye, and R. L. Watts, 2003, "Decentralization of the firm: Theory and evidence," *Journal of Corporate Finance*, Vol. 9, pp. 3–36.

DeAngelo, L. E., 1981, "Auditor independence, low balling, and disclosure regulation," *Journal of Accounting and Economics*, Vol. 3, pp. 113–127.

Easterbrook, F. H., 1984, "Two agency-cost explanations," *American Economic Review*, Vol. 74, pp. 650–659.

Fama, E. F., and M. C. Jensen, 1983, "Agency problems and residual claims," *Journal of Law and Economics*, Vol. 26, pp. 327–349.

Jensen, M. C., 1986, "Agency costs of free cash flows, corporate finance, and takeovers," *American Economic Review*, Vol. 76, pp. 323–329.

Jensen, M. C., and W. Meckling, 1995, "Specific and general knowledge and organizational structure," *Journal of Applied Corporate Finance*, Vol. 8, No. 2, pp. 4–18.

Mayers, D., and C. W. Smith, Jr., 1981, "Contractual provisions, organizational structure, and conflict control in insurance markets," *Journal of Business*, Vol. 54, No. 3, pp. 407–434.

Myers, S., 1977, "Determinants of corporate borrowing," *Journal of Financial Economics*, Vol. 4, pp. 147–176.

Rozeff, M. S., 1982, "Growth, beta, and agency costs as determinants of dividend payout ratios," *Journal of Financial Research*, Vol. 5, pp. 249–259.

Smith, C. W., Jr., 1986, "Investment banking and the capital acquisition process," *Journal of Financial Economics*, Vol. 15, pp. 3–29.

Smith, C. W., Jr., and J. B. Warner, 1979, "On financial contracting: An analysis of bond covenants," *Journal of Financial Economics*, Vol. 7, pp. 117–161.

Smith, C.W., Jr., and R. L. Watts, 1982, "Incentive and tax effects of executive compensation plans," *Australian Journal of Management*, Vol. 7, No. 2, pp. 139–157.

Wakeman, L. M., 1981, "The real function of bond rating agencies," *Chase Financial Quarterly*, Vol. 1, pp. 18–26.

Watts, R. L., 1977, "Corporate financial statements: A product of the market and political processes," *Australian Journal of Management*, Vol. 2, pp. 53–75.

PART V

EVIDENCE OF MARKET DISCIPLINE FOR COUNTRIES

Chapter 17

Capital Controls: Mud in the Wheels of Market Discipline

Kristin J. Forbes*
Council of Economic Advisers and Massachusetts Institute of Technology, Sloan School of Management

1. Introduction

In the early and mid-1990s, most international economists and Washington-based policymakers supported rapid capital account liberalization for emerging markets. Liberalization was expected to have widespread benefits. For example, it was predicted to increase capital inflows, thereby financing investment and raising growth. It could facilitate the diversification of risk, thereby reducing volatility in consumption and income. Liberalization could also increase market discipline, thereby leading to a more efficient allocation of capital and higher productivity growth. Many countries followed this advice and removed their capital account restrictions.

The initial results were generally positive—increased capital inflows, investment booms, and impressive growth performance. In the last decade, however, this positive view of capital account liberalization has been widely questioned. Several countries that had recently removed capital account restrictions, such as Mexico, Thailand, Korea, Russia, and Argentina, experienced severe financial crises. These experiences, especially when combined with the recent backlash against globalization, caused many people to question the benefits of unrestricted capital flows in emerging markets. Does capital account liberalization lead to inefficient investment and asset market bubbles? Could controls on capital flows have prevented these crises, or at least reduced their virulence? Even the International Monetary Fund (IMF), formerly the bastion of capital market liberalization, has cautiously begun to support certain capital controls, especially taxes on capital inflows.[1]

These concerns have been bolstered by the inconclusive macroeconomic evidence on the benefits of capital account liberalization and the costs of capital controls. Although there is an extensive literature on this subject (discussed in more detail in section 2), the lack of agreement across studies, methodologies, and data sources is remarkable. In a recent survey of capital account liberalization, Eichengreen (2002) summarizes his conclusions: "Capital account liberalization, it is fair to say, remains one of the most controversial and least understood policies of our day ... empirical analysis has failed to yield conclusive results." In a recent review of the empirical evidence on globalization, Prasad et al. (2003) conclude: "... if financial integration has a positive effect on growth, there is as yet no clear and robust empirical proof that the effect is quantitatively significant."

Many skeptics interpret these inconclusive macroeconomic results as evidence that the theoretical benefits of capital account liberalization may be elusive, possibly due to a range of market imperfections. A closer look at individual countries that have removed their capital controls, however, suggests that capital account liberalization may actually have substantial benefits, but these benefits are extremely difficult to measure at the macroeconomic level (especially in a cross-country framework). Most countries that remove their capital controls simultaneously undertake a range of additional reforms and undergo widespread structural changes, so that it is extremely difficult to isolate the specific impact of removing the controls. Accurately measuring one of the most important benefits of capital account liberalization—increased competition and market discipline that leads to a more efficient allocation of capital and higher productivity growth—is extremely complicated. Moreover, the benefits of removing capital controls may vary substantially across countries based on factors such as: their institutional development, the strength and depth of their financial system, and the quality of their corporate governance.

Instead, a potentially more promising way to assess the effect of capital account liberalization may be to focus on more detailed microeconomic evidence on how capital controls have generated specific distortions in individual countries. Several recent studies have adopted this approach, with much more conclusive results than the macroeconomic, cross-country studies. Johnson and Mitton (2002) show that the Malaysian capital controls provided a shelter for government cronyism and reduced market discipline. Forbes (2003) shows that the Chilean capital controls made it more difficult for smaller firms to obtain financing for productive investment. Desai et al. (2002) show that capital controls reduced the amount of foreign direct investment by U.S. multinationals and created additional distortions as U.S. companies attempted to evade the controls. Li et al. (2004) show that capital controls reduced market discipline and lowered the efficiency of stock market prices.

Although this literature examining the microeconomic effects of capital controls is only in its infancy, the combination of results is compelling. These papers use diverse methodologies to examine very different aspects of capital controls in a range of countries and time periods, yet each finds a consistent result; capital controls have significant economic costs and lead to a misallocation of resources. Even if it is difficult to capture these effects at the macroeconomic level during periods when countries undergo rapid structural reform, this misallocation of resources is bound to reduce productivity and potential growth rates. Tobin (1978) argued that a tax on currency transactions would act as "sand in the wheels" of international financial markets. In comparison, given this new microeconomic evidence that capital controls may lead to a misallocation of capital through a number of different channels, a more accurate rendition may be that capital controls are not just "sand," but rather "mud in the wheels of market discipline."

The remainder of this paper is as follows. Section 2 briefly reviews the inconclusive macroeconomic, empirical evidence on capital controls. Section 3 discusses, in more detail, several recent microeconomic studies showing how capital controls can cause "mud in the wheels of market discipline." Section 4 weighs these costs of capital controls relative to the potential benefit of reduced vulnerability to crises. Section 5 concludes.

2. The Inconclusive Macroeconomic Evidence on Capital Controls

The theoretical literature suggests that there are a number of potential benefits from capital account liberalization. Prasad et al. (2003) survey this literature and describe four direct benefits: the augmentation of domestic savings, a reduction in the cost of capital through better global allocation of risk, the transfer of technological and managerial know-how, and the stimulation of domestic financial sector development. It also describes three indirect benefits: the promotion of specialization, the commitment to better economic policies, and a signaling of friendlier policies for foreign investment in the future. Capital account liberalization, however, can also have important costs. For example, by increasing market discipline and integration with global financial markets, removing capital controls can increase a country's vulnerability to banking and currency crises. As seen in the 1990s, these crises can be severe and have substantial economic and social costs.

The macroeconomic literature, however, has had limited empirical success in consistently showing that capital account liberalization has any of these effects.[2] The most common testing approach has been to evaluate if reducing capital controls is correlated with higher economic growth. The contrasting results of the two most cited studies in this literature capture the general inconsistency. Rodrik (1998) finds no significant relationship between capital account openness and growth, while Quinn (1997) uses a different measure of capital account openness and finds a significant positive relationship. A recent evaluation of this literature by Prasad et al. (2003) yields the same inconclusive results. Figure 17.1 replicates a key graph of the paper. It shows no significant relationship between financial openness and the growth in real per capita income across countries—even after controlling for a series of the standard variables in this literature.[3] In fact, of the 14 recent studies on this subject surveyed in Prasad et al. (2003), 3 find a positive effect of financial integration on growth, 4 find no effect, and 7 find mixed results.

There are a number of possible explanations for these conflicting results and lack of consensus. First, it is extremely difficult to accurately measure capital account openness. Simple empirical statistics measuring policies and regulations can not accurately capture the complexity and effectiveness of liberalization. De facto measures of integration (such as capital flows or foreign asset holdings) are also problematic, since some countries with large capital inflows still maintain relatively strict capital controls (such as China), while other countries with relatively unrestricted capital accounts receive fairly little foreign capital (such as many African

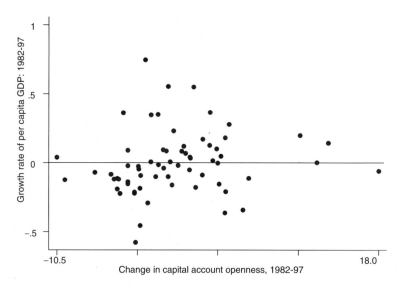

Notes: Growth is measured by growth in real per capita gross domestic product (GDP). Conditioning variables are: initial income, initial schooling, average investment/GDP, political instability, and regional dummies
Source: Prasad et al. (2003).

Figure 17.1: Conditional Relationship between Financial Openness and Growth, 1982–97

nations). Second, different types of capital flows and capital controls may have different effects. For example, recent work suggests that the benefits of foreign direct investment to growth may be greater than those of portfolio flows. Controls on capital inflows may be less harmful since they can be viewed as a form of prudential regulation, while controls on capital outflows may be interpreted as a lack of government commitment to sound policies and/or a lack of attractive domestic investment opportunities.

Third, the impact of removing capital controls could depend on a range of other, hard-to-measure factors. For example, recent work suggests that countries are more likely to benefit from capital account liberalization if they have stronger institutions, better corporate governance, and more effective prudential regulation. Fourth, the sequence in which different types of capital controls are removed may determine the aggregate impact. For example, lifting restrictions on offshore bank borrowing before freeing other sectors of the capital account may increase the vulnerability of a country's banking system (as seen in Korea in the mid-1990s). Finally, there may be "threshold effects" that are difficult to capture in linear regressions. More specifically, countries may need to attain a certain level of financial market integration or of overall economic development before attaining substantial benefits from lifting capital controls.

Despite these imposing challenges to measuring the cross-country impact of capital account liberalization, several papers have focused on narrower aspects of this issue and generated more conclusive and promising results. For example, recent work shows that stock market liberalizations in emerging markets lead to increased investment and a lower cost of capital.[4] Other recent work suggests that the impact of capital account liberalization is closely related to the quality of governance and institutions.[5] Given the numerous channels by which capital account liberalization could affect an economy, it is not surprising that focusing on particular aspects of this relationship can yield more conclusive results. Further narrowing the investigation to specific countries and experiences with capital controls may be even more productive.

3. Mud in the Wheels: Microeconomic Evidence of the Distortions from Capital Controls

Given these myriad difficulties in assessing the impact of capital account liberalization, potentially even more promising than the approaches used in these cross-country studies is to focus on the microeconomic impact within specific countries. Although case studies inherently have the shortcoming that it is difficult to control for other events that occur simultaneously, this approach can avoid many of the problems (discussed above) with the macroeconomic, cross-country literature. Moreover, this approach can facilitate a much more detailed measurement of exactly how capital account liberalization affects the allocation of resources and creates specific market distortions. The next four subsections discuss recent studies that have used very different methodologies to examine specific microeconomic effects of capital controls. Despite the range of experiences and approaches, each clearly identifies a significant cost of capital controls. The accumulation of these costs and distortions suggests that capital controls may act as "mud in the wheels of market discipline."

3.1 Protection for Cronyism in Malaysia

In September of 1998, soon after the peak of the Asian crisis, Malaysia imposed controls on capital outflows. Some predicted dire effects, such as scaring foreigners from investing and doing business in Malaysia for years. Others predicted that the capital controls would have the benefit of giving the Malaysian government "breathing room" to enact reforms that would facilitate recovery and raise long-run growth. A few years later, two papers (presented at the same conference) used macroeconomic data to assess the impact of these capital controls. Kaplan and Rodrik (2002) argued that the capital controls had positive macroeconomic effects, while Dornbusch (2002) argued that they had no significant effect. These contradictory views of one specific country's experience with capital controls mirrors the disagreements in the broader macroeconomic literature.

Johnson and Mitton (2002), however, use a very different, microeconomic approach to analyze the impact of the Malaysian capital controls. It examines how the Asian crisis and the announcement of the capital controls affected stock returns for individual Malaysian companies. The analysis splits the sample of firms into those with political connections to senior government officials (such as Prime Minister Mahatir), and those without political connections. The paper finds that in the initial phase of the crisis, before the capital controls were enacted, politically connected firms experienced a greater loss in market value than firms without political connections. When the controls were put into place, politically connected firms experienced a relatively greater increase in market value. These results suggest that the Asian crisis initially increased financial pressures on Malaysian firms, improving market discipline and reducing the ability of governments to provide subsidies for favored firms. When the capital controls were put into place, however, investors expected that the Malaysian government would have more freedom to help favored firms and engage in cronyism. In other words, the capital controls reduced market discipline and provided a shelter for government cronyism.

Moreover, the empirical estimates in Johnson and Mitton (2002) suggest that this cost of the Malaysian capital controls was substantial. In the initial phase of the crisis (from July 1997 to August 1998), politically connected firms lost about $5.7 billion in market value due to the fall in the expected value of their connections. When the controls were enacted in September 1998 (and market values were substantially lower), politically connected firms gained about $1.3 billion in market value due to the increased value of their connections. Another calculation indicates that at the end of September 1998, after the capital controls had reduced market discipline, political connections were worth about 17 percent of the total market value for connected firms.

3.2 Increased Financial Constraints for Smaller, Publicly Traded Firms in Chile

Another well-known example of capital controls is the encaje, a tax on capital inflows adopted by Chile from 1991 through 1998. An extensive literature has examined the macroeconomic effect of these capital controls, with a range of results.[6] For example, some papers argue that the controls reduced country vulnerability to external shocks, while others claim that they had no effect on vulnerability. There is somewhat more agreement (albeit not unanimous) that the controls lengthened the maturity of capital inflows, with no significant effect on their volume. Assessing the macroeconomic impact of the capital controls is complicated by Chile's rapid growth, ambitious economic reforms, and sound policy environment during this period. Despite these difficulties, however, there is fairly widespread agreement that the encaje generated some small economic benefits for Chile, with minimal economic costs. This assessment has prompted a number of countries to consider enacting similar controls on capital inflows.

A closer look at the microeconomic evidence, and especially how these capital controls impacted different types of firms, however, suggests that this assessment is overly optimistic. Forbes (2003) examines how the encaje affected investment and financial constraints for different types of publicly traded firms in Chile. The results show that the capital controls generated a number of distortions—such as an increase in companies listing abroad through American depository receipts (ADRs) in order to avoid the tax. Most important, an extensive empirical analysis indicates that the encaje significantly increased financial constraints for smaller, publicly traded companies, but not for larger firms. In other words, the capital controls made it relatively more

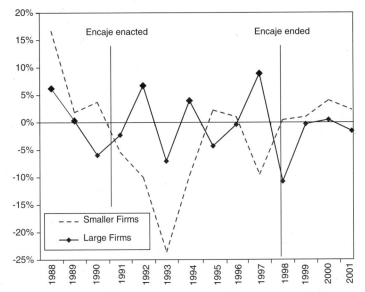

Source: Forbes (2003).

Figure 17.2: Growth in Investment/Capital Ratios for Chilean Firms

difficult and expensive for smaller companies to raise financing. Figure 17.2 (replicated from the paper) shows investment growth for publicly traded Chilean firms around the time of the capital controls, without controlling for all the variables in the more formal empirical analysis. Investment growth was higher for smaller firms both before and after the encaje (which is a standard result in the finance literature). During the period that the capital controls were in place, however, investment growth plummeted for smaller companies and was generally lower than for large companies.

Therefore, the results in Forbes (2003) suggest that capital controls may have created a number of microeconomic distortions in Chile, such as making it more difficult for smaller companies to obtain financing for productive investment.[7] This inefficient allocation of capital and resources undoubtedly reduced productivity and growth in Chile. These costs of capital controls could be particularly important for emerging markets in which small and new firms are often important sources of job creation and economic growth.

3.3 Reduced Investment and Distortionary Behavior by U.S. Multinationals
While the previous two subsections discuss the microeconomic effects of capital controls on domestic firms, another potentially important impact of capital controls is on foreign investment. Theory suggests that foreign investment can bring numerous benefits to host countries, such as increasing the capital stock and transferring technology and skills, all of which would raise investment, productivity, and growth.

Desai et al. (2002) attempt to measure the effect of capital account liberalization on foreign direct investment by examining the behavior of U.S. multinational firms in countries with and without capital controls. It shows that capital controls distort the asset allocation, financing, transfer pricing, and divided policies of U.S. multinationals. For example, capital controls in host countries reduce investment by multinationals by roughly 20 percent, and U.S. firms operating in countries with capital controls tend to overinvest in physical assets and underinvest (by as much as 40 percent) in financial assets. The paper also shows that when countries liberalize their capital accounts, these distortions tend to be reversed. For example, capital account liberalization is associated with large increases in multinational investment, particularly in local financial assets.

Moreover, Desai et al (2002) show that capital controls can cause U.S. multinational affiliates to distort prices in order to circumvent the controls. More specifically, foreign affiliates adjust prices by which they "trade" with their U.S. parents so that they run "trade deficits" about 4 percent to 6 percent larger than in countries without capital controls. The magnitude of this distortion is comparable to that which would occur if the foreign country raised taxes by about 20 percent to 50 percent. Therefore, this paper suggests that not only will capital controls distort the amount and type of foreign direct investment available to host countries, but they can also generate additional distortions as companies attempt to evade the controls and extract profits.

3.4 Reduced Efficiency in Stock Market Pricing

Capital controls may not only distort the behavior of multinational affiliates and locally owned companies, but can also affect the efficiency of domestic equity markets by reducing competitive pressure, market discipline, and the information content of stock prices. More specifically, by making it more difficult for foreigners to invest in domestic stock markets, capital controls could limit this valuable source of information and liquidity. As discussed above in the context of Malaysia, capital controls can insulate markets and reduce market discipline by providing a shelter for cronyism and other non-competitive activities. Capital controls might also limit the ability of potentially successful companies to raise additional financing, thereby restraining their ability to invest and grow.

Li et al. (2004) examine the extent to which individual stock prices move up and down together in specific countries—that is, "synchronicity"—to attempt to measure some of these effects. High levels of comovement and low levels of firm-specific variation in prices suggest that stock prices are less efficient. In other words, when stock prices are driven more by aggregate, country-level news instead of by firm-specific variables and information, there is less market discipline. This paper uses several different measures to show that greater openness in capital markets (but not in goods markets) is correlated with greater firm-specific content in stock prices, and therefore with more market discipline and pricing efficiency. This relationship is magnified in countries with strong institutions and good governance.

One set of results, although not a focus of Li et al. (2004), is particularly relevant to this assessment of the relationship between capital controls and market discipline.[8] Around the time of the Asian crisis, the firm-specific variation in stock prices increased significantly in most Asian countries and remained high for an extended period. This pattern is graphed for Korea in figure 17.3, and is typical for most open economies in the region. In Malaysia, the firm-specific component of stock prices also increased significantly after the Asian crisis, but then fell sharply after its capital controls were imposed (as also shown on figure 17.3). Although not a definitive test, this indicates that the Asian crisis increased market discipline and the firm-specific content in stock prices, while the Malaysian capital controls appear to have suppressed market discipline and reduced the efficiency of stock market prices.

4. But … Can Capital Controls Reduce Vulnerability to Crises?

The four studies discussed above suggest that capital controls can create a number of microeconomic distortions and therefore reduce productivity and growth. Despite these potentially serious costs, supporters of capital controls argue that this policy can yield benefits that outweigh these costs. The most frequently cited benefit is that capital controls reduce country vulnerability to currency and banking crises. The series of emerging markets that liberalized their capital accounts, and subsequently experienced a crisis in the 1990s, is often cited to support this argument. Capital controls, by placing "mud in the wheels of market discipline" may render countries less vulnerable to external shocks and therefore reduce their susceptibility to crises.

This is not surprising since capital controls share many similarities to most standard regulations—such as labor market regulations that make it more difficult to fire workers. Regulations on both capital flows and labor markets can create safer, less volatile markets, whether in the form of more stable capital flows or workers less likely to lose their jobs. Both regulations also have a cost, however, whether in the form of lower levels of investment or lower aggregate employment, both of which

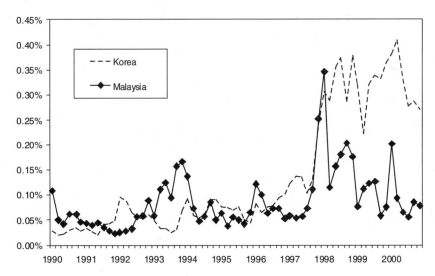

Note: Higher levels of firm-specific variation in stock prices indicate greater pricing efficiency.
Source: Based on data from Li et al. (2004).

Figure 17.3: Firm-Specific Variation in Stock Prices

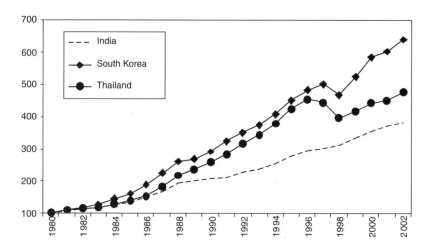

Note: Income per capita is gross domestic product per capita in international dollars, adjusted for PPP.
Source: Original data from World Bank, World Development Indicators, available at http://
www.worldbank.org/data/.

Figure 17.4: Income per Capita in Select Asian Countries, Normalized to 100 in 1980

reduce efficiency and economic growth. To evaluate the overall desirability of a specific regulation, it is necessary to weigh the costs against the benefits. Therefore, any
accurate evaluation of capital controls needs to weigh the potential costs discussed
throughout this paper against the potential benefit of reduced vulnerability to crises.

A thorough evaluation of this trade-off is beyond the scope of this paper, but figure
17.4 provides some anecdotal evidence. The figure graphs an index of real income per
capita (adjusted for purchasing power parity—PPP) in India, Korea, and Thailand from
1980 through 2002.[9] Income is normalized to 100 in 1980 in order to equalize income
levels at the start of the period. All countries maintained fairly stringent capital controls
in 1980, but then Korea and later Thailand began to liberalize their capital accounts in
the late 1980s and early 1990s. Growth increased as capital flowed into Korea and
Thailand and investment boomed. In 1997, however, both Korea and Thailand experienced severe financial crises. Between 1997 and 1998, income per capita fell by about
7 percent in Korea and 12 percent in Thailand. India, which maintained fairly stringent
capital controls throughout this period, actually had a small increase in income per
capita and emerged relatively unscathed from the Asian crisis.

Despite the crisis, however, Korea and Thailand still have substantially higher
income levels than India on the graph—even after correcting for initial income levels
in 1980. The figure suggests that in Korea, the Asian crisis was only a short-term
deviation from a higher long-term growth rate. Despite the plunge in income during
the crisis, the rapid recovery almost compensated for growth lost during the crisis. As
a result, Korean income per capita is now close to where it would have been if growth
had continued at trend and was not interrupted by the crisis. Granted, Thailand has

been slower to recover from the Asian crisis, and income per capita did not recover to its pre-crisis levels until 2001. Despite this severe crisis and prolonged recovery, however, average income levels in Thailand are still substantially higher than in India—despite starting at the same normalized level in 1980. All in all, the graph indicates that although crises can have severe economic costs, the short-term impact on income levels may be small compared to the long-term benefits of higher growth rates.

Granted, even if countries with open capital accounts tend to grow faster, on average, than countries with capital controls, some individuals and governments may still chose to restrict capital flows and reduce the chance of disruptive crises. This is similar to some countries' preferences for more regulated labor markets and greater job stability, even at the cost of higher unemployment and lower economic growth. In the case of capital account liberalization, however, this trade-off is less clear. Although recent experience suggests that emerging markets with liberalized capital accounts have recently been more vulnerable to crises, the empirical evidence is less definitive. In fact, Glick and Hutchinson (2000) find a positive—instead of negative—correlation between capital controls and the occurrence of currency crises in both a bivariate and multivariate analysis.

A closer look at the case study evidence suggests that this empirical evidence of a positive relationship between capital controls and crises is not surprising. Countries with macroeconomic imbalances (and which are therefore more vulnerable to crises), may choose to impose capital controls in order to avoid difficult economic reforms, or to avoid capital outflows that may trigger a crisis. Developed countries, or emerging markets with sound macroeconomic environments, are not only less likely to experience crises, but also less likely to enact capital controls and forego the benefits of free capital flows. Countries with closed capital accounts can still experience domestic financial crises and banking crises. Therefore, although capital account liberalization may increase country vulnerability to crises in some cases, the relationship between capital controls and financial crises is not straightforward.

5. Conclusions

Although the theoretical literature suggests that there could be substantial benefits to emerging markets from capital account liberalization, the empirical macroeconomic literature has had limited success in consistently identifying these benefits. There are a series of compelling reasons why it may be difficult to measure the aggregate impact of capital controls in a range of very different countries that often undergo a variety of structural changes simultaneously with liberalization. A more useful approach may be to focus on more narrow empirical analyses that can measure the specific effects of capital account liberalization at the microeconomic level.

The series of papers surveyed above indicates that focusing on microeconomic data, and especially individual case studies of specific effects of capital controls, yields much stronger evidence of the resulting economic distortions and costs. The Malaysian capital controls provided a shield for crony capitalism. The Chilean capital controls increased financial constraints and limited investment in smaller, publicly traded companies. U.S. firms tend to reduce investment and adopt a range of distortionary practices in countries with capital controls. Stock market pricing tends to be less efficient in countries with capital controls. Even though none of these papers attempts to aggregate these microeconomic effects into estimates of an economy-wide cost of capital controls, they clearly suggest that capital controls can lead to a misallocation of resources through several different channels. The accumulation of these different costs of capital controls indicates that they may act as "mud in the wheels of market discipline" and significantly depress productivity and growth.

Potentially offsetting these costs, capital controls may have the benefit of reducing country vulnerability to currency and banking crises. Although the short-term impact of crises on income levels can be severe, this effect is generally small when compared to the long-term benefits of higher growth rates possible with liberalized capital accounts. Moreover, the benefits of capital account liberalization may be smaller, while the risk of severe crises may be greater, for countries with weak institutions and poor corporate governance.

Mud in the wheels of a cart will slow down movement toward your destination. If mud in the wheels also weighs down the cart, minimizing the chance of the cart being overturned, some people may choose the weighted-down, slower vehicle. Moreover, if the cart has a weak frame and the wheels are only held together by the dried mud, it may be prudent to strengthen the wheels and ensure that a minimum frame is in place before removing the mud and moving rapidly. Given a certain level of structural integrity in the cart, however, most people would probably chose to take the mud out of the wheels, even if it slightly increases the risk of a spill, in order to more quickly arrive at their destination. Similarly, capital controls act as "mud in the wheels of market discipline." They create a number of microeconomic distortions and inefficiencies that can substantially reduce long-term growth rates. Capital account liberalization may increase the risk of crises, especially for countries with weak institutions, but can also substantially raise productivity growth and overall standards of living.

*Kristin J. Forbes is a member of the President's Council of Economic Advisers. She is on leave from the Massachusetts Institute of Technology's Sloan School of Management, where she is the Mitsubishi Career Development Chair and associate professor of international management.

Notes

1. For example, Fischer (2002), the former First Deputy Managing Director of the IMF, writes: "The IMF has cautiously supported the use of market-based capital inflow controls, Chilean style." Eduardo Aninat, a Deputy Managing Director of the IMF, recently stated: "… in some circumstances, these controls on capital inflows can play a role in reducing vulnerability created by short-term flows. …" (Druckerman, 2002).

2. For excellent surveys of this literature, see Eichengreen (2002) or Prasad et al. (2003).

3. The control variables include: initial income, initial schooling, average investment/gross domestic product, political instability, and regional dummies.

4. For example, see Henry (2000) and Bekaert and Harvey (2000).

5. For example, see Klein (2003) and Gelos and Wei (2002).

6. Simone and Sorsa (1999) is an excellent survey of the empirical literature on the Chilean capital controls.

7. Recent work by Gallego and Hernández (2002) also shows that the Chilean capital controls affected a range of firm-level variables, with differential effects on small and large companies.

8. These results were removed from the published version of the paper but are available in the working paper.

9. I do not include China on this graph, since it is not a clear case of an open or closed capital account over this period. Although China maintains some strict capital controls—such as on capital outflows—it has also substantially liberalized restrictions on other capital movements—such as on inflows of foreign

References

Bekaert, Geert, and Campbell Harvey, 2000, "Foreign speculators and emerging equity markets," *Journal of Finance,* Vol. 55, April, pp. 565–614.

Desai, Mihir, C. Fritz Foley, and James Hines, 2002, "Capital controls, liberalizations, and foreign direct investment," Harvard Business School and University of Michigan, working paper.

Dornbusch, Rudiger, 2002, "Malaysia's crisis: Was it different?," in *Preventing Currency Crises in Emerging Markets*, Sebastian Edwards and Jeffrey Frankel (eds.), Chicago: University of Chicago Press.

Druckerman, Pamela, 2002, "Some warm to use of capital controls," *Wall Street Journal,* October 24.

Eichengreen, Barry, 2002, "Capital account liberalization: What do cross-country studies tell us?," *The World Bank Economic Review,* Vol. 15, No. 3, pp. 341–365.

Fischer, Stanley, 2002, "Financial crises and reform of the international financial system," National Bureau of Economic Research, working paper, No. 9267.

Forbes, Kristin, 2003, "One cost of the Chilean capital controls: Increased financial constraints for smaller traded firms," National Bureau of Economic Research, working paper, No. 9777.

Gallego, Francisco, and Leonardo Hernández, 2002, "Microeconomic effects of capital controls: The Chilean experience during the 1990s," Massachusetts Institute of Technology and Central Bank of Chile, working paper.

Gelos, Gaston, and Shang-Jin Wei, 2002, "Transparency and international investor behavior," National Bureau of Economic Research, working paper, No. 9260.

Glick, Reuven, and Michael Hutchinson, 2000, "Stopping 'hot money' or signaling bad policy? Capital controls and the onset of currency crises," Federal Reserve Bank of San Francisco and University of California, Santa Cruz, working paper.

Henry, Peter, 2000, "Do stock market liberalizations cause investment booms?," *Journal of Financial Economics,* Vol. 58, October, pp. 301–334.

Johnson, Simon, and Todd Mitton, 2002, "Cronyism and capital controls: Evidence from Malaysia," *Journal of Financial Economics,* Vol. 67, February, pp. 351–382.

Kaplan, Ethan, and Dani Rodrik, 2002, "Did the Malaysian capital controls work?," in *Preventing Currency Crises in Emerging Markets,* Sebastian Edwards and Jeffrey Frankel (eds.), Chicago: University of Chicago Press.

Klein, Michael, 2003, "Capital account openness and the varieties of growth experience," National Bureau of Economic Research, working paper, No. 9500.

Li, Kan, Randall Morck, Fan Yang, and Bernard Yeung, 2004, "Firm-specific variation and openness in emerging markets," *Review of Economics and Statistics,* forthcoming.

Prasad, Eswar, Kenneth Rogoff, Shang-Jin Wei, and M. Ayhan Kose, 2003, "Effects of financial globalization on developing countries: Some empirical evidence," International Monetary Fund, occasional paper, No. 220.

Quinn, Dennis, 1997, "The correlates of changes in international financial regulation," *American Political Science Review,* Vol. 91, September, pp. 531–551.

Rodrik, Dani, 1998, "Who needs capital-account convertibility?," in *Should the IMF Pursue Capital Account Convertibility?,* Peter Kenen (ed.), *Essays in International Finance,* No. 207, Princeton: Princeton University Press.

Simone, Francisco Nadal De, and Piritta Sorsa, 1999, "A review of capital account restrictions in Chile in the 1990s," International Monetary Fund, working paper, No. 99/52.

Tobin, James, 1978, "A proposal for international monetary reform," *Eastern Economic Journal,* Vol. 4, July/October, pp. 153–159.

Chapter 18

Equity Integration in Times of Crisis

Robert P. Flood*
International Monetary Fund

and

Andrew K. Rose
University of California, Berkeley

The objective of this paper is to implement an intuitive and simple-to-use measure of asset-market integration on stock market data. In particular, we are interested in asking whether equity market performance is affected by financial crises. We examine two important financial crises: the aftermath of Russia/Long-Term Capital Management in the autumn of 1998, and the Asian crisis in late 1997. In both cases, we find that stock market integration is adversely affected by the crisis, but only temporarily.

1. Defining the Problem

What does *asset-market integration* mean? We adopt the view that financial markets are integrated when assets are priced by the same stochastic discount rate. More precisely, we define security markets to be integrated if all assets priced on those markets satisfy the pricing condition:

$$1) \qquad p_t^j = E_t(m_{t+1} x_{t+1}^j),$$

where: p_t^j is the price at time t of asset j, $E_t()$ is the expectations operator conditional on information available at t, m_{t+1} is the intertemporal marginal rate of substitution (MRS), for income accruing in period $t + 1$ (also interchangeably known as the discount rate, stochastic discount factor, marginal utility growth, pricing kernel, and zero-beta return), and x_{t+1}^j is income received at $t + 1$ by owners of asset j at time t (the future value of the asset plus any dividends or coupons). We rely only on this standard and general intertemporal model of asset valuation; to our knowledge this Euler equation is present in all equilibrium asset-pricing models.

Our object of interest in this study is m_{t+1}, the marginal rate of substitution, or, more precisely, estimates of the *expected* marginal rate of substitution, $E_t m_{t+1}$ The MRS is the unobservable DNA of intertemporal decisions; characterizing its distribution is a central task of economics and finance. The discount rate ties pricing in a huge variety of asset markets to peoples' saving and investment decisions. The thrust of this paper is to use asset prices and payoffs to characterize important aspects of its distribution. We are especially interested in whether the properties of the MRS are systematically different during periods of financial turbulence.

The substantive point of equation 1 is that all assets share the same marginal rate of substitution. There is no asset-specific MRS in an integrated market (indeed, that's our definition of a "market"), and no market-specific MRS when markets are integrated with each other. Learning more about the MRS is of intrinsic interest, and has driven much research (for example, Hansen and Jagannathan, 1991, who focus on second moments). Measures of the expected MRS also lead naturally to an intuitive test for integration. In this paper, we use a simple test for the equality of $E_t m_{t+1}$ across sets of assets. This is a necessary (but not sufficient) condition for market integration. We focus in particular on whether market integration varies systematically between periods of market tranquility and crisis.

2. Methodology

We use the fact that in a well-functioning integrated market, the MRS prices all assets held by the marginal asset holder. Indeed what we *mean* by asset market integration is that the same MRS prices all the assets. In other words, if we could extract m_{t+1} (or rather, its expectation) independently from a number of different asset markets, *they should all be the same if those markets are integrated.* As Hansen and Jagannathan (1991) show, there may be many stochastic discount factors consistent with any set of market prices and payoffs; hence our focus on the *expectation* of MRS, which is unique.

Consider a generic identity related to equation

2) $$p_t^j = E_t(m_{t+1} x_{t+1}^j) = COV_t(m_{t+1}, x_{t+1}^j) + E_t(m_{t+1})E_t(x_{t+1}^j),$$

where $COV_t()$ denotes the conditional covariance operator. It is useful to rewrite this as

3) $$x_{t+1}^j = -[1/E_t(m_{t+1})]COV_t(m_{t+1}, x_{t+1}^j) + [1/E_t(m_{t+1})]p_t^j + \varepsilon_{t+1}^j,$$
$$x_{t+1}^j = \delta_t(p_t^j - COV_t(m_{t+1}, x_{t+1}^j)) + \varepsilon_{t+1}^j,$$

where $\delta_t \equiv 1/E(m_{t+1})$ and $\varepsilon_{t+1}^j \equiv x_{t+1}^j - E_t(x_{t+1}^j)$, a prediction error.

We then impose two restrictions:

1) *Rational expectations*: ε_{t+1}^j is assumed to be white noise, uncorrelated with information available at time t, and

2) *Covariance model*: $COV_t(m_{t+1}, x_{t+1}^j) = \beta_0^j + \Sigma_i \beta_i^j f_{i,t}$, for the relevant sample,

where: β_0^j is an asset-specific intercept, β_0^j is a set of I asset-specific factor coefficients and $f_{i,t}$ a vector of time-varying factors.

With our two assumptions, equation 3 becomes a panel-estimating equation. We exploit *cross-sectional* variation to estimate (δ), the coefficients of interest that represent the expected risk-free return and are time varying but common to all assets. These estimates of the MRS are the focus of our study. We use *time-series* variation to estimate the asset-specific "fixed effects" and factor loadings (β), coefficients that are constant across time. Intuitively, these coefficients are used to account for asset-specific systematic risk (the covariances).

Estimating equation 3 for a set of assets $j = 1, \ldots, J_0$ and then repeating the analysis for the same period of time with a different set of assets $j = 1, \ldots, J_1$ gives us two sets of estimates of (δ), a time-series sequence of estimated discount rates. These can be compared directly, using conventional statistical techniques, either one by one, or jointly. Under the null hypothesis of market integration, the two sets of (δ) coefficients are equal. We choose our data to focus on periods of time where integration may be expected to break down, that is, periods of financial stress.

3. Discussion of the Technique

We make only two assumptions. Both are conventional in the literature, though most of the entire field uses stronger versions of them. While both assumptions can reasonably be characterized as "mild" in the area, it is worthwhile to elaborate on them further.

It seems unremarkable to assume that expectations are rational for financial markets, at least in the very limited sense above. We simply assume that asset-pricing errors are not *ex ante* predictable at high frequencies. This seems eminently reasonable, even during periods of crisis.

The more controversial assumption is that the asset-specific covariances (of payoffs with the MRS) are either constant or depend on a small number of factors. Nevertheless, this is certainly standard practice. Rather than develop our own factor model, we start our analysis by relying on the well-known three-factor model famously deployed by Fama and French (1996). (For our Asian empirics, we use a model with two asset-specific effects; an intercept and a time-varying factor suggested by the famous capital asset pricing model (CAPM), namely the market return.) We defend our strategy on three grounds. First, in the applications below, we need to maintain the covariance model for only a month or two at a time. It seems intuitively plausible to imagine that the change in an asset's covariance structure does not change much for samples of this length. Second, the literature also makes this assumption, but for much longer spans of time. For instance, Fama and French (1996) assumed that their model worked well for thirty years. Finally, we show below that the key results are insensitive to the exact factor model. This is important; if the technique were sensitive to the factors used to model (δ), then the integration measure would be no more useful than any of the individual factor models. Indeed, if the measure were factor-model sensitive, it would be preferable to use the factor model itself as the object of measurement.

While we focus on equation 3, there are other moments that would help characterize the MRS, (δ); see for example, Hansen and Jagannathan (1991). We concentrate on this one for four reasons. First, as the first moment, it is the natural place to check first. Second, it is simple to estimate. Third, our estimates and results are robust to the factor model that conditions the measurements. Finally, the measurements are discriminating for market integration, yet they confirm our prior beliefs and previous research. In the examples below, our measure never rejects internal market integration for portfolios of Standard & Poor's (S&P) stocks priced in the New York Stock Exchange (NYSE) during periods of tranquility, or for Korean stocks priced in Seoul. Nevertheless, we *can* reject integration for short periods of financial stress in the NYSE. Further, we reject integration strongly—by an order of magnitude—between the Korean and Japanese markets.

Our methodology has a number of strengths. First, it is based on a general intertemporal theoretical framework, unlike other measures of asset integration such as stock market correlations (see the excellent discussion in, for example, Adam et al. 2002). Second, standard asset-pricing models are completely consistent with our methodology, and the exact model does not seem to be important in practice. Third, we do not need to model the MRS directly. The MRS need not be determined uniquely, so long as its expectation is unique. Fourth, our strategy requires only two assumptions; we need not assume, for example, complete markets, homogeneous investors, or that we can model "mimicking portfolios" well. Fifth, the technique requires only accessible and reliable data on asset prices, payoffs, and time-varying factors. Sixth, the methodology can be used at very high frequencies and at low frequencies as well. Seventh, the technique can be used to compare expected discount rates across many different classes of assets including domestic and foreign stocks, bonds, and commodities. Next, the technique is easy to implement and can be applied with standard econometric packages; no specialized software is required. Finally, the technique is focused on an intrinsically interesting object, the expected marginal rate of substitution.

A comparison of our technique with those already extant in the literature is available in a longer version of this paper, which is freely available on the Internet.

4. The Russia/LTCM Crisis of 1998

The New York Stock Exchange can reasonably be considered to be the largest and most liquid stock exchange in the world, certainly for the last decade. It is thus a demanding forum in which to check whether our technique can reveal signs of financial turbulence, and where we begin.

The financial crisis of 1998 began with the Russian devaluation and unilateral debt restructuring of August 18 1998. Interest rate spreads for emerging markets and much of the corporate sector rose thereafter, especially following the near failure of Long-Term Capital Management (LTCM). The rescue of LTCM was announced on September 23. The crisis subsided after a loosening of monetary policy throughout much of the Organization for Economic Cooperation and Development that began in late September with an American monetary policy loosening on September 29. This was widely criticized as being inadequate, and was followed on October 15 and November 17 by others.[1]

The American stock market peaked in mid-July and bottomed out in late August, about twenty percent below its peak (though volatility was particularly high from mid-September through mid-October). Still, much of the action had been in bond markets. Between mid-August and early October, government bond yields fell by about 110 basis points (implying price gains of between 6 percent and 11 percent for benchmark 7–10 year bonds). A number of spreads also rose during this period, including the spread between "on-the-run" and "off-the-run" Treasuries (a standard measure of liquidity; this widened from less than 10 basis points to over 35 basis points in mid-October).

We now examine at some length the integration of the U.S. stock market during this interesting episode of turbulence.

5. Implementing Our Technique

We begin by estimating a model with asset-specific intercepts and the three time-varying factors used by Fama and French (1996). In practice, we divide through by lagged prices (and redefine residuals appropriately):

$$4) \qquad x_{t+1}^{j} / p_{t-1}^{j} = \delta_{t}((p_{t}^{j} / p_{t-1}^{j}) + \beta_{0}^{j} + \beta_{1}^{j} f_{1,t} + \beta_{2}^{j} f_{2,t} + \beta_{3}^{j} f_{3,t}) + \varepsilon_{t+1}^{j},$$

for assets $j = 1, ..., J$, periods $t = 1, ..., T$. That is, we allow (δ_{t}) to vary period by period, while we use a "three-factor" model and allow (β^{j}) to vary asset by asset. We normalize the data by lagged prices since we believe that $COV_{t}(m_{t+1}, x_{t+1}^{j} / p_{t-1}^{j})$ can be modeled by a simple factor model with time-invariant coefficients more plausibly than $COV_{t}(m_{t+1}, x_{t+1}^{j})$, and to ensure stationarity of all variables. The three Fama–French factors are: 1) the overall stock market return less the Treasury bill (T-bill) rate, 2) the performance of small stocks relative to big stocks, and 3) the performance of "value" stocks relative to "growth" stocks. Further details and the data set itself are available at French's website.[2] For sensitivity analysis, we also examine other simpler covariance models.

Equation 4 can be estimated directly with non-linear least squares. The degree of non-linearity is not particularly high; conditional on (δ_{t}) the problem is linear in (β^{j}) and vice versa. We employ robust (heteroskedasticity and autocorrelation consistent "Newey West") covariance estimators.

We use a moderately high frequency approach. In particular, we use one-month spans of daily data. Using daily data allows us to estimate the coefficients of interest (δ_{t}) without assuming that firm-specific coefficients (β^{j}) are constant for implausibly long periods of time. Still, we see no reason why higher- (and/or lower-) frequency data could not be used.

6. The Data Set

Our data set is drawn from the "U.S. Pricing" database provided by Thomson Analytics. We collected closing rates for the first (in terms of ticker symbol) one hundred and twenty firms from the S&P 500 that did not go ex-dividend during the months in question (September through November). The absence of dividend payments allows us to set $x_{t+1}^j = p_{t+1}^j$ (and does not bias our results in any other obvious way). The data set has been checked for outliers.

We are most interested in the period of financial turbulence of October 1998. Still, so as to generate a reasonable comparison set, we separately examine September, October, and November. Also, we perform our analysis for the same three months for four consecutive years: 1996 through 1999. We go back two years rather than one since the stock market turbulence of October 1997 may be of independent interest (the Dow Jones industrial average posted its biggest loss ever on Oct 27, 1997). Thus we use comparable months from 1996 and 1998 as our "control sample" with which to compare our results for 1997 and especially 1998, and also compare October with September and November.

We group our 120 firms into twenty portfolios of six equally weighted firms each, arranged simply by ticker symbol. We use portfolios rather than individual stocks for the standard reasons of the finance literature. In particular, as Cochrane (2001) points out, portfolios' betas are measured with less error than individual betas because of lower residual variance. They also vary less over time (as size, leverage, and business risk change less for a portfolio of equities than any individual component). Portfolio variances are lower than those of individual securities, enabling more precise covariance relationships to be estimated. And of course portfolios are what investors tend to use (especially those informed by finance theory!).

7. Results

We start by combining data from all 20 portfolios to estimate the time-varying marginal rate of substitution (that is, estimates of $\delta_t \equiv [1/E_t(m_{t+1})]$). We provide time-series plots of the estimated deltas along with a plus/minus two standard error confidence interval in figure 1, one graphic for each of ten months. (We do not provide graphics for October 1998 and 1999 for reasons discussed below.) Each month is estimated separately, so as to ensure that the portfolio-specific covariance models are assumed to be constant for only a month at a time.

There is one striking feature of the graph. In particular, the time-series variation in delta is high, consistent with the spirit of Hansen and Jagannathan (1991). While the discount rate moves around the value of unity, it fluctuates considerably. That is, the MRS does not seem to be close to constant at a daily basis. Further, this volatility does not seem to be constant over time. For example, the stock market turbulence of October 1997 shows up clearly. Since short-term interest rates in the United States during this period of time were quite low and stable, it is easy to reject the hypothesis that the MRS derived from American equity markets equals the sluggish and low (but positive) short-term American interest return.

Still, it is inappropriate to dwell on the characteristics of figure 18.1 at this point, since the graphics are implicitly based on the assumption that the American stock market is integrated, and hence delivers a single estimate of $\{\delta_t\}$. Is the latter in fact true?

It is simple to test for stock-market integration using the strategy outlined above. One simply estimates $\{\delta_t\}$ from two different samples of assets over the same period

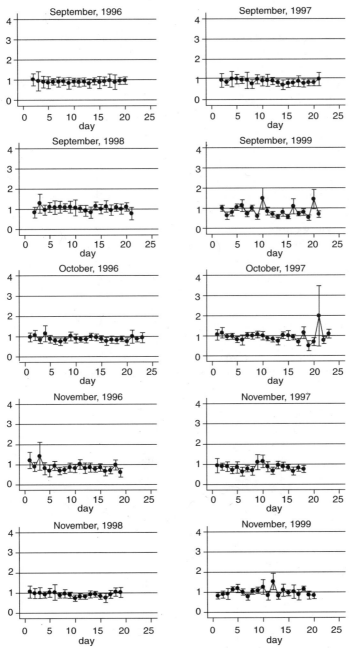

Note: The vertical lines intersecting the data points indicate the two standard error confidence levels.

Figure 18.1: Estimates of Expected Discount Rate from LTCM/Russia Crisis

of time, and compares them. Consider September 1996. When we estimate equation 4 from the first ten portfolios, we obtain a log-likelihood of 631.79. When we estimate precisely the same equation using data from the (mutually exclusive) other set of ten portfolios, we obtain a log-likelihood of 602.95. Finally, when we pool observations from all twenty portfolios, we obtain a log-likelihood of 1,217.39. This combined estimate of equation 4 only differs from the two separate estimates of equation 4 in that a single vector of $\{\delta_t\}$ is estimated instead of two different estimates of the same vector (the portfolio-specific slopes and intercepts (β^j) are unconstrained). If the NYSE is integrated, the single combined estimate of $\{\delta_t\}$ should be equal to (and more efficiently estimated than) the two different estimates of $\{\delta_t\}$. Statistically, under the hypothesis of normally distributed errors and integration, twice the difference between the combined and separate log-likelihoods is distributed as a chi-square with degrees of freedom equal to the dimensionality of $\{\delta_t\}$; a likelihood ratio (LR) test. Since there were 19 business days in the month, $-2*[(631.79 + 602.95) - 1217.39] =$ 34.7 should be drawn from the $\chi^2(19)$ distribution under the null of integration and normally distributed errors. As 34.7 is at the .02 tail of the $\chi^2(19)$ distribution, the null hypothesis of integration and normally distributed error is (marginally) rejected.

Such an interpretation is unfair to the hypothesis of market integration, since it is being maintained jointly with the assumption of normality. It is well known that asset prices are not in fact normally distributed; Campbell, Lo, and MacKinlay (1997). Rather, there is strong evidence of fat tails or leptokurtosis. Accordingly, it is more appropriate to use a bootstrap procedure to estimate the probability values for the likelihood ratio tests.

The bootstrap procedure I employ is as follows. We estimate the deltas from all twenty portfolios, under the null hypothesis of integration. This gives us an estimate of $\{\epsilon\}$. We then draw randomly with replacement from this vector to create an artificial

A. Fama-French Factor Model (intercepts, 3 time-varying factors)

	September	October	November
1996	34.7 (.33)	26.6 (.83)	32.3 (.40)
1997	39.7 (.17)	37.5 (.39)	32.2 (.05)
1998	34.4 (.40)	55.5 (.02)	27.6 (.56)
1999	16.6 (.97)	57.1 (.00)	30.3 (.43)

B. One-Factor Model (intercepts, market return factor)

	September	October	November
1996	24.2 (.55)	25.9 (.64)	41.2 (.05)
1997	29.6 (.34)	36.3 (.26)	29.7 (.19)
1998	25.4 (.49)	53.1 (.01)	22.6 (.61)
1999	15.9 (.95)	24.7 (.65)	26.3 (.42)

Note: Likelihood-ration test statistics (bootstrap P-value).

Table 18.1: Integration inside the American S&P 500

vector of $\{\varepsilon\}$ which we then use to construct an artificial regressand variable $\{x\}$. Using this artificial data, we then generate a likelihood ratio test by estimating the model from the first set of 10 portfolios, the second set of 10 portfolios, and the combined set of 20. We then repeat this procedure a large number of times to generate an empirical distribution for the LR test statistic.

Table 18.1, panel A records the likelihood-ratio tests of integration inside the American stock market. The top panel records 12 test statistics, one for each of the different sample months. The lower the statistic, the more consistent with the null hypothesis of stock market integration. The bootstrapped p-values for the hypothesis are tabulated in parentheses. Only two of the test statistics are high (the p-values are too low), indicating rejection of the null at conventional significance levels for the Octobers of 1998 and 1999.[3] That is, the NYSE seems to be integrated except for the crisis period of October 1998 and also October 1999.

8. Sensitivity Analysis

Two questions of interest emerge immediately. The first is the curious rejection of integration for October 1999; the second is the more important one, and concerns the sensitivity of our results to the precise covariance model employed. We handle them simultaneously.

Thus far we have relied on the Fama-French model of asset covariances. That is, the covariance of each asset's return with the MRS is characterized by four parameters: an intercept (β_0^j) and factor loadings on the market return minus the T-bill rate (β_1^j), the difference between small and large stock returns (β_2^j), and the difference between returns of stocks with high and low book to market ratios (β_3^j). Are our results sensitive to the number of factors used? It turns out that the answer is negative.

In table 18.1, panel B we provide test statistics (and bootstrapped p-values) to examine tests of integration within the S&P, but using only the return on the market instead of the three Fama-French factors (while retaining the portfolio intercepts as well). The test statistics and conclusions are essentially unchanged, with one exception; October 1999. For that sample period, the high test statistic falls to a level wholly consistent with integration. In fact, the high value for 10/99 in table 18.1, panel A depends critically on an anomalous movement of the SML (returns of small stocks relative to those of large stocks) over two consecutive days in mid-October 1999. Since this is a sensitive finding that stems from a non-traditional factor, we do not take it that seriously. And it is reassuring to us that the vast majority of our findings are robust with respect to the exact covariance model deployed.

Indeed, our findings are more robust than implied by table 18.1. A longer version of this paper (available on the Internet) goes further and drops the market factor from our covariance model, leaving only portfolio-specific intercepts (β_0^j) but no time-varying factors. Again, the results are essentially unchanged (indeed, the actual values of the test statistics are little affected!). The same is true when no portfolio-specific terms at all are used. This robustness is encouraging since it demonstrates the insensitivity of our methodology to even drastic perturbations in the exact factor model employed.

We conclude that the American stock market seems to have been dramatically affected by the crisis of October 1998. Compared with the months and years immediately

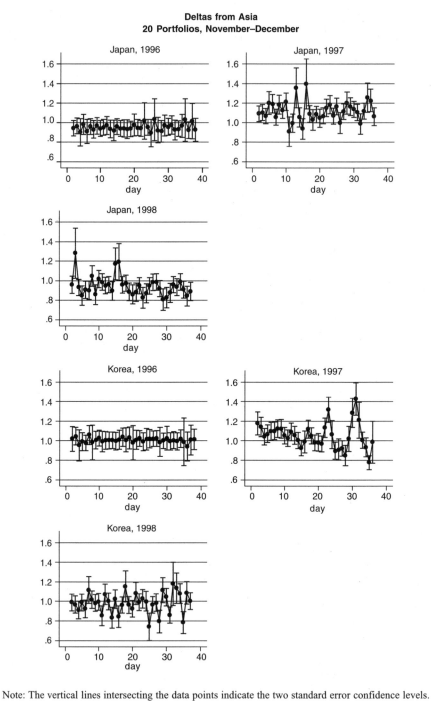

Deltas from Asia
20 Portfolios, November–December

Note: The vertical lines intersecting the data points indicate the two standard error confidence levels.

Figure 18.2: Estimates of Expected Discount Rate from Asian Crisis

before and after the period, there is a substantive but transient drop in market integration. This finding seems both sensible and robust.

9. The Asian Crisis

We now apply our methodology to examine the Asian crisis of 1997. The Asian crisis is often viewed as starting in early July 1997, and subsiding in early 1998. We focus on Korea, the largest of the directly affected economies, and one of the most severely affected. While bad Korean economic news arrived in the spring and summer of 1997, the most dramatic events took place in the late autumn of 1997.[4] After a relatively calm summer and early autumn (certainly compared with events further South), the won was attacked beginning on November 6. This quickly led to a collapse of the Korean stock market, and rippling effects elsewhere in Asia and abroad. The IMF package of early December 1997, international assistance and a decisive Korean policy response started to turn things around by the end of the year, though the real effects continued through 1998.

Our Asian data set is drawn from Datastream. Since Tokyo and Seoul are in the same time zone, we collected closing rates for the first (in terms of ticker symbol) 400 stocks from the Tokyo stock exchange and the first 360 stocks from the Korean stock exchange that did not go ex-dividend during the months in question (November and December, 1996 through 1998). We converted Korean prices in won into Japanese yen using a matched nominal exchange rate. Again, we have checked the data set for outliers and excluded holidays, and again we group our firms into twenty portfolios each for both Japan and Korea, arranged simply by ticker symbol. As the single time-varying factor, we use the first-difference in the natural logarithm of the stock market index (the Nikkei 500 for Tokyo, and the Korea SE Composite or "KOSPI" for Seoul). So for each of our (twenty Japanese and twenty Korean) portfolios, the covariance of payoffs with the discount rate is parameterized by a portfolio-specific intercept and also a sensitivity with respect to the appropriate (Japanese/Korean) market return. That is, we estimate:

$$4') \qquad x_{t+1}^j / p_{t-1}^j = \delta_t((p_t^j / p_{t-1}^j) + \beta_0^j + \beta_1^j f_{1,t}) + \varepsilon_{t+1}^j.$$

Estimates of the marginal rate of substitution (that is, $\{\delta_t\}$) for Japan and Korea are provided in figure 18.2. For each country, three time-series plots of the estimated deltas along with a plus/minus two standard error confidence interval is provided, one graphic for each year. Each plot thus spans a two-month interval (though the plots look similar when they are estimated on samples of a single month).

As with figure 18.1, the time-series volatility in delta is high. This is especially true of 1997 (the Korean crisis of December 1997 is readily apparent), though the other years also show a lot of variation. Still, an even more striking feature of the graphics in figure 18.2 is that the Japanese and Korean sets of $\{\delta_t\}$ do not look similar. This is especially true of 1997, though the 1998 series also look quite different. Of course, if the two markets are integrated, then only a single expected marginal rate of substitution should characterize both markets.

	November	December	November–December
1996	32.18 (.19)	27.3 (.32)	50.8 (.26)
1997	33.3 (.20)	27.0 (.29)	51.6 (.23)
1998	54.1 (.13)	10.5 (.97)	31.7 (.92)

Notes: One-factor model (intercepts, domestic market return factor).
Likelihood-ration test statistics (all p-values =.00).

Table 18.2: Integration inside the Korean Stock Exchange

To confirm this ocular impression, we now compute analogues to the likelihood ratio tests of integration presented in table 18.1. Where table 18.1 focused on the internal integration of American stocks traded on the NYSE, tables 18.3 and 18.4 check the cross-market integration of Japanese and Korean stocks.

Before we examine the degree of international integration, it is important to check for the degree of internal (domestic) financial integration. After all, if American stock exchanges can be disrupted by financial crises, less-liquid Asian ones can be as well! Thus table 18.2 is an analogue to table 18.1 in that it tests for internal integration of the Korean stock exchange during the height of the financial crisis of 1997, as well as the years before and after. Surprisingly (at least to us), there is no indication of any breakdown in financial integration from the likelihood ratio tests (which again use bootstrapped p-values). This is true when we examine November and December separately, and also when we pool the data across the two months.

Still, the real question of interest to us concerns international integration; do the Korean and Japanese stock exchanges share a common expected MRS? As we expect from figure 18.2, the answer is decisively negative in table 18.3. In this table, we estimate equation 4' but impose equality across the two sets of $\{\delta\}$. (The portfolios of, for example, Japanese stocks, are each parameterized with a portfolio-specific intercept, and a coefficient on the aggregate Japanese index.) The likelihood ratio tests of market integration are an order of magnitude larger than those in table 18.1 or table 18.2, and reject the hypothesis of market integration at all reasonable significance levels. They jump considerably during the crisis of 1997, but from already enormous levels in 1996. They then fall in 1998, but only back to the huge levels experienced before. That is, the Korean and Japanese stock markets become less integrated during the financial crisis of late 1997, but they are never integrated during the period we consider.

Under the null hypothesis of integration, equation 4' is not strictly correct since both Japanese and Korean stocks should be affected by both the aggregate Japanese and Korean markets (or a composite of the two). We allow for this by estimating:

	November	December	November–December
1996	389.9	259.2	640.3
1997	639.1	1716.2	2,480.5
1998	269.3	591.3	876.3

Notes: One-factor model (intercepts, domestic market return factor).
Likelihood-ration test statistics (all p-values =.00).

Table 18.3: Integration between Korea and Japan

	November	December	November–December
1996	439.0	261.8	645.6
1997	626.5	1,595.1	2,401.1
1998	284.7	519.0	814.3

Notes: Two-factors model (intercepts, domestic and foreign market return factors).
Likelihood-ration test statistics (all p-values =.00).

Table 18.4: Integration between Korea and Japan

4″) $$x_{t+1}^{j} / p_{t-1}^{j} = \delta_t ((p_t^{j} / p_{t-1}^{j}) + \beta_0^{j} + \beta_1^{j} f_{1,t} + \beta_2^{j} f_{2,t}) + \varepsilon_{t+1}^{j},$$

where the second factor represents the foreign aggregate market return (Korea for the Japanese portfolios, Japan for the Koreans). The analogues for this model are tabulated in table 18.4 and deliver similar point-estimates and identical conclusions to those of table 18.3. This is no surprise, since the message throughout is that the hypothesis of international integration is grossly at odds with the data.

10. Summary and Conclusions

This paper developed a simple method to test for asset integration, and then applied it within and between equity markets during times of crises. The technique relies on estimating and comparing the expected riskless returns implied by different sets of assets. Our technique has a number of advantages over those in the literature and relies on just two relatively weak assumptions: 1) rational expectations in financial markets; and 2) covariances between discount rates and returns that can be modeled with a small number of factors for a short period of time.

If our integration findings hold up to further scrutiny, the interesting question is not whether financial markets with few apparent frictions (such as the Seoul and Tokyo stock exchanges) are poorly integrated but why? What are the mechanisms that seem to break down during periods of market stress such as those that affected the New York Stock Exchange during the financial crisis of 1998? We leave such important questions for future research.

*Robert P. Flood is senior economist in the Research Department at the International Monetary Fund. Andrew K. Rose is the B.T. Rocca, Jr. Professor of International Business in the Haas School of Business at the University of California, Berkeley, a National Bureau of Economic Research research associate, and a Center for Economic Policy Research research fellow. The authors thank Pedro Rodriguez for assistance with the data. Professor Rose thanks the Bank of Japan for hospitality during the course of this research. The data sets, sample E-Views programs and output, and a current version of this paper are available at http://faculty.haas.berkeley.edu/arose.

Notes

1. See for example, the International Monetary Fund's *World Economic Outlook and International Capital Markets Interim Assessment* of December 1998.

2. http://mba.tuck.dartmouth.edu/pages/faculty/ken.french/data_library.html

3. Hence the missing graphics of figure 1.

4. Nouriel Roubini's *Global Macroeconomic and Financial Policy Site* is the standard background reference and is available at www.stern.nyu.edu/globalmacro.

References

Adam, Klaus, Tullio Jappelli, Annamaria Menichini, Mario Padula, and Marco Pagano, 2002, "Analyse, compare, and apply alternative indicators and monitoring methodologies to measure the evolution of capital market integration in the European Union," manuscript.

Campbell, John Y., Andrew W. Lo, and A. Craig MacKinlay, 1997, *The Econometrics of Financial Markets*, Princeton: Princeton University Press.

Chabot, Benjamin, 2000, "A single market? The stock exchanges of the United States and London: 1866–1885," University of Michigan, working paper.

Chen, Zhiwu, and Peter J. Knez, 1995, "Measurement of market integration and arbitrage," *Review of Financial Studies*, Vol. 8, No. 2, pp. 287–325.

Cochrane, John H., 2001, *Asset Pricing*, Princeton, NJ: Princeton University Press.

Fama, Eugene, and Kenneth R. French, 1996, "Multifactor explanations of asset pricing anomalies," *Journal of Finance*, Vol. 51, No. 1, pp. 55–84.

Hansen, Lars Peter, and Ravi Jagannathan, 1991, "Implications of security market data for models of dynamic economies," *Journal of Political Economy*, Vol. 99, No. 2, pp. 225–262.

Roll, Richard, and Stephen A. Ross, 1980, "An empirical investigation of the arbitrage pricing theory," *Journal of Finance*, Vol. 35, No. 5, pp. 1073–1103.

Chapter 19

Assessing the Evidence on Market Discipline for Countries

Andrew G. Haldane*
Bank of England

1. What's Different about Countries?

This session of the conference differs from the others in focusing on the effects of market discipline on countries (or the sovereign) rather than on private financial or nonfinancial firms. In what ways might market discipline operate differently for countries? And what implications does this have for incentives and design mechanisms?

Sovereigns are sovereign. They are, quite literally, a law unto themselves. Unlike companies, it is a matter of choice for sovereigns whether they subject themselves to the discipline of market forces. As a result, the incentives problem is more acute for countries than for private firms. How best can we discipline an ultimately sovereign entity?

In practice, the official community has charged a supra-national agency—the International Monetary Fund (IMF)—with this task. There are broadly two ways in which the IMF has sought to enhance discipline over countries' macroeconomic policies. In defining these two mechanisms, it is useful to draw on Bliss's (2004) taxonomy between *ex ante* discipline (pre-crisis) and *ex post* discipline (post-crisis).

In promoting *ex ante* discipline, the primary vehicle used by the IMF has been a myriad set of codes and standards of best public policy practice which has emerged over recent years. Transparency about compliance (or otherwise) with these codes and standards can serve as a potentially powerful disciplining force over countries. In other words, codes plus transparency reinforce the market forces disciplining countries *ex ante*.[1]

In promoting *ex post* discipline, the IMF has tended to use the carrot of official sector lending in tandem with the stick of IMF conditionality. In other words, official sector (rather than market) discipline has tended to be used by the IMF after a crisis has struck. Market discipline alone is, in these circumstances, typically deemed to be too severe. Indeed, that is one rationale for the IMF's very existence.

How successful have these two approaches proven in practice? The *ex post* discipline of IMF conditionality appears to have a mixed record, even when the pill has been sugared with large amounts of official financing. Over the period 1992–98, almost 70 percent of IMF stand-by arrangements (SBAs) suffered "interruptions" and over 40 percent suffered "irreversible interruptions" (Ivanova et al., 2003). Put differently, one in every four IMF program conditions has not been implemented historically.

As a direct consequence of these failures, repeated and prolonged use of IMF resources has proven the rule rather than the exception. Over the period 1971–2000, 51 countries were prolonged users of IMF resources, in the sense of having had an IMF program for seven out of ten years (IMF, Independent Evaluation Office, 2002). Taken together, this evidence suggests that attempts to discipline sovereigns using official measures have a somewhat checkered history. Has market discipline been able to ride to the rescue?

2. Market Discipline and Countries—The Evidence

In the aftermath of the Asian crises, the official sector began devising codes and standards defining best practices in many fields of public policy. These included data, auditing and accounting, corporate governance, supervision and regulation of banks, insurance companies, and securities firms, and transparency of monetary, fiscal, and financial policies. There are now over 80 such codes and standards.

The IMF, acting in tandem with other official agencies, has begun assessing countries' compliance with twelve core codes and standards in the so-called Reports on the Observance of Standards and Codes (ROSCs). Over 400 ROSC modules have been completed for around 94 countries (more than half of the IMF's membership). Perhaps more importantly, 302 of these ROSC modules have also been published. Complementing these initiatives, 135 countries have now submitted to publish their Article IV country consultations (the IMF's annual health check); and 52 countries have signed up to more detailed evaluations of their financial vulnerability through the so-called Financial Sector Assessment Program (FSAP). Progress has not been confined to the official sector. Recently, there has been a private sector-led initiative to develop the use of standards and codes for country evaluation purposes—so-called e-standards.

All of this is tangible progress towards greater information and improved analysis and transparency about the policy risks countries may be running, each of which are necessary conditions for enhanced market discipline. None, however, are sufficient. For example, effective market discipline additionally requires a response from market participants to the signals they have received. What evidence is there of such an effect?

A body of evidence is beginning to emerge to suggest that transparency does reap rewards. Given the shortness of the sample since the Asian crises, this evidence is necessarily tentative. But it paints a broadly consistent qualitative picture: country transparency lowers the cost and may increase the quantum of capital flowing to emerging markets. On borrowing costs, the Institute for International Finance (2002), in an early study, found that countries not complying with the IMF's Special Data Dissemination Standard (SDDS) were charged a hefty interest premium relative to compliant countries, even after controlling for other factors.

More recently, a study by the IMF (Glennerster and Shin, 2003) has looked at the effects of a broader range of transparency initiatives—for example, ROSC and Article

IV publication—on borrowing costs. It finds a significant effect, economically and statistically, which tends to lower spreads by roughly 5 percent to 20 percent. Recent work at the Bank of England has found similar, if slightly smaller, such effects. Quantity side evidence in general corroborates this conclusion. Gelos and Wei (2002) consider the behavior of U.S. equity funds investing in emerging markets. They find that portfolio flows tend to be affected significantly by the degree of transparency within these markets, whether from the official sector in the policies they pursue or from the private sector in the (legal and accounting) standards they abide by. Transparency appears capable of delivering a lower cost of capital for countries, which for most of them should prove a significant incentive.

3. Can Official Discipline Complement Market Discipline?

One open policy question is whether anything could be done to enhance complementarities between the twin tools of official discipline (where the record is patchy) and market discipline (where the record is more encouraging, despite it being early days). For example, could the IMF devise an official lending facility which better harnessed market forces to help support official discipline?

The current configuration of IMF facilities is not well suited to this task. The staple IMF facility is the SBA. This offers bridging finance to countries which have already hit problems, with strings attached (conditionality). In order words, standard IMF facilities provide little if any ex ante incentive for countries to put their house in order ahead of crisis. They are long on ex post need and short on ex ante incentives.

In 1999, the IMF created a new facility which aimed to achieve a better balance between ex ante incentives and ex post need—the contingent credit line (CCL). It offered a line of credit to countries satisfying a number of ex ante criteria—including SDDS compliance—and in this way aimed to strengthen incentives for better policy ahead of problems striking. In the event, the CCL has had no takers and seems unlikely to be renewed as a facility at its next review date (November 2003).

The apparent failure of the CCL does not suggest, however, that the task of using IMF facilities to support market discipline is a fruitless one. The current CCL was, with hindsight, rather too long on ex ante incentives relative to ex post need. But a recast CCL could seek out the middle ground between the polar extremes of the SBA and the CCL, thereby better balancing ex post and ex ante incentives.

Such a facility would prospectively be attractive to a number of countries aiming to graduate from IMF lending, but which at the same time would like some foreign exchange insurance cover during this (possibly lengthy) transition phase. Brazil and Mexico are two countries in such a transition phase. So too are a number of the emerging markets across Southeast Asia. To date, the latter set of countries have purchased self-insurance, by stockpiling foreign currency reserves. Such behavior is widely perceived to have had costs, both for the countries in question and for the international financial system more broadly. A well-designed contingent IMF fund could help mitigate those costs, by harnessing the complementary forces of market and official discipline.

4. Do Capital Markets Exert the Right Amount of Discipline?

Market discipline is of course no panacea. If we think of market discipline as a risk-based tax on countries, then there is no cast-iron guarantee that the market will set this tax optimally to induce remedial responses from the borrower. Market tax rates may, for example, be excessively volatile or be levied at the wrong rate, relative to country-specific measures of risk.[2]

There is some evidence of both such frictions in practice. For example, figure 19.1 plots a measure of financial market expectations of default probabilities in Brazil since the beginning of 2001 at a one- and five-year horizon. These probabilities are extracted from credit default swap prices, given an assumed recovery rate. They map pretty much one-for-one into country borrowing costs.

The gyrations in these implied probabilities are striking. Having flat-lined for over a year at very low levels, default probabilities shot up to around 60 percent for around 6 months in the second half of 2002, before reverting back to their previously low levels soon after. While there was an important Brazilian election in the second half of 2002 which helps account for these patterns, it is difficult to reconcile the scale of these movements with that single event. With hindsight, borrowing costs seem to have been excessively volatile, first on the upside and then on the downside, relative to underlying country risk.

A more formal means of controlling for movements in country-specific risk is shown in figure 19.2 which plots average emerging market borrowing costs against average credit ratings of the same countries. On average over time, these two series have had a pretty close relationship, as might be expected. But significant deviations have occurred, especially over the past year. Over that period, borrowing spreads have fallen from around 40 percent above their historical mean to almost 40 percent

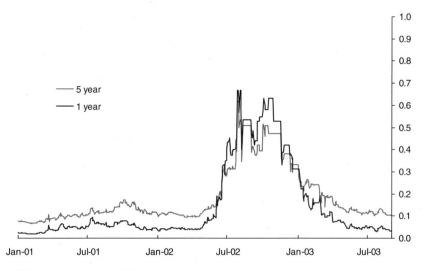

Note: Using a recovery rate of 25 percent.

Figure 19.1: Brazil Default Probabilities

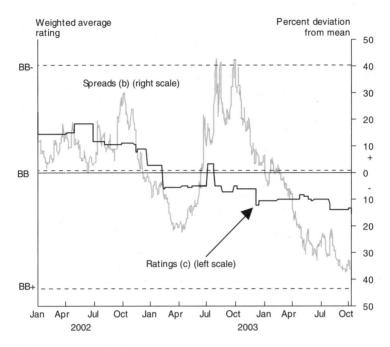

Figure 19.2: Spreads' Ratings

below it. At the same time, average country ratings have improved only very marginally. Again, there is evidence first of a significant overshooting and more recently of a significant undershooting of borrowing costs.

Figure 19.3 attempts a more systematic breakdown of the factors contributing to recent movements in emerging market borrowing spreads; it is based on an econometrically estimated model (Ferrucci, 2003). Specifically, the contributions to recent movements in spreads are decomposed into a fundamentals-based component (country-specific risk), a component attributable to supply-side or external factors (such as developed country interest rates), and an unexplained component.

Fundamental factors indeed help account for some of the fall in emerging market borrowing spreads since, say, mid-2002. But the largest part of that fall cannot be explained by either fundamental or supply-side factors. The same is true of the run-up in spreads during the first half of 2002. Taken together, this evidence strongly suggests a degree of excess-volatility in the behavior of borrowing costs: Market "tax rates" have in general been too volatile given underlying movements in country risk.

What about the *level* of market "tax rates"? One factor that might consistently distort the level of borrowing costs is the expectation of the official safety net, operating through the IMF. We would expect this moral hazard distortion to be greater, the more systemically (or geopolitically) important the country in question. Figure 19.4 presents some evidence to suggest these distortions have historically been non-trivial.

It looks at the impact of "news" about IMF interventions on borrowing costs in the country that is the subject of the intervention and on emerging market borrowing

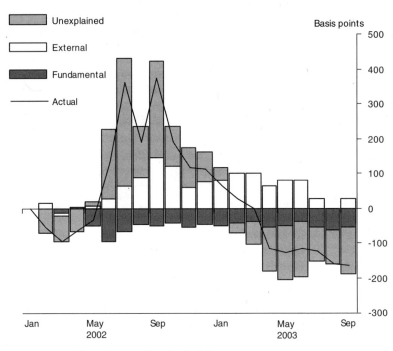

Sources: J. P. Morgan Chase & Co. and Bank calculations.

Figure 19.3: Contribution to Changes in Spreads

costs in general (see Haldane and Scheibe, 2003, for a detailed discussion). Twenty-six IMF intervention events are considered, starting with the Mexico bailout in 1995 and ending with the IMF package for Brazil in the fall of 2002. Spreads fell following the vast majority of these IMF interventions, on average by between 5 percent and 10 percent across the 26 events. This is consistent with some undermining of the market disciplining effects of borrowing costs as a result of the operation of the international safety net. The level of the market "tax-rate" has historically proven too low, at the same time as the volatility of these tax-rates has proven too high.

5. What Trade-Offs Do Emerging Markets Face?

Financial liberalization plainly confers a number of lump-sum efficiency benefits. The paper by Forbes (2004) nicely assimilates some of the recent literature on the size of these benefits. On some micro estimates, these efficiency gains are non-trivial.

Against these benefits need, however, to be weighed some of the instability costs of liberalization. Liberalization opens up economies to a wider and deeper constellation of potential shocks, with attendant instability costs. Moreover, there are good theoretical and empirical reasons for believing these instability costs may be particularly pervasive and acute for emerging countries. In other words, for these sets of countries the efficiency-stability trade-off may be a very real one.

Theoretical support for this proposition can be found in the work of, for example, Allen and Gale (2000). They consider the stability of different types of financial network (national or international) in the face of different sizes of shock. They reach two important conclusions. First, the most stable financial networks are the polar extremes of financial autarky and perfect financial integration. The former is stable because the system is in effect immunized against shocks; the latter is stable because the system is in effect self-insured against shocks—network interconnections serve as a shock absorber.

Interestingly, however, intermediate degrees of financial integration are the least stable of the financial regimes. Intermediate regimes are still prone to shocks, but system interconnections are not sufficiently well developed to defuse these. Indeed, to the contrary, these interconnections potentially serve as a shock transmitter; they are the bringer of bad news to other nodes in the network. As a consequence, system behavior is highly non-linear in response to shocks along the transition path to full integration, with the middle ground especially fragile. That is a sobering message for emerging markets embarking on a journey of capital account liberalization.

Second, these non-linearities are most prominent when there is an imbalance between the size of the shock in relation to size of the system as a whole—when you have, if you like, big fish operating in small ponds. That is an apt description of the situation facing many emerging markets in the early throes of liberalization. To illustrate the imbalance, consider a hypothetical portfolio shock. This involves a minuscule portfolio reallocation of 1 basis point (one hundredth of one percentage point) by institutional investors in the Group of 10 plus the European Union countries. What would be the effects of such a portfolio shift?

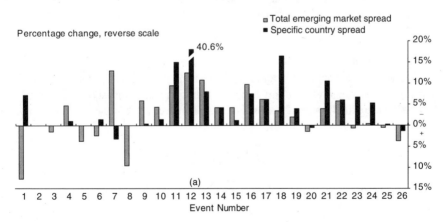

(a)

a) Event number 12 is the Russian "non-intervention" event on 17 August 1998, therefore these bars are reversed in value, that is, spreads increased by 40.6 percent.
Source: J. P. Morgan Chase & Co. and Bank calculations

Figure 19.4: Borrowing Spreads and IMF Packages

Argentina	4.4%
Brazil	1.0%
Hong Kong	0.6%
Thailand	11.0%
Poland	21.4%
India	1.9%
Korea	6.2%

Source: Borio, Chincarini, and Tsatsaronis (1997).

Table 19.1: Effect of 1 basis point Portfolio Shift by G10.EU Institutional Investors on Market Capitalisation in Selected Emerging Markets (%, end 1997)

Table 19.1 shows its impact as a share of the market capitalization of some selected emerging markets; these ready-reckoners are taken from the study by Borio, Chincarini, and Tsatsaronis (1997). These numbers are not small. At one extreme, such a tiny portfolio adjustment would amount to over one fifth of the Polish stock market.

It is also possible to guesstimate, albeit roughly, what impact these portfolio reallocations might have on equity prices. For that, we use the ready-reckoner estimated by Froot, O'Connell, and Seasholes (1998) for the effects of portfolio flows on emerging equity market prices. These estimates, while no more than ballpark figures, are based on proprietorial information on equity portfolio flows collected by State Street Bank. Using these order flow ready-reckoners gives the estimated price effects shown in table 19.2. While not to be taken too literally, the striking feature of these estimates is their size. This underscores the fact that imperfect degrees of financial integration, taken together with the big-fish-small-pond dynamic, may make for non-trivial instabilities for emerging markets. For some countries, these instability costs could legitimately dwarf the permanent benefits of liberalization.

6. Measuring Integration within and between Markets

Whatever pace of financial integration emerging markets choose, there is an interesting methodological question about how market integration is best measured. The paper by Flood and Rose (2004) presents a novel means of answering this question. It estimates

Argentina	70%
Brazil	6%
Hong Kong	10%
Thailand	177%
Poland	343%
India	18%
Korea	99%

Sources: Author's calculations.

Table 19.2: Effect of 1 basis point Portfolio Shift by G10/EU Institutional Investors on Equity Prices in Selected Emerging Market (%, end 1997)

cross-asset and cross-market stochastic discount factors. The null of perfect integration is rejected if these estimated marginal (risk-adjusted) rates of substitution are unequal across assets or markets ($\delta \neq 1$). The paper finds this to be the case at crisis time.

One of the attractions of this approach is that it places few theoretical restrictions on the data—for example, on the form of the stochastic discount factor. The data are allowed to speak for themselves. In essence, the approach relies on only two key assumptions: the choice of conditioning factors for the risk-correction is assumed to be appropriate; and agents are assumed to form rational expectations. Of these, the former assumption is always likely to be a bone of contention, while the latter is generally viewed as benign. But it is the second assumption which, in this situation, it is useful to explore.

Rational expectations are founded on the assumption that agents are able to form priors about the distribution of the underlying stochastic variables. That assumption may be questionable at times of crisis. There may be uncertainty in the sense of Knight (1921), as distinct from risk, about the evolution of the economy. In those situations, the fundamental asset pricing equation needs to be modified thus:

$$p_t^i = E_t\left(m_{t+1}^* x_{t+1}^i\right)$$

where $m_{t+1}^* = z_{t+1} m_{t+1}$.

The conventional stochastic discount factor, m_{t+1}, now needs to be premultiplied by a further stochastic factor, z_{t+1}. Theory will in general place restrictions on z_{t+1}, for example, regarding the form of Knightian uncertainty and the degree of uncertainty (as distinct from risk-) aversion of agents (see Epstein and Wang, 1994, and Hansen, Sargent, and Tallarini, 1999).

The presence of Knightian uncertainty affects the asset pricing formula in two important ways. First, the mean of the stochastic discount factor is biased downwards compared with the case without uncertainty. This is sometimes given the interpretation of "pessimistic expectations" (Epstein and Wang, 1994). Knightian uncertainty leads agents to more heavily discount future returns. Second, it gives rise to a degree of indeterminacy in asset prices. Under uncertainty, asset prices can fluctuate in a band for given fundamentals and still satisfy the asset pricing equation.

Both of these features have echoes in the empirical estimates of Flood and Rose (2004). They find estimates of δ which are significantly in excess of unity—consistent with a lower discount factor and hence with "pessimistic expectations." They also find that estimates of δ wobble around about unity—consistent with some degree of price-indeterminacy within some given range for fundamentals. In short, both of the empirical findings taken by Flood and Rose as consistent with imperfect market integration could alternatively be interpreted as evidence of perfect market integration in the presence of heightened Knightian uncertainty at crisis time. Further restrictions would be needed to unravel these alternative hypotheses given their observational equivalence in the data.

*Andrew G. Haldane is head of international finance at the Bank of England. The views expressed within are not necessarily those of the Bank of England. The author is grateful to Catherine Hovaguimian for comments.

Notes

1. I assess the evidence on the potency of this effect below.

2. See Polk and Sapienza (2002) for a consideration of the real effects of distorted asset prices.

References

Allen, F., and D Gale, 2000, "Financial contagion," *Journal of Political Economy*, Vol. 108, pp. 1–33.

Bliss, R., 2004, "Market discipline: Players, processes, and purposes," *Market Discipline across Countries and Industries*, Cambridge, MA: MIT Press.

Borio, C. V., L. Chincarini, and K. Tsatsaronis, 1997, "Institutional investors, asset management, and financial markets," Bank for International Settlements, mimeo.

Epstein, L., and T. Wang, 1994, "Intertemporal asset pricing under Knightian uncertainty," *Econometrica*, Vol. 62, No. 3, pp. 283–322.

Ferrucci, G., 2003, "Empirical determinants of sovereign emerging market economies bond spreads," Bank of England, working paper.

Flood, R., and A. Rose, 2004, "Equity integration in times of crisis," *Market Discipline across Countries and Industries*, Cambridge, MA: MIT Press.

Forbes, K., 2004, "Capital controls: Mud in the wheels of market discipline," *Market Discipline across Countries and Industries*, Cambridge, MA: MIT Press.

Froot, K., P. O'Connell, and M. S. Seasholes, 1998, "The portfolio flows of international investors," National Bureau of Economic Research, working paper, No. 6687.

Gelos, R. G., and S. Wei, 2002, "Transparency and international investor behaviour," International Monetary Fund, working paper.

Glennerster, R., and Y. Shin, 2003, "Is transparency good for you, and can the IMF help?," International Monetary Fund, working paper, No. WP/03/132.

Haldane, A. G., and J. Scheibe, 2003, "IMF lending and creditor moral hazard," Bank of England, working paper.

Hansen, L-P., T. J. Sargent, and T. D. Tallarini, 1999, "Robust permanent income and pricing," *The Review of Economic Studies*, Vol. 66, pp. 873–907.

Institute for International Finance, 2002, *Action Plan*, Washington, DC.

International Monetary Fund, Independent Evaluation Office, 2002, *Evaluation of the Prolonged Use of Fund Resources*, available at www.imf.org.

Ivanova, A., M. Mayer, A. Mourmouras, and G. Anayiotos, 2003, "What determines the implementation of IMF-supported programs?," International Monetary Fund, working paper, No. WP/03/8.

Knight, F., 1921, *Risk, Uncertainty and Profit*, Boston: Houghton Miflin.

Polk, C., and P. Sapienza, 2002, "The real effects of investor sentiment," Northwestern University, mimeo.

PART VI

CURRENT STATE OF CORPORATE GOVERNANCE

Chapter 20

U.S. Corporate Governance: What Went Wrong and Can It Be Fixed?

Franklin R. Edwards*

Columbia University Business School

1. Introduction

The front-page corporate scandals that erupted in the U.S. economy beginning in 2001—Enron, WorldCom, Tyco, Adelphia, HealthSouth, and others—have undermined confidence in the U.S. business system and raised questions about the effectiveness of corporate governance in the United States.[1] While some may see these scandals, and the related financial irregularities, as simply the products of a few dishonest or unethical corporate managers caught up in the collapse of the stock market bubble that began in 2000, the pervasiveness of the corporate misconduct suggests otherwise—that there was a massive failure of U.S. corporate governance. This paper explores why this failure occurred and what can be done to improve our governance system.

Public distrust of corporate executives has increased sharply in the last few years for several reasons. One is the egregiously excessive chief executive officer (CEO) compensation paid to many CEOs, especially to those presiding over poorly performing firms with collapsing stock prices. In 2001, Larry Ellison, CEO of Oracle, received $706 million from stock options as his software company sputtered and its stock fell precipitously. Soon afterward the disclosure of the large perks given to General Electric's former CEO Jack Welsh made front-page news, reinforcing a growing distrust in the motives of corporate managers. Then there was Jeffrey Barbakow, CEO of Tenet Healthcare, who made $190 million in the fiscal year ending mid-2002, during which time much of his firm's earnings was being generated by a massive Medicare fraud perpetrated by Tenet Healthcare. And even more outrageous, if possible, was the $71 million paid to Dennis Kozlowski, Tyco's former CEO, while he was allegedly looting Tyco of some $600 million.

The final coup de grâce, perhaps, was the recent and embarrassing disclosure of New York Stock Exchange's CEO Dick Grasso's lofty compensation structure and his subsequent forced resignation, putting the New York Stock Exchange's (NYSE) own governance structure in the spotlight—particularly troubling given the central role that the NYSE plays in determining and regulating the corporate governance standards of major corporations.

A second reason for public distrust has been the increased incidence of corporate "reporting failures." Earnings restatements increased markedly during the past ten years. In the period 1990–97 there were 49 restatements a year by publicly traded companies, compared to 91 in 1998, 150 in 1999, and 156 in 2000.[2] More generally, the number of *financial* restatements have risen sharply in recent years: 92 in 1997, 102 in 1998, 174 in 1999, 201 in 2000, 225 in 2001, and a projected 250 in 2002.[3] These have fostered a view that earnings management (or "manipulation") has become a part of the U.S. business culture, and, not surprisingly, have left the impression that U.S. business executives cannot be trusted to tell the truth. A recent Gallup poll of how the public views the CEOs of large U.S. corporations is hardly reassuring: CEOs were rated slightly ahead of car dealers in public trust, and well below military officers.[4]

The most disturbing aspect of the recent corporate misconduct was the collective failure of our corporate governance mechanisms to detect these financial misstatements and the related corporate misconduct early enough to prevent the corporate debacles that occurred. Why were corporate boards not more diligent in ferreting out this misconduct, and in demanding more managerial accountability and more accurate disclosure? Where were the "gatekeepers"—the auditors, securities analysts, credit rating agencies, and the firm's own investment bankers and lawyers? Why did auditors acquiesce to financial reporting that, at best, can be viewed as incomplete and misleading, or, at worst, as just outright fraud? And why, only a few days before Enron's bankruptcy, did 16 out of 17 securities analysts covering Enron have either "buy" or "strong buy" recommendations on its stock?[5] When the entire market was questioning Enron's reporting, how can we explain the steadfastness of these analysts' recommendations? And where were the firm's owners, especially the large institutional investors? At the peak of the market, sixty percent of Enron stock was held by large institutional investors.[6] Why didn't they demand more information about Enron's extensive off-balance-sheet activities, and about how Enron was generating its earnings, instead of simply acquiescing to whatever Enron reported? Finally, why did corporate managers behave as they did? Was there a sudden outburst of greed and unethical conduct among corporate managers, or is there a fundamental misalignment of manager and shareholder incentives that was not present in prior years? Clearly, responsibility for what happened must be parceled out among all of the participants in our corporate governance system: managers, corporate boards, gatekeepers, and shareholders.

It is also not a palatable defense to argue that our system of corporate governance, whatever its flaws, is nevertheless superior to those of other countries.[7] Whether or not this is true, recent corporate scandals have certainly illuminated aspects of our system that can be improved upon. The benefits of better corporate governance appear to be substantial.[8] This paper both reviews corporate governance mechanisms employed in the United States to determine why they may have failed and explores measures that might be taken to enhance their effectiveness. A fundamental aspect of this review is an examination of the motivations and incentives of participants in the corporate governance system to determine whether their incentives are aligned with those of shareholders and investors, and to examine remedies that have been proposed to better align these interests.

2. The Structure of Corporate Governance in the United States

Corporate governance is comprised of a multifaceted set of legal and institutional mechanisms designed to safeguard the interests of corporate shareholders and to reduce the agency costs that derive from the separation of ownership (shareholders) from control (managers and/or controlling shareholders). Fundamental to corporate governance are mechanisms that provide shareholders with information about the activities and operations of corporations, and legal rules that establish the respective responsibilities of managers and boards of directors as well as the penalties attached to irresponsible behavior.

A first line of defense, so to speak, are federal securities laws that empower owners (shareholders) by requiring corporate disclosure sufficient to make the operations of corporations transparent to them. If shareholders come to believe that a company is being managed improperly or inefficiently, they can decide not to buy the company's stock or to sell it if they already own it. Either way, badly performing managers are subjected to "market discipline" which may change the way that they operate their companies. In addition, federal securities laws empower shareholders more directly by providing a proxy voting system that allows them to elect corporate directors and to impose their collective will with respect to "material" changes in the organization or operations of the company. The proxy system, however, is cumbersome and exorbitantly expensive for shareholders except, perhaps, for those who hold very large stakes in a company.

Corporate law (consisting largely of state-based corporate law until the recent Sarbanes–Oxley Act) is a second line of defense. State law and the certificate of incorporation endows corporations with perpetual life and establishes a governance structure for the corporation, assigning rights and duties to shareholders, directors, and managers. These rights and duties, as interpreted and honed by a long line of court cases, have resulted in managers and directors (and controlling shareholders) owing various fiduciary duties to shareholders—specifically, duties of care, loyalty, and candor. Breaches of these duties can result in shareholder suits against managers and directors to stop certain actions from occurring (such as the sale of the company) or for damages stemming from actions that are not in the interests of shareholders. State corporate law, therefore, attempts to better align the interests of managers and directors with those of shareholders by imposing various legal obligations on managers and directors and then penalizing them if they fail to meet those obligations.

A third governance mechanism is executive compensation. Shareholders and their elected directors may choose to employ an incentive compensation structure for both managers and directors that better aligns their interests with those of shareholders. In particular, in recent years executive compensation has been increasingly tied to the company's stock performance by granting managers either stock options or restricted stock. Prior to the 1990s little use was made of equity-based compensation schemes, but during the 1990s equity-based pay, and particularly stock options grants, increased dramatically. Of the $11.2 million increase in *average* CEO pay during the 1990s (from $3.5 million in 1992 to $14.7 million in 2000), stock options valued at the time of the grant alone accounted for $6.4 million of this amount (stock options grew from $800,000 to nearly $7.2 million). By 1999, 94 percent of S&P 500 companies were granting stock options to their top executives, and the grant-date value of these options accounted for 47 percent of total CEO compensation. Further, stock options are now given to a broad range of executives and employees. This stands in sharp contrast to executive pay packages in other countries, which have typically employed far lesser amounts of equity-based pay.

Supplementing the foregoing governance mechanisms are two "market disciplinary" mechanisms: "gatekeepers" and "hostile takeovers." The term "gatekeepers," broadly viewed, has come to mean the auditors, credit rating agencies, securities analysts, underwriters, and lawyers who protect the interests of shareholders by monitoring the corporation and corporate insiders, and by "certifying" the accuracy of corporate reporting and the legality of corporate behavior. Gatekeepers can be thought of as independent, skilled, professionals who are interposed between the corporation and investors and who perform a certification function imposed either by the law (such as auditors) or by market convention (such as securities analysts). According to conventional theory, gatekeepers can be relied upon to perform their respective roles honestly and effectively because they are independent of the corporations they monitor and because their business success depends critically on their credibility and reputation. The desire to build and maintain a strong reputation with investors and creditors, arguably, should align the incentives of gatekeepers with those of investors and creditors, rather than with those of corporate managers. In addition, the threat of private litigation should deter gatekeepers from fraudulent or reckless behavior.

Hostile takeovers are the ultimate market response to corrupt or inefficient managers and to a general failure of other corporate governance mechanisms to correct these problems. Takeovers replace entrenched and inept managers with new managers capable of increasing stockholder value, and typically employ measures to better align manager interests with those of shareholders (such as incentive compensation schemes). As a corrective mechanism, however, hostile takeovers are typically a blunt and costly mechanism. By definition, they always encounter stiff resistance from entrenched managers aided by laws that usually permit them to erect formidable takeover defenses, making hostile takeovers an attractive option only when agency costs are especially large. There also is the possibility that hostile takeovers can be used to "greenmail" companies rather than to increase efficiency. Nonetheless, because the mere threat of a hostile takeover may be a significant deterrent to lazy and inept managers, hostile takeovers remain an important component of an effective system of corporate governance.

3. What Went Wrong?

Most of the recent corporate scandals are characterized by either the willingness of corporate managers to inflate financial results, either by overstating revenues or understating costs, or to divert company funds to the private uses of managers (that is, looting the company). Prominent examples of fraudulent "earnings management" are WorldCom's intentional misclassification of as much as $11 billion in expenses as capital investments—perhaps the largest accounting fraud in history; Enron's creation of off-balance-sheet partnerships to hide the company's deteriorating financial position and to enrich Enron executives; and HealthSouth's overbilling of Medicare and fraudulent accounting practices. Examples of just plain looting may be Adelphia and Tyco, where top executives allegedly stole millions of dollars from their companies and then tried to cover it up.

If nothing else, the pervasiveness of this kind of managerial misconduct raises the following questions about the motivations and incentives of American business managers and about the effectiveness of American corporate governance.

1. Is there a fundamental misalignment of managerial and shareholders' interests in the United States, and, if so, what are the causes of this misalignment? Or, stated somewhat differently, does the incentive structure that American managers typically face motivate them to engage in the kind of financial fraud and earnings mismanagement that has characterized recent corporate scandals, and what is the source of this perverse incentive structure?[9]

2. Why did internal governance mechanisms, such as corporate boards, audit committees, and compensation committees, either condone or, more likely, fail to penetrate the fog of misinformation and fraud that shrouded managerial misconduct and allowed managers to deceive shareholders and investors? Are the incentives of board members the same as those of shareholders, or are they conflicted in significant ways?

3. Why did the gatekeepers—auditors, credit rating agencies, securities analysts, investment banks, and lawyers—not uncover the financial fraud and earnings manipulation that occurred, and alert investors to potential discrepancies and problems long before the consequences came crashing down on them in the form of plummeting stock values? Are the incentives of gatekeepers consistent with those of shareholders and investors?

4. Finally, why were not shareholders themselves more vigilant in protecting their interests, especially large institutional investors? What are the motivations and incentives of the money managers who run these institutions?

3.1 Managerial Incentives, Executive Compensation, and Earnings Misreporting

Why do managers engage in earnings misreporting in the short run when they know that the true state of the company's operations must eventually be revealed, either by the collapse of the firm or by their inability to continue to deceive investors? Further, why has the incidence of misreporting increased during the 1990s? There must, obviously, be benefits that managers can reap in the short-run that make such deceptive behavior rational. An obvious benefit of misreporting is that managers get to keep their jobs longer, but this benefit existed long before the 1990s and probably does not explain the increased incidence of misreporting during the 1990s. An answer may be that the benefits from misreporting increased during the 1990s, and therefore the incentive to misreport increased, because of the dramatic shift in the compensation structure of American executives towards equity-based compensation. In particular, in 1989 only 4 percent of the median CEO pay of the S&P 500 industrial companies was equity-based—96 percent was salary and cash bonuses. By 2001, equity-based pay had jumped to 66 percent of the median CEO compensation.[10] Further, a greater use of stock options grants by companies' accounts for most of this increase. As a consequence, the sensitivity of CEO pay (as well as the pay of other executives) to short-term corporate performance increased substantially in the 1990s, as did the benefits and incentive to report (or misreport) favorable company performance.

Equity-based pay is certainly part of the Enron story. The compensation of Enron executives was closely linked to shareholder value, and its executives had a substantial portion of their compensation at risk (as much as 70 percent according to Enron's own compensation committee report). As such, Enron executives had a strong incentive to make every effort to increase earnings and the company's stock price. While this may arguably result in a better alignment of interests of managers and shareholders, it may also have the unintended effect of creating strong temptations for managers to engage in transactions that circumvent accounting rules in order to misrepresent the financial condition of the company and boast stock prices.

In view of the recent corporate scandals, therefore, we may want to revisit the use of equity-based compensation to motivate managers, and, in particular, whether a different pay structure could be used to reduce the incentives for managers to inflate earnings. While the rationale behind equity-based compensation is enticing—to motivate managers and better align manager and stockholder interests, there may be better ways to structure pay packages to obtain these benefits without also getting the bad effects. In particular, longer vesting periods and greater use of "restricted" stock (for example, options holders could receive restricted stock) may better align managerial interests with the long-run value of the firm. In addition, a more sensible accounting treatment of stock option grants that requires them to be treated as an expense on financial statements may eliminate the "perceived" cost advantage of options to corporations (and boards) and may increase transparency and market discipline. Prompt disclosure of stock selling by managers also may enable the market to better assess the motivations of managers who exercise stock options and quickly sell the stock they receive.[11] Requiring more stock ownership by executives relative to their cash salaries also may be useful.

Although the Sarbanes–Oxley Act[12] does not address executive compensation as such, it does attempt to mitigate the incentives of corporate managers to inflate short-term earnings by requiring the forfeiture of "... incentive-based or equity-based compensation ..." to the corporation during the 12-month period following the filing of an inflated earnings report if the corporation later restates its earnings.[13] In addition, under threat of criminal prosecution, it requires that the chief executive officer and chief financial officer of every publicly held firm certify in every periodic report filed with the Securities Exchange Commission (SEC) "that information contained in the periodic report fairly presents, in all material respects, the financial condition, and results of the issuer."[14]

Finally, as response to concerns about "excessive" pay unrelated to firm performance, Sarbanes-Oxley requires greater public disclosure of compensation and benefits received by corporate executives, makes more explicit the responsibilities that compensation committees of boards have in determining and reviewing executive compensation plans, and requires that compensation committees be comprised solely on independent directors. In addition, as of June 30, 2003, SEC-approved NYSE and Nasdaq listing requirements require shareholder approval (or a vote) to approve stock option grants and other equity-based compensation plans as well as material changes in these plans.

3.2 Corporate Boards

Why have corporate boards not been more alert to the kinds of managerial behavior that brought about the recent corporate scandals? Again, Enron is illustrative of the problem. As boards go, Enron's was a "Dream Team," stacked with sophisticated and distinguished individuals, and with experts in finance, investing, and accounting. Its directors had significant ownership stakes in Enron as well, so their interests should have been aligned with those of Enron's shareholders.[15] Its 14-member board had only two internal executives, Chairman of the Board and former CEO Kenneth Lay and President and CEO Jeffrey Skilling. The other twelve directors consisted of five CEOs, four academics, a professional investor, the former president of Enron's wholly owned subsidiary Belco Oil & Gas (an affiliated director), and a former UK politician. On paper, at least, 86 percent of Enron's board might be considered to be "independent," considerably higher than for most U.S. companies.[16]

Enron's board structure also was everything one could have wanted: subcommittees for compensation and management development, audit and compliance, nominating and corporate governance, and finance, and these committees were all comprised of outside directors (except for the finance committee which had one affiliated director). In addition, the audit committee had a state of the art charter making it "... overseer of Enron's financial reporting process and internal controls ...," had "... direct access to financial, legal, and other staff and consultants of the company," and had the power to retain other (outside) accountants, lawyers, or whatever consultants that it deemed appropriate.[17] Even the corporate culture at Enron seemed ideal. In a 1999 speech on the Conference on Business Ethics, Chairman Kenneth Lay said: "A strong independent and knowledgeable board can make a significant difference in the performance of any company. ... It's not an accident that we put strength of character first. Like any successful company, we must have directors who start with what is right, who do not have hidden agendas and [who] strive to make judgments about what is best for the company and not about what is best for themselves or some other constituency."

Yet detailed examinations of what happened at Enron after its collapse arrived at conclusions about board performance strikingly at odds with the picture painted above. The Senate Subcommittee on "The Role of the Board of Directors in Enron's Collapse" concluded that there was a fiduciary failure of the board (a breach of its duties of care, loyalty, and candor?) because it allowed Enron to engage in high-risk accounting, inappropriate conflict of interest transactions, extensive undisclosed off-the-books activities, inappropriate public disclosure, and excessive compensation.[18]

The *Powers Report* concluded that "The board cannot be faulted for failing to act on information that was withheld, but it can be faulted for the limited scrutiny it gave to [many] transactions, [such as those] between Enron and the LJM partnerships" (p. 148). Whether or not these are fair assessments of the board's performance, Enron does make clear that high-powered equity-based compensation schemes combined with opaque financial disclosure policies create strong incentives to manipulate financial results, and that in this environment corporate boards must be especially vigilant about monitoring financial results and financial controls and about monitoring and approving transactions where there are actual or potential conflicts of interest. It is fair to say, I believe, that the Enron board did not meet this higher standard of care.

Why did the Enron and other corporate boards fail? And can we do anything to prevent this from happening again? The Sarbanes–Oxley Act and the new NYSE governance rules seek to improve board performance by increasing the role of independent directors on boards and by requiring boards to adhere to specific processes and procedures, and by tightening the definition of what constitutes an "independent" director. In addition, to enhance market discipline greater disclosure is now required of off-balance sheet arrangements and other transactions that have obfuscated company financial statements and misled investors.

In effect, the Sarbanes–Oxley Act reforms have codified and given teeth to what was generally viewed as "best board practice" prior to the recent corporate scandals, and by doing so is attempting to change the corporate culture about what board responsibilities are and about what is expected of boards and directors. The objective is to narrow the scope for corporate misconduct in the future by increasing the responsibilities and powers of corporate boards, and possibly by increasing director liability for misconduct. It remains to be seen, however, whether Sarbanes–Oxley will succeed in changing the traditional culture of collegiality and the "go along" atmosphere that pervaded most corporate boards in the past, and which Warren Buffett, in his annual letter to Berskshire Hathaway shareholders, summed up well when he confessed he had often been silent on management proposals contrary to shareholders interests while serving on 19 boards since the 1960s. Most boards, he said, had an atmosphere where "collegiality trumped independence."[19] To change the traditional culture I would go even further than Sarbanes–Oxley and require that the jobs of CEO and chairperson of the Board be separated and that the board be chaired by an independent director.

The judiciary also has been moving in the direction of increased liability for directors.[20] Of particular note is the recent decision in re: Walt Disney Company, where the Delaware Court of Chancery permitted a stockholder suit against the directors of Walt Disney to proceed to trial in response to a complaint that the directors breached their fiduciary duties by permitting what can only be viewed as an excessive termination payment (valued at $140 million) to departing (after little over a year) Disney executive Michael Ovitz.[21] The Court said: "The sheer size of the payout ... pushes the envelope of judicial respect for the business judgment of directors in making compensation decisions."

3.3 Gatekeepers

It is also important to increase market discipline of corporations. While greater transparency—better accounting rules and disclosure—is an essential part of this goal, it is equally important that information be used effectively by shareholders and investors. An important function of "gatekeepers"—external auditors, credit rating agencies, securities analysts, investment banks, and lawyers—is to provide verification or certification services to investors. In particular, an auditor certifies the accuracy of an issuer's financial statements; a debt rating agencies certifies the creditworthiness of an issuer; a securities analyst provides objective assessments of a corporation's earnings prospects and general competitiveness; an investment bank provides a "fairness opinion" in merger situations with respect to the value of a firm or its securities, and as an underwriter of initial public offerings implicitly pledges its reputation with respect to the issuer's credibility; and an attorney for an issuer provides its opinion to the underwriters that all material information of which it is aware concerning the issuer has been properly disclosed. Theoretically, investors should place more credibility in gatekeepers than in their clients or issuers because gatekeepers have more to lose and less to gain by deceiving investors than do issuers. In particular, by deceiving investors they could jeopardize the reputational capital they built up over many years and by providing services to many different clients.

What, then, explains the collective failure of gatekeepers to detect and expose the questionable financial and accounting decisions that led to the collapse of Enron, WorldCom, and other "misreportings" or accounting frauds? According to one view gatekeepers can be expected to perform their monitoring roles diligently and honestly because their business success should depend on their credibility and reputation with the ultimate users of their information—investors and creditors. Lacking this credibility, why would firms employ auditors and credit rating agencies? Further, if gatekeepers provide fraudulent or reckless opinions, they are subject to private damage suits by those damaged by relying on their misleading opinions.

An alternative view, of course, is that the interests of gatekeepers may be more closely aligned with those of corporate managers than with investors and shareholders because it is the firm, after all, that hires, pays for, and fires the gatekeepers, and not the investors or creditors. Auditors are hired and paid by the firms they audit; credit rating agencies are typically retained and paid by the firms they rate; lawyers are paid by the firms that retain them; and, as we have recently learned through embarrassing lawsuits brought against high-profile investment banks, the compensation of security analysts (who work primarily for investment banks) is closely tied to the amount of related investment banking business that their employers (the investment banks) do with the firms that their analysts evaluate.[22] It is not much of an exaggeration, I believe, to say that firms that hire gatekeepers are paying them for favorable evaluations, not unbiased evaluations. Gatekeepers certainly know this, and that if they give unfavorable evaluations they are unlikely to be retained again.

Thus, because most gatekeepers are inherently conflicted, they may not always act in the interests of investors and shareholders. This conflict is also more serious than may at first appear because in many cases, such as auditing firms, clients of gatekeeper firms are typically associated with a single partner of the firm. The loss of a client, therefore, while perhaps a relatively minor loss of income for the gatekeeper firm, can mean a devastating loss in income and reputation to that partner, and may adversely effect his or her position at the firm. Further, it seems likely that gatekeeper conflict of interest has gotten worse during the 1990s because of the increased cross-selling of consulting services by auditors and credit rating agencies, and by the cross-selling of investment banking services.[23] According to one recent survey, large corporations now pay consulting fees to their auditors that are on average more than three times the audit fees they pay.[24] In contrast, in 1990, 80 percent of the clients of the Big Five auditing firms received no consulting services from their auditing firms, and only one percent of those clients paid consulting fees in excess of their auditing fees.[25]

Increased cross-selling also may reduce market discipline by gatekeepers by making it easier for clients to threaten to fire uncooperative gatekeepers. For example, firing an auditor might subject the firm to intense public scrutiny and result in public disclosure of the reasons for the auditor's dismissal or resignation, and may even invite SEC intervention.[26] But it is far easier and less visible for a firm to threaten to reduce its use of the auditor's consulting services in retaliation for an unfavorable opinion. This can be a powerful incentive for auditors and other gatekeepers to provide compliant opinions. Further, increased cross-selling may potentially make it rational for gatekeepers to engage in behavior that is very profitable in the short (or intermediate) term but "reputation-depleting" in the long run.

Finally, an argument can be made that during the 1990s the deterrent effect of legal liability for gatekeepers declined as well, further reducing market discipline.[27] Prior to the 1990s, auditors, for example, faced a real risk of civil liability from class action suits. But during the 1990s Supreme Court decisions together with the Private Securities Litigation Reform Act of 1995 and the Securities Litigation Uniform Standards Act of 1998 significantly reduced the threat of private litigation.[28]

Thus, to make gatekeepers more effective, we need to reduce their conflicts of interest and their incentive to provide compliant opinions, and/or increase the threat of market discipline through greater legal liability if they fail to adequately represent the interests of investors and creditors. To accomplish this, I believe there needs to be more limits put on the cross-selling of consulting and tax services by auditing firms[29] and credit rating agencies, mandatory "term limits" for auditing firms,[30] the separation of security analysis from core investment banking services, and "noisy exit" provisions for lawyers.

In addition, we need to revisit the liability system that applies to gatekeepers. The current "fault-based" (or negligence) regime has proven to be costly and ineffective. It may be time to consider replacing it with a "strict liability" regime with limits or caps. A strict liability regime would impose strict liability on gatekeepers for material misstatements and omissions in offering documents and financial statements and remove due diligence-based defenses. It would force gatekeepers to take measures to prevent issuer misconduct without requiring a costly inquiry into whether the gatekeepers satisfied inexact standards of conduct (that is, reasonable care or due diligence defenses). But without limits such a system would obviously be draconian.

However, there are a variety of ways to limit the liability of gatekeepers.[31] An important task for the future is to determine if one of these strict liability regimes is likely to work better than what we now have, which does not appear to work at all.

3.4 Owners and Institutional Shareholders

Another important dimension of market discipline is getting owners and particularly institutional shareholders—pension funds, mutual funds, banks, life insurance companies, and endowment funds—to take a more active role in monitoring and disciplining corporate misconduct. As large owners, institutional investors should have a greater incentive to monitor corporations and should be better able to overcome the information asymmetries and agency costs associated with diffuse stock ownership. Yet, institutional investors, even though holding large positions in firms like Enron, Tyco, Global Crossing, and WorldCom, collectively failed to protect their investors from huge losses incurred as a consequence of managerial misconduct in these firms.

Getting institutional investors to be more effective corporate monitors is undoubtedly a critical part of any hope we may have of empowering shareholders and increasing market discipline. Together, institutional investors hold about 55 percent of the outstanding equity (market value) of all U.S. firms, up from 34 percent in 1980 and just 12 percent in 1960; and in the largest 1,000 U.S. firms they own more than 61 percent of the outstanding equity. They also account for 75 percent of the trading in NYSE-listed stocks.[32] Is also seems likely that institutional ownership will continue to grow in the future. With respect to the relative importance of the different institutions, in terms of *assets owned*, their respective shares are private pension funds: 27 percent, investment companies or mutual funds: 23 percent, insurance companies: 15 percent, and public pension funds: 14.5 percent. In terms of *assets managed*, however, investment companies are by far the largest: they manage almost 36 percent of total institutional assets, compared to 20 percent for private pension funds, 18 percent for both insurance companies and banks, and 6 percent for public pension funds.

Other than a few public pension funds, however, institutional investors have not played an active role in monitoring corporations. To a large extent they have been content to do nothing or simply sell the stock of companies where they disagree with management's strategy. This behavior could be viewed as a rational response to managerial misconduct, since any other course of action would arguably be more costly and less rewarding for the shareholders and beneficiaries of the institutions. But another view is that institutional fund managers have conflicts of interests that incentivize them against direct action to prevent corporate misconduct. The fact that institutional fund managers customarily support entrenched corporate managers against dissident shareholders suggests that their interests may be more aligned with those of corporate managers than with shareholders (or owners).

What are these conflicts? One source of conflict is the compensation structure of most fund managers—typically a flat percentage of assets under management, which makes their compensation depend largely on the amount of assets under management. This provides a strong incentive for them to grow the assets of the fund. They are rewarded for increasing the funds under management, and penalized for losing funds that they already have. This has created a significant conflict for mutual fund managers because, during the 1990s, retirement funds originating with corporations have grown substantially and have become their most important source of "stable" funds. Pension assets now constitute more than 20 percent of total mutual fund assets, up from 5 percent in 1990. Mutual fund managers are unlikely to engage in corporate governance actions that antagonize corporate managers for fear of losing these pension funds.[33] Second, there is an inherent conflict embedded in the corporate culture which discourages private pension fund managers from active corporate governance. Corporate managers effectively control their own pension funds, and few of them want to meddle in the affairs of other companies for fear of provoking a similar reaction by the pension funds controlled by those companies.

The law also discourages institutional investors from acquiring large positions in companies and taking a direct interest in corporate affairs For example, the "five and ten" rule in the Investment Company Act of 1940 is a clear attempt to limit mutual fund ownership, and Section 16(b) of the Securities and Exchange Act of 1934 (the "short-swing profits" rule) discourages mutual funds from taking large equity positions and from placing a director on a portfolio company's board of directors.[34] Also, the Employee Retirement Income Security Act (ERISA) and standard trustee law poses significant legal risks to private pension fund managers who acquire large blocks of stock or are active in corporate governance.[35]

Thus, making institutional investors more active and more effective corporate monitors cuts at the heart of our cultural and legal foundations and involves complex legal, structural, and philosophic issues, starting with whether we even want to encourage institutional investors to take larger ownership positions in firms and to pursue activist governance strategies. What, after all, are the motives and incentives of fund managers, and are these likely to be consistent with those of shareholders? Does not institutional activism introduce still another non-transparent principal-agent relationship, fraught with potential conflicts and monitoring problems? And, if we do encourage more institutional activism, do we want to encourage active ownership by all institutions, or just some? In particular, public pension funds may be conflicted by private interest groups or political interests. Finally, what structural and legal changes must be made to change the culture of institutional passiveness and bring about more activism? Of course, if we give up on making institutional investors more effective shareholders, which shareholders will have the incentive and power to monitor corporate managers? Simply selling the shares of underperforming firms may not be enough.

At minimum, we need to remove incentives that institutional fund managers now have to support corporate managers. A positive step towards accomplishing this is the new SEC requirement that mutual funds have to disclose annually all their proxy votes during the previous twelve months. This requirement should be extended to all institutional investors. Greater transparency of how fund managers use their proxy votes will at least subject them to scrutiny by their own investors and beneficiaries. We should also review the governance structure of institutional investors themselves.[36] In particular, we need to be assured that the directors of mutual funds are competent and represent the interests of mutual fund shareholders, and that they are truly independent of fund management companies. A good start would be to require that a mutual fund board be comprised entirely of "independent" directors and make the definition of "independence" the same as that employed in the Sarbanes–Oxley Act or in the New York Stock Exchange listing requirements.

4. Conclusion

The eruption of corporate accounting scandals and related financial irregularities in the last few years, together with the subsequent revelation of widespread corporate misconduct among American firms, has raised fundamental questions about the effectiveness corporate governance in the United States, and in particular about why there was a collective failure of our corporate governance mechanisms to prevent or at least alert shareholders and investors to impending problems.

To some degree, responsibility for recent corporate misconduct must be allocated to the failure of several components of our business and governance system: 1) corporate managers; 2) corporate boards; 3) gatekeepers; and 4) shareholders, and especially institutional investors. In many cases corporate managers failed in their fiduciary duties to shareholders, and were seemingly motivated more by self-aggrandizement and outright greed than by a desire to benefit the corporation and its owners. Corporate boards also failed to represent the interest of shareholders effectively, largely because they either were ignorant of what was going on or did not want to rock the "go along" collegial atmosphere typical of most boardrooms. And where were the "gatekeepers?" Why did the Enron and WorldCom auditors and lawyers not understand what was going on and demand more disclosure and candor, and why did virtually every securities analyst fail to see the potential for significant problems in the financial statements (and the associated incomprehensible footnotes) put out by these firms? Finally, shareholders themselves, and especially institutional investors, must bear some of the responsibility for what happened. Rather than actively scrutinizing the behavior of corporate managers and boards, they were largely content to take a passive approach to their investments.

This paper reviews key components of corporate governance in the United States to determine why these mechanisms may have failed, and discusses steps that have recently been taken to correct these deficiencies as well as some additional steps we might want to take to further improve corporate governance. In specific, the paper reviews recent trends in executive compensation in the United States and the implications for managerial incentives, the effectiveness of corporate boards, and the role and effectiveness of "gatekeepers" and institutional investors.

An overriding conclusion of this review, not surprisingly, is that all of our corporate governance mechanisms are beset by significant conflicts of interest, and that these conflicts may have become more severe in recent years because of changes in our corporate and financial system. As a consequence, it may be time for a comprehensive review of the U.S. governance system to determine whether additional measures can be taken to mitigate these conflicts.

*Franklin R. Edwards is the Arthur F. Burns Professor of Economics and Finance at Columbia University Business School

Notes

1. Lacayo and Ripley (2000), pp.32–33.

2. Moriarty and Livingston (2001), pp.53–57.

3. U.S. Senate (2002), pp. 4–5.

4. Keen (2002), p. 2A.

5. Partnoy (2002), p. 115.

6. Healy and Palepu (2002).

7. Holmstrom and Kaplan (2003) and Denis and McConnell (2003).

8. Gompers, Ishii, and Metrick (2001).

9. By earnings mismanagement I mean not only reporting that is illegal or inconsistent with accepted accounting standards but also statements that while within accepted legal and accounting standards are primarily meant to deceive investors about the company's true financial condition.

10. Hall and Murphy (2003).

11. Financial Economists Roundtable (2003). In addition, stricter accounting standards that reduce the ex ante opportunities to engage in misreporting would also help to curb misreporting, as would a requirement that companies and their auditors have to report a "true and fair view" of the company's financial condition. See Benston and Hartgraves (2002), pp. 105–127.

12. This statute is entitled the "Public Company Accounting Reform and Investor Protection Act of 2002," 15 U.S.C. sec. 7201 et seq., 107 Pub. L. No. 204, 116 Stat. 745 (hereafter referred to as simply the Sarbanes–Oxley Act).

13. Sarbanes–Oxley Act, Section 304. This provision applies only if the earnings restatement is the product of "misconduct."

14. Sarbanes–Oxley Act, Section 906 codified as 18 U.S.C. sec 1350. The SEC recently announced that employee benefit plan reports and 8-K reports are exempt from certification.

15. The beneficial ownership of the outside directors reported in the 2001 proxy ranged from $266,000 to $706 million. See Gillan and Martin (2002), p. 23.

16. Enron's Proxy Statement, News Release, May 1, 2001. Subsequent to Enron's collapse, the independence of some of Enron's directors was questioned by the press and in Senate hearings because some directors received consulting fees in addition to board fees, Enron had made donations to groups with which some directors were affiliated and had also done transactions with entities in which some directors played a major role.

17. Gordon (2002), pp. 1399–1427.

18. Permanent Subcommittee on Investigations, Committee on Governmental Affairs, United States Senate, 2002, July 8.

19. Strauss and Hansen (2003), p. B. 01.

20. For a brief historical summary of relevant court decisions, see Coffee (2003a), pp. 51–56.

21. Delaware Court of Chancery, 2003, "In Re: The Walt Disney Company Derivative Litigation," Consolidated C.A. No. 15452, May 28.

22. Citigroup paid $400 million to settle government charges that it issued fraudulent research reports; and Merrill Lynch & Co. agreed to pay $200 million for issuing fraudulent research in a settlement with securities regulators, and also agreed that in the future its securities analysts would no longer be paid on the basis of the firm's related investment banking work.

23. Coffee (2003b). See also Coffee (2002) and Coffee (2003c).

24. Stewart and Countryman (2002), p. C-1.

25. Public Oversight Board, Panel on Audit Effectiveness (2002), p. 102.16J.

26. See Item 4 ("Changes in Registrants Certifying Accountant") of Form 8-K.

27. See Coffee (2002), pp. 25–27.

28. *Ibid.*, pp. 25–57.

29. Section 201 of the Sarbanes–Oxley Act already specifies eight types of professional services which the auditor of a public company may not perform for its audit client, and also authorizes the Public Company Accounting Oversight Board (PCAOB) to prohibit additional services if it determines that they may compromise the auditor's independence. I favor even greater limits on non-auditing services.

30. Sarbanes–Oxley requires that the senior partner in charge of each audit be changed every five years, but not the auditing firm.

31. For alternative views on this issue, see Coffee (2003a) and Partnoy (2001), pp. 491, 540.

32. Cox and Thomas (2002), p. 855.

33. While active corporate governance may arguably raise portfolio returns and enhance mutual fund performance, and therefore attract new funds, this relationship is hardly as direct and predictable as the one described above.

34. Requires that at least 50 percent of the value of a fund's total assets satisfy two criteria: an equity position cannot exceed five percent of the value of a fund's assets, and the fund cannot hold more then ten percent of the outstanding securities of any company.

35. Roe (1994).

36. See proposal of the International Corporate Governance Network on "Principles of Shareholder Stewardship."

References

Benston, George, and Al Hartgraves, 2002, "Enron: What happened and what we can learn from it," *Journal of Accounting and Public Policy*, Vol. 21, pp. 105–127.

Coffee, Jr., John C., 2003a, "Gatekeeper failure and reform: The challenge of fashioning relevant reforms," Columbia Law School, working paper, No. 237, September, pp. 51–56.

_____, 2003b, "What caused Enron? A capsule social and economic history of the 1990s," Columbia University Law School, working paper, No. 214, January 20.

_____, 2003c, "Corporate gatekeepers: Their past, present, and future," Duke Law School, working paper, no. 7.

_____, 2002, "Understanding Enron: It's about the gatekeepers, stupid," *Business Law*, Vol. 57, No. 1403.

Cox, James D., and Randall Thomas, 2002, "Leaving money on the table: Do institutional investors file claims in securities class actions?," *Washington University Law Quarterly*, Vol. 80, No. 4, p. 855.

Denis, Diane, and John McConnell, 2003, "International corporate governance," European Corporate Governance Institute, working paper, No. 05/2003, January.

Financial Economists Roundtable, 2003, "The controversy over executive compensation," Chicago, November.

Gillan, Stuart, and John Martin, 2002, "Financial engineering, corporate governance, and the collapse of Enron," University of Delaware, Center for Corporate Governance, working paper, No. 2002-001, p. 23.

Gompers, Paul A., Joy L. Ishii, and Andrew Metrick, 2001, "Corporate governance and equity prices," Harvard Business School, working paper, July.

Gordon, Jeffrey N., 2002, "What Enron means for the management and control of the modern corporation: Some initial reflections," *University of Chicago Law Review*, Vol. 69, No. 3, Summer, pp. 1399–1427.

Hall, Brian, and Kevin Murphy, 2003, "The trouble with stock options," National Bureau of Economic Research, working paper, No. w9784, June.

Healy, Paul, and Krishna Palepu, 2002, "Governance and intermediation problems in capital markets: Evidence from the fall of Enron," Harvard Business School, Negotiation, Organizations, and Markets, research paper, No. 02-27, August.

Holmstrom, Bengt, and Steven Kaplan, 2003, "The state of U.S. corporate governance: What's right and what's wrong?," *Journal of Applied Corporate Finance*, Vol. 15, No. 3, Spring.

Keen, Judy, 2002, "Anxiety rearranges poll numbers," *USA Today*, July 30, p. 2A.

Lacayo, Richard, and Amanda Ripley, 2000, "Persons of the year," *Time Magazine*, Vol. 160, No. 27, December 30, pp. 32–33.

Moriarty, George B., and Phillip B. Livingston, 2001, "Quantitative measures of the quality of financial reporting," *Financial Executive*, Vol. 17, No. 5, July/August, pp. 53–57.

Partnoy, Frank, 2002, "Financial Oversight of Enron: the SEC and Private Sector Watchdogs," statement before the United States Senate Committee on Governmental Affairs, 107th Cong., S. Hrg. 107-376, January 24, p.115.

_____, 2001, "Barbarians at the gatekeepers?: A proposal for a modified strict liability regime," *Washington University Law Quarterly*, Vol. 79, pp. 491, 540.

Public Oversight Board, Panel on Audit Effectiveness, 2002, "Report and recommendations, exposure draft," Washington, p. 102.16J.

Roe, Mark J., 1994, *Strong Managers, Weak Owners: The Political Roots of American Corporate Finance*, Princeton, N.J.: Princeton University Press.

Stewart, Janet Kidd, and Andrew Countryman, 2002,"Local audit conflicts add up: Consulting deals, hiring practices in question," *Chicago Tribune*, February 24, p. C-1.

Strauss, Gary, and Barbara Hansen, 2003, "Special report: Bubble hasn't burst yet on CEO salaries despite the times; top executives cash in even as stockholders lose out," *USA Today*, March 31, p. B. 01.

U.S. Senate, Committee on Banking, Housing, and Urban Affairs, 2002, "Financial statement restatements: Trends, market impacts, regulatory responses and remaining challenges," report to the chairman, United States General Accounting Office, October, No. GAO-03-138, pp. 4–5.

Chapter 21

Corporate Governance in Europe: Competition versus Harmonization

Marco Becht*
*European Center for Advanced Research in Economics and Statistics,
Université Libre de Bruxelles, and European Corporate Governance Institute*

and

Colin Mayer
*Saïd Business School, Oxford University, Center for Economic Policy Research,
and European Corporate Governance Institute*

1. Overview

Several issues have featured prominently in recent corporate governance debates in Europe. These include a European Commission Action Plan on improving corporate governance and proposals for reforming European company law. A common question to emerge from these debates is the extent to which regulation should be harmonized across member states of the European Union or diversity should be allowed to persist or even encouraged.

Underlying this is the diverse forms of corporate arrangements that exist in Europe. Not only are continental European companies very different from the textbook models of the UK and U.S. but they are also very different from each other. Attempts at harmonizing regulatory rules concerning the corporate sector strike at the heart of these differences. Some people view this as a good thing, arguing that the differences are impediments to the promotion of integrated European markets, and a source of inefficiency and rigidity. Others believe that the differences reflect deep-rooted historical, political and social factors with which the Commission cannot and should not interfere.

There are two sets of policies under current consideration that capture this controversy particularly well. The first is the proposed European Directive on takeovers. The second is the set of European Court of Justice rulings on freedom of establishment, coming out of Article 48 of the Treaty of Rome. What is interesting about these two issues is that they both attempt to address corporate diversity in Europe but do so in diametrically opposing ways.

Section 2 provides a stylized map of corporate control arrangements in Europe. It describes the different models of corporate ownership and control that exist today. The relative merits of these have been much discussed, and section 3 sets out the theoretical advantages and drawbacks of each. New policies for improving the functioning of the various governance models have been proposed and are described in section 4. Section 5 considers the debates on a takeover directive and freedom of establishment and argues that the outcome of these will have fundamental implications for the future of the European corporation. Section 6 concludes and summarizes the article.

2. Two Models

The economics and finance literature distinguishes two basic models of corporate control and governance: the *blockholder model* (B) and the widely held *corporation model* (W). In the blockholder model an individual, a group of individuals, or an organization command many or most of the votes at the corporation's shareholder meetings. The blockholder has the power to appoint and/or remove the board of directors and the blockholder-appointed board appoints and/or removes the chief executive officer (CEO).[1] In contrast, the widely held corporation has a broad equity base with many small shareholders who, individually, command a small number of votes. The incumbent board nominates the new board, which is confirmed by the passive mass of small shareholders in a vote. Formally the board appoints the CEO. In practice, the CEO appoints the board, putting incumbent managers in control of the widely held corporation.

2.1 Alternative Forms of Ownership

In practice, each of the main models takes two different forms. In the blockholder model blocks of votes can be acquired with a proportional amount of capital (one-share-one-vote; Model B1) or with a less-than-proportional amount, through legal devices that give blockholders more than one vote for each euro invested (one-share-more-votes; Model B2). Prominent examples are equity capitalizations with non-voting shares, shares with multiple voting rights or issuance of certificates without votes. The most complex of these devices are "pyramids" or "control cascades" that combine companies to control chains. At each level of the chain the controlling blockholder brings in outside capital while keeping control, thereby reducing the cost of control.

For widely held companies, there are those open to hostile takeovers (Model W1) and those that are not (Model W2). In companies that are open to hostile bids, an outsider can purchase shares to form a controlling block, moving the company from the widely held to the blockholder model. The incumbent board (and/or CEO) is forced to hand control to the blockholder. In well-defended companies, share blocks cannot be assembled without board and/or CEO approval. Takeover defenses in widely held companies include devices like voting right restrictions, share transfer restrictions, staggered boards, and "poison pills."

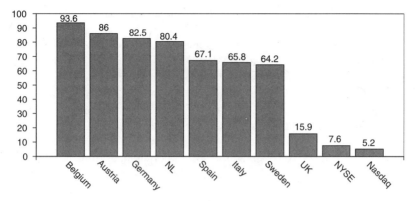

Source : Barca and Becht (2001), *The Control of Corporate Europe*, OUP.

Figure 21.1: Percentage of Listed Companies with a Blocking Minority of at Least 25%

2.2 National Characteristics

The use of the different models varies across the European Union and the United States. Most corporations in continental Europe are dominated or controlled by blockholders. Figure 21.1 shows the percentage of listed firms in seven continental European companies with a single shareholder or block of shareholders commanding more than 25 percent of votes in a firm. It shows that in between 80 percent and 95 percent of listed firms in Austria, Belgium, Germany, and the Netherlands, there is a single shareholder that commands more than 25 percent of votes. In Italy, Spain and Sweden, the figure is around two-thirds of companies. In contrast, in the UK the figure is 16 percent and in the U.S. between 5 percent and 7 percent.

Figure 21.2 shows the equivalent figures for majority control. It shows that in a majority of Austrian, Belgian, German, and Italian companies there is a single majority shareholder or voting block of shareholders. In the Netherlands, Spain, and Sweden it is between 25 percent and 40 percent of companies. In the UK and U.S. it is around

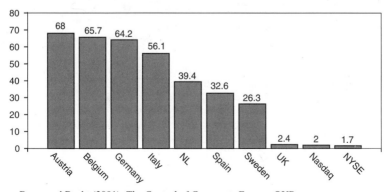

Source : Barca and Becht (2001), *The Control of Corporate Europe*, OUP.

Figure 21.2: Percentage of Listed Companies under Majority Control

2 percent. Concentration of ownership is appreciably higher on the Continent than in the UK or U.S.

In most countries, the principle of one-share-one-vote applies but exceptions to this are found in the Nordic countries (shares with multiple voting rights) and the Netherlands (certificates, priority shares), where deviations from one-share-one-vote play an important role.[2] While widely held corporations are found in the United States, the United Kingdom, and Japan, the United Kingdom is the only country where most corporations are open to hostile takeovers. In the United States most incumbent boards can rely on a range of devices that give them the power to prevent hostile acquisitions; in Japan, a network of cross-holdings shields corporations from unfriendly challenges to insider control.[3] Widely held corporations in continental Europe are also frequently shielded from hostile takeovers. One example of this is Banco Santander Central Hispano (BSCH) S.A. that uses a combination of voting right restrictions and delayed appointments to the board and key board positions to impede the ability of raiders to gain control (see figure 21.3).

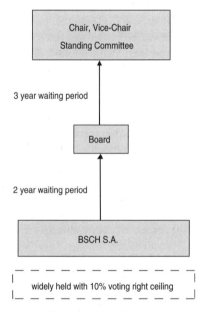

Note: The takeover defenses at BSCH combines a 10 percent voting right restriction with waiting periods for gaining access to important board positions. A potential raider must have been a shareholder for two years to gain a board seat and a member of the board for three years before becoming eligible for election to key positions, like the chairmanship, vice-chairmanship, or the powerful standing committee. The arrangement is secured through a 70 percent supermajority amendment, allowing a 30 percent coalition to prevent a raider from removing the statutory defenses from the statutes. BSCH voluntarily dismantled these defensive structures in June 2003.

Source: Company Statutes, company web site at www. bsch.es.

Figure 21.3: Former Control Structure of Banco Santander Central Hispano S.A.

2.3 Convergence

There is considerable change in progress. There is evidence of declining significance of pyramidal structures. The Agnelli group, for example, has disposed of companies operating in chemicals and cement. In Germany, voting right restrictions have been eliminated and some cross-shareholdings involving banks are being unwound following changes in their tax treatment. In Spain, the significance of the state has declined with privatizations. Some state control has been maintained through golden shares but these have not been widely applied. In Sweden, cross-shareholdings have largely disappeared and dual-class shares have been eliminated in many firms. There has been more intervention by minority shareholders in, for example, blocking the merger between Volvo and Renault. However, significant differences in systems remain.

3. Which Model Is Superior?

The blockholder model and the widely held model are the poles of a classic economic trade-off. There are costs and benefits associated with each model of corporate control. Theory does not suggest that one model is superior.

The widely held model provides diversification opportunities, spreading corporate risk over a large investor base. It is also associated with greater secondary market liquidity and, as a result, a lower cost of equity. But the potential costs of the widely held model are considerable. Boards are "unaccountable" and/or captured by a CEO who pursues "visionary" projects, like acquisition programs financed through equity issues to their broad shareholder base. At the same time there is a lack of monitoring at the shareholder and the board level.

The most obvious way of solving the problems of the widely held model is a move to the blockholder model. Large shareholders, at least in theory, have the power to monitor management, either directly or through boards they appoint. However, there are also potential costs. Boards are captured by blockholders, who might pursue their own aims, not those of all shareholders. For example, blockholder-controlled boards (and CEOs) might engage in transactions with companies the blockholder owns at non-market prices, at the expense of minority shareholders. By definition, blockholder-controlled companies (at least those of the "one-share-one-vote" variety) have a narrower equity base and lower secondary market liquidity. To increase secondary market liquidity, blocks must be sold, moving the company into the widely held regime.

It has also been suggested that different forms of corporate ownership are suited to different types of activity. Blockholder models are able to offer stakeholders in the firm greater commitments and take longer-term horizons than widely held firms. On the other hand, they offer less flexibility for corporate restructurings. In newly emerging technologies, where the ability to innovate and restructure are important, the widely held model may offer advantages, while the blockholder model may be better suited to more traditional industries, which require long-term investments and participation by several related parties. In addition, different models may be needed at different stages of development. Developing and transition economies in earlier stages of development may benefit from the long-term commitments of the blockholder model before moving to the widely held form.

4. Improving the Models

Numerous policy measures have been suggested to improve the functioning of the widely held and blockholder models.[4]

4.1 Widely Held Model

In the widely held model, dispersed shareholders do not have enough "voice" in important decisions. A straightforward policy is to raise the effectiveness of voice mechanisms and to reduce their cost, for example by allowing corporate voting by mail and/ or electronic voting. Proxy solicitation concentrates voting power temporarily, for example through proxy fights.

Board capture by the CEO is a well-known potential problem of the widely held corporation. The standard remedy is an increase in the autonomy of the board from the CEO, for example through the appointment of non-executive and, preferably, independent directors. Particularly sensitive issues like remuneration, audit, and nomination for election to the board are delegated to committees staffed with a majority of independent directors. It is suggested that the roles of chairman and CEO should be separated in unitary board systems that combine them (by law in France and practice in the United States). On issues where board autonomy is deemed to fail, the corporate charter or the law can prescribe that decisions are put to a shareholder vote. Shareholders might also nominate directors for election to the board.

A preferred route in the United States has been to increase directors' liability. For example, the Sarbanes–Oxley legislation introduced in 2002 has increased the liability of CEOs and chief financial officers. The open-ended contract between shareholders, boards, and the CEO is not only enforced via corporate elections, but also through the courts. In Europe shareholder suits are much less common than in the United States.

In theory, facilitating hostile takeovers is yet another way of reducing the potential cost associated with the widely held model. Hostile takeovers discipline management ex post by removing them from the helm of the company and ex ante by threatening the removal of poor management. Introducing a "market for corporate control" in continental Europe via a Takeover Directive has been a policy priority for the European Commission (see section 5).

4.2 Blockholder Model

The main problem of the blockholder model is that power is exerted at the expense of minority shareholders. A direct approach to reducing this power has been suggested by the Organization for Economic Cooperation and Development's Principles of Corporate Governance (1999), which recommend the appointment of directors independent of the CEO and blockholders. The trouble with this is that it is difficult to make directors independent if they can be removed by a blockholder at will.

An alternative route imposes outright limits on the voting power of blockholders. For example, to protect minority shareholders early corporate charters imposed voting right ceilings or one-member-one-vote rules. The restriction can also operate at board level, by preventing blockholders from removing directors without the approval of minorities. The trouble is that these measures also protect boards (and management) from hostile bids, weakening the potential for this to act as a disciplinary device.[5]

5. European Union Policy

5.1 European Commission's Takeover Directive

The European Commission has placed considerable importance on the implementation of a European Takeover Directive. It regards it as central to the reconstruction of corporate Europe the replacement of poor management, the breaking of traditional ties dominated by the private interests of families and large corporate groups, and the integration of European financial markets.

The Commission has taken as its role model for a Takeover Directive the regulatory system that exists in the UK. In contrast to other European countries, the UK has an active market in takeovers with few impediments to acquisitions. Its regulatory system is enshrined in the Takeover Code that lays down the rules by which takeovers are conducted, the requirement on bidders to disclose purchases of share blocks, to notify the market of their intentions in regard to potential acquisitions, to make tender offers once a certain percentage of shares (30 percent) has been accumulated, to offer all shareholders the same price as that offered to the sellers of blocks of shares, and to squeeze out minorities once a certain percentage of shares (90 percent) have been tendered.

These rules have been successful at creating a well-functioning and orderly takeover market and the Commission regards them as appropriate to the operation of takeovers throughout Europe. However, its attempt to introduce legislation to this effect collapsed when a vote in the European Parliament failed to gain a majority.

The problem that the Commission has encountered in trying to implement the Takeover Directive is the diverse nature of ownership and control patterns of European companies described above. As a consequence, there is considerable variation across countries in the extent to which firms are vulnerable to takeovers. Far from creating a level playing field, it was felt that the Takeover Directive would produce an unbalanced market with the companies of some countries being vulnerable to hostile bids from companies that were themselves protected against bids. Reciprocity therefore became a condition for the acceptance of the Takeover Directive by some member states.

The Commission's response following recommendations made by a committee chaired by Jaap Winter was to attempt to break down some of the barriers to acquisitions that exist in Europe. The proposal was to introduce a breakthrough provision by which acquirers could surmount at least some of the restrictions on takeovers, for example in relation to voting right restrictions. The difficulty that was encountered was, as described above, different anti-takeover devices are employed to different degrees across Europe. Dual class shares, for example, are commonplace in Sweden and pyramid structures in Germany. Unless all takeover barriers are eliminated, then the removal of some is inevitably regarded as showing preference to certain countries over others. That has been the response to the Commission's proposals with particularly heated debates between Germany and Sweden over breakthrough proposals.

The latest suggestion is the inclusion of an explicit reciprocity clause that states that bidders will have to succumb to the breakthrough provision to make them vulnerable to acquisition as well. Of course, even this does not achieve full reciprocity since blockholder controlled companies will not be vulnerable. Full reciprocity requires widely held voting rights throughout Europe. As it stands, a reciprocity condition would diminish rather than extend the market for corporate control because imbalances would make it possible for most targets to contest reciprocity.

The reciprocity debate illustrates the fundamental issues involved in trying to introduce a takeover market in Europe. It is one thing to have a set of rules that lay down the procedures by which takeovers are organized. It is another to attempt to interfere with the ownership structures of European corporations. The Commission sees ownership and changes in ownership as being concerned with the exercise of corporate control and takeovers as a more appropriate form of corporate control than that currently exerted by blockholders motivated by private interests. Existing structures should therefore be swept aside in favor of a takeover market.

In contrast, some member countries regard their system of corporate ownership and control as being closely embedded in both their productive systems and social arrangements. According to this view, ownership and control patterns reflect fundamental differences in industrial, social, and political structures across countries. The failure of the Commission to make headway on the Takeover Directive is symptomatic of the difficulties and inappropriateness of attempting to impose harmonization in the area of corporate legislation. Europe has diverse corporate and financial systems that are a source of potential strength, not weakness, and should not be thrown away for the neatness of uniformity.

5.2 Freedom of Establishment

On this basis the appropriate direction is exactly the opposite of that which the Commission is seeking in harmonizing legislation, namely to promote freedom of mobility of corporations across national boundaries. In marked contrast to the inertia on takeover harmonization, this is an area in which there have been substantial developments that will have far-reaching consequences for the whole of the corporate structure of Europe. These developments have not involved the European Commission but the European Court of Justice. Article 48 of the Treaty of Rome extends entitlement to freedom of establishment to companies or firms formed in accordance with the law of a member state and having their registered office, central administration, or principal place of business within the Community. In other words, companies incorporated in one member state have the same rights to operate in any other member state.

This has been challenged by a number of member states concerned that restrictions that they impose on companies operating in their countries can be circumvented through incorporation in another member state. For example, some countries impose capital requirements on all corporations to protect creditors and employees, and other countries do not. In particular, there has been an active debate on the real seat principle, namely whether there have to be significant operations in a company's country of incorporation. In a series of landmark cases (Centros, Überseering, and most recently Inspire

Art) the European Court of Justice has affirmed freedom of establishment and rejected the real seat notion.[6]

These cases open up the possibility of competition between member states for incorporation equivalent to that of competition between states in the U.S. The debates in the U.S. on whether competition in incorporation gives rise to runs to the top or bottom, whether there is effective competition in incorporation, and the empirical evidence on effects of reincorporation are all therefore now directly relevant to Europe.[7]

However, there is an important distinction between what is happening in Europe and what is already active in the U.S. While incorporation and reincorporation involves competition between states within a system in the U.S., as noted before, financial and corporate systems in Europe are very different. Competition within Europe is therefore between systems rather than within a system and is more analogous to product differentiation than perfect competition. Different corporate and financial systems promote different types of activities.

The attraction of competition is that it allows for a better matching of companies to the systems best suited to their activities. For example, companies that require access to market sources of finance may benefit from the shareholder-oriented corporate and regulatory code in the UK whereas companies seeking longer-term relations with banks and employees may opt for systems that provide greater protections to these parties.

One area in which competition can be detrimental is in terms of the operation of systems. If, for example, long-term relations between investors and firms require restrictions on the ability of firms to exit from such relations, then intensified competition can undermine their operation. In other words, there may be externalities that give rise to detrimental effects of competition. There has been a debate in Europe on whether freedom of mobility should apply to exit of firms from countries as well as entry into countries or whether countries should be able to restrict the exit of firms. Another case, involving the *Daily Mail* in the UK, has pointed to the ability of countries to limit exit, in this case in relation to the settlement of tax liabilities. Without a cross-border merger directive, it is in any event difficult for firms to be able to reincorporate in the way in which they use establishment and mergers into subsidiaries in the U.S. to effect cross-state reincorporation.

In the absence of a clear understanding of the merits of different systems, and in the presence of significant social and political obstacles to harmonization, freedom of mobility and competition between member states offers much more prospect for reform in Europe than harmonization. It is the rulings of the European Court of Justice that have received little publicity to date rather than the headline grabbing directives from the European Commission that are most likely to transform the landscape of corporate Europe over the next few decades.

5.3 Regulatory Competition versus Harmonization

The interesting question that this raises is what will be the result of competition. The prevailing view is that the winner will be the UK. This is consistent with the UK government siding with parties favoring freedom of establishment in the above European Court of Justice cases. The UK is currently viewed as having the preferred system of corporate governance. It combines the desirable features of U.S. markets without their excesses and avoids the sclerosis of continental European systems. The Cadbury Committee established codes of good corporate governance that are now enshrined in rules and legislations around the world.

The UK system of corporate governance has good standards of information disclosure, reliable auditing that is based on a substance-over-form principle, and increasing separation of the roles of chairman and chief executive officer of corporations. There is an active market in corporate control and increasingly institutional investors are taking an active role in monitoring their investments and making their views known where they have misgivings. It therefore encapsulates all of the principles of good governance that are currently being discussed.

The main reason why companies may be expected to migrate to the UK is to escape the restrictive social obligations that are frequently included in their domestic corporate legislation. Employee representation on boards and worker councils are the most widely discussed examples of these. While UK corporate law does not prevent companies from including worker representation in their charters, it does not require it. It is therefore less prescriptive than much continental European legislation in this area.

But the fundamental difference between countries relates to the issue with which we started—markets for corporate control. While hostile takeovers are accepted in the UK, they are not in many other European countries. Companies that wish to protect themselves from market control may therefore find other countries more attractive locations for incorporation. The central issue then boils down to whether firms seek the flexibility of the market oriented UK system, together with its market control mechanisms, or the more stable arrangements on the Continent.

To date, the concentrated ownership structures, the interlocking webs of shareholdings, and the involvement of families on the Continent have proved to be remarkably resilient. For some firms, the attraction of stable, committed owners will dominate considerations of flexibility and access to markets. According to the varieties-of-capitalism thesis, this will suit certain types of organizations and activities but not others.

The outcome of competition may not therefore be the Delaware-takes-all phenomenon that has been observed in the U.S. Some companies may migrate to the UK and it is likely that London will consolidate its position as the preferred location of corporate headquarters. But other firms may prefer to operate in different environments, in which case, the outcome will be an appropriate matching of companies with legal and corporate systems.

6. Conclusions

Europe displays a rich tapestry of corporate governance, ownership, and control arrangements. There are merits and deficiencies of each and a variety of ways in which their operation can and should be improved. However, the main issue facing policymakers in Europe is the degree to which that diversity should be tolerated or restricted. There is a natural tendency amongst policymakers to harmonize regulation. It is neater, it avoids problems of runs to the bottom, and it allows imposition of best practice. And therein lies of the heart of the issue. Is there a system of best practice in corporate governance that should be imposed across Europe? If, as many people believe, best practice is closer to the market systems of the UK and U.S. than the insider systems of continental Europe, should the latter be swept aside in favor of the former? If so, how should this be done, and what rules are most likely to produce this outcome?

The attempted introduction of a European Takeover Directive illustrates one approach. Most of continental Europe has serious impediments to takeovers, a takeover market would help to restructure European corporations, integrate European financial markets, and replace bad management, and the UK takeover code reflects best practice. The appropriate approach therefore is for the European Commission to introduce legislation along the lines of the UK takeover code together with rules that allow existing impediments to takeovers to be surmounted.

There is a second approach that provides an interesting contrast to the European Commission's on takeovers. By upholding the principle of freedom of establishment, the European Court of Justice is encouraging companies to select between systems, and member states to compete in the design of their regulatory rules. Far from centralizing and imposing best practice, this allows firms to choose and member states to identify best practice for themselves.

There are several attractions of this approach. The first is that we simply know very little about best practice and it is foolish to select a model that might turn out to be inappropriate or inadequate in a few years' time. Secondly, if there is best practice, then it may vary across countries, time, and activities. What is suited to one economy is quite different from another. What is suited to one firm is quite different from another. And in particular, what is suited to one period is quite different from another when technologies and economic circumstances change. According to this view, diversity of corporate governance systems should be regarded as a strength, not a weakness, of the European financial systems. Regulation should promote diversity, not stifle it. It should not be picking winners, but encouraging the market to identify winners and push out the frontier of best practice, precisely along the lines of freedom of establishment.

Europe is potentially on the verge of undertaking one of the most interesting experiments in corporate and regulatory history. It is of more fundamental significance than competition between states in the U.S. because of the diversity of corporate sectors and financial systems that exist in Europe. The outcome of this experiment will have far-reaching consequences for the future competitiveness of corporate Europe. As academics, we should follow this experiment with acute interest. As policymakers, we should view this as an opportunity to provide real innovation in the design of regulation. And as captains of industry, we should regard this as an opportunity to select regulatory arrangements that promote, rather than undermine, corporate activities.

*Marco Becht is a professor of finance and economics at Université Libre de Bruxelles (ULB), a resident fellow at the European Center for Advanced Research in Economics and Statistics (ECARES) at ULB, and the executive director of the European Corporate Governance Institute. Colin Mayer is the Peter Moores Professor of Management Studies at the Saïd Business School, director of the Oxford Research Center at Oxford University, and associated with the Center for Economic Policy Research and the European Corporate Governance Institute.

Notes

1. In some countries the ability of blockholders to appoint, remove, or influence boards is limited by company law (Germany, Holland) or listing rules (in the United Kingdom). In Belgium a blockholder commanding 50 percent of the votes (plus one vote) can remove the board at any time (*ad nutum*), bringing the Belgian system very close to the stylized description of the blockholder model.

2. The model is also used to a limited extent in France (double voting rights after voting shares are held for a certain number of years) and Germany (non-voting stock is commonly issued by mid- and small-cap family-controlled firms).

3. While individually the holdings are small, together they provide a formidable defense.

4. See, for example, European Commission (2003).

5. See Becht, Bolton, and Roëll (2003) for further details.

6. See appendix I for complete references and www.ecgi.org/mobility for links to the full-text judgements and opinions.

7. A flavor of these debates can be found in Bebchuk (1992), Cary (1974), Macey and Miller (1987), Romano (1985), Roe (2003), and Wymeersch (2003).

Appendix I

European Court of Justice Rulings on Mobility
Judgment of the Court (Second Chamber) of July 10, 1986.

Case: D. H. M. Segers v Bestuur van de Bedrijfsvereniging voor Bank- en Verzekeringswezen, Groothandel en Vrije Beroepen. Case No: Case 79/85.

Judgment of the Court of September 27, 1988.

Case: The Queen v H. M. Treasury and Commissioners of Inland Revenue, ex parte Daily Mail and General Trust plc. Case No: Case 81/87.

Judgment of the Court of March 9, 1999.

Case: Centros Ltd v Erhvervs- og Selskabsstyrelsen. Case No: Case C-212/97

Judgment of the Court of November 5, 2002.

Case: Überseering BV v Nordic Construction Company Baumanagement GmbH (NCC). Case No: Case C-208/00

Judgment of the Court of September 30, 2003

Case: Kamer van Koophandel en Fabrieken voor Amsterdam v. Inspire Art Ltd. Case No: Case 167/01.

References

Bebchuk, Lucien, 1992, "Federalism and the corporation: The desirable limits on state competition in corporate law," *Harvard Law Review*, Vol. 1435.

Becht, Marco, Patrick Bolton, and Ailsa Roëll 2003, "Corporate governance and control," European Corporate Governance Institute, working paper in finance, No. 2, available at http://papers.ssrn.com/sol3/papers.cfm?abstract_id=343461, also *Handbook of the Economics of Finance*, North Holland, forthcoming.

Cary, William, 1974, "Federalism and corporate law: Reflections upon Delaware," *Yale Law Journal*, Vol. 663.

European Commission, 2003, "Communication from the Commission to the Council and the European Parliament," *Modernising Company Law and Enhancing Corporate Governance in the European Union—A Plan to Move Forward*, Vol. 284, No. 01, available at http://europa.eu.int/eur-lex/en/com/cnc/2003/com2003_0284en01.pdf.

Macey, Jonathan, and Geoffrey Miller, 1987, "Towards an interest-group theory of Delaware corporate law," *Texas Law Review*, No. 469.

Roe, Mark J., 2003, "Delaware's Competition," *Harvard Law Review*, Vol. 117, available at http://ssrn.com/abstract=354783.

Romano, Roberta, 1985, "Law as a product: Some pieces of the incorporation puzzle," *Journal of Law, Economics, and Organization*, Vol. 225.

Wymeersch, Edy, 2003, "The transfer of the company's seat in European company law," European Corporate Governance Institute, law working paper, No. 08/2003 and 40 CMLR, p. 661.

Chapter 22

Evolving Corporate Governance in Japan

Hugh Patrick*
Columbia University

Corporate governance is a global hot topic. In Japan, committees consider, academics study, polls are taken, models compete, and rhetoric abounds. Still, while considerable change is underway, it is partial and inertia is powerful. It is premature to determine how key questions will be answered. Will companies shift from primary priority for employees and other inside stakeholders to greater emphasis on realizing value for those largely ignored stakeholders, the shareholders? Will outside directors play an essential role on corporate boards? Will capital markets provide a major source of external governance, a role once assigned to "main banks"? Will a market for corporate control emerge? Will market discipline become effective?

It is essential to understand the context with which corporate governance is changing and not changing. Governance in Japan evolved in two major states—prewar "Anglo-Saxon type" capitalism (Okazaki, 2001) and postwar "Japanese welfare" capitalism (Dore, 2000) and is now entering a third stage.

Until the end of World War II, Japanese companies were controlled by their owners, typically founders or their family successors. Some firms grew large; others failed or were taken over in an active market for corporate control. Most finance was internal or based on new share issuance; banks did not play a significant monitoring role. By the early 1930s successful family-controlled business groups (zaibatsu) had become a major feature of the Japanese big business industrial organization, as is the case today in Korea, Thailand, Malaysia, Indonesia, and other Asian economies. Each major zaibatsu family used a holding company and developed cadres of professional managers to monitor and to manage its industrial companies. The hierarchical governance of zaibatsu was effective, both in the performance of component companies and in the ability to take over under-performing non-group firms (Okazaki, 2001).

Government controls over the economy beginning in the mid 1930s substantially altered the economic system, and postwar Allied Occupation reforms reinforced a fundamental change in corporate governance. The government took over zaibatsu shares in companies at a pittance, imposed capital levies (often paid in corporate stock) on the wealthy, and wartime guarantees of corporate borrowing were abrogated. The shares were sold first to employees and then to other individuals.

In the atmosphere of zaibatsu dissolution and occupation economic democratization reforms, management successfully argued that ownership and management should be separated, and that an independent management should reduce the status of (equity) capital and raise that of labor. Management claimed to be the mediator, serving the public interest. However, initially union leaders and management mistrusted each other. This was in part because occupation reforms led to development of what became a highly politicized labor union movement. Strikes and other contentious confrontations persisted until the 1950s. Then new labor leaders gave priority to economic objectives, notably job security and wage increases, in an economy that was growing rapidly. By the mid 1950s what has been termed the postwar system of closely integrated economic institutions, including the corporate governance system, was in place.

Japan's corporate governance system is now in a third phase. It is more market-oriented and has substantially greater transparency and increased weight for shareholder interest relative to employee interests. Still, it is significantly different from the Anglo-American model, and is probably closer to the continental European approach than to U.S. practice.

1. The Postwar Economic System

Over the course of Japan's high-growth era, from the early 1950s to the mid-1970s, a highly complementary, rather tightly linked set of economic institutions characterized as the postwar economic system, developed and evolved. In practice, this was a big business system, focusing on the listed companies that are the locus of public discourse on corporate governance. Privately owned small and medium enterprises were a lesser part of the system, substantively and symbiotically, even though they provided the major share of output and employment.

The system was a rational economic and institutional response to conditions in the 1940s and 1950s, especially the opportunities for rapid growth as a low-income, well-educated, follower economy. The key elements were the permanent employment system of labor–management relations, enterprise unions, separation of ownership and management control, stable shareholdings, main bank external finance, and supportive government policies and regulations. As Aoki (2000) well analyzes, conceptually the system was founded on "contingent governance": Control was entrusted to managers contingent on sound financial performance, and the main bank had the responsibility to lead the restructuring of any firm in distress.

1.1 Labor–Management

In the high-growth era, enterprise unions and management forged a win–win game in which workers made a no-strike commitment and accepted rapid technological changes and the development of firm-specific skills in exchange for permanent employment and seniority-based annual wage increases and promotions. Management and union leadership came to work closely together. Management realized that employees were, together with banks, the most important stakeholders. The relatively few instances in which a chief executive officer (CEO) and top management lost the trust of employees led to internal crisis and his resignation (Nitta, 2001).

In return for employee (and public) acceptance of management as the responsible power, top management compensation was good but not outrageous—some 10 times to 20 times employee average wages. Managers also were rewarded with large expense accounts and excellent retirement benefits, and enjoyed prestige and high social status. When times became so difficult, as they have over the past decade, that the work force had to be reduced, it has been done by a negotiated combination of attrition, early retirement with special benefits, and transfer of workers to subsidiary or other related firms rather than with layoffs.

Management control has been internal, hierarchical, and perpetual. Stereotypically, the president of a company, in consultation with colleagues, selects a successor on becoming chairman after serving as CEO for six to eight years. Boards have been large, a reward to the most successful managers in the seniority-based system. The external labor market for senior executives is virtually nonexistent; managers try to remain in power until well-compensated retirement, which may involve a senior position in a subsidiary. Corporate performance is of course important; metrics include firm size and relative ranking, revenue growth rate, and reputation, as well as profitability.

1.2 Ownership and Control

Japan is the most extreme case of separation of ownership and control of listed companies. In general, management controls and shareholding is dispersed or passive. There are some relatively young companies that are controlled by their founders or successor families. There also are a number of spin-offs that are controlled by their parents, as well as a few foreign-controlled firms. Accordingly, one must be cautious of studies of corporate behavior that do not distinguish among types of firms. This chapter focuses on the large majority of companies in which ownership and control are separated.

The system is one of entrenched managerial autonomy and corporate governance by strong norms of managerial self-restraint. Of course company management is not completely autonomous. It is constrained by four major stakeholders, in order of importance: its customers, as is true everywhere; its employees, especially those on the managerial track; its creditors, particularly its banks; and its shareholders. Management has to ensure adequate performance to keep all the stakeholders reasonably content.

Japanese management has two fundamental, interrelated goals. The first is to maintain management independence and autonomy in a self-selected, self-perpetuating management system. The second is to ensure the independent survival of the firm in perpetuity. Bankruptcy and liquidation is the worst possible outcome; selling the firm (usually termed merger) is the second worst. Japanese managers are not unique in their desire for autonomous control and power. What is unique was that the early postwar economic and political environment enabled them to shape the evolving system to their great benefit.

Management preached the ideology that the company is a community which serves society, with responsibilities and reciprocal obligations in particular to its employees and its business and financial partners (Learmount, 2002; see also Dore, 2000). One result was a system of cozy back-scratching, some might say collusion, among the management of Japan's large industrial companies, financial institutions, and the government bureaucracies—particularly the Ministry of Finance. The system was opaque, with minimal disclosure; forbearance was the policy stance, since growth made it possible to write off mistakes and difficulties easily; and allocation of regulatory rents and budget redistribution to lagging sectors could solve other problems.

Profit maximization has virtually never been articulated by a Japanese manager as a primary objective. Indeed, for many Japanese, profit maximization is not an accepted value; it connotes antisocial, selfish behavior. In the early 1990s when Japanese senior managers were asked whose interest should be given first priority, inside stakeholders or shareholders, 97.1 percent responded stakeholders. This also was the reply of 82.7 percent of German and 78.0 percent of French senior managers. In contrast, only 24.4 percent of senior managers in the U.S. and 29.5 percent in the UK responded similarly (Yoshimori, 1995, cited in Allen and Gale, 2000, p. 113). When asked to choose between layoffs or dividend reduction, Japanese managers overwhelmingly (97.1 percent) preferred employment maintenance, unlike the U.S. (10.8 percent) and the UK (10.7 percent). Germany was 59.1 percent and France, 60.4 percent.

While the objective is not maximization of profits or shareholder value, in practice good profits are necessary to buy off all stakeholders. This was well understood by Japanese management in the 1960s and 1970s when corporate growth was rapid and profit rates were high. However, in the 1980s focus on operating profits faded and return on corporate assets (ROA) declined significantly. The continuing rise in land and stock prices, culminating in the boom of the late 1980s, flooded companies with paper capital gains. These not only provided the resources to continue satisfying stakeholders but shifted management attention away from operating profits, while continuing ever-more investment in plant and equipment and research and development (R&D). Furthermore, they generated managerial self-confidence in the system that at times crossed over to hubris. Then the huge twin bubbles of stock and urban real estate prices burst at the beginning of the 1990s.

1.3 Stable Shareholding

The foremost management priority regarding shareholding was to ensure that a controlling interest was held by friendly companies—suppliers, customers, and especially financial institutions—that would not intervene in management and otherwise be passive unless called on to block a takeover. The horizontal financial keiretsu epitomized this system, which embodied considerable cross-shareholding among companies, but stable shareholding was implemented by virtually every company. At least equally important, shareholding reinforced ongoing business relationships.

1.4 The Role of Banks

Until the 1980s, bank loans were the dominant source of much-needed external finance for large companies as well as small. Relationship banking, epitomized by the main bank system, was the norm. The main bank relationship was a "more or less informal set of regular practices, institutional arrangements, and behavior that constitute a system of corporate finance and governance" (Aoki and Patrick, 1994, p. xxi).

The main bank was presumed to have access to privileged information from its clients and to monitor corporate performance and behavior on behalf of all creditors. Banks could and did intervene to replace managers (Sheard, 1994), substituting for missing external markets for corporate control. However, there were few cases of large-firm failure or even major difficulties until the 1990s (Sheard, 1994, Hoshi and Kashyap, 2001, chapter 5).

Japanese banks are controlled by their management. Their shares are dispersed among a wide range of client firms, none with a significant ownership position. Even for the banks at the core of the Big Six financial keiretsu, where group ownership was 20 percent to 30 percent, group firms have abstained from substantial monitoring.

In the postwar system, the monitors of bank corporate governance were Ministry of Finance regulators. Highly risk averse since the 1927 banking crisis, their policy was that no bank should fail. They achieved this by restrictions on capital market development, wide regulated spreads between deposit and loan interest rates, and a convoy system in which all banks were to grow at about the same rate and the strong were to rescue the weak. It came to be very costly and even dangerous because of the forbearance it engendered (Hoshi and Patrick, 2001).

For decades the operating profits of banks have been extraordinarily low. Since the 1990s, losses on loans have been partly offset by realizing capital gains on relationship holdings of corporate shares, but depressed share prices have produced an ironic twist. Banks that repurchased relationship shares now often have losses on them!

1.5 System Overview

The postwar economic system and, indeed, Japanese society are imbued with networks of strong embedded relationships—between suppliers and assemblers, sellers and buyers, banks and borrowers, management and employees, bureaucrats and businessmen, bureaucrats and politicians, politicians and support groups, and among schoolmates. In a rapidly growing economy, good relationships build trust, reduce transaction costs, and provide incentives for specific investments and R&D activities among networks of firms. Because Japanese do not much trust outsiders—whether other Japanese or foreigners—individuals and institutions invest great time and effort to build these relationships. They become embedded in normal economic intercourse and significantly reduce the cost of doing business. The norms of relationships replace the rule of law, which mainly protects outsiders who rely more on contracts and the courts (Milhaupt, 2001). Embedded relationships lock the participants into each other; over time these become reputational, even moral, commitments. The downsides of relationships are the loss of flexibility and susceptibility to moral hazard. Breaking these relationships without strong reason means serious reputation loss; exit is difficult. Japanese managers have found it hard to terminate supplier relationships and virtually impossible to lay off workers outright.

The system worked well when the economy and companies grew rapidly. All stakeholders were being rewarded, mistakes were papered over, and the few firms that fell into distress were readily handled by their main bank and the government. While opaque, the corporate and public governance systems were widely trusted and accepted. However, successful catch-up growth eventually undermined the system.

In the 1970s, domestic saving began to exceed business investment; credit became easy. Financial deregulation, first of interest rates and then of the bond market, undermined the regulatory system, and prudential regulation was not developed to replace it. The bursting of the immense urban real estate and stock market bubbles in 1990–91 created huge balance-sheet problems for corporations and financial institutions. Business and government responded poorly in the 1990s, engaging in delay and forbearance in the vain hope that the economy would soon recover. Japan's mediocre growth, about 1.1 percent since 1992, and spreading public awareness of corporate and bureaucratic problems and misbehavior, led to significant erosion of confidence in management and in the postwar governance system (Fukao, 2003). It has come to be more widely accepted that good corporate governance and good economic performance have to be founded on disclosure, transparency, and competitive markets. The noblesse oblige that yoked the business and bureaucratic elites to a growing economy is now selfish vested interest that chokes Japan's recovery.

2. Changes in the Corporate Governance Environment

Japan is slowly but substantially transforming its corporate governance system, a process begun in the early 1990s. Each of the major elements is changing—company top management, labor–management relations, shareholders, the main bank system, capital markets, outside auditors, and government policy. Given space limitations, I focus on the current state of corporate governance without much discussion of the process of change. For my evaluation of the contemporary Japanese economy see Patrick (2003).

2.1 Government Policy

Change has been driven significantly by government bureaucrat-led reforms of corporate and related laws and institutions. The rules of the game have changed substantially, much more comprehensively so far than the way the game is actually being played. Milhaupt (2003), on which the following paragraphs are based, well describes and analyzes the formal institutional environment for corporate governance today, which has become significantly more flexible and enhancing of disclosure and transparency. He appropriately focuses on the major changes in corporate law, especially on amendments to the commercial code.

Milhaupt categorizes these legal changes into two groups: flexibility enhancing amendments and monitoring enhancing amendments. Firms now have greater organizational flexibility in rewarding employees and in mergers, divestitures, and reorganizations. They can issue stock options. They can use share exchanges in a more permissive mergers and acquisitions system. The prohibition on holding companies has been eliminated, thereby promoting spinoffs, mergers, corporate reorganizations, and more diverse employment arrangements among the subsidiaries of a holding company. Firms can now buy back their shares, and issue tracking shares. The Civil Rehabilitation Act, roughly comparable to U.S. Chapter 11 of the bankruptcy code, makes possible more effective reorganization procedures, including prepackaged bankruptcies.

The legal basis for better monitoring has strengthened substantially, with important implications. The prohibitive filing fee for stockholder derivative suits against management was eliminated in 1993. The traditional insider statutory auditor system is a key institution of corporate governance; its basic function is to monitor compliance with the law. The statutory auditor system has been strengthened. Now the board of audit must have at least three members, including at least one outsider, and by 2005 at least half of the members must be outside auditors.

Reforms of corporate boards are significant in principle, if not yet in practice. Instead of the statutory auditor system, companies now can opt for a committee system of board organization based on the U.S. model, replacing statutory auditors with board committees for audit, nomination, and compensation (Nakamura, 2003). A majority of committee members must be independent directors. An executive officer system has been established for the senior managers who run the company operations but typically no longer serve on the board. This enables the board to focus on oversight and strategy, as distinct from internal supervision and operational decision-making.

Corporate accounting standards and requirements have been revised significantly to bring them into broad conformity with international standards, thereby substantially enhancing transparency. Now required are cash flow statements, mark-to-market of financial assets, and reporting of pension liabilities on balance sheets. Consolidated accounting has been tightened. Spring 2003 legislation enhances Financial Supervisory Agency (FSA) regulatory oversight and monitoring of the accounting industry, despite its desire to preserve self-regulation.

The Big Bang legislation of 1996 aimed to make capital markets "free, fair, open, and competitive," and follow-on laws and newly created institutions have helped to accelerate the process of bank and corporate restructuring. These include the RCC (Resolution and Collection Corporation), the IRCJ (Industrial Revitalization Corporate of Japan), and the Civil Rehabilitation Law. The government reorganized and strengthened financial system regulatory oversight by splitting it off from the Ministry of Finance to the newly created FSA.

2.2 Shareholding and Shareholders

The pattern of shareholding is substantially different now than a decade ago. The most dramatic changes have been the declining share of commercial bank and life insurance company ownership, and the rise of foreign institutional investors and trust banks.

With declining share prices, very low dividend rates, and particularly the new mark-to-market rules, commercial banks have been under great balance-sheet and profitability pressure to sell their stockholdings. This has been somewhat offset by a desire to maintain established relationships with major long-term clients. In any case, as table 22.1 shows, from March 1991 to March 2003 commercial bank and life insurance companies' shares of listed companies' stock declined sharply. Trust banks increased the share substantially, primarily reflecting their pension fund management business. For all three groups, most of the change is since the 1996 Big Bang. Foreign holdings have been volatile but rising—going from 4.7 percent in 1991 to 17.7 percent in 2003.

Even more revealing and important are the declines in stable shareholding (down over 18 percentage points) and cross-shareholding (down almost 11 points). These declines are also mostly since 1996. Banks and industrial companies have sold shares in each other, though apparently the former much more than the latter. The story for

A. Shareholders	1991	1996	2003
Financial institutions	43.0	41.1	39.1
Commercial banks	15.7	15.1	7.7
Trust banks	9.8	10.3	21.4
Life insurance companies	12.0	11.1	6.7
Other financial institutions	5.5	4.6	3.3
Securities companies	1.7	1.4	0.9
Industrial companies	30.1	27.2	21.5
Japanese individuals	20.4	19.4	20.6
Foreigners	4.7	10.5	17.7
Government	0.3	0.3	0.2
B. Stable and cross shareholding[a]			
Stable shareholding (total)	45.6	43.4	27.1
Cross shareholding (total)	18.0	17.1	7.4
Banks	15.7	15.0	7.7
cross-shareholding	7.4	7.4	3.7
Life insurance companies	11.9	11.2	6.7[a]
Industrial companies	14.0	13.5	10.0
cross-shareholding	9.6	8.8	3.2
related companies	3.7	4.1	6.9
Other financial institutions	4.0	3.7	2.7
cross-shareholding	0.9	0.9	0.5

[a] Estimated.

Notes: Data are for March for the year shown (March 1991 is the end of fiscal 1990, and so forth.). Stable shareholders are financial institutions and industrial corporations that hold shares on a long-term basis for businesses and managerial relationship reasons. Cross-shareholding is a subset of firms holding each other's shares, typically banks and their corporate clients.

Sources: Nippon Life Insurance Research Institute, National Stock Exchanges.

Table 22.1: Distribution of Listed Company Shareholding (in percent)

industrial companies is more mixed; they have reduced cross-shareholding with banks, but have substantially increased holdings in related firms, in part because of newly listed subsidiaries. Even so, in a 1999 survey of 731 responding companies (out of 1,307) listed on the Tokyo Stock Exchange first section, over 98 percent (719) indicated they had stable shareholders. For almost two-thirds, stable holders had more than half of all shares (Nitta, 2001).

The changing patterns of stock ownership and the new institutional environment and rules have made meaningful shareholder activism possible for the first time. One important form has been shareholder derivative suits. As in the U.S., this litigation is driven mainly by lawyer fees; shareholders have obtained few direct gains (West, 2001). However, the successful suit in 2000 against Daiwa Bank directors, resulting in an award of $775 million in damages, has had a huge shock effect. The threat of shareholder suits has significantly altered the mind-set of corporate directors and audit firms, even though business and Keidanren have now successfully lobbied for legal limitations on director liability.

Foreign investors, who have focused on blue-chip Japanese companies, particularly those with better corporate governance, also are having an impact. Japanese CEOs have begun engaging in investor relations, traveling regularly to the U.S. to meet with institutional investors. For a sample of 1,100 nonfinancial companies listed on the first section of the Tokyo Stock Exchange in the 1990s, Ahmadjian and Robbins (2003) show that the greater the percentage of a firm's shares held by foreigners, the more likely it is to engage in the profit-enhancing activities of employee downsizing and asset divestiture. While the causal flow is not clear, they find no significant relationship between downsizing in one year and changes in foreign ownership the next; nor was foreign ownership likely to increase in troubled firms.

2.3 The Main Bank System

The heyday of the main bank system was in the 1960s and 1970s; it had weakened even prior to the late 1980s asset bubble. The burst bubble was disastrous for banks, corporate borrowers, and home owners; a huge amount of paper wealth was destroyed. From its December 1989 high to October 2003, the Nikkei 225 stock index was down almost 75 percent and had been even lower. Nationwide land prices have declined for 12 consecutive years since 1991: by 39.7 percent for residential land, 65 percent for commercial land, and even more in major urban regions.

The main bank system—indeed the entire banking system—was subject to a severe stress test and, given the balance-sheet effects of the huge decreases in asset values, not surprisingly were found seriously wanting. Nonperforming loans (NPLs) have overwhelmed banks; despite write-offs of some four times their capital, banks have not yet overcome their NPL difficulties. Banks do not have sufficient capital to absorb the costs of supporting the restructuring of their distressed large corporate borrowers. Their commitments have become an albatross around the necks of main banks; they certainly no longer can be effective monitors. At the extreme, zombie main banks and their zombie industrial clients are locked in a deep embrace, both staying alive by rolling over and even increasing loans, something made feasible by the extraordinary low interest rate structure.

Politicians, government bureaucrats, and bank management are all responsible for Japan's banking mess. To have been effective, main bank responsibility for restructuring distressed client companies required strong Ministry of Finance and Bank of Japan support and much larger injections of government capital than occurred. While the myth of the 1980s was that land prices would never decline, the myth of the 1990s was that the economy would soon naturally return to its growth path.

Forbearance and procrastination have prevailed because of a perverse incentive structure: politicians do not want to be accused of using more taxpayer money to bail out rich bankers; regulators do not want to admit past mistakes; bank managers do not want to lose their jobs and pensions. The 2003 Resona Bank bail out provides a new and better model for bank restructuring. The government injected sufficient capital that Resona can write off its NPLs and restore operational effectiveness; management was replaced; a U.S.-style corporate board system with outside directors was installed; and employment is being cut and wages sharply reduced. Importantly, the Resona crisis was caused by an external auditor's tough stance. The main downside was that shareholders received a windfall rather than sharing the costs. Such makeshift and partial government policies have made for widespread moral hazards in the financial system.

It is a mistake to think that bank-business relationships will become arm's-length, and thus highly unlikely that a main bank system with preemptive effective monitoring of large companies will be created. Instead, serious monitoring is being undertaken by Japan's capital markets, although this is still in its early stages.

2.4 Capital Markets

Japan's capital markets are now quite well developed in some respects, but market discipline and monitoring are not yet strong. Financial deregulation culminated in the implementation of the Japanese Big Bang policy of the late 1990s to develop capital markets. Foreign financial institutions are active participants. Institutional gatekeepers—securities analysts, credit rating agencies, investment banks, and knowledgeable financial media—are increasing in number and activity. Accounting standards and auditing requirements and procedures have been strengthened. The rules and their regulation are solid. Stock prices now have an important signaling effect for investors and for company managers. However, in the mediocre growth environment, viable companies are repaying debt, and the supply of equity or bond issues is limited.

A merger and acquisition market has been developing, both between Japanese firms and with foreign firms. The most notable industries involved are banking, where mergers have created four mega-banks, and automobiles, where only two domestically controlled assemblers (Toyota and Honda) remain of eight a decade ago. However, virtually all mergers have been friendly. There have not yet been any successful hostile takeover bids or shareholder proxy fights. But, unlike a decade ago, they are now thinkable. The failure of Yoshiaki Murakami, a shareholder activist, to win a second, widely publicized proxy fight against Tokyo Style Company in spring 2003 is suggestive both of continuing obstacles and future trends. Tokyo Style is an apparel company with huge cash reserves and a stock price below its cash-equivalent holdings. Despite the economic logic of a huge dividend or a major stock buy-back, the company's banks and domestic institutional investors sided with management.

Japanese institutional investor activism in corporate governance is nascent but gradually increasing. Even more than in the United States, Japanese institutional investors vote with management. The U.S. pension fund CalPERS is actively promoting its corporate governance guidelines in Japan, but it has no Japanese counterpart yet. The closest is the increasingly active Pension Fund Association. It has promulgated guidelines for its 1700 members which emphasize shareholder value and urge members to vote proxies accordingly.

In 2002, CalPERS invested $200 million in a corporate governance-oriented fund with Shuhei Abe's SPARK Asset Management Company and, in 2003, $200 million in the $1 billion U.S.-based Taiyo Fund with Wilbur Ross to employ friendly approaches to corporate governance to build value in listed Japanese companies.

Morningstar Japan has created an index of 150 socially responsible firms. While their quantitative impact is limited, these activities receive considerable publicity and are influencing the mindset of market participants.

West (2001) and Milhaupt (2001) have noted the quite successful activist role of a nonprofit corporate reform organization called Shareholder Ombudsman, which has been involved in high-profile shareholder derivative suits, and has negotiated substantial monetary settlements and management commitments to improve practices. This organization has not sought publicity, but Milhaupt argues that managers cannot afford to ignore it.

The capital market still has major lacunae. As the Tokyo Style case attests, there is not yet a market for corporate control. This is despite the fact that a number of companies have a market capitalization below their ready break-up value. Persistent stable shareholding is part of the reason. Another has been the ongoing predilection of domestic institutional investors to support incumbent management regardless of its performance. Further, the corporate bond market does not price risk adequately. Spreads are quite narrow, a high yield (junk) bond market is only nascent, and banks have not yet developed a loan market charging higher rates to riskier borrowers. Their dilemma is that, should they set interest rates realistically based on creditworthiness, many of their borrowers would go bankrupt. Neither the banks nor the politicians can afford that.

2.5 The Permanent Employment System

Poor economic growth and the need by firms to cut costs, downsize, and restructure have sharply reduced the demand for labor, while the supply has continued to increase. Unemployment has risen to an unprecedented 5.3 percent; but that is not the full story. Participation rates have fallen as potential workers have withdrawn from, or never entered, the labor force. Part-time workers have gone from 4.7 million in 1990 to 12 million today, some 23 percent of those employed. Firms have had to go beyond the traditional adjustments of overtime reduction, elimination of contract and temporary employees, and dispatch of workers to affiliated firms.

For many companies, downsizing requires more than attrition. For legal and reputational reasons, firms have not been able simply to lay off workers. Rather, they have pressured worker early retirement or "voluntary" separation by providing buyouts. The specifics have been worked out in close consultation with the enterprise unions, and there has been virtually no overt labor strife, despite substantial discontent. This gradualist, expensive approach reflects management's continuing commitment to its regular employees. Senior managers have been particularly concerned about their eventual successors—employees on the management track. This process of downsizing of employment is seen by some as the deinstitutionalization of the permanent employment system (Ahmadjian and Robinson, 2001). Others argue that the system is adjusting but has not fundamentally changed (Kato, 2001).

It is too early to determine what will happen to the permanent employment system. Wages and promotions will be based more on merit rather than seniority. Many of today's young college graduates do not believe that a company's permanent employment commitment is credible; they expect to shift from one company to another over time as opportunities emerge. I think the permanent employment system will persist in modified form, in part because the inevitable reductions in the number of Japanese of labor force age, a demographic given, will create labor shortages by the end of this decade if the economy succeeds in achieving sustained growth.

2.6 Outside Auditors

In addition to its statutory auditors, companies are required to use outside auditors to certify their financial statements. Auditing firms can no longer afford to be accommodating of management interests. The Enron and Arthur Andersen collapses shocked Japan's auditing profession. Closer to home, in early 2002 Ohta-Showa Audit Company had to pay a substantial fine to the Financial Services Authority for its mishandling of Long-Term Credit Bank audits. Under revised rules, since March 2003 auditors are required to declare whether a client faces serious risk of going bankrupt within a year, and can be sued if they mislead shareholders.

The May 2003 decision of the auditors not to allow a full five years of Resona Bank deferred tax assets to count as capital was dramatic. It meant that Resona was below the 4 percent minimum capital requirement for domestic banks. Unable to raise further capital privately, Resona had to request a capital injection from the government, with all that entailed. Suddenly auditors became major players in the governance of distressed banks and other companies.

3. Corporate Management Responses

Japanese management is on the defensive. Its leadership and corporate governance are under challenge due to sustained poor performance, exacerbated by some highly publicized scandals. What has emerged is a lively debate and a fascinating clash of views and policy proposals between a few business leaders who actively seek to change Japanese corporate governance to a much more market-based, American-type system and those leaders, skeptical of American corporate governance in practice, who want to improve the existing Japanese system. The debate centers on two issues: For whose interests does the company exist; and who should be responsible for monitoring the company's operations?

Yoshihiko Miyauchi, chairman and CEO of Orix, epitomizes those pushing for a major transformation of Japanese corporate governance. In 1999 he stated: "We aim at a stockholder's capitalism that brings long-run benefits to stockholders, not short-term ones as in the United States" (Takahashi, 1999). He has arranged programs to train Japanese in their proper roles and responsibilities as potential outside directors. Not surprisingly, the leaders of some of the blue chip companies in which foreign shareholding is highest are among the most outspoken proponents of change. At the same time, some of Japan's most successful companies are headed by defenders of the current system. Thus, Hiroshi Okuda, chairman of Nippon Keidanren (the Japanese Business Federation) and former president of Toyota Motor Corporation, and Fujio Cho, current president of Toyota, affirm that a company's primary commitment is to its employees. Toyota, however, is such an exceptionally successful company that some argue it cannot be a role model. Nonetheless, other business leaders such as Fujio Mitarai, president of highly successful Canon Inc., also defend the current system.

One test will be the number of companies that choose to shift to the new option, as of April 2003, of a committee-based board embodying a significant role for outside directors. In their first opportunity (in most cases the June 2003 shareholder annual meetings), 36 firms adopted the committee-style system; 5 have more outside than internal directors, and in another 5 the numbers are equal. Some companies indicated they switched in order to enhance transparency and attract foreign investors. Others, such as Hitachi, did so to reinforce control over group firms; current or former executives from the parent company are being made as outside directors of 18 listed group companies. Several of the companies have come under foreign control (Nikkei net Interactive).

Some business leaders suggest the number of companies adopting the committee-based system will be about 125 by 2005. That will still be small relative to the total of some 2,500 listed companies. About 24 percent of Japanese listed companies surveyed now have at least one outside director and that number will increase; nonetheless managers continue to be very reluctant to share much power with outsiders. And, as in all countries, an ongoing issue is how independent outside directors really are.

The trend to reduce board size sharply and create an executive officer system is accelerating. Even Toyota reduced its board by more than half in 2003. As of early 2003, 34.2 percent of listed companies have adopted the executive officer system (Michael Solomon Associates, 2003). However, establishing this system is motivated predominantly by efforts to increase management oversight efficiency; it has a limited effect on corporate governance. Many firms and their peak organization Nippon Keidanren are focusing on improvements in internal auditing, control, and ethical behavior, which are termed internal corporate governance (Ito, 2003).

Overall, corporate governance reform seems to have been driven primarily by legal and institutional reforms rather than a fundamental change in management mindset, at least so far. So, whether it wants to or not, management has to be much more responsive to shareholder interests due to greater disclosure and auditing requirements, the threat of being sued, and the embarrassment of a hostile proxy fight.

In fiscal 2002, 783 firms announced plans to buy back up to ¥9.7 trillion ($88.2 billion at ¥110/dollar) of their shares and actually repurchased ¥2.8 trillion. Close to 800 firms have announced repurchases during fiscal 2003 of ¥7.3 trillion. Nippon Life, Japan's largest insurance company, has taken an activist position, pressing firms with cash surpluses to carry out buy-back programs and to increase dividends, threatening to raise the issue at the 2004 shareholder meetings. Some firms are beginning to use stock options to align managerial and shareholder interests; however, given unattractive American experience, they are cautious. It will be some time before stock options become important in aligning management and shareholder interests.

Aside from those companies and financial institutions in severe financial distress, Japanese management remains firmly entrenched. Firms going through restructuring or workouts will see some management personnel changed. Their corporate governance will surely improve. But, unless the firms become foreign-controlled, it is not likely their fundamental commitments to regular employees and internal directors will change substantially.

The moral hazards of the Japanese corporate governance system are quite different from those common in the U.S. Thus, for example, Japanese firms do not pay extravagant compensation to top management. While American managers may steal from the company, Japanese managers steal *for* the company. One form of moral hazard in Japan is that middle management expends considerable effort to protect the CEO and senior management from exposure of company mistakes or personal scandal. This opaqueness has its costs, as gangster blackmail has demonstrated. There are two fundamentally more important moral hazards. First, management has had a proclivity to invest surplus cash in new projects, seemingly regardless of profitability. Second, managers of firms in serious difficulty keep current employees far too long, thereby significantly eroding the value of the company, the firm's future, and the prospects for both current and future employees. And, as the company deteriorates, they do not replace themselves with managers who are given a mandate to carry out the needed reforms.

4. Conclusion

The answer to all the questions posed at the start of the chapter is "to some extent, and in quite Japanese ways." This is because there is no monolithic Japanese corporate governance system today and there will not be in the future. Different firms will have different corporate governance systems, depending on their histories, ownership patterns, and leaders. This chapter is about the large subset of listed firms in which ownership and control are separated. Within this group, the variance of corporate governance arrangements will be substantially wider than in the past.

First, one major lesson of the past decade for Japanese management is that it is essential to restore the early postwar understanding that profitability is very important. Often better corporate governance is a code phrase for better corporate profitability. Only by earning profits can management buy off employees, shareholders, and other stakeholders, and thereby stay in power. All firms will come to give substantially greater weight to shareholder interests, but only a few firms will make maximization of shareholder value a primary objective. The important weight given to the interests of regular employees will persist. This will be reinforced by the return to labor market tightness as the economy achieves its growth potential and as labor force numbers decline absolutely.

Second, one or even several outside directors will come to serve on most corporate boards, but in only a few companies will they constitute a majority. The value of outside directors will continue to be founded on their independent views and judgment based on their own career experiences and their relationships, aside from the token symbolism for good corporate governance. I doubt that more than a modest minority of Japanese companies will adopt the U.S.-style committee-board system, since it bestows far greater power on outside directors.

Third, the main bank system has been found wanting in the severe stress test it has undergone from the early 1990s, and it is unlikely to play a major monitoring role again for most listed companies. Of course, some companies with traditional relationship affiliations, symbolized by the keiretsu, will continue to rely significantly on bank finance, though the degree of bank monitoring power and capability is uncertain. Regulatory forbearance and expanded safety nets not only for depositors but apparently shareholders have exacerbated and lengthened the duration of financial system weakness.

Fourth, a market for corporate control will emerge, and that will have important psychological effects. What is needed is the first success. There are a number of potential prospects. Hostile bids will have to be led by Japanese; behavior by the creditor banks will be one key. However, rather than a plethora of overt hostile take-over bids, I anticipate that concerned parties will negotiate arrangements to improve corporate performance and governance.

Fifth, financial market discipline has never been strong, kept weak first by successful growth and now by Japan's persistent lack of aggregate demand and poor economic performance. Nonetheless, there have been and will continue to be significant improvement in capital market institutions and investments, and prices are coming to play a significant monitoring role. Most directly benefiting will be the overlapping group of companies with large foreign institutional shareholding, subject to international competition, and adopting the committee board system.

The greatest improvements in Japanese corporate governance thus far have been substantially enhanced disclosure and transparency. These have been mandated by legal reforms. Capital markets still have a long way to go to have significant monitoring impact on most companies.

I do not expect the institutions of the postwar economic system to collapse or disappear. My judgment as to what will happen includes the following. The permanent employment system will rely less on seniority, more on merit, but the corporate commitment to permanent employment (to age 60) will endure. Employees may feel less committed to the firm than before, but commitment will increase with years of service; labor markets for middle-aged and older employees are not likely to become a great deal more flexible. Good relations between management and worker representatives will continue to be important, pragmatic, and relatively harmonious. Companies will still want to maintain good relationships with banks and vice versa; bank provision of financial services will increase even as their loans decrease. Unless a company does so poorly that it is taken over, its self-perpetuating management system will continue to be entrenched.

Japan is not going to embrace the Anglo-American governance model: After all, it is under attack at home and how the reformed system will work is not clear. Rather, I think Japanese firms will, slowly, continue to adopt (adapt) market-oriented approaches while seeking to retain the goals, if not the practices, of the postwar economic system. In short, the wise Japanese management today is engaging in corporate government reforms that do not fundamentally reduce its entrenchment, while enabling the firm—and thus *all* its stakeholders—to be more successful in the long run.

*Hugh Patrick is director of the Center on Japanese Economy and Business at Columbia University. Parts of the section on the postwar economic system are based on Patrick (2002).

References

Ahmadjian, Christina L., and Gregory E. Robbins, 2003, "A clash of capitalisms: Foreign shareholders and corporate restructuring in 1990s Japan," paper.

_____, 2001, "Safety in numbers: Downsizing and the deinstitutionalization of permanent employment in Japan," *Administrative Science Quarterly*, pp. 622–654.

Allen, Franklin, and Douglas Gale, 2000, *Comparing Financial Systems,* Cambridge: MIT Press.

Aoki, Masahiko, 2000, *Information, Corporate Governance and Institutional Diversity: Competitiveness in Japan, the United States, and the Traditional Economies,* Oxford: Oxford University Press.

Aoki, Masahiko, and Hugh Patrick (eds.), 1994, *The Japanese Main Bank System: Its Reliance for Developing and Transforming Economies*, Oxford: Oxford University Press.

Dore, Ronald, 2000, *Stock Market Capitalism: Welfare Capitalism—Japan and Germany Versus the Anglo-Saxonso*, Oxford: Oxford University Press.

Fukao, Mitsuhiro, 2003, "Japan's lost decade and weakness in its corporate governance structure," in *Japan's Economic Recovery: Commercial Policy, Monetary Policy, and Corporate Governance*, Robert M. Stern (ed.), Northampton, MA: Edward Elgar, pp. 289–327.

_____, 1995, *Financial Integration, Corporate Governance, and the Performance of Multinational Companies*, Washington: The Brookings Institution.

Hoshi, Takeo, and Anil Kashyap, 2001, *Corporate Financing and Governance in Japan: The Road to the Future*, Cambridge: MIT Press.

Hoshi, Takeo, and Hugh Patrick (eds.), 2001, *Crisis and Change in the Japanese Financial System*, Boston: Kluwer Academics.

Ito, Kazuhide, 2003, "Japan's solution for the recent corporate scandals: corporations' positive actions for reinforcing ethical behavior," *Japan Economic Currents*, Washington: Keizai Koho Center, Vol. 29, February.

Kato, Takao, 2001, "The ending of lifetime employment in Japan?: Evidence from national surveys and field research," *Journal of the Japanese and International Economies,* Vol. 15, pp. 489–514.

Learmount, Simon, 2002, *Corporate Governance—What can be learned from Japan*, Oxford: Oxford University Press.

Michael Solomon Associates, 2003, "Interview with Takushi Shimoda, Managing Director, Tokyo Stock Exchange," *Japan Corporate Governance Report*, No. 5, March–April.

Milhaupt, Curtis J., 2003, "A lost decade for Japanese corporate governance reform?: What's changed, what hasn't, and why," Columbia Law School, Center for Law and Economics, working paper, July 9.

_____, 2001, "Creative norm destruction: The evolution of non-legal rules in Japanese corporate governance," *University of Pennsylvania Law Review*, Vol. 149, June, pp. 2083–2129.

Nakamura, Nobuo, 2003, "Corporate governance in Japan: Today and tomorrow," *Japan Economic Currents*, Washington: Keizai Koho Center, Vol. 34, July, pp. 6–10.

National Stock Exchanges (Zenkoku Shoken Torihikisho), 2003, "Heisei 14-nenndo kabushiki bunpu jokyo chosa chosa kekka: Shiryo-hen (A survey of distribution of shareholding: Fiscal year 2002)," June 16, available at www.nse.or.jp/j-bunpu.htm.

Nikkei net Interactive, 2003, "36 listed firms to adopt U.S.-style corporate governance as of June," June 15, at www.nni.nikkei.co.jp/ac/feat/ectrends/ectrends00545.html.

Nitta, Michio, 2001, "Corporate governance Japanese style: Roles of employees and unions," *Social Science Japan*, Tokyo: Institute of Social Sciences, University of Tokyo, Vol. 20, March.

Nippon Life Insurance (NLI) Research Institute, 2003, Mochiai jyoukyou chousa: 2002 nendo han (A survey of cross shareholdings: Fiscal year 2002), September 18, at www.nli-research.co.jp.

Okazaki, Tetsuji, 2001, "The role of holding companies in pre-war Japanese economic development: Rethinking zaibatsu in perspective of corporate governance," *Social Science Japan Journal*, Vol. 4, No. 2, pp. 243–268.

Patrick, Hugh, 2003, "Whither the Japanese Economy," *Annual Report 2002–2003*, Columbia Business School, Center on Japanese Economy and Business.

_____, 2002, "Corporate governance, ownership structure, and financial crises: experience of East Asian countries," *The Finance Crisis and Beyond*, Chiho Kim (ed.), Seoul: Korea Deposit Insurance Corporation.

Sheard, Paul, 1994, "Main banks and the governance of financial distress," in *The Japanese Main Bank System: Its Reliance for Developing and Transforming Economies*, Masahiko Aoki and Hugh Patrick (eds.), Oxford: Oxford University Press, pp. 188–230.

Takahashi, Hirosuki, 1999, "Corporate governance in Japan: Reform of top corporate management structure," *JEI Report*, Japan Economic Institute, No. 28a, July 23.

West, Mark D., 2001, "Why shareholders sue: The evidence from Japan," *Journal of Legal Studies*, Vol. 30, June.

Chapter 23

Quis Custodiet Ipsos Custodes? Controlling Conflicts of Interest in the Financial Industry?

Eugene N. White*
Rutgers University and National Bureau of Economic Research

Can the market adequately control conflicts of interest in the financial industry? [1]The recent corporate scandals that emerged in the wake of the 2000 stock market collapse elicited strong policy responses that imply markets are relatively ineffective. The objective of these changes is to head off any further loss of investors' confidence in the financial system. Although these reforms have been presented as costless, there are trade-offs, as many will reduce or eliminate the synergies that formed the current financial architecture. If the existing governance and incentive structures failed to serve investors well, can the government ensure that there is better vigilance at a low cost to efficiency?

1. Synergies and Conflicts of Interest: A Package Deal

Reliable information is essential for markets to perform their economic function of channeling funds to individuals and firms with the greatest productive opportunities. But a key problem of ensuring that information is accurate is the asymmetric relationship between lenders and borrowers. One party to a financial contract has less accurate information than the other party, posing a potential impediment to the efficient functioning of the financial market.

Managers of a corporation have better information about its returns and risk than do the purchasers of its securities or bank loan officers. This information asymmetry leads to the two basic problems of adverse selection and moral hazard. Adverse selection arises before a transaction when managers who may divert funds to less productive uses are most likely to seek external funds. As their selection makes it more likely that investments will perform poorly, investors who cannot screen out bad from good investments may decide not to invest. Moral hazard occurs after the financial transaction has taken place when managers are able to misallocate funds because investors cannot adequately monitor their behavior. Investors respond to this predicament by reducing their funding.

Individual investors could conduct their own screening and monitoring of managers, but they face substantial problems. If they become well informed, investors will be subject to free-rider behavior by others who observe their decisions. Their effectiveness is further diminished by economies of scale and scope in the collection of information. One solution is for investors to delegate the task of screening and monitoring to financial institutions that can specialize and gain the economies of scale and scope. Analysts in investment banks can advise clients on what securities to buy; auditors may opine on accuracy of the accounts presented by management, and rating agencies will rank the relative riskiness of securities. In addition to these fee-based services from agents, intermediaries can invest funds from the public in a diversified portfolio constructed with their private information. However the essential problem of monitoring arises again, as investors using the services of financial institutions need to monitor and screen these watchmen. A financial institution must convince its customers that it is adequately monitoring its employees. If markets work efficiently, then the intermediary should be able to signal that it is doing its job by building a reputation or requiring managers put their funds at risk. (Diamond, 1991, and Ramakrishnan and Thakor, 1984.)

In most theoretical literature, financial institutions are treated as though each type of institution focuses on solving one kind of informational asymmetry. Yet, the information that any one institution possesses is useful beyond the provision of one service. For example, banks have long-term customer relationships, from which they obtain reusable confidential information about firms' resources, cash flows, and other characteristics. A close long-term relationship induces customers to reveal more confidential information. Financial institutions also gain a cost advantage because they can exploit cross-sectional information across customers. Thus, they become low-cost producers of information for complementary financial services.

These synergies or economies of scope offer substantial benefits, but they also create potential costs in the form of conflicts of interest. Although conflicts of interest appear in almost all economic relationships, the following definition is used in this paper:

> Conflicts of interest arise when a financial service provider, or an agent within such a service provider, has multiple interests which create incentives to act in such a way as to misuse or conceal information needed for the effective functioning of financial markets.

Combinations of financial services under one roof open the door to conflicts of interest. If individuals or firms can successfully exploit conflicts of interest, they benefit from the information asymmetries vis-à-vis customers and prevent markets from channeling funds to the most productive investments. Yet, exploitation of a conflict of interest will, once recognized, reduce the reputation of an institution. The existence of a conflict does not necessarily mean it will be exploited if the institution places a high value on its reputation. Public policy remedies may not be required to control the exploitation of conflicts. However, even if there is exploitation, intervention to reduce conflicts needs to be balanced against the reduction in the economies of scope. In this paper, these issues are examined for two conflicts, one in investment banking and the other in auditing.

2. Conflicts between Underwriting and Research

Benefiting from economies of scale and scope, investment banks jointly provide financial services that bridge informational asymmetries in the primary and secondary capital markets. They float new and seasoned securities, advise on mergers and acquisitions, act as brokers or dealers, provide research, and make markets. The conflict of interest in investment banking that has received most recent attention has been the conflict between providing research to investors and underwriting initial public offerings. By identifying and monitoring what companies are worthy of investment, research analysts reduce the problems of adverse selection and moral hazard. The investment bank that serves as the lead underwriter for a syndicate acts as the delegated monitor for individual investors and the rest of the syndicate, collecting the vital information on the firm desiring the IPO. The lead underwriter gains an information advantage, which is greatest at the beginning. Its research analysts who have been part of the discovery process should be able to offer better buy/sell recommendations and superior forecasts of the firm's performance. Furthermore, the lead underwriter usually is the dominant market maker. Information synergies from underwriting, research, and market making thus provide a rationale for combining these distinct financial services.[2] The success of an investment bank's combination of these activities will contribute to its reputation and future prospects.

However, by serving two clients, a conflict of interest arises. Issuers may benefit from optimistic research while investors seek unbiased research. If the incentives for these two activities are not appropriately aligned, there will be a temptation for employees on one side of the firm to distort information to the advantage of their clients and the profit of their department. To manage this conflict of interest it is necessary to set appropriate compensation for research analysts, but this is difficult because the information they generate for investors is not a purely private good and cannot be limited to the firm's clients. Thus, it is not surprising that brokerages do not typically charge clients for research (Dugar and Nathan, 1995). A further problem arises in the evaluation of analysts' performance because they provide multiple services. During the recent boom, some stock prices moved far away from fundamentals, enhancing the reputations of analysts who correctly picked stocks at the expense of those who focused on accurate forecasts of earnings.

Although compensation rules vary among firms, an analyst's external reputation is important for compensation. External reputation is influenced by the *Institutional Investor*'s polls (Stickel, 1992) that rank analysts on buy/sell recommendations, earnings forecasts, reports, and overall service. Analysts' reputation is important not just for brokerage customers, but it is also considered a vital marketing tool for investment banks in the initial public offering (IPO) market. A survey of chief executive officers (CEOs) and chief financial officers (CFOs) whose firms issued IPOs in the 1990s reported that three-quarters considered the reputation of the research department and its analysts in the selection of a lead underwriter (Galant, 1992). Analysts' support is often considered part of an implicit understanding between underwriter and issuer. Finally, analysts' focus on the evolution of industries gives them a highly specialized knowledge, enabling some to help underwriters by screening companies that are coming to market.

If analysts are compensated in part by underwriting departments, there is a strong conflict of interest potential for analysts. The conflict of interest will be most acute if the IPO market is highly profitable relative to brokerage, inducing them to bias their reports in favor of issuers. The short-term payoff for an analyst may outweigh the benefits of investing in a long-term reputation in a soaring market, with a temptation to seize the firm's reputational rents by promoting "hot" issues.

The conditions of the boom market of the 1990s appear to have been ideal for tempting analysts to exploit the conflict of interest. Technology stocks dominated the IPOs and the quality of companies going to market underwent a change (Ritter and Welch, 2003). Most IPO companies had several years of established positive earnings from the 1960s to the 1980s, but the number of issuers with negative earnings soared to nearly 80 percent in 1999 and 2000. They may have had long-term potential, yet stock prices were moving away from their conventional relationships with fundamentals. Investors seem to have ignored these standard signals, giving more attention to target prices and other information, raising the reputation of the most optimistic analysts.

With IPO markets booming, media attention focused on analysts' pronouncements. There appears to have been pressure on them to join in the optimistic promotion of stocks. For example, in late 1998, most analysts held that Amazon.com was overvalued at $240; Jonathan Cole of Merrill Lynch believed $50 to be a reasonable price. Henry Blodget at Oppenheimer and Co. set a price target of $400. When Amazon.com surpassed it, he was hailed as a guru; Cole departed and Merrill Lynch hired Blodget. Rewards for optimism seem to have pervaded the industry. In a study of the movement of analysts from job to job to higher- or to lower-status brokerage houses, Hong and Kubik (2003) found that while analysts were rewarded for the relative accuracy of earnings forecasts, those who were more optimistic than the consensus were also more likely to experience favorable job separations, and promotions for optimism became more important by the late 1990s.

Analysts influence investors, and their buy/sell recommendations are treated as "new" information, moving the market (Womack, 1996). But, it is not clear that the analysts intended to deceive customers. While analysts made far more buy than sell recommendations in the boom, the ratio scarcely change after the collapse of the bull market. More importantly, many research-only houses where there was no potential conflict also had far more buy than sell recommendations.[3] What evidence is there that analysts tried to exploit conflicts of interest? The answer to this question should be found in the differential behavior of analysts at underwriting and non-underwriting banks. Owing to their key position, lead underwriters' analysts' reports should carry extra weight and their predictions should be unbiased and more accurate than those of other analysts. Consequently, the market should react more to their announcements than to reports of other analysts. However, if they are biased, underwriter analysts will issue relatively more positive recommendations for firms that trade poorly in the IPO aftermarket. Furthermore, if the market recognizes the potential conflict of interest, then investors should discount underwriter analysts' recommendations relative to non-underwriter analysts.

For 1990 and 1992, Michaely and Womack (1999) examined the "buy" recommendations of lead underwriter and other analysts for IPOs after the Securities and Exchange Commission's (SEC) twenty-five day post-IPO "quiet period." They found that in the month after the quiet period, lead underwriters' analysts made 50 percent more buy recommendations than other firms' analysts for the same securities, suggesting some conflict of interest. But, stock prices of firms recommended by lead underwriting banks declined during the quiet period, while other banks' picks rose. The market recognized the difference in the quality of information. The excess return at the recommendation date is 2.7 percent for underwriters' analysts and 4.4 percent for other analysts. Considering a two-year holding period from the IPO date, the performance of other analysts' recommended issues was 50 percent better than the performance of underwriters' recommendations. Finally, the same investment banks made better recommendations on IPOs when they were not the lead underwriter, implying that it not a difference in analyst's ability but an underwriter bias.[4] The finding that the market discounts analyst optimism is also supported by survey data. Boni and Womack (2002) found that 86 percent of the professional money managers and buy-side analysts said that they discount the recommendations and reports of analysts when there is an investment banking relationship between the bank and the company analyzed.

While many in the market recognized the presence of conflicts of interest and the potential for their exploitation, the debate on the appropriate policies has been largely foreclosed by the "Global Settlement" reached on December 20, 2002, by the SEC, the New York Attorney General, National Association of Securities Dealers, North American Securities Administrators Association, New York Stock Exchange, and state regulators with the ten largest investment banks.[5] The five key terms of the agreement were: 1) Firms are required to sever the links between research and investment banking, including analyst compensation for equity research and analysts' accompanying investment banking personnel on road shows. 2) The practice of spinning is banned. 3) Each firm is required to make public its analyst recommendations, including its ratings and price target forecasts. 4) For a five-year period, brokerage firms will be required to contract with no less than three independent research firms to provide research to their customers. Regulators will chose an independent consultant "monitor" for each firm to procure independent research to ensure that investors get objective investment advice. 5) Total fines of $1.4 billion will be levied that are partly for retrospective relief, independent research, and investor education.

This settlement has some good and some alarming features. One general aim seems to be to make analyst information a public good. If research is socialized, firms will have less incentive to compete for customers by the quality of their research. By taxing the firms to fund independent research, they will be induced to cut back on their own internal analysis and lower its quality. Some separation between analysts and underwriters with firewalls is appropriate, but complete separation is mistaken. The failed attempt to separate commercial and investment banking under the Glass–Steagall Act shows that this remedy is extreme. Given that the market already discounted lead underwriters analysts' recommendations, firms were subject to some market discipline. Separation means that firms will have to have a separate staff for underwriting to perform the analysis, raising costs, losing some economies of scope. As exploitation of conflicts of interest was not uniform across the industry, firms can be disciplined by loss of reputation and litigation where conflicts were exploited by individual firms. One intervention—banning spinning—is probably appropriate as it will ensure that insiders do not take advantage of outsider investors, exploiting the lack of information about how shares are distributed.

In general, the global settlement relies on separation and the socialization of research as remedies. Alternative remedies would be to increase the ability of the market to discipline firms by increasing disclosure to investors of underwriting relationships, complementing this with supervisory oversight where disclosure would result in the loss of proprietary information, as in the case of mergers and acquisitions.

3. Conflicts of Interest between Auditing and Consulting

Auditors are another key group of watchmen needed to overcome the informational asymmetry between shareholders and managers. To reassure investors, managers provide a set of accounts to demonstrate how they have used the firm's resources. This presentation of information does not eliminate the inherent agency problem. To ensure the reliability of these accounts, auditors can provide an independent assessment of the accounts prepared by managers and attest to the quality of information. The information collected by an audit firm has many potential uses beyond an audit report. Auditors have branched into new consulting services, notably tax advice, accounting, management information systems, and strategic advice, commonly referred to as management advisory services (MAS). These complementary services have economies of scope, but they create two potential sources of conflict of interest: 1) auditors may bias their opinions to limit any loss of fees in the "other" services, and 2) auditors may be called upon to evaluate tax and financial structures that were designed by their non-audit counterparts. Both conflicts may lead to biased audits, with the result that less information is available in financial markets. As in investment banking, individuals or firms can benefit from the exploitation of these conflicts of interest because of the reputational capital that auditing firms have built up with investors.

Currently, audit opinion is expressed in a report attesting to whether the financial statements provide a "fair presentation" or "true and fair view" of the performance and position of a firm. To form judgments, investors require standards for comparisons, which were originally developed in the nineteenth century by professional accounting societies that evolved into the American Institute of Certified Public Accountants (AICPA). Until the New Deal, there was no federal regulation of accountants and auditors. The collapse of the stock market in 1929 led to the passage of the Securities Act of 1933 that required companies offering shares to the public to submit regular financial statements certified by an independent public or certified accountant. The Securities Exchange Act of 1934 created the SEC, which was given jurisdiction over the accounting profession and its rules. The SEC delegated its accounting and auditing rule-making authority to private standard-setting bodies with self-regulation and SEC oversight. In financial accounting, the task of setting standards was delegated to AICPA committees, which evolved into the Financial Accounting Standards Board (FASB). For auditing, the AICPA retained its standard-setting role in the Auditing Standards Board. The rules for auditing govern the conduct of an audit, the nature of the reports, and provide monitoring by peer reviews and the Public Oversight Board. As a result of the auditing scandals, much of this standard-setting and oversight has been taken over by the government. The Sarbanes–Oxley Act of 2002 established the Public Company Accounting Oversight Board (PCAOB). Under the SEC's oversight, the PCAOB will register accounting firms and establish rules for auditing, conduct inspections and investigations with the power to hold disciplinary proceedings, and impose sanctions. The PCAOB has indicated its intention to take over the rule-making authority for auditing standards, while leaving accounting rules in the hands of the FASB.

Investors highly value the information provided by auditors. Empirical evidence reveals that favorable opinions issued by audit firms with a strong reputation are valued more than those issued by firms with weaker reputations. Mansi, Maxwell, and Miller (2003) found that the use of a big-six auditor reduces the rate of return required by investors for a firm and that this effect is almost three times larger for non-investment grade issuers where information asymmetries are greater. Respect for audit reports is so great that there is acknowledged to be an "expectations gap." McEnroe and Martins (2001) discovered that there is large difference between the perception of what an audit opinion is intended to convey and what it actually accomplishes.[6] Many users of audits believe that an unqualified audit opinion indicates that the entity is financially sound and that there is no fraud or illegal activity. These expectations are widely held, in spite of the fact that in the U.S. the audit opinion only indicates that management's presentation of the financial information is a fair presentation of the position and performance of the company and conforms to the generally accepted accounting principles (GAAP).

In this environment, audit failures, particularly those appearing to arise out of perceived conflicts of interest caused a demand for reform. The conflict most frequently discussed in the popular financial press arises from an auditor providing non-audit services. As in the case of research and underwriting, the conflicts of interest arise because services were combined to exploit economies of scope. Auditing firms are natural consultants because they gather and assess a wide array of information that enables them to evaluate managements' accounting decisions. Such expertise has natural information synergies with consulting services. This alliance of activities was furthered as corporate accounting systems became computerized, and auditing firms soon specialized in computerized management information systems. In the early 1980s, auditing firms emerged as powerhouses of the consulting business, with the largest entering the ranks of the top ten of global consulting firms. The leading firm was Andersen Consulting, which was almost solely a systems-oriented consulting firm.[7]

Are these situations where there is a potential conflict of interest widely exploited by the industry? Prakash and Venable (1993) found that audit clients have incentives to limit non-audit purchases from incumbent auditors. Their conjecture is that a perceived reduction in auditor independence reduces audit credibility, adding agency costs for companies as the value of the auditors' monitoring role is reduced. More recently studies have examined whether auditor's fees for MAS are associated with abnormal accruals, used as a proxy for earnings management and biased reporting. Frankel, Johnson, and Nelson (2002) find that non-audit fees are positively associated with small earnings surprises and the magnitude of discretionary accruals. Antle, Gordon, Narayanamoorthy, and Zhou (2002) used a UK data sample, where there is greater disclosure of audit and non-audit fees, and saw no significant effect of abnormal accruals on audit fees or non-audit fees. In addition, they discovered that higher fees for non-audit services decreased abnormal accruals and interpreted this finding as evidence that non-audit services improve financial management. De Fond et. al. (2002) also found no evidence that non-audit service fees impair auditor independence. Auditors were more likely to issue qualified audits to clients that pay higher audit fees, consistent with a risk-based propensity to audit more. This finding was supported by Bell, Landsman, and Shackleford (2001) who ascertained that risky clients have higher fees because of extra effort expended by auditors.

These studies point to auditors expending more effort to address aggressive or risky accounting decisions made by clients. Although conflicts of interest have long been a concern, there appears to be no systematic patterns of exploitation. Yet, the rapid growth of MAS activities, followed by the spectacular audit failures, have produced demands that auditing be separated from non-auditing services. Congress responded to this perceived problem in Section 201 of the Sarbanes–Oxley Act of 2002, which makes it unlawful for registered public accounting firm to provide any non-audit service to an issuer contemporaneously with the audit including: bookkeeping, financial information systems design, appraisals, actuarial services, internal audit outsourcing, management functions, broker, dealer, investment advisor, investment banker, legal services, and any other service that the PCAOB determines are impermissible. This drastic measure will eliminate not only potential conflicts of interests and but also economies of scope. However, research suggests that conflicts of interest may not have been an overwhelming problem for audit firms. Instead the loss of auditor independence, the use of the partnership form for multi-product firms and litigation risk may have been the most important ingredients in the recent audit failures.

Auditing firms have been primarily organized as partnerships; and until the 1980s, the managing partners, governance structure, and profitability were dominated by the audit side of the firms. In the 1990s, MAS activities and revenues grew dramatically and audit profits were under increased competitive pressure and litigation risk (Healy and Palepu, 2001; Palmrose, 1988, 1991). The partnership structure meant that non-audit partners had to share their growing revenues with audit side and incur increased risk. Power struggles erupted, and the battle was most intense at Arthur Andersen. In these struggles, audit partners were pressured to increase revenues, and the dominance of local offices by single clients played an important role. Many of Arthur Andersen's largest failed clients, Enron, WorldCom, Qwest, and Global Crossing, were the largest companies in their local regions. The manager of a regional or city office would be wary of taking a negative stance on an audit that would risk losing the client. The loss of an Enron or WorldCom account would have been devastating to a local office and its partners even if it were only a small part of firm-wide revenues and profits. Whether this problem was systemic is unclear. For example, Reynolds and Francis (2000) analyzed the influence of large clients on office-level auditor reporting decisions and found no evidence of it influencing accruals. They and De Fond et. al. (2002) found the evidence consistent with auditors reporting more conservatively for larger clients because these clients pose greater litigation risk and hence more reputational risk.

Concern over preservation of an audit firm's reputation is the driving factor behind litigation risk. Class action lawsuits, filed on behalf of shareholders, beginning in the 1970s, claimed that declines in share prices were caused by faulty auditing (Palmrose, 1991). Litigation defeats imposed financial penalties and higher insurance costs, plus a loss of reputation. As a result, audit firms focused attention on reducing litigation risk, assessing the risk of their practices and clients. The national offices of audit firms began to perform risk assessments of clients and practices to manage these costs. Firms adjusted their activities to protect themselves from litigation. Auditors and corporations sought and relied upon an increased codification of auditing and accounting standards. The adherence to these rules facilitated a legal defense of compliance with rules (Dye, 1993). Auditors shifted their focus from opining on whether financial statements fairly present the "true" financial condition and performance of the company to compliance with the detailed GAAP rules. Managers were able to argue now that audit opinions should concentrate on compliance with the rules, shifting attention from performance and obscuring the true economic condition of companies. The focus on GAAP rules thus was another vital part of the debacle at Enron and other companies.

In addition to these problems, the decline of auditor independence threatens the effectiveness of audits. In principle, firms have an audit committee of the board of directors that is supposed to monitor auditing to prevent any conflict of interest between the auditors and management. However, audit committees were rarely in complete charge. Executive officers have often become the primary decision-makers, selecting the audit firm and negotiating the fees. This conflict of interest can only be remedied by a change in the governance structures.

While the Sarbanes–Oxley Act addresses some issues, the emphasis on separation by function is not the key and may well lower the effectiveness of auditors. It is unlikely that the proscription of non-auditing services, would have prevented the recent audit failures. The market can impose considerable discipline, as Arthur Andersen paid the ultimate price by its demise. To bolster the drive for reputation, some reforms are necessary. As Section 301 of the Sarbanes–Oxley Act recognizes, the corporate governance structure of companies needs to be altered so audit committees hire and determine the compensation of auditors, not management. A fundamental change is also required to shift auditors away from focusing on the adherence to detailed prescriptive accounting rules. The continued focus on the codification of accounting and auditing standards will not improve the quality of auditors' reports and may lead to more manipulative innovations to hide companies' true conditions. Lastly audit firms themselves need to adjust their internal governance and compensation structures to limit the problem of large client dominance of local offices and from competition between audit and non-audit services. Firms can devise their own structures, but the PCAOB may help by monitoring and encouraging the development and use of best-practice compensation and performance measurement structures.

4. Remedies for Conflicts of Interest

Is market discipline sufficient to control conflicts of interest? Market discipline hits firms hard with pecuniary penalties and promotes the development of institutional structures that limit conflicts and signal the firm's intent to the public. Litigation is an important part of market discipline. It is particularly effective as exploitation of conflicts is not uniform across the financial industry. While litigation may be the appropriate response to discipline specific firms and individuals as part of an overall market solution, legal liabilities and penalties need to be carefully designed, as demonstrated by the behavior of audit firms seeking to avoid the litigation risk from class action lawsuits.

Market-based solutions may not work if the market is unable to obtain sufficient information to punish firms that are exploiting conflicts of interest. To address this failure, there are four classes of interventions: 1) mandatory disclosure for increased transparency, 2) supervisory oversight, 3) separation by function, and 4) socialization of information. However, each of these remedies interferes with the combination of financial services, from which firms gain economies of scope, thereby imposing a potentially high cost on market efficiency. Perhaps, the most potent example of a misplaced remedy is the separation of commercial and investment banking by the Glass–Steagall Act (Crockett, Harris, Mishkin, and White, 2003). The separation imposed a high cost; and only after a long struggle, was the act was reversed in 1999. Market discipline that forced institutional changes on banks worked fairly well before 1929. The repeal of Glass–Steagall moved back to a greater emphasis on disclosure and oversight that were originally recommended by contemporary experts.

Mandatory disclosure to increase transparency is the least intrusive remedy. Disclosure that reveals whether a conflict of interest exists may help investors to judge how much weight to place on the information delivered by each firm. Yet, mandatory disclosure may be insufficient. Financial firms may hide relevant information and disclosure may reveal too much proprietary information. These problems suggest that the more intrusive approach, some supervisory oversight, may be needed. Supervisors can observe proprietary information about conflicts of interest without revealing it to a financial firm's competitors and can take actions to prevent financial firms from exploiting conflicts of interest.

If the market cannot get sufficient information from disclosure or supervisory oversight is ineffective, one may contemplate the more extreme solution of enforcing the separation of financial institutions by function. Separation by function has the goal of ensuring that "agents" are not placed in the position of responding to multiple "principals" so that conflicts of interest are reduced. Moving from less stringent separation of functions (different in-house departments with firewalls between them) to more stringent separation (different activities in separately capitalized affiliates or prohibition of the combination of activities in any organizational form) lessens conflicts of interest. Sometimes, firms may adopt these solutions independently—as did American universal banks in the 1920s—to signal that they are controlling conflicts. However, stringent separation of functions—as selected by the Glass–Steagall Act—may seriously reduce synergies of information collection, thereby preventing financial firms from taking advantage of economies of scope in information production.

The most radical response to conflicts of interest is to socialize the provision or the funding source of information. The argument for this approach is that information is a public good and so may need to be publicly supplied. Of course, the problem with this approach is that a government agency or publicly funded entity may not have the same strong incentives as private financial institutions to produce high quality information, thus reducing the flow of essential information to financial markets. While conflicts may not be entirely prevented by mandatory disclosure and supervisory oversight, the case for separation by function or socialization of information is hard to make given the costs imposed on the financial system.

In evaluating remedies, it is important to remember that the many types of agents who provide information to the financial markets have a range of access to information. Analysts have the least access, and rating agencies have more. Auditors probably have the most privileged private access followed by government regulators charged with supervisory oversight. This gradient of access to information should reflect the ability of agents to discover the true financial condition and performance of the firms that they observe. Agents' ability to discover this information will also be determined by their compensation and the other incentives provided to them.

Although these agents provide some overlapping information, one is not a substitute for another. This lack of substitution is not solely because they provide different types of information or signals to the public. These agents are all subject to various pressures and conflicts of interest that may diminish their ability to perform their task of discovery. Analysts may be well compensated and have substantial research resources at their disposal, but they may be too favorable to the firms if their bank is an underwriter and they have the least access to proprietary information. Ratings agencies are more insulated from conflicts of interest and have better access to information; but enjoying an oligopoly, their research effort may be reduced. Auditors enjoy superior access to proprietary information and operate in a competitive industry, but the value of their opinions may be reduced by conflicts of interest and a litigation-risk induced focus on rules rather than principles. Finally, regulators/supervisors may have the best access to proprietary information, yet their capacity to monitor is limited by the resources they have been allocated and political pressures for forbearance.

To ensure that the capital markets are adequately served, it is necessary to have multiple agents working to reduce the information asymmetries. One may become less useful at one point in time, but maintaining the quality of information delivered by these different agents engaged in overlapping work is more likely to provide sufficient monitoring of companies. Remedies should increase the effectiveness of these agents rather than constrain or co-opt them.

*Eugene N. White is a professor of economics at Rutgers University and a research associate at the National Bureau of Economic Research. The quotation in the title translates to "Who Watches the Watchmen?" and is taken from Juvenal (55–127 A.D.) *Satires*.

Notes

1. This paper is based on a forthcoming monograph, Crockett, Harris, Mishkin, and White (2003). We analyzed four conflicts of interest in the financial services industry, but only two are discussed in detail here.

2. For one theoretical treatment of how synergies arise between brokerage and underwriting, see Stefanadis (2003).

3. The predominance of buy recommendations may be the result of censoring, not overoptimism. If analysts censor by discontinuing coverage of a stock or failing to update their forecasts, then the observed average buy recommendations and earnings forecasts will be higher than the unobserved means.

4. Dugar and Nathan (1995) find additional evidence that investors are not completely fooled by optimistic analysts.

5. The firms are Bear Stearns, Credit Suisse First Boston, Deutsche Bank, Goldman Sachs, J.P. Morgan, Lehman Brothers, Merrill Lynch, Morgan Stanley, Salomon Smith Barney, and UBS Warburg.

6. Practitioners emphasize that accounting is not a precise measurement system, and there is no system of rules that can be written to eliminate the need for judgment (Wallman, 1996).

7. Andersen Consulting became Accenture, which had an initial public offering in 2001.

References

Antle, Rick, Elizabeth A. Gordon, Ganapathi Narayanamoorthy, and Ling Zhou, 2002, "The joint determination of audit fees, non-audit fees, and abnormal accruals," Yale University, Yale ICP, working paper, No. 02-21.

Bell, Timothy B., Wayne R. Landsman, and Douglas A. Shackleford, 2001, "Auditors' perceived business risk and audit fees: Analysis and evidence," *Journal of Accounting Research*, Vol. 39, June, pp. 35–44.

Boni, Leslie, and Kent Womack, 2002, "Solving the sell-side research problem: Insights from buy-side professionals," University of New Mexico, working paper.

Chan, Louis K. C., Jason Karceski, and Josef Lakonishok, 2003, "Analysts' conflict of interest and biases in earnings forecasts," National Bureau of Economic Research, working paper, No. 9544, March.

Crockett, Andrew, Trevor Harris, and Frederic Mishkin, and Eugene N. White, 2003, *Conflicts of Interest in the Financial Services Industry: What Should We Do About Them?*, Geneva/London: International Center for Monetary and Banking Studies and the Center for Economic Policy Research.

DeFond, M., K. Raghunandan, and K. R.Subramanyam, 2002," Do non-audit service fees impair auditor independence? Evidence from going concern audit opinions," *Journal of Accounting Research*, Vol. 40, September, pp. 1247–1274.

Diamond, Douglas, 1991, "Monitoring and reputation: The choice between bank loans and directly placed debt," *Journal of Political Economy*, August, pp. 689–721.

Dugar, Amitabh, and Siva Nathan, 1995, "The effect of investment banking relationships on financial analysts' earnings forecasts and investment recommendations," *Contemporary Accounting Research*, Vol. 12, No. 1, Fall, pp. 131–160.

Dye, Ronald A., 1993, "Auditing standards, legal liability, and auditor wealth," *Journal of Public Economy*, Vol. 101, December, pp. 887–914.

Frankel, Robert M., Marilyn F. Johnson, and Karen K. Nelson, 2002, "The relation between auditors' fees for nonaudit services earnings management," *The Accounting Review*, Vol. 77, supplement, pp. 71–105.

Galant, Debbie, 1992, "Going public," *Institutional Investor*, Vol. 26, No. 4, April, p. 127.

Healy, Paul M., and Krishna G. Palepu, 2001, "Information asymmetry, corporate disclosure, and the capital markets: A review of the empirical disclosure literature," *Journal of Accounting and Economics*, Vol. 31, September, pp. 405–440.

Hong, Harrison, and Jeffrey D. Kubik, 2003, "Analyzing the analysts: Career concerns and biased earnings forecasts," *Journal of Finance*, Vol. 58, No. 1, February, pp. 313–351.

Mansi, Sattar A., William F. Maxwell, and Darius P. Miller, 2003, "Does auditor quality and tenure matter to investors? Evidence from the bond market," Virginia Tech, working paper, April.

McEnroe, John E., and Stanley C. Martens, 2001, "Auditors' and investors' perceptions of the expectations gap," Accounting Horizons, December, pp. 345-358.

Michaely, R., and K. L. Womack, 1999, "Conflict of interest and the credibility of underwriter analyst recommendations," *Review of Financial Studies*, Vol. 12, pp. 653–686.

Palmrose, Zoe-Vonna, 1991, "Trials of legal disputes involving independent auditors: Some empirical evidence," *Journal of Accounting Research*, Vol. 29, supplement, pp. 149–185.

_____, 1988, "An analysis of auditor litigation and audit service quality," *The Accounting Review*, Vol. 63, January, pp. 55–73.

Prakash, Mohinder, and Carol F. Venable, 1993, "Auditee incentives for auditor independence: The case of non audit services," *The Accounting Review*, Vol. 68, January, pp. 113–133.

Ramakrishnan, Ram T. S., and Anjan V. Thakor, 1984, "Information reliability, and a theory of financial intermediation," *Review of Economic Studies*, Vol. 51, No. 3, July, pp. 415–432.

Reynolds, J. Kenneth, and Jere R. Francis, 2000, "Does size matter? The influence of large clients on office-level auditor reporting decisions," *Journal of Accounting and Economics*, Vol. 30, December, pp. 375-400.

Ritter, Jay R., and Ivo Welch, 2003, "A review of IPO activity, pricing, and allocations," *Journal of Finance*, Vol. 57, No. 4, August, pp. 1795–1826.

Stefanadis, Chris, 2003, "Tying and universal banking," Federal Reserve Bank of New York, March.

Stickel, S., 1992, "Reputation and performance among security analysts," *Journal of Finance*, Vol. 47.

Wallman, Steven M. H., 1996, "The future of accounting, part III: Reliability and auditor independence," *Accounting Horizons*, Vol. 10, December, pp. 76–97.

Womack, Kent L., 1996, "Do brokerage analysts' recommendations have investment value?," *Journal of Finance*, Vol. 51, No. 1, March, pp. 137–167.

PART VII

INTERACTION OF MARKET DISCIPLINE AND PUBLIC POLICY

Chapter 24

The Role and Limitations of Financial Accounting and Auditing for Market Discipline

George J. Benston*
Emory University

Investors (debt and equity holders) might discipline the managers of enterprises in two ways. First, the amount and cost of resources that managers can play with depend on the price investors demand for transferring or withdrawing funds to or from the managers' enterprises. Second, investors discipline managers by the rewards (for example, compensation) or punishments (for example, dismissal) they or their agents offer to or impose on the managers, based on the managers' past and expected future performance.

The two aspects of market discipline are based on investors being able to obtain reliable information about the enterprises' and their managers' performance and on being able to act effectively on that information. In this paper, I will not be concerned about the latter issue, even though it is a vitally important aspect of corporate governance. Accounting and auditing, the subject of this paper, deals with the first issue—information from which investors' decisions might be made.

1. The Role of Audited Financial Statements

For hundreds of years, managers of enterprises have used internal double-entry accounting systems, from which they or their employees produce budgets, analyses of past and future decisions, and financial statements—balance sheets, income statements, and (more recently) statements of cash flows. The financial statements can provide important sources of information for owners of the enterprises and potential investors. They have reason, though, to question the truthfulness of the managers' statements, because dishonest and incompetent managers have incentives to produce false or misleading information. The cost of this moral hazard, if it cannot be overcome, is borne by capable and honest managers and owners. If owners do not trust the managers' reports, they are likely to pay them less, constrain their decision-making authority, or dismiss them. Owners also bear the cost of moral hazard when they borrow funds, because potential creditors who doubt the veracity of the financial reports are likely to demand a higher interest rate to compensate them for the additional risk or insist on collateral, covenants, and guarantees. Outside equity investors, particularly in corporations, who cannot efficiently administer and monitor risk-reducing terms, will not invest or invest only where they are willing to trust promises by the controlling owners and have reason to expect returns that are sufficiently high to compensate them for the risk. Perhaps for this reason, newly chartered and closely held corporations usually are funded with bank loans and equity contributed by inside shareholders. Initially, therefore, trustworthy financial statements tended to be produced primarily for the benefit of creditors. These financial statements then played an important role in convincing outside equity investors to invest in corporations that often were controlled by others.

Managers can assure investors that their company's financial statements are trustworthy by having the numbers audited by accounting experts who have strong reputations for probity, independent public accountants (IPAs).[1] But, how can investors trust the IPAs, who prior to enactment of the Sarbanes–Oxley Act of 2002, were hired and fired by the audited company's board of directors (or the chief executive officer with a compliant board)? I previously suggested that IPAs could be trusted, for two reasons (Benston, 1979). One is that CPAs, such as myself, are people of superior ability and moral rectitude. Indeed, although this is a self-serving observation that clearly is not universally accurate, it is true that the early IPAs were chosen to audit financial statements because they had such reputations. The other reason that is more important for CPA firms particularly (rather than individual IPAs), is that the value of the firm and the fortunes of its partners would be severely damaged if it became known to or even suspected by investors that the CPA firms might be suborned by dishonest, opportunistic managers who wanted them to directly or indirectly (by doing a poor audit) participate in its fraud on investors. Although some CPA firms might compromise their professional responsibility for such a client in order to continue to earn audit and consulting fees, the potential cost of earnings from other clients would in all likelihood greatly exceed that benefit.

Independent public accountants attest that financial statements are prepared in accordance with generally accepted accounting principles (GAAP) and audited in accordance with generally accepted auditing standards (GAAS), for several reasons. First, GAAP and GAAS offer investors an efficient means of understanding the meaning of the numbers presented in financial statements and the rules governing the recognition of income, expense, assets, liabilities, and cash flows are specified.[2] Second, at least until recently (when fair-value accounting not restricted to market values was adopted for financial assets), GAAP restricted managers' ability to manipulate the reported numbers extensively. Third, because all CPAs subscribe to GAAP, managers' ability to shop for more compliant IPAs is curtailed.

In my 1979 article, I predicted that large CPA firms, particularly, would tend to conduct effective audits and would not participate in a fraud on investors, if for no other reason than the firm would take too great a chance of incurring even greater losses. I was both wrong and right. I was wrong, because it appears that one of the (then) big-five CPA firms, Arthur Andersen, either allowed some of its partners to conduct poor audits or participate with Enron and with other firms (for example, Waste Management, Sunbeam) in producing grossly misleading financial statements. I was right, because, as a result, when those misstatements were discovered, Arthur Andersen was first weakened and then destroyed.

2. Hypotheses on the Reasons for the Current Apparent Misdeeds of CPA Firms That Gave Rise to the Sarbanes–Oxley Act of 2002

I offer five, not necessarily mutually exclusive, hypotheses that speak to the extent of and reasons for the recent financial statement manipulations and frauds by corporate offices and the apparent failure of their external auditors to shield investors from those misleading financial statements.

1. IPAs' misdeeds are not as extensive or as grave as they appear to be as a result of the extensive publicity about some well-known corporations, particularly Enron.

2. Stock options awarded to managers in the 1990s by compliant boards of directors substantially enhanced managers' incentives to inflate reported net income to increase or sustain stock prices.

3. The rewards to CPA firms from consulting caused them to overlook or even participate in managers' financial statement misstatements.

4. Inadequacies in the structure and application of GAAS and GAAP are responsible for IPAs having to attest to financial statements that are potentially misleading to investors.

5. The Securities and Exchange Commission (SEC) has not imposed sufficient costs on CPA firms and, particularly, on individual IPAs when misleading or fraudulent financial reports were discovered, to adequately dissuade them from conducting poor or dishonest audits and attesting to such reports.

3. Were the Misdeeds Not As Extensive or As Grave As They Appear to Be?

From news stories, it would appear as if a very large number of corporations have had to restate their financial statements as a result of material errors, omissions, and misstatements. These corporations include such well-known and previously highly respected companies as Enron, Adelphia, Global Crossing, WorldCom, Qwest, Rite Aide, IBM, Sunbeam, Waste Management, Xerox, Merck, PeopleSoft, Tyco, Cendant, and HealthSouth. But, about 12,000 corporations file annual financial statements with the SEC. To what extent have corporations generally published grossly inadequate or fraudulent financial statements? Importantly for this paper, were the restatements a result of errors or frauds not caught by IPAs, IPAs' participation with managers in producing numbers that had to restated, a consequence of IPAs having caught the misstatement, or a change in the SEC's or Financial Accounting Standard Board's (FASB) interpretation of GAAP that required a restatement?

The first aspect of the issue—the prevalence of misstated financial reports—has been examined by two kinds of studies, some which determined the extent of restatements, and some which analyzed the SEC's reports of misleading and fraudulent financial reports. The Financial Executives International (2001) (FEI) examined several databases for all mentions of restatements due to irregularities or errors for 1977 to 2000. The FEI found 224 restatements between 1977 and 1989 (17 per year on average), 392 during 1990 to 1997 (49 a year) and 464 during 1998 to 2000 (155 per year). The peak is 1999, with 207, of which 57 were due to SEC objections to the way software companies accounted for in-process research and development (IPR&D). The FEI identifies the other restatements as due to increased scrutiny by the SEC following the publicly expressed concern about accounting manipulations by its then chairman, Arthur Levitt (1998) and the SEC's newfound insistence that corporations correct past statements for discovered errors rather than write the error off over future periods. Thus, the substantial increase in the number of restatements in recent years appears due more to change in the SEC's practices than to deterioration of corporate accounting practices.

Palmrose and Scholz (2002) similarly but more extensively (in that they picked up more small companies) studied restatements over 1995 to 1999. They found an increasing number of announced restatements over the five years studied: 44, 48, 90, 106, and 204, 492 in all. Most of these were smaller companies (asset size mean is $1,075 million, but median is $89 million). Revenue misstatement was the most pervasive reason for the restatements (37 percent), although several other reasons almost always were present. The most important of the other reasons are merger-related items (29 percent), most of which (19 percent) are adjustments to IPR&D write-offs.

The General Accounting Office's (GAO) database search over January 1, 1997, through June 30, 2002, came up with 845 publicly traded companies that announced restatements involving accounting irregularities (GAO, 2002). These, the GAO (p. 76) states, "include 'aggressive' accounting practices, intentional and unintentional misuse of facts applied to financial statements, oversight or misinterpretation of accounting rules, and fraud ... regardless of its [the restatement's] impact on the restating company's financials." The number increased each year, from 83 in 1997 to 195 in 2001 and 110 in the first six months of 2002; the reasons for the restatements are consistent with other studies.

The SEC issues *Accounting and Auditing Enforcement Releases* (AAERs) that report actions it has taken against specific companies that, it alleges, violated its accounting regulations. Beasley et al. (1999) studied a random sample of 204 of the nearly 300 AAERs issued between 1987 and 1997. Most of the companies criticized were relatively small (72 percent had assets below $100 million), had weak boards of directors, and were charged with a fraud that involved a senior corporate officer. Half of the instances involved improper revenue recognition, 18 percent overstated assets, 18 percent overstated liabilities, and 12 percent misappropriated assets (the categories are overlapping). The SEC explicitly named external auditors in 56 cases, of which 9 (35 percent) were from major IPA firms. In 26 of these (46 percent) auditors were found to have performed substandard audits. Beasley et al. do not report any actions taken against individual IPAs or their firms.

Finally, the SEC examined its enforcement actions over the five years ending July 31, 2002 (SEC, 2003). It conducted 227 enforcement investigations of "fraud and other improper conduct," which specified 380 "bad" practices. Improper revenue recognition (again) was identified as the most important (33 percent), followed by improper expense recognition (27 percent), inadequate disclosures in the MD&A (management discussion and analysis) and in other parts of the statement (11 percent), improper accounting in connection with business combinations (6 percent), failure to disclose related party transactions (6 percent), and inappropriate accounting for non-monetary and roundtrip transactions (5 percent).

The FEI study finds that losses in market values over the three days surrounding announcements of restatements were relatively small before 1998—an average of $0.9 billion a year. But, in 1998, 1999, and 2000, these annual losses were $17 billion, $24 billion, and $31 billion, mostly due to the top 10 firms in each year making restatements. However, in total, the losses for all the corporations making restatements were less than 0.2 percent of their total market value. The GAO study of 689 restatements for which stock price data were available finds a three-day market-adjusted loss of 10 percent of those corporations' capitalization or a total of $97 billion. This loss, though, is only 0.11 percent of the total market capitalization of listed corporations.

The extent to which IPAs could have, but did not, prevent corporations from having to restate their financial statements is not revealed by the studies reviewed. Nor do the studies reveal whether the restatements resulted from IPAs finding misstatements that otherwise would not have been disclosed, whether they resulted from frauds that even a well-done audit would not have found, or whether restatements were a consequence of poor audits or tacit or explicit complicity of IPAs with their clients to deceive investors.

The Beasley et al. study, though, did find 26 instances of poor or fraudulent audits. Additional evidence can be gleaned from two of the other studies. Palmrose and Scholz (2002) found that auditors were sued in fourteen percent of the restatements they studied. The GAO's (2002, p. 59) analysis of 150 AAERs issued between January 2001 and February 2002 found that cease and desist actions were taken against 39 CPAs and nine CPA firms. The GAO also presents 16 "case studies" that detail the reasons for and effects of restatements. In three cases the auditors discovered the violations. In three cases revaluations were the result of changed interpretations of GAAP. The remaining ten of involved important and substantial violations of GAAP (for example, liabilities not reported, improper recognition of income, expensing costs that should have been capitalized, falsification of expenses, and rampant self dealing by management). From the GAO's descriptions, it appears to me that an effective auditor should have caught these misstatements.

Thus, although the losses can be substantial (particularly recently) for investments in some companies that restate their financial statements, losses to investors who hold diversified portfolios appear to be small overall. Only some of these losses could have been prevented had IPAs been more diligent and audits more effective. The potential savings to investors should be contrasted against the additional costs of such audits that would be imposed on all publicly traded corporations.

From the available studies, I conclude that there is support for the hypothesis that IPAs generally have been effective gatekeepers in preventing managers from producing financial statements designed to mislead investors, with some important exceptions (notably, Arthur Andersen). "Bad" statements, though, have been produced by an economically important subset of corporations in recent years. In several of these cases, auditors have been either lax or complicit.

4. Did Stock Options Enhance Managers' Incentives to Inflate Reported Net Income?

Managers usually want reported net income to increase, because this growth demonstrates that they are performing well, which tends to increase their compensation and job security. When they own stock or stock options they additionally share in the gains when reported net income reflects or affects stock prices. Stock options awarded in large amounts to chief executive officers (CEOs) during the 1990s may have been an important impetus for some CEOs to manipulate or falsify reported net income. Hall and Murphy (2003, p. 4) document that "[t]he average real pay for S&P 500 CEOs skyrocketed in the 1990s, growing from $3.5 million in 1992 to $14.7 million in 2000. Most of the increase reflects the escalation in stock options valued at time of grant, which grew nine-fold from an average of about $800,000 in 1992 to nearly $7.2 million in 2000. (In contrast, other components of total compensation merely tripled during the period.)"

Stock options granted to senior managers increased substantially after 1993, in part (or in large measure) because Section 162(m) of the Internal Revenue Code, adopted in 1994, prohibits deduction of compensation paid to "proxy-named executives" (usually the five highest paid officers) in excess of $1 million, unless it is "performance based." Options served to circumvent the limitation. In addition, GAAP does not require corporations to record the cost to shareholders of compensation in the form of options.

Apparently for both reasons, some boards of directors awarded CEOs and other senior officers enormous numbers of options. Hall and Murphy (2003, p. 30) observe: "The perception that options are nearly free to grant is readily acknowledged by practitioners and compensation consultants, but is usually dismissed by economists because it implies systematic suboptimal decision-making and a fixation on accounting numbers that defies economic logic." Furthermore, the fair value of the options is reported in footnotes, as is their effect on fully diluted shares outstanding and earnings per share. Consequently, they argue, stock analysts and investors can easily adjust reported net income for the cost of options.

However, at least two types of evidence support the conclusion that the accounting treatment of the cost of options has been of great importance to CEOs and boards of directors. Carter and Lynch (2003) find that corporations accelerated the repricing of options (due to lower stock prices) just before the FASB required expensing when options were repriced, after which this previously common practice declined sharply. Corporations apparently gave up a practice that, presumably, enhanced employees' performance incentives, rather than record an expense that did not affect cash flows. The other bit of evidence is the substantial, successful, and probably costly political pressure by CEOs to keep the FASB from requiring companies to expense the fair value of options, as described by Levitt (2002, p. 108). If inclusion of the cost of stock options in the income statement rather than in a footnote makes no difference, how can corporate pressure to keep stock options from being expensed be explained?

The hypothesis that stock options drove corporate managers to doctor their financial reports has not been adequately tested, to my knowledge. Such a test would involve examining the financial statements of corporations that were issued after their senior managers were compensated with relatively high numbers of stock options. A control sample would include corporations of similar size in similar industries where stock options were not used extensively to compensate senior managers. The hypothesis would be supported if corporations where senior managers held relatively large numbers of stock options compared to the control sample later issued financial statements with accounting irregularities (for example, materially overstated net income and understated liabilities) that might have misled investors, such that the price of the corporations' stock increased substantially more than expected, given their prior (beta) relationship with stock prices generally (usually termed an "abnormal" residual return). It also would be useful to examine situations where materially misleading financial statements were not associated with abnormally greater residual returns. (The GAO study (2002) provides a list of companies that restated their financial statements, but these include restatements that did not materially affect the reported numbers.)

A somewhat limited study provides some support for the hypothesis. Kedia (2003) compares a sample of 224 corporations of the 845 determined by the GAO (2002) as having announced restatements due to accounting irregularities for which ExecuComp has compensation data on the five most highly paid executives. She does not determine which of the GAO-identified corporations made material changes to their financial statements, examine the stock price effect of the restatements, or provide information about the 621 corporations not included in the ExecuComp data. Kedia compares the 224 corporations with a control group of all firms that did but are not included in the GAO study for which the compensation data are available from the same data source. She finds a statistically and, to some extent, economically significant positive relationship between GAO-reported restatements and an increase in the value of top-managers' stock options. This relationship does not hold, though, when managers own relatively high amounts of their corporations' stock. Kedia cites three other unpublished studies that, she writes, also find a significant positive relationship between executive stock options and restatements.

Thus, there is some evidence that stock options influenced overly aggressive accounting by CEOs and chief financial officers (CFOs). Left to be explained is why the "restatement" companies' IPAs did not prevent publication of misleading numbers, either by refusing to attest that the statement was prepared in accordance with GAAP or by resigning from the engagement, assuming that the restatements were necessary to correct misstatements that served to inflate reported net income.

5. Did Consulting Fees Cause IPAs to Acquiesce to Managers' "Bad" Financial Statements?

Non-audit consulting by large CPA firms has increased substantially. In 1990, 12 percent of the revenue from SEC audit clients of the Big 5 audit firms was derived from consulting; the percentage increased to 32 percent in 1999. (Over this period tax increased from 17 percent to 20 percent.) However, 75 percent of these clients in

1999 received no consulting services from their auditors (80 percent in 1990). (See Panel on Audit Effectiveness, 2000, p. 112.) Critics of non-audit consulting by CPA firms, though, could point to instances of substantial amounts of consulting income earned by the external auditors of major corporations. In 2000, Arthur Andersen received $27 million from Enron for non-audit services and $25 million for audit services. Levitt (2002, p. 138) describes several much more "egregious" instances, but does not indicate whether their auditors attested to misleading financial statements. He then says, somewhat disingenuously: "I'm not suggesting that each of these audit firms has compromised its independence. But I have to wonder if any individual auditor, working on a $2.5 million audit contract, would have the guts to stand up to a CFO and question a dubious number in the books, thus possibly jeopardizing $64 million in business for the firm's consultants."

In fact, Levitt (2002, pp. 117–139) believes strongly that IPAs' independence was compromised to the detriment of investors. He says (p. 129): "No auditor would ever admit that he allowed bad numbers because he wanted to bring more consulting business to the firm. But the ascendancy of consulting and the coincidence of accounting misdeeds, company restatements, and billions in shareholder losses were too striking to dismiss as happenstance." Levitt describes (p. 128) "a no-holds-barred public relations and lobbying campaign to stop us ((the SEC) from prohibiting an auditing firm from providing a range of services to its clients)." CPA firms, he says (p. 129), "argued that the rules were unnecessary. The SEC, they said, had not proven that any auditor had compromised himself in order to win or keep a consulting contract."

The CPA firms were correct with respect to the evidence. The Panel and Audit Effectiveness (2000, Chapter 5) considered the issue at some length. It conducted its own analysis of audit practices and concluded: "The Panel is not aware of any instances of non-audit services having caused or contributed to an audit failure or the actual loss of auditor independence." Indirect evidence on this issue appears in several academic research papers. Frankel et al. (2002) found that higher ratios of non-audit to total fees, disclosed in corporate proxy statements as required by the SEC, were positively associated with the absolute amount of discretionary accruals (that is, accruals above or below the amount expected, given a corporation's sales, plant and equipment, etc.) and with the likelihood that reported earnings would equal or slightly exceed analysts' forecasts. They assume that these variables indicate "earnings management." It is not clear why these metrics should be meaningful measures of accounting irregularities that are harmful to investors. Furthermore, "non-audit fees" include payments for tax preparation and advice, a service that external auditors have traditionally provided and still may provide, which diminishes the conclusions about non-audit fees that might be drawn from this work. Furthermore, several papers report contrary results. Ashbaugh et al. (2003) control for firm performance, after which there no longer is a significant relationship between non-audit fees and non-discretionary accruals and analysts' forecasts. Larker and Richardson (2003) more correctly examine total fees as well as audit and non-audit fees separately, and use a latent-class model to divide the sample into clusters with similar characteristics that might influence their accruals. They also analyze negative and positive accruals separately. They find a positive relationship for one cluster that includes only for 8.5 percent of their sample. That cluster is characterized by corporations that, relative to the other corporations in the other two clusters, have smaller market capitalization, lower book-to-market ratios, lower institutional holdings, and higher insider holdings, which leads the authors to conclude (p. 28): "Thus, corporate governance is a key factor for understanding accrual choices, as opposed to these choices simply being a function of fees paid to auditors." For the other clusters, they find a consistently negative significant relationship between the fees paid to auditors and accruals. Assuming that accruals do, indeed, indicate managerial manipulation of reported net earnings, this finding is consistent with auditors who face riskier or more difficult audit situations both charging higher fees and constraining management. In any event, their findings are contrary to those reported by Frankel et al.[3]

Additional research indicates that non-audit fees are not associated with other measures of "bad" financial statements. DeFond et al. (2002) find no association between the issuance of a qualified audit opinion on financially distressed corporations and the provision of non-audit services. Kinney et al. (2003) use proprietary data (from which they can separate tax from other non-audit services). They find a negative association of fees for tax services and restatements and no consistent relationship between other non-audit fees and restatements. DeFond et al. (2002, p. 1253) also report that a study by Palmrose (1999) of 1,071 legal and regulatory actions taken against the Big Five audit firms and their predecessor firms from 1960 through 1995 "finds no instances of lawsuits against auditors that allege non-audit services impair independence."

It is possible, of course, that (as Levitt asserts) some IPAs allow opportunistic clients to misstate reported accounting data in ways that are misleading to investors. The reports of the Neil Batson, court-appointed examiner in bankruptcy in re: Enron (2002, 2003), describe Arthur Andersen's complicity with Enron's managers in aggressively applying specific GAAP rules to produce materially misleading financial statements that inflated net income and assets, understated debt, misreported sources of revenue, reported tax savings as revenue before taxes, and overstated cash flow from operations. What is not known is whether Andersen's acts were a consequence of the substantial audit fees alone or the substantial non-audit fees the firm received and wanted to continue receiving, or whether the auditors simply got too close to management and not only lost the skepticism required by GAAS, but became active participants in management's view of how Enron's operations should be presented to investors. Because of the extensive investigation by the examiner in bankruptcy, much is known about Enron's accounting. Investigations of other corporations, the managers of which are charged with manipulating and misstating financial statements, are needed to see if the practice of Arthur Andersen at Enron are unique or widespread.

Overall, though, the empirical evidence to date overwhelmingly indicates no positive relationship between non-audit fees paid to IPAs and poor audits or misleading financial statements. I conclude, therefore, that this hypothesis is not supported.

6. Were Inadequacies in the Structure and Application of GAAS and GAAP Responsible for IPAs Having to Attest to Financial Statements That Are Potentially Misleading to Investors?

Independent public accountants rarely have been found to have conducted fraudulent audits—knowingly overlooking or disregarding evidence of managers misappropriating shareholders' resources or falsifying the accounting records (Benston, 2003a). However, auditors have been charged with conducting poor and incompetent audits, such that they failed to discover material frauds and misstatements. For example, it is difficult to understand how the external auditors of WorldCom could have failed to discover that billions of dollars of expenses were capitalized or why the auditors of HealthSouth did not learn that billions of dollars of sales were created with false accounting entries.

One explanation of why some IPAs conduct inadequate audits is that audits are a "loss leader," wherein CPA firms bid low and charge less for an audit contract in order to obtain and keep lucrative consulting contracts. Aside from the evidence just reviewed that does not find a positive association between non-audit fees and "bad" financial statements, this explanation is inconsistent with what is known about CPA firms' rewards from auditing and consulting. Antle and Gitenstein (2000) analyzed the financial records of the (then) big-five CPA firms and found that, while the per-hour rate for consulting is higher than the rate for auditing (assurance engagements), the present value to CPA firms of audit fees is considerably greater, because the net cash flow from audits is steadier and continues for a longer time. Furthermore, the expected costs to CPA firms from lawsuits based on fraudulent or deliberately inadequate audits are likely to far exceed the benefits.[4]

However, it is possible that some CPA firms might (perhaps mistakenly) risk doing inadequate audits in the belief that the probability is very high that their clients are honest and that statements conform to GAAP, such that the savings in audit costs exceed the expected cost of lawsuits and loss of reputation, because these events are unlikely to occur.

I suggest two other explanations for poor audits. One is the increasing use by IPAs of analytical auditing, wherein numbers proposed for financial statements are examined via ratio and other analyses to determine situations where they are "out of line." CFOs who are "cooking the books" often were previously employed by the CPA firm that audits their records, or by similar CPA firms, know the analytical methods used, and can adjust the records to make it appear as if there were no problems. The second, related explanation is that relatively few auditors actually use or fully understand the value of statistical sampling to determine the accuracy and reliability of a client's accounting records. The GAAS (SAS 39) only suggests the use of statistical sampling. Without sampling, it is difficult to see how IPAs can have a meaningful basis for determining whether the numbers used in an analytic model are correct and the extent to which a corporation's statements are materially incorrect.

Violations of some basic GAAP requirements have been important reasons for "bad" financial statements. Mulford and Comiskey (2002) describe many such violations, based on their examination of reports by the SEC, the press, and corporate financial filings. The largest proportion of these involved misstatements of revenue, including fictitious sales and shipments, booking revenue immediately for goods and services sold over extended periods, keeping the books open after the end of an accounting period to record revenue on shipments actually made after the close of the period, recording sales on goods shipped but not ordered and on goods ordered but not shipped, recognizing revenue on aggressively sold merchandise that was returned ("channel stuffing"), recording revenue in the year received even though the services were provided over several years, booking revenue immediately when the goods were sold subject to payment over extended periods where collectibility was unlikely, shipments to a reseller that was not financially viable, and sales subject to side agreements that effectively rendered sales agreements unenforceable.

Expenses also were misrecorded. Some involved booking promotion and marketing expenses to a related, but not consolidated, enterprise and recognizing revenue on shipments, but not the cost and liability of an associated obligation to repay purchasers for promotion expenses. Several corporations took "big bath" write-offs when a new CEO took over. Warranty and bad debt expenses were understated. Aggressive capitalization and extended amortization policies were used to reduce current-period expenses.

Assets were overstated by such means as recording receivables for which the corporation had established no legal right, such as claims on common carriers for damaged goods that were not actually submitted, and those that it probably could not collect. Inventories were overstated by overcounts and by delaying write-downs of damaged, defective, overstocked, and obsolete goods. Declines in the fair market values of assets (for example, debt and equity securities) were delayed, even though the chances of recovery were remote. Liabilities were understated, not only for estimated expenses (such as warranties), but also for accounts payable, taxes payable, environmental clean-up costs, and pension and other employee benefits.[5]

The GAO's (2002, appendices 5 through 20) sixteen cases studies also describe violations of GAAP that resulted in materially misleading financial statements. As noted earlier, in six cases the auditors either discovered the violation or the violation resulted from changed interpretations of GAAP. In two cases (Sunbeam and Waste Management) Arthur Andersen's engagement partners allegedly were aware of serious violations of GAAP and, nevertheless, gave unqualified opinions. Why the auditors of the eight remaining cases did not discover the violations of GAAP and either prevent publication of the statements or resign from the engagement is not explained.[6]

I believe that two important aspects of GAAP, in addition to violations of GAAP, are responsible for some important "bad" financial statements: rules-based rather than principles-based application of GAAP, and fair-value accounting.

The current rules-based approach has permitted, indeed, encouraged, managers and their consultants to design accounting procedures that are in technical accordance with GAAP, even though they are contrary to the substance or spirit of GAAP and result in misleading financial statements. Enron was a master of that approach.[7] Accountants not only find it difficult to challenge the use of such procedures, but also (at least as revealed by the examiner in [Enron's] bankruptcy) propose or assist in their design. In this sense, the practice of public accounting has become quite similar to tax practice, with clients demanding and accountants providing expertise on ways to avoid the substantive requirements of GAAP while remaining in technical compliance.[8]

There are several reasons for this rules-based approach. First, auditors believe that they can avoid losing lawsuits, if they can show that they did in fact follow the rules. Second, there is the fear of losing a client by refusing to attest to accounting procedures that do, after all, technically conform to GAAP. Third, government agencies such as the SEC tend to establish or support rules and then demand strict adherence to them. This protects the agencies from claims of favoritism and arbitrariness, forestalling political interference. Last, but by no means least, GAAP has been criticized because it permits managers some degree of choice under some circumstances. The FASB was created in 1973 largely in response to concern about excessive accounting flexibility. Its well-funded full-time professional staff and directors have fulfilled their mandate and have developed a very large set of detailed rules designed to limit alternative means of compliance with GAAP.

Fair-value accounting gives managers considerable scope for overstating revenue and assets, when used to revalue assets for which there are no reliable relevant market prices. The FASB and SEC, in fact, have been moving increasingly towards incorporating fair values in GAAP. Energy trading contracts must be recorded at fair values, even when these can be determined only by discounting the present value of expected cash flows over as much as ten years. Derivatives must be stated at fair values, even when they are not traded and, necessarily, are marked to model rather to market. Other financial assets must be stated at fair value when they are transferred to a special purpose entities (SPE), even when the transferor effectively controls the SPE.

Opportunistic corporate managers also can take advantage of the fair-value procedures of the AICPA's *Investment Company Guide* to manipulate the value of non-traded equity securities. The AICPA requires investment, business development, and venture-capital companies to revalue financial assets held (presumably) for trading to fair values, even when these values are not determined by arm's-length market transactions. In such instances, the values can be based on "independent" appraisals and on models using discounted expected cash flows.[9] Enron (and probably many other corporations) specified that its holdings of wholly owned subsidiaries and thinly traded equities of companies it established were "merchant" investments to which the AICPA's investment-company fair-value rule could be applied. It then valued those investments as equal to the present value of its estimates of cash flows that the assets might generate. For example, Enron formed a joint 20-year venture with Blockbuster, Inc., called Braveheart, to provide movies on demand to television viewers. Unfortunately, Enron did not have the technology to deliver the movies and Blockbuster did not have the rights to the movies to be delivered. Nevertheless, as of December 31, 2000, Enron assigned a fair value of $125 million to that investment and a profit of $53 million from increasing the investment to its fair value, even though no sales had been made, based on discounted cash flows that might be generated from its capturing substantial numbers of viewers in several markets. Enron recorded additional revenue of $53 million from the venture in the first quarter of 2001, although Blockbuster did not record any income from the venture and dissolved the partnership in March 2001. In October, Enron had to reverse the $110.9 million in profit it had earlier claimed, an action that contributed to its loss of public trust and subsequent bankruptcy.

External auditors who (unlike Arthur Andersen) are suspicious of fair values, are faced with a very difficult problem. How can they argue against managers who presumably know their businesses and insist that their estimates of the amounts and probability distribution of expected cash flows are correct? After all, the managers should know their business better than auditors! If the estimates turn out to be incorrect (as is likely), the managers can point out that the actual numbers are within the range of the projected possibilities. Furthermore, conditions could have unexpectedly changed, making it very difficult for the external auditors or investors to determine whether or not the managers deliberately misestimated the net cash flow and discount rate.

Based on the foregoing and other examples from Enron presented in Benston (2003b), I conclude that there is support for the hypothesis that shortcomings in GAAS (not requiring statistical sampling, where feasible) and GAAP (emphasis on rules rather than principles and on fair-value accounting that is not limited to reliable, market-derived relevant numbers) probably is responsible for at least some "bad" financial statements.

7. Have the Costs Imposed on CPA Firms and on Individual IPAs That Attested to "Bad" Financial Statements Been Insufficient?

I earlier argued that the costs to CPA firms of doing poor audits and allowing clients to produce misleading financial statements should be sufficient to deter them from such behavior (Benston, 1979 and above). At least in some important instances (for example, Enron), I was wrong. I now believe that my mistake was that I incorrectly expected that, although an individual partner might find it worthwhile to give in to or "work with" a client to keep the account, other partners would realize an individual's incentive and monitor and control this form of sub-optimization. I still do not understand why Arthur Andersen not only did not adequately monitor its Houston partner, David Duncan, but also allowed Enron to dismiss Andersen auditors who disagreed with Enron's accounting, and gave Duncan, rather than the head office in Chicago, veto power over decisions as to what was and was not allowable under GAAP. However, I now better understand why an individual partner would be tempted to do whatever was necessary to keep a client happy.

Some CPA-firm partners manage only one or a few very large clients, often because they acquired these clients for the firm or because of the magnitude of the audits. Consequently, a large part of their compensation and position in their firm depends on keeping and increasing billings to a specific client. If the client demands the partner's acquiescence to aggressive interpretations and applications of GAAP that result in possibly misleading financial statements, partners who refuse will bear substantial costs if, as a result, the client leaves. Alternatively, if the partner gives in to the client, three events might occur. First, the aggressive accounting turns out to be right and the financial statements do not appear to be misleading. Second, although the financial statements are criticized, the partner is not blamed because, technically, the statements were prepared in accordance with GAAP. Third, if the financial statements are criticized by the SEC or the CPA firm is sued, the compliant partner will be defended rather than disciplined by the firm. Should CPA firms fire or otherwise punish a partner for having supervised and approved an incompetent or inadequate audit or agreed too readily to client demands, the firm would be admitting its collective guilt to regulators and present or potential plaintiffs. It would not be surprising, therefore, if some IPAs decide that, for them personally, the immediate cost of losing a major client outweighs the probable cost of giving in to that client's demands.

However, if individual IPAs believed that they would be denied the right to attest to statements filed with the SEC or lose their CPA certificates should their clients' financial statements be found to be "bad" by the SEC or a court, I believe they would be much more likely to refuse the clients' demands for inadequate audits or attestations of misleading financial statements. In Benston (2003a) I review the ways that state and federal authorities could discipline individual CPAs and evidence on the extent to which punishments for attesting to fraudulent and materially misleading financial statements have been imposed. The record indicates that punishments are rare. Pursuant to its Rule of Practice 203(e), the SEC can fine and bar IPAs from practice before it who attested to financial statements that significantly violated GAAP or who supervised audits that depart significantly from GAAS. But, it has imposed such penalties infrequently, as I have documented (Benston, 2003A).

It also is important to note that partner-in-charge and confirming partner on an audit do not individually sign the attestation statement, which shields errant IPAs from criticism.

8. The Sarbanes–Oxley Reforms

Sarbanes–Oxley imposes some changes that might improve the effectiveness of market discipline with respect to audited financial statements. I group these into those that affect boards of directors and managers and those that affect IPAs.

The board of directors' ability to enhance IPAs' independence from managers has been increased. Section 301 of the act mandates that the board's audit committee must include only independent directors, at least one of whom must be a "financial expert."[10] The audit committee is given power and responsibility over the external auditors. It must be directly responsible for the appointment, compensation, retention, and oversight of the work of the corporation's IPAs (called registered public firms by the act). It also must be given the resources its members believe are necessary to fulfill its obligations, including hiring its own counsel and experts.

The act also imposes obligations on corporate senior officers and on directors. Pursuant to Section 302, the CEO and CFO must certify the "appropriateness of the financial statements and disclosures contained in the periodic report, and that those financial statements and disclosures fairly present, in all material respects, the operations and financial condition of the issuer." Section 303 of Act makes it unlawful for any officer or director to fraudulently influence, coerce, manipulate, or mislead any auditor for the purpose of rendering the financial statements materially misleading. If financial statements must be restated due to "material noncompliance" with financial reporting requirements, the CEO and CFO must reimburse the corporation for incentive-based compensation received or profits from the sale of shares in the corporation during the preceding twelve months (Sections 304 and 305).

Independent public accountants who audit the financial statements of SEC registrants are now regulated by a newly created agency, the Public Company Accounting Oversight Board (PCAOB). The board has five full-time "financially literate," well-paid members, two of whom must be or have been CPAs and the remaining three must not be or have been CPAs. The PCAOB reports to the SEC, but is funded separately with fees imposed on public companies (issuers). Public accounting firms that audit issuers' statements must register with the PCAOB; hence, they are called registered public accountants (RPAs). Under Section 103, the PCAOB shall establish, or adopt, by rule, "such auditing and related attestation standards, such quality control standards, and such ethics standards to be used by registered public accounting firms in the preparation and issuance of audit reports ... as may be necessary or appropriate in the public interest or for the protection of investors." It conducts annual inspections of RPAs that audit more than 100 issues, and every three years for all others. It has authority to conduct investigations and disciplinary proceedings, and impose sanctions, subject to review and modification by the SEC.

Registered public accountants must have a second partner review and approve audit reports and adopt quality control standards (§103; these practices were previously employed by CPA firms that conducted audits of SEC registrants). The lead audit or reviewing partner must rotate off the audit every five years (§ 203; this practice was often, but not universally, followed). The issuer cannot employ as CEO or CFO (or person in an equivalent position) a person employed by the company's audit firm during the one-year period preceding the date of the initiation of the audit (§ 206).

One change that probably will be detrimental to investors is the prohibition of an RPA providing nine specified non-audit services contemporaneously with the audit (tax-related services are not prohibited). As provided for in Section 201, these include: bookkeeping or other services related to the audit client's accounting records or financial statements; financial information systems design and implementation; appraisal or valuation services and fairness opinions; actuarial services; internal audit services; management function, such as acting as a director or officer or performing decision-making, supervisory, or ongoing monitoring; human resources, such as searching for executives, engaging in psychological testing, acting as a negotiator on the audit client's behalf, and recommending hires; broker–dealer services; and legal services. Consequently, investors in corporate shares will no longer benefit from economies of scope that probably were achieved when these services were provided in conjunction with an audit. Furthermore, it will now be less difficult for the four remaining major RPAs to collude to increase audit fees, because they will no longer be able to offer lower consulting fees as a means of disguised competition. The evidence reviewed earlier indicates that investors will achieve no offsetting benefits.

9. Conclusions

Overall, I conclude that financial statements produced in accordance with GAAP and audited by IPAs in accordance with GAAS has generally been an effective aid for imposing market discipline on the managers of publicly traded corporations. Traditional accounting has provided investors with useful indicators of the way their resources have been used and served to constrain misuse of those resources by managers. The accounting measure of economic performance—periodic recognition of revenue to which expenses are matched, based on market transactions that give rise to reliable, not-readily manipulated numbers, applied with a conservative bias—has provided investors with trustworthy numbers. The numbers reported in the balance sheet and statement of cash flows also provide investors with numbers that often can be used effectively to estimate economic values. In most instances, the trustworthiness of the numbers can be determined only by an audit conducted by an IPA, which usually have yielded trustworthy financial reports.[11]

Recent scandals involving financial statements of well-known corporations that revealed grossly misleading and possibly fraudulently produced numbers, accompanies with audits that did not uncover and correct these problems, have raised doubts about the validity and usefulness of audited financial statements. I delineated and examined five hypotheses that might explain why these accounting problems have surfaced in recent years. First, I conclude that the problems, as indicated by restatements and SEC criticism, have increased, but still represent a relatively small proportion of the statements produced by publicly traded corporations. Second, stock options granted to some managers may have increased their incentives to inflate reported net income, but this does not explain why some IPAs attested to the validity of these statements and the statements of other corporations. Third, fees from collateral consulting services do not appear to be the reason for poor audits, misleading, or fraudulent statements. Fourth, some inadequacies in GAAS and GAAP appear to have been responsible for "bad" financial statements. With respect to GAAS, increasing use of less costly analytical auditing techniques, perhaps driven by competition among external auditors, may have allowed some managers to get away with fraudulently prepared accounting records. Although statistical sampling of those records probably would have been effective in uncovering the frauds, this has not been a GAAS requirement. I find that GAAP has been deficient in two regards. One is the emphasis on rules rather than on the basic principles. The other is the increasing move toward fair-value accounting for assets that is not limited to reliable, relevant market values. This has allowed opportunistic managers to overstate reported net income and assets. Fifth, insufficient discipline by the SEC of individual IPAs who attest to "bad" financial statements has been an important exacerbating factor. Provisions of the Sarbanes–Oxley Act should reduce the impact of stock options and might impose higher costs on errant individual IPAs. However, they will increase the cost of audits by prohibiting CPA firms from providing consulting services to audit clients, while failing to correct the limitations of GAAS and GAAP, and, and impose additionally higher costs on investors in the form of fees. Whether the benefits from the Act exceed the costs is yet to be seen.

Finally, investors should realize that: 1) financial statements can provide only some numbers that are useful for investment decisions; and 2) that the numbers reported cannot be free of managerial manipulation, although the extent of manipulation can be limited and, to a substantial extent, recognized and adjusted. Recognition of these limitations of accounting is essential, if audited financial statements are to be useful for imposing market discipline on corporate managers.

*George J. Benston is the John H. Harland Professor of Finance, Accounting, and Economics at the Goizueta Business School of Emory University.

Notes

1. Although all except junior IPAs are certified public accountants (CPAs), not all CPAs are IPAs. All CPA firms, though, are IPAs.

2. Space limitations required removal of even a limited description of these rules; see Benston (2003b).

3. Antle et al. (2002) use a simultaneous equations procedure, and also find a negative relation for both U.S. and UK firms over 1992 to 2000.

4. Palmrose and Scholz (2002) found that more than half of litigation against IPAs they studied involved fraud. They cite several other studies with similar findings.

5. Also see Shilit (2002) for a similar and somewhat overlapping description of what he calls "accounting shenanigans" and Benston (2003b) for summaries of other studies that provide data on the percentage of apparent GAAP violations in restated financial statements and in statements criticized in the SEC AAERs.

6. In response to §703 of the Sarbanes–Oxley Act, the SEC produced the *Study and Report on Violations by Security Professions*, which covers calendar years 1998 to 2001. During this period enforcement actions were taken against 1,713 persons or organizations, including 75 "other," a category that includes accounting firms, exchanges, investment companies, and persons associated with investment companies. No other breakdown is given and nothing is mentioned about violations by or actions taken against public accountants or CPA firms.

7. See Benston and Hartgraves (2002) and Batson (2002, 2003) for descriptions of the very complicated procedures adopted by Enron. Also see Benston (2003a) for additional descriptions of how Enron followed the letter, but not the intent, of GAAP to produce misleading financial statements.

8. The Sarbanes–Oxley Act of 2002, which prohibits auditors from offering their clients with a wide range of non-audit services, allows them to provide tax preparation and advice.

9. The AICPA has issued a Proposed Statement of Position that would limit application of investment-company accounting to investment companies, no owner of which owns 20 percent of its financial interests (*Clarification of the Scope of the Audit and Accounting Guide Audits of Investment Companies and Equity Method Investors for Investment in Investment Companies,* dated, December 17, 2002). If adopted it would become part of GAAP for fiscal years beginning after December 15, 2004. (The original effective date was December 15, 2003).

10. It is interesting to note that Enron's audit committee more than met these requirements. Five of its six members were actively involved in finance or energy and the sixth was president of a major medical facility. Its chair (Robert Jaedicke) was a retired distinguished accounting professor and former dean of a major business school, and one member (Wendy Gramm) was former chair of the Commodity Futures Trading Commission.

11. See Benston (2003b) for a discussion and analysis on which this conclusion is based.

References

Antle, Rick, and Mark H. Gitenstein, 2000, "Analysis of data requested by the Independence Standards Board from the five largest accounting firms," unpublished report presented to the Independence Standard Board, February 17.

Antle, Rick, Elizabeth A. Gordon, Ganapathi Narayanamoorthy, and Ling Zhui, 2002, "The joint determination of audit fees, non-audit fees, and abnormal accruals," Yale University, working paper.

Ashbaugh, Hollis, Ryan LaFond, and Brian W. Mayhew, 2003, "Do non-audit services compromise auditor independence?," *The Accounting Review*, Vol. 78, pp. 611–639.

Batson, Neal, 2003, "Second interim report of Neal Batson, court-appointed examiner," United State Bankruptcy Court, Southern District of New York, In re: Chapter 11 Enron Corp., et al., Debtors, Case No. 01-16034 (AJG), Jointly Administered, January 21.

_____, 2002, "First interim report of Neal Batson, court-appointed examiner," United State Bankruptcy Court, Southern District of New York, In re: Chapter 11 Enron Corp., et al., Debtors, Case No. 01-16034 (AJG), Jointly Administered, September 20.

Beasley, Mark S., Joseph V. Carcello, and Dana R. Hermanson, 1999, *Fraudulent Financial Reporting: 1987–1997: An Analysis of U.S. Public Companies, Research Commissioned by the Committee of Sponsoring Organizations of the Treadway Commission*, Jersey City, NJ: AICPA (American Institute of Certified Public Accountants).

Benston, George J., 2003a, "The regulation of accountants and public accounting before and after Enron," *Emory Law Review*.

_____, 2003b, *The Quality of Corporate Financial Statements and Their Auditors before and After Enron*, Washington, DC: Cato Institute for Policy Analysis.

_____, 1979, "The market for public accounting services: Demand, supply, and regulation," *The Accounting Journal*, 1979-80, Vol. 2, Winter, pp. 2–46; republished in the *Journal of Accounting and Public Policy*, 1985, Vol. 4, pp. 33–79.

_____, 1976, *Corporate financial disclosure in the UK and the USA*, London and New York: Saxon House and Lexington Books.

Benston, George J., and Al L. Hartgraves, 2002, "Enron: What happened and what we can learn from it," *Journal of Accounting and Public Policy*, Vol. 21, pp. 105–127.

Carter, Mary Ellen, and Luann J. Lynch, 2003, "The consequences of the FASB's 1998 proposal for stock option repricing," *Journal of Accounting and Economics*.

DeFond, Mark L., K. Raghunandan, and K. R. Subramanyam, 2002, "Do non-audit service fees impair auditor independence? Evidence from going concern audit opinions," University of Southern California, working paper.

Financial Executives International, 2001, "Quantitative measures of the quality of financial reporting," FEI Research Foundation, PowerPoint presentation, available at www.fei.org.

Frankel, Richard M., Marilyn F. Johnson, and Karen K. Nelsen, 2002, "The relation between auditor's fees for non-audit services and earnings management," *The Accounting Review*, supplement, Vol. 77, pp. 71–105.

General Accounting Office, 2002, *Financial Statement Restatements: Trends, Market Impacts, Regulatory Responses, and Remaining Challenges*, Washington, DC, No. GAO-03-138, October.

Hall, Brian J., and Kevin J. Murphy, 2003, "The trouble with stock options," *Journal of Economic Perspectives*, Vol. 17, pp. 49–70.

Kedia, Simi, 2003, "Do executive stock options generate incentives for earnings management? Evidence from accounting restatements," Harvard Business School and Ohio State University, working paper, September.

Kinney, William R., Zoe-Vonna Palmrose, and Susan W. Scholtz, 2003, "Auditor independence and non-audit services: What do restatements suggest?," University of Texas at Austin, working paper.

Larker, David F., and Scott A. Richardson, 2003, "Fees paid to audit firms, accrual choices, and corporate governance," University of Pennsylvania, The Wharton School, working paper October 9.

Levitt, Arthur, with Paula Dwyer, 2002, *Take on the Street*, New York: Pantheon Books.

_____, 1998, "The numbers game," remarks to New York University Center for Law and Business, available at www.sec.gov/news/speech/speecharchive/1998/spch220.txt, September 28.

Mulford, Charles W., and Eugene E. Comiskey, 2002, *The Financial Numbers Game: Detecting Creative Accounting Practices*, Hoboken, NJ: John Wiley & Sons, Inc.

Palmrose, Zoe-Vonna, 1999, "Empirical research in auditor litigation: Considerations and data," American Accounting Association, *Studies in Accounting Research*, No. 33.

Palmrose, Zoe-Vonna, and Susan Scholz, 2002, "The circumstances and legal consequences of non-GAAP reporting: Evidence from restatements," paper presented at a conference sponsored by *Contemporary Accounting Research*.

Panel on Audit Effectiveness, 2000, *Report and Recommendations,* Shawn F. O'Malley (chair), Stamford, CT: The Public Oversight Board, available at www.probauditpanel.org. , August 31.

Rich, Wiley D., 1935, *Legal Responsibility and Rights of Public Accountants*, New York: American Institute Publishing Co.

Securities and Exchange Commission (SEC), 2003, *Report Pursuant to Section 704 of the Sarbanes-Oxley Act of 2002*, Washington, DC, January.

Shilit, Howard, 2002, *Financial Shenanigans: How To Detect Accounting Gimmicks & Fraud in Financial Reports,* second edition, New York: McGraw-Hill.

Weirich, Thomas, 2000, "Analysis of SEC accounting and auditing enforcement releases," in *Panel on Audit Effectiveness: Report and Recommendations*, Stamford, CT, appendix F, pp. 223–228.

Chapter 25

Fair Values and Financial Statement Volatility

Mary E. Barth*
Graduate School of Business,
Stanford University and
International Accounting Standards Board

1. Introduction

There is an increasing use of fair values as the measurement objective in financial statements. Currently, fair values are used to measure some assets and liabilities, but there is a trend for standard-setters to propose using fair values more pervasively. This is because standard-setters, and others, believe that fair values provide the most relevant information to financial statement users. There also is an extensive academic literature supporting this view (see, for example, Barth, Beaver, and Landsman, 2001, for a review). Some concerns about the use of fair values focus on the reliability of their estimation. Others focus on the implications of the increased volatility in financial statement amounts that is likely to result from the increased use of fair values. These concerns are related in that estimation error is one source of financial statement volatility. This paper seeks to identify the sources of volatility in financial statement amounts that is attributable to using fair values as the measurement basis. It then discusses each source to determine whether the volatility is useful information to investors and, if not, what standard-setters can do to mitigate it and, if so, what standard-setters can do to enhance users' understanding of it.

It is widely accepted that if financial statement amounts are based more on fair values, the amounts will change more from period-to-period than they would in a system based more on historical cost. The recognized amounts in question include summary amounts, such as net income and equity book value, as well as individual line items in the balance sheet and income statement. Because historical cost-based amounts change little from period-to-period, historical cost-based amounts are thought of as less volatile.[1] In a fair values-based accounting system, one expects recognized amounts to change each period, leading to increased volatility. This arises because fair values summarize the stream of expected future cash flows; a change in expectation relating to any of the cash flows changes the fair value. However, it is important to understand the sources of volatility because financial statement volatility *per se* is not an indication of flawed financial reporting. The world is a volatile place and, thus, volatility in financial statement amounts should be expected. Advocates of using fair values as the measurement basis in accounting are quick to point out that historical cost-based amounts may be less volatile, but that is the result of masking underlying economic volatility not the result of superior financial reporting.

Volatility is a concern for entities presenting their financial statements to the extent that users rely on financial statement information to aid them in assessing the economic volatility, or risk, of the entity's operations. In fact, a primary objective of financial reporting is to provide users with information relating to the uncertainty and timing of future cash flows. Thus, providing information about inherent volatility is key to complete financial reporting. However, to the extent that capital providers price the perceived risk, the entity's cost of capital will increase as volatility increases. Priced risk includes not only systematic risk, but also information risk (Barry and Brown, 1985, 1986; Easley and O'Hara, 2003). There is a large literature in accounting documenting that markets are quite efficient at processing publicly available information (see, for example, Beaver, 1998). However, there also is evidence that investors do not understand fully accounting amounts (for example, Sloan, 1996; Xie, 2001; and Barth and Hutton, 2004) and some information is not publicly available. Thus, if the financial statements overstate economic volatility, there is a chance that investors and other users of financial statements will assess a risk premium to the entity's cost of capital that is higher than that justified by the economic situation facing the entity.

Volatility is a particular concern for bank supervisors, such as the Basel Committee, because they are charged with ensuring the stability and soundness of the financial system. The objective of financial statements, as articulated in the International Accounting Standards Board's (IASB) *Framework for the Preparation and Presentation of Financial Statements* (IASB, 2001), is to provide information about the financial position, performance, and changes in financial position of an entity that is useful to a wide range of users in making economic decisions. Although such financial statements serve the common needs of a variety of users, it would be unsurprising if financial statements do not serve all of the needs of all users, including bank supervisors. However, these users should be able to use financial statements as a basis for their analysis and requirements.

The remainder of this paper is organized as follows. The next section identifies the sources of volatility in financial statement amounts. The following section relates these sources of volatility to relevance and reliability, the two primary characteristics of accounting amounts that standard-setters consider in deciding what should be recognized in financial statements. The next section offers some suggestions as to what standard-setters can do to aid financial statement users in understanding the effects of each source of volatility, and the final section provides concluding remarks.

2. Sources of Financial Statement Volatility

Volatility from period-to-period in financial statement amounts derives from several sources. The most obvious is the entity's activities during the period and changing economic conditions that are reflected in the financial statements. Using fair values as a measurement basis in accounting is intended to reflect better this economic volatility than using historical cost-based amounts. However, there are several sources of volatility in financial statement amounts that derive from using fair value amounts for financial statement recognition.

Before analyzing the results of using fair values as the measurement basis in financial statements, it is important to clarify what the term "fair value" means to accounting standard-setters. The IASB defines fair value as the amount for which an asset could be exchanged, or a liability settled, between knowledgeable, willing parties in an arm's length transaction (IASB, 2003a). There is only one fair value for any particular asset or liability.[2] The definition of fair value does not require the presence of a deep and liquid market for fair values to be well defined. Thus, fair values should not be confused with some underlying "true" value, the determination of which is illusive in the presence of imperfect or incomplete markets. Rather, the definition, and its elaboration in accounting standards, specifies how to estimate fair value when a market does not exist. The key feature of this definition of fair value is that it comprises estimates of cash flows that market participants could obtain from the asset or liability. That is, it does not include estimates of entity-specific cash flows, discounted at the rate of interest market participants would expect to receive for bearing the risks inherent in those cash flows, that is, the discount rate does not include entity-specific risk preferences. Thus, one would not expect the market value of the entity's equity to equal the sum of the fair values of its assets and liabilities.

It is also important to note that the following discussion focuses on the effects of using fair values to measure assets and liabilities. This is not to ignore volatility in net income. Rather, this is because the IASB's *Framework* (IASB, 2001), and that of other standard-setters, including the Financial Accounting Standards Board (FASB), defines income and expenses as changes in assets and liabilities—they are not measured directly. Thus, accounting measurement focuses on measuring assets and liabilities. Accordingly, when assets and liabilities are volatile, so is net income. However, because income and expenses are measured as changes in assets and liabilities, net income volatility can be larger or smaller than asset and liability volatility, depending on the correlation between the changes.[3]

The first two sources of volatility relate to the accounting for individual assets and liabilities, rather than to the combined effect of accounting for different assets and liabilities. One is *estimation error volatility* and the other is *inherent volatility*. To see these sources of volatility, consider an asset or liability to be measured, x. In a fair values-based accounting system, x can be thought of as the fair value of the asset or liability. This presumes that standard-setters have concluded that fair value is the object of measurement.[4] The mean of x is $\bar{x}$ and the variance of x is σ_x^2. Thus, at any point in time, the realization of x is drawn from a distribution. The variance of x, σ_x^2, is its inherent volatility. Usually, accountants do not observe x and need to estimate it. Thus, the amount recognized in the financial statements is

$$X = x + \varepsilon,$$

where ε is the estimation error, which has a variance of σ_ε^2. In a simple setting, ε has mean zero, which indicates that the recognized amount, X, is an unbiased measure of x.

In such a setting, the estimation error, $X - x$, equals ε and σ_ε^2 is the estimation error volatility of x. Assuming X and x are uncorrelated, $\sigma_x^2 = \sigma_x^2 + \sigma_\varepsilon^2$. So, the volatility of the recognized amount, X, is greater than the volatility of the underlying amount, x. For example, if x is the fair value of a debt security, X could be the market price of the debt, obtained from a thinly traded market. In this case, X likely measures x with error, but X could be an unbiased measure of x.

In more complex settings, X is not unbiased and the nature of the bias affects the specification of the estimation error volatility. One reason for bias and, thus, another source of estimation error volatility is model misspecification. That is, we do not have well-developed models to estimate fair values of all assets and liabilities. For example, currently there are no formulas for estimating the value of employee stock options. The Black–Scholes (1973) formula is based on assumptions that typically do not hold for employee options, such as transferability. Thus, using the Black–Scholes (1973) option pricing formula to estimate the value of employee options likely introduces biases of an unknown, probably nonlinear, form.[5]

The IASB and the FASB currently are jointly developing a fair-value hierarchy, which indicates that when a price for the asset or liability exists in deep and liquid markets, that price is the asset or liability's fair value. When such markets do not exist, the fair values must be estimated as what the price would be if such a market did exist. In such a case, fair values are the present value of expected future cash flows associated with the asset or liability, discounted at a market rate. Because future cash flows are unknown, they involve estimation of uncertain outcomes. Thus, estimation error is a natural and unavoidable byproduct of the estimation process. Even if the estimates are unbiased, the actual cash flows likely will differ from the estimates. For fair values obtained from market prices, estimation error volatility is small. For fair values obtained through estimation, estimation error volatility reflects the precision of the estimates.

Inherent volatility is the volatility of x itself, that is, σ_x^2. The higher the variance of x, the more likely it is that next period's x will differ from this period's x. That difference creates volatility in the financial statements, but it is economic volatility, which financial statements should reflect. The issue is not how precisely can one measure x; the issue is that x is a random variable with a nonzero standard deviation. This is not a result of the accounting process—it is economic reality. The future realization of x, which financial statement users ultimately are interested in, depends on future states of the world yet to occur. Because x is volatile, the measurements of x are also volatile. Thus, inherent volatility is not an accounting problem per se. However, some argue that recognizing in financial statements a measure of the realization of x at a particular point in time has the potential to mislead financial statement users. That is, for highly volatile x, the measure of the x realization on any particular date is unlikely to be predictive of future x, and not predictive enough to be useful in financial reporting. This perspective implicitly places more weight on the variance of the x distribution than on the mean, perhaps, overweighting the implications of a particular realization of x for predicting future realizations. As discussed below, information about both the mean and the variance can be important to financial statement users.

The third type of volatility is *mixed-measurement volatility*. Mixed-measurement volatility arises because currently there is no common measurement objective for all assets and liabilities. That is, some assets and liabilities are measured at historical cost, some are measured at the lower of cost or a current value, some are measured at fair value, and some are not recognized at all.[6] As a result, the effects of economic events are not fully recognized in financial statements for all assets and liabilities. An example of this is when assets are recognized at fair value and fixed rate liabilities are recognized based on historical cost. In this situation, when there is an increase in market interest rates, the values of assets decrease and this decrease is recognized in the financial statements. The values of the liabilities decrease, but this decrease is not recognized. Thus, an interest rate increase has a relatively larger negative effect on the financial statements, that is, lower net assets and lower net income, than it would if assets and liabilities were both measured either using fair values or using historical cost. Similarly, a decrease in market interest rates has a relatively larger positive effect. This resulting increased volatility is a direct result of a mixed-measurement accounting system.

3. Relation to Relevance and Reliability

Relevance and reliability are two fundamental characteristics of financial statement information. In financial accounting, relevance means that the information is capable of making a difference to users' decisions by helping users form predictions about the outcomes of past, present, or future events or to confirm or correct expectations (FASB, 1980). Thus, relevance is an information notion. Accountants seek to measure items that are relevant to users' economic decisions. Reliability is the extent to which the measure of the item represents what it purports to represent. Thus, reliability is a measurement notion. The IASB's *Framework* (IASB, 2001) as well as that of the FASB and other standard-setters, makes clear that for a given level of relevance, the most reliable amount is the one that should be recognized. Conversely, conditional on a(n) (unspecified) threshold of reliability, the most relevant amount should be recognized.

Turning to the three sources of financial statement volatility, estimation error volatility relates to reliability. An accounting amount is reliable if it is verifiable, representationally faithful, and neutral. Verifiability is the extent to which different measurers would arrive at the same amount. This assumes, as above, that there is an underlying amount, x, that accountants want to measure. Standard-setters refer to this amount as the measurement objective. Thus, in the notation used above, one measurer estimates x as $X_1 = x + \varepsilon_1$, another estimates it as $X_2 = x + \varepsilon_2$, etc., where ε_i are the realizations of ε. Thus, the variance of ε captures verifiability, an important element of reliability—the lower σ_ε^2, the greater the reliability of X.

Inherent volatility relates to relevance. The higher σ_x^2, the greater the relevance of x.[7] As noted above, relevance is an information notion, not a measurement notion. Relevance is really about x, not about X. From an information perspective, inherent volatility, that is, σ_x^2, reflects relevance because when the fair value of an asset or liability has higher inherent volatility, it is more difficult to predict the fair value at any point in time. Thus, knowing the current fair value has greater potential to make a difference to users for economic decisions. However, inherent volatility does not reflect all dimensions of relevance. For example, the realized amount itself captures dimensions of relevance—one would expect assets and liabilities with larger fair values to be more relevant than those with smaller fair values. Thus, it is important to financial statement users to have information about the asset or liability's current value, as well as its inherent volatility.

Inherent volatility also relates to reliability. Interestingly, the higher σ_x^2, the greater the reliability of X. This is because another dimension of reliability is representational faithfulness, that is, the extent to which the measure, X, represents what it purports to represent, x. Assuming X and x are positively correlated, which should always be the case, σ_x^2 reflects the covariance between X and the underlying asset or liability fair value, x, that is, X's representational faithfulness. For example, if $X = x + \varepsilon$, as assumed above, and X and ε are uncorrelated, $\text{cov}(X, x) = \sigma_x^2$. Thus, viewing σ_x^2 as $\text{cov}(X, x)$, the higher σ_x^2, the greater the reliability of X, all else equal. One concern about fair-value accounting is that all else is not equal—in particular a concern is that σ_ε^2 for a fair values-based X is greater than for a historical cost-based X. However, as BCS show, it is σ_x^2 relative to σ_ε^2 that is important, not the absolute amounts of σ_ε^2 and σ_x^2 considered separately. Thus, the measurement error volatility cannot be considered in isolation from the relevance of x, the object of measurement.[8]

Mixed-measurement volatility has no direct relation to relevance or reliability of particular assets or liabilities. For each asset and liability, standard-setters who established the present accounting rules presumably concluded that the measure prescribed was the best combination of relevance and reliability. However, a mixed-measurement accounting model generally impairs relevance and reliability of net income or other amounts comprising components that are measured using different attributes. This problem is the prime reason for hedge accounting. It also has caused standard-setters to strive to use the same measurement attribute for more assets and liabilities; attempting to solve this problem is one of the driving forces behind the increased use of fair value accounting. As a way for firms to mitigate mixed-measurement volatility, the IASB's revised standard on financial instruments permits firms to designate at inception any financial asset or liability as measured at fair value, with changes in fair value recognized in net income (IASB, 2003b).

4. What Can Standard-Setters Do to Help Users?

Financial statement amounts, whether based on fair values or historical costs, reflect the measure of assets, liabilities, and equity at a point in time, and income and expense over the financial reporting period. The amounts can be thought of as attempting to recognize measures of the realizations of the x distribution. Concerns over volatility in financial statements should not be confused with concerns that these recognized amounts are not useful for financial statement users. Rather, one should think of the concerns as reflecting that financial statements have, historically, focused on the current values of assets and liabilities, that is, measures of the realizations of x. The increased use of fair values as a measurement basis has highlighted the fact that financial statements provide little information about the variance of the x distribution. Increased use of fair values will result in financial statements reflecting more inherent volatility and, likely, more estimation error volatility. Thus, information is needed in addition to information about the realizations of x, not instead of it.

Financial statements comprise not only the primary statements, that is, the balance sheet, income statement, statement of changes in equity, and cash flow statement, but also the footnotes that accompany them. Thus, financial statements can provide information through recognition or disclosure. Although disclosure is not a substitute for recognition, it can be a complement. Users need to understand estimation error volatility because it reflects information uncertainty, which they need to factor into their risk assessments. They need to understand inherent volatility because it reflects the underlying riskiness of the entity's cash flows and, thus, it has direct implications for risk assessment. Although it is difficult empirically to distinguish these, as noted above, a primary objective of financial reporting is to provide users with information relating to the uncertainty and timing of future cash flows. Thus, providing information about inherent volatility is key to complete financial reporting. Financial statement users also need to understand how mixed-measurement volatility arises so that they can adjust for it. This is because mixed-measurement volatility is simply an artifact of the accounting system and does not reflect a risk that should be priced by capital providers or be a concern of regulators.

Relating to estimation error volatility, users need information about the variance of ε, the error in estimating x. To this end, standard-setters can require disclosure of whether recognized fair values are obtained directly from market prices, or based on assumptions obtained from markets, or whether they are based on management's estimates of future cash flows, or other non-market-based assumptions. This reflects the thinking behind the IASB's and FASB's fair value hierarchy that fair values estimated using market prices or other market-based assumptions are likely to be more reliable. This also reflects the motivation for the disclosure requirements in IAS 32, *Financial Instruments: Presentation and Disclosure* (IASB, 2003c), which distinguish recognized fair values based on the extent of market inputs into their estimation.

To the extent fair-value estimates are based on the entity's estimates of future cash flows and other non-market-based assumptions, standard-setters can require disclosure of the likely variation in reasonable estimates of those cash flows or assumptions. An example of such a disclosure is the range of reasonably possible pension actuarial assumptions. They also can require disclosures relating to variation in X attributable to σ_ε^2. That is, how the recognized amount would be affected by reasonable alternative estimates of underlying cash flows or assumptions. An example of such a disclosure is how the firm's pension liability would be affected by a change in the actuarial assumption.

Relating to inherent volatility, the objective is to provide information about the volatility of x, the fair value of interest. To achieve this objective, standard-setters could require disclosure of value-at-risk, which is the maximum percentage value of the asset or liability that could be lost during a fixed period, for example, one day, within a specified confidence level, for example, 95 percent. They also could require disclosure of estimated inherent volatility or a history of past measures of realizations, that is, past Xs. All of these would give financial statement users information about the inherent volatility of the asset's or liability's fair value. Providing financial statement users with information about inherent volatility historically has not been a focus of financial statements. As noted above, financial statements focus on the realizations of x, as measured by X. However, the increased use of fair values in financial statements has highlighted the fact that to serve users' needs financial statements need to include information about the variance of x as well.

Relating to mixed-measurement volatility, standard-setters can help financial statement users by developing standards that eliminate it as much as possible. This is the motivation behind hedge accounting and the fair value option in International Accounting Standard (IAS) 39 *Financial Instruments: Recognition and Measurement* (IASB, 2003b). Hedge accounting is intended to eliminate mixed-measurement volatility; it is not intended to account for economic hedges. The fair value option in IAS 39 is intended to eliminate mixed-measurement volatility, at least for financial instruments. However, it is unlikely that all mixed-measurement volatility can be eliminated. Even using fair values to measure all recognized assets and liabilities is unlikely to achieve this goal. There likely will be economic assets and liabilities that are not recognized in financial statements as long as the frameworks used for financial reporting include definitions of financial statement elements, that is, assets and liabilities, and reliability constraints. Thus, standard-setters can aid users' risk assessments by providing disclosures that highlight accounting policies and how these affect recognized amounts. These requirements are largely in place today. However, users must have sufficient accounting training to comprehend fully the implications for mixed-measurement volatility of an entity's accounting policies.

5. Concluding Remarks

There is an increasing use of fair values in financial statements. One of the concerns over using fair values stems from the increase in volatility of financial statement amounts that is inevitable with using more fair values. This paper identifies three sources of financial statement volatility that are associated with using fair values in financial reporting—estimation error volatility, inherent volatility, and mixed-measurement volatility. Mixed-measurement volatility derives from using fair values for some assets and liabilities and historical cost-based amounts for others. Using a common measurement objective would reduce substantially mixed-measurement volatility. Thus, the increased use of fair values will help eliminate this source of volatility in financial statements. However, increased use of fair values likely is associated with two additional sources of financial statement volatility. In particular, estimation error volatility is unavoidable when using fair values because most fair values are not observable from market prices and must be estimated. Although obtaining more precise estimates of fair values should be a goal, standard-setters can require firms to provide information about estimation error volatility to aid financial statement users in assessing the attendant information risk. Several recent IASB standards have begun to do just that.

Inherent volatility derives from economic, not accounting, forces. Thus, inherent volatility is what financial statements should reflect. It is not an accounting problem, other than to ensure users have the information about it they need. Standard-setters cannot, nor should they strive to, eliminate or mask inherent volatility. Rather, they should require disclosure of information about the volatility inherent in the values of an entity's assets and liabilities. Such disclosures might include value-at-risk or a history of realized amounts. Requiring this type of information in financial statements is relatively new. Exactly what disclosures are needed and how the information comprising the disclosures should be obtained are open questions. Another open question is how such information should be presented. Is information scattered throughout financial statement footnotes the most useful presentation or should standard-setters attempt to develop a method of summarizing such information, similar to the way in which assets and liabilities and income and expenses are summarized in the primary financial statements. Devising such summary information is an ambitious task for standard-setters and for researchers—there is no obvious way to aggregate information about volatility.

Users of financial statements need to understand the various sources of financial statement volatility so that they can assess the riskiness of the firm. Investors, creditors, and regulators are concerned about volatility, but masking it does not serve users needs. Rather, effort should be expended on measuring it as precisely as possible and providing information about it to financial statement users.

*Mary E. Barth is the Atholl McBean Professor of Accounting and senior associate dean for academic affairs in the Graduate School of Business at Stanford University. She is also a member of the International Accounting Standards Board. The author appreciates the helpful comments and suggestions from Bill Beaver, Greg Clinch, and Wayne Landsman.

Notes

1. It is important to note that using historical costs as the measurement basis also can induce volatility into financial statements. This arises when a transaction or other event results in recognizing in a single period a gain or loss that accrued economically over several periods. For example, when an appreciated long-term asset is sold, the gain is recognized in income in the period of the sale, whereas the gain was attributable to unrecognized increases in the asset's value that accrued over several years. This volatility arises from delayed recognition of economic events.

2. The IASB and FASB are in the process of developing guidance on how to estimate fair value. Part of that effort focuses on whether fair value is an entry or exit value notion, that is, how transactions costs affect fair values. At present, the definition of fair value is silent on this point. However, exit values should not be confused with liquidation values; the only different between entry and exit values should be transactions costs.

3. To see this, recall that the volatility, or variance, of the difference between two random variables equals the sum of their variances, minus two times their covariance. $\sigma^2_{x-y} = \sigma^2_x + \sigma^2_y - 2\sigma_{x,y}$. Thus, for uncorrelated variables, the variance of the difference is the sum of the two variances. Consistent with this, Barth (1994) shows that the variance of changes in fair values that are recognized in income can be substantially larger than the variance of the underlying assets and liabilities. This can result in income and expenses having substantially less reliability than the related assets and liabilities. See Section 3 for a discussion of how volatility relates to reliability.

4. More generally, x can be thought of as the object of interest to financial statement users, for example, the entity's payoff or the series of expected future cash flows. In this setting, x is what financial statement users seek to forecast. In this more general setting, because fair values are defined, as described above, as the present value of expected future cash flows, fair value is a measure of the underlying x, not the object of measurement.

5. It is for this reason that the FASB's Statement of Financial Accounting Standards No. 123 requires entities to use expected option life rather than its contractual life when estimating the fair value of employee stock options and the forthcoming IASB standard on Share-Based Payment will encourage entities to use lattice pricing models when the assumptions of the Black–Scholes (1973) formula are likely not to hold.

6. For example, under International Financial Reporting Standards, held-to-maturity investments and many liabilities are measured at cost, inventory and long-term assets are measured at lower of cost or a current value, and many financial instruments are measured at fair value.

7. This interpretation of relevance is consistent with Kirschenheiter (1997) and Barth, Clinch, and Shibano (BCS, 2003). Kirschenheiter (1997) characterizes relevance as the covariance between X and x and BCS characterizes it as σ_x^2. In BCS, as above, these two characterizations are equivalent. Both studies characterize reliability as σ_ε^2.

8. Often relevance and reliability are thought to be trade-offs; more (less) relevant measures are less (more) reliable. However, this is not necessarily the case when one factors in the representational faithfulness dimension of reliability. For example, if one believes that fair values are the most relevant measure, then x is fair value. Historical cost is not reliable, despite our ability to measure it precisely, because it has very low representational faithfulness. That is, cov (X, x) can be low when X is a historical cost measure and what we are interested in measuring, x, is fair value, diminishing the reliability of historical cost. Thus, one should not equate measurement precision, that is, σ_ε^2, with reliability; cov (X, x) is another important dimension of reliability.

References

Barry, C. B., and S. J. Brown, 1986, "Limited information as a source of risk," *Journal of Portfolio Management*, Winter, pp. 66–72.

_____, 1985, "Differential information and security market equilibrium," *Journal of Financial and Quantitative Analysis*, Vol. 20, pp. 407–422.

Barth, M. E., 1994, "Fair value accounting: Evidence from investment securities and the market valuation of banks," *The Accounting Review*, Vol. 69, pp. 1–25.

Barth, M. E., W. H. Beaver, and W. R. Landsman, 2001, "The relevance of the value relevance literature for accounting standard setting: Another view," *Journal of Accounting and Economics*, Vol. 31, pp. 77–104.

Barth, M. E., G. Clinch, and T. Shibano, 2003, "Market effects of recognition and disclosure," *Journal of Accounting Research*, Vol. 41, pp. 581–609.

Barth, M. E, and A. P. Hutton, 2004, "Analyst earnings forecast revisions and the pricing of accruals," *Review of Accounting Studies*, forthcoming.

Beaver, W. H., 1998, *Financial Reporting: An Accounting Revolution*, third edition, Engelwood Cliffs, NJ: Prentice-Hall.

Black, F., and M. Scholes, 1973, "The pricing of options and corporate liabilities," *The Journal of Political Economy*, Vol. 81, pp. 637–654.

Easley, D., and M. O'Hara, 2003, "Information and the cost of capital," Cornell University, working paper.

Financial Accounting Standards Board, 1984, "Recognition and measurement in financial statements of business enterprises," *Statement of Financial Accounting Concepts No. 5*, Stamford, CT.

_____, 1980, "Qualitative characteristics of accounting information," *Statement of Financial Accounting Concepts No. 2,* Stamford, CT.

International Accounting Standards Board, 2003a, *International Financial Reporting Standards*, London, UK.

_____, 2003b, "International Accounting Standard IAS 39," *Financial Instruments: Recognition, and Measurement*, London, UK.

_____, 2003c, "International Accounting Standard IAS 32," *Financial Instruments: Recognition, and Measurement*, London, UK.

_____, 2001, *Framework for the Preparation and Presentation of Financial Statements*, London, UK.

Kirschenheiter, M., 1997, "Information quality and correlated signals," *Journal of Accounting Research*, Spring, pp. 43–59.

Sloan, R. G., 1996, "Do stock prices fully reflect information in accruals and cash flows about future earnings?," *The Accounting Review*, Vol. 71, pp. 289–315.

Xie, H., 2001, "The mispricing of abnormal accruals," *The Accounting Review*, Vol. 76, pp. 357–373.

Chapter 26

Enron and Effective Corporate Governance

Charles M. Elson*
University of Delaware

The bankruptcy of the famed Enron Corporation has proven not only to have been a seminal business event, as rarely does a company as large and well-positioned as Enron fail, but has proven a watershed event in American corporate law and governance, inspiring numerous reforms in the corporate legal and regulatory regimes. The seminal question, however, and the one critical to understanding the reforms demanded and enacted is why—why did the company collapse—or, more directly, who is responsible for this failure and what could have been done to have avoided it. A number of commentators have concentrated on the failure of the gatekeepers—those objective outside monitors such as the auditors, the rating agencies, and the investment analysts, who it is argued either acquiesced in, did little to prevent, or even missed altogether the problematic activity of company management that led to the collapse.[1] Reforming the conduct and structure of these gatekeepers it is suggested, is necessary to prevent a repeat of Enron and to restore public confidence in our financial markets. I cannot quibble with much of this argument. Clearly the outside monitors failed miserably in their responsibilities. They were either incredibly negligent or sufficiently coopted by Enron management to have lost all objectivity and efficacy. So what can be done? I believe that while creating better outside monitors may be helpful, the real key to the prevention of Enron-type scandals is centered and dependent on the inside monitors—the company's directors. As corporate insiders, they are in the best position to observe the corporate management—the secret, though, is making them objective and engaged monitors.

But how? This is where an examination of classical corporate governance theory becomes relevant and helpful. Under traditional theory, the board acts as an active management monitor for shareholder benefit. It must decide when to engage and when to terminate a management team and acts to provide supportive management oversight in between these two points. Central to this active monitoring are the concepts of independence and equity. To fulfill their oversight responsibilities effectively, directors must be independent of management and holders of a personally meaningful

equity stake in the enterprise. Independence is a critical element in meaningful monitoring. Independence, which involves the absence of any economic ties to management or the company itself other than equity ownership, provides a director with the
distance and objectivity necessary to examine management action in the most effective manner. Economic relationships with management, including consulting, service
provision, or other indirect arrangements, may cloud judgment and make it more
difficult to review management conduct objectively. A lack of independence lends to
ineffective monitoring because it makes a director either too comfortable with management and its representations, or due to relational concerns, unable to effectively
disengage to objectively review management conduct. A good distance from company management allows the kind of reflective review of management conduct that
public shareholders expect and is necessary to long-term corporate success.

Additionally, director independence is not only important for its impact on director conduct, but management activity as well. The watchwords are accountability and
responsibility. All of us must need to feel accountable to someone. The idea of responsibility to a watchful intermediary spurs thoughtful decision-making and reflection on management's part. This cannot occur unless the intermediary is in fact
independent of the examined party. This is why the concept of the independent board
is so critical to modern governance theory.

Coincident and complementary to its emphasis on director independence, modern governance theory has also emphasized the need for directors to hold an equity
stake in the corporation. While independence promotes objectivity, the board also
must have an incentive to exercise that objectivity effectively. Granting board members equity ownership in the corporation may help achieve this goal. When management appoints the board, and directors have no stake in the enterprise other than their
board seats, there is simply no personal pecuniary incentive to engage in the active
monitoring of management. As directors shirk their duty to monitor management
actively, stockholder interests are left unprotected. The most effective way to incentivize
directors to address their responsibilities from the perspective of the shareholders, to
whom they are responsible, is to make them stockholders as well. By becoming equity
holders, the outside directors assume a personal stake in the success or failure of the
enterprise. When directors are active equity participants, they have an incentive to
monitor management's performance more effectively, since poor monitoring may have
a direct negative impact upon their personal financial interests.

Of course, where stock ownership is insubstantial when compared to the other
private benefits associated with being a director, the motivational impact is bound to
be minimal. For example, in many large public corporations, outside directors do
have a nominal equity stake in the company, but receive far more substantial compensation in the form of annual fees, which often exceed $90,000, in exchange for atten-
dance at a few board meetings per annum. Such a compensation system, of course, is
wholly inadequate to promote the kind of personal incentive necessary to create an
active board. To have any sort of favorable impact on director behavior, the amount of
stock that each director holds must be substantial. Therefore, to align director and shareholder interests and promote effective monitoring, director fees should be paid primarily in restricted company stock. It is important to note that while equity ownership

provides the incentive to monitor, it alone does not provide the proper objectivity to foster effective oversight. Independence creates this objectivity, and that is why modern governance theory demands both equity ownership and independence. Independent directors without equity ownership may be objective, but they have little incentive to engage in active oversight. Equity ownership provides the incentive to exercise objective oversight. On the other hand, equity holding directors who are not independent may have the proper incentive but lack the necessary objectivity. Independence and equity ownership, acting in tandem, are the keys to effective corporate governance.

How does this emphasis on director independence and equity relate to the board failure at Enron? The answer is most straightforward. The Enron directors lacked independence from management. They may have held company equity, but without the appropriate independence from Enron management, lacked the necessary objectivity to perceive the numerous and significant warning signals that should have alerted them to the alleged management malfeasance that led to the company's ultimate meltdown and failure.

These signs included five specific concerns that should have induced greater board probing of management initiatives. The first involved the management's request that the board waive, on two specific occasions, the company's code of ethics that prohibited officer conflict of interest transactions. The now infamous waivers allowed the debt shifting, off-balance-sheet transactions that were alleged to have been designed to mask the company's true precarious financial situation from investors. The second warning signal involved massive sales of company stock by numerous high-level insiders. Management stock sales are never viewed as a good sign of the company's future prospects and should have alerted the board of potential problems. The third, fourth, and fifth signals involved company's auditors—Arthur Andersen. Andersen had been initially engaged as Enron's external auditor. Its role, however, expanded dramatically. Operating in a climate dominated by numerous authorities, including the chairman of the Securities and Exchange Commission calling for substantial reform of the auditor/company relationship, Enron's relationship with Andersen was problematic in several respects. In addition to its role as the company's auditor, Andersen was also providing substantial amounts of consulting services to Enron, in one year billing approximately $27,000,000 for its consulting activities. As this was occurring, there was substantial criticism being directed at this sort of auditor/client consulting, as it was argued that this led to compromised audits. Additionally, Andersen was not only providing external auditing services, but was also functioning as the company's internal auditor. This kind of activity also faced great criticism as it was argued that co-mingling these two oversight responsibilities, internal and external audit, would compromise the effectiveness of both. Finally, senior members of the Enron finance department had been hired directly from Arthur Andersen. This practice too had been critiqued on the grounds that it had the potential of creating unwelcome pressure on the external auditor because of the relationships that existed between former and present firm employees.

These five warning signals, obvious to an outsider, were all missed by the Enron board. Had the directors asked questions about these actions, perhaps they would have discovered and appropriately responded to the management misdeeds that hastened the company's collapse. So why did the board miss these signs? They were a highly respected, intelligent, and influential group. What went so wrong to have rendered them ineffective proximate monitors? Simply stated, they lacked the appropriate independence from management to have had the objectivity to appreciate the severity of the warnings that they were receiving.

A large number of the Enron directors, despite the fact that they were technically outsiders—not full-time employees of the company—still had numerous financial or quasifinancial relationships with the company and its management that compromised their independence and consequent objectivity. Several directors had direct consulting relationships with the company for which they were well compensated. Others were officers of charitable organizations that were the beneficiaries of significant donations from Enron or members of company management. Some had business dealings with the company. A few had been directors for so many years, that their board seats appeared to have become company-sponsored sinecures. Although under the existing Securities and Exchange Commission or New York Stock Exchange requirements most of these directors would have been classified as independent, in fact they were not, at least not in the sense that corporate governance theorists would consider appropriate. Independence means no significant financial relationships at all with the company or its management. The problem with these types of relationships is that they compromise one's objectivity. They create a bond with company management that makes it more difficult to review management's actions objectively and dispassionately. That is, I believe, what happened to the Enron directors. The relationships that they had with company management created a comfort level in them vis-à-vis management that made it possible for them to simply explain away or to miss completely the various warning signs before them. Their independence deficit did not necessarily make them bad actors, only much less sensitive ones and, as such, wholly ineffective.

Their failings, however, should not suggest that inside monitors can never be effective, and that reliance on an outside monitor is more appropriate. They failed not due to their position within the organization, but their lack of independence. Had they been truly independent of management, as well as significant equity holders in the company, the Enron tale might have had a happier ending. The lesson of Enron is not that inside monitors are generally ineffective, but that for inside monitors to be inspired and successful monitors of management to protect shareholders value, they must be independent, which gives them objectivity and equity holders, which gives them the incentive to exercise the objectivity that independence brings.

*Charles M. Elson is the Edgar S. Woolard, Jr., Chair in Corporate Governance and director of the John L. Weinberg Center for Corporate Governance at the University of Delaware. This paper is based upon an earlier version published in the *Wake Forest Law Review*, Vol. 38, No. 3.

Notes

1. See Coffee (2003) describing the role of corporate gatekeepers during the 1990s, and Macey (2003) describing the different types of objective monitors and their roles.

References

Coffee, Jr., John C., 2003, "What caused Enron?: A capsule social and economics history of the 1990s," *Cornell Law Review*, Vol. 89.

Macey, Jonathan R., 2003, "Efficient capital markets, corporate disclosure, and Enron," *Cornell Law Review*, Vol. 89.

Chapter 27

Interaction of Market Discipline and Public Policy: Discussion

Shyam Sunder*
Yale University

The remarks in this paper consist of two parts. The first part concerns the linkages established in the three excellent papers among accounting, corporate governance, and market discipline. The second part discusses the possible uses and abuses of market discipline to define and develop efficient accounting institutions. Several speakers have referred to the choice of whether we look at the glass of market discipline to be half full or half empty. Experience with the promise and failure of market discipline in accounting suggests that we would be best off if we keep an open mind, and assess the efficient application of market discipline on a case-by-case basis. Neither general reliance on, nor the avoidance of, the market discipline offers the prospect of developing efficient accounting institutions.

1. Accounting, Corporate Governance, and Market Discipline

Benston examines five hypotheses about the recent reports of inappropriate corporate financial reports. First, perhaps these failures are not as important or excessive as they appear to be. It is unlikely that the frequency of such failures can be efficiently reduced to zero. The question posed by this hypothesis can be addressed only in relation to an appropriate—and as yet elusive—standard for the optimal number of failures complicated by the problem of changing environment and enforcement policies. It is true that the number of corporate financial restatements increased markedly after 1998. However, this increase cannot be attributed to idiosyncratic change in the behavior of the Securities and Exchange Commission (SEC) without careful examination of the factors that may have led to such the changes in SEC's enforcement policy in the first place. It is possible, indeed likely, that SEC reacted to an increase in abuses in corporate financial reporting. Whether an average 0.1 percent to 0.2 percent loss in the market value of all firms during the few days surrounding the announcement of accounting restatements is an acceptable trade-off for the cost of additional auditing remains an open question. The evidence establishes, beyond reasonable doubt, that the late nineties saw an unprecedented rise in the frequency of such restatements.

Evidence on the second hypothesis yields some support for the idea that executive stock options lead chief executive officers (CEO) and chief financial officers to adopt aggressive accounting practices. It is reassuring to learn that, as elsewhere in economics, compensation systems yield no free lunch. Attempts to motivate managers and align their incentives with the shareholder interest through performance-contingent compensation carry a cost of their own—the risk of corrupting the accounting system which is operated and controlled by the managers.

Benston rejects a third hypothesis that the consulting fees, through their influence on incentives of independent accountants, may have caused the accounting failures. I do not disagree with the data, or the inference drawn from it. He does not consider the possibility that the failure of the accounting market may have caused the accountants to resort to consulting in the first place. Under this alternative hypothesis, the oft-repeated cause and effect relationship between consulting and accounting failures is reversed.

The fourth hypothesis is that inadequacies of generally accepted accounting principles (GAAP) and generally accepted auditing standards (GAAS) may have caused the financial reporting failures. Benston concludes that the principles-based (instead of rules-based) accounting standards and statistical sampling in auditing might have saved the day. I am skeptical on both accounts.

Rules versus principles, in spite of its rhetorical appeal, is a false dichotomy. No rule-maker sets out to write detailed rules instead of broad principles, or to choose form over substance. With best of intentions, rule-makers get drawn into making detailed rules. The answer lies not in the incentives and behavior of individuals but in the institutional structures we create to write and enforce standards.

Under pressure from their clients, auditors return to the rule-maker for clarifications. It is difficult and costly to say no to a client, and the rule-makers exist to make more rules. It does not take long to move from "Thou shalt not steal" to "Thou shalt not steal X, Y, and Z," etc. It is not fair to set up a rule-making body such as the Financial Accounting Standards Board and then to criticize it for writing rules which are too detailed. Without structural changes, any rule-maker would be driven in the same direction with time and resources.

Whether the technical device of statistical sampling can help auditors to detect errors and fraud efficiently depends on their willingness to use such devices. Statistical sampling has been available to the auditors for some time; it is all too easy for an unwilling auditor to appear to use statistical sampling without extracting its benefits of efficiency. Statistical sampling cannot help an auditor who does not want to detect errors in fraud.

Finally, Benston examines the hypothesis that punishment imposed on errant auditors is insufficient and infrequent, and reaches an affirmative conclusion. I agree. I am less sanguine than Benston and Elson are about the beneficial effects of recent reforms. The newly created Public Company Accounting Oversight Board will have little permanent effect on ensuring that auditors deliver high quality work. The inherent quality of auditors' work is unobservable ex ante, and barely observable ex post after great cost and delay.

Barth's paper suggests the motto that measurement should be as precise as possible, but no more. No reasonable person should disagree. Yet, the old images of accountants burning midnight oil to match accounts to the last penny has not faded away, and many the accuracy of bookkeeping is easily confused with the accuracy of accounts. Consequently, many people hold an exaggerated view of how precise accounting is and ought to be. Accounting rule-makers are constantly hounded by those who ask: Why can't you accountants just tell the simple truth?

The problem is that what is true is not simple; what is simple is not true. If you don't believe it, ask yourself how much wealth you have.

Over the recent decades, accounting theoreticians have worked out the difficult trade-offs that are possible on the Pareto frontier between our conflicting desires to produce financial reports which are more relevant as well as less error prone. Our wish to cross such frontiers is understandable. But standards and statutes, no matter how much power of enforcement lies behind them, cannot annul the laws of economics.

Elson's comments focus on the key issue of corporate governance and carefully analyze elements of both director independence as well as equity ownership needed to support better governance. I agree with his analysis and suggestions. However, the governance theory has emphasized independence at the expense of other, equally important, factors such as directors' competence, knowledge and experience, connections, trust in the eyes of the CEO, and most of all, a positive motivation to protect the minority shareholders—the small investor who is not in the room and cannot price protect himself or herself. In corporate governance debates, independence of the directors from the senior management is promoted at the expense of these other considerations.

Some other features of the directors-independent-of-managers model of corporate governance being popularized these days raise questions about its potential effectiveness in addressing the governance problem. With the directors and officers' insurance policies bought by publicly held firms, directors have little liability to shareholders. Despite frauds amounting to billions of dollars, not a single non-executive director of a corporation has been charged with wrongdoing. While voting to select the directors, shareholders have little choice but to vote for the slate proposed by the nominating committee. They have no information about the past performance of the individual directors in governance of the corporation. Without choice or information, the shareholder voting as a governance mechanism is largely an exercise in futility except in those rare cases where a well-publicized proxy fight is on.

In spite of all the attention showered on it in the recent years, the corporate governance problem is hardly new. The British East India Company, the first major multinational corporation chartered in 1601, faced severe governance problems throughout the two and a half centuries of its existence. The minutes of its Court of Governors are replete with not-always-successful efforts to solve the governance problem over long distances that had not yet been spanned by telecommunications or air travel. In spite of their promise, the modern communications do not seem to have made much difference. The problem arises from human nature, not technology, and has no easy fixes.

2. Uses and Misuses of Market Discipline in Accounting

In banking, the use of market discipline to address the governance problems has a long history, and is taken for granted today. The idea is relatively new to accounting, and it is possible to use the market discipline to devise better practice, standards, and institutions of accounting. To this end, I shall mention a few possible uses, and an example of misuse of market discipline in accounting.

Development of better accounting rules and standards can be facilitated by allowing two or more sets of rule-makers compete openly for the allegiance and royalty revenues of the reporting firms who are left free to choose any one set of standards for their financial reports. At a small additional cost of competing rule-makers, corporations could save hundreds of billions of dollars each year in lowered cost of capital. Comparability of results does not obtain even when a single set of rules is applied across different economic environments. Market reactions to firms that choose different standards will inform better decisions by rule-makers. Allowing competition among sets of standards increases the chances that each firm will choose to report by rules that minimize its own cost of capital, giving rise to different sets of accounting rules for different kinds of firms and different kinds of economic environments.

Instead of creating a chain of watchmen to "watch the watchman," implicit in the recent legislation to create the Public Company Accounting Oversight Board, we could resort to help from market discipline. Removal of the mandatory audit requirement of the SEC would allow better-run companies to use auditing as a costly signal to convey a sense of confidence in their information to the shareholders. Some proposals for the use of market discipline include combining the audit function with insurance and allowing reporting firms to buy any amount of fair financial representation insurance from a company that will conduct its own audit to limit its own exposure to risk.

A third example of the use of market discipline in accounting concerns executive stock options. Under this proposal, the firm would be free to attribute any value to the incentive options granted to the employees. This value will be announced and expensed in the financial reports and deducted from the tax return of the firm. The firm would be obligated to sell similar options to its shareholders at a price equal to this value; the market will ensure that any undervalued options get diluted down to the stated value.

The 1970s changes in the public policy to push for more competition in the market for audit services is an example of misdirected use of market discipline. Until the 1970s, the U.S. government had refrained from pushing for greater competition in markets for professional services (for example, doctors, lawyers, dentists, and accountants) for the fear that such action may cause failures in markets where the customers could not observe the quality of the services provided. By the mid-seventies, theoretical arguments by Stigler and others about the robustness of competition had eased such qualms. The Supreme Court decision on Bates vs. the Bar of the State of Arizona in 1977 led the U.S. Department of Justice to force professional associations to remove anticompetitive provisions (for example, no advertising, no solicitation of competitors' clients or employees, etc.) from their respective codes of ethics. The unobservability of the quality of services rendered in auditing is extreme; unlike the results of the endeavors of doctors and lawyers, the consequences of auditors' efforts are rarely observable ex post. The increased competition led to a rapid decline in the price and quality of audit services within a short period of time. The major accounting failures of the past few years can be traced back to this misguided attempt to use market discipline in a market which could not be sustained under the forces of competition.

To summarize, careful use of market discipline can effectively address many problems of accounting and auditing that have surfaced in the recent years. It would be prudent to have such use guided by economic analysis. Ideological commitment to market discipline independent of the specific circumstances can be just as harmful as ignoring the market forces.

*Shyam Sunder is the James L. Frank Professor of Accounting, Economics, and Finance at the Yale School of Management.

PART VIII

INTERACTION OF MARKET DISCIPLINE AND PUBLIC POLICY

Chapter 28

Can the Unsophisticated Market Provide Discipline?

Gerard Caprio*
World Bank

and

Patrick Honohan
World Bank

1. Introduction

Despite significant upgrading of bank regulations and supervisory capacity and expertise, there has been little evident improvement in bank failure experience worldwide over the past decade. In addition, cross-country evidence suggests that systems that are overregulated by discretionary official supervisors—ostensibly in the interests of prudence—underperform along a number of dimensions. Perhaps most interestingly, an approach based on strengthening official supervision was found at best to have no significant effect on the development of the financial sector; at worst, except in the most institutionally advanced countries, the effect went the other way (increased supervisory powers associated with less financial sector development). Instead, evidence from a cross-country survey suggests that banking systems work better where market discipline is fostered by strict accounting and auditing rules, use of international rating agencies by banks, and avoidance of deposit insurance (Barth, Caprio, and Levine, 2003).

How much reliance can one place on market forces where the liquidity, transparency, and other underlying characteristics of markets is deficient? Specifically, which elements of market discipline work better in immature environments? Most practitioners think that, as markets plainly do not function well in low-income countries, then it must be the case that market discipline also does not work, and that therefore these countries need to rely more heavily on capital and bank supervision, the two pillars stressed in the approach of the Basel Committee. Is this presumption correct?

This paper provides new data on the changing degree to which the prerequisites for market discipline are in place. Using this data and proxies for the degree of banking vulnerability, we will provide some evidence on the presence of prerequisites for the different flavors of market discipline—that provided by large depositors, by debt and equity holders, and by specialized information firms such as rating agencies and auditors—in different countries and on their possible effectiveness. However market discipline does function, empirical evidence indicates that it does a better job compared with reliance on official supervision. While attempts to improve the latter no doubt should and will continue, there is much to be said in favor of building on strengths. Accordingly, the last section of the paper addresses policy considerations regarding what can be done to improve the functioning of market discipline.

To summarize our findings, there is no systematic tendency for low-income countries to lack the prerequisites for market discipline. Offsetting factors to the weaker market and formal information infrastructures are 1) the less complex character of banking business in low-income countries; 2) the growing internationalization of these markets through the presence of foreign banks, and through international trading of the debt and equity of locally controlled nongovernment banks; and 3) the smaller size of the business and financial community. On the other hand, continuing dominance by public sector banks in some countries limits the likely development of market monitoring, clearly a cause for concern, given the disappointing record of governments around the world as monitors of their self-owned banks.

Among the different channels of market discipline, low-income countries are best positioned to exploit depositor discipline if the government avoids the chilling effects of blanket guarantees and the like. Because depositor discipline is effectively in the hands of a small number of large depositors, the information requirements for depositor discipline may be more easily satisfied in an economy where the financial and business elite is small, as it is in many of the lower income countries.

Though local institutional deficiencies can appear to be a limiting factor, the effectiveness of discipline through debt and equity markets in low-income countries is enhanced by the increasing tendency for privately controlled banks in developing countries to make their equity available for depository receipt (DR) trading on international markets, and to issue internationally traded debt. The use of information intermediaries (accounting firms and rating agencies) is also growing rapidly in low-income countries, but their independent ability to contribute to market discipline seems rather limited given the heightened conflicts of interest in small business communities and the modest resources that are typically devoted to ratings.

Although market monitoring appears to be better developed in low-income countries, relative perhaps to expectations, it still is the case that more can and should be done to strengthen it. Although we find some evidence that countries where there is greater scope for local monitoring (because their banking systems are not predominantly government-owned or foreign-owned) do employ policies friendly to market discipline, it is of some concern that there has been some drop in the use of such policies overall.

Importantly, we do not suggest that current or prospective levels of market monitoring would be sufficient to protect small developing countries from banking crises, as these result in part from the greater nominal, real, and financial volatility that these economies suffer (World Bank, 2001). However, we do think that strengthening market monitoring will help both in limiting the cost of crises and in reducing the likelihood of crises that originate from within the banking sector.

2. Where Are the Preconditions in Place? Cross-Country Evidence

Evidence concerning the effectiveness of the various flavors of market discipline, though strongly suggestive of a potential role in disciplining bank insiders in various contexts, is fragmentary both in terms of country coverage and in terms of the channels of effect examined. That risky banks may pay more for their sources of funds is hardly a discovery with earth-shattering policy implications. That the promulgation of a credible official blanket deposit guarantee may weaken this link is by now almost axiomatic. Ideally we would know which particular forms of market discipline are materially effective in different institutional environments and whether the adoption of discipline-relaxing policy stances makes a material difference. The needed evidence relates both to elements of the political and policy environment, which can act as a negative, discipline relaxing, force (for example by guaranteeing depositors or substituting state ownership for private), and the market and administrative institutional requirements (including legal and regulatory requirements).

In this section we show how these environmental aspects, relevant for the effectiveness of market discipline, can vary in practice from country to country, and show that although some aspects are correlated with gross domestic product (GDP) per capita, this is not the whole story.

2.1 The Environment—Developing Countries Look Different

Contrasts between developing and advanced economies in the ownership structure of banks and other financial service providers, in the degree to which wealth and information can be concentrated among a relatively small business elite and the typical lack of scale that results in high information acquisition costs by those outside this elite group, can drastically affect the relative effectiveness of different types of market discipline—that coming from large depositors, from equity or debt holders, or from specialist information firms.

Of these points, ownership can most easily be quantified. The importance of foreign strategic ownership and of government ownership varies substantially even for countries at the same overall level of development and of financial sophistication and these overall ownership structure issues are arguably among the most decisive in determining whether or not market discipline—of whatever flavor—is likely to flourish.

Where banks are government-owned, the implicit depositor guarantee is strong, at least to the extent that the government itself is considered creditworthy.[1] Banks in developing countries that are branches or subsidiaries of banks based in advanced economies will typically be subject more to the market discipline of their home country—at least so far as group performance is concerned. Even where ownership is based in developing countries, host country market discipline will typically take a backseat to market discipline in the home country.

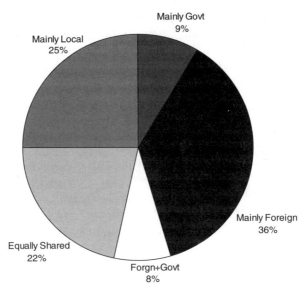

Notes: Mainly government (foreign, private) means more than 60% of total assets in this form;
Foreign+Government means these two together hold more than 70%. Equally shared is a residual category.
Source: World Bank Regulation and Supervision Survey.

Figure 28.1: Predominant Ownership of Reporting Banking System (Percent of Reporting Jurisdictions)

The extent to which many developing country banking systems are dominated by government- or foreign-controlled banks is not widely recognized. The World Bank Regulation and Supervision Survey asks for data on the market share of majority government-owned banks and of majority foreign-owned banks.[2] Analysis of the responses reveals that the median share, for developing countries, of these two categories taken together is 68.1 percent. Two in every five developing country banking systems have 85 percent or more in these two categories, and the lower quartile is over 94 percent. The remainder (31.9 percent for the median, 15 percent for two-fifths of countries, and 6 percent for the lower quartile) represents an upper bound on the share of the banking system for which it is domestic market discipline that is chiefly relevant (see figure 28.1). It has to be said that several of the jurisdictions covered in the survey with mainly foreign-owned banks are small offshore centers; nevertheless, the mean population size of countries dominated by government-owned and foreign-owned banks is larger than that of the other countries, so this is not simply a small country phenomenon. And the true figure for privately controlled banks is undoubtedly lower, when account is taken, for example, of 1) banks with minority government stakes where the public sector's total shareholding (including other public sector institutions such as social insurance funds and other state-owned financial intermediaries) exceeds 50 percent; 2) joint venture banks with government and foreign partners between them holding more than 50 percent; and 3) effective control by government or foreign banks albeit with less than 50 percent.

2.2 Preconditions—By Flavor of Discipline and Income Level

We can attempt to quantify some of the preconditions for market monitoring, using in particular data from the second (2003) wave of the World Bank's regulatory survey (of which the first wave results are discussed in Barth, Caprio, and Levine, 2001, 2003) and combining this with other sources of information. We begin with updated information on the overall "private sector monitoring" index proposed by Barth, Caprio, and Levine and summarizing the extent to which the private sector is empowered to exercise market discipline. This private sector monitoring index captures elements of the preconditions for each of the flavors of market discipline we have discussed.[3]

Unsurprisingly, we find that this index is higher, the higher the fraction of the banking system that is in local private hands (figure 28.2, panel A). In other words, those countries that have predominantly government-owned or foreign-owned banking systems have

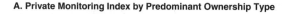

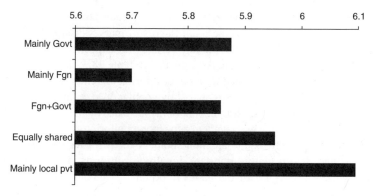

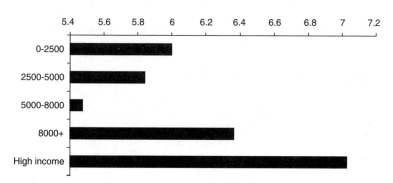

Source: World Bank Regulation and Supervision Survey; for definition of predominant type of ownership see note to figure 1.

Figure 28.2: Private Monitoring Index

lower values of this index. This can be seen as fitting, to the extent that their banks do not need *local* market discipline. On the other hand, there is no apparent correlation between the market monitoring index and per capita income (figure 28.2, panel B). Yes, the high-income economies have a higher average value than the developing countries as a group, but within the latter, the average value actually declines as one moves from the lowest income categories. Overall, then, data for the private sector monitoring index does not suggest a systematic tendency for the preconditions for market discipline to be more absent at lower income categories.

Barth, Caprio, and Levine (2003) found that the private monitoring index was negatively correlated with a variety of measures of banking risk. Here we use just one additional (inverse) measure of risk, De Nicoló's Z (De Nicoló et al., 2003). This is computed for each country as the average ratio for the largest banks of accounting capital to the standard deviation of bank earnings. The bivariate correlation between the private monitoring index and the risk measure Z is quite strong (see table 28.3, equation 1.1 below—lower values of Z imply higher risk), though as discussed below this relation is not very robust.

More speculatively, we can attempt to isolate components of the environment that are particularly relevant to each of the main flavors of market discipline. Table 28.1 proposes an allocation. For example, the key variable for depositor monitoring is absence of official depositor protection. As indicated in table 28.3, depositor discipline would also be particularly facilitated by a better information environment among the largest depositors, here crudely approximated by population size (the smaller the better). Likewise, better accounts, and accountability of bank management[4] is also assigned as likely to be particularly relevant to depositor monitoring of bank management.

Turning to discipline by equity and bond holders, the percentage of private banks that are listed will be especially important. Finally, for information specialists to be effective, it will be necessary for the banks to be rated (we count how many of the largest ten banks are rated) and for adequate auditing requirements (we measure this by asking if external audit by a certified auditor is compulsory). The mean values for these variables, as measured using data from the Regulation Survey, are shown in table 28.2.

Type of precondition:	Market and administrative institutions	Political and policy stance
Source of discipline		
Depositors	Accountability of bank management Size of country (small)	Deposit protection (low)
Equity and bond holders	Percentage of private banks listed	Government ownership share (low)
Information firms	Number of banks rated Auditing requirements	Foreign ownership share (high)

Table 28.1: Suggested Assignment of Preconditions to Different Sources of Discipline

Income level	<$2,500	$2,500-$5,000	$5,000-$8,000	>$8,000
Accountability of bank management	2.71	2.72	2.72	2.91
Small size of country	11	8	10	4
Percentage of private banks listed	0.33	0.45	0.50	0.69
Number of banks rated	0.6	3.8	2.0	4.1
Auditing requirements	0.72	0.78	0.63	0.82
No deposit protection	0.56	0.26	0.32	0.09
Government ownership share	0.09	0.29	0.25	0.13
Foreign ownership share	0.43	0.33	0.46	0.52

Note: For definition of variables employed see note to table 3.
Source: World Bank Regulation and Supervision Survey, except income level (measured in PPP, 2001) and size (population in millions): World Development Indicators.

Table 28.2: Indicators of Selected Preconditions by Income Level (Developing Countries, Mean Values)

Using data on these variables in regressions explaining allocation, we note that the key specific preconditions for depositor discipline and that provided by equity holders are again correlated with Z and with the correct sign (table 28.3, equations 1.2 and 1.3). The presence of a formal deposit insurance scheme is used for depositor discipline, and an approximate[5] share of the privately owned banking system that has a stock exchange listing for the equity holders. On the other hand, the number of rated banks is not significant (equation 1.4), in line with our expectation that the role of specialized information firms may be a weaker channel, especially for a sample that includes such a high proportion of developing countries. Of the available proxies other institutional indicators proposed in table 1, only the size variable (population) proves to be significant (table 28.3, equation 1.7) and it has the expected sign: small countries performing better.

It needs to be noted, of course, that these bivariate correlations are not very robust, and as such can be taken as suggestive only. This is not surprising, given the very indirect character of the proxies employed. In particular, gross national product (GNP) per capita is an even stronger (inverse) predictor of banking risk (table 28.3, equation 2.2), and it displaces the private sector monitoring index—though this remains close to significant at the 10 percent level when included.[6] More important, there is no evidence of an interactive term (table 28.3, equations 2.3 and 2.5): There is no indication of a systematically different private sector monitoring index is equally effective in reducing risk in rich and poor countries.

Assessing the degree to which these preconditions are satisfied in different countries, it proves *not* to be the case that the preconditions are systematically less present in poorer countries.

Take depositor discipline. As already mentioned, depositors do require basic disclosures of accounting information and for the bank managers to be accountable for the accuracy of this information. Our summary variable for bank management accountability[7] can vary from 0 to 3, though most countries score 2 or 3, and we find (table 28.2) that

(A.) Correlation of banking risk with the preconditions for different flavors of market discipline

| Equation: | 1.1 | | 1.2 | | 1.3 | | 1.4 | | 1.5 | | 1.6 | | 1.7 | |
| Dependent var. | Bank risk Z | | Bank risk Z | | Bank risk Z | | Bank risk Z | | Bank risk Z | | Bank risk Z | | Bank risk Z | |
Explanatory var.	Coeff.	t-Stat	Coeff.	t-Stat	Coeff.	t-Stat	Coeff.	t-Stat	Coeff.	t-Stat	Coeff.	t-Stat	Coeff.	t-Stat
Constant	-1.77	1.3	2.63	8.9***	1.70	3.3***	2.35	3.4***	1.04	0.6	6.02	2.5**	3.84	8.5***
Private Monitoring Index	0.712	3.4***												
No deposit insurance			1.26	2.1**										
Listed % of pvt banks					2.35	2.6**								
Number banks rated							0.115	1.2						
Bank accounts									0.680	1.1				
Auditing											-3.12	-1.3		
Population size (log)													-0.374	2.4**
R-squared / NOBS	0.125	85	0.052	85	0.082	76	0.029	48	0.015	49	0.020	48	0.066	85
Adjusted R-squared	0.114		0.040		0.070		0.008		0.003		0.008		0.054	
S.E. of regr./DW	2.27	1.95	2.36	1.81	2.38	1.72	2.57	1.23	2.42	1.83	2.40	1.81	2.34	1.64
Log likel./Method	-189.1	LS	-192.6	LS	-172.8	LS	-112.3	LS	-192.3	LS	-194.0	LS	-191.9	LS

Table 28.3: Regression Results

(B.) Interaction of index of private market discipline with per capita income and ownership structure in affecting banking risk

Equation:	2.1		2.2		2.3		2.4		2.5		2.6	
Dependent var:	Bank risk Z		Bank risk Z		Bank risk Z		Bank risk Z		Bank risk Z		Bank risk Z	
Explanatory var.	Coeff.	t-Stat	Coeff.	t-Stat	Coeff.	t-Stat	Coeff.	t-Stat	Coeff.	t-Stat	Coeff.	t-Stat
Constant	−1.77	1.3	1.64	4.2***	−0.543	0.4	1.613	4.2***	2.12	0.8	1.03	2.0*
Private Monitoring Index	0.712	3.4***			0.359	1.6			−0.058	0.1		
GNP per cap (x 100)			0.817	3.5***	0.708	3.0***			−1.154	0.7	0.652	2.4**
PvtMon x GNP p.c.							0.124	4.0***	0.281	1.2		
PvtMon x Privatebanks											0.243	2.0*
R-squared / NOBS	0.125	85	0.138	80	0.167	80	0.169	80	0.181	80	0.168	72
Adjusted R-squared	0.114		0.127		0.141		0.159		0.149		0.144	
S.E. of regr./DW	2.27	1.95	2.17	1.46	2.19	1.45	2.14	1.44	2.15	1.44	2.22	1.38
Log likel./Method	−189.1	LS	174.7	LS	−168.1	LS	−173.3	LS	−172.7	LS	−158.1	

Notes: The dependent variable bank risk is measured by De Nicoló's Z, which is the average for banks in each country of each bank's return on assets plus accounting capital all divided by the standard deviation of returns (cf. De Nicoló et al., 2003). Data kindly provided by Gianni de Nicoló. Except where mentioned, the explanatory variables are zero-one dummies based on the second (2003) wave of the World Bank's Regulation and Supervision Survey, and employing essentially the same definitions as proposed by Barth, Caprio and Levine (2001). Private Monitoring Index is the composite private monitoring index discussed in the text. "No deposit insurance" is coded "0" if there is an explicit insurance system and that depositors were wholly compensated (to the extent of legal protection) the last time a bank failed; coded "1" otherwise. "Listed % of pvt banks" is an approximation to the share of the privately owned part of the banking system consisting of banks with a stock market listing. It is a composite indicator based on data from three sources: It divides the aggregate assets of listed banks and bank holding companies (source Bankscope) by the percentage of total banking assets (source IFS), and expresses the result as a percentage of the share of non-government and non-state-owned banks in total banking assets from the Regulation Survey. "Number banks rated" is the number among the largest ten banks which is rated by an international rating agency. "Bank accounts" ranges from 0 to 3 depending on whether interest accrued but unpaid is excluded from bank earnings, whether consolidation of group accounts is required, and whether bank directors are legally liable for misleading information. "Auditing" means external audit by a certified auditor is compulsory. Private Banks is the percentage share of banking assets in banks that are not owned by government or by foreign banking groups. GNP per cap is gross national product per capita in purchasing power parity (PPP) terms, hundreds of U.S. dollars; population size is in millions; both 2001, Source: World Development Indicators. Two cross product terms with the Private Monitoring Index (PvtMon) are also employed.
***, **, and * indicate significance at the 1%, 5%, and 10% levels, respectively.

Table 28.3: Regression Results (continued)

the variation of the mean value here by countries in different income classes is relatively small, going from 2.71 in the lowest quartile of developing countries to 2.77 in high-income countries (upper middle-income countries score highest: 2.91 on this measure). Additionally however, there is the point that informal sources of depositor information are likely to be much better where the number of large depositors, whether individual or corporate, is small (cf. the Scottish analogy, above). While we do not have systematic data on the number of large depositors for many of our sample countries, it is clearly an offsetting positive factor that strengthens potential depositor discipline in the poorer countries on average. The negative prerequisite is the absence of deposit protection. Using the simple existence of an explicit deposit insurance scheme as a proxy for this, we find that fewer of the poor countries have such schemes and to that extent the negative preconditions are more often present in poor countries (table 28.2).

Turning to discipline by debt and outside equity holders, considering the availability of stock market listings to be an indicator of one precondition for this kind of discipline, we see (table 28.2) that the estimated share of total banking assets in listed entities does seem to increase as income levels go up, and indeed there is a significant positive correlation (R=0.27) between this index and per capita GNP. However, when the percentage of total assets in listed firms is expressed as a proportion of banking assets not in government or foreign bank hands, the correlation becomes insignificant (R=0.18). Once more, then, the positive preconditions are not systematically weaker in poor countries.

The role of rating agencies does appear to be greater in rich countries. The number of rated banks increases significantly with per capita income, even when normalized by the share of non-government, non-foreign bank-owned banks in the system.

Thus, when the data, fragmentary though it is, is interpreted through this prism, we can find surprisingly little evidence of systematic difference in the extent to which most positive and negative prerequisites for market discipline are present as between poor and rich, large and small countries. To be sure, systemic crises caused by macroeconomic, exchange rate, or fiscal instability tend to swamp the discriminating function of the market as between banks that are soundly run and the rest, and these events are more prevalent in poor and small economies.

Against this background, it is interesting to examine whether the prerequisites for market discipline that are under government control have been strengthened in recent years. Table 28.4 compares indicators of bank regulation and supervision from the first World Bank survey, with most observations from 1998 or 1999, and the second survey, which was taken in early 2003. Focusing on the original 107 countries responding in the first survey, this table shows the responses grouped by countries at different income levels.

The changes that stand out the most are for the low-income countries, where there has been a significant increase in the stringency of capital regulations and the overall index of capital regulation, a slight decline in official supervisory powers, but a substantial jump in prompt corrective action powers.[8] Interestingly, low-income country supervisors' discretion to forbear actually increased somewhat—in other words, they have the ability to take prompt corrective action powers, but are not as constrained as they were previously. The one supervisory variable that was found by

Means		High income	Upper middle	Lower middle	Low income
Overall capital stringency	*Survey I*	**3.92**	3.29	**3.12**	3.11
	Survey II	3.79	**3.45**	3.09	**4.40**
Capital regulation index	*Survey I*	**5.61**	5.05	4.42	4.47
	Survey II	5.45	**5.23**	**4.70**	**5.60**
Official supervisory power	*Survey I*	**10.79**	**11.33**	**11.19**	**11.37**
	Survey II	10.39	10.36	10.48	10.90
Prompt corrective action	*Survey I*	1.49	2.71	1.85	2.47
	Survey II	**1.63**	**3.00**	**2.39**	**4.10**
Supervisory forbearance	*Survey I*	**1.87**	1.29	**1.38**	**1.72**
discretion	*Survey II*	1.75	**1.55**	1.17	1.40
Liquidity / Diversification	*Survey I*	**1.92**	**2.10**	**2.00**	**1.68**
Index	*Survey II*	1.55	1.55	1.13	1.20
Private Monitoring Index	*Survey I*	**7.08**	**7.10**	**6.73**	**5.47**
	Survey II	6.87	6.36	6.04	5.40

Notes: In each case, the higher value as between the two surveys is shown in **bold**. Countries are classified by income level into high, upper-middle, lower-middle, and low income using standard World Development Indicators classifications, 2003.
Source: World Bank Regulation and Supervision Survey.

**Table 28.4: Trends in Bank Regulation and Supervision
Surveys Carried Out in 1998–99 (Survey I) and 2003 (Survey II)**

Borio, Caprio, and Levine to have some positive impact on the development of the financial sector and on limiting the occurrence of banking crises, namely requirements that banks diversify their risks, actually decreased in all the countries, including in the low-income countries, where small economic size and insufficient diversification could be a critical issue. Thus it would appear all the more important for authorities to try to strengthen market discipline. Unfortunately, according to the survey, the private monitoring index has decreased somewhat. Part of this decline reflects some spreading of deposit insurance (the absence of which raises this index).

Beyond the information that is available, it follows that markets need the incentive to act. Depositors' incentives to monitor the health of the banks in which they put their money is reduced to the extent that they are credibly insured, and the greater is this insurance. Perhaps the best illustration of this was the study by Demirgüç-Kunt and Huizinga (2004), which found that in countries with explicit deposit insurance, banks that were expanding their lending portfolio rapidly did not pay much of the increased cost for their funds, whereas in countries without explicit deposit insurance, the cost of funds rose smartly as banks attempted to expand. Moreover, most developing countries that offer deposit insurance appear to underprice it substantially (Laeven, 2002), and a number have exceptionally generous deposit insurance ceilings, with some even offering blanket deposit insurance for all deposits. Scaling back deposit insurance coverage, thereby increasing the share of deposits that are not insured, should increase monitoring by those uninsured, while still protecting small depositors, who in most cases possess little comparative advantage in monitoring banks. Thus deposit insurance ceilings of about one to two times per capita GDP—about the norm in higher income countries—likely have little cost in reducing the effective degree of market monitoring that is conducted.

3. Conclusions

Market discipline on banks can help alert regulators to risky or self-serving behavior by bank insiders; it can also act directly on insider incentives. But market discipline is unlikely to emerge in the absence of relevant market and information infrastructures, and where explicit or implicit government guarantees stifle the incentive for depositors, debt and outside equity holders, or information specialists to exercise such discipline.

The widespread belief that market discipline on managers and controlling shareholders of privately owned banks cannot be effective in less developed financial environments was questioned. For one thing, many of the privately owned banks in the developing world are foreign-owned. As such, the foreign private sector in the home countries—typically more developed—of these banks, will also be exercising discipline. Besides, the quality and relevance of information available to large depositors on the probity and skills of local bank management is arguably higher in less sophisticated settings—and relatively higher than that available to official regulators. In general, we find more reason to think that market discipline works certainly better in lower income countries than pre-existing beliefs generally held. Countries should build on any success in this area by limiting the role of explicit deposit guarantees, reducing state ownership of banks where it is prevalent, and by not putting all their eggs in the supervisory basket. Greater disclosure, for example, of how risk taking is rewarded and how rating agencies earn their fees would support the development of better market monitoring. More broadly, it seems that greater emphasis on the third pillar in the Basel II Accord than on the refinements of the risk-weighting system of the first pillar may be warranted for most developing countries.

*Gerard Caprio is director of the financial policy and strategy group in the Financial Sector Operations Vice Presidency and Patrick Honohan is a senior advisor of the Financial Sector Operations and Policy Department at the World Bank. The findings, interpretations, and conclusions expressed in this paper are entirely those of the authors. They do not necessarily represent the views of the World Bank, its executive directors, or the countries they represent. This paper draws on data from a wider effort to assess bank regulatory issues; the cooperation of Jim Barth, Maria Carkovic, Cindy Lee, Ross Levine, Ying Lin, and Guillermo Noguera, and the helpful comments of our discussant, Charles Freedman and other participants at the Chicago conference are acknowledged.

Notes

1. This will differ depending on the currency denomination of deposits.

2. Unless otherwise noted, data on banking, market and regulatory conditions in this and the following section is based on preliminary results from the second (2003) wave of the World Bank's Regulation and Supervision Survey in which data for 133 jurisdictions has now been collected.

3. The methodology for computing the summary index of private monitoring is as described in Barth, Caprio, and Levine, 2001. As such it covers bank accounting rules, auditing and disclosure requirements, rating of banks, deposit insurance, and subordinated debt.

4. Here measured by an index whose value is higher depending on whether interest accrued but unpaid is excluded from bank earnings, whether consolidation of group accounts is required, and whether bank directors are legally liable for misleading information.

5. Because of issues of aggregation and double counting, this measure is a fairly rough approximation. See note to table 4 for its construction.

6. Several authors (La Porta et al., 1999, and Barth, Caprio, and Levine, 2001) have previously noted the difficulties presented by including GNP per capita, potentially an endogenous variable, in regressions along with determinants of banking risk. Clearly there is a risk that the independent role of such determinants as the private monitoring index could be masked by such inclusion.

7. This again follows the definition of Barth, Caprio, and Levine and includes treatment of interest accrued but not received, existence of consolidated accounting for groups and legal liability of directors.

8. Official supervisory powers, as disaggregated by Barth, Caprio, and Levine (2001) cover a broad array of powers, some related to the ability to implement prompt corrective action, others at supervisors' ability to force restructuring and reorganization, or to declare insolvency.

References

Barth, James R., Gerard Caprio, Jr., and Ross Levine, 2003, "Bank regulation and supervision: What works best?," *Journal of Financial Intermediation.*

_____, 2001, "The regulation and supervision of bank around the world: A new database," in *Integrating Emerging Market Countries into the Global Financial System*, Robert E. Litan and Richard Herring (eds.), *Brookings-Wharton Papers on Financial Services*, Washington: Brookings Institution Press, pp.183–240.

Beck, Thorsten, Aslı Demirgüç-Kunt, and Ross Levine, 2003, "Law, endowments, and finance," *Journal of Financial Economics.*

Demirgüç-Kunt, Aslı, and Harry Huizinga, 2004, "Market discipline and deposit insurance," *Journal of Monetary Economics*, forthcoming.

De Nicoló, Gianni, Philip Bartholomew, Jahanara Zaman, and Mary Zephirin, 2003, "Bank consolidation, internationalization, and conglomeration: Trends and implications for financial risk," International Monetary Fund, working paper, No. 03/158, July.

Hellman, Thomas, Kevin Murdock, and Joseph Stiglitz, 2000, "Liberalization, moral hazard in banking, and prudential regulation: Are capital requirements enough?," *American Economic Review*, Vol. 90, March, pp.147–165.

Kroszner, Randall, 1997, "Free banking: The Scottish experience as a model for emerging economies" in *Reforming Financial Systems: Historical Implications for Policy*, Gerard Caprio, Jr., and Dimitri Vittas (eds.), New York: Cambridge University Press.

Laeven, Luc, 2002, "Pricing of deposit insurance," World Bank, policy research working paper, No. 2871.

Lamoreaux, Naomi, 1994, *Insider Lending: Banks, Personal Connections, and Economic Development in Industrial New England*, New York: Cambridge University Press.

La Porta, Rafael, Florencio Lopez-de-Silanes, Andrei Shleifer, and Robert W. Vishny, 1999, "The quality of government," *Journal of Law, Economics, and Organization*, Vol. 15, No. 1, pp. 222–279.

World Bank, 2001, *Finance for Growth: Policy Choices in a Volatile World*, New York: Oxford University Press.

Chapter 29

How Can the Invisible Hand Strengthen Prudential Supervision? and How Can Prudential Supervision Strengthen the Invisible Hand?

Richard J. Herring*
University of Pennsylvania, The Wharton School

1. Introduction

The Basel Committee has placed market discipline in a symmetrical position, alongside minimum capital standards and the supervisory review process, as one of three complementary pillars in the proposed new capital adequacy framework (Basel II). The reality of the proposal, however, falls short of this rhetorical symmetry. The space allocated to market discipline in the most recent restatement of the proposal (Bank for International Settlements, 2003) is less than a tenth of the overall proposal. Moreover, the attention to market discipline is, at best, incomplete. The proposal focuses exclusively on disclosure, which is arguably a necessary, but surely not a sufficient condition for effective market discipline. Nonetheless, a properly formulated market discipline policy, strengthened by an appropriate supervisory review process, holds the promise of greatly enhancing the safety and soundness of the financial system without imposing the heavy compliance costs inherent in the complex capital charges laid out under pillar 1.

In this paper, I will examine the case for market discipline in principle and consider concerns raised about the operation of market discipline in practice. Then I will consider the pillar 3 proposal to improve disclosure and conclude with a consideration of how enhanced market discipline could achieve the Basel Committee's (Bank for International Settlements, 2001, p.1) stated objective of "strong incentives on banks to conduct their business in a safe, sound, and efficient manner including an incentive to maintain a strong capital base as a cushion against potential future losses arising from risk exposures."

2. The Case for Market Discipline versus Official Discipline

Although I will later argue that market discipline and official regulation and supervision can and should be complementary policies, I will first consider the case in which they are alternative ways of achieving financial stability. In order to make the best possible case for market discipline I will make several very strong (and demonstrably dubious) assumptions. These will be relaxed in the following section when we consider the operation of market discipline in practice.

First, assume banks have transparent risk and capital positions so that it is easy for market participants to evaluate the adequacy of capital relative to risk exposures for each bank. Second, assume that market participants have the incentive to process this information because they believe they will suffer loss in the event that a bank should default. Third, assume that market participants are able to process this information to achieve unbiased estimates of each bank's probability of default and employ these estimates to price claims or adjust quantities to reflect each bank's probability of default.[1] Fourth, assume that banks respond to an increase in the price and/or a reduction in the availability of funds by reducing exposures to risk or increasing capital.[2] Under such circumstances banks will be deterred from taking imprudent actions by market discipline exerted through an increase in the price or reduction in the quantity of funds. Indeed, the anticipation of an adverse market response may often be sufficient to deter imprudent behavior.

In principle, any claimant on the bank who satisfies the first three assumptions may exercise effective market discipline. This might include depositors, bondholders and shareholders as well as counterparties of the bank in the over the counter (OTC) and other interbank markets. Kwast et al. (1999) describe these price and quantity sanctions on the bank as "direct influence." The disciplinary influence of these transactions, however, may extend beyond the pricing of a particular transaction with the bank.

Even though they do not conduct direct transactions with the bank, other market participants also exercise influence over the bank and may rely to some extent on observations of market prices or quantity sanctions in evaluating the bank. For example, the financial press, securities analysts, ratings agencies, and the supervisory authorities may all make use of the prices in primary or secondary markets to assess the prospects of a bank. Kwast et al. (1999) describe this as "indirect influence" because it is exercised by an entity that was not party to the original transaction. Indirect influence may be even more powerful than direct influence. For example, a fall in share prices on the secondary market will affect managers to the extent that their compensation is tied to share prices and may even lead to a hostile takeover bid.[3] And, the supervisory authorities could initiate prompt corrective action measures in response to market signals.

Of course, mechanisms of market discipline can extend beyond price and quantity sanctions that are the usual object of analysis. For example, bondholders may negotiate covenants designed to constrain the bank's leverage, ownership structures, dividend policy, or asset substitution possibilities and counterparties may demand additional collateral. Similarly, shareholders, through their ability to elect the board of directors, have a voice in corporate governance and, *in extremis*, may choose to wrest corporate control from the incumbent management team.

Much of the power of market discipline derives from the ability of the price system to aggregate information from a diversity of sources and price transactions at which funds are allocated and risks are exchanged.[4] But an efficient price system presumes a considerable amount of financial infrastructure that should not be taken for granted. For example, it requires reliable accounting practices that reflect the true state of a bank's balance sheet and risk exposures and timely disclosure of this information to market participants. In addition, it requires a legal framework and judicial system that will enforce financial contracts with reasonable predictability and without undue delay.

This ideal system of market discipline has many attractive features relative to the kind of official oversight that most countries have devised. Market discipline is forward-looking and inherently flexible and adaptive. Market surveillance is continuous, impersonal, and non-bureaucratic. Motivated by the objective of maximizing risk-adjusted profits, market participants have strong incentives to draw information from whatever sources they find relevant and process the information using whatever model seems appropriate to price risk-taking properly and to withdraw funding promptly when a bank's risk profile seems excessive relative to its ability to bear loss.

In contrast, official oversight is usually rule-based, episodic, bureaucratic, and slow to change. This is particularly troublesome in a rapidly evolving financial environment characterized by financial innovations. As Evanoff and Wall (2001) observe, supervisors can acquire access to proprietary data, but they are more constrained by law, regulation, and data availability to keep models constant for long periods. Official discipline tends to be more intrusive and burdensome. Official sanctions are difficult to fine-tune to small variations in risk-taking, giving rise to significant compliance costs for regulated firms and potentially important distortions in the allocation of financial capital and real resources.

Moreover, efforts to shift from traditional, rule-based regulation and supervision to more flexible, market-mimicking regulation may impose even greater compliance costs. One aim of the pillar 1 capital charges is to make capital adequacy regulation more sensitive to market judgments about risk as embodied in external and internal ratings of default risk. Leaving aside the important questions of whether the officials have gotten the absolute and relative risk weights right (Altman and Saunders, 2001), the enormous complexity of the pillar 1 capital charges raises a serious question about whether efforts to make regulation and regulatory sanctions more risk sensitive justifies the additional compliance costs.

Regulators and supervisors have an objective function that differs from that of most market participants. The precise nature of that objective function is subject to dispute although it certainly is more complicated than the maximization of risk-adjusted profits. From a public interest perspective, officials are assumed to take a systemic view of banking problems and act to minimize spillover costs to the rest of the economy. Regulation and supervision are intended to cause banks to change their preferred behavior to minimize the externalities of banking panics. From the perspective of public choice theory, however, several less public-spirited motives may influence regulatory behavior even though official actions may be cloaked in the rhetoric of the public interest. Public choice theory views regulation as the outcome of efforts of interest groups, politicians, and bureaucrats to use the political process for their own personal benefit by taking advantage of the significant agency problems between the taxpayer principals and regulator agents (Kane, 2001 and 2002).

In order to guard against the arbitrary use of regulatory and supervisory power, most countries subject disciplinary decisions by officials to some sort of judicial or administrative review. This places a burden on official oversight that does not encumber market discipline. In order to discipline a bank, a supervisor must not only know that a bank is taking excessive risk, but also the supervisor must be able to prove it to the satisfaction of the reviewing body—perhaps beyond a reasonable doubt. This leads to a natural tendency to delay disciplinary measures until much of the damage from excessive risk-taking has already been done and impedes the deployment of regulatory sanctions that are finely calibrated to small changes in risk-taking. It also leads officials to react mainly to what has already happened (and is, therefore, objectively verifiable) rather than acting on the basis of expectations about what may happen (which are inherently subjective and disputable).

One of the principal merits of market discipline is that bank directors and managers are faced with the burden of proving to the market that the bank *is not* taking excessive risks rather than subjecting officials to the burden of proving, in a review process, that the bank *is* taking excessive risks. This surely places the burden where it belongs and facilitates better corporate governance by making clear that the directors and managers of a bank are responsible for its risk exposures and ability to bear loss, not the regulatory and supervisory authorities.

In summary, ideal market discipline can ensure that bank directors and managers take full account of the bank's risk exposures in operating the bank. Impersonal market forces, unencumbered by the bureaucratic processes that characterize the supervisory and regulatory process, should be able to monitor the insolvency risk of banks more efficiently and discipline banks that take excessive risks more promptly than the official sector. Moreover, the substitution of market discipline for official discipline would eliminate compliance costs, which are often heavy, and would facilitate a more efficient allocation of resources.

3. Concerns about Market Discipline in Practice

It is convenient to organize the concerns about the way market discipline works in practice with regard to the four conditions for ideal market discipline because most concerns can be related to doubts about whether one or more of the conditions for ideal market discipline are met.

3.1 Lack of Transparency

Concerns about the transparency of bank operations and risk positions find support in the fundamental theory about the role of banks. As providers of finance to borrowers who cannot gain access to the securities markets, banks specialize in holding illiquid, imperfectly marketable claims that are very difficult for outsiders to value. In addition, the increasing importance of trading and especially the development of the OTC derivatives business, has raised concerns that even if one could obtain a true snapshot of a bank's condition, it could change drastically within hours. Morgan (2000) has shown that these theoretical concerns about the transparency of bank risk-taking have empirical validity. His study of bond ratings has shown that the ratings agencies disagree more about ratings for banks (and insurance companies) than for any other kind of firm.

Disclosure is incomplete as evidenced by the fact that in nearly every country, regulators and supervisors require the disclosure of considerable information of presumed relevance to the current and future condition of the bank that is not shared with the market. Moreover, the data available to the market is backward-looking and released only with a lag—even though some of the most sophisticated institutions are, in effect, marking themselves to market every day for internal management purposes.

Accounting conventions often seem to conceal as much as they reveal about the current and future condition of the bank. In many countries bank accounting is a peculiar mix of accrual, historical cost, and mark-to-market accounting that can facilitate income smoothing and, indeed, the concealment of deteriorating credit quality through evergreening.[5] Moreover, the distinction between the banking book and trading book, based not on the objectively verifiable nature of the financial instrument, but upon the unobservable intent of bank management, invites "gains trading" or the selective realization of capital gains and deferral of the recognition of capital losses.[6]

One way to address these concerns is through mandatory disclosure of information concerning a bank's current condition and prospects. This is the approach taken by the Basel Committee that will be discussed below. Of course, mandatory disclosure requirements are likely to be a second-best approach since they are an attempt by officials to anticipate what the market should want to know about an institution, moderated by a sense of what is politically acceptable to banks. Disclosure requirements tend to be rigid, slow to adapt to market changes and may produce considerable, irrelevant information and, therefore, impose unnecessary compliance costs on banks.

Disclosures demanded by the market, on the other hand, are likely to be more efficient and more relevant since they will address precisely the information market participants believe they need to evaluate the bank. And so, it is useful to ask why market demand does not elicit sufficient information. One possibility is that market participants feel protected by the safety net in varying degrees and thus do not press their demands for adequate information. Similarly, under these conditions, banks would not perceive any clear advantage in providing such information because it would have little, if any, impact on their operating costs. This leads to the next concern about market discipline in practice—that market participants may lack a compelling motive to discipline banks.

3.2 Inadequate Incentives to Discipline Banks

For market discipline to be an effective force for controlling a bank's risk of insolvency, at least some market participants must have an incentive to demand information and monitor and evaluate that bank's probability of default. Fear of loss is perhaps the most powerful means of motivating market participants to price claims on the bank to compensate for the expected probability of default. In principle, fear of loss is relevant for all holders of claims on a bank, but in practice the incentive has often been dulled for most creditors of large, internationally active banks by policies of official support aimed at safeguarding financial stability.

Explicit deposit insurance relieves insured depositors of the fear of loss.[7] More-over, the enhanced prudential supervision required to protect the deposit insurer may convey the impression that official oversight has been substituted for market oversight. Indeed, on-site bank examination and the practice of sharing confidential information concerning the soundness of the bank with official supervisors creates an impression that official supervision is the first-line of defense against imprudent risk-taking and implies a quasi-official certification of the soundness of a bank. This may add to politi-cal pressures to provide broader assistance that extends beyond explicit deposit insur-ance in the event an institution experiences financial distress. In many countries officials have often provided what amounts to implicit insurance for most or all creditors through forbearance of prudential rules, liberal discount window lending, guarantees, official capital infusions, or the arrangement of assisted mergers in which an acquiring institu-tion purchases some of the assets and assumes all of the liabilities of a faltering institu-tion. Direct official support for holders of equity claims is rare (but not unknown).

To the extent that claimants on the bank expect to be protected by an official safety net in the event that the bank falters, the potentially strong connection between a bank's portfolio risk and leverage choices and funding costs is weakened. The pow-erful motivation for market discipline provided by the fear of loss is undermined. The ratings agency has attempted to assess the likelihood that individual banks would receive official support should this become necessary. As the analysts at Fitch ob-serve (Andrews, Moss, and Marshall, 2002, p. 1) "… whether or not banks default on their financial commitments is often a function not only of their intrinsic creditwor-thiness but also of the readiness and capacity of some outside agency, usually the state, either to support them by some form or subsidy, perhaps based on a guarantee, and/or to rescue them it they get into trouble." Hoggarth, Jackson, and Nier (2003) have examined the correlation between the Fitch Support Ratings and the average capital ratio (the leverage component of overall risk) and found a strong negative correlation, which is consistent with the hypothesis that a greater likelihood of offi-cial support reduces the force of market discipline on bank risk-taking.

In order to restore an incentive for market discipline, it is essential that at least some uninsured counterparties of the bank perceive a risk of loss. Given the time inconsistency issue referred to above, officials face a challenge in making a credible commitment not to bail out large institutions that may be considered systemically important. The U.S. attempted to achieve this with the Federal Deposit Insurance Corporation Improvement Act reforms in 1991. In particular, Congress instituted a system of prompt corrective action to enforce capital requirements and remove the option of forbearance. In addition, the Federal Deposit Insurance Corporation (FDIC) is mandated to choose the method of resolution that is least costly to the deposit insurance fund of all possible methods for meeting the FDIC's obligation to protect insured depositors subject to a systemic risk exception. This will normally forestall bailouts of uninsured creditors.

Flannery and Rangan (2002) provide evidence that this change in policy in the United States may have succeeded in strengthening market discipline on U.S. bank holding companies. They attribute the substantial buildup in capital at large U.S. banks, well above regulatory minimums, to enhanced incentives to monitor and price default risk. The new Fitch Support Ratings for U.S. banks are consistent with this hypothesis as well. The analysts at Fitch have assigned even the largest U.S. banks the lowest support rating indicating, "support from an outside source is possible, but cannot be relied upon."

3.3 Biased Prices and Destabilizing Flows

Assuming that market participants have sufficient incentives to discipline banks, some observers have raised concerns about the quality of market discipline in practice. In the face of growing evidence that market prices reflect actual or prospective bank risk to some extent,[8] attention has shifted to potential errors in such prices. Some of these concerns involve whether default risk is factored into market prices appropriately. Other concerns involve the disruptive nature of quantity sanctions that are often deployed instead of price sanctions.

Three kinds of questions center around market prices: 1) Do market prices reflect default risk correctly? 2) Do they respond to changes in risk-taking ex ante? 3) Do they undermine the stability of the banking system?

The first concern about market prices is that even if they accurately reflect the probability that a bank will default, they will reflect only the anticipated, private costs of default, not the social costs. Market participants lack incentives to take a systemic view of the probability that a bank may default and therefore may be willing to accept a higher probability of default than is socially optimal. While this concern is part of the fundamental rationale for prudential supervision, its contemporary relevance is open to doubt. Currently most major U.S. banks maintain capital ratios that are well above regulatory minimums, indeed, even above the standards necessary to earn a regulatory designation of "well capitalized." Thus it appears that the market demands a higher degree of safety than the regulators.

Option pricing theory (Merton, 1974) implies that both bond and equity prices incorporate market expectations of the probability of default. Indeed, in a frictionless world, with complete markets, theses probabilities would be identical. But comparisons of implicit default probabilities extracted from bond prices and equity prices are far from perfectly correlated (Bliss and Flannery, 2002). Hancock and Kwast (2001) have shown that inferences about the probability of default based on debt instruments issued by a particular bank may differ from instrument to instrument or across different data series for the same instrument.

Extraction of default probabilities from equity prices requires several very strong assumptions that may not always hold. On the surface, it appears much more straightforward to extract default probabilities from debt instruments. Unfortunately, several factors in addition to the probability of default affect yields and spreads in bond markets. Elton et al. (2001) have examined spreads in rates between (nonfinancial) corporate and government bonds across rating classes and attempted to identify the portion that can be accounted for by expected default loss, the tax premium (which arises because corporate bonds are subject to state and local taxes while U.S. Treasury obligations are not), and a risk premium to compensate investors for the higher systematic risk associated with corporate debt. While default risk is significant, it accounts for a smaller proportion of the spread than the tax premium and risk premium.

Similarly, Collin-Dufresne, Goldstein, and Martin (2001) attempted to explain *changes* in spreads based on proxies for credit risk and liquidity. They find default risk explains only about one quarter of the variations in the changes in spreads. While liquidity factors explain a bit more of the remaining variation, most of it is explained by a component that is unrelated to firm-specific or macroeconomic factors.

Like regulatory models to identify problem banks (Evanoff and Wall, 2001), market price signals (and the techniques used to extract default probabilities from them) are subject to both type I errors (prices incorporate a default premium that is too high relative to the true probability of default) and type II errors (prices incorporate a default premium that is too low relative to the true probability of default). Type I errors can impose unwarranted costs on banks and lead to misguided regulatory actions. Type II errors can also lead to a misallocation of financial and real capital. Flannery (2001) has observed that optimal supervisory policy will minimize the social costs of anticipated type I and type II errors. Unfortunately, we are a long way from being able to specify the social costs or the respective sizes of the two kinds of errors with any precision.

3.4 Responses to Changes in Ex Ante Risk-Taking

We argued above that ideal market discipline responds to increases in risk *ex ante*, before the dangers of excessive risk-taking have been realized, and rewards banks promptly for reductions in risk. In practice, however, the market response to increased risk is too often *ex post*, after losses have occurred, rather than *ex ante*, when riskier positions are taken. (This may be a consequence of the first concern, inadequate *ex ante* disclosure of risk exposures. But it may sometimes be the reaction to an unanticipated risk.)

Similarly, once established, risk premiums tend to be sticky. When default premiums ratchet up, it takes a very long time for them to return to normal levels even though a bank may take dramatic corrective action. This is observable in interbank markets with regard to the phenomenon of tiering.[9] When concerns arise regarding the creditworthiness of a particular bank or group of banks, these banks will be obliged to pay a higher spread over the base rate. Typically, banks will remain in that tier above the benchmark rate for a very long time. While sticky, *ex post* sanctions are less efficient in disciplining bank risk-taking than *ex ante* sanctions that can influence bank decisions before losses are incurred, they are not without value. The anticipation of sticky, *ex post* sanctions by banks may also be a powerful deterrent to imprudent risk taking *ex ante*.

3.5 Destabilizing Flows

The main traditional concern about market discipline was recently articulated by Arnold Schilder (2002, p. 4), chairman of the Accounting Task Force of the Basel Committee on Banking Supervision: "Once the risks start to materialize, and the market is aware that the bank's position is weakened, it may react excessively. Banks may then be subjected to high interest rates or ultimately be excluded from the market, possibly even regardless of their performance. This could spread to other banks and jeopardize the stability of the banking system." The concern is less that market discipline won't work, than that it will work too disruptively, with potentially heavy spillover costs for the banking system.

Some observers find support for this view in the history of banking in the United States in the nineteenth century. During the nineteenth century, banks in the U.S. and many other countries were disciplined mainly by the market, with government oversight limited basically to the chartering function. In some respects the system functioned well. Brokers and other arbitrageurs established discounts on the notes of individual banks that broadly reflected default probabilities. Banks, in turn, competed in building reputation and capital strength. Indeed, banks advertised and maintained very high capital ratios. But the system was also plagued by periodic banking panics and bank failures that amplified shocks to the real economy. Whether these panics were a consequence of the inherent defects of the regime of market discipline or a reflection of the inflexibility of the supply of currency is debatable. But the subsequent erection of the various components of the safety net is based on the premise that market discipline was at least partly to blame.

These concerns apply less to market discipline through price sanctions than to market discipline through quantity sanctions. The fundamental problem is that banks find it costly to reduce the scale of their balance sheets rapidly and so a herd-like withdrawal of funding in response to bad news may cause such substantial losses that even a well-capitalized institution may be forced to default. Short-term financial claims give the holder the opportunity to run in the event that concerns arise regarding a bank's solvency. And once a run begins, all others who can redeem their claims at face value have an incentive to do so. Thus quantity sanctions tend to be like a binary switch that is turned either off or on. This is market discipline at work, but it is discipline so harsh that it is likely to be lethal rather than instructive.[10]

In contrast, price discipline tends to be less disruptive and more like a rheostat. If a bank is forced to pay a higher price for its funds, its profits will suffer, but it should have time to make appropriate adjustments in its leverage and scale of operation or risk exposures without incurring a fire-sale loss on forced liquidation of its assets. Price sanctions are administered mainly through long-term claims.

These considerations suggest that market discipline is less likely to be destabilizing if it is channeled through holders of long-term claims on the bank—either equity or long-term, subordinated debt—who cannot impose quantity sanctions. As noted earlier, there are theoretical reasons to believe that the prices of both equity and debt contain information about the market expectations regarding the probability of default. Although the interpretation of either becomes difficult when a bank is very near the point of default because the value of the put option implicit in the price of equity rises sharply so that the value of equity may increase with an increase in the volatility of the bank's assets and deep discount, low quality bonds tend to be priced more like equity. Nonetheless, either equity prices or subordinated debt should yield useful information until the point at which default is perceived to be imminent.

Most attention[11] has been focused on subordinated debt as a preferred channel of market discipline, but the liquidity of equity markets is generally substantially more robust than that of secondary debt markets and so equity prices may be more informative. Both may provide useful information. Mandatory, periodic issues of subordinated debt could provide a powerful source of direct discipline, while equity prices may be a more reliable source of information for indirect discipline.[12]

3.6 Market Discipline May Not Influence Bank Behavior

The preceding section has considered circumstances in which market discipline may be destabilizing. In this section we consider the opposite extreme, the circumstances when it may be ineffectual. Berger (1991) raised this issue when he noted that it was important not only to assess whether the prices of liabilities reflected risk perceptions, but also whether such price changes influenced bank behavior.

This problem is most likely to arise when a bank feels securely protected by the safety net, but the market perceives that some categories of claims may be subject to loss. If the bank has easy access to insured deposits, then any increase in default premiums demanded on uninsured liabilities (or equity) may simply lead to a substitution of insured deposits rather than a reduction in portfolio risk or leverage.

The concern is also raised with regard to direct market discipline if new issues of securities are a relatively small component of the cost of funds. Under such circumstances, even if market prices fully reflect expected probabilities of default, they may have so little impact on the bank's average cost of funds that the disciplinary impact is negligible. The concept of indirect market discipline, however, opens the range of possibilities for increases in the default premium to influence bank behavior even if the bank makes no new issues of securities at the less favorable price. As noted above, equity prices may have a direct impact on bank management even if the bank issues no new shares. Similarly, to the extent that the financial press, security analysts, ratings agencies, and the supervisory authorities monitor secondary market prices to assess the current condition and prospects for a bank, indirect market discipline may be quite powerful. Indeed, if the supervisory authorities wish to increase the influence of market discipline they can do so quite readily by linking supervisory and regulatory sanctions to secondary debt or equity prices.

More broadly, most of the concerns about the operation of market discipline in practice can be dealt with by suitable changes in regulation or supervision. If market participants lack sufficient information to price default risk, then disclosure can be improved. If market participants lack incentive to price default risk because they expect to be protected by the safety net, then the supervisory authorities need to develop ways to deal with systemic risk without protecting some categories of market participants, particularly holders of subordinated debt and equity. If quantity sanctions by market participants are thought to be too destabilizing, then market discipline can be channeled through holders of long-term claims who cannot engage in herd-like behavior. The Basel Committee's efforts to enhance market discipline, however, focus exclusively on improving disclosure, and so we will turn to disclosure policy in the next section.

3.7 Pillar 3

Pillar 3 would require the disclosure of substantially more information than banks currently disclose. Specific required disclosures include the scope of capital requirements across the holding company, the terms and conditions of all capital instruments, and exposures to credit, market, operational, and interest rate risk. Banks that qualify for the internal ratings based procedures determining capital charges under pillar 1 will be required to disclose inputs into their credit rating models. Qualitative disclosures are to be made annually, capital disclosures, semi-annually, and capital adequacy disclosures, quarterly. In addition, banks are to make quarterly disclosures of any information subject to rapid change.

Enforcement of disclosure requirements would depend primarily on "moral guidance" or "dialogues" with bank management with the possibility of official sanctions. But additional capital would not be imposed when disclosures are inadequate (although to the extent that additional disclosure is a prerequisite for use of the investment review board approach there is an implicit capital benefit for improved disclosure). Moreover, if a bank believes that a mandatory disclosure would reveal proprietary data, it may omit the disclosure and include a statement about why it is omitted. This could lead to substantial variation in disclosures. No audit of pillar 3 disclosures is required unless otherwise subject to legal requirements and so the quality of disclosures may also be subject to substantial variations.

Unfortunately, considerable risk-relevant data has been omitted from required disclosures. These include foreign/domestic currency breakdowns of assets and liabilities and exposures to sovereign borrowers, publicly controlled corporations, and commercial real estate, all of which have a played a central role in banking crises in the recent past. And comparability of data remains constrained by national differences in accounting, provisioning, and statistical standards.[13]

In one key respect, Basel II represents a retreat from a level of transparency achieved by the original Accord. One of the principal achievements of the original Accord was a straightforward (if deeply flawed) way of comparing the capital adequacy of internationally active banks. Many banks chose to report their tier 1 capital ratios, although it was not required. Even though these ratios are based on accounting conventions and supervisory standards that vary across countries, they did provide a crude measure of capital adequacy. Despite the expanded disclosures regarding capital instruments and ratios, that will no longer be true. Banks are provided with so many options under the pillar 1 capital charges, including the use of internal models, and are potentially subject to additional, but not necessarily disclosed, capital charges under pillar 2, in addition to many other details subject to national discretion, that it is no longer possible to compare capital adequacy across institutions in a straightforward manner. Thus, although the Basel Committee may have made progress in terms of the range and quantity of data disclosed, the comparability of data remains a concern.

4. Concluding Comment on the Relative Advantages of Enhanced Market Discipline

In order to enhance market discipline, the Basel Committee should not only improve disclosure standards but also strengthen the motives for a least some claimants to exercise discipline over banks and amplify the impact of market discipline by linking it to supervisory actions. This enhanced market discipline would in turn strengthen prudential regulation and supervision.

Additional disclosure will have little impact unless at least some market participants have an incentive to collect, analyze, and monitor the new data. For several banks, including some of the largest, most internationally active banks, there is reason to doubt that the strength of the motive for market participants to exercise discipline over debt instruments. For example, Fitch (July 2003) rates over 400 internationally active banks as having an "extremely high" or "high probability of external support"—roughly equal to the number for which external support, "although possible, cannot be relied upon." This is a problem that can and should be fixed. Indeed, if pillar 2 had been tightened to include a genuine prompt corrective action component, substantial progress would have been made.

What is needed, ultimately, are better resolution tools so that even a very large institution can be resolved with minimal systemic spillovers. It should be possible in the event of insolvency to eliminate the claims of shareholders, replace managers, and imposes losses on at least some uninsured creditors, without disrupting the essential operations of the bank. The bridge bank model in the United States holds promise as a way of accomplishing these objectives while providing sufficient time for the supervisory authorities to make an optimal disposition of the bank, either through piecemeal liquidation or merger. Unfortunately, market discipline is likely to be less effective than it should be until creditors are persuaded that a credible resolution process is in place for every major, internationally active bank.

Concerns about the disruptive nature of quantity sanctions are a plausible reason to focus market discipline on holders of long-term claims and in this regard subordinated debt and equity may both play a useful role. The concern that direct discipline through these channels is slight because new issues are relatively infrequent can be addressed in two ways. First, regular issues of subordinated debt can be required. Although this does impose additional transactions costs on the issuing bank, the issuing costs are less than those of issuing new equity and probably less than the compliance costs associated with the more intrusive forms of regulation and supervision that could be removed. Second, indirect market discipline can amplify direct market discipline.

Supervisors can enhance market discipline by linking supervisory actions to secondary market information. A wide range of responses is possible. If there is substantial skepticism about the quality of market information, it could be used to help allocate examination resources so that banks subject to adverse market signals receive more frequent and intense examinations. But if there is more confidence in the accuracy of market signals, prices could also be used to trigger standard debt covenants such as progressively greater restrictions on bank dividend policies, management fees, deposit insurance premiums, or capital requirements. Indeed, the full set of prompt corrective action measures could be linked to levels of default premiums implicit in market prices.

This enhanced market discipline holds substantial promise of strengthening the financial system more effectively and at lower cost than the current Basel II proposal. The Basel II proposal seems unlikely to accomplish its laudable, stated objectives of eliminating regulatory capital arbitrage and aligning regulation with best practices in credit risk management. It will not eliminate incentives for regulatory arbitrage because the risk weights, despite their complexity, still do not reflect risk accurately. It fails to align regulation with best practices in credit risk management because it obliges banks to implement procedures that fail to take account of portfolio diversification, one of the most important tools for dealing with risk. Moreover, Basel II does not address the fundamental problem that measures of regulatory capital are based on accounting conventions that vary substantially from country to country and can be easily manipulated by banks that wish to boost their regulatory capital without increasing their capacity to bear loss. Finally, the extraordinary complexity of Basel II will impose heavy compliance costs and make it very difficult to monitor the enforcement of capital requirements.

In contrast, enhanced market discipline provides a simple but effective way to enhance the effectiveness of capital regulation at much lower cost. Indeed, enhanced market discipline is much more likely to accomplish the stated objectives of Basel II. First, it will deter regulatory arbitrage. Regulatory risk weights that diverge from actual risks may give banks an incentive to engage in transactions to reduce risk-weighted assets without reducing exposure to risk. But market participants will not be misled by regulatory risk weights. What matters to holders of subordinated debt and equity is the bank's overall exposure to risk of insolvency. If they perceive that a transaction increases a bank's exposure to risk, the bank will be penalized by the market and, to the extent that regulators rely on market signals to monitor risk, by the regulators as well.

Second, institutions that employ best practices in risk management, which will surely evolve over time, will be able to deploy capital more efficiently and have better control over their risk of insolvency. Rather than impede advances in risk management as Basel II threatens to do by prescribing a specific approach to risk management, holders of subordinated debt are likely to reward institutions than can quantify and control their overall exposures to risk more effectively. Unlike the Basel II approach that prescribes a particular approach to risk measurement and management, the market will reward the adoption of whatever improvements in risk management prove to be effective. In addition, market participants who perceive themselves to be at risk of loss are likely to be an effective force for enhancing disclosure that will augment the pillar 3 requirements.

Finally, market discipline will help reduce the distortions introduced by the reliance of regulators on accounting measures of capital. Holders of risky claims are likely to increase pressures for the adoption of market value accounting because market values, not accounting values are relevant for assessing the risk of insolvency. Moreover, holders of subordinated debt are unlikely to be deceived by gains trading and under-provisioning that can boost regulatory capital without enhancing an institution's capacity to bear loss.

Enhanced market discipline is also likely to improve the performance of the supervisory authorities. The secondary market price of subordinated debt provides a highly visible signal of the riskiness of a bank and, because holders of subordinated debt stand in line for repayment after the deposit insurance authority, they have a strong motive to press for prompt corrective action to minimize losses at a failing institution.

Cast in the most favorable light, the Basel II proposal is an attempt to align regulation with market estimates of risk. But this raises a logically prior question: Why invest in an enormously complicated way to mimic the market, when it is much easier to harness market discipline in support of safety and soundness objectives?

*Richard J. Herring is the Jacob Safra Professor of International Banking at the Wharton School of the University of Pennsylvania.

Notes

1. The first four assumptions will assure the existence of what Bliss and Flannery (2002) call market monitoring.

2. This corresponds to the Bliss and Flannery (2002) notion of market influence. It is difficult to measure because the anticipation of an adverse market response should be an important disciplinary force that will dissuade management from initiating imprudent action. Of course, actions not taken cannot be observed. See Hamalainen, Hall, and Howcroft (2001) for a far-ranging survey of market discipline.

3. Hoggarth, Jackson, and Nier (2003) cite the case of Nat West, which was subject to a takeover bid when the report of relatively modest shortfall in profits because of an error in pricing options led to a fall in shareholder prices and a successful takeover bid. In most markets, regulatory inhibitions stifle the market for corporate control which could, otherwise, be a very powerful source of market discipline.

4. Andrew Crockett (2001) made this point eloquently in his lecture on the distinction between microprudential and macroprudential objectives.

5. Evergreening is the practice of making additional, negative net present value loans to borrowers who are unable to repay in order to avoid the necessity of reporting a loan as nonperforming. Of course, not all loans to borrowers who are experiencing repayment difficulties are negative net present value (Herring, 1989). That's why the practice is so difficult for outsiders to monitor.

6. See Carey (1993).

7. Unless deposit insurance is structured to include a deductible or an element of coinsurance and the authorities employ resolution techniques that actually may impose losses on depositors.

8. See, for example, Flannery (1998), Evanoff and Wall (2001), Swidler and Wilcox (2002), and the references therein for evidence regarding U.S. banks. See Sironi (2003), Nier and Baumann (2003), and Hoggarth, Jackson, and Nier (2003) for evidence regarding European banks.

9. In the late 1990s Japanese banks were subject to tiering in international interbank markets because of concerns about their solvency.

10. Still, one should not dismiss the demonstration effect altogether. Napoleon's notion of a hanging an admiral "pour encourager les autres [to encourage others]," was probably an effective, if draconian, teaching tool.

11. See, for example, Horvitz (1986), Evanoff and Wall (2000), and U.S. Shadow Financial Regulatory Committee (2000). Herring (2003) contains an analysis of the Shadow proposal in the context of a broader assessment of Basel II.

12. See Bank for International Settlements (2003) for a recent survey of subordinated debt and equity markets in the member countries of the Basel Committee.

13. In addition to these points, the staff of the IMF (Kohler, 2003) noted that "Significant additional benefits can be achieved through use of standard formats for presentation of metadata (textual descriptions of data), Internet-based data collections systems, application of extensible markup language (XML) techniques, flexible database construction, and data gateways."

References

Altman, Edward, and Anthony Saunders, 2001, "An analysis and critique of the BIS proposal on capital adequacy and ratings," *Journal of Banking and Finance*, Vol. 25, No. 1.

Andrews, David, Jim Moss, and David Marshall, 2002, "Fitch Ratings' bank support rating definitions revised," *Fitch Criteria Report*, July 29, pp. 1–5.

Bank for International Settlements, 2003, "Public disclosures by banks: Results of the 2001 Disclosure Survey," Basel Committee on Banking Supervision, report, May.

_____, 2001, "Working paper on pillar 3—Market discipline," Basel Committee on Banking Supervision, working paper, September.

Berger, Allen N., 1991, "Market discipline in banking," *Proceedings of Conference on Bank Structure and Competition*, Federal Reserve Bank of Chicago.

Bliss, Robert R., and Mark J. Flannery, 2002, "Market discipline in the governance of U.S. bank holding companies: Monitoring vs. influencing," *European Finance Review*, Vol. 6.

Board of Governors of the Federal Reserve System, 2000, "The feasibility and desirability of subordinated debt," report by the Board of Governors of the Federal Reserve System and the Secretary of the U.S. Department of the Treasury, submitted to the Congress, December.

Carey, Mark S., 1993, "Snacking and smoothing: Gains trading of investment account securities by commercial banks," Board of Governors of the Federal Reserve, working paper, July.

Collin-Dufresne, Pierre, Robert S. Goldstein, and J. Spencer Martin, 2001, "The determinants of credit spread changes," *Journal of Finance*, December, Vol. 56, No. 6.

Crockett, Andrew, 2001, "Market discipline and financial stability," speech at a conference on Banks and Systemic Risk at the Bank of England, London, pp. 23–25.

Elton, Edwin J., Martin J. Gruber, Deepak Agrawal, and Christopher Mann, 2001, "Explaining the rate spread on corporate bonds," *Journal of Finance*, Vol. 56, No. 1, February, pp. 247–277.

Evanoff, Douglas D., and Larry D. Wall, 2001, "Sub-debt yield spreads as bank risk measures," *Journal of Financial Services Research*, Vol. 20, No. 2/3.

_____, 2000, "Subordinated debt as bank capital: A proposal for regulatory reform," *Economic Perspectives*, Federal Reserve Bank of Chicago, Second Quarter, pp. 40–53.

Fitch, Inc., 2003, "Launch of Fitch's bank support rating methodology," *Criteria Report*, July 22.

Flannery, Mark J., 2001, "The faces of 'market discipline'," *Journal of Financial Services Research*, Vol. 20, No. 2/3, October/December.

_____, 1998, "Using market information in prudential bank supervision: A review of the U.S. empirical evidence," *Journal of Money, Credit, and Banking*, Vol. 30, No. 3, August.

Flannery, Mark J., and Kasturi P. Rangan, 2002, "Market forces at work in the banking industry: Evidence from the capital buildup of the 1990s," University of Florida, working paper, September.

Hamalainen, Paul, Maximilian J. B. Hall, and Barry Howcroft, 2001, "A framework for implementing market discipline in financial regulatory design," Loughborough University, Banking Center, research paper, December.

Hancock, Diana, and Myron Kwast, 2001, "Using subordinated debt to monitor bank holding companies: Is it feasible?," *Journal of Financial Services Research*, Vol. 20, No. 2/3, October/December, pp. 147–188.

Herring, Richard J., 2003, "The subordinated debt alternative to Basel II," University of Pennsylvania, Wharton School, working paper.

_____, 1989, "The economics of workout lending," *Journal of Money, Credit, and Banking*, Vol. 21, February, pp. 1–15.

Hoenig, Thomas, 2003, "Should more supervisory information be publicly disclosed?," *Economic Review*, Federal Reserve Bank of Kansas City, Third Quarter, pp. 5–14.

Hoggarth,G., P. Jackson, and E. Nier, 2003, "Banking crises and the design of the safety net," paper presented at the Ninth Dubrovnik Economic Conference, Dubrovnik, June 26–28.

Horvitz, P. M., 1986, "Subordinated debt is key to new bank capital requirement," *American Banker*, December 31.

Kohler, Horst, 2003, "Letter to Jaime Caruana to comment on the third consultative paper on Basel II," International Monetary Fund, posted on the BIS website, July 31.

Kane, Edward J., 2002, "Using deferred compensation to strengthen the ethics of financial regulators," *Journal of Banking and Finance*, Vol. 26, September, pp. 1919–1933.

_____, 2001, "Relevance and need for international regulatory standards," in *Brookings-Wharton Papers on Financial Services*, R. E. Litan and R. J. Herring (eds.),Washington: Brookings Institution Press, pp. 87–116.

Kwast, Myron L., et al., 1999, "Using subordinated debt as an instrument of market discipline," report of a Study Group on Subordinated Notes and Debentures, Board of Governors of the Federal Reserve System, staff study, No. 172, December.

Merton, Robert, 1974, "On the pricing of risky debt: The risk structure of interest rates," *Journal of Finance,* Vol. 29, pp. 449-470.

Morgan, D. P., 2000, "Rating banks: Risk and uncertainty in an opaque industry," Federal Reserve Bank of New York, staff reports, No. 105; *American Economic Review,* forthcoming.

Nier, Erlend, and Ursel Baumann, 2003, "Market discipline and financial stability: Some empirical evidence," *Financial Stability Review*, June.

Schilder, Arnold, 2002, "Accounting standards, transparency, and supervision," *BIS Review*, Vol. 64, November.

Sironi, Andrea, 2003, "Testing for market discipline in the European banking industry: Evidence from subordinated debt issues," *Journal of Money, Credit, and Banking*, Vol. 35, No. 3, June.

Swidler, Steven, and James Wilcox, 2002, "Information about bank risk from option prices," *Journal of Banking and Finance*, May.

U.S. Shadow Financial Regulatory Committee, 2000, *Reforming Bank Capital Regulation: A Proposal by the U.S. Shadow Financial Regulatory Committee, AEI Studies on Financial Deregulation*, Washington, DC: AEI Press, March.

Chapter 30

Healing with Destabilizing 'Market Discipline'

Daniel Cohen*
École Normale Supérieure, Cepremap, and Center for Economic Policy Research

and

Richard Portes
London Business School, Columbia Business School, l'Ecole des Hautes Etudes en Sciences Sociales, and Center for Economic Policy Research

1. Towards Efficient Market Discipline ex Ante, Orderly Workouts ex Post

1.1 Orderly Workouts: SDRM and CACs

The widespread debt crisis of the 1980s became 'the lost decade' for Latin America, and the banks ultimately had to accept substantial write-offs. The Asian crisis of 1997–98 was devastating at the time and is still not over for Indonesia. The Russian default of August 1998 was settled relatively quickly, but even quicker were the shock waves it sent out to the financial markets—with some role in the failure of Long-Term Capital Management, a sharp rise of all emerging market bond spreads, and the subsequent Brazilian exchange rate crisis. Dealing with country debt crises is always very messy, often protracted, and very costly to both debtor and creditors.

There are alternatives. After the Mexican crisis of 1994–95, Jeffrey Sachs (1995) proposed an international bankruptcy regime modeled on Chapter 11 of the U.S. bankruptcy code. Eichengreen and Portes (1995) argued instead for a combination of contractual and institutional changes that would not require an international bankruptcy court. The Group of Ten (G-10) deputies issued a report in May 1996 that endorsed the latter route. Nothing was done, because the G-10 left any action to the initiative of market participants. But the lenders had already expressed their opposition to any measures that would, as they put it, "make default easier". It should instead be as "painful and messy" as possible, they said, in order to deter any violation of the sanctity of contracts.

This is one aspect of "market discipline" that we shall not explore in this paper. It is clear, however, that this argument is wrong. If the debtor perceives default as infeasible or unacceptably costly, even when an objective assessment would say it is unavoidable, then we see "gambles for resurrection": policies with some small chance of getting out of the hole but a high probability of a failure that exacerbates the difficulties. The Argentine debt exchange in summer 2001 is an excellent example, perhaps the costliest such gamble in history. On the other hand, if default is too easy, then we do get moral hazard.

The discussions on the international financial architecture that followed the Asian crisis of 1997–98 revived the debate, but the results were the same as before: no change. The crises in Turkey and Argentina were handled in much the same way as the Asian crises—a pre-crisis period of exchange rate rigidity, endorsed by the International Monetary Fund (IMF), followed by big bailout packages when trouble came. Only the debacle and default of Argentina broke the pattern, and the consequences have been disastrous for that country, if not for the international financial system. And all these episodes have weakened the IMF and its authority.

There are now signs of serious change in the framework for crisis resolution and debt restructuring. Stanley Fischer (1999) proposed that the IMF act as international lender of last resort (ILLR). In November 2001, Anne Krueger, his successor as first deputy managing director of the IMF, advocated a sovereign debt restructuring mechanism (SDRM) to facilitate a declaration of insolvency for an over-indebted country along the lines of Chapter 11 of the U.S. Bankruptcy Code (Krueger, 2001). One institutional manifestation of the Fischer proposal is the contingent credit line (CCL) facility, which would enable a country affected by a contagion crisis to draw on additional lines of credit. No country, however, has as yet made use of this facility. The proposal in this paper has some kinship with it, but we believe it is better designed to meet a specific market failure and should be more attractive to borrowers.

The Krueger proposal has also not been implemented. Despite subsequent revisions that reduced the role of the IMF (Krueger, 2002), the SDRM would still require an international treaty or amendment of the IMF Articles of Agreement. John Taylor, U.S. undersecretary of the Treasury for international affairs, had meanwhile responded with a version of the proposals for contractual changes that had appeared in 1995–96 (Taylor, 2002). At the autumn 2002 IMF annual meetings, a 'two-track' approach was confirmed: further work on the SDRM, with the intention of getting to an operational proposal by spring 2003, side-by-side with efforts to make actual progress on collective action clauses (CACs). But at the April 2003 meetings, the proposal was shelved, specifically because it would have required an amendment to the articles (IMF, 2003).

Both these proposals (ILLR and SDRM) are too ambitious to constitute a realistic agenda for reform. An ILLR must have at its disposal either the resources to inject an indeterminate quantity of fresh liquidity or perfect information regarding solvent and insolvent financial intermediaries. As the latter assumption is virtually ruled out by the very nature of financial crises, the former is tantamount to giving the IMF the means to create liquidity ex nihilo. Such a transfer of monetary sovereignty, which was extremely difficult to implement in the European case, seems totally unrealistic on a world scale. If there is to be a world LLR, it is rather for the large central banks (the Federal Reserve, the European Central Bank, and the Bank of Japan) to play this role.

Anything along the lines of the Fund's SDRM proposal is infeasible for the same political reason. Setting up an international court with authority over the handling of sovereign debt would entail a substantial transfer of sovereignty, in order to give the court the statutory basis for suspending legal procedures against a country. Nevertheless, there is no doubt that the Krueger initiative dramatically changed the terms of the discussion and at the least gave impetus to the adoption of CACs (see our discussion in Cohen and Portes, 2003).

1.2 "Market Discipline" Can Destabilize ex Ante

These policy developments reflect a reality that is admittedly complex in itself but which raises one simple and essential question. When financial crises erupt, the action taken by the IMF cannot ignore the underlying causes. It is not possible to treat in the same manner a country that is the victim of an unforeseeable loss of market confidence and a country where the macroeconomic indicators have long been unsatisfactory and which therefore is borrowing at abnormally high interest rates. Note that here we deal only with "emerging market" economies. Whereas their cost of capital in international markets has risen and become more volatile in recent years, the very poor countries have no market access whatsoever.

It is for dealing with situations in which a country is suffering from a lack of confidence unjustified by any major deterioration in its fundamentals that the ILLR approach would be useful. It is for dealing with situations in which the debt no longer bears a relation to the fundamentals that the procedures involving bankruptcy or debt reduction are essential. Correctly applying such a distinction is very difficult under pressure of time, when the crisis erupts. This is partly because there will always be doubts over the motives prompting investors to withdraw their confidence. The doubt regarding the nature of crises explains the risk of moral hazard. Because it is not always possible to distinguish the "good" debtors which have been unlucky from the "bad" which have continued to implement unsustainable policies, intervention by the IMF has continually swung between too much and too little. It was to circumvent these difficulties that the Meltzer Commission (2000) proposed confining the Fund's scope for action to only those countries that "prequalify" based on strict criteria of indebtedness and transparency. But this proposal offers nothing for the countries that would fall outside the scope of such prequalification, and this is hardly feasible.

Just as for orderly workouts, analytical economics offers tools for understanding and dealing with financial instability. One key reason why the distinction between confidence crises and crises of fundamentals is difficult to make is that the former often rapidly turn into the latter: If interest rates rise, debt can rapidly be subject to a snowball effect, which then becomes self-fulfilling with regard to the fundamentals themselves. This is the argument used by Williamson (2002) to characterize the Brazilian crisis: The debt is at a level made unsustainable by high interest rates but which would rapidly be brought down to an equilibrium level (recalling the government's primary surpluses) by low interest rates. Economics is familiar with such multiple equilibria: Low rates represent one equilibrium, high rates another.

This is a market imperfection, because we cannot be confident that the unaided market will choose the "good equilibrium" over the "bad equilibrium." We see here a fundamental flaw in the process of market discipline. We propose a policy intervention to deal with this structural weakness in the mechanisms of international capital flows. This is based on a simple taxonomy that enables us to break down the origin of crises into three components: a crisis of confidence (spreads and currency crisis), a crisis of fundamentals (real growth rate), and a crisis of economic policy (primary deficit). The policy would seek to short-circuit confidence crises, partly by using IMF support to improve ex ante incentives.

There are many differences between sovereign and corporate debt (Eichengreen and Portes, 1995; Cohen and Portes, 2003). One of the most important arises from a country's lack of transferable collateral. If its market access is blocked by a confidence crisis, then it may be endogenously obliged to default, in effect fulfilling the initial fear. Self-fulfilling debt crises are a phenomenon whose theoretical rationale has been explored in the literature (Calvo, 1988; Cole and Kehoe, 1996, 2000). The intuitive rationale is quite simple: Perception of high risk raises the spread, which in turn raises the debt service burden, which in turn provokes the debt crisis. This may happen as a rational equilibrium if the fundamentals out of which a country can service its debt depend partly on its creditworthiness. If default reduces the amount that a country can service (even reduces this ability to nothing in the case of outright default), then lenders that expect that nothing will be paid do indeed get nothing. This is less likely in the case of corporate debt if default amounts, say, to changing the management of the firm. Any mechanism that is geared towards maintaining ex post efficiency of debt workouts is then bound to reduce the risk of a confidence crisis. In particular, a mechanism which guarantees an efficient debt write-off ex post can eliminate the risk of a confidence crisis (Cohen, 2003). This is one of the key advantages of an orderly workout mechanism: By guaranteeing that ex post resolution of the crisis is efficient, it deters the emergence of ex ante confidence crises. Our proposal offers a different way of avoiding market destabilization leading to the "bad equilibrium."

In addition to the theoretical literature on self-fulfilling debt crises, there are at least two areas of empirical work that are relevant to our story, but which we shall not explore here. First, we have a literature on whether country spreads are accurate predictions of default and recovery rates—that is, what are the ex post returns to sovereign debt? In fact, *in the aggregate*, and going back to the 19th century, *lenders have not mispriced* sovereign debt: the ex post average real rate of return is remarkably stable, at around 2 percent to 3 percent, for lending in the periods before 1913 (Lindert and Morton, 1990), 1920–29 (Eichengreen and Portes, 1986), and 1970–2000 (Klingen et al., 2003). But the averages conceal very wide variation between large losses and high returns. Second, there are studies of the *determinants* of country spreads (for example, Kamin and Kleist, 1999; Grandes, 2003; Uribe and Yue, 2003) and the relation of spreads to sovereign ratings (for example, Cantor and Packer, 1995, 1996; Afonso, 2003). These conclude that there is some relationship between spreads and a country's fundamentals, but it is not tight, nor is that between spreads and ratings, and global factors (like U.S. interest rates) have a strong influence on each country's spread, independently of its fundamentals and policies.

Overall, this literature does not give a reassuring picture of how market discipline operates for individual countries, even if despite crises and defaults, lenders to sovereigns have earned approximately the risk-free rate on average ex post.

2. The Financial Crises of the 1990s Are Different from Those of the 1980s

In the period leading up to 1982, when Mexico suspended payment on its debt, spreads were very low, rarely exceeding 200 basis points to 250 basis points, as most bankers at the time thought that countries do not default. Spreads on both Mexican and Brazilian debt did rise in the few months before the debt moratoria, but the syndicated bank lending of the 1970s and early 1980s showed no signs of recollection of the 1930s. Although spreads did vary somewhat with the characteristics of the borrower, there was no perceptible market discipline. The bulk of the financial crises involved syndicated loans with very low spreads, and the average real rate of interest on sovereign borrowing in the 1970s was negative. The debt crisis of the 1980s was not anticipated by the lenders. The resolution of the crisis took several painful years, during which Latin American economies stagnated—to the point where income per capita returned to the late 1960s level, in what has often been called a lost decade.

The nature of the debt crises changed in the 1990s. The agents are now different. Corporate borrowers have joined sovereign debtors. Lenders are different, too: bondholders rather than bank loan syndicates. The 1980s story according to which high public deficits created high debt, and eventually interest rate rises brought major crises, is not the only one at hand. Confidence crises, through exchange rates or through interest rates, create new scenarios. Crises are more complex: the Asian crises, the Mexican crisis, the Russian crisis give a range of cases that are difficult to subsume under one story. Some crises were expected, some were unexpected, and quite often, in each case, for good reasons.

As examples of "foretold" crises, take the cases of Argentina and Ecuador; at the other extreme, take Korea or Mexico (table 1, panels A and B). From the comparison of these two cases, it is fairly clear that Argentina and Ecuador were fundamentally insolvent, at least with respect to one of the two criteria which are commonly used: debt-to-export ratio above 200 percent and/or debt-to gross domestic product (GDP) ratio above 50 percent (note, however, that it takes both indicators to anticipate a crisis, on which more later). Huge spreads were paid, and at the time when the crisis erupted, no lender could claim that it was taken by surprise. Yet despite this apparent market discipline, many lenders were taken by surprise; and the discipline of higher spreads had little perceptible effect on the policies of Argentina or its creditors. Argentina was able to borrow at excessive spreads, which simply worsened its fiscal position and exacerbated the crisis and its consequences. This is a case where a write-down of the debt is needed, in order to return as soon as possible to sustainable growth.

Case 2 is exactly the opposite. No major macroeconomic disequilibria were observable, insofar as the outstanding stocks were concerned; spreads were correspondingly low. In the case of Mexico, however, it is clear that the large current-account deficit was creating liquidity pressures. On the other hand, Korea failed by none of these criteria. Indeed, its weakness came from elsewhere, that is, the short-term nature of its debt. As the current account demonstrates, however, there was no particular need for a major exchange rate adjustment.

In case 3 (table 30.1, panel C), the sovereign risk pertains to the nature of the debtor. Despite good macroeconomic performance, creditors could examine the macroeconomics and perceive the risk of defaults that the shaky government or the shaky banking system could create. The spreads were correspondingly high.

Let us summarize the discussion so far in table 30.1, panel D. Compared to the 1980s, then, it does not appear to be the case that large disequilibria went unnoticed by the markets. As we now discuss, the high-debt/low-spread cell is empty. In this sense, market discipline improved.

A. Case 1
Foretold crises: Argentina, Ecuador (data two years before the crisis)

	Argentina	**Ecuador**
D/X	380%	250%
D/GDP	36%	85%
Spreads (basis points)	623	597
Current account (% of GCP)	–5%	–11%

B. Case 2
Unexpected crises: Mexico, Korea (two years before the crisis)

	Mexico	**Korea**
D/X	180%	76%
D/GDP	35%	25%
Spreads (basis points)	367	106
Current account (% of GDP)	–7.2%	–1.9%

C. Case 3
Foretold crises without apparent macroeconomic disequilibria
(two years before the crisis)

	Turkey	**Russia**
D/X	194%	121%
D/GDP	54%	26%
Spreads	738	800
Current account	–0.7%	+0.7%

D. Summary

	High debt	**Low debt**
Low spread	None	Case 2
High spread	Case 1	Case 3

Table 30.1: Characteristics of Crises

3. Debt Crises of the 1990s: A Taxonomy

We present in the appendix the list of countries which signed a program with the IMF during the nineties. We distinguish three groups of countries according to the nature of the program. Group A ("hard crises") includes all countries which have experienced one EFF (extended fund facility); Group B includes all (other) countries which have experienced more than one SBA (standby agreement) in a row (intermediate crises); Group C includes all countries which have experienced only one SBA (short crisis).

Except for a few cases to which we shall return, the three groups behave as one would expect. Debt is high in group A, moderate in group B, low in group C. More specifically, the debt-to-GDP ratio is significantly higher in group A, where it stands at 75 percent, on average. In both groups B and C it is a little over 50 percent, which is the conventional wisdom threshold for a risk of debt crisis (see Cohen, 2003). While the debt-to-GDP ratio is a good predictor for being in A rather than in B or C, the debt-to-export ratio is instead a discriminating factor for being in B or C: it stands at 200 percent for group B (again, 200 percent is the conventional wisdom number); it stands well below on average for group C, at about 150 percent.

There are a few exceptions to this broad pattern. In group A we find Russia, which despite good macroeconomic data had to resort to an EFF, in the face of its inability to raise foreign funds (as reflected by the huge spread paid on the debt). A similar story comes from Colombia, a country where internal politics and the sheer instability in stability of the state are the critical problem, more than any macroeconomic imbalance. In group B there are a few exceptions to the rule that debt-to-GDP is high, but this is often the case with countries such as Brazil or India where it is the debt-to-export ratio which is very high (well above the 200 percent threshold); again this is the not-so-surprising case of relatively closed countries for which both indicators are needed to assess the overall solvency of the country. The only exception in group B is Uruguay, where both ratios are relatively low and which appears to be a *prima facie* case of contagion from the two risky neighbors. In group C, Nigeria is a mirror image of Brazil or India: high debt-to-GDP but low debt-to-export, which is easily explained by the outward orientation determined by oil exports.

An additional statistic shows the share of public debt in GDP for each of the three subgroups. Public debt represents 90 percent, 80 percent, or 70 percent in groups A, B, or C.

The key to our story is the spread paid on the debt. All countries in group A and B paid high spreads well before (at least two years before) the crisis occurred. At the other extreme all countries in group C were paying low spreads even one month before the crisis exploded. Their crises were basically unpredictable, or if predicted, not expected to last very long.

We can summarize these findings so far as follows: *Major crises (types A and B) are old-style crises: high debt (in the sense of either D/GDP above 50 percent or D/X above 200 percent) and mostly public. They are predictable at least two years ahead of time.*

4. The High-Spread/High-Debt Crisis

Let us now shed some light on the nature of the debt dynamics. The self-fulfilling story is one in which a high spread causes high debt rather than the other way around.

Although this phenomenon is theoretically plausible, it is not easy to show empirically that it is indeed convincing. In order to shed some light on this debate, we have decomposed the debt dynamics into the following identity:

Increase of the Debt-to-GDP ratio = real interest rate × Debt-to-GDP ratio
– Growth rate of the economy × Debt-to-GDP ratio
– Primary Surplus/GDP.

The real interest rate is the nominal rate (risk-free rate + spread) adjusted for the deviation of the exchange rate from purchasing power parity (PPP). The dynamics are computed from 1990 up to the year of the debt crisis itself. We present this decomposition below by dividing each of the three terms of the right-hand side by the left-hand side (the sum adds to one). We reach the results shown in table 30.2.

The first term is roughly interpreted as a confidence premium, the second term as a measure of the underlying fundamentals and the third term as a measure of the policy choices. We see that on average, the growth component (second column) is the critical factor behind the dynamics of debt. The confidence premium factor (first column) is the second important item, while the deficit itself appears to play the least important role. This confirms, if not the self-fulfilling theory according to which the confidence term would account for all of the debt dynamics, at least the idea that confidence risks do indeed levy a substantial charge on the country's resources.

	Interest	Growth	Deficit
Argentina	0.16	–0.51	0.33
Brazil	0.47	–0.51	0.01
Colombia	0.01	–0.99	–0.01
Korea	0.22	–0.26	0.52
Ecuador	0.42	–0.54	–0.04
India	0.35	–0.49	0.16
Indonesia	0.10	–0.73	0.17
Malaysia	–0.07	–0.49	0.44
Mexico	–0.45	–0.51	0.04
Pakistan	–0.25	–0.45	0.30
Panama	0.07	–0.40	–0.54
Papua	0.51	–0.37	0.12
Peru	0.25	–0.73	–0.02
Philippines	–0.46	–0.07	–0.47
Russia	0.50	–0.50	0.00
Thailand	–0.06	–0.33	0.61
Turkey	0.52	–0.10	–0.39
Uruguay	–0.85	0.00	0.14
Venezuela	–0.41	–0.08	–0.51
Zimbabwe	0.29	–0.50	–0.20

Table 30.2: Debt Dynamics

Overall we can then say that the debt crises of the nineties are a combination of three factors of equal importance: a self-sustained dimension by which the interaction of interest rates and the fiscal position (often also exchange rates) create a perverse dynamics that is in part self-fulfilling; a risk that arises from weak fundamentals; and finally a term that arises from the primary deficits and the lack of internal discipline.

This decomposition suggests two policy implications and one hope. Given the role of policy mismanagement in debt dynamics, we believe that early corrective devices would be quite useful in avoiding spiraling debt. Given the fact that bad "fundamentals" are also a major part of the story, we conclude that debt write-off may also be needed. Finally, the role of the confidence term suggests that efficient measures (taken ex ante and ex post) could alleviate the importance of that term.

5. How to Prevent Market Discipline from Creating a Confidence Crisis

5.1 Prequalification Alone Is Not Credible

Until very recently, the Fund could make six different types of loan: 1) the traditional standby (SBA); 2) the SRF (supplementary reserve facility) introduced in 1998; 3) the CCL (contingent credit line) created in 1998 but never used and now discarded; 4) the EFF (extended fund facility) created in 1975 to provide long-term help for countries whose financing problems have a "structural" cause; 5) the PRGF (poverty reduction and growth facility), the means by which the Fund helps the poor countries; and 6) the CCCF (compensatory and contingency financing fund), created in the 1960s and intended for countries subject to a crisis in their terms of trade that is temporary in nature (or regarded as being temporary).

The EFF was created when the financial markets were mostly inaccessible to the developing countries, even to the middle-income countries that we would now call "emerging market countries." Williamson (2001) proposed its abolition. He also argued for abolishing the CCL: Countries are reluctant to use it and want to avoid signaling to the financial markets that they are afraid of a speculative attack of the kind that they could easily trigger off in trying to avert it. Another drawback of the CCL facility is that it is supposed to be "automatic" for countries meeting certain eligibility criteria, yet the Fund has been averse to making it fully automatic, and the final agreement for access to the CCL remains dependent on an ad hoc decision. "Virtually automatic" is a long way from "absolutely automatic" in the field of financial flows. For such reasons, the IMF executive board has just pronounced formally the demise of the CCL (November 2003).

Williamson opted for a single so-called crisis window, combining those of the SRF and the CCL, making it possible to face up to crisis situations. In addition, there would be another CCFF window designed for countries undergoing shocks that are outside their control, natural disasters, or commodity price shocks.

A critical question is whether the crisis window should be open to all. A good start to the question of how to avoid confidence crisis is the discussion, revived by the Meltzer report (Lerrick and Meltzer, 1999; Meltzer Commission, 2000), which relates to the prequalification of countries entitled to draw on lines of credit from the Fund. The criteria for prequalification could possibly include some of those involved in eligibility for the granting of CCL. This is in principle interesting, in that it encourages countries to adopt reasonable behavior ex ante and rewards them ex post by actual support from the Fund.

The prequalification criteria discussed in the Meltzer report include: freedom of capital movements, adequately capitalized commercial banks, transparent statistics for official and officially guaranteed debt, and a balanced budget. Williamson rightly criticizes the report's demand for the requirement of free movement of capital, but underlines the importance of transparent criteria as regards banking (the Basel Core Principles) and taxation. The discussion in this case would center on the question of whether norms of the Maastricht type (deficit below 3 percent) are needed or whether discretionary assessment by the Fund would suffice. This tends to raise also the more general question of "rating." Should the Fund add its own voice to those of the existing bodies?

This idea of prequalification is obviously weakened by the time-inconsistency of such a policy. It is hard to imagine that the international financial community would disregard Turkey or Argentina on the grounds that these countries had not previously prequalified. The associated idea that the Fund should commit itself in advance never to exceed certain "presumptive limits" on its lending (for example, a given multiple of quotas) is also attractive. It sets a prior limit on the system of maximum guarantees granted to the countries and should therefore limit the amount of reckless lending. But again, it is hard ex post—even assuming the resources exist—to limit the supply in a credible manner. In fact, the case in which the commitment not to intervene beyond the quota of available resources is credible is the only case in which one would prefer it not to be: when a systemic crisis strikes a whole region, with the action by the Fund exposed to quantitative limitations dictated by the scarcity of its own resources. And yet this is perhaps the only case in which the supply of credit could be capable of being "unlimited" or at least very substantial, if the Fund were to be helped to play the role of lender of last resort.

In order to derive a positive conclusion from the debate, it seems essential to us that prequalification should commit a country, in a constructive manner, to take measures that ensure its solvency or minimize the risk of crisis. Presumptive limits, on the other hand, can hold only if there is an alternative to unacceptably messy defaults (see Cohen and Portes, 2003).

5.2 A Lender of First Resort

Let us start by discussing a "pure" confidence crisis, where market discipline is dysfunctional: the case where fears of default create high spreads and raise debt to unsustainable levels. Take a situation in which creditors realize that a country could be safe if only it could borrow at low rates. Assume however that the problem is simply one of coordination. If all creditors could agree on lending at the riskless rate, the country would indeed be safe and the fear of default could be overcome. On the other hand, in the very nature of self-fulfilling crises, if one creditor expects other creditors to lend at punitive rates, then it would have to join the crowd and also charge the high rate. In such circumstances, one might apply a method which is common in the field of venture capital and which amounts to allowing an individual investor to make an offer that is conditional on other investors' commitments (Chamon, 2002). Assume for instance that an investor is allowed to post a willingness to purchase a specified quantity of a bond issued by a country at a given spread, but could retract its offer if the country fails to convince other subscribers. In that case the individual investor does not need to worry about other investors' reluctance. Either the subscription is entirely subscribed at the "good" spread and the "good" equilibrium is reached, or it is not and the individual investor does not get trapped into an equilibrium in which he would be alone in lending at the riskless rate.

There is a great merit to this suggestion, which makes it possible to trace out the supply curve of the market, at a given spread. But it is only a static solution to a fundamentally dynamic problem. Indeed, the core of the problem is quite often that creditors are worried by the action of the debtor, not only for the present but also for the future. The fact that a debtor could be tempted to raise its risk profile in the future is one key reason for the reluctance of creditors to commit themselves at low spreads (Cohen, 1991). In order to solve this dynamic problem, what is really needed is a commitment mechanism that allows a given debtor to rule out borrowing at excessive spreads, not only today but for the future as well.

The simplest way to proceed would be as follows. Assume that the country manages to commit itself *not* to borrow at punitive rates. Think for instance of a kind of "usury law" that the country would apply to itself, forbidding it to borrow above a given interest threshold, say a spread over 300 basis points. In the model of self-fulfilling debt crises of the kind that is analyzed in Cole and Kehoe (1996) and Cohen (2003), a debtor that is the victim of a confidence shock usually wants to get out of the danger zone by taking stringent actions. We find it useful for a country to be able to commit itself to implement such behavior. Before we return below to how the mechanism could actually be implemented, one can see the merits of such a commitment. If it could be made credible, then it would avert the self-fulfilling spiral that we alluded to before. Furthermore, by raising the stakes of maintaining a good reputation, this is a mechanism that can ease the policy choices of a country: It would politically facilitate the early resolution of debt crises. This would be a positive interaction between policies and market discipline.

To summarize, the reason why a commitment on spreads is important is twofold. First, the informational content of spreads is quite rich, as we argued above. Second, spreads are a symptom and a cause of future troubles.

Let us now investigate what it takes to make such a mechanism credible. Assume that a country initially borrows at low spreads: Think of Mexico today, and assume that a new shock (fall in the price of oil …) suddenly lowers the market's assessment of its creditworthiness. If the country accepts higher spreads, it "gambles for resurrection" by taking the chance that things will eventually settle down, or simply buys time in order to make internal adjustments. The problem with this option is that the debt may meanwhile spiral upwards, making it more difficult ex post to get the country to act decisively. For a country that is committed, say, to a 300 basis point to 400 basis point spread, the IMF should work with the country on an analysis of the cause of the problem and of the remedies which could resolve it. A program would then be designed, which, if agreed upon by the country, could grant access to IMF money if needed.

Nothing should be automatic in this process. Countries signal ex ante their willingness to avoid the snowball effect of rising spreads and rising debts and seek to avoid it at an early stage. But IMF support remains conditional on taking appropriate measures, so that it is not a free lunch. Furthermore, IMF money could be granted at a rate that incorporates a spread, say of 300 basis points, so that countries will not necessarily want to tap IMF resources.

One may fear that the informational content of spreads will be reduced as they become a policy variable (a version of Goodhart's law). It is true that lenders, being aware of the fact that countries will take actions against rising spreads, will change their pricing policy. If, as a result, spreads become lower, this is in itself a good thing as it reduces the snowball effect. But it is very unlikely that they could fail to detect a country that becomes insolvent. Indeed, actions to correct imbalances are voluntary, not automatic. Lenders must then keep track of a debtor's solvency. But the policy may achieve the role of making self-fulfilling spread crises if not impossible, at least less likely.

The merit of this approach is that it allows the country to take very early corrective actions, with the support of IMF loans. By acting early the measures should not be daunting. By showing its willingness to act, the country further boosts its reputation, not too late as is often the case, but early on: when the country can still see the benefit of raising its profile in the eyes of international investors.

In our view this mechanism would be an appropriate, feasible and effective replacement for the contingent credit line facility. The CCL was created to help "first-class policy" countries to face confidence shocks. As Stanley Fischer emphasized, such countries do not need to be "perfect." They need to obey international standards such as the Basel Committee's Core Principles for Banking Supervision, the code on Transparency in Monetary and Financial Policies, etc. The country must have enjoyed "constructive relations with its private creditors and be taking appropriate measures to limit its external vulnerability," the latter including exchange rate viability and the absence of arrears on sovereign debt. The idea is to create a "first-class" policy straitjacket that discriminates between the implementation of good and bad policies and eradicates the moral hazard risk.

The problem, however, is that the practical balance between the straitjacket and the flexible response to confidence crises does not appear to have been found. No country ever used the CCL. They feared that to ask for it would send a wrong signal to the market, and despite the quasi-prequalification clauses, they could never be quite sure that they would get it, which could make things even worse. Our mechanism would be reserved for countries that have never defaulted on their claim in order to avoid the high-risk strategy. It would be based on spreads and perhaps on other additional measures of solvency. The reason why we attach so much importance to spreads is that they both reveal a problem and contribute to creating it.

Daniel Cohen is a professor of economics at École Normale Supérieure, a research fellow at Cepremap, and a codirector of the Center for Economic Policy Research. Richard Portes is a professor of economics and chair of the Economics Faculty at the London Business School and the Joel Stern Visiting Professor of International Economics at Columbia University. He is also directeur d'etudes at l'Ecole des Hautes Etudes en Sciences Sociales and the founder and president of the Center for Economic Policy Research. This paper draws on material in the authors' report (Cohen and Portes, 2003) prepared for the Conseil d'Analyse Economique (CAE). They are very grateful to Laurence Bloch and Jean Pisani-Ferry for their help and their comments on their work. They have also benefited from comments at a CAE meeting, as well as comments from Ted Truman.

A. Crisis A (crisis = 1 EFF (Extended Fund Facility))

(t): year of agreement date of prog.			Debt/GDP			Debt/Exp			Public debt as share of long-term debt[c]
			(t–2)	(t–1)	(t)	(t–2)	(t–1)	(t)	(t)
Algeria	May 95	EFF	54.2	74.3	84	219.5	277	265.6	100.0
Argentina	Feb 98	EFF	35.8	38.7	48.5	331.2	362.4	380.4	74.8
Colombia	Dec 99	EFF	34.9	34.5	42.1	186.6	225.4	217.2	62.7
Egypt	Sept 93	EFF	100.2	78	67.2	240.4	180.6	181.9	97.8
Gabon	Nov 95	EFF	99.8	113	102.8	144.6	160.6	148.9	100.0
Indonesia[a]	Aug 98	EFF	58.3	65.3	167.9	219.3	206.9	262	57.6
Jamaica	Dec 92	EEF	122.8	132.9	147.4	189.8	184.9	173.5	99.2
Jordan	Feb 96	EFF	132.4	126.2	121.7	185.7	167.6	151.7	99.6
Pakistan	Oct 97	EFF	49.4	45.7	47.5	252.2	249.7	263.9	92.3
Panama	Dec 97	EFF	68	68.3	65.3	83.0	76.4	75.4	97.4
Peru	June 99	EFF	50.1	53.8	57.8	321	332.4	320.6	85.6
Philippines	June 94	EFF	61.2	64.9	59.9	187.1	187.3	161	93.2
Russia[b]	March 96	EFF	37.9	35.3	29.7	156.7	129.6	119.5	100.0
Yemen	Oct 97	EFF	178.1	137.6	76.7	190.5	174.6	103.6	100.0
Zimbabwe	Sept 92	EFF	38.2	41.1	62.9	159.6	172.4	219	91.5
Average			74.8	74.0	78.8	204.5	205.9	203.0	90.1

Notes: [a]political and economic consequences of the Asian crisis
[b]plus an SRF (Supplemental Reserve Facility) component in 07/98
[c]3-year average
[d]Brazil, Turkey and Uruguay also benefited from SRF combined with SBA (2 for Brazil, 1 for Turkey and Uruguay)
[e]3 SBA spread over the 1990s. Data in (t) are averages for the period 1990–2000
[f]Malaysia has not asked for IMF aid. July 97 is the date of the floating of the currency.

Appendix: Taxonomy of Debt Crises

B. Crisis B (crisis = 2 or 3 consecutive SBA)

(t): year of agreement date of prog.		Debt/GDP (t–2)	(t–1)	(t)	Debt/Exp (t–2)	(t–1)	Public debt as share of long-term debt[c] (t)
Brazil[d]	Dec 98	2SBA	23.5	24.1	31.4	302.5	291.6	372.8	55.8
Costa Rica	Aug 91	3SBA	91.2	68.8	74.6	236.2	179.4	174.8	91.5
Dominican Rep.	Aug 91	2 SBA	63.3	64.9	61.9	164.9	195.8	197.5	97.3
El Salvador	July 95	3SBA	29.4	27.6	27.7	92.9	83.7	82.7	99.7
Ecuador[e]	Dec 91	3SBA	97.5	97.5	97.5	291.3	291.3	291.3	97.4
India	Jan 91	2 SBA	26	26.7	32.5	318	330.9	317.2	97.8
Papua N.G.[e]	July 91	3SBA	69.2	69.2	69.2	119.5	119.5	119.5	60.7
Turkey[d]	Dec 99	2 SBA	47.1	47.1	54.3	157	155.8	194	67.8
Uruguay[d]	March 99	3SBA	33.5	34.9	36.8	138.5	159.8	174.9	94.0
Average			53.4	51.2	54.0	202.3	200.9	213.9	84.7

C. Crisis C (crisis = 1 SBA)

(t): year of agreement date of prog.		Debt/GDP (t–2)	(t–1)	(t)	Debt/Exp (t–2)	(t–1)	Public debt as share of long-term debt[c] (t)
Korea	Dec 97	25.4	27.4	32.8	76.1	83.8	84.9	61.6
Indonesia	Nov 97	64.6	58.3	65.3	226.7	219.3	206.9	62.0
Malaysia[f]	July 97	40.6	41.3	49.8	39.9	41.8	49.3	55.4
Mexico	Feb 95	33.6	34.4	61.1	195.1	179.4	172.5	82.5
Nigeria	Aug 00	103.4	93.4	92.9	257.7	189.9	146.8	99.0
Thailand	Aug 97	50.5	51.3	62.6	112.1	120.2	122.7	37.0
Venezuela	July 96	65.18	47.1	50.18	190.87	157.11	128.58	93.1
Average		54.7	50.5	59.2	156.9	141.7	130.2	70.1

Notes: [a]political and economic consequences of the Asian crisis
[b]plus an SRF (Supplemental Reserve Facility) component in 07/98
[c]3-year average
[d]Brazil, Turkey and Uruguay also benefited from SRF combined with SBA (2 for Brazil, 1 for Turkey and Uruguay)
[e]3 SBA spread over the 1990s. Data in (t) are averages for the period 1990–2000
[f]Malaysia has not asked for IMF aid. July 97 is the date of the floating of the currency.

Appendix: Taxonomy of Debt Crises (continued)

References

Afonso, A., 2003, "Understanding the determinants of sovereign debt ratings," *Journal of Economics and Finance*, Vol. 27, pp. 56–74.

Bank for International Settlements, 1996, "The resolution of sovereign liquidity crises," report of G-10 deputies, Basel, Switzerland.

Calvo, G., 1988, "Servicing the public debt: The role of expectations," *American Economic Review*, Vol. 78, pp. 647–661.

Cantor, Richard, and Frank Packer, 1996, "Determinants and impact of sovereign credit ratings," *Economic Policy Review*, Federal Reserve Bank of New York, Vol. 2, No. 2, October, pp. 37–53.

_____, 1995, "Sovereign credit ratings," *Current Issues in Economics and Finance*, Federal Reserve Bank of New York, Vol. 1, No. 3.

Chamon, M., 2002, "Are debt crises self-fulfilling?," Harvard University, mimeo.

Cohen, D., 2003, "How to avoid self-fulfilling debt crises?," École normale supérieure, mimeo.

_____, 2001, "The HIPC initiative: True and false promises," *International Finance*, Vol. 5.

_____, 1991, *Private Lending to Sovereign States*, Cambridge, MA: MIT Press.

Cohen, D., and R. Portes, 2003, "Crise souveraine: Entre prévention et résolution [Sovereign crisis: Between prevention and resolution]," Conseil d'Analyse Economique, report, No. 43, in French.

Cole, H., and T. Kehoe, 2000, "Self-fulfilling debt crises," *Review of Economic Studies*, Vol. 67, pp. 91–116.

_____, 1996, "A self-fulfilling model of Mexico's 1994–95 debt crisis," *Journal of International Economics*, Vol. 41, pp. 309–330.

Eichengreen, B., and R. Portes, 1995, *Crisis? What Crisis? Orderly Workouts for Sovereign Debtors*, London: Center for Economic Policy Research.

_____, 1986, "Debt and default in the 1930s: Causes and consequences," *European Economic Review*, Vol. 30, pp. 599–640.

Fischer, S., 1999, "Reforming the international financial system," *Economic Journal*, Vol. 109, pp. 557–576.

International Monetary Fund, 2003, "Report of the managing director to the International Monetary and Financial Committee on a statutory sovereign debt restructuring mechanism," available at www.imf.org/external/np/omd/2003/040803.htm.

Grandes, M., 2003, "Convergence and divergence of sovereign bond spreads: Lessons from Latin America," École Normale Supérieure, mimeo.

Kamin, S., and K. von Kleist, 1999, "The evolution and determinants of emerging market credit spreads in the 1990s," Bank for International Settlements, working paper, No. 68.

Klingen, C., B. Weder, and J. Zettelmeyer, 2003, "How private creditors fared in emerging debt markets 1970–2000," International Monetary Fund, mimeo.

Krueger, A., 2002, "New approaches to sovereign debt restructuring," International Monetary Fund, paper.

_____, 2001, *International Financial Architecture for 2002: A New Approach to Sovereign Debt Restructuring*, Washington, DC: American Enterprise Institute, November 26.

Lerrick, A., and A. Meltzer, 2001, "Blueprint for an international lender of last resort," Carnegie-Mellon, mimeo.

Lindert, P., and P. Morton, 1990, "How sovereign debt has worked," in *Developing Country Debt and Economic Performance, Vol. 1*, J. Sachs (ed.), Chicago: University of Chicago Press.

Meltzer Commission, 2000, "Final report," Washington, DC, available at www.bicusa.org/usgovtoversight/meltzer.htm.

Sachs, J., 1995, "Do we need an international lender of last resort?," Princeton University, Graham Lecture.

Taylor, J., 2002, "Sovereign debt restructuring: A U.S. perspective," press release, Washington, DC, at www.treas.gov/press/releases/po2056.htm.

Uribe, M., and V. Yue, 2003, "Country spreads and emerging countries: Who drives whom?," Duke University, mimeo.

Williamson, J., 2002, "Is Brazil next?," Institute for International Economics, International Economics Policy Brief.

_____, 2001, "The role of the IMF: A guide to the reports," Institute for International Economics, May.

Chapter 31

Comments on Market Discipline and Public Policy

Charles Freedman*
Carleton University

Of the three papers I have been asked to discuss this morning, the first two, by Caprio and Honohan and Herring, deal with the potential role of market discipline in banking, while the third, by Cohen and Portes, deals with the destabilizing role of capital flows in emerging economies. I will therefore discuss the first two papers on banks together and then the paper on sovereign debt in emerging economies.

The papers by Caprio and Honohan and Herring illuminate a number of the issues that have been at the center of this conference. Implicit in their focus on the role of market discipline in banking as opposed to market discipline more generally in financial markets and in nonfinancial markets is the classic question: "Are banks (or, for that matter, all deposit taking financial institutions) different from other types of firms, and do they need special treatment from the perspective of supervisory discipline and market discipline?" As was discussed in the first session of this conference, the traditional answer to this question has focused on a number of aspects of banking—the importance of protecting small depositors, the difficulty of evaluating nonmarketable bank assets, the moral hazard involved once deposit insurance has been introduced, and what has come to be known as the macroprudential or systemic risk or systemwide consequences of bank failures. One aspect of the latter issue has been the possibility and impact of bank runs, given the liquid nature of many bank deposits. But attention has also been paid in this context to the specialized infrastructure that the banks provide for granting credit, particularly in developing economies and for small- and medium-sized enterprises in all economies, and to the impact on the economy as a whole of generalized stresses and problems in the financial sector.

The distinction between banks, on the one hand, and financial markets and nonfinancial entities, on the other, is not based on the fact that banks are supervised and regulated and nonbanks are not. Indeed, there is a wide range of laws and practices that apply to all corporations (for example, laws regarding bankruptcy, fraud, securities issues, and treatment of minority shareholders, and practices related to accounting and disclosure). Rather, the distinction is between ex ante or preventive regulation, which attempts to prevent certain kinds of behavior from occurring, and ex post or remedial regulation, which attempts to penalize inappropriate activity after the fact (Chant, 1987).

Preventive regulation tends to be applied to those entities where inappropriate behavior would result in outcomes to others that could not readily be compensated for after the fact. For example, drug companies are regulated in a preventive fashion and are not allowed to sell new products until they have undergone testing and received approval from the authorities. This is because remedial regulation (that is, compensation after the fact) is seen as insufficient to guard against the potentially catastrophic outcomes of death or severe impairment of the users of these products. The producers of most other products are typically subject only to a remedial regulatory regime, relying largely on law suits by the aggrieved parties as a key mechanism to penalize inappropriate behavior.

With banks and other financial institutions, the view has been that the consequences of their inappropriate behavior to those who use the services of these entities could not be adequately addressed by a remedial regime. Hence, these entities are subject to preventive regulations in the form of supervision in an attempt to reduce the probability of such inappropriate behavior occurring.

The different treatment of banks because of their supposedly special characteristics (liquid liabilities, non-marketable assets, and pervasive role in the financial system with the consequent systemic and systemwide effects of failure) leads to a number of questions. First, and most fundamental, are banks still special and do they need to be subject to different types of discipline? Second, can market discipline replace supervision entirely or in part? Third, even if market discipline cannot replace supervision, can it complement it? Fourth, and relatedly, what are the mechanisms through which market discipline operates to influence the behavior of financial institutions and/or supervisors? Fifth, what empirical evidence can be adduced to throw light on these questions?

There are also a number of more technical subsidiary questions that require consideration. Will the information needed for market discipline be forthcoming as a result of market pressures or should it be mandated by the supervisors? If the latter, how does one know that the benefits of making the required information available will exceed the costs to the institutions of providing it? In cases of entities where financial positions change rapidly (for example, hedge funds), how useful is a periodic snapshot of their financial position? How does one make the financial statements as meaningful as possible and comparable across institutions? Will the available information be used effectively?

Both of the papers on banking examine these and other issues and provide thoughtful and balanced analyses of the potential role of market discipline. The Caprio–Honohan paper brings to bear insights from cross-country experience, particularly in emerging economies, and focuses largely on the empirical evidence, while the Herring paper approaches the issues mainly from analytic and descriptive perspectives. Both papers examine in detail the mechanisms through which market discipline is supposed to affect behavior and some of the questions that have been raised regarding the effectiveness of these mechanisms. In the remaining time at my disposal, I will assess some of the arguments and counterarguments and try to draw my own conclusions as to the weight of the evidence.

First, the mechanisms. Market discipline can operate through its effects on prices and quantities. It operates on the behavior of managers and/or via the information provided to other agents, such as supervisors. Many types of market discipline operate in both of these ways. For example, a widening spread on subordinated debt can result in increased costs to the bank when it issues new subordinated debt, as a signal to supervisors that there is a perception in the market that the bank is now riskier than it had been previously, and as a signal to others who transact with the bank to demand higher risk premia (in the case of depositors) or to impose lower limits and/or to demand more collateral (in the case of counterparties). In practice, problems in a bank may be signaled first by the behavior of large counterparties in reducing the limits on the positions they are prepared to take in transactions with a bank in interbank, foreign exchange, and derivative markets, or by increasing the amount of collateral they demand to protect themselves on such transactions. This type of market discipline by counterparties, which shows up anecdotally rather than in published or easily accessible data form, may provide important information for supervisors and is worth trying to integrate into the analysis of market discipline. Indeed, in the current environment, it may be the most important form of market discipline in banking.

How useful are the various types of market discipline described in the papers likely to be in practice? Both papers seem to argue that market discipline will be of use in and of itself as well as an aid (or complement) to supervisory discipline. Nonetheless, especially in the Caprio–Honohan paper, the implicit conclusion seems to be that most of the benefits will come directly from the market discipline and only secondarily from its complementarity with supervisory discipline. And it is this implicit conclusion that I do not find persuasive, partly because of my interpretation of some of the developments that have taken place over recent years and partly because some of the various strands of market discipline are not fully articulated and, as we all know, the devil is in the details.

Let me begin with the role of uninsured depositors. Both papers correctly point out that the existence of high levels of deposit insurance and, more importantly, a perception that major institutions will be bailed out lessens the effectiveness of the role of depositors as a mechanism for market discipline. More generally, the assessment by uninsured depositors of the likelihood of their coming out whole is a function both of the riskiness of the bank and the expected behavior of the authorities, since it is in the hands of the latter as to how an institution in difficulty will be treated. And, based on their past history, it will be difficult for the authorities in many countries to be credible in asserting that no bank is too big to fail and that uninsured depositors will bear losses. What would be needed to enhance market discipline by depositors, in my view, would be a very carefully articulated and publicly disclosed set of arrangements that involve prompt corrective action by supervisors, and mechanisms for continuity in the economic operations of a failing bank (say by a bridge bank) while the uninsured depositors are haircutted. Such arrangements would have to be in place in advance, since it would be almost impossible to introduce them in a crisis, and in any case they would not have the desired effect on depositors unless depositors understood that this was the expected outcome of a bank failure.

That said, if such arrangements were in place, there would be the risk of what Herring has called destabilizing flows, with the possibility of excessive reaction by depositors (and other creditors) to perceived weaknesses in a bank. Other papers in this conference have treated this type of quantity sanction as a useful action or threat to induce appropriate behavior by managers of banks. But Herring raises the concern that such a quantity adjustment might be excessive, that is, very large and very abrupt. The type of run that he is concerned about results from the nature of bank balance sheets, with considerable amounts of short-term or demand liabilities, and difficulty in assessing credit risk on a significant portion of bank assets due to the non-marketability of these assets. Given the relatively small loss of income to depositors from shifting their claims from a bank that may be weak to one that is perceived to be stronger and the potentially large losses associated with maintaining deposits at the weaker bank, it is not surprising that there could be runs on those banks that resembled in some way the bank in difficulty. And it may not be an easy task to distinguish illiquidity from insolvency. Indeed, some observers, such as Charles Goodhart, have argued that is very difficult even for central banks in their lender of last resort role to make this distinction in practice. All the more so for the ordinary depositor who has less access to bank data than the authorities.

Herring argues that "market discipline is least likely to be destabilizing if it is channeled through holders of long-term claims on the bank—either equity or long-term subordinated debt—who cannot impose quantity sanctions." But it is not clear to me how one could limit it in this way without guaranteeing that all depositors would be made whole. And such an action would, of course, make it easier for a bank in difficulty to continue to operate unless and until its supervisor stepped in to force it to exit from the sector or to be recapitalized.

Caprio and Honohan make the interesting point that uninsured depositors in low-income developing countries may be very knowledgeable about the riskiness of the local, indigenous banks because economic power and wealth are concentrated within a relatively small business elite in such countries. I think that this and some of the other evidence they adduce regarding the nature of the environment in such countries does lend credence to their view that one should not dismiss the role of market discipline in such countries simply because of their stage of development. That said, it would be helpful on a technical level if they went beyond the bilateral regressions in their empirical work and used multiple regression analysis to determine which of the explanatory market discipline factors are most closely associated with banking risk. One further distinction that might be of interest in their table 4 on trends in bank regulation and supervision is whether these trends have been different in countries where supervision is the responsibility of a separate entity from those in which supervision is lodged in the central bank.

I was also unclear about the implications to be drawn regarding the size of the foreign-owned bank sector in a country. Caprio and Honohan argue that this pushes market discipline from the host country to the home country. Is this a good thing or a bad thing? And is it as true for subsidiaries as it would be for branches? Given that their private monitoring index actually declines and then rises as one goes up the income scale, does that mean that a very low-income country is worse off relying on market discipline for foreign-owned banks from countries with slightly higher income but better off for foreign-owned banks from countries with a much higher income? Or is this a case where income levels are correlated with foreign ownership and where multiple regression analysis might give an explanation for the nonlinear relationship between the private monitoring index and income levels?

A requirement that banks issue a certain amount of subordinated debt has been widely discussed as a mechanism by which increased market discipline can be imposed on banks. Both papers note the difficulty of drawing inferences from movements in the interest rate spreads on subordinated debt because such movements can reflect changes in liquidity factors and the macroeconomic situation, as well as firm-specific default risk. Given the thinness of subordinated debt markets and the difficulty of drawing inferences from changes in the spreads on outstanding subordinated debt, Caprio and Honohan suggest that the emphasis be put on a requirement for periodic new issues of such debt with short maturities. This raises a number of questions. In contrast to Herring, who wishes to emphasize the role of long-term subordinated debt because of the possibility of destabilizing flows, Caprio and Honohan want to rely on more frequent short-term issues. But what happens if the market dries up for new issues in general, or for new issues of riskier banks? Is there mandatory exit or recapitalization of the bank in such circumstances, or is there discretion on the part of the supervisor to defer such action? Or would the inability of a bank to issue subordinated debentures in a difficult market situation simply be a signal to supervisors to look more closely at that institution?

Another important issue is whether one should rely upon the market to elicit the data needed to facilitate market discipline or whether data disclosure should be mandated by the authorities. While the former position, that the market will be able to determine what data are needed and to induce financial institutions to provide such data, seems logical on the surface, I expect that requirements mandated by the authorities will play a role in bringing about the disclosure of the relevant data. For one thing, to get data that permits comparisons across banks, both the types of data released and the timing of the releases have to be similar across banks.

One consideration that would have to be kept firmly in mind, in deciding on disclosure of particular types of data is whether the benefits to the markets of obtaining such data exceed the costs to the banks of providing them. A further issue is whether a snapshot of data, say quarterly, gives sufficient information regarding financial institutions that change their positions frequently. And will the market have the incentives to make full use of the available data, given the costs of using the data and the widespread belief in an implicit guarantee? In a different context, the large databases of country information gathered and made available by the International Monetary Fund (IMF) seem to have been accessed much less by lenders to these countries than might have been expected. A further issue worth addressing is whether there should be increased disclosure by supervisors of supervisory information.

Of particular interest in the context of emerging economies is the attempt by Caprio and Honohan to integrate the theoretical arguments regarding the mechanisms for market discipline, political economy considerations (which may be especially important in emerging economies), market prerequisites, and empirical evidence. This is a very welcome addition to the literature. And their conclusion that the environmental conditions in developing countries are more conducive to market discipline than had previously been generally believed gives one reason for optimism. Moreover, they give useful and practical advice on how to improve the infrastructure further.

That said, some of the proposals for more market discipline in both papers need to be fleshed out further in terms of the mechanics and details of operation. I continue to believe that the primary benefit of the increased use of market discipline will be via its signalling effect to supervisors to pay more attention to those institutions where there are warning signals. These mechanisms will also be helpful, of course, in providing incentives to banks to act in such a way as to avoid being singled out in this way for increased attention by supervisors and by markets.

Despite my questions and some disagreements with the authors, I found these two papers very interesting and their insights valuable in pushing forward the future role of market discipline. What I would conclude is that we should try to make increasing use of market discipline mechanisms at the same time as we try to improve the quality of supervisory regimes, especially in emerging economies. The latter would involve training of staff along with increased independence of the supervisory system and increased transparency as to how supervisors are carrying out their responsibilities.

The Cohen–Portes paper is very different from the two papers just discussed. Whereas they take the perspective that market discipline will, by and large, help to bring about good results through both direct and indirect mechanisms, the Cohen–Portes paper starts from the position that the destabilizing elements of market discipline outweigh (and by considerable margin) the benefits of market discipline when it comes to emerging market sovereign borrowers. In particular, their concern is with the way in which a liquidity or confidence problem, by leading to a sharp rise in interest rate spreads, can rapidly turn into a solvency problem. Or, to put it slightly differently, there may be a good equilibrium with low spreads and a solvent borrower, and a bad equilibrium with high spreads and an insolvent borrower, and to quote the authors, "we cannot be confident that the unaided market will choose the 'good equilibrium' over the 'bad equilibrium'." The authors propose as a solution to this problem an arrangement whereby countries with good fundamentals (that is, decent growth rates) and good policy (that is, a supportive fiscal stance) commit themselves not to borrow above a given spread, say 300 basis points above the riskless rate (which I assume to be the rate on U.S. Treasuries). If markets demand spreads from the country that are above this ceiling, they will be able to turn to the IMF for funding at that ceiling spread.

There are a few points I would like to raise about the analysis before turning briefly to the policy approach recommended in the paper. The authors take the view that lenders have difficulty distinguishing between countries with liquidity problems and those with solvency or default problems. While this certainly was true on some occasions in the past, my impression is that markets have become more discriminating in the more recent period and that indiscriminate herding by lenders has become less of a problem (although it is not nonexistent).

It would be helpful in their discussion of debt if the authors clarified whether they were discussing externally held debt, or debt denominated in foreign currencies, or total debt, and whether and how the different forms of debt affect their analysis. Moreover, their equation analyzing the effects of the various causal factors on the change in debt ratios and their discussion of the snowballing effect of high spreads on the debt ratio seems implicitly to assume that the average spread on country debt adjusts very quickly to a change in the spread on issues of new debt (or the marginal spread). And this probably is the case where countries largely borrow at short term or, if they borrow at long term, the debt is denominated in foreign currencies and hence the cost of servicing and repaying the debt increases when the country's currency is devalued or depreciates. As a technical point in this context, I am not sure that I understand the implications of the definition by the authors of the real interest rate as the nominal rate (presumably on foreign currency debt) adjusted by the deviation of the exchange rate from purchasing power parity (PPP). This seems to imply that exchange rates move back to PPP in the very short term, an assumption that is at variance with much recent history. It is also the case that it is not just spreads that matter and that the riskless world or U.S. real rate matters as well. We have seen the pressures on emerging economies that developed when world real rates rose.

One way of breaking the link between marginal and average spreads is to develop domestic markets in longer-term debt and to lengthen the average term of the debt outstanding. Higher spreads caused by a temporary liquidity problem would then have much less impact on the debt ratio of a sovereign borrower. This is one reason why so much attention is now being paid in the international community to the prerequisites needed and the mechanics required to develop such markets in emerging economies.

The authors are also critical of the proposal to put limits on IMF lending. I would just note in this context that proposals for presumptive limits can allow for breaching such limits in certain circumstances but, as in Federal Deposit Insurance Corporation Improvement Act in the United States, exceptions to the presumptive limits could require special approval (such as, for example, super-majority voting).

I would now like to make a couple of points on the innovative policy recommendation in the paper regarding the commitment by "good" sovereign borrowers to a ceiling on the spreads that they are prepared to pay. It presumes that the IMF is more adept than the private sector at distinguishing between liquidity and solvency problems and will not err on the side of generosity (possibly in response to political pressures). As I noted earlier, I think that markets have recently shown increased capacity to make such distinctions, and the increased information being made publicly available by debtor countries should help us move further in this direction. I also remain concerned about the credibility of a country's commitment not to borrow at spreads above a certain level, particularly given that the IMF support remains conditional.

I would conclude by noting an alternative solution that has been proposed in a joint paper by the Bank of England and the Bank of Canada for both solvency and liquidity problems—namely a temporary standstill arrangement (Haldane and Krueger, 2001.) The latter would force lenders and borrowers to come together and reach agreement on any necessary restructuring or reprofiling of the country's finances. "Bank holidays" are often a more effective way of dealing with liquidity runs than lending into arrears.

*Charles Freedman is scholar in residence at Carleton University, Ottawa, Canada. The author would like to thank Clyde Goodlet and John Murray of the Bank of Canada for helpful comments on earlier draft of these remarks.

References

Chant, John, 1987, "Regulation of financial institutions—A functional analysis," Bank of Canada, technical report, No. 45, January.

Haldane, Andy, and Mark Kruger, 2001, "The resolution of international financial crises: Private finance and public funds," Bank of Canada, working paper, No. 2001-20, November.

PART IX
POLICY PANEL

Chapter 32

Reestablishing Market Discipline as Part of Bank Regulation

Charles W. Calomiris*
Columbia Business School

1. Introduction

A major problem confronts microeconomic empirical studies that try to measure the *potential* role of market discipline over banks by using information about the way markets for bank debt penalize risk (through either withdrawals of debt or higher pricing of bank debts). The problem is that the government safety net (deposit insurance, Fedwire, and implicit guarantees) remove much of the incentive of debt holders to discipline banks. Thus, the potential role of debt market discipline in a counterfactual world in which some bank debts would be carefully designed so as not to enjoy safety net protection (U.S. Shadow Financial Regulatory Committee, 2000) may be much greater than empirical studies of today's bank debt markets indicate.

That criticism applies to studies of virtually all forms of currently uninsured debts, and even to long-maturity subordinated debts. Uninsured debts may be protected by the deposit insurer, if it finds that doing so provides what it regards as the least-cost means of resolution of the financial institution's problems, or if the government decides to protect uninsured debts, as it is permitted to do in the United States under the Federal Deposit Insurance Corporation Improvement Act. Furthermore, delays in intervening to close a bank may give uninsured debt holders precious time to permit their debts to mature and exit the bank prior to closure. Until the policy environment is reformed to ensure that uninsured debts are truly at risk (U.S. Shadow Financial Regulatory Committee, 2000), it is likely that estimates of potential market discipline based on current market behavior will substantially underestimate the role that market discipline can play in bank regulation.

Another problem with reliance on microeconomic evidence is that doing so may underestimate the cost of market discipline. Those who are skeptical about the merits of heavy reliance on market discipline sometimes express concern that too much market discipline may be a problem from a macroeconomic perspective. To the extent that market discipline punishes banks excessively it may lead to unwarranted withdrawals of deposits (and, in extreme cases, to sudden "bank runs"), which could have important systemic effects on other banks, and on the aggregate supply of credit. Those effects and their costs would not be captured by microeconomic studies that focus only on the responses of debt pricing or debt withdrawals to underlying risk.

I propose that the way to deal with these two deficiencies—the effects of safety nets in limiting observed discipline, and the need to take account of the macroeconomic, systemic consequences of potentially excessive discipline—is to look carefully at both the microeconomic and macroeconomic consequences of market discipline over banks in environments where market incentives to apply discipline were strong. That approach entails looking beyond the current experience of the Group of Seven (G-7) economies, and focusing instead on historical cases, and cases from a few contemporary economies, where policy encouraged robust market discipline.

When one does so, the clear message that emerges from the evidence is that debt market discipline is a very powerful force for punishing losses or the risk of losses. A second important lesson is that market discipline has been wielded with great precision. The notion that market discipline produces chaotic bank runs is simply not true, either as a description of the history of banking in the United States or elsewhere, or as a description of current market discipline.

Finally, an empirical examination of the operation of a market disciplined banking system provides unique insight about market reactions to loss and to the risk of loss. Does market discipline create incentives for banks to maintain higher equity capital and lower asset risk, ex ante, or does it instead operate mainly after the fact, to force banks to adjust their equity capital and asset risk ex post to adverse shocks? The evidence clearly shows that market discipline exerts its influence both ex ante and ex post. Ex ante, banks operating under market discipline satisfied market-determined risk-based capital standards; banks with higher asset risk were forced by the market to maintain higher equity. Ex post, banks that suffered losses were penalized by withdrawals and higher costs of debt, which encouraged them to reduce asset risk and cut dividends to restore market confidence.

The strong incentives that market discipline creates for banks to react to losses with reduced asset risk and retentions of earnings are a key benefit from market discipline. In the wake of bank losses today, regulators often forbear, and in doing so, make banking systems vulnerable to eventual collapse. Market discipline was unforgiving, and thus forced banks to respond to losses aggressively and quickly. Those responses explain why systemic banking collapse was so rare historically, in contrast to modern day experience. Safety nets create a tolerance for bad risk management, ex ante, and an incentive for those who suffer losses to double their bets, ex post. In an earlier session at this conference, Malcolm Knight noted that banks today seemed not to manage "macro" risk very well, and he questioned whether market discipline was wise enough to prevent cycles of banking system collapse produced by waves of excessive market exuberance followed by excessive market pessimism. The history of market discipline, however, suggests that the absence of market discipline has been the most important contributor to poor management of macro risk, and to systemic banking sector collapses. From the standpoint of systemic risk in banking, it is far more important that bankers and market participants be scared than that they be smart.

I begin by briefly reviewing historical evidence about the operation of market discipline, banking panics, and systemic banking collapses. I then consider the rationale for restoring a modicum of market discipline in banking systems today, and consider the regulatory changes that would be necessary to reestablish market discipline.

2. What Does a Disciplined Banking System Look Like?

For more than two millennia, banks have structured themselves in a way that promotes market discipline. The reliance on short-term debt, and the use of first-come, first-served rules of payment to depositors, provided uniquely strong incentives for informed depositors to monitor banks, and for banks to do their utmost to maintain depositor confidence about their capital adequacy and risk management (Calomiris and Kahn, 1991).

It is a common, and mistaken, perception that this exposure to depositor discipline promoted systemic collapse. Many economists and policymakers believe, for example, that banks were more prone to failure under the disciplined historical environment than they are in the present environment, and many point to the banking panics in the United States during the nineteenth century, and the banking difficulties of the Great Depression of the 1930s, as evidence of historical banking fragility.

Historical evidence actually points to very different conclusions. By the mid-nineteenth century, the United States was unique among countries in the incidence of banking panics, defined as moments of widespread withdrawal by depositors from the banking system (Bordo, 1985; Calomiris, 2000). But, as disruptive as the pre-World War I banking panics of 1873, 1884, 1890, 1893, 1896, and 1907 were to the operation of the U.S. system, they were brief episodes, and involved few important bank failures (Calomiris, 2000). Of all these episodes, the greatest incidence of bank failure occurred during the 1893 panic, in which the negative net worth of banks represented roughly one-tenth of one percent of U.S. gross domestic product (GDP) (Calomiris, 2003). By modern day standards, that failure experience would hardly be noticed. Since the late 1970s, over a hundred episodes have occurred in which countries have experienced waves of bank failure with resolution costs in excess of one percent of GDP, and more than a score of those episodes produced resolution costs in excess of ten percent of GDP.

That recent experience is unprecedented. During the pre-World War I era, banking system collapses were rare. I have been able to document only four episodes worldwide from 1880 until 1913 that resulted in banking sector resolution costs in excess of one percent of GDP: Argentina in 1890, Italy in 1893, Australia in 1893, and Norway in 1900. None of these cases produced resolution costs in excess of ten percent of GDP, and only two of them (Argentina and Australia) produced costs in excess of three percent of GDP. Of the four cases, the Italian and Argentine cases were directly traceable to incentive problems produced by safety net guarantees (liability insurance for the Banca Romana, and mortgage guarantees for Argentine banks). During the Great Depression, banking system losses were also smaller than during many of the episodes of the last twenty years. In the U.S., the resolution costs of bank failures during the Depression was less than four percent of GDP.

The reason that losses from bank failures were smaller historically was because bank lending contracted quickly in the wake of shocks to the system, reducing the risk of banking sector collapse. Banks suffering asset losses also cut their dividends to retain equity capital, to reassure depositors that the risk of loss to depositors was low. Banks that failed to cut loans and dividends enough to restore depositor confidence saw deposit costs rise, and saw their deposits leaving for safer destinations in other banks.

Consider, for example, the experience of U.S. banks during the Great Depression. During the boom of the 1920s, New York banks raised their ratio of loans relative to the sum of cash and government securities from 2.1 in 1922 to 3.3 in 1929. That rising risk on the asset side, however, was offset by a rise in the ratio of equity to assets, which rose (in market value terms) from 18 percent in 1922 to 33 percent in 1929 (Calomiris and Wilson, 2004). When the shocks of the Great Depression hit banks, New York banks responded quickly and dramatically. By 1933, the ratio of loans to cash and government securities had fallen to 1.0, and by 1940, it stood at 0.3. Dividends of New York banks fell from $392 million in 1929 to $162 million by 1940. Few New York banks failed during the Depression. Cross-sectional regression analysis shows that rising default risks in banks that failed to reduce asset risk and cut dividends resulted in outflows of deposits—the market discipline that forced banks to be prudent.

Similarly, in Chicago, banks that suffered the most during the Depression also saw severe contractions in their retail deposits, and were forced to rely increasingly on high-priced sources of funds from other institutions (Calomiris and Mason, 1997). More generally, throughout the country, banks that failed tended to be those that were unable to recover deposit market confidence in the wake of severe shocks to their assets (Calomiris and Mason, 2003a). Calomiris and Mason (1997, 2003a) find that bank failures were generally traceable to fundamental weakness, rather than "panic" or illiquidity, on the part of banks. For the most part, during the Depression, market discipline seems to have been applied selectively to weak institutions.

Because market discipline produced a contraction of lending, it contributed to the severity and duration of the Depression. Calomiris and Mason (2003b) find that states in which shocks to banks were especially severe saw the biggest declines in lending, and they trace the effect of the decline in the supply of loans in producing unusually severe contractions in output.

Argentina provides a modern day example of a similar role of market discipline in promoting effective bank risk management, with similar consequences for the supply of lending in the wake of bank losses. Calomiris and Powell (2001) review regulatory policies and bank behavior in Argentina during the 1990s. Weak banks that were unable to bolster capital and cut risk in the wake of losses suffered rapid deposit withdrawals, and sometimes were forced to fail. The operation of deposit market discipline, and the prospect of failure (due to the absence of government bailouts) encouraged prudent risk management. As during the Great Depression, deposits and loans contracted dramatically during the 1995 crisis in Argentina, which contributed to the contraction in economic activity.

A clear lesson of the experiences reviewed above is that market discipline produces a contraction in the supply of credit. Like *any* effective form of prudential regulation, market discipline results in the management of risk and equity capital to produce adequate equity capital relative to asset risk. Adequate equity relative to asset risk is achieved through a combination of reduced dividends, reduced lending, and other reductions in asset risk (for example, reduced exposure to market risks).

Some critics of market discipline complain that it works too well as a form of prudential regulation. Reductions in the supply of loans, critics argue, worsen the severity of recessions, and result in unnecessary economic distress. When considering such criticisms, however, it is important to bear two points in mind.

First, any attempt to limit the "procyclicality" of prudential regulations (whether in the form of forbearance from meeting equity capital guidelines, or government protection of banks to offset the effects of market discipline) necessarily increases the risk of banking sector collapse. That is true not only because of the immediate effect on bank risk from relaxing such constraints, but more importantly, because banks often will game the regulatory system to take full advantage of such protection by expanding their risks at the expense of the taxpayers.

Second, theory and empirical evidence suggest that forbearance does not achieve its intended results of making loans available to creditworthy borrowers, or of mitigating the macroeconomic cyclical consequences that would attend the contraction of credit produced in a disciplined banking system. Banks that have experienced problems often use government protection to pursue "resurrection risk-taking," doubling their bets by using government support to offer increased protection to unproductive crony borrowers, or to increase foreign exchange risk in a desperate attempt to reverse their fortunes. These high-risk strategies tend not to produce resurrection, and are wasteful of taxpayer resources in the process. In fact, for these reasons, forbearance and government support of weak banks tend to exacerbate the cyclical severity of recessions (Beim and Calomiris, 2001; Honohan and Klingebiel, 2000; Boyd et al., 2000; and Cull et al., 2000). Thus, it is not true that forbearance or the mitigating of market discipline works as a form of countercyclical policy; on the contrary, because of the ways banks respond to those policies, they typically deepen financial collapse and recessions.

3. Why Regulators Need Markets

Having established that market discipline works as a means of enforcing prudential risk-based equity capital standards, that it does so with little risk of unwarranted "panic" side effects or other disruptions, and that the adverse macroeconomic effects of market discipline are not avoided by forbearance, I now turn to the question of whether regulatory actions, in the absence of market discipline, can achieve the same results.

From a theoretical perspective, there are two reasons why supervision and regulation without market discipline will tend to be deficient. First, market participants may have better access to information, or be better skilled at interpreting the meaning of information, than regulators or supervisors. For example, one of the reasons that Argentine bank regulators were keen to increase the role of market discipline over banks in the 1990s was the belief that market participants (who were themselves active participants in derivatives markets) had better real time information about banks' derivatives exposures than did supervisors. Second, market participants face different incentives than regulators and supervisors in their use of information. Market participants with their own money on the line will tend to be far more reliable in their willingness to impose discipline. A consistent theme of the past two decades of supervisory and regulatory behavior around the world is that supervisors and regulators often face strong incentives to forbear. Unlike market participants, they are not playing with their own money. Furthermore, supervisors and regulators are often paid little, and in many countries, are susceptible to bribes. And supervisors may suffer adverse consequences from performing their jobs properly. Bankers can appeal to politicians to exert political pressure on regulators and supervisors, who may risk losing their jobs if they do not agree to forbear. Finally, the heavy reliance on book value capital requirements (which depend for their effectiveness on the recognition of losses by banks and their supervisors) as the primary tool of prudential regulation provides a convenient means for supervisors and regulators to avoid imposing discipline on banks by simply postponing the recognition of problems.

In an important empirical study of regulatory practice around the world, Barth, Caprio, and Levine (2002) examine the relative effectiveness of market discipline versus other prudential regulations as a means of promoting banking sector stability. They find that market discipline is uniquely effective, and find no significant effects from other forms of regulation in reducing banking sector risk.

4. How to Reestablish Market Discipline

Having argued that market discipline is uniquely valuable as an element of prudential regulation, I now turn to the question of how it might be reestablished. One means of doing so would be to eliminate the government safety net for banks through the outright repeal of deposit insurance. While I believe that it is true that there is no legitimate argument in favor of deposit insurance as an economic mechanism (Calomiris, 2000), in general, I do not favor deposit insurance repeal as the means of introducing market discipline into the banking system, for one simple reason: Typically, repealing the safety net is simply not credible. As has been illustrated over and over again, politicians find it difficult to impose losses on small savers. More importantly, politicians are willing to use the excuse of helping small savers to justify their wholesale protection of crony capitalists through bank bailouts and guarantees of all bank deposits.

Reinstating market discipline, then, is a policy challenge that must take into account both the economics of "mechanism design" and the politics of credible regulation. The trick is to find ways to promote effective market discipline in a way that is politically robust—that is, in a way that is not likely to fall prey to political pressures that could be brought to bear by bankers, depositors, or populist politicians before the market has a chance to impose its discipline on banks.

Candidate policies include: 1) "narrow banking," 2) increasing reliance on "internal models" of risk that use market measures of asset values and asset risk, and 3) an array of "hard" and observable market-determined constraints that banks must satisfy as part of their regulatory compliance (including, but not limited to, a subordinated debt requirement as part of the bank's prudential risk-based minimum capital requirement). In my view, only the third approach has much of a chance of succeeding.

Narrow banking refers to the idea of insuring only transactional deposits of banks, and requiring insured deposits to be backed entirely by low-risk assets (Treasury bills). Insured deposits and the assets that back them would be housed in a separate narrow bank subsidiary within the broader bank. The idea is to limit the abuse of safety net protection by segregating the assets that back transaction deposits from other assets. The problem with this approach is that it presumes, unrealistically, that de jure uninsured deposits would be uninsured de facto, as well. There is much evidence to suggest the contrary. Banks often correctly anticipate that they will receive government protection even in the absence of a deposit insurance system. Indeed, one could argue that the absence of any protection invites ad hoc protection to occur on a broader basis than it would if a credible, limited system of protection were in existence.

A second option, currently favored by the Basel Committee and U.S. bank regulators, is to require large banks to adopt internal models of their risk, using market information and sophisticated approaches for measuring risk that capture the bank's exposure to loss from a variety of influences. Enthusiasts of this approach point out that it seems to offer a desirable combination of objectivity and flexibility in the measurement and regulation of bank risk. The problem, however, is that the measurement of risk relied upon by supervisors and regulators remains unobservable to the market. Models are developed by banks and approved by regulators. The tendency for regulators to forbear limits the desirability of this approach. Forbearance would take the form of permitting banks to adopt unrealistic assumptions about the measurement of risk that would be hard to hold supervisors or regulators accountable for, ex post. The internal models approach may make sense as a complement to imposing market discipline (in the presence of market discipline, internal models may be helpful as a supervisory tool), but it cannot substitute for market discipline.

The third, and final, regulatory option is to incorporate "hard" market constraints into the regulatory process. One such hard constraint would be to require that banks maintain a minimum amount of credibly uninsured (subordinated) debt as part of their capital structure. Because banks would always be on this financing margin, even if the amount of the unprotected debt were small, it would provide an important indicator of market opinion about banks, and one that would not be subject to the political pressures that give rise to forbearance. The U.S. Shadow Financial Regulatory Committee (2000) discusses in detail the challenges to constructing a credible subordinated debt requirement and ways of overcoming those challenges.

This is not the place to review in detail the argument for a minimum subordinated debt requirement, or to discuss the important question of how its form could vary across countries. Rather, I would make three points. First, without some form of credibly uninsured debt as a continuing feature of bank financing decisions, supervisors and regulators will lack the benefit of market opinions about bank risk when those opinions are needed most. Banks that are not required to employ uninsured debt as a financing tool will choose to avoid it, particularly at moments when it is needed most (when banks become weak), since banks will prefer not to advertise the market's low opinion about them to their regulators.

Second, subordinated debt is only one of many potentially useful hard and observable constraints that could be adopted as part of the regulatory process. In Argentina during the 1990s, other hard, observable constraints, which depended on market information, were also employed (Calomiris and Powell, 2001). For example, minimum equity capital requirements were set as a function of loan interest rates. The higher the loan interest rate charged by the bank, the higher the amount of equity capital required to back the loan. Equity capital requirements for market risk also reflected explicit value-at-risk measures, which were based on observable market volatilities. Finally, banks' regulatory liquidity requirements could be met, in part, in the form of standby arrangements with foreign banks, which meant that positive market perceptions about a local bank translated directly into reduced regulatory compliance costs. The point is that there are many ways to bring hard, observable market pricing into the regulatory process. A minimum subordinated debt requirement will work better if is accompanied by other measures that provide additional, independent market assessments of bank risk, and translate those assessments into credible prudential actions.

Third, subordinated debt, or other forms of hard, observable constraints, should not be seen as a substitute for supervision and prudential regulation, but rather as a means for making supervision and regulation more effective. Regulators and markets are complementary processors of information. Regulators have access to information about banks not available to markets, and vice versa. The primary gains from incorporating market discipline into the regulatory process are to give additional information to regulators and supervisors, and to increase the accountability of regulators and supervisors by creating objective, observable measures of bank condition that discourage regulatory forbearance.

5. What Market Discipline Is Not

Some regulators now pay lip service to the need for market discipline, but define market discipline in ways that are unlikely to be effective. For example, the Basel Committee's definition of market discipline—its "third pillar" of prudential regulation—revolves around disclosure standards. Disclosure of information certainly is a prerequisite to market discipline, but it does not follow that regulatory disclosure standards are either a necessary or a sufficient condition for market discipline.

Clearly, disclosure standards are not sufficient for establishing market discipline. If debt market participants have no debt at risk of loss, then they face little incentive to pay attention to information disclosed by banks, and therefore, such disclosure may have no effect on prudential management of asset risk or equity capital. Furthermore, disclosure standards may be superfluous in an environment where market participants hold risky bank debt, since in that environment, banks will face strong incentives to provide meaningful information to markets about their risks even if they are not required to do so by regulators. The history of market discipline in banking predates by centuries any regulatory disclosure requirements, suggesting that markets have been able to get the information they need when banks raise risky debt in the market, even in the absence of disclosure standards.

Another false definition of market discipline relates to the regulatory use of debt ratings by private ratings agencies. Regulators increasingly require the use of ratings when measuring the riskiness either of bank assets or of bank liabilities. But ratings are not a reliable measure of risk, and they become especially unreliable when regulators try to use them for that purpose. Normally, in the absence of regulatory requirements, the constituency for a rating is the holder of the security being rated. The demand for a ratings agency's services depends crucially on its reputation with debt holders, which provides an incentive for honest, critical ratings. But when ratings are used to satisfy regulatory requirements, the constituency for the rating is often the bank (either as a holder of the rated asset, or as an issuer of the rated liability), and the ratings agency's incentives will be quite different. Now, it will be rewarded for helping the bank to avoid a costly regulatory constraint by underestimating the default risk of the rated debt. Evidence from a variety of experiences suggests that the regulatory use of ratings can lead to "grade inflation," and in some cases, even produce a race to the bottom among ratings agencies (Cantor and Packer, 1994; Calomiris, and Powell, 2001).

6. Conclusion

Banking systems used to depend primarily on the behavior of bank debt holders to encourage the prudential management of risk and equity capital by bankers. Market discipline worked effectively to limit risk-taking by banks, and provided strong incentives for proper risk management by banks. In recent decades, government protection of banks has resulted in the reduction, and in some cases, the elimination of the risk of loss to market participants that hold bank debt. In many countries, the burden of disciplining banks has fallen entirely on supervisors and regulators, and they have proven themselves unwilling or unable to substitute adequately for the discipline of the market.

It would be desirable and feasible to reestablish the role of market discipline in bank regulation through the use of "hard," observable, market-determined regulatory constraints as part of prudential bank regulation. Disclosure rules and reliance on ratings agencies' opinions, by themselves, cannot produce market discipline. There is no substitute for the information that can be obtained, and the discipline that results, from the behavior of market participants placing their own funds at risk.

*Charles W. Calomiris is the Henry Kaufman Professor of Financial Institutions at Columbia Business School.

References

Barth, James R., Gerard Caprio, Jr., and Ross Levine, 2002, "Bank regulation and supervision: What works best?," National Bureau of Economic Research, working paper, No. 9323.

Beim, David O., and Charles W. Calomiris, 2001, *Emerging Financial Markets*, New York: McGraw Hill-Irwin.

Bordo, Michael D., 1985, "The impact and international transmission of financial crises," *Rivisti di Storia Economica*, Vol. 2, pp. 41–78.

Boyd, John, Pedro Gomis, Sungkyu Kwak, and Bruce Smith, 2000, "A user's guide to banking crises," World Bank, conference paper.

Calomiris, Charles W., 2003, "Victorian perspectives on the banking crises of the 1990s," Columbia Business School, working paper.

_____, 2000, *U.S. Bank Deregulation in Historical Perspective*, Cambridge, UK: Cambridge University Press.

Calomiris, Charles W., and Charles M. Kahn, 1991, "The role of demandable debt in structuring optimal banking arrangements," *American Economic Review*, June.

Calomiris, Charles W., and Joseph R. Mason, 2003a, "Fundamentals, panics, and bank distress during the Great Depression," *American Economic Review*, December.

_____, 2003b, "Consequences of bank distress during the Great Depression," *American Economic Review*, June, pp. 937–947.

_____, 1997, "Contagion and bank failures during the Great Depression: The June 1932 Chicago banking panic," *American Economic Review*, December, pp. 863–883.

Calomiris, Charles W., and Andrew Powell, 2001, "Can emerging market bank regulators establish credible discipline? The case of Argentina, 1992–99," in *Prudential Supervision: What Works and What Doesn't*, Frederic S. Mishkin (ed.), Chicago: University of Chicago Press, pp. 147–196.

Calomiris, Charles W., and Berry Wilson, 2004, "Bank capital and portfolio management: The 1930s capital crunch and scramble to shed risk," *Journal of Business*, forthcoming.

Cantor, Richard, and Frank Packer, 1994, "The credit rating industry," *Quarterly Review*, Federal Reserve Bank of New York, Vol. 19, Summer–Fall, pp. 1–26.

Cull, Robert, Lemma Senbet, and Marco Sorge, 2000, "Deposit insurance and financial development," World Bank, conference paper.

Honohan, Patrick, and Daniela Klingebiel, 2000, "Controlling fiscal costs of banking crises," World Bank, conference paper.

U.S. Shadow Financial Regulatory Committee, 2000, *Reforming Bank Capital Regulation: A Proposal by the U.S. Shadow Financial Regulatory Committee*, Washington, DC: AEI Press.

Chapter 33

Comment on Policy

Christine M. Cumming*
Federal Reserve Bank of New York

Let me begin by thanking the Federal Reserve Bank of Chicago and the Bank for International Settlements for this excellent conference on market discipline and for inviting me to participate in this final panel.

I'd like to highlight some themes from the last two days by comparing the current corporate governance crisis with another recent crisis, the asset quality problems in the banking system in the early 1990s. The asset quality problems then severely affected the condition of the banking system. The problems began with mistakes in credit judgment, a failure to take appropriate note of the buildup of exposures across the market, and the concentration of exposures with similar risk characteristics at many individual banks. Breakdowns in risk management and internal controls at these banks compounded the problems.

Today's corporate governance crisis inelegantly lumps together under a single rubric a wide-ranging set of problems that have surfaced over the last two years. These problems have in common lapses in professional standards at institutions whose business depends on trust, including many leading financial institutions and corporations. Several speakers noted yesterday that lapses also have occurred in firms that play a due diligence role in financial markets, such as accountants, lawyers, analysts, and rating agencies, the "gatekeepers" in our financial system.

Speakers at this conference have presented evidence that a loss of public confidence in chief executive officers and concerns about ethical integrity are real. A study of corporate governance issues (Conference Board Commission on Public Trust and Private Enterprise, 2003) presents evidence on this latter point. It cites results from a KPMG "Organizational Integrity Survey" conducted in 2000, before the current crisis began. The survey found that 60 percent of employees surveyed observed violations of law or company standards at least "sometimes" in a 12-month period.[1]

The prominent role of ethical lapses is a large part of what makes the corporate governance crisis so uncomfortable. The asset quality problem involved bad judgment, inadequate risk management, and flawed internal control systems at center stage.

Ethical lapses no doubt also played a role, but not a prominent one. In contrast, the undeniable recent rise in restatements and Securities and Exchange Commission and criminal investigations puts ethics center stage. The strong reaction to these developments affirms the view that the vast majority of people in our business places are honest and ethical and see the need to address the risk of an erosion in integrity in our markets.

So what is the way out? Our experience with major problems with asset quality in the early 1990s could be instructive. That crisis proceeded in three stages.

First, there was an intense period of problem identification and cleanup in the form of recognizing problem loans. Banks wrote off exposures when necessary, and mobilized their workout staffs when some eventual recovery still seemed possible.

Second, the passage of Federal Deposit Insurance Corporation Improvement Act (FDICIA) in late 1991 represented an important milestone. This law was no compliment to bankers or their regulators for a job well done. Given the magnitude of the perceived failures, Congress stepped in with a series of minimum standards to make sure a comparable problem could not recur.

Third and very important, as problem identification ended and FDICIA implementation began, bank managers began a voluntary reform process. The process began because the managers of virtually every large surviving bank said "never again." As a result, they made major improvements to credit risk management, built up loan review staffs, and strengthened the analysis of risk and return at the business line and transaction level. These reforms went well beyond FDICIA requirements and represented the seeds of the risk management revolution in banking.

A comparable reform process took place as supervisors sought to upgrade the examination and surveillance process. The thinking that led to risk-focused examinations just a few years later began in those early post-FDICIA years. Here, too, supervisors modernized the supervision process well beyond FDICIA requirements.

Central to both reform processes was the willingness of bank managers and supervisors to acknowledge the severity of the problem. Managers and supervisors could be said to "own the problem." From the negative currents of the crisis, an affirmative and innovative direction emerged that has served the industry and the financial system well.

We can identify the same three phases in the current corporate governance crisis. We've had a period of problem identification and repair. For example, the requirement that management certify their financial statements in mid-August 2002 was probably helpful, providing a window of opportunity to get accounting problems disclosed, one strand of the governance-related problems. The stream of revelations, however, has continued into the fall, so the close of this phase remains uncertain.

The Sarbanes–Oxley Act represents the sort of second-phase framework legislation in this crisis that FDICIA represented in the asset quality crisis. As several noted yesterday, Sarbanes–Oxley largely codifies good governance practice. Charles Elson in particular noted that the corporate governance changes in Sarbanes–Oxley were in train, if slowly, from the mid-1990s. The corporate governance crisis simply accelerated movement in an established direction.

It is the third phase of private, voluntary reform that still needs to gain traction. Individual firms have taken the lead in making specific corporate governance reforms, but it appears that no groundswell of announcements from other corporations followed.

Of course, important changes are likely to occur, but it's notable that in these instances, some official body or their stand-in is providing the push. Many large corporations will end up with a lead director and outside directors will meet periodically without management present, given the New York Stock Exchange's new requirements. The latter especially is a potentially powerful reform. The Financial Accounting Standards Board, as we heard at this conference, will likely promulgate a standard on expensing options. More indirectly relevant to corporate governance, the Jobs and Growth Act of 2003 has increased incentives to pay dividends, an important discipline on firms. Paying dividends represents a continuing commitment to the shareholders to make cash payments, a stronger commitment than the occasional buyback of shares.

In measuring how strong the third wave of private, voluntary reform, executive compensation is probably the bellwether issue. The Conference Board Commission tackles the issue head on, beginning the discussion with:

> The Commission shares the public's anger over excessive executive compensation, especially to executives of failed or failing companies, and finds that compensation abuses have contributed to a dramatic loss of confidence in the governance of American publicly held corporations—with visible and damaging financial market effects.[2]

Michael Jensen earlier in this conference provided a thoughtful assessment of the intoxicating, but ultimately dangerous firm-level dynamics created by excessive increases in stock prices. Compensation is a major channel of that dynamic. Imagine the impact if 100 leading corporations adopted Michael Jensen's suggestion to address the problem: that stock options be eliminated altogether in executive compensation.

The question remains: Who owns the problem?

Owning the problem is important because an industry-initiated reform process backed by "never-again" conviction is likely to be far more efficient than government regulation. As Clifford Smith pointed out yesterday, regulation in an area as firm-specific and internal as corporate governance is likely to involve opportunity cost losses far greater than the costs of simply complying with the regulations. Those opportunity costs have to be all the larger in today's fast-paced economy, with its short product cycles and rapid changes in competitive leadership.

There may be a greater social opportunity loss, however. That is the opportunity to turn the very negative currents evident today into an affirmative industry-driven movement for change that could make real breakthroughs in governance methodologies and structures. This conference has highlighted several possible areas of reform.

The discussion has surfaced questions about realistic expectations for the role of directors given the existing resources available to them. Should the resources be expanded and how? Do parts of the director's role need to be rethought? The discussion has several times raised questions about the corporate governance of institutional investors, a much neglected topic. What are the responsibilities of institutional investors to investors? What internal mechanism for overseeing executive management is appropriate for such investors and how does that vary by type of institutional investor? What disclosures are appropriate? The discussion has raised several possibilities for data collection and dissemination at both the market-wide and the firm level to enhance transparency and aid sound governance and risk management practices.

Finally, the conference has devoted attention to the need for reform in the accounting industry. An enormous opportunity exists to modernize the profession, instill a renewed sense of mission in the next generation of accountants, and catalyze intellectual breakthrough in the discipline.

This conference opened with the transparency and governance of banks. The FDICIA required larger banks to adopt many of the reforms recently enacted in Sarbanes–Oxley. In explaining the success of banks in weathering this past recession, separating the effects of better governance from those of many other improvements since the early 1990s, notably higher capital and more sophisticated risk management, is probably impossible, but there is little doubt that they helped. Based on that experience, it seems reasonable to expect real improvement in the corporate sector more broadly.

The value of strong corporate governance in banks and other financial institutions offers an antidote to the too-big-to-fail problem. Most large financial institutions have substantial franchise value beyond the balance sheet. Franchise value is most obvious for retail banking operations, where there is a well-developed market in deposits and the kind of brand and customer stickiness that are easily identified as intangibles. But wholesale businesses, especially payments and custody businesses, have similar qualities to varying extents, as reflected in fairly well developed markets for some of them.

Franchise value probably holds up well in the early phases of a bank's financial or asset quality problem. As a financial company deteriorates, of course, these intangibles deteriorate, as high-quality customers move to other providers and customers and counterparties adopt defensive, just-in-case strategies in their relationship with the firm.

Effective corporate governance can take account of this phenomenon. In the U.S., the board of directors of a financial institution is required to act in the interest of the shareholders. Given the growth of markets for financial businesses and financial institutions, that is, the market for corporate control, the board and management confronting rising bank distress should feel obligated to carefully consider which options maximize shareholder interest, and act on those options promptly. An infrastructure of investment bankers, accountants, and others is available to provide information to help the board and management make an informed decision. The need for a strong market in corporate control is one of Hal Scott's prerequisites for market transparency, along with capital instruments and legal mechanisms for bankruptcy and foreclosure.

Our U.S. experience has provided a series of stunning examples of the cost, and it is huge, when corporations and other institutions damage their reputation in an advanced economy. These examples have received global press attention. They make instructive case studies. I suspect a careful analysis of bond and equity prices at the security-by-security level would demonstrate the reputation cost effects that Luigi Zingales suggested we should try to identify.

How we tackle the reforms we make here in the U.S. will thus have global spillovers. And much is at stake. This conference contained a number of papers that presented evidence of the actual gains from greater market transparency in emerging market economies where transparency is increasing and the potential gains where it is not.

Whether we muddle through or break through our problems, especially those that have a large component of ethical lapses, the result matters in a political economy dimension. As market reforms have taken place all over the world and regulatory and institutional barriers have come down, some ongoing skepticism has persisted about the humanity and the morality of what to many looks like Darwinian competition.

In that sense, we need to recognize that, as many at this conference have stated, no system of incentives and controls are simultaneously foolproof and viable. Human judgment is a crucial component of any governance system. With many of us involved in educating young people for their professional careers or training them as they begin working, we all have a role to play. We need to focus on the individual and the formation of his or her values in the higher education process and in the business or professional setting.

*Christine M. Cumming is the executive vice president and director of research at the Federal Reserve Bank of New York. The views in this comment are those of the author and do not represent the views of the Federal Reserve Bank of New York or the Federal Reserve System.

Notes

1. Conference Board Commission on Public Trust and Private Enterprise (2003), pp. 22–23.

2. ibid., p. 9.

Reference

Conference Board Commission on Public Trust and Private Enterprise, The, 2003, "Findings and recommendations," New York, January.

Chapter 34

Market Discipline—Interaction with Public Policy

Patricia Jackson*
Bank of England

Pillar 3, aimed at enhancing market discipline, is an important part of the Basel Committee proposals for a new risk-based capital standard. This raises the question of what the role of the authorities is in what is essentially a private sector process. It also raises the question whether more reliance on enhanced market discipline could reduce the need for the advanced risk measurement processes proposed in Basel II.

1. The Role of Market Discipline

Market discipline would help to make the financial system more robust if it changed the behavior of the market participants ex ante. If the threat of an adverse market reaction to a significant increase in risk taking relative to capital discouraged risky behavior then the system could be safer. Some firms clearly would still take large risks and, in terms of the system, an early reaction by the market is preferable to a sudden and severe reaction.

Effective market discipline relies on several conditions being met (Hoggarth, Jackson, and Nier 2003a):

• The market must have information to assess riskiness.

• Those in the market with a claim must be at risk of loss if the firm fails.

• The cost to the firm of an adverse market view must be significant.

There are three main channels for market discipline for a bank: the equity market through the cost of capital and, for the management, the threat of takeover; the bank's counterparties through their setting of the size and price for lines/exposures; and subordinated debt. Individual depositors will react too late to be a main channel and for most banks subordinated debt is a relatively small percentage of liabilities, although a significant part of tier 2 capital. Bliss and Flannery (2002) did not find any evidence that an increase in subordinated debt yield spreads changed bank asset allocation. Of the three routes, the equity market and a bank's counterparties are probably the most important. With these two routes, the better the information, probably the earlier the reaction to any build up in risk.

2. The Role of the Authorities

Given that this is a market process, what is the role of the authorities? This can be divided into several parts. The first is ensuring that public sector policies do not undermine market discipline. In terms of the conditions for effective market discipline set out above, clearly public safety nets affect the second condition. If markets believe banks are too big to fail, or that banks in general might be bailed out, then those with a claim on the bank may not feel at risk of loss. But public policies also affect the third condition. If insurance for deposits is broad, including, for example, wholesale counterparties, the costs to a firm of an adverse view will be substantially reduced, especially where funding of deposit insurance is not risk based. This is likely to enable higher risks to be run relative to capital. The negative effects of deposit protection are well understood (for example, Merton, 1977).

Baumann and Nier (2003) looking at 729 banks from 32 countries show that banks fully funded from insured deposits will have an equity to assets ratio 2 percentage points lower than the mean of 10.5 and banks which benefit from government support over one percentage point lower.

Creating the right environment for market discipline should influence the general structure of safety net policies and also the handling of financial crises. In a financial crisis the authorities will face a trade-off. The immediate costs imposed by the crisis may be reduced by the introduction of wide safety nets but at the cost of increasing the likelihood of future crisis by damaging market discipline. There is evidence that unlimited deposit protection reduces the output costs of resolving banking crises while increasing the likelihood that a country experiences a crisis. See Hoggarth, Jackson, and Nier (2003b).

All these elements are related with the public sector's own influence on market discipline. But does the public sector also have a more general role in enhancing market discipline? There may be changes that can be made to the institutional framework that could make market discipline more effective. The Baumann and Nier study also shows that lack of disclosure can enable banks to run higher risks. Why is there a public sector role here? In other words, why does market pressure not lead to adequate information disclosure? Banks when considering information disclosure focus on the private costs not the public benefits. Currently banks in some countries do not release core information such as their tier 1 ratio. Tier 1 capital is the component able to absorb losses prior to default and therefore essential to assess riskiness. There is some evidence that shareholders attempt to free ride on the regulators assuming that they are assessing riskiness leaving the equity market to focus on earnings—reducing the amount of information they need. This may well be shortsighted given that regulators do not guarantee that banks will not fail. Counterparties would use the information if they had it but may not always penalize their counterparts for lack of information disclosure on the off chance that they might be more risky.

There may also be coordination issues. Banks are concerned that deluging market analysts with information not released by other banks may be misinterpreted and may lead to greater share price volatility. Nonstandard disclosure is difficult to assess. Banks currently disclose information on value at risk of the trading portfolios under different confidence intervals and holding periods, making comparison almost impossible. Many banks release quantities of qualitative information but this is difficult to interpret. The more difficult the information is to assess, the higher the costs for analysts and the more that reactions might not be correct.

Public policy can therefore have a role in both ensuring that core information is disclosed to the market and standardizing the statistics that are shown. This is the approach that the Basel Committee is adopting in pillar 3 of Basel 3. Pillar 3 sets out the core information items that banks must disclose. The composition of capital (for example, tier 1 and innovative instruments within it) will have to be disclosed. Other important elements, like the exposure to an interest rate shock and information on the credit books, will also have to be disclosed. The committee has streamlined the proposals but some banks still argue that it will be difficult for analysts to interpret. But a settled set of data, meeting standards determining the content, should be far easier to assess than the plethora of pieces of partial information currently released on bases that vary bank by bank. There is another criticism that is directed exactly at this standardization. That banks may have other more important items which should be released given the structure of their portfolios, but this can still be provided as an additional element. Clearly banks can offer more information if they wish to and offer a gloss to the core statistics.

In any public policy in this area, the costs and benefits of requirements need to be considered. It is this process that has led to some streamlining of the Basel III proposals and a focus on minimum standards for core information disclosure.

Some commentators have argued that although pillar 3 minimum disclosure is important, the more complex credit risk measurement in Basel II is not necessary—indeed, one could be the substitute for the other. However, a very important part of Basel II is the establishment of a new language of risk—probability of default (PD), loss given default (LGD), and exposure at default on commitments (EAD)—according to set standards. This new language of risk in the internal ratings approach enables comparable credit risk disclosure to be made. For banks not on the internal ratings approach for credit risk disclosure will largely be limited to areas like provisions and past due assets, by region and type of industry. In contrast, for institutional review board (IRB) banks, loans by PD band and default outturns by main portfolios—corporate, sovereign, interbank, and retail—will be possible. For advanced IRB banks which set their own LGDs, weighted average loss given default by band will also be disclosed. This will be a huge advance in terms of information on credit risk. Currently a few banks release information on loans by band and for those that do there is no standardization in terms of what the bands mean. The information is also difficult to interpret because banks do not necessarily release information on their whole portfolio which can be misleading. Many banks release qualitative information on credit books but this is even more difficult to interpret. The advanced credit risk capital approaches are therefore a precondition for effective disclosure at this juncture.

*Patricia Jackson is the special advisor responsible for coordinating research projects on financial stability at the Bank of England.

References

Basel Committee on Banking Supervision, 2003, "The New Basel Capital Accord," Bank for International Settlements, consultative document, April.

Baumann, Ursel, and Erlend Nier, 2004, "Disclosure, volatility, and transparency," *Economic Policy Review*, Federal Reserve Bank of New York, forthcoming.

_____, 2003, "Market discipline, disclosure, and moral hazard in banking," *Proceedings of the 2003 Conference on Bank Structure and Competition*, Federal Reserve Bank of Chicago.

Bliss, Robert, and Mark Flannery, 2002 "Market discipline and the governance of U.S. bank holding companies: Monitoring versus influencing," *European Finance Review*, Vol. 6, No. 3, pp. 361–395.

Hoggarth, Glenn, Patricia Jackson, and Erlend Nier, 2003a, "Market discipline and financial stability," *The Future of Domestic Capital Markets in Developing Countries*, Robert E. Litan, Michael Pomerleano, and V. Sundararajan (eds.), Washington: Brookings Institution Press.

_____, 2003b, "Banking crises and the design of safety nets," paper presented to the 9th Economic Conference, Dubrovnik, Croatia.

Merton, Robert C., 1977, "An analytic derivation of the cost of deposit insurance loan guarantees," *Journal of Banking and Finance*, Vol. 1, pp. 3–11.

Conference Program

Market Discipline: The Evidence across Countries and Industries

Cosponsored by
Federal Reserve Bank of Chicago and Bank for International Settlements

October 30, 2003 – November 1, 2003
Federal Reserve Bank of Chicago
Chicago, Illinois USA

Thursday, October 30, 2003

12:30 pm – 1:20 pm   Registration

1:20 pm   **Welcome**
Malcolm D. Knight, General Manager,
Bank for International Settlements

Charles Evans, Senior Vice President
and Director of Research,
Federal Reserve Bank of Chicago

1:30 pm   **Session I: Theory of Market Discipline**

Moderator:
George G. Kaufman, Loyola University Chicago
and Federal Reserve Bank of Chicago

Papers:
*Market Discipline in Banking:
Where Do We Stand?*
Jean-Charles Rochet, Toulouse University

*Market Discipline: Players, Processes,
and Purposes*
Robert R. Bliss, Federal Reserve Bank of Chicago

*Market Discipline for Financial Institutions
and Sovereigns*
Hal S. Scott, Harvard Law School

Discussant:
Kostas Tsatsaronis, Bank for International
Settlements

3:30 pm   Break

3:50 pm   **Session II: Evidence of Market
                         Discipline in Banking**

Moderator:
Anil Kashyap, University of Chicago

Papers:
*Market Discipline of U.S. Financial Firms:
Recent Evidence and Research Issues*
Mark Flannery, University of Florida
Stanislava Nikolova, University of Florida

*Bank Market Discipline and Indicators
of Banking System Risk: The European Evidence*
Reint Gropp, European Central Bank

*Weakening Market and Regulatory Discipline
in Japanese Financial System*
Mitsuhiro Fukao, Keio University

*Market Discipline in Emerging Economies:
Beyond Bank Fundamentals*
Eduardo Levy-Yeyati, Universidad Torcuato Di Tella
Maria Soledad Martinez Peria, World Bank
Sergio L. Schmukler, World Bank

Discussant:
David Llewellyn, Loughborough University

6:00 pm   Reception

7:00 pm   Dinner and Keynote Speaker

                           Moderators:
                           Claudio Borio, Bank for International Settlements
                           Thomas Jones, Vice Chairman, International
                           Accounting Standards Board

Friday, October 31, 2003

7:30 am   Breakfast and Keynote Speaker

                           Moderator:
                           Michael H. Moskow, President,
                           Federal Reserve Bank of Chicago

                           Anne Krueger, First Deputy Managing Director,
                           International Monetary Fund

8:50 am   ## Session III: Evidence of Market
                           Discipline in Other Industries

                           Moderator:
                           David Marshall, Federal Reserve Bank of Chicago

                           Papers:
                           Market Discipline in Insurance and Reinsurance
                           Scott E. Harrington, University of South Carolina

                           *Conflicts of Interest and Market Discipline among
                           Financial Services Firms*
                           Ingo Walter, New York University

                           Market Discipline and Corporate Control
                           Clifford W. Smith, Jr., University of Rochester

                           Discussant:
                           Luigi Zingales, University of Chicago

10:30 am   Coffee

10:45 am   **Session IV: Evidence of Market Discipline for Countries**

Moderator:
Charles Evans, Senior Vice President and
Director of Research, Federal Reserve Bank
of Chicago

Papers:
*Capital Controls: Mud in the Wheels
of Market Discipline*
Kristen Forbes, Member-Designate,
President's Council of Economic Advisers

Equity Integration in Times of Crisis
Robert P. Flood, International Monetary Fund
Andrew K. Rose, University of California
  at Berkeley

Discussant:
Andrew Haldane, Bank of England

12:30 pm   Lunch and Keynote Speaker

Moderator:
Michael H. Moskow, President,
Federal Reserve Bank of Chicago

Malcolm D. Knight, General Manager,
Bank for International Settlements

2:00 pm   **Session V: Current State of Corporate Governance**

Moderator:
David Mayes, Bank of Finland

Papers:
*U.S. Corporate Governance: What Went Wrong
and Can It Be Fixed?*
Franklin R. Edwards, Columbia University

*The Agency Costs of Overvalued Equity
and the Reform of Corporate Governance*
Michael C. Jensen, Monitor Group
and Harvard University

Current Issues in European Corporate Governance
Marco Becht, Universite Libre de Bruxelles
Colin Mayer, Oxford University

Evolving Corporate Governance in Japan
Hugh Patrick, Columbia University

*Quis Custodiet Ipsos Custodes? Controlling
Conflicts of Interest in the Financial Industry*
Eugene N. White, Rutgers University

4:00 pm   Break

4:15 pm   **VIa: Interaction of Market Discipline
                 and Public Policy**

Moderator:
Randall Kroszner, University of Chicago

Papers:
*The Role and Limitations of Financial
Accounting and Auditing for Market Discipline*
George J. Benston, Emory University

Fair Values and Financial Statement Volatility?
Mary Barth, Stanford University

*The Enron Failure and Corporate Governance
Reform*
Charles M. Elson, University of Delaware
Christopher J. Gyves, Wake Forest University
   School of Law

Discussant:
Shyam Sunder, Yale University

6:00 pm   Reception

7:00 pm   Dinner and Keynote Speaker

                           Moderator:
                           Jack B. Evans, The Hall-Perrine Foundation
                           Susan Schmidt Bies, Member, Board of Governors
                           of the Federal Reserve System

Saturday, November 1, 2003

7:30 am   Breakfast and Keynote Speaker

                           Moderator:
                           Malcolm D. Knight, General Manager,
                           Bank for International Settlements

                           Jaime Caruana, Governor, Bank of Spain,
                           and Chairman, Basel Committee
                           on Banking Supervision

8:50 am   **Session VIb: Interaction of Market
                           Discipline and Public Policy**

                           Moderator:
                           James Nelson, Federal Reserve Bank of Chicago

                           Papers:
                           *Can the Unsophisticated Market Provide
                           Discipline?*
                           Gerard Caprio, World Bank
                           Patrick Honohan, World Bank

                           *Can the Invisible Hand Strengthen Prudential
                           Supervision?*
                           Richard J. Herring, University of Pennsylvania

                           Dealing with Destabilizing 'Market Discipline
                           Daniel Cohen, École Normale Supérieure
                           and Cepremap
                           Richard Portes, London Business School
                           and Columbia University

                           Discussant:
                           Charles Freedman, Carleton University

10:35 am   Coffee Break

10:50 am   ## Session VII: Policy Panel

Moderator:

William C. Hunter, University of Connecticut
and Federal Reserve Bank of Chicago

Charles Calomiris, Columbia University
Christine Cumming, Federal Reserve Bank
of New York
Lawrence Harris, Securities and Exchange
Commission
Patricia Jackson, Bank of England and
Basel Committee on Banking Supervision

12:30 pm   Buffet Lunch and Adjournment

Organizing Committee: Claudio Borio, Bank for International
Settlements
William C. Hunter, University of Connecticut
and Federal Reserve Bank of Chicago
George G. Kaufman, Loyola University
Chicago and Federal Reserve Bank of Chicago
Kostas Tsatsaronis, Bank for International
Settlements

Index

Accounting
  consistent standards for, 30–31
  corporate governance and, 341–343 (*see also* Corporate governance)
  disclosure and, 18–22
  GAAP and, 164, 293, 295, 304, 308, 311–315, 342
  IPA misdeeds and, 304–316
  pension plans and, 20–22
Accounting and Auditing Enforcement Releases (AAERs), 306–307
Adelphia, 193, 237, 305
Agency, 49n19
  conflicts of interest and, 175–186
  examiners and, 41–42
  hostile takeovers and, 40–41
  insurance and, 159–171
  principal problem and, 42–45
  too-big-to-fail issue and, 138, 152, 420
Aggregation, 82, 408
  capital controls and, 205–207
  macroprudential regulation and, 56–57
  risk-taking and, 12–13
  self-fulfilling crises and, 384–385
Agnelli group, 259
Ahmadjian, Christina L., 279
Allen, F., 231
Allen, L., 91
Amazon.com, 290
A. M. Best ratings, 165–166, 168
American depository receipts (ADRs), 202–203
American Institute of Certified Public Accountants (AICPA), 292–293, 314
American Stock Exchange (AMEX), 94
Analysts, 219–221
  investment influence of, 290–292
  rewards to, 290
  role of, 22–23
  See also Models
Andersen Consulting, 293
Andrews, David, 368
Antle, Rick, 294
Aoki, Masahiko, 272
Argentina, 197, 382, 390, 409–412
Arthur Andersen, 294–295, 307, 315, 337
Asahi Bank, 125, 131

Auditing, 18, 131
  conflicts of interest and, 292–296
  consulting fees and, 309–311
  CPA firms' misdeeds and, 305–311
  expectations gap and, 293
  financial statements role and, 303–305
  Japan and, 280
  loss leader, 312
  net income inflation and, 308–309
  Sarbanes-Oxley Act and, 304–305, 319n8
Banca Romana, 409
Banco Santander Central Hispano, 258
Bank for International Settlements, xi, 3, 5, 11–15, 427
Bank holding companies (BHCs), 42
Banking, 43, 49n10, 63–67
  auditors and, 18
  Bank Recapitalization Act and, 122
  black box approach and, 147–156
  board interlocks and, 177
  bridge bank model and, 374
  CAMEL ratings and, 92–93
  capitalization influence and, 92–93
  changes in, 55
  Chicago panic and, 91–92
  CHIPS and, 73
  collective action clauses (CACs) and, 9, 73–76, 381–383
  conflicts of interest and, 175–185
  conglomeration and, 96
  credit risk profile and, 29
  debt prices and, 90–92, 95 (*see also* Debt)
  deposit insurance and, 46–47, 50n28, 71, 121–125, 260, 349, 359, 368, 399–400, 412–413
  destabilizing flows and, 369–372, 400
  developing countries and, 349–361
  disclosure and, 18–20, 53n16, 367
  distinctions in, 397–402
  emerging economies and, 135–144
  equity prices and, 92
  Europe and, 101–117
  evaluation of, 89–90
  evergreening and, 367, 376n5
  examiners and, 41–42
  failure and, 46–47, 60

Banking (continued)
    Financial Revitalization Act and, 122
    foreclosure and, 71–72
    fundamentals and, 135–144
    government-owned, 138, 351–352
    Great Depression and, 410
    improvement of, 72–73
    indicators for, 108–109
    inference dangers and, 92
    information and, 62, 423–426
    institutional factors and, 136–138
    interest rates and, 139–141
    Japan and, 119–133, 272–273, 277–278
    legal issues and, 71–72
    liability structure and, 59–60
    loan-loss reserve and, 92
    low-income markets and, 349–361
    macroprudential regulation and, 56–57
    market indicators and, 62, 94–96
    measuring vulnerability of, 349–361
    narrow, 412–413
    New Basel Capital Accord and, 25–33, 55
    nonperforming loans and, 277
    policy influences and, 148, 151
    private monitoring index and, 353–360
    prompt corrective action (PCA) and, 39–40,
        45, 57, 61
    ratings downgrades and, 106–109
    regulatory methods for, 56–58
    Resona Bank rescue and, 125–127
    restructuring and, 71–72
    risk-management and, 18–20, 136, 138–142
    Russian default and, 113
    safety nets and, 408, 412
    SEC and, 59
    spread and, 104–105
    stakeholder monitors and, 149–151
    supervisory review and, 27, 57–58, 93–94
    transparency limits and, 58–59
    World War I era and, 409
    Y-9 reports and, 45
Bank of Canada, 403
Bank of England, 403
Bank of Japan, 121, 129
Bank Recapitalization Act, 122
Bankruptcy, 164–165, 181, 425
    bailout packages and, 381–383
    ILLR and, 382–383
    SDRM and, 381–383
Barbakow, Jeffrey, 237
Barclay, M. J., 191
Barth, James R., 412
Barth, Mary E., 80, 323–333, 343, 353, 431
Basel Capital Accord, 13, 20, 413

    New Capital Accord and, 25–33 (*see also*
        New Basel Capital Accord)
    prompt correction action (PCA) and, 57
    supervisory action and, 57–58
Basel Committee on Banking Supervision
    (BCBS), 5, 55, 87, 102–103, 363, 390,
    392
Batson, Neil, 311
Baumann, Ursel, 424
Beasley, Mark S., 307
Becht, Marco, 255–267, 431
Belgium, 103
Bell, Timothy B., 294
Benston, George J., 303–321, 342–343, 431
Berger, Allen N., 88, 135, 372
Bergman, William, 44
Berskshire Hathaway, 244
Bhattacharya, Sudipto, 56
Bies, Susan Schmidt, xii, 17–23, 432
Big Bang legislation, 275
Big Five, 246
Big Six, 273
Billet, M., 91–92
Birchler, U., 107
Black, Fisher, 43–44, 59, 95, 326
Bliss, Robert R., 82, 88, 424, 427
    banking and, 60–61
    discipline aspects and, 37–53, 225
Blockholder model, 256–261
Blodget, Henry, 290
Board interlocks, 177–178
Bondholders, 43
    market information and, 60–61
    player relationships and, 46–47
    See also Investment indicators for, 94–96
BOPEC, 93
Bordo, Michael D., 409
Borio, Claudio, 57, 232, 429, 433
    developing countries and, 349, 353–354, 359
    Europe and, 109–110, 112, 114
Brazil, 8, 387
Brewer, Elijah, 167
Brickley, J. A., 189
Bridge bank model, 374
Bulow, Jeremy, 76
Calomiris, Charles W., 59, 433
    discipline reestablishment and, 407–416
    Europe and, 102, 106
    U.S. financial firms and, 91, 93
CalPERS, 278–279
Calvo, G., 384
CAMEL (capital adequacy, asset quality,
    management, earning, and liquidity)
    ratings, 92–93, 108

Campbell, John Y., 218
Canada, 73, 403
Cannella, Albert A., 41
Canon, Inc., 281
Capital, 70–71, 408
  bank evaluation and, 89–93, 122 (*see also* Banking)
  insurance and, 159–171
  Japan and, 278–279
  liberalization and, 197–199
  New Basel Capital Accord and, 25–33
  price response and, 90–91
  restoration measures and, 129–131
  tier 1, 424–425
  tier 2, 424
  See also Investment
Capital asset pricing model (CAPM), 213
Capital control, 209–210
  crises vulnerability and, 205–207
  Japan and, 271–272
  liberalization and, 197–208
  macroeconomic evidence on, 199–201
  microeconomic evidence on, 201–205
  prices and, 204–205, 207–208
Caprio, Gerard, 349–362, 397–402, 412, 432
Cargill, T., 92
Carletti, Elena, 59
Carter, Mary Ellen, 308
Caruana, Jaime, xii, 25–33, 432
Casualty insurance, 160, 162, 165–168
Caveat emptor approach, 176
Cendant, 305
Certificates of deposit (CDs), 90, 92, 168
Certified public accountants (CPAs)
  AICPA and, 292–293, 314
  costs imposed upon, 315–316
  GAAP applications and, 304, 308, 311–318
  misdeeds of, 304–316
  Sarbanes-Oxley Act and, 305, 316–317
Chamon, M., 391
Chant, John, 398
Chief executive officers (CEOs). *See* Management
Chile, 4–5, 198, 202–203, 207
China, 199
Chincarini, L., 232
Cho, Fujio, 280
Christie, A. A., 189
Churning, 179
Civil Rehabilitation Act, 274–275
Clearing house interbank payments system (CHIPS), 73
Cochrane, John H., 216
Cohen, Daniel, 381–396, 402–403, 432

Cole, H., 384, 391
Cole, Jonathan, 290
Cole, Rebel, 167
Collective action clauses (CAC), 9, 73–76, 381–383
Collin-Dufresne, Pierre, 370
Comiskey, Eugene E., 312
Committee on the Global Financial System (CGFS), 14
Conference Board Commission on Public Trust and Private Enterprise, 417, 419
Conflicts of interest, 299–300
  auditors and consultants, 292–296
  board interlocks and, 177–178
  churning and, 179
  clients and, 178–179
  cross-selling and, 179
  disclosure and, 179
  exploitation of, 176, 182–185
  failure to execute and, 179
  front-running and, 178
  Glass-Steagall Act and, 296
  guilt and, 175
  information misuse and, 178
  investor loans and, 178
  IPOs and, 289–290
  judiciary abuse and, 177
  laddering and, 180
  late-trading and, 180
  margin lending and, 179
  principal transactions and, 176–177
  privacy and, 179
  research and, 180, 289–292
  retail financial services and, 178–179
  self-dealing and, 178
  shifting bankruptcy risk and, 181
  solutions for, 296–298
  spinning and, 178
  strategic financial profiles and, 181–182
  stuffing and, 179–180
  suitability and, 179
  synergies and, 287–289
  taxonomy for, 176–177, 185
  tying and, 177
  underwriting and, 289–292
  wholesale financial markets and, 176–181
Conglomeration, 96
Consulting, 292–296
Contingent credit line (CCL), 227, 382, 389
Cooper, K., 102
Corporate governance, 72, 250–253, 417
  accounting and, 341–343
  blockholder model and, 256–261
  conflicts of interest and, 287–298

Corporate governance (continued)
  corporate boards and, 243–244
  earnings misreporting and, 241–243
  Enron and, 193, 237–238, 242–244, 247,
      250n16, 294–295, 305, 315, 335–339
  ERISA and, 248
  Europe and, 255–267
  executive scandals and, 237–243, 294–295
  FDICIA and, 418, 420
  financial statements and, 305–318, 323–332
  gatekeepers and, 238, 240, 245–247
  Glass-Steagall Act and, 296
  harmonization and, 263–264
  IPOs and, 289–291
  Japan and, 269–283
  managerial incentives and, 241–243
  NYSE and, 244, 247, 249, 419
  OECD and, 260
  owners and, 247–249
  Private Securities Litigation Reform Act, 246
  public trust and, 237–239
  regulatory competition and, 263–264
  ROAs and, 272
  Sarbanes-Oxley Act and, 23, 239, 243–244,
      249, 293–296, 418, 420
  SEC and, 242, 248
  shareholders and, 247–249
  stock options and, 308–309
  takeovers and, 272
  U.S. structure of, 239–240
  voting rights and, 256–261
  widely held model and, 256–261
Corporations
  accounting standards and, 30–31
  BHCs and, 42
  bonding mechanisms and, 191
  buyouts and, 279
  conflicts of interest and, 175–186, 287–300
  conglomeration and, 96
  consultation issues and, 29
  control and, 72, 187–194
  current practices in, 28–31
  disclosure and, 18–22
  financial statements and, 305–318, 323–332
  hostile takeovers and, 40–41
  IPOs and, 289–291
  Japan and, 269–284
  legal issues and, 192
  net income inflation and, 308–309
  organizational architecture and, 188–191
  pension plans and, 20–22
  principles and, 30
  proprietary information and, 29–30
  public information and, 29

  restructuring and, 71–72
  rules and, 30
  Sarbanes-Oxley Act and, 305, 316–317
  voting rights and, 256–261
Costs, 423
  agency, 40–42, 49n19
  bankruptcy and, 164–165
  conflict of interest and, 183
  control changes and, 164–165
  counterparties and, 87
  financial distress, 163–165
  hostile takeovers and, 40–41
  incomplete contracting and, 40
  insurance and, 159–171
  investment, 88
  IPA/CPA fines and, 315–316
  issuance, 143n7
  liberalization and, 197–199
  stakeholder monitors and, 149–151
Covitz, Daniel M., 61, 94–95
Credit risk. See Risk-management
Cross-selling, 179
Cumming, Christine M., 417–421, 433
Currency, 143n3, 281
Curry, T., 93
Dahl, D., 93
Daiwa Bank, 125, 276
Danzon, Patricia, 160
D'Avolio, G., 58
DeAngelo, Harry, 167
DeAngelo, Linda, 167, 191
Debt, 384, 402–403
  Argentina and, 382
  bankruptcy and, 164–165, 181, 381–383, 425
  CACs and, 9, 73–75
  dynamics of, 387–389
  Europe and, 103–104
  foreclosure and, 71–72
  high-spread, 387–389
  insurance and, 165, 168
  lender of first resort, 390–392
  lender of last resort, 382–383
  mandatory requirements and, 102–103
  narrow banking and, 412–413
  prices and, 90–91, 95
  prudential supervision and, 410–411
  quantities, 91–92
  ratings downgrades and, 108–109
  restructuring and, 71–72
  SDRMs and, 74–75, 381–383
  subordinated, 46, 59–62, 64n23, 69, 103–
      104, 108–109, 143n7, 150, 168, 401,
      412–414
  See also Economic crises

Décamps, Jean-Paul, 58–59
Default. *See* Bankruptcy; Economic crises
Defined-benefit pension plans, 20–22
Defond, Mark L., 294–295, 311
Demirgüç-Kunt, Asli, 359
Deposit insurance, 71, 399–400, 412–413
  developing counties and, 349, 359
  Europe and, 260
  Japan and, 122–125
  prudential supervision and, 368
  purpose of, 46–47, 50n28
Deposit Insurance Law, 121–125
Derivatives markets, 44, 48n9, 399, 411–412
Desai, Mihir, 198, 203–204
Destabilizing flows, 369–372
DeYoung, Robert, 42, 60
Diamond, Douglas, 288
Disclosure, 18–22, 53n16, 80, 419
  banking and, 367
  misleading, 179
  pillar 3 and, 372–373
  See also Information
Docking, D., 92
Dore, Ronald, 271
Dugar, Amitabh, 289
Duncan, David, 315
Dye, Ronald A., 295
Easterbrook, F. H., 191
East India Company, 343
Economic crises, 14, 408
  Argentina and, 382, 410
  Asian crisis and, 221–223
  bankruptcy code and, 381
  Brazil and, 381
  changes in nature of, 385–387
  Chicago panic and, 91–92
  collective action clauses (CACs) and, 9, 73–76, 381–383
  confidence and, 389–392
  corporate scandals and, 237–243
  firm value and, 89
  Great Depression and, 60, 409–410
  high-spread, 387–389
  IMF assessments and, 8–9, 225–233
  integration and, 211–224
  Japan and, 119–121, 125–132
  Korea and, 385–386
  lender of first resort, 390–392
  liberalization and, 230–232
  Mexico and, 381, 385–386, 391
  Russia and, 214–215, 318, 385–387
  savings and loans, 61
  self-fulfilling, 384–389
  too-big-to-fail issue and, 138, 152, 420

  Turkey and, 382
  World War I era and, 409
Economic issues, 14–15
  devaluation and, 4
  financial statements and, 305–318, 323–332
  IMF and, 5–7
  incentives and, 14–15
  interest rates and, 139–141
  New Basel Capital Accord and, 25–33
Edwards, Franklin R., 237–253, 430
Eichengreen, B., 381, 383
Ellison, Larry, 237
Elmer, P., 92
Elson, Charles M., 335–339, 343, 431
Elton, Edwin J., 369
Emerging Market Bond Index (EMBI), 139
Employee Retirement Income Security Act
  (ERISA), 248
Enron
  auditing and, 305, 315
  conflicts of interest and, 294–205
  consultation fees and, 337
  corporate control and, 193, 237–238, 242–244, 247, 250n16, 335–339
Entrepreneurship, 4
Epermanis, Karen, 168
Equations
  asset price, 211–212, 233
  debt to GDP ratio, 388
  estimation error, 325
  indicator variable, 105
  integration model, 211–212, 215, 221, 223
  probit model, 105
  spread, 104–105
Equilibrium, 383–385
Equity, 40, 408
  call models and, 95–96
  corporate governance and, 237–243 (*see also* Corporate governance)
  developing countries and, 349–361
  European markets and, 103–104
  IMF assessments and, 225–233
  insurance and, 159–171
  integration and, 211–223
  interest rates and, 414
  labor market and, 41, 49n15
  loan-loss reserve and, 92
  low-income markets and, 349–361
  player relationships and, 46–47
  price evidence and, 92
Ethics. *See* Corporate governance; Legal issues
Europe
  blockholder model and, 256–261
  corporate governance and, 255–267

Europe (continued)
   distance-to-default for, 104, 111–113
   equity markets and, 103–104
   freedom of establishment and, 262–263
   harmonization and, 263–264
   insurance and, 159–171
   market indicators and, 105, 108–109
   ratings downgrades and, 106–109
   regulatory competition and, 263–264
   risk-management and, 104–113
   Russian default and, 113
   sub-debt and, 103–104
   Swiss deposit insurance and, 107
   takeovers and, 256–257, 261–262
   Treaty of Rome and, 255–256
   widely held model and, 256–261
European Commission Action Plan, 255
European Court of Justice, 255–256, 262–263
European Takeover Directive, 261–262
European Union, 105, 261–264
Evanoff, Douglas D., 91, 365, 370
Evans, Charles, 427, 430
Evans, Jack B., 432
Evergreening, 367, 376n5
Examiners. *See* Regulation
Ex ante approach, 370, 408
   destabilization and, 383–385
   SDRM and, 381–383
   versus ex post, 225–233
Expectations gap, 293
Exposure at default (EAD), 425
Extended fund facility (EFF), 389
Fama, Eugene, 40, 189, 213
Farrell, Kathleen A., 41
Federal Deposit Insurance Corporation (FDIC),
   46–47, 71, 349, 368, 403
Federal Deposit Insurance Corporation Improve-
   ment Act (FDICIA), 18, 40, 42, 57, 73, 418,
   420
Federal Reserve Bank of Chicago, xi, 3, 427
Feldman, R., 93
Fenn, George, 167
Ferguson, Roger, 27
Financial Accounting Standards Board (FASB)
   auditing and, 305, 308, 314
   conflict of interest and, 293
   role of, 21–22
   volatility and, 326–327, 329, 331n2, 332n5
Financial Executives International (FEI), 306–
   307
Financial holding companies (FHCs), 91
Financial Rehabilitation Commission, 119
Financial Revitalization Act, 122, 124
Financial Sector Assessment Program (FSAP), 6, 14

Financial Stability Forum (FSF), 14
Financial statements
   estimation error and, 325–326
   fair values and, 323–332
   misleading, 305–318 (*see also* Corporate
      governance)
   relevance and, 327–328
   Sarbanes-Oxley Act and, 305, 316–317
   volatility and, 323–330
Financial System Stability Assessments
   (FSSAs), 6
Finland, 108
First Capital Corporation, 167
First Executive Corporation, 167
Fischer, Stanley, 382
Fissel, G., 92
Fitch ratings, 106, 108–109, 368–369, 374
Flannery, Mark J., 60, 424, 428
   discipline process and, 38, 42, 147–148,
      150–151
   prudential supervision and, 368–370
   U.S. financial firms and, 87–100
Flood, Robert P., 211–224, 430
Forbes, Kristin J., 197–210, 430
Foreclosure, 71–72
Franchise value, 163–164
Francis, Jere R., 295
Fraser, Donald, R., 41, 102
Freedman, Charles, 397–404, 432
Freixas, Xavier, 56
French, Kenneth R., 213
Front-running, 178
Froot, K., 232
Fukao, Mitsuhiro, 119–133, 149, 151–152, 428
Furfine, C., 90
Galant, Debbie, 290
Gale, D., 231
Gambles for resurrection, 382
Gelos, R. G., 227
General Accounting Office (GAO), 306–307,
   309, 313
General Electric, 237
Germany, 103, 259, 261
Gilson, Stuart, 167
Glass-Steagall Act, 296
Glennerster, R., 226
Global Crossing, 247, 294, 305
Globalization, 10, 400–401
   American depository receipts (ADRs) and,
      202–203
   corporate governance and, 269–283
   currency risk and, 143n3
   developing countries and, 135–144, 349–
      361

Globalization (continued)
  Europe and, 101–117
  IMF and, 225–233
  Japan and, 119–133
  liberalization and, 197–208, 230–232
  low-income markets and, 349–361
  private monitoring index and, 353–360
  Resona Bank rescue and, 125–127
  Russian default and, 113
  Treaty of Rome and, 255–256
Goldberg, L., 91
Goldstein, Robert S., 370
Goodhart, Charles, 400
Gordon, Elizabeth A., 294
Government, 8
  bank ownership and, 351–352
  IMF and, 5–7
  insurance and, 161–162
  Japan and, 121–125, 129–132, 274–275
  liberalization and, 197–208
  market hostilities of, 3–5
Gramm-Leach-Bliley legislation, 37, 91, 96
Grasso, Dick, 237–238
Great Depression, 60, 409–410
Greece, 108
Gropp, Reint, 71, 93, 95, 428
  discipline's black box, 147–148, 150–152,
    154
  Europe and, 101–117
Gross domestic product (GDP), 409
Group of Seven, 408
Group of Ten, 381
Gunther, J., 93
Gyves, Christopher J., 431
Haldane, Andrew G., 73, 225–234, 403, 430
Hall, Brian J., 308
Hall, J., 90–91
Hancock, D., 94, 104
Hansen, Lars Peter, 214
Harrington, Scott E., 159–173, 429
Harris, Lawrence, 433
Hawke, Jerry, 27
HealthSouth, 237, 305
Healy, Paul M., 294
Herring, Richard J., 363–379, 400
Hirata, Satoshi, 131
Hitachi, 281
Hoggarth, Glenn, 368, 423–424
Hokkaido Takushoku Bank, 120–121, 124, 127
Hong, Harrison, 290
Honohan, Patrick, 349–362, 397–402, 432
Hoshi, Takeo, 273
Hostile takeovers, 40–41
Hudgins, S., 91

Huizinga, Harry, 359
Hunter William C., 433
IBM, 305
Ideal Mutual, 167
Illinois, 410
Immunity laws, 73–76
Incentives, 14–15
  bank failures and, 49n10
  CEOs and, 41
  corporate governance and, 187–194, 241–243
  liability structure and, 59–60
  New Basel Capital Accord and, 25–33
  regulators and, 45
  risk-taking and, 12–13
Independent public accountants (IPAs)
  consulting fees and, 309–311
  costs imposed upon, 315–316
  GAAP applications and, 304, 308, 311–318
  misdeeds of, 304–316
  Sarbanes-Oxley Act and, 305, 316–317
  trust of, 304
India, 206, 387
Indonesia, 269
Industrial Revitalization Corporation Japan
    (IRCJ), 127, 275
Industry. *See* Corporations
Information, 423
  Argentina and, 411–412
  banking and, 60–62
  conflicts of interest and, 287–289 (*see also*
    Conflicts of interest)
  cost and, 38
  credit risk and, 425–426
  inference dangers and, 92
  insurance and, 159–171
  market influences and, 88–89
  misuse of, 178
  New Basel Capital Accord and, 101, 135, 142,
    372–373
  objective, 59
  price response to, 90–91
  prompt corrective action (PCA) and, 61
  proprietary, 29–30
  risk-management and, 109–113, 136, 138–142
    (*see also* Risk-management)
  SDDS and, 226
  tier 1 and, 424–425
  Y-9 reports and, 45
Inherent volatility, 325–328
Initial public offerings (IPOs), 289–291
Institutional Investor's polls, 289
Insurance, 5, 171–173, 349
  bankruptcy and, 164–165
  catastrophes and, 160

Insurance (continued)
  compulsory, 163
  control changes and, 164–165
  deposit, 46–47, 50n28, 71, 121–125, 260, 349,
    359, 368, 399–400, 412–413
  downgrades and, 168–169
  European Union and, 159
  financial distress costs and, 163–165
  franchise value loss and, 163–164
  governmental guarantees and, 161–162
  intermediaries and, 164
  judgement proof buyers and, 163
  life, 161
  policy implications for, 169–170
  property/casualty, 160, 162, 165–168
  ratings and, 165–166
  risk sensitivity of demand and, 161–163
  sub-debt and, 168
  transparency and, 162–163
Integration, 232–233
  Asian crisis and, 221–223
  defining asset-market, 211–212
  methodology for, 212–219
  OECD and, 214–215
  Russia/LTCM crisis and, 214–215
  sensitivity analysis and, 219, 221
Interest
  equity effects and, 414
  insurance and, 160–161
  prices and, 135, 139–141
  rate distribution and, 139–141
  vector analysis of, 144n18
International Accounting Standards Board
    (IASB), 5–6, 21–22, 326–330, 331n2
International Association of Insurance Advisors
    (IAIS), 5
International Fiscal Association (IFA), 6
International Monetary Fund (IMF), xi-xii, 387,
    391–392, 401–403
  Article 4 and, 6–9
  contingent credit lines and, 227
  country assessments and, 225–233
  crisis handling and, 8–9
  ex ante v. ex post approach and, 225–233
  FSAPs and, 6, 14
  historical perspective and, 3–5
  as lender of last resort, 382
  liberalization and, 197
  organization of, 5–7
  role of, 3–10
  ROSCs and, 226
  safety nets and, 70
  SDDS and, 226
  stand-by arrangements and, 226

  technical assistance and, 6–7
  transparency and, 7–8
International Organization of Securities
    Commissions (IOSCO), 5
Investment, 80–82
  analyst influence and, 290–292
  auditor influence and, 292–296
  bank evaluation and, 89–90
  black box approach and, 147–156
  conflicts of interest and, 287–289 (*see also*
    Conflicts of interest)
  corporate governance and, 237–243 (*see
    also* Corporate governance)
  costs of, 88
  expectations gap and, 293
  information for, 22–23, 60–61, 94–96
  integration and, 211–223
  interest rates and, 139–141
  Japan and, 272, 275–279
  market indicators and, 60–61, 94–96
  monitoring and, 88
  one-share-one-vote principle and, 256–261
  pension plans and, 20–22
  ROAs and, 272
  safety nets and, 14–15, 69–70, 73–74
  stakeholder monitors and, 149–152
  systemic risk and, 136, 138–142
  takeovers and, 40–41
  See also Markets
Italy, 409
Ivanova, A., 226
Iyo Bank, 121
Jackson, Patricia, 368, 423–426, 433
Jackson, William, 167
Jagannathan, Ravi, 214
Jagtiani, Julapa, 60, 90–91
Japan, 149, 151–152, 214
  Allied Occupation and, 269–270
  auditors and, 280
  banking and, 122, 125–127, 131, 272–273,
    277–278, 280
  Big Bang legislation and, 275
  capital control and, 271–272
  Civil Rehabilitation Act and, 274
  corporate governance and, 269–283
  currency issues and, 281
  Deposit Insurance Law and, 122–125
  financial crisis of, 119–121, 221–223
  Financial Revitalization Act and, 122
  investment and, 275–279
  IRCJ and, 127, 275
  policy changes in, 274–280
  postwar economic system of, 270–274
  prompt corrective action (PCA) and, 153

Japan (continued)
  RCC and, 275
  regulation absence in, 127–129
  restoration measures for, 129–132
  ROAs and, 272
  safety net for, 121–122
  takeovers and, 272
  World War II era and, 269–270
  zaibatsu dissolution and, 269–270
Jensen, Michael, 40, 189, 191, 431
Jobs and Growth Act, 419
Johnson, Simon, 198, 201–202
Jones, Thomas, 6, 17, 429
Jordan, J., 92
Joye, M. P., 189
Judgement proof, 163
Judiciary abuse, 177
Kahn, Charles M., 59, 409
Kane, Edward J., 366
Kaplan, Ethan, 201
Kashyap, Anil, 273, 428
Kato, Takao, 279
Kaufman, George G., 427, 433
Kehoe, T., 384, 391
Kinney, William R., 311
KMV Corporation, 104, 108
Knight, Malcolm, xii, 5, 11–15, 408, 427
Korea, 70, 269, 385–386
  Asian crisis and, 221–223
  capital controls and, 197, 204, 206
  equity integration and, 214
Kozlowski, Dennis, 237
Krainer, J., 93, 95
Kroszner, Randall, 431
Krueger, Anne, xii, 3–10, 382, 429
Krueger, Mark, 73, 403
Kubik, Jeffrey D., 290
Kwast, Myron L., 94, 104, 364
Labor market, 41, 49n15
Laddering, 180
Laeven, Luc, 359
Landsman, Wayne R., 294
Lang, William W., 42
Larker, David F., 310
Late-trading, 180
Lay, Kenneth, 243
Learmount, Simon, 271
Lee, D. Scott, 41
Legal issues
  Bates v. Bar of the State of Arizona, 344–345
  Civil Rehabilitation Act, 274–275
  conglomeration and, 96
  Elliot Associates case, 75–76

  foreclosure and, 71–72
  Glass-Steagall Act, 296
  Gramm-Leach-Bliley legislation, 37, 91, 96
  Private Securities Litigation Reform Act, 246
  restructuring and, 71–72, 74
  Sarbanes-Oxley Act, 23, 243–244, 295–296
    (*see also* Sarbanes-Oxley Act)
  Securities Act, 292
  sovereign immunity laws and, 75–76
  Treaty of Rome, 255–256
Lemieux, C., 90–91
Lender of first resort, 390–392
Lender of last resort, 382–383
Lerrick, A., 389
Levine, Ross, 349, 353–354, 359, 412
Levitt, Arthur, 306, 308, 310
Levonian, Mark, 59, 61
Levy-Yeyati, Eduardo, 135–149, 151–153, 428
Li, Kan, 198, 204
Liability structure, 59–60
Liberalization, 197–199, 208
  benefits of, 230–232
  crises vulnerability and, 205–207
  macroeconomic evidence and, 199–201
  microeconomic evidence and, 201–205
Life insurance, 161
LJM, 244
Llewellyn, David T., 147–156, 428
Lloyd's of London, 167
Lo, Andrew W., 218
Loans. *See* Debt
Long-Term Capital Management (LTCM), 45, 214–215, 217
Long-Term Credit Bank of Japan, 122, 124, 127
Lopez, J., 93, 95
Loss given default (LGD), 425
Lowe, P., 109–110
LTCB, 120, 122
Lynch, Luann J., 308
Maastricht Treaty, 105, 390
Mächler, A., 107
MacKinlay, A. Craig, 218
Maechler, A., 91
Malaysia, 198, 201–202, 204–205, 207, 269
Management
  agency and, 40–42, 49n19
  annual fees for, 336
  bridge bank model and, 374
  CAMEL ratings and, 92–93
  capital controls and, 197–210
  collective action clauses (CACs) and, 9, 73–76, 381–383
  conflicts of interest and, 287–289 (*see also* Conflicts of interest)

Management (continued)
  consulting fees and, 309–311
  corporate governance and, 237–254 (*see also*
    Corporate governance)
  counterparties and, 87
  derivatives dealers and, 48n9
  equity holders and, 40–41
  examiners and, 41–42
  financial statements and, 305–318, 323–332
  Japan and, 270–271, 279–280
  net income inflation and, 308–309
  New Basel Capital Accord and, 26–27
  organizational architecture and, 46–47, 189–
    191
  player relationships and, 46–47
  private monitoring index and, 353–360
  public choice theory and, 365–366
  ratings downgrades and, 106–107
  restructuring and, 71–72
  risk and, 11–12 (*see also* Risk-management)
  stock options and, 308–309
  supervisory action and, 27, 57–58, 88–89, 425
Management advisory services (MAS), 292, 294
Mansi, Sattar A., 293
Margin lending, 179
Market discipline
  advantages of, 373–376
  agency and, 40–42, 49n19
  appearance of, 409–411
  banking and, 55–67 (*see also* Banking)
  black box of, 147–156
  capital instruments and, 70–71
  collective action clauses (CACs) and, 9, 73–
    76, 381–383
  components of, 38–39
  confidence and, 389–392
  conflicts of interest and, 175–186
  debt prices and, 90–92 (*see also* Debt)
  definitions of, 48n1, 69, 88–90, 102–103, 414–
    415
  direct, 58–60, 62
  emerging economies and, 135–144
  equilibrium and, 383–385
  Europe and, 101–117
  ex ante approach, 225–233, 370, 381–385
  ex post approach, 225–233, 381–383
  Gramm-Leach-Bliley legislation and, 37
  IMF and, 3–10
  impediments to, 151–154, 197–210
  improvement of, 72–76
  incentives and, 14–15
  insurance and, 159–173
  investor information and, 22–23 (*see also*
    Information)

Japan and, 119–133
  legal issues and, 71–72
  New Basel Capital Accord and, 25–33
  official discipline and, 364–366
  pension plans and, 20–22
  players in, 42–47
  policy and, 82–84 (*see also* Policy)
  reasons for increasing, 39–40
  reestablishment of, 412–414
  requirements for, 80–82
  risk-taking and, 11–14
  role of, 423–426
  safety nets and, 69–70, 408
  scale and, 12–14
  sovereigns and, 73–76
  transparency and, 58 (*see also* Transparency)
Market Discipline: The Evidence across
  Countries and Industries (conference), xi–
  xii
Markets
  confidence and, 389–392
  corporate control and, 72
  derivative, 44, 48n9, 399, 411–412
  devaluation and, 4
  developing countries and, 349–361
  equity, 103–104
  European, 101–117
  government hostilities and, 3–5
  IMF and, 5–7
  indicators for, 94–96, 105, 108–109
  influence of, 88–89
  information and, 411–412
  integration and, 211–224
  Japan and, 119–133, 275–277
  labor, 41, 49n15
  low-income, 349–361
  monitoring and, 88
  over-the-counter, 364, 366–367
  panics and, 410–411 (*see also* Economic
    crises)
  pension plans and, 20–22
  private monitoring index and, 353–360
  retail, 178–181
  sub-debt, 46, 59–62, 103–104
  tax rates and, 229
  transparency and, 58–59
  wholesale, 176–181
Marshall, David, 368, 429
Martens, Stanley C., 293
Martin, J. Spencer, 370
Mason, Joseph R., 91, 410
Maxwell, William F., 293
Mayer, Colin, 255–267
Mayers, D., 191

Mayes, David, 149, 430
McDill, K., 91
McDonough, William, 26–27
McEnroe, John E., 293
Meckling, William H., 40, 189
Meltzer Commission, 383, 389
Merck, 305
Merrill Lynch, 290
Merton, Robert C., 44, 59, 369, 424
Mexico, 197, 381, 385–386, 391
Michaely, R., 291
Milhaupt, Curtis J., 273–274, 279
Miller, Darius P., 293
Mission Insurance Group, 167
Mitton, Todd, 198, 201–202
Mixed-measurement volatility, 326–328
Miyauchi, Yoshihiko, 280
Mizuho Financial Group, 132
Models, 93–94, 412
  Black-Scholes, 43–44, 59, 95, 326
  blockholder, 256–261
  bridge bank, 374
  capital asset pricing, 213
  debt-put, 95–96
  equity-call, 95–96
  integration, 211–224
  probit, 105–106
  widely held, 256–261
Moody ratings, 106, 165–166
Morgan, Donald P., 89, 367
Mortality risk, 161
Moskow, Michael H., 429-430
Moss, Jim, 368
Mulford, Charles W., 312
Murphy, Kevin J., 308
Mutual Benefit Life, 167
Myers, Stuart, 59, 190
Narayanamoorthy, Ganapathi, 294
Nathan, Siva, 289
Nelson, James, 432
Netherlands, 103, 258
New Basel Capital Accord, 25, 37, 117
  accounting standards and, 30–31
  approaches to, 27–28
  industry practices and, 28–31
  information and, 101
  management of, 26–27
  market-driven solutions and, 28
  pillar 3 and, 135, 142, 372–373, 414, 423–426
  prudential regulation and, 363–377
  stability and, 26–27
  status of, 31–33
  supervisory review and, 27

New York, 410
New York Stock Exchange (NYSE), 94, 193, 214, 218
  corporate governance and, 244, 247, 249, 291, 419
  Global Settlement and, 291
  Grasso and, 237–238
Niehaus, Greg, 160
Nier, Erleng, 368, 423–424
Nigeria, 387
Nikolova, Stanislava, 87–100, 147–148, 150–151, 428
Nippon Credit Bank, 120, 122, 127
Nippon Keidanren, 277, 280–281
Nitta, Michio, 271, 276
Nonperforming loans (NPLs), 277
O'Connell, P., 232
Okazaki, Tetsuji, 269
Okuda, Hiroshi, 280
One-share-one vote principle, 256–261
Oppenheimer and Co., 290
Oracle, 237
Organization for Economic Cooperation and Development (OECD), 214–215, 260
Orix, 280
Ovitz, Michael, 244
Ownership. *See* Management
Padoa, Schioppa, T., 110
Palepu, Krishna G., 294
Palmrose, Zoe-Vonna, 295, 306–307, 311
Panel and Audit Effectiveness, 310
Patrick, Hugh, 269–285, 431
Penn Central, 40–41
Pension Fund Association, 278–279
pension plans, 20–22
PeopleSoft, 305
Peria, Maria Soledad Martinez, 135–149, 151–153, 428
PHICO Insurance Company, 167
Poland, 232
Policy, 82–84
  agency costs and, 40–42
  Bank Recapitalization Act and, 122
  corporate governance and, 341–343 (*see also* Corporate governance)
  developing countries and, 349–361
  entrepreneurial approach and, 4
  European Union, 261–264
  FDICIA and, 40
  Financial Revitalization Act and, 122
  Gramm-Leach-Bliley legislation and, 37
  Great Depression and, 410
  IMF and, 3–10
  improvements for, 72–76

Policy (continued)
   Japan and, 269–284
   liberalization and, 197–208, 230–232
   low-income markets and, 349–361
   Maastricht Treaty and, 390
   macroeconomic stability, 5
   narrow banking and, 412–413
   New Basel Capital Accord and, 25–33 (*see also* New Basel Capital Accord)
   private monitoring index and, 353–360
   prompt corrective action (PCA) and, 39–40, 45, 57
   proprietary information and, 29–30
   public information and, 29
   recommendations for, 97, 113–114, 131–132, 154–155, 264–265, 373–376, 397–404, 417–421
   rules vs. principles, 27–28, 30
   safety nets and, 14–15, 69–70, 73–74
   Sarbanes-Oxley Act and, 23, 420
   standards for, 27–31
   supervisory action and, 57–58
   too-big-to-fail issue and, 138, 152, 420
Portes, Richard, 381–396, 402–403, 432
Portugal, 108
Poverty reduction and growth facility (PRGF), 389
Prakash, Mohinder, 294
Prasad, Eswar, 199
Prices
   biased, 369–370
   capital control and, 204–208
   debt, 90–91, 95
   default risk and, 368–369
   destabilizing flows and, 369–372, 400
   equity, 92
   information response and, 90–91
   integration model and, 211–223
   interest rates and, 135, 139–141
Principal transactions, 176–177
Pritzker family, 51n31
Privacy, 179
Private monitoring index, 353–360, 401
Private Securities Litigation Reform Act, 246
Probability of default (PD), 425
Probit model, 105–106
Prompt corrective action (PCA), 61
   banking and, 39–40, 45, 57, 152–153
   discipline's black box and, 148, 152
   Japan and, 153
Property insurance, 160, 162, 165–168
Proprietary information, 29–30
Prowse, Stephen, 42
Proxy voting, 17

Prudential supervision, 363
   biased prices and, 369–370
   destabilizing flows and, 369–372
   incentives and, 367–369
   macro, 56–57, 110
   market *versus* official discipline and, 364–366
   micro, 56, 110
   pillar 3 and, 372–373
   risk-management and, 410–411
   transparency and, 366–367
Public choice theory, 365–366
Public Company Accounting Oversight Board (PCAOB), 18, 293–294, 317, 342, 344
Purchasing power parity (PPP), 206, 388, 403
Quinn, Dennis, 199
Qwest, 294, 305
Rajan, Raghuram, 89
Ramakrishnan, Ram T. S., 288
Rangan, Kasturi P., 368–369
Regulation
   accounting standards and, 30–31
   agency costs and, 40–42
   auditors and, 18
   Bank Recapitalization Act and, 122
   bridge bank model and, 374
   capital controls and, 197–210
   collective action clauses (CACs) and, 9, 73–76, 381–383
   corporate governance and, 237–254, 263–264 (*see also* Corporate governance)
   Deposit Insurance Law and, 122–125
   developing countries and, 349–361
   disclosure and, 18–22
   discretionary, 349
   ERISA and, 248
   Europe and, 101–117
   examiners and, 41–42
   ex ante, 225–233, 370, 381–385
   FDIC and, 46–47, 71
   FDICIA and, 40, 42, 57, 418
   Financial Revitalization Act and, 122
   Global Settlement and, 291
   improvement of, 72–76
   incentives for, 45
   information and, 411–412
   Japan and, 119–133
   low-income markets and, 349–361
   narrow banking and, 412–413
   New Basel Capital Accord and, 25–33 (*see also* New Basel Capital Accord)
   player relationships and, 43, 46–47
   principles and, 30
   prompt corrective action (PCA) and, 39–40, 45, 61

Regulation (continued)
prudential, 56–57, 110, 363–377, 410–411
public choice theory and, 365–366
reasons for, 56–58
reestablishment approaches for, 407–415
restructuring and, 71–72
risk-management and, 44–45 (*see also* Risk
management)
role of, 423–426
rules and, 30
safety nets and, 14–15, 69–70, 73–74, 408
Sarbanes-Oxley Act and, 23, 418, 420
SEC and, 23, 59 (*see also* Securities and
Exchange Commission (SEC))
Shadow Financial Regulatory Committee,
73, 95, 165, 413
sovereigns and, 73–76
supervisory action and, 57–58, 93–94
Y-9 reports and, 45
Reliance, 167
Renault, 259
Reports on the Observance of Standards and
Codes (ROSCs), 6, 8, 226
Research, 289–292
Resolution and Collection Corporation, 275
Resona Bank, 125–127, 131, 277–278
Restructuring, 71–72, 74
Return on assets (ROAs), 272
Reynolds, J. Kenneth, 295
Richards, A., 106–107
Richardson, Scott A., 310
Risk-management, 11, 39, 408, 413, 423
black box approach and, 147–156
CAMEL ratings and, 92–93
capital controls and, 197–210
capitalization influence and, 92–93
conflict of interest and, 175–185
credit risk profile and, 29
currency convertibility and, 143n3
destabilizing flows and, 369–372
disclosure and, 18–20
equity holders and, 43–44
Europe and, 101–117
ex ante, 370
Federal Reserve and, 45
financial innovations and, 18–20
incentives for, 12–13
insurance and, 159–171
integration and, 211–224
interest rates and, 139–141
liability structure and, 59–60
lower issue effects and, 104–105
macroeconomic factors and, 136
market information and, 60–61

New Basel Capital Accord and, 25–33
perception of, 12–13
private monitoring index and, 353–360
prompt corrective action (PCA) and, 39–40
prudential supervision and, 363–377
ratings downgrades and, 106–107
regulators and, 44–45
safety nets and, 14–15, 69–70, 73–74
scale and, 12–14
spread and, 104–105
sub-debt yields and, 61
systemic issues and, 136, 138–142
Rite Aid, 305
Ritter, Jay R., 290
Robbins, Gregory E., 279
Rochet, Jean-Charles, 55–67, 84, 155, 427
Rodrik, Dani, 199, 201
Rose, Andrew K., 211–224, 430
Rozeff, M. S., 191
Russia, 385–387
capital controls and, 197
European banking and, 113
Long-Term Capital Management crisis and,
214–215, 217
Sachs, Jeffrey, 381
Safety nets, 14–15, 83, 408, 412
distortion of, 69–70
Japan and, 121–122
sovereigns and, 73–74
Sanyo Securities, 120–121
Sarbanes-Oxley Act, 23, 418, 420
auditors and, 304–305, 319n8
conflicts of interest and, 293–296
IPAs and, 305, 316–317
SEC and, 316–317
U.S. corporate errors and, 239, 243–244, 249
Saunders, Anthony, 95
Schilder, Arnold, 370
Schmidt, J., 93
Schmukler, Sergio L., 135–149, 151–153, 428
Scholes, Myron, 43–44, 59, 95, 326
Scholz, Susan, 306–307
Scott, Hal S., 69–77, 82, 420
Seasholes, M. S., 232
Securities Act, 292
Securities and Exchange Commission (SEC), 23,
59, 341
AAERs of, 306–307
auditing errors and, 305, 313–317
conflicts of interest and, 291
consulting fees and, 309–310
corporate control and, 191, 242, 248
creation of, 293
enforcement investigations and, 306–307

SEC (continued)
    FASB and, 314
    fraudulent reports and, 305–307
    GAAP and, 311–318
    PCAOB and, 344
    Sarbanes-Oxley Act and, 316–317
Self-dealing, 178
September 11 attacks, 112
Shackleford, Douglas A., 294
Shareholders. *See* Investment
Sheard, Paul, 273
Shin, Y., 226
Shocks. *See* Economic crises
Shrieves, R., 93
Sironi, A., 104–105
Skilling, Jeffrey, 243
Smith, Adam, 38
Smith, Clifford W., Jr., 187–194, 419, 429
Sorescu, Sorin M., 42
Sovereign debt restructuring mechanism
    (SDRM), 74–75, 381–383
Sovereigns, 70, 73–76
Spain, 259
Special Data Dissemination Standard (SDDS),
    226
Spinning, 178
Spread, 104–105
Stakeholder monitors, 149–152
Standard & Poor's (S&P) ratings, 22–23, 106
    corporate governance and, 242
    insurance and, 165–166
    integration and, 214, 219
State-owned enterprises (SOEs), 76
State Street Bank, 232
Stickel, S., 289
Stiroh, Kevin J., 89
Stock indicators, 94–96
Stock options, 308–309
Stuffing, 179–180
Subordinated debt, 46, 59–62, 64n23, 401, 414
    European markets and, 103–104
    insurance and, 168
    issuance cost and, 143n7
    narrow banking and, 412–413
    ratings downgrades and, 108–109
    stakeholder monitors and, 150
Sumitomo Mitsui Financial Group, 131
Sunbeam, 305
Sunder, Shyam, 341–345, 431
Super-majority voting, 403
Supervisory review, 27, 57–58, 88–89, 425
Sweden, 108, 259, 261
Swindle, S., 92
Synergy, 287–289

Systemic risk. *See* Risk-management
Takahashi, Hirosuki, 280
Takeovers, 40–41, 72
    Europe and, 256–257, 261–262
    Japan and, 272
Tax rates, 229
Taylor, John, 73, 382
Technology, 19, 26
Tenet Healthcare, 237
Terrorism, 112
Thailand, 197, 206–207, 269
Thakor, Anjan V., 56, 288
Tobin, James, 198
Tokyo Stock Exchange, 127, 276
Tokyo Style Company, 278–279
Toyota Motor Corporation, 280–281
Trade. *See* Markets
Transit Casualty, 167
Transparency, 366–367
    costs and, 38
    crisis handling and, 8–9
    IMF and, 7–9
    imposing more, 58
    insurance and, 162–163
    limits of, 58–59
    New Basel Capital Accord and, 25–33
    player relationships and, 46–47
    principles and, 30
    rules and, 30
Treaty of Rome, 255–256
Tsatsaronis, Kostas, 79–84, 232, 428, 433
Turkey, 70, 382, 390
Tyco, 193, 237, 247, 305
Tying, 177
UFJ Bank, 131–132
Underwriting, 289–292
Unicover, 167
United Kingdom, 3–4, 74, 103, 105
    corporate governance and, 263–264
    East India Company and, 343
    one-share-one-vote principle and, 258
United States, 413
    American depository receipts (ADRs) and,
        202–203
    blockholder model and, 256–261
    bridge bank model and, 374
    corporate governance and, 237–253
    insurance and, 159–171
    Japan and, 282
    widely held model and, 256–261
U.S. Federal Reserve
    pension plans and, 21
    price response and, 90–91
    risk-management and, 45

U.S. Shadow Financial Regulatory Committee, 73, 95, 165, 413
U.S. Supreme Court, 344
U.S. Treasury, 369
Usury law, 391
Venable, Carol F., 294
Vesala, J., 108
Vives, Xavier, 59
Volatility, 323–330
Volvo, 259
Voting, 256–261, 403
Wakeman, L. M., 191
Wall, Larry D., 91, 365, 370
Walt Disney Company, 244
Walter, Ingo, 175–186, 429
Warga, A., 94
Waste Management, 305
Watts, R. L., 189, 191
Wei, S., 227
Welch, Ivo, 94, 290
Wellons, Philip, 70
Welsh, Jack, 237
West, Mark D., 279

Whidbee, David A., 41
White, Eugene N., 287–300, 431
Widely held model, 256–261
Williamson, J., 383, 389
Wilson, Berry, 93, 410
Wilson, Harold, 4
Winter, Jaap, 261
Womack, K. L., 291
World Bank, xi, 6, 352–353
WorldCom, 193, 237, 247, 294–295, 305
World War I era, 409
World War II era, 269–270
Xerox, 305
Y-9 reports, 45
Yamaichi Securities, 120–121
Zaibatsu dissolution, 269–270
Zanjani, George, 168
Zhou, Ling, 294
Zimbabwe, 4
Zimmerman, J. L., 189
Zingales, Luigi, 420, 429
Zurich, 4